Physics for CSEC®

2nd Edition

John Avison
Louise Petheram
David Henry
Devinesh Neeranjan

OXFORD
UNIVERSITY PRESS

OXFORD
UNIVERSITY PRESS

Great Clarendon Street, Oxford, OX2 6DP, United Kingdom

Oxford University Press is a department of the University of Oxford. It furthers the University's objective of excellence in research, scholarship, and education by publishing worldwide. Oxford is a registered trade mark of Oxford University Press in the UK and in certain other countries

First published by Nelson Thornes Ltd in 2007
Second edition published by Nelson Thornes Ltd in 2014
This edition published by Oxford University Press in 2014

British Library Cataloguing in Publication Data
Data available

978-1-4085-2511-1

10 9

Printed in India by Multivista Global Pvt. Ltd

Acknowledgements

Cover photograph: iStockphoto
Illustrations: Tech-Set Ltd, Gateshead
Page make-up: Tech-Set Ltd, Gateshead

Thanks are due to David Henry and Devinesh Neeranjan for their contributions in the development of this book.

Contents

Introduction

Physics for CSEC® has been written to meet the requirements of the Caribbean Secondary Education Certificate in Physics. The contents provide complete coverage of the Physics syllabus specified by the Caribbean Examinations Council, with the content tailored exactly to the Caribbean syllabus.

During the preparation of this book invaluable advice and information was provided by two very experienced Caribbean physics teachers, David Henry and Devinesh Neeranjan. Their guidance has also helped to ensure that the book reflects the needs of students and teachers across the Caribbean and places applications and principles of Physics in a Caribbean context.

The School-Based Assessment [SBA] of practical skills has been addressed by providing details of the requirements of the scheme, fully supported by many suggestions for its successful implementation in schools. This book lends itself to the needs of the SBA by adopting a practical approach to most topics.

Key facts and important topics are emphasised throughout the book, helping you to focus on the most important aspects of physics when preparing for the examination. Additionally there are lots of worked examples to show how calculations can be done, and these are followed up with practice exam-style questions at the end of each unit. If you work through all the suggested tasks and questions you should be well prepared for the examination.

The accompanying student CD has interactive activities, multiple-choice practice questions and many other useful features to make learning more interesting and to help you understand concepts fully. You will also find a glossary of key terms and answers to the practice exam-style questions.

Physics is an interesting and vital subject which helps you understand the universe you live in and how everyday things work. We hope you will enjoy reading and using this book and that you may be inspired to study physics at a higher level.

Section A

A1 Physical quantities

Quantities with units and symbols, SI

	Symbol for the quantity	Quantity	Unit for the quantity	Symbol for the unit
Length, mass and time	l	length	metre	m
	A	area	square metre	m^2
	V	volume	cubic metre	m^3
	m	mass	kilogram	kg
	d or ρ	density	kilogram per metre cubed	$kg\,m^{-3}$
	t	time	second	s
	T	period	second	s
	f	frequency	hertz (= $second^{-1}$)	Hz
Force and pressure	F	force	newton	N
	W	weight	newton	N
	M	moment of a force	newton metre	N m
	p	pressure	pascal (= $N\,m^{-2}$)	Pa
Mechanics and motion	s	distance, displacement	metre	m
	W	work	joule (= newton metre)	J
	E	energy	joule	J
	E_P	potential energy	joule	J
	E_K	kinetic energy	joule	J
	P	power	watt (= joule per second)	W
	v or u	speed, velocity (u = initial)	metre per second	$m\,s^{-1}$
	c	speed of waves, light	metre per second	$m\,s^{-1}$
	a	acceleration	metre s^{-2}	$m\,s^{-2}$
	g	acceleration of free fall	metre s^{-2}	$m\,s^{-2}$
	g	gravitational field strength	newton per kilogram	$N\,kg^{-1}$
	p	momentum	kilogram metre s^{-1}	$kg\,m\,s^{-1}$
	p	impulse	newton second	N s
Heat and temperature	E_H	heat energy	joule	J
	θ or T	temperature	degree Celsius, kelvin	°C, K
	C	heat capacity	joule per kelvin	$J\,K^{-1}$
	c	specific heat capacity	joule $kg^{-1}\,K^{-1}$	$J\,kg^{-1}\,K^{-1}$
	L	latent heat	joule	J
	l	specific latent heat	joule per kilogram	$J\,kg^{-1}$
Electricity	Q	electric charge	coulomb	C
	I	electric current	ampere	A
	E	electromotive force (e.m.f.)	volt (= joule per coulomb)	V
	V	potential difference (p.d. or voltage)	volt	V
	R	resistance	ohm	Ω
	C	capacitance	farad	F
	W	electrical energy or work	joule	J

The International System of Units, SI

Base units

The international system of units has seven fundamental or base quantities from which all other physical units can be derived (see table on page 3).

This system of units is a development of the metric system of measurements and has been adopted in many countries to help standardise all measurements internationally.

Fundamental quantity	Base SI unit
mass	kilogram
length	metre
time	second
current	ampere
temperature	kelvin
amount of substance	mole
luminous intensity	candela

Notes:

- It is important to use the correct upper or lower case letters for the symbols. E.g. K (upper case) is kelvin but k (lower case) is kilo.
- Roman (upright) letters are used in printing for unit symbols while italic (sloping) letters are used for quantities.
- Avoid writing plurals of unit symbols by adding an 's' because the symbol 's' stands for seconds.

Changing units

Equations usually use SI units, so sometimes you will need to change grams into kilograms, centimetres into metres, minutes into seconds and so on. To do this, you need to know the conversion factor. For example:

1000 g = 1 kg, so 45 g = 0.045 kg

100 cm = 1 m, so 215 cm = 2.15 m

1 min = 60 s, so 3 min = 180 s

Sometimes conversions will be a little more complicated.

1 square metre (1 m^2) = 100 cm × 100 cm = 10 000 cm^2,
so 1 cm^2 = 1 ÷ 10 000 = 0.0001 m^2

Derived units

All other units are derived from these base units. Three important and useful examples are given below.

Derived quantity	Defining equation	Unit derived from base SI	Special equivalent SI name
Force (*F*)	force = mass × acceleration	$kg \times m\,s^{-2}$	newton: 1 N = 1 $kg\,m\,s^{-2}$
Work (*W*)	work = force × displacement	$kg\,m\,s^{-2} \times m = kg\,m^2\,s^{-2}$	joule: 1 J = 1 N m
Voltage or potential difference (*V*)	$\text{voltage} = \frac{\text{energy transferred}}{\text{charge}}$	$= \frac{kg\,m^2\,s^{-2}}{A\,s}$	volt: 1 V = 1 $J\,C^{-1}$

Changing units for derived units

If you need to do conversions for derived units, it is easier to start from the base units. For example, speed is calculated by dividing distance by time; if you need to calculate a speed in metres per second ($m\,s^{-1}$) it is easier to change distances into metres and times into seconds before you do the calculation.

Decimal places and significant figures

'Decimal places' are the number of places occupied by figures after the decimal point. For example 6.45 is a number written to '2 decimal places'. Writing a value to more decimal places *does not* make it more accurate. If you can only measure distances to the nearest centimetre (0.01 m), then any average values you calculate should also only be given to the nearest centimetre (0.01 m).

Significant figures tell us about precision. Zeros at the front of a number are not included, but those in the middle are. 6472 is a number written to 4 significant figures, so is 0.6472, so is 6072. 6472 is written as 6470 to 3 significant figures, 6500 to 2 significant figures (round up or down to the nearest number with just 2 non-zero digits), 6000 to 1 significant figure (round up or down to the nearest number with just 1 non-zero digit).

Worked example

How many decimal places and significant figures does the number 56.34 have?

56.34 has two figures after the decimal point so has two decimal places.
It has four non-zero figures so is written to four significant figures.

Key fact

Standard form

The standard mathematical method of indicating very large or very small amounts of a quantity is to show it in standard form or scientific notation.

In standard form, the decimal point always appears after the first significant (non-zero) number. The number of times the number must be multiplied or divided by ten to have the correct value is written as a power of ten, called the exponent.

Examples:
330 is 3.3×10^2
0.022 is 2.2×10^{-2}

Prefixes: large and small amounts

One method of indicating very large or small amounts is to use the standard metric prefixes given in the table. Again it is important to use the correct upper or lower case letters. E.g. M (upper case) means 'multiply by a million' while m (lower case) means 'divide by a thousand'!

		Prefix	Symbol	Example	
multiple	10^{12}	tera	T	terametre	Tm
	10^9	giga	G	gigawatt	GW
	10^6	mega	M	megajoule	MJ
	10^3	kilo	k	kilogram	kg
submultiple	10^{-1}	deci	d	decibel	dB
	10^{-2}	centi	c	centimetre	cm
	10^{-3}	milli	m	milliampere	mA
	10^{-6}	micro	μ	microcoulomb	μC
	10^{-9}	nano	n	nanosecond	ns
	10^{-12}	pico	p	picofarad	pF

Summary questions

1 What is the difference between a base unit and a derived unit?

2 Write the value 4200 $\text{J kg}^{-1}\text{K}^{-1}$ in standard form.

3 Write 289.341 to each of the following numbers of significant figures.
a 5 **b** 4 **c** 3 **d** 2 **e** 1

4 Write each of the following numbers in standard form.
a 4200 **b** 300 000 000 **c** 384 400

A2 Measuring

Human beings have always been extremely curious about their surroundings. We ask many varied questions about the world and the things we see and experience around us. Most of the answers that physicists can give boil down to information about three basic ideas, which we call length, mass and time. It is important that we learn how to measure these quantities accurately.

A2.1 Length, area and volume

Objectives

By the end of this topic you will be able to:

- use a variety of instruments to measure length
- use measuring, formulae and estimation to find the area of regular and irregular shapes
- find the volume of regular and irregular solids using both measurement and the displacement method
- use sensitivity, accuracy and range to assess the suitability of instruments
- explain how to minimise parallax errors.

Units of measurement

Units of length, displacement or distance

The SI unit of length, displacement or distance is the metre. We often use multiples and submultiples of the metre.

▼ Common multiples and submultiples of the metre

Unit		Equivalent in metres	
1 kilometre (km)	=	1000 m	or 10^3 m
1 centimetre (cm)	=	0.01 m	or 10^{-2} m
1 millimetre (mm)	=	0.001 m	or 10^{-3} m
1 micrometre (mm)	=	0.000 001 m	or 10^{-6} m
1 nanometre (nm)	=	0.000 000 001 m	or 10^{-9} m

Measuring length

When we need to measure a length we must choose a measuring instrument that is suitable for the length to be measured and will give the required accuracy.

Length to be measured: range	Measuring instrument	Best accuracy: sensitivity
several metres	steel tape measure	1.0 mm
about 1 cm to 1 m	ruler	0.5 mm
about 1 mm to 1 cm	vernier callipers	0.1 mm
about 0.1 mm to 2 or 3 cm	micrometer screw gauge	0.01 mm

How do we decide what accuracy is needed?

In an experiment, aim for a similar accuracy in all the measurements you take. 1% or 1 part in 100 parts is a good accuracy to aim for.

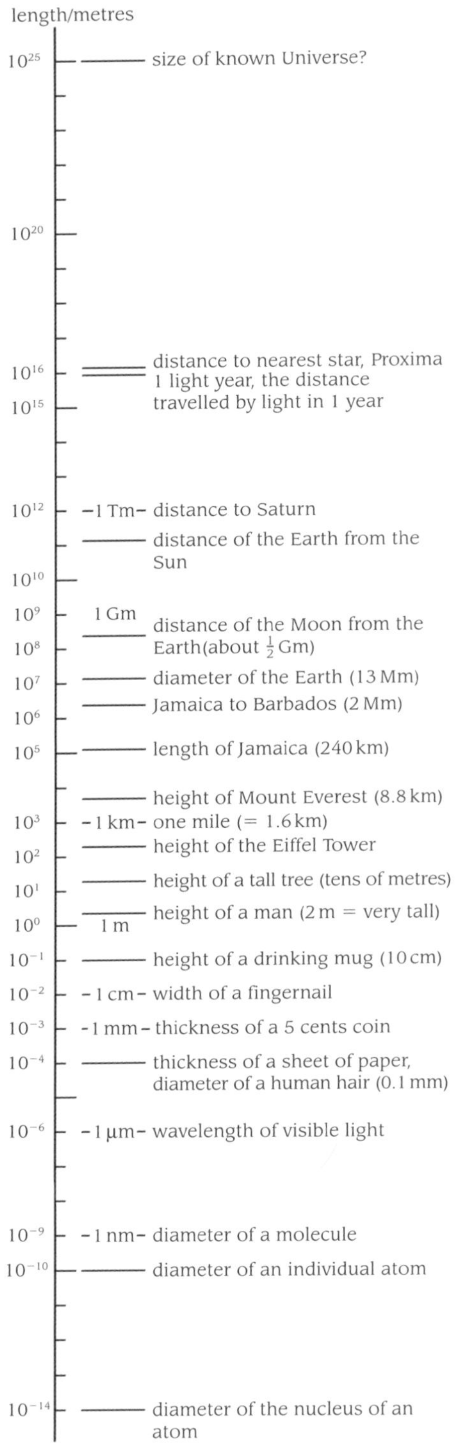

▲ **Figure 2.1.1** Lengths in the Universe

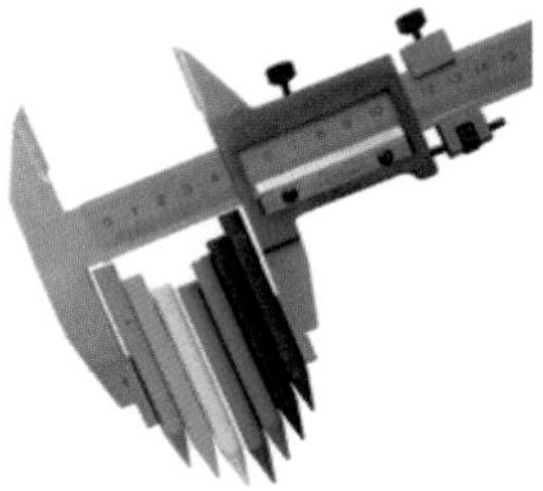

▲ **Figure 2.1.3** Using a vernier calliper

For example, for a wire of diameter of about 1 mm:

- a micrometer measures to the nearest 0.01 mm (accuracy of 0.01 mm in 1 mm, which is 1%)
- vernier callipers measure to the nearest 0.1 mm (accuracy of 0.1 mm in 1 mm, which is 10%).

Therefore, for this diameter wire, a micrometer is a better choice than vernier callipers.

Using a ruler

Figure 2.1.2 shows three ways in which errors are sometimes made when lengths are measured with a ruler.

1 Avoid a gap between the ruler and the object to be measured or you will be guessing the position of both ends of the object on the scale of the ruler.

2 Avoid end errors. Take care to line up the end of the object with the zero of the scale.

3 Avoid parallax errors. Position your eye vertically above the scale.

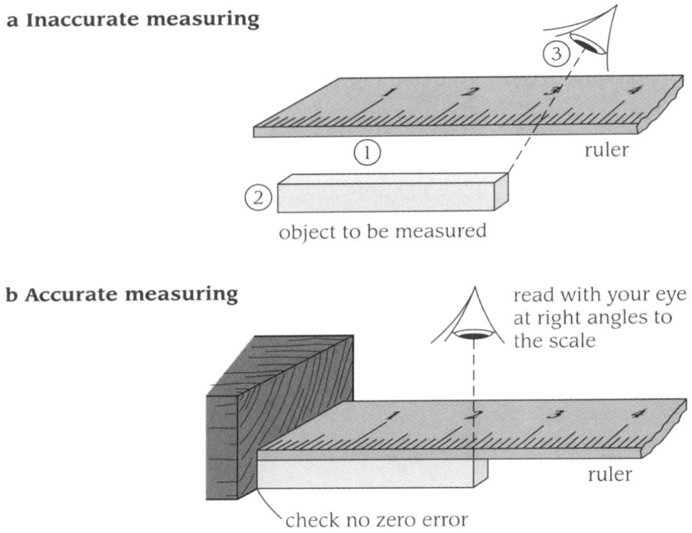

▲ **Figure 2.1.2** Using a ruler

Using vernier callipers

- Find an object to measure and close the jaws of the callipers until they just grip it.

The main scale is usually numbered in centimetres, but has millimetre divisions.

- Read the main scale opposite the zero mark on the sliding jaw, obtaining a reading to 1/10 cm or 1 mm accuracy.

The name vernier refers to the special scale on the sliding jaw, which gives readings to tenths of a millimetre. The vernier scale has 10 divisions, which are slightly smaller than millimetres (actually 0.9 mm). This scale gives readings to 0.1 mm or 0.01 cm.

- To read the vernier scale, look for the mark on the vernier scale, which is exactly lined up with a mark on the main scale.

The number of this mark on the vernier scale is the reading for the tenths of millimetres. In Figure 2.1.4, the fourth vernier mark is lined up giving a reading of 0.4 mm or 0.04 cm to be added to the main scale reading of 3.2 cm.

Diameter = 3.2 cm + 0.04 cm = 3.24 cm.

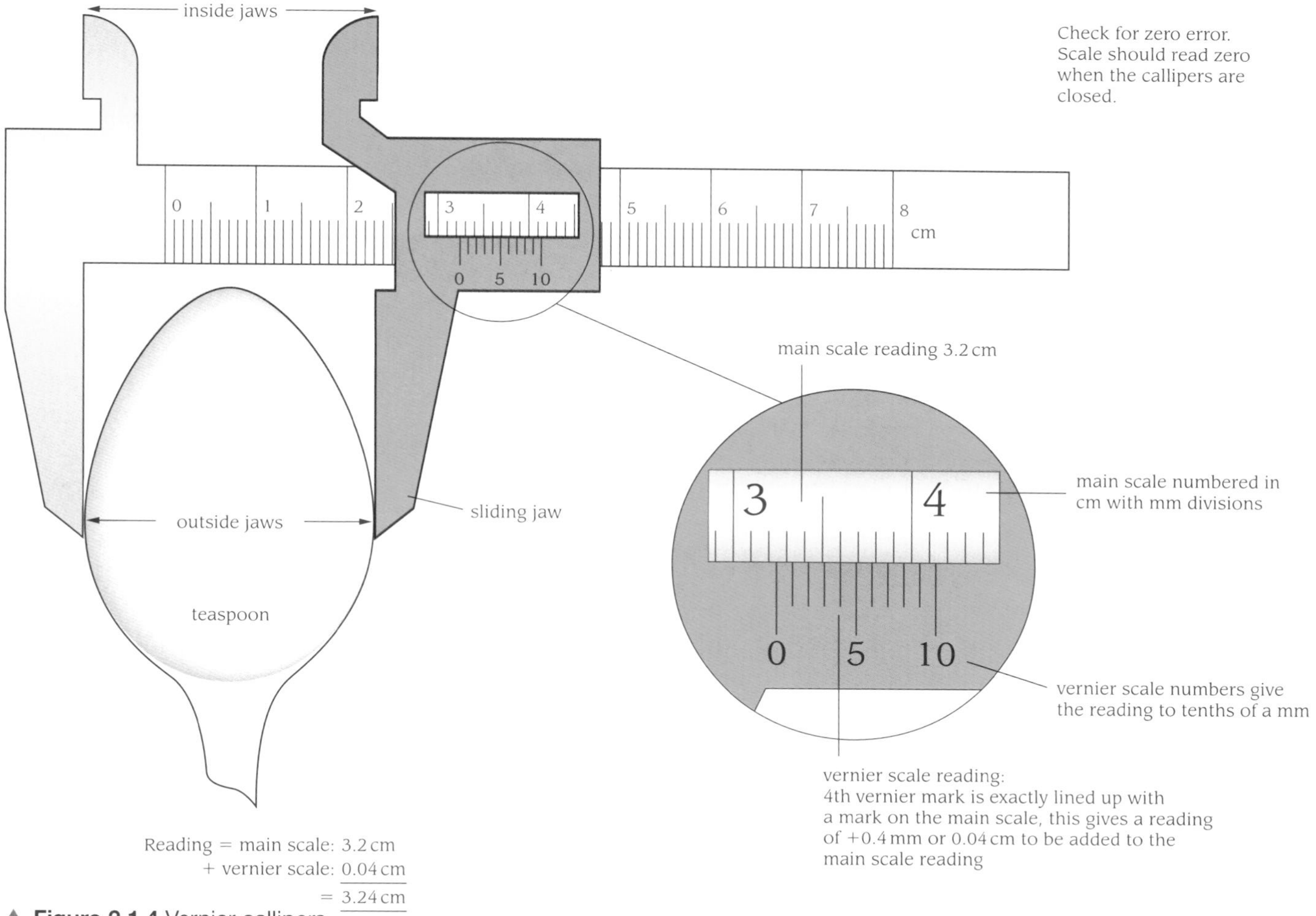

▲ **Figure 2.1.4** Vernier callipers

Using a micrometer screw gauge

- Hold an object between the open jaws and screw them closed using the ratchet.

The ratchet will slip when the grip of the jaws is just tight enough to give an accurate reading.

The main scale, marked along the sleeve, is numbered in mm and has mm and $\frac{1}{2}$ mm marks.

- Read this scale at the edge of the thimble.

The ratchet turns the rotating thimble, one revolution of which opens or closes the gap between the jaws by $\frac{1}{2}$ mm. A scale, which has 50 divisions, is marked around the edge of the thimble. In each complete revolution of the thimble its movement of $\frac{1}{2}$ mm along the sleeve is divided into 50 parts. So each division on the thimble scale is:

$$\frac{0.5\ \text{mm}}{50} = 0.01\ \text{mm, i.e. a hundredth of a millimetre.}$$

- Read the number of hundredths of mm on the thimble scale opposite the centre line of the sleeve scale.

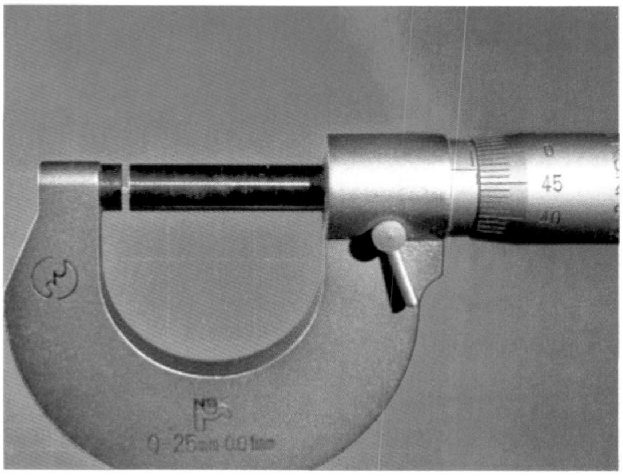

▲ **Figure 2.1.5** A micrometer screw gauge

Worked example

What does the micrometer in Figure 2.1.6 read?

The sleeve scale reads 7.5 mm and the thimble scale reads 35/100 mm = 0.35 mm:

diameter of pencil = 7.5 mm + 0.35 mm = 7.85 mm.

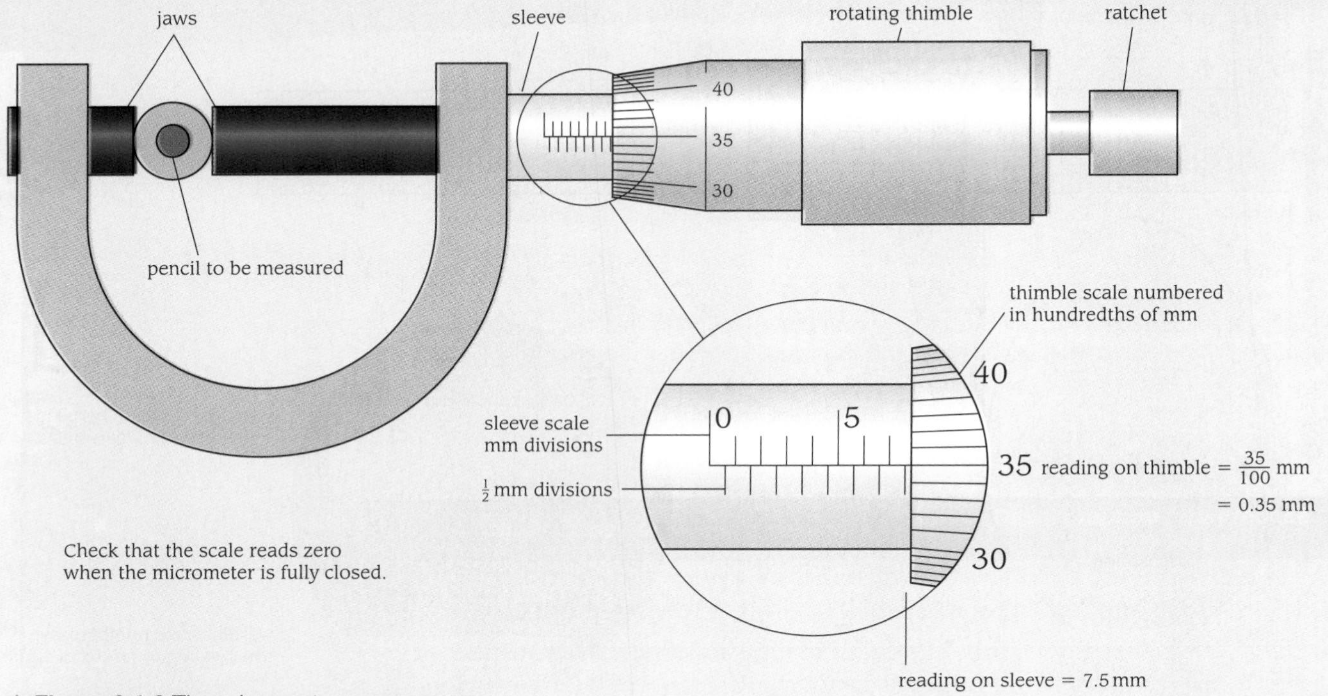

▲ **Figure 2.1.6** The micrometer screw gauge

Units of area

When we need to calculate the area of a surface we can use standard formulae for particular shapes. (For example, rectangle $A = lb$, disc $A = \pi r^2$.) Whatever the shape, the SI unit of area is the square metre, written m^2. Sometimes, in questions on pressure for example, we use square centimetres, written cm^2, and it is often necessary to convert them to square metres.

As there are 100 cm in 1 m,

there are 100 cm × 100 cm = 10 000 cm^2 in 1 m^2.

So 1 m^2 = 10^4 cm^2.

Measuring area

Finding the area of regular shapes by formula

Rectangle:

$$\text{area} = \text{length} \times \text{breadth}$$

In Figure 2.1.7, area = 5 cm × 3 cm

= 15 square centimetres = 15 cm^2

The area of a triangle = $\frac{1}{2}$ × base × height

The area of a disc = π × radius squared = πr^2

The surface area of a sphere = $4\pi \times r^2$

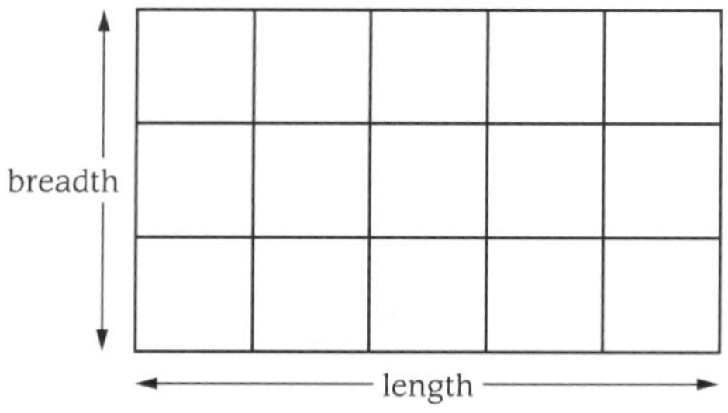

▲ **Figure 2.1.7** The area of a rectangle

Finding the area of irregular shapes

To find the area of an irregular shape, divide it up into small squares of known area and count the squares. When squares are only partly filled, match up pairs which together make a full square. Using smaller squares increases the accuracy of this method.

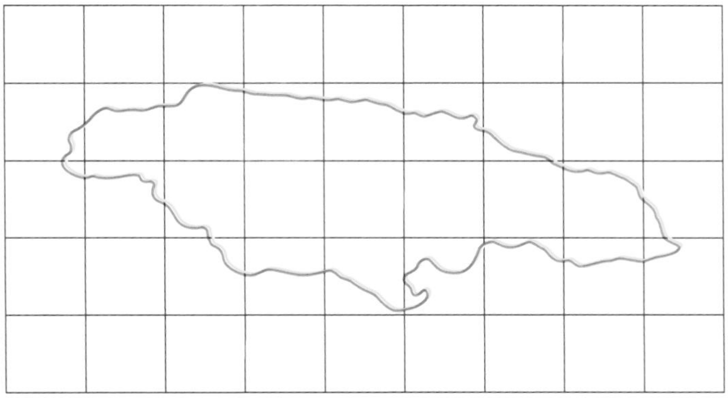

▲ **Figure 2.1.8** Finding the area of Jamaica

Worked example

Measuring the area of an irregular shape

Estimate the area of Jamaica by counting the squares on the map in Figure 2.1.8. The lines are drawn 30 km apart.

The number of full squares is about 12.

Each square has an area $= 30\,\text{km} \times 30\,\text{km} = 900\,\text{km}^2$.

So the area of Jamaica $= 12 \times 900\,\text{km}^2 = 10\,800\,\text{km}^2$.

Units of volume

For regularly shaped solids such as rectangular blocks we can also calculate their volumes using standard formulae. The SI unit of volume is the cubic metre, written m^3. One cubic metre is a rather large volume and gives high values for densities, so we often use cubic centimetres, written cm^3, for practical measuring.

As there are 100 cm in 1 m,

there are $100\,\text{cm} \times 100\,\text{cm} \times 100\,\text{cm} = 1\,000\,000\,\text{cm}^3$ in $1\,\text{m}^3$.

So $1\,\text{m}^3 = 10^6\,\text{cm}^3$.

Measuring volume

Solids and liquids have almost constant volumes but a great variety of shapes. This makes measuring volumes quite difficult except for regular shaped solids such as rectangular blocks, cylinders and spheres. The table summarises the basic methods used for measuring the volumes of solids and liquids.

Volume to be measured	Instruments
Regular shaped solid object	Ruler, callipers or micrometer using a formula
Irregular shaped solid object	Displacement can and measuring cylinder
Liquids (large volumes)	Measuring cylinder
Liquids (small or accurate volumes)	Calibrated burette or flask

The SI unit of volume is the cubic metre (or $1\,\text{m}^3$). The volume of a cube of sides 1 metre is very large and we often use the cubic centimetre (cm^3) as a more convenient unit.

$1\,\text{cm}^3$ is equivalent to 1 millilitre (or 1 ml).

$1\,\text{cm}^3 = 10^{-2}\,\text{m} \times 10^{-2}\,\text{m} \times 10^{-2}\,\text{m} = 10^{-6}\,\text{m}^3$

and $1\,\text{m}^3 = 10^6\,\text{cm}^3 = 1\,000\,000\,\text{cm}^3$.

Finding the volume of regular shaped solids by formula

$$\text{Volume of a rectangular block} = \text{length} \times \text{breadth} \times \text{height}$$

$$V = lbh$$

$$\text{Volume of a cylinder of radius } r = \text{height} \times \text{area of end}$$

$$V = h(\pi r^2)$$

$$\text{Volume of a sphere of radius } r\text{: } V = \tfrac{4}{3}\pi r^3$$

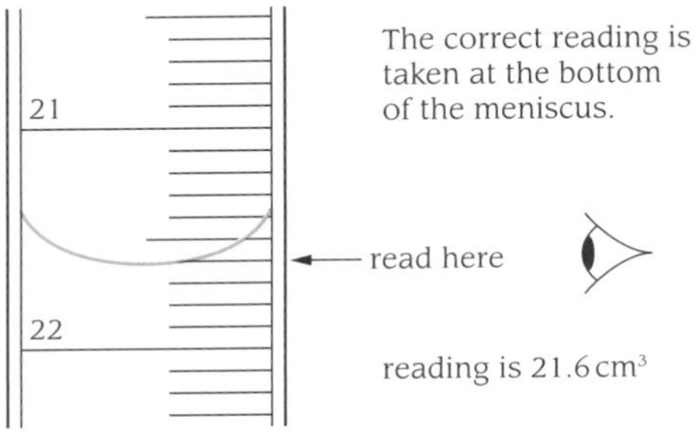

▲ **Figure 2.1.9** Reading a meniscus

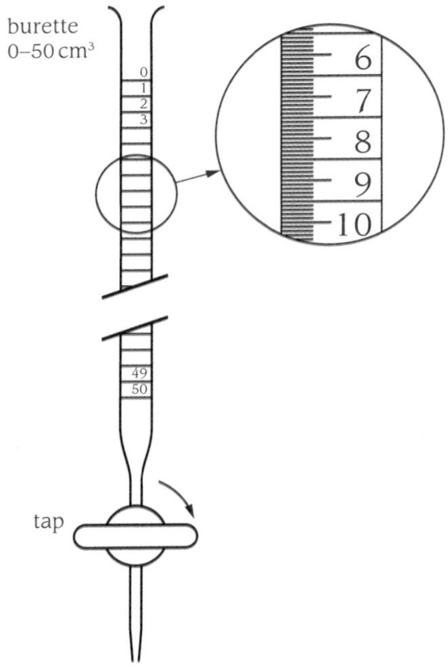

▲ **Figure 2.1.10** Reading a burette

▲ **Figure 2.1.11** Reading the scale on the pipette gives the volume of liquid contained in the pipette.

Measuring the volume of a liquid

Reading a meniscus

Looked at from a side view, the surface of a liquid inside a vertical tube is not a straight line. A liquid surface curves at the edges where the liquid 'wets' the glass. This curved surface is called the meniscus.

Correct readings are taken:

- when the instrument is vertical or resting on a horizontal surface
- when the reading is taken at the bottom of the meniscus, and
- when your eye is level with the meniscus.

Using a burette

- Check that the tap is closed.
- Using a filter funnel in the top, pour in the liquid to be measured to a point above the top zero mark.
- Remove the funnel.
- Carefully open the tap to allow the liquid to run out slowly until the level drops exactly to the zero mark.
- To obtain an accurate volume of liquid, run out liquid until the required reading is reached on the burette. Note that the burette scale reads downwards.

Using a measuring cylinder

Large or small volumes of liquid can be measured using a measuring cylinder but this instrument is less accurate than a burette. Although the scale reads upwards, remember to read the liquid level at the bottom of the meniscus. Note whether the graduations are marked in steps of 1 cm^3, 5 cm^3 or larger.

For accurate readings, check that the measuring cylinder is dry and that it is standing on a level surface.

Measuring the volume of an irregular shaped solid

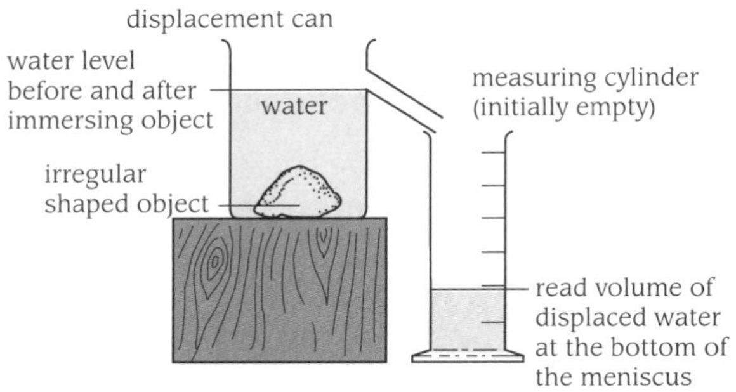

▲ **Figure 2.1.12** Measuring the volume of a small irregular shaped object

A simple method of measuring the volume of any shape or size of solid object uses a **displacement can**.

- Choose a displacement can which is large enough to take the whole object covered with water.
- Fill the can until water overflows from its spout.
- Place an empty measuring cylinder under the overflow spout and then gently lower the object.

The volume of water displaced and collected in the measuring cylinder equals the volume of the solid object.

If no displacement can is available, you can use any large graduated container such as a measuring cylinder, which is wide enough to take the object. Partly fill the measuring cylinder with water and take a reading of the water volume. Insert the object and take another volume reading. The difference between the two readings gives the volume of the irregular shaped object.

Solid objects that float

A metal object such as a brass weight can be used as a 'sinker'. By attaching a sinker, the floating object can be pulled down below the surface of the water in a measuring cylinder or displacement can.

- Find the volume of the sinker alone.
- Find the volume of object plus sinker.
- Subtract readings to find the volume of the object alone.

Summary questions

1 Name two instruments used to measure length.

2 How could you find the volume of an irregularly shaped object that floats?

3 What does a burette measure?

Things to do

- Select the instruments you would use to measure the following items.
- State why you have chosen each instrument and give the range of measurements possible with the instrument and its sensitivity.

a) The thickness of a human hair

b) The diameter of a table-tennis ball

c) The area of a window pane

d) The inside diameter or bore of a water pipe

e) The diameter of a bolt when deciding the size of hole to drill for it

f) The volume of liquid in a juice bottle

g) The volume of a glass stopper

A2.2 Mass, density and time

Mass

The mass of an object, being dependent only on the amount of matter it contains, is the same wherever it is. For example, an astronaut has the same mass on Earth, on the surface of the Moon or inside a spaceship. He needs the same size push to get him moving wherever he is.

Units of mass

The SI unit of mass is the kilogram. Note that the symbol is kg with a lower case 'k' for kilo (= 1000). There is a standard 1 kg mass made of platinum–iridium alloy kept at Sèvres near Paris at the International Office of Weights and Measures. All other masses are, in theory, measured by comparison with this standard mass.

▼ Common multiples and submultiples of the gram

Unit	Equivalent in: kilograms (kg)	grams (g)	
1 tonne (t)	1000 kg = 10^3 kg	10^6 g	
1 kilogram (kg)	SI unit of mass	1000 g	= 10^3 g
1 gram (g)	0.001 kg = 10^{-3} kg	1 g	= 10^0 g
1 milligram (mg)	10^{-6} kg	0.001 g	= 10^{-3} g
1 microgram (μg)	10^{-9} kg	10^{-6} g	

Objectives

By the end of this topic you will be able to:

- use a beam balance to measure mass
- calculate density using density $= \frac{\text{mass}}{\text{volume}} = \rho \frac{m}{V}$
- define density as mass per unit volume
- measure density of liquids and both regular and irregular solids
- investigate the factors which might affect the period of a simple pendulum.

Exam tip

In everyday language we talk about mass and weight as though they are the same thing. They are not. Weight is a force. The weight of something on Earth is a measure of how hard its mass is pulled downwards by the Earth's gravity. You will learn more about weight in unit A4.

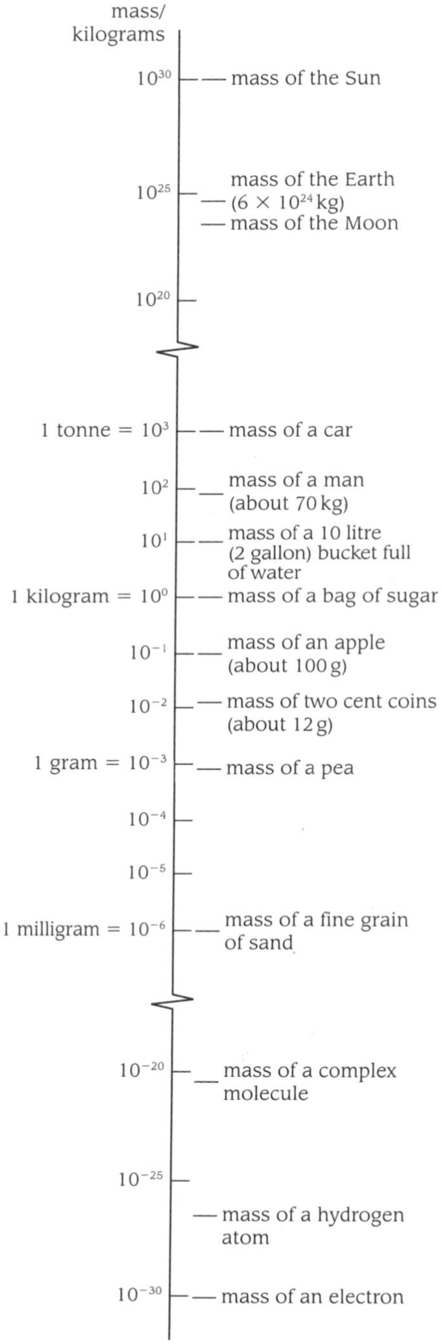

▲ **Figure 2.2.2** Masses in the Universe

Measuring mass

Figure 2.2.1 shows a balance being used to find an unknown mass by comparing it with a standard mass. The beam is balanced when both masses are the same. Mass can also be found using an electronic balance or a spring balance.

These ways of measuring mass actually measure weight, that is how hard something is pulled by gravity.

The beam balance works because if the masses on each side are the same, they are pulled equally hard, so the beam balances.

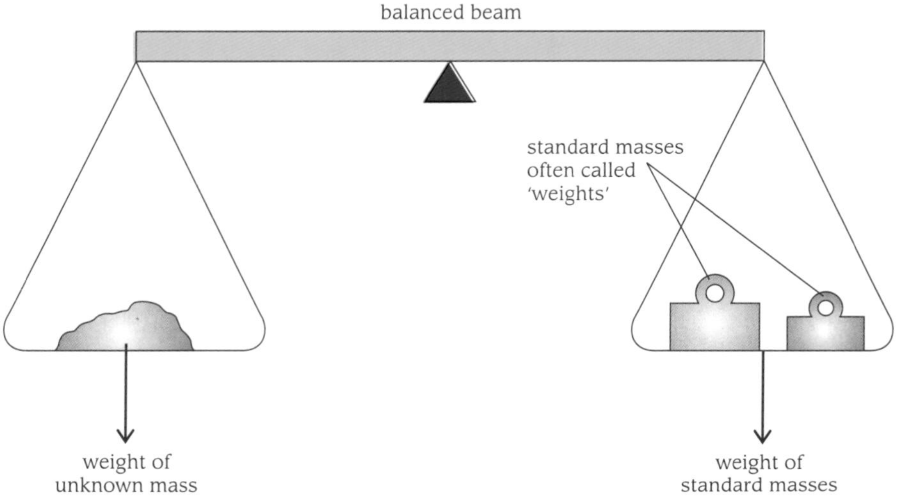

▲ **Figure 2.2.1** Finding an unknown mass

The spring balance and electronic balance both record how hard an object is pulled by the Earth's gravity. The larger the object's mass, the harder it is pulled. Away from Earth, where the gravity is different, the balances would give the wrong reading.

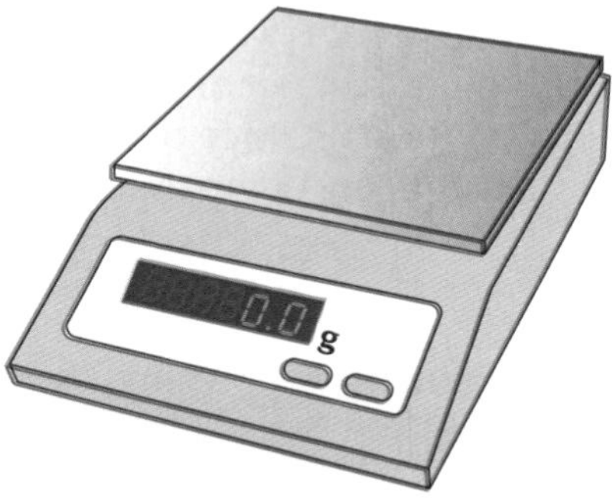

▲ **Figure 2.2.3** Electronic balance

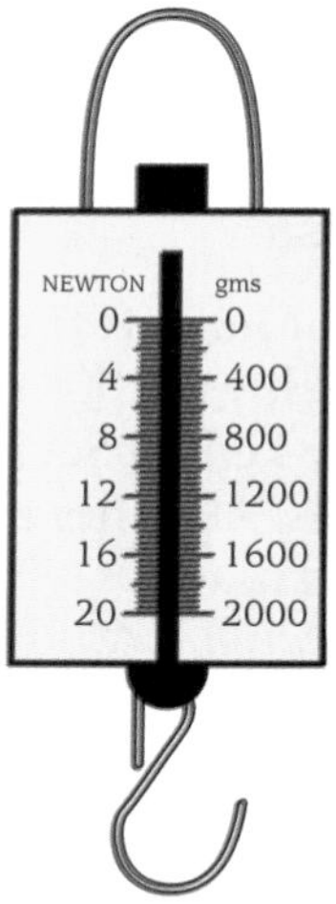

▲ **Figure 2.2.4** Spring balance

To find the mass of a liquid, measure the mass of an empty, dry container and subtract this from the mass of the same container with the liquid in it.

Density

The samples in Figure 2.2.5 have equal volumes of 1 cubic centimetre each. When we compare the masses of equal volumes of substances we are comparing their **densities**.

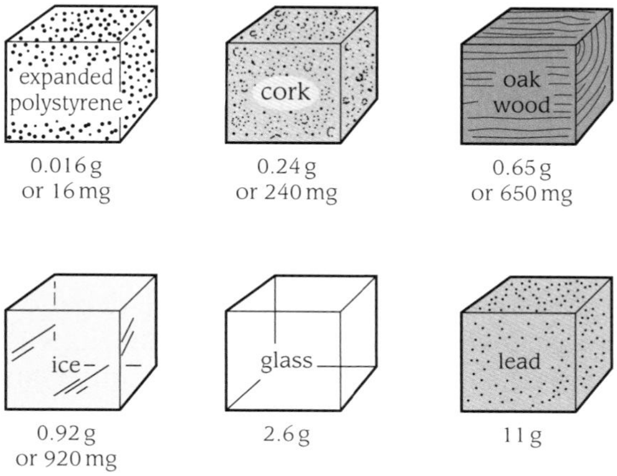

▲ **Figure 2.2.5** Comparing masses of a cubic centimetre of various substances

In dense substances matter is compressed or closely packed, but in a substance of low density matter is loosely packed or expanded (as in expanded polystyrene).

The density of a substance is defined as its mass per unit volume.

$$\text{density} = \frac{\text{mass}}{\text{volume}} \qquad \rho = \frac{m}{V}$$

- The Greek letter ρ (rho) is the symbol used for density but d is also used sometimes.
- The units of density in SI are kilogram per cubic metre or kg m^{-3}.
- It is often convenient to use gram per cubic centimetre or g cm^{-3}.

Changing density

Density tells us about how the matter in a substance is arranged. The density only changes if the substance changes. So, pure water has exactly the same density whether it is in a cup or in a swimming pool. It only changes if something else, such as salt, is mixed in with the water. (Or if the water is heated or cooled – see Unit B8.)

Measuring density

All that is needed to find the density of a particular substance is the measurement of the mass and volume of an object made of that substance.

If you are asked to describe how to find the density of a substance, explain how you would measure both the volume and the mass of a suitable sample and why you would use the instruments you suggest.

To find the volume of an irregular solid, place the solid in a displacement can and measure the volume of the water it displaces. This is also the volume of the irregular solid.

To measure the density of a liquid, find the volume using a measuring cylinder or burette, and the mass by subtracting the mass of the empty container from the mass of the container with the liquid in it.

Worked example

Calculating density

A glass stopper has a volume of 16 cm^3 and a mass of 40 g. Calculate the density of glass in g cm^{-3} and kg m^{-3}.

Using: $\rho = \frac{m}{V}$

$$\rho = \frac{m}{V} = \frac{40\text{ g}}{16\text{ cm}^3} = 2.5\text{ g cm}^{-3}$$

Converting the units:

$$\rho = \frac{m}{V} = \frac{40\text{ g}}{16\text{ cm}^3}$$
$$= \frac{4.0 \times 10^{-2}\text{ kg}}{1.6 \times 10^{-5}\text{ m}^{-3}}$$
$$= 2.5 \times 10^{3}\text{ kg m}^{-3}$$

The density of the glass is 2.5 g cm^{-3} or 2.5×10^3 kg m^{-3}.

Worked example

Calculating volume

Calculate the volume of a block of expanded polystyrene of mass 400 g if its density is 16 kg m^{-3}.

The mass (400 g) must be converted to kilograms to match the density units:

m = 400 g = 0.40 kg.

The rearranged density formula gives:

$$V = \frac{m}{\rho} = \frac{0.40}{16} = 0.025\text{ m}^3$$

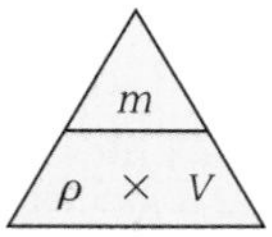

Worked example

Calculating mass

Calculate the mass of a gold coin of volume 2.1 cm^3.
(The density of gold is 19 g cm^{-3}.)

Rearranging the density formula we have

$m = \rho \times V = 19 \times 2.1 = 40$ g

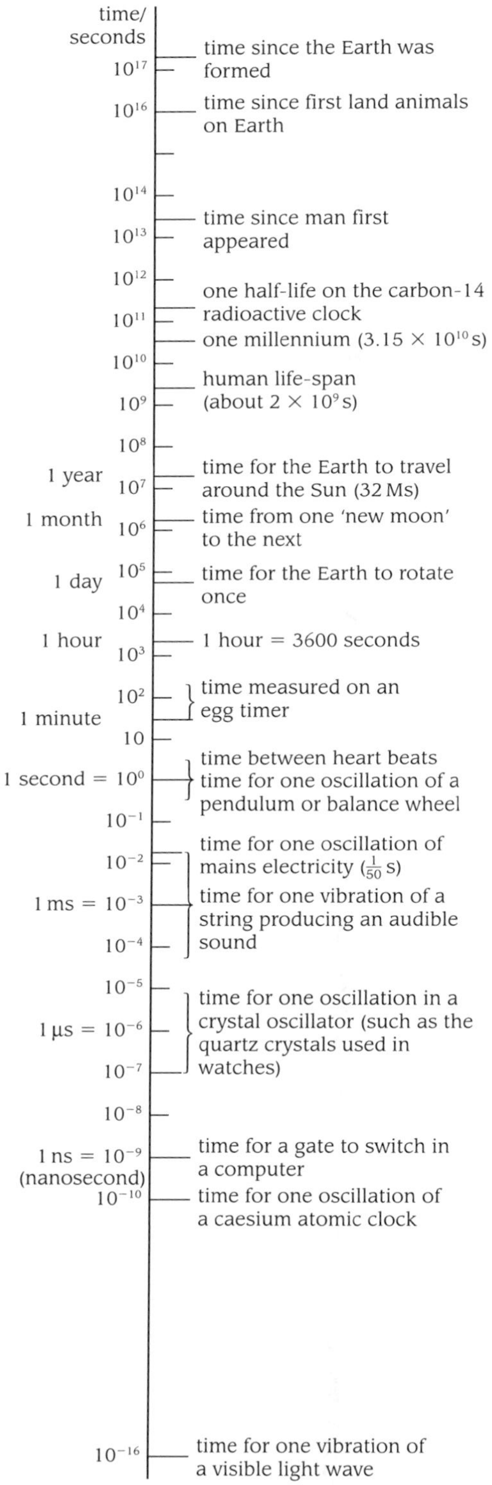

▲ **Figure 2.2.6** Some times and some 'clocks'

Things to do

- Select the instruments you would use to measure the following items.
- State why you have chosen each instrument and give the range of measurements possible with the instrument and its sensitivity.
  a) The density of chocolate
  b) The density of milk
  c) The density of a wine bottle cork stopper

Time

Methods of telling the time, or measuring time, all depend on some regular event, either natural or devised. The Sun has provided us with a natural clock that counts in years, as the Earth travels in orbit around it, and in days, as the Earth rotates on its own axis. The sundial was devised to divide up the day using the sun-cast shadow of a rod as a slowly moving pointer across a dial. But we needed clocks that ran in the dark and clocks that were accurate. As technology developed we needed clocks of ever greater accuracy until now our computers need clocks that measure time in fractions of a millionth of a second.

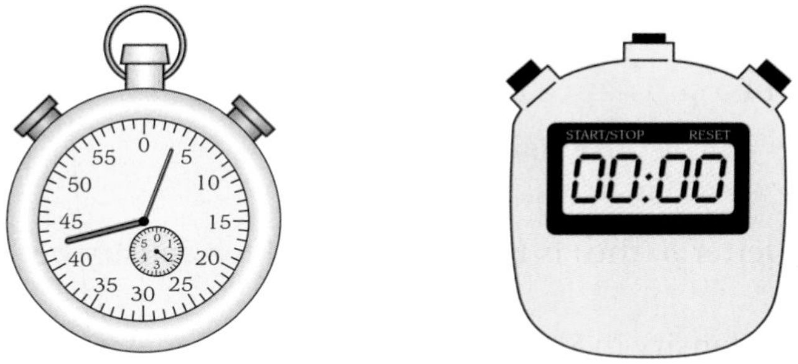

▲ **Figure 2.2.7** Analogue and digital stopwatches

Definition of the second

- We now use an atomic clock to give us an unvarying time standard against which other clocks are checked.
- The atomic clock chosen is the caesium-133 atom, which emits electromagnetic radiation of a precise and unvarying frequency.

The second is defined as exactly 9 192 631 770 time periods of the caesium-133 atomic oscillator.

(You do not need to know this definition!)

Measuring time

Different kinds of clocks are needed because of the wide range of times that we try to measure. Some particularly useful 'clocks' are the following:

a) The oscillations of a crystal such as the quartz crystal used in watches

b) The oscillations of electrons in an electric circuit such as the 50 hertz frequency of the mains electricity supply, which is used to drive clocks and electric motors at a constant speed

c) The rotation of the Earth on its axis

Time intervals, Δt

On many occasions in physics experiments we shall need to measure time intervals rather than the time of day or 'clock time'. A time interval is the length of time between the beginning and end of some event.

If we write t as the symbol for the time of day or 'clock time' then we need a different symbol for a time interval.

The symbol Δt is used for a time interval or change of time.

The Δ symbol is a Greek capital D, which we use to stand for difference. So Δt is the time difference between the beginning and end of an event.

Timing a pendulum

- Set up a pendulum as shown in Figure 2.2.8 with a length l of 50 cm.
- Fix a pointer opposite the position of the bob when it hangs at rest.
- Set the pendulum swinging and check with a protractor that the angle of swing on each side is not more than about 10°. (For a pendulum 50 cm long, the bob should be displaced no more than 10 cm to one side.)
- Sit in front of the pendulum so that your eye is level with the bob and at right angles to its swing.
- As the bob passes the pointer, start the stopwatch.
- When it next passes the pointer going in the same direction, stop the stopwatch and read the time interval.

For a 50 cm long pendulum the correct time for one oscillation, which you have just measured, is 1.4 seconds. How accurate was your timing?

- Repeat the timing several times.
- By how much do your measurements vary?
- How could you reduce the effect of the human reaction time and so obtain a more accurate result?
- Try timing twenty oscillations instead of just one.
- Repeat the timing of twenty oscillations and find an average value.

The time for one complete oscillation of a pendulum is called its period, T. Timing 20 or 50 oscillations and dividing by 20 or 50, gives a more accurate value of T because the error in timing due to your reaction time is also divided by 20 or 50.

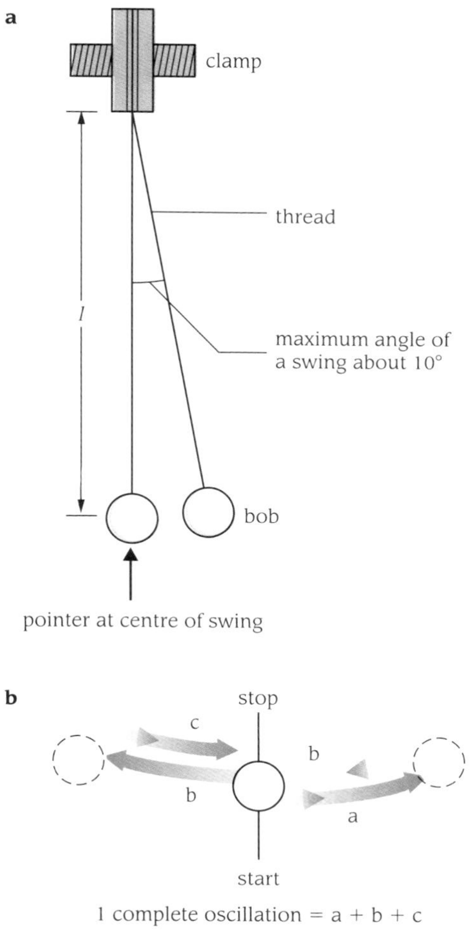

▲ **Figure 2.2.8** Timing a pendulum

What factors affect the period of a pendulum?

- Using the methods explained above, investigate how the following factors affect the period of a pendulum.
  1. The length of the pendulum from the point of suspension to the centre of the bob.
  2. The mass of the pendulum bob (length kept constant).
  3. The amplitude (or angle) of the swing of the pendulum.
- Tabulate the results in a table, varying the length, the mass of the bob and the angle of swing each in turn.
- In the case of the length of the pendulum, calculate also the square root of the length.
- Draw graphs of T against l, of T^2 against l, and of T against $\sqrt{l}$, where T is the period of the pendulum and l is the length.
- What does your graph show?

Length l/m	0.5	0.4	0.3
Time for 20 oscillations t_1/s			
Time for 20 oscillations t_2/s			
Average time 20 oscillations t/s			
Period T/s			
Period² T^2/s²			
Square root of length $\sqrt{l}/\sqrt{m}$			

Results of your investigations

1 The straight-line graphs of T^2 against l and T against $\sqrt{l}$, are both ways of showing that the period T is proportional to $\sqrt{l}$, i.e., if we make a pendulum four times longer it takes twice as long to make each oscillation.

2 Changing the mass should have no effect on the period.

3 For accurate results, keep oscillations small, less than about 10°.

! Key fact

The period T of a pendulum can be calculated from the formula:

$$T = 2\pi\sqrt{\frac{l}{g}}$$

where l is the length of the pendulum and g (= $10\,\mathrm{m\,s^{-2}}$) is the acceleration due to gravity.

Summary questions

1 Give two differences between mass and weight.

2 Give the formula for density.

3 How would making a pendulum longer affect its period of oscillation?

Objectives

By the end of this topic you will be able to:

- discuss possible sources of error in any measurements you make including those made with digital instruments
- suggest ways of reducing errors in your measurements
- assess the suitability of instruments for minimising errors on the basis of their sensitivity, accuracy and range.

A2.3 Errors

Sources of errors

Errors don't just happen when someone makes a mistake reading an instrument. The error in a measurement is the difference between the value someone reads and the true value. Most errors are either random or systematic.

Random errors

Random errors average out over several readings. All the readings will be scattered around the true value. Random errors occur:

- because the quantity being measured may not be uniform, e.g. a tree trunk circumference may vary in different places
- where a human response factor is involved, e.g. when timing a pendulum, or recording when a ball hits the ground you may sometimes stop the stopwatch too early, sometimes too late.

Systematic errors

Systematic errors do not average out over several readings. All the readings will be displaced from the true value. Systematic errors may be difficult to spot and may even be dangerous. They may occur because:

- an instrument has an incorrect zero setting, e.g. the pointer on a meter always reads too high or too low
- an instrument is incorrectly calibrated, e.g. when a clock runs too fast

- a thermometer reads too low
- the measuring equipment itself changes the quantity being measured
- reading an instrument from an incorrect position introduces a parallax error.

Non-linear scales

Non-linear scales have graduations that are not evenly spaced. They are difficult to read accurately and values in-between graduations are hard to estimate. Avoid scales like these if you can!

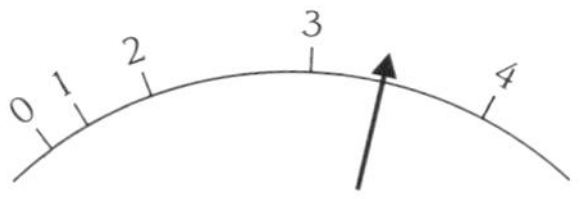

▲ **Figure 2.3.1** A non-linear scale

> **Key fact**
>
> What you should do when taking readings:
> - Record readings in a table.
> - Write down all readings, not just average values.
> - Include zero readings from instruments.
> - Always give the units in which the measurements are made.
> - Use a consistent number of decimal places for your readings. For example, measurements of length read from a millimetre scale might be: 12.0 mm, 11.5 mm, 12.5 mm, 11.0 mm, etc.

How to make your measurements more accurate

- Random errors can be reduced by taking more readings of the same measurement.

  An average or mean value is more accurate and more reliable than a single reading.

$$\text{mean value} = \frac{\text{sum of individual readings}}{\text{number of readings taken}}$$

- Use an instrument that has a suitable range and precision. Such an instrument will allow you to read its scale more accurately, giving more significant figures in your reading and avoiding guessing values between scale graduations.
- Choose an instrument or a measuring scale where the values you measure cover as much of the range as possible. So if you are measuring currents that vary from 0 A to 0.9 A, a scale of 0 to 1 A would be a good choice, a scale from 0 to 10 A would not be.

The range chosen for the current measurement in Figure 2.3.2 (0 to 5 A) was unsuitable because the deflection of the pointer was too small. This range was not sensitive enough and introduced a larger error or uncertainty in the reading. The reading (0.5 A) is accurate to only 1 significant figure. If a 0 to 1 A range had been selected so that, on the upper scale, the values represented 0.2, 0.4 up to 1.0 A, the pointer would have moved half way across the scale and the reading would have been accurate to 2 significant figures, perhaps 0.52 A.

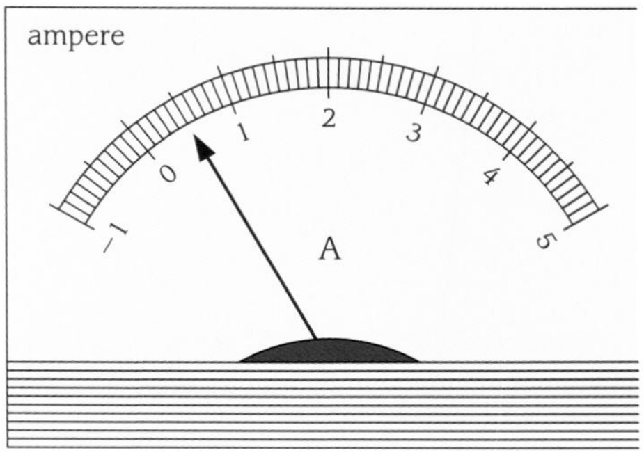

▲ **Figure 2.3.2** A linear scale

How to avoid or reduce systematic errors

- Read instruments correctly, e.g. avoiding parallax errors. If two people read the same instrument, ensure they read from the same place.
- Use more than one technique to measure the same quantity.
- Check instruments by substituting other ones for the same measurement.
- Check instruments by looking for zero errors. This can apply to all pointer-and-scale analogue instruments as well as to digital instruments.

Random versus systematic errors

- A result is described as 'accurate' if it is free from systematic errors.
- A result is said to be 'precise' if the random error is small.

A digital reading is not exact just because it gives a numerical value. There is always an uncertainty about the next digit, which does not show. The value shown on the scale in Figure 2.3.4 could be anywhere between 3.355 and 3.365. So the error in this reading is ± 0.005. You do not need to show errors in your readings, but you do need to be able to say where and why errors might occur.

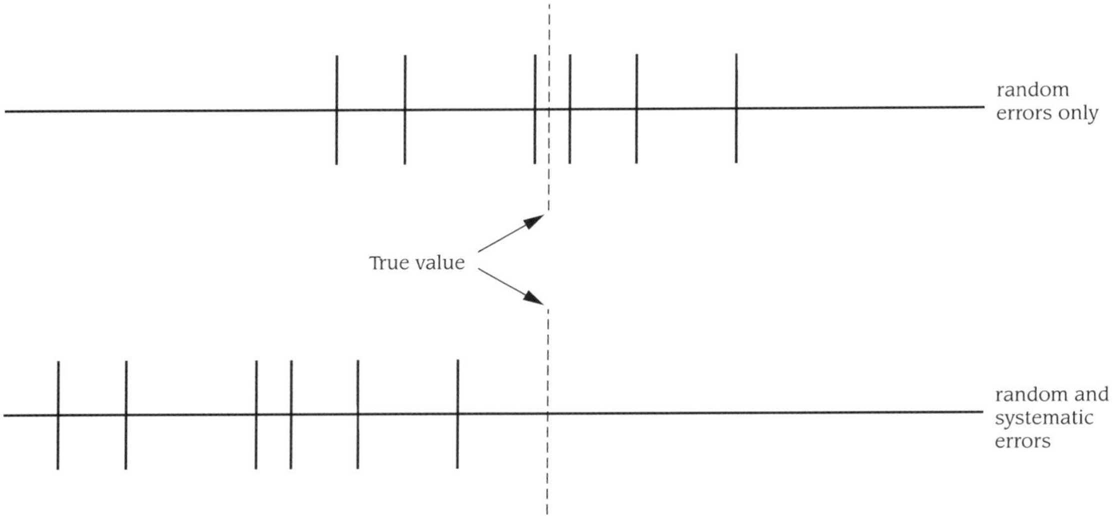

▲ **Figure 2.3.3** Random and systematic error distributions

▲ **Figure 2.3.4** A digital scale

Summary questions

1. Give one example of something that might cause a systematic error.
2. Explain what is meant by a precise reading.

A3 Graphs

Graphical representation of readings or data provides a clear, easily interpreted visual report of an experimental investigation.

Graphs can show trends and relationships between physical quantities, which are not always immediately obvious from a list of figures.

Graphs are an important aspect of analysing and reporting all experimental and research work in science and it is important that you know and understand how to draw a good graph and interpret it correctly.

A3.1 How to draw a graph

Objectives

By the end of this topic you will be able to:

- plot, interpret and use graphs of experimental data
- draw a line of best fit for a set of plotted values, and understand the reasons why a 'best fit' line gives the best average value of the gradient or intercept
- determine the gradient and intercept of a straight-line graph.

What to plot?

- Sometimes you are told what to plot, e.g. the instruction might be to plot displacement against time. In this case, you plot displacement on the vertical or y-axis and time on the horizontal or x-axis.
- When the choice is up to you, there is a general rule that the independent variable is plotted on the x-axis and the dependent variable on the y-axis. The independent variable is the quantity that changes independently itself like time or that causes the other variable to change. So time is always plotted on the x-axis. The dependent variable changes in response to the change in the other variable.
- Sometimes what we decide to plot is chosen so that it will produce a straight-line graph. A straight-line graph is easier to recognise and to obtain results from, e.g. when investigating Boyle's law for the volume of a gas (page 144) we choose to plot volume against 1/pressure to give a straight-line graph confirming the inverse relationship between volume and pressure.
- Label your graph to state clearly what is plotted against what.

Key fact

Plotting the points

- It must be clear to your teacher or the examiner exactly where each point is plotted after you have drawn the best fit line on your graph.
- Use a cross (either + or ×) or draw a small circle around your point ⊙ to make it clear. The advantage of using a + cross is that each line of the cross can be drawn in line with the exact value read from an axis.
- If one or two points obviously look as if they do not follow the line of the other points, check that you have plotted them correctly and possibly go back to your experiment and take those readings again.
- If there are big gaps in your plotted points, particularly at one end of the graph, attempt to obtain more readings from your experiment to plug those gaps.

Choosing sensible scales for the axes

- It is important to use as much of the graph paper as possible when plotting a graph. As a guide, if you can double either scale without your points going off the page, you should. This might involve turning the page round through 90°.
- Scales should always be easy to use and the values of intermediate lines on the graph paper easy to calculate. Avoid any multiples of awkward numbers like 3 for scale divisions and be careful when small divisions are worth 2.
- Label both axes with the physical quantity and with its units, e.g. time/s or velocity/m s^{-1}.

Summary questions

1 Which axis would you use for an independent variable?

A3.2 Drawing the 'best fit' straight line

- Using a ruler and a sharp pencil, draw a straight line that best represents the trend of the points you have plotted. This may not pass through every point but it is more important that points slightly off the straight line are scattered symmetrically on both sides of the line, all along the line.
- If $y = 0$ when $x = 0$ and no possible measurement error is involved, then the best fit line should be chosen to pass exactly through the origin.

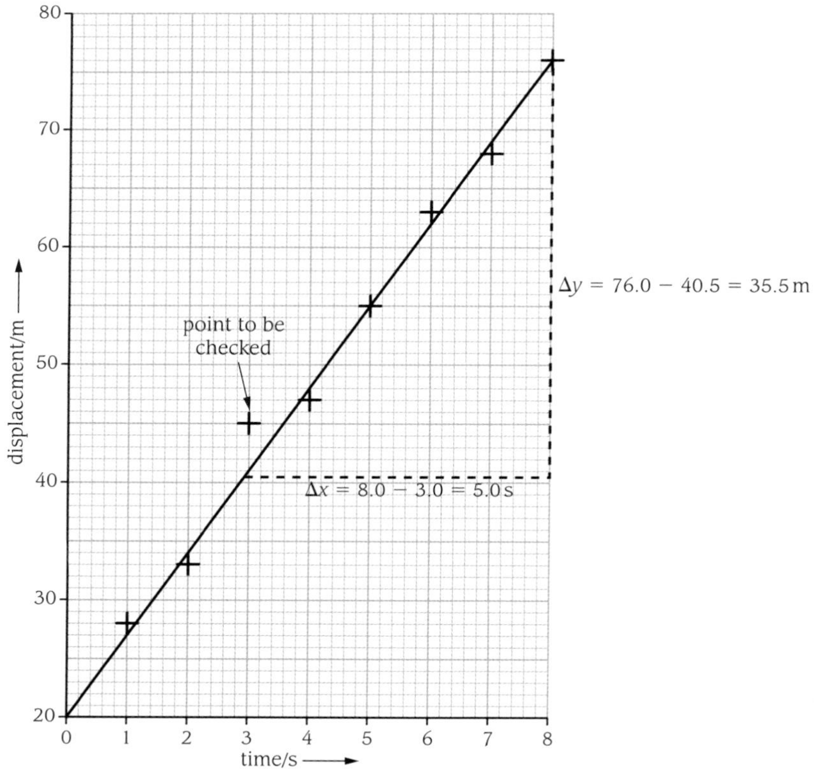

▲ **Figure 3.2.1** Graph of displacement against time. Note: there is an initial displacement of 20 at time = 0 s.

Why do we use a 'best fit' line?

- Drawing a 'best fit' line is a process which finds a good average from a set of values which have some random variations.
- It is better than an arithmetic mean because it can ignore results which are too far off the straight line and give greater weighting to those which fit it well.
- It can identify results which are obviously incorrect and allow the readings to be repeated or checked.
- It provides an accurate method of extracting numerical results from a set of data.

▼ Data for the displacement against time graph

independent variable: x-axis — *dependent variable: y-axis*

Time/s	Displacement/m
0	20.0
1.0	28.0
2.0	33.0
3.0	45.0*
4.0	47.0
5.0	55.0
6.0	63.0
7.0	68.0
8.0	76.0

*If possible, this experimental value should be checked as the point lies too far off the 'best fit' straight line.

Summary questions

1 How could drawing a line of 'best-fit' be used to help identify incorrect readings?

A3.3 Finding the gradient of a graph

Why do we often want to find the gradient of a graph?

- The gradient often gives the numerical value of a quantity that is required, e.g. if we plot displacement (y-axis) against time (x-axis), the gradient gives the velocity.
- Draw a large triangle against the straight line.
- Write down the values you obtain from your graph for Δy and Δx. In an examination, marks may be awarded for these.
- Make sure you show the units of the gradient in your answer. The units of the gradient are the units of the y-axis divided by the units of the x-axis, so for the displacement–time graph in Figure 3.2.1, the units of the gradient will be m/s or $\mathrm{m\,s^{-1}}$.

Key fact

When finding a gradient

- The sides of the triangle represent the changes: Δy and Δx.
- It should not be possible to double the length of both Δy and Δx. If you can, your triangle is too small for best accuracy.
- It helps to select exact scale graduations giving easy-to-read values on the x-axis as you will be dividing by the value of Δx.

$$\text{gradient} = \frac{\text{change in quantity on } y\text{-axis}}{\text{change in quantity on } x\text{-axis}}$$

$$\text{gradient} = \frac{\Delta y}{\Delta x} = \frac{\Delta\text{displacement}}{\Delta\text{time}}$$

$$\text{gradient} = \frac{76.0 - 40.5}{8.0 - 3.0} = \frac{35.5\,\text{m}}{5.0\,\text{s}}$$

$$\text{gradient} = \text{velocity} = 7.1\,\mathrm{m\,s^{-1}}$$

Summary questions

1 Why should a large triangle be drawn to calculate the gradient?

A3.4 Finding an intercept on a graph

Intercepts are the values obtained where the graph cuts an axis.

- The reading obtained from the y-axis intercept is the value of the y-variable when the x-variable is zero, e.g. the value of the velocity recorded at time zero.
- The reading obtained from the x-axis intercept is the value of the x-variable when the y-variable is zero, e.g. the time at which the velocity became zero.
- You may have to extend the line drawn on your graph so that it cuts an axis. This process is called extrapolation.
- A warning! The axes of your graph must start at the origin. If the scale does not start at zero, the value you read will not be the intercept.

Key fact

Data obtained from the graph of velocity against time

Intercepts

- *y*-intercept = value of velocity at time t = zero.
- *y*-intercept = 36.0 m s^{-1}.
- *x*-intercept = value of time when velocity reaches zero.
- *x*-intercept = 3.25 s.

Area under the graph

- This area is triangular.
- Area = $\frac{1}{2}$ × height × base
  $\frac{1}{2}$ × height = average velocity
  base = time taken to stop
- Area = average velocity × time
  = distance travelled.
- Area = $\frac{1}{2}$ × 36.0 m s^{-1} × 3.25 s
  = 58.5 m.
- Note that by using the values on the scales in seconds and m s^{-1}, we obtain the distance travelled in metres.

Counting squares

- If you count the 1 cm squares under this graph, each square, 1 cm × 1 cm would represent 5 m s^{-1} × 0.5 s, or 2.5 m.
- There are about 23 1 cm^2 squares.
- The distance travelled = 23 × 2.5
  = 57.5 m.

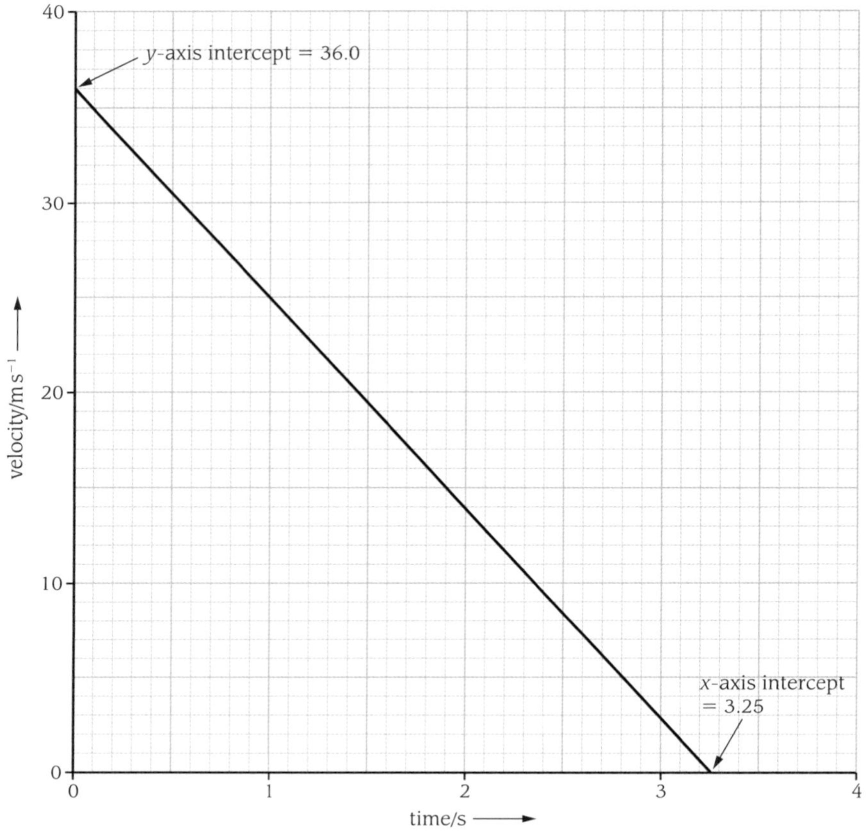

▲ **Figure 3.4.1** Graph of velocity against time

Summary questions

1 What does the *y*-intercept on a distance–time graph give?

A3.5 Finding the area under a graph

The area under a graph can sometimes give useful information, e.g. the area under a speed or velocity against time graph gives the distance travelled.

- For straight-line graphs, such as Figure 3.5.1, divide the area into rectangles and triangles and find the area of each.
- For curved graphs count squares and estimate parts of squares making up the equivalent of whole squares.
- When you count squares, you must multiply the number of squares by a scale factor to give the value of the total area in correct units. The scale factor depends on the scales used on each axis.

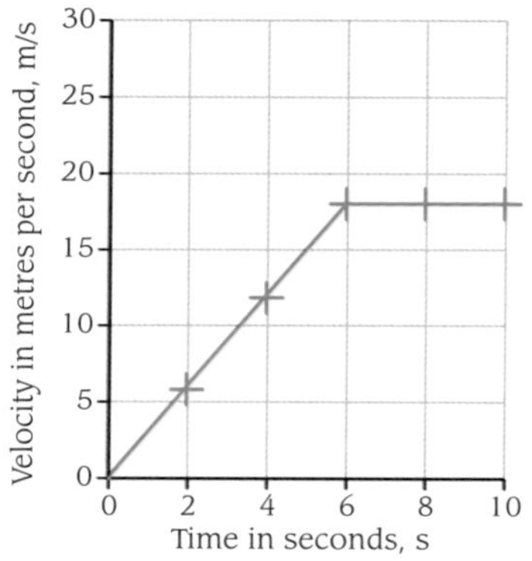

▲ **Figure 3.5.1** Distance–time graph

Summary questions

1 Describe two ways you could find the area under a graph.

2 Which way would you use for a curved graph?

A3.6 Drawing curved graphs

If you plot your values on a graph and they seem to make a curve, not a straight line, do not join up the dots with straight lines. Instead, draw a smooth curve, which may not pass exactly through every point.

- Your smooth curve shows the trend in the readings. A flexicurve or 'French curve' may help you draw a smooth curve.
- Check readings that do not fall exactly on the curve.

Interpreting a curved graph

The graph of the motion of a falling object in Figure 3.6.1 shows how its velocity (measured downwards) changes with time.

What can we deduce from this graph?

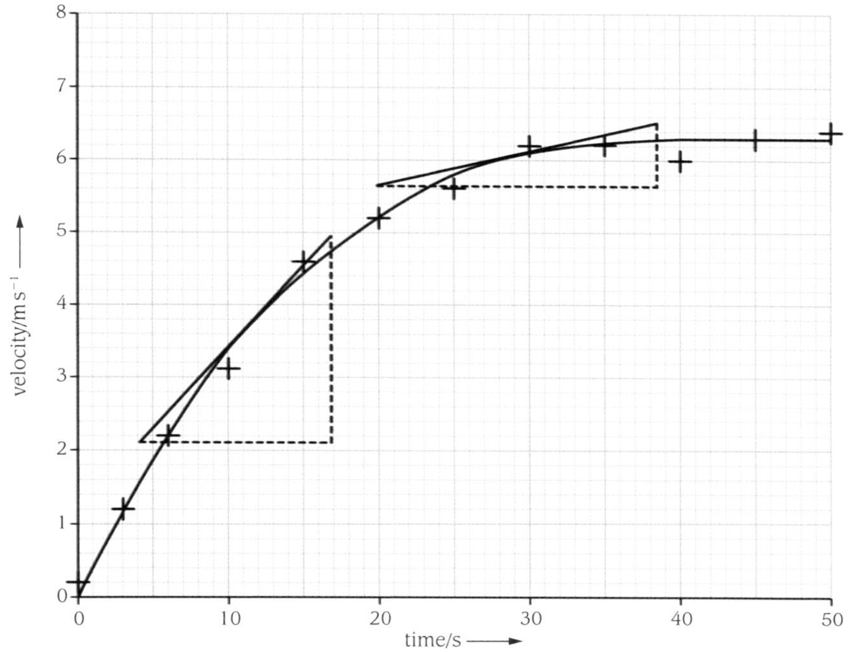

Figure 3.6.1 Graph of velocity against time

Gradient

You do not need to be able to find the gradient of a curve.

The gradient of the curve in Figure 3.6.1 changes. Lines, called tangents, drawn against the curve can be used to find the gradient at any particular point. The gradient of the curve in Figure 3.6.1 gradually decreases to zero.

$$\text{gradient} = \frac{\text{change of velocity}}{\text{change of time}} = \frac{\Delta v}{\Delta t} = \text{acceleration}$$

We can conclude that the acceleration of the falling object decreases to zero. This is an illustration of a falling object reaching its terminal (maximum) velocity.

Summary questions

1 Does the gradient of a curved graph remain constant or change?

▼ Data for the curved velocity against time graph

independent variable: x-axis Time/s	*dependent variable: y-axis* Velocity/m s^{-1}
0.0	0.2
3.0	1.2
6.0	2.2
10.0	3.1
15.0	4.6
20.0	5.2
25.0	5.6
30.0	6.2
35.0	6.2
40.0	6.0
45.0	6.3
50.0	6.4

Key fact

Drawing conclusions from graphs

- When you have drawn your graph it is important to draw a conclusion and state what it shows.
- The fact that a graph is a straight line confirms a directly proportional relationship between the two quantities plotted on the axes, **provided the graph passes through the origin.**
- A curved graph tells you that the quantity represented by its gradient changes in a certain manner. (See the curved graph in Figure 3.6.1.)
- The gradient or intercept found by taking values from the graph will be a conclusion. It is important to give these values their correct units.
- Your conclusion might involve a comparison with an expected theory or value. For example, how does your value for the acceleration of a freely falling object compare with the accepted value of 9.8 m s^{-2}?

Practice exam-style questions

1 Read this micrometer screw gauge.

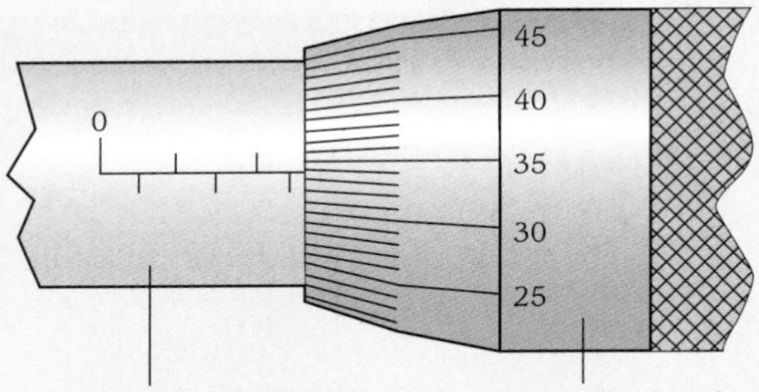

sleeve reading =

thimble reading =

total reading =

2 Read the diameter of the ball measured with this vernier calliper.

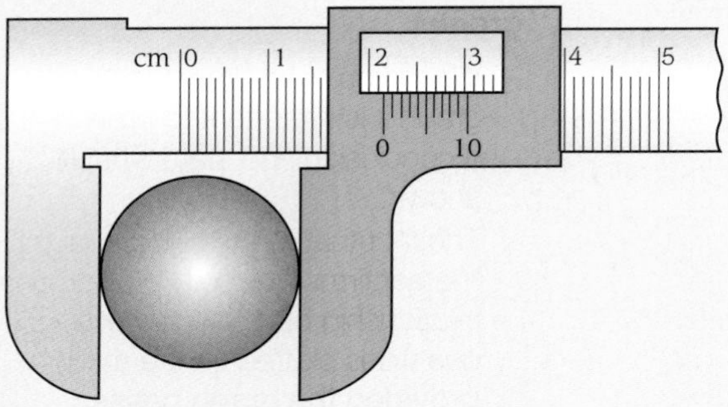

main scale reading =

vernier scale reading =

total reading =

3 Read this vernier scale.

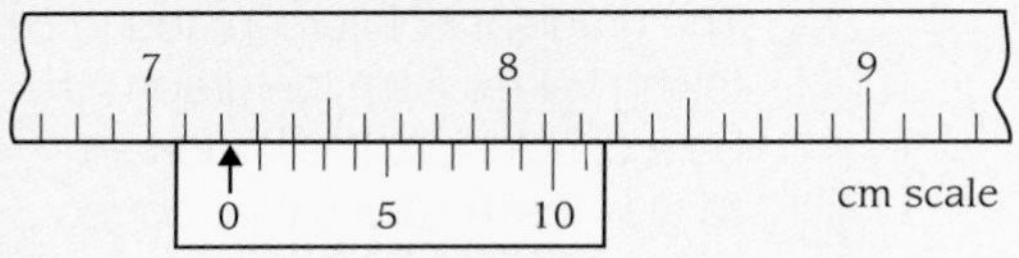

main scale reading =

vernier scale reading =

total reading =

4 A student carried out an experiment using a simple pendulum to measure the acceleration due to gravity, *g*. Her results are tabulated below.

Time for 10 oscillations	28.2	23.8	20.1	16.2	12.0
Time period, *T*/s	2.82				
Length, *l*/m	1.96	1.44	1.00	0.64	0.36
$\sqrt{l}$ in $\sqrt{m}$	1.40				

a) Copy and complete the table of results.

b) Plot a graph of time period, *T* against $\sqrt{l}$.

c) Draw the best fit straight line through the points on your graph.

d) Find the gradient (slope) of the line.

e) Calculate the acceleration due to gravity, *g*, using the equation:

$$g = \frac{4\pi^2}{\text{gradient}^2}$$

f) How does your result compare with the accepted value of 9.81 m s^{-2}?

5 A pile of 500 sheets of paper has a mass of 2.0 kg. The pile is 300 mm long, 200 mm wide and 50 mm thick. Calculate:

a) the thickness of one sheet

b) the mass of one sheet

c) the volume of the pile

d) the density of the paper.

6 In experiments to measure the relative density of various liquids, the masses given in the table below were obtained for three liquids, a, b and c. Calculate the relative densities of these liquids.

	Mass of empty flask/g	Mass of flask full of liquid/g	Mass of flask full of water/g
a)	220	1020	1220
b)	130	730	630
c)	60	1460	160

7 The table shows readings taken while loads were being added to a spiral spring.

Load/N	Length/mm	Extension/mm
0	10.2	0
2.0	12.3	
4.0	14.5	
6.0	16.5	
8.0	18.5	
10.0	20.7	
12.0	22.9	
14.0	24.8	
16.0	28.0	

a) Copy and complete the table.

b) Plot a graph of extension against load.

c) Find the gradient of the graph.

d) Calculate the spring constant. (spring constant = 1/gradient)

e) Use your graph to find the length of the spring when the load is 15.0 N.

f) Use your graph to find the load required to produce an extension of 6.0 mm.

8 The graph of distance against time in the figure below shows the motion of an accelerated object.

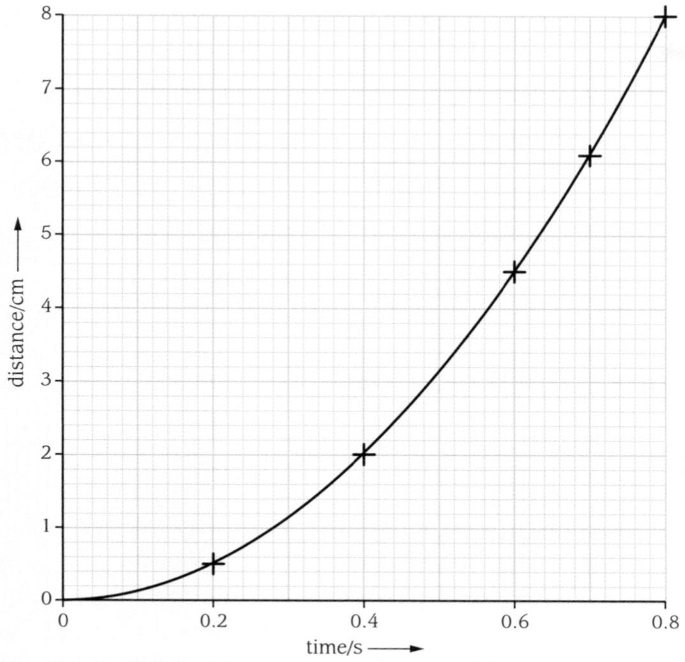

The table below gives some of the data used to plot the distance against time graph.

Distance, *s*/cm	Time, *t*/s	t^2/s^2
0	0	0
	0.2	
	0.4	
	0.6	
	0.7	
	0.8	

a) From the graph, find corresponding values of the distances, *s*, for the times indicated and enter them in a copy of the table.

b) Calculate corresponding values for t^2 and complete your table.

c) Plot a graph of *s* against t^2.

d) Find the gradient of your graph.

e) Find the object's acceleration, *a*, in $m\,s^{-2}$. (acceleration is given by: $a = 2 \times$ gradient)

9 A car accelerates from rest. The table shows how the speed of the car varies over the first 30 s of motion.

Time/s	0	5.0	10.0	15.0	20.0	25.0	30.0
Speed/m s^{-1}	0	16.5	22.5	24.5	25.5	26.0	26.0

a) Draw a graph of speed against time.

b) Use your graph to find the following:

i) the maximum speed reached by the car

ii) the speed of the car after 7.5 s

iii) the distance travelled by the car in the first 10 s.

10 The results given in the table below show how the temperature of a substance, cooling from the liquid phase to the solid phase, varied with time.

Time/minutes	Temperature/°C
0	98
2	86
4	75
6	72
8	71
10	70
12	70
14	70
16	69
18	68
20	66
22	62
24	56
26	47
28	40
30	36

a) Plot a graph of temperature against time.

b) State the temperature at which the substance changes from liquid to solid.

c) Explain why the temperature remains constant for several minutes.

d) Explain why the curve is steepest at first.

e) Explain why the curve becomes less steep after 26 minutes.

11 An empty displacement can weighs 340 g. When it is completely filled, it holds 500 cm^3 of water and weighs 840 g.

a) Calculate the density of water.

b) A large glass marble is added to the displacement can. 20 cm^3 of water overflows into a beaker, and the displacement can now weighs 872 g. Calculate the density of glass.

A4 Forces

We use and feel forces all the time but we are not always consciously aware of them. Forces that push and pull and get things moving or slow things down are easy to spot, but forces that hold things still and keep things balanced are less obvious. Whatever its effect, a force is the action of one object on another object.

Objectives

By the end of this topic you will be able to:

- recognise and describe a force and show it on a diagram
- say what causes a force, what it acts on and what effect it has
- measure forces using a spring balance
- explain how friction is caused and can be reduced
- state the relationship between mass and weight.

A4.1 Finding out about forces

What is a force?

A force is a 'push or pull', which one object applies to another object. A force acting on an object can make the object start or stop moving, or change speed or change direction. It can also make an object change shape. When several forces act at once on an object, the resultant force is the single force that would have the same effect. Sometimes the effects of the different forces cancel out; then the forces are said to be balanced.

A force is a vector quantity. It has both magnitude (size or strength) and direction. A scalar quantity only has size. To describe a force you must give both the size of the force and the direction in which it acts.

Representing a force by an arrow

We draw the arrows to represent forces so that:

- it is clear which object the force acts on
- the tail-end of the arrow begins where the force pushes or pulls
- the arrow points in the direction of the force
- the length of the arrow indicates the magnitude or strength of the force (this is important when we are adding forces and using scale drawings).

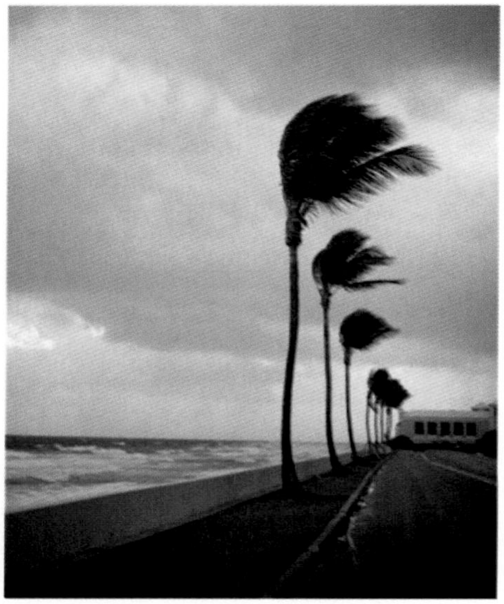

▲ **Figure 4.1.1** Here you can see the effect of the force but not the force itself

Types of force

Forces always involve an interaction between two objects. When the objects are joined together or are in contact, the forces are known as contact forces.

When forces act over a distance without any direct connection they are called non-contact forces. The regions over which non-contact forces act are called fields.

Contact forces	Non-contact forces
frictional forces tension in strings, ropes, wires, springs (normal) reaction forces between objects in contact with each other expansion force of compressed spring expansion force of heated object upthrust force on floating object	gravitational attraction between Earth and Moon magnetic fields of magnets and electric currents (these affect magnetic materials and other current-carrying conductors, and are how electric motors and generators work)

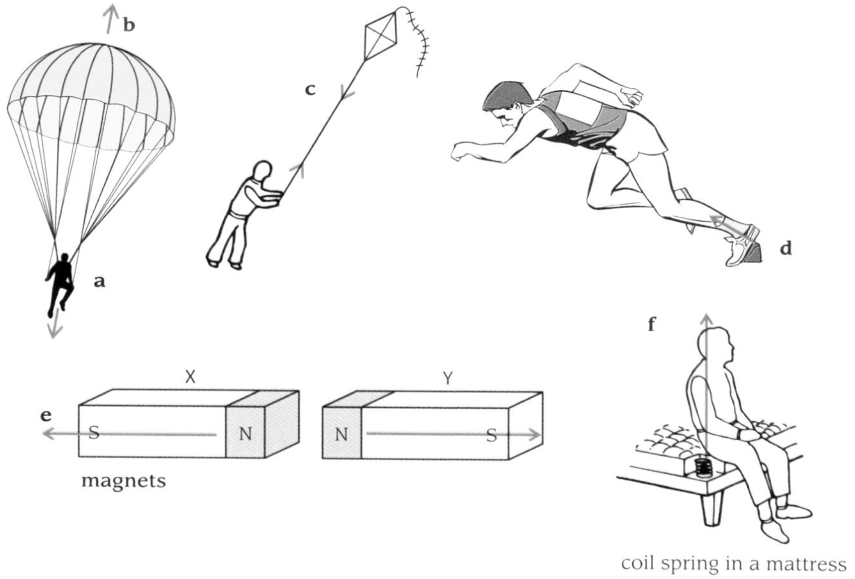

▲ **Figure 4.1.2** Forces

Study each diagram in Figure 4.1.2 and decide:

i) the name or cause of the force shown by the arrow
ii) the object on which the force acts
iii) whether the force is a contact force or a non-contact force and whether it 'pushes' or 'pulls' and the effect of the force.

The arrows in the diagrams in Figure 4.1.2 show:

a) the man's weight, a non-contact force. It is the downward force on the man due to the pull of gravity of the Earth.
b) the air resistance or drag, a contact force. Air molecules push against the inside of the parachute, opposing the motion of the parachute.
c) the tension in the string, a contact force. At one end tension pulls on the child, on the other end it pulls on the kite.
d) the contact force of the starting block. This is a forwards force, which helps the sprinter start moving.
e) the magnetic force, a non-contact force. Like poles repel, so the magnets push each other apart.
f) the expansion force of a compressed spring, a contact force. The spring pushes upwards on the sitter. This balances the downward force, which is the weight of the sitter.

Key fact

FRICTION

Frictional forces:
- are a reaction to other forces
- oppose motion
- cause wear and damage
- generate heat and waste energy
- are necessary for grip (e.g. for walking or driving).

Causes of friction
- Friction is caused by points of contact on the surfaces obstructing movement, and by molecular forces of attraction at these points of contact.

Ways of reducing friction
- Make surfaces smoother.
- Use a lubricant such as oil or grease.
- Use wheels or rollers.
- Fit ball-bearings on axles.
- Streamline shapes of vehicles.

Mass and weight

Unfortunately in everyday language we often use the word 'weight' when strictly we should use 'mass' and we talk about 'weighing' an object when we are finding its mass.

The pull of the Earth on an object is called its weight.

This pull or weight is caused by what we call 'gravity'. The weight of an object varies a little from place to place on the surface of the Earth; on the Moon the weight is only $\frac{1}{6}$ of its value on the Earth. In deep space, away

▲ **Figure 4.1.3** The streamlined shape of this vehicle reduces the drag force of the air.

from all gravity, an object has no weight at all. The link between mass and weight is that at a particular place the weights of objects are proportional to their masses.

The mass of an object is a measure of the matter in it and depends on the number of atoms it contains and the size of those atoms.

Mass	Weight
Measured in kilograms (kg)	Measured in newtons (N)
A measure of the amount of matter in an object	The pull of the Earth on the object
A scalar quantity	A vector quantity (a pull is a force and has direction)
Constant everywhere	Changes slightly when an object moves to different places on the Earth; reduces to zero in deep space
Can be measured by comparison with a standard mass or by measuring weight assuming that mass and weight are proportional at a particular place	Can be measured by the extension of a spring balance or by comparison with another weight on a beam balance

Measuring forces

Strong forces have a larger magnitude than weaker forces. The unit of force is the **newton (N)**. Figure 4.1.5 shows a range of forces from about one hundredth of a newton (0.01 N) to one hundred newtons (100 N).

- Lift each object and feel its weight.

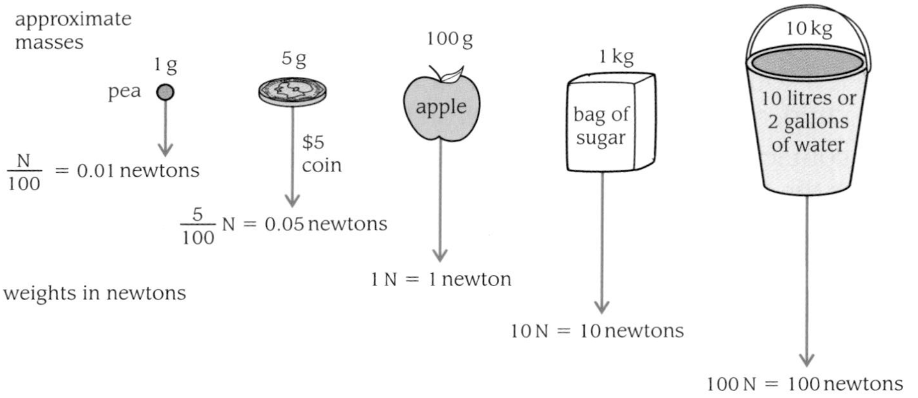

▲ **Figure 4.1.5** Forces measured in newtons

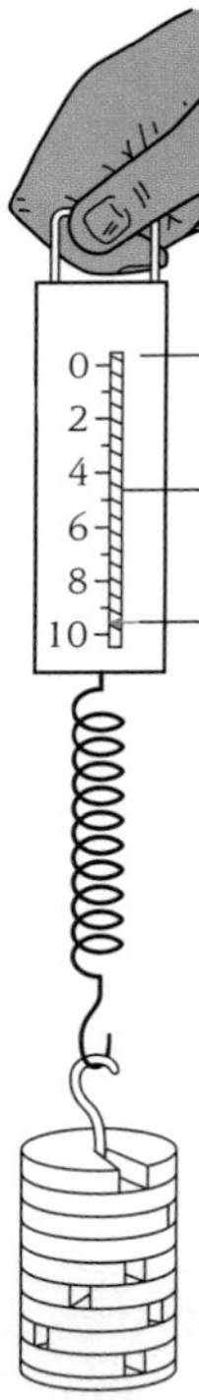

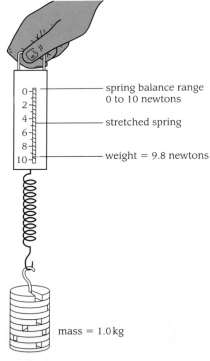

▲ **Figure 4.1.4** Measuring weight on a spring balance

The downward force due to gravity is called weight. The weight of a small apple is about 1 N. On Earth there is a downward force due to gravity of about 10 N on each kilogram of mass.

Worked example

A block of wood has a mass of 340 g. What is its weight?

340 g = 0.340 kg, so weight = 0.340 × 10 = 3.4 N

Using a spring balance to measure forces

Spring balances are calibrated using known forces to stretch or compress their springs. Since spring balances measure forces, they should be calibrated in newtons but they often have scales in grams or kilograms. (This is so that they can also be used to find masses on Earth. The readings in grams or kilograms are correct only on the surface of the Earth.)

The Earth's gravitational pull on an object of mass 1 kg is approximately 10 N at the Earth's surface.

We say that the strength of the Earth's gravitational field, g, at the surface of the Earth is 10 newtons per kilogram.

Weighing in different places

The weight of a given mass is different in different places, because the force due to gravity changes. A mass has about $\frac{1}{6}$ the weight on the Moon that it has on Earth because the strength of gravity on the Moon is only about $\frac{1}{6}$ its strength on Earth. Weight is calculated using the formula,

$W = mg$, where W = weight, m = mass, g = acceleration or field strength due to gravity.

Note that an astronaut in deep space holding the top of the spring balance with one hand and pulling the hook with the other could still stretch the spring and get a measure of his strength because in this case gravity is not involved.

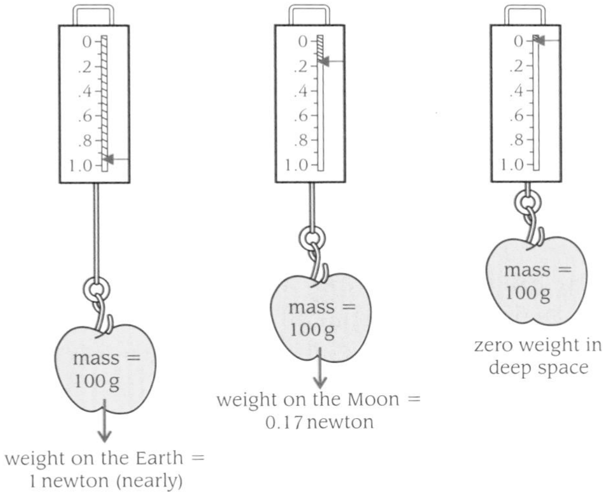

▲ **Figure 4.1.6** Weighing in different places

Worked example

What is the weight of a girl of mass 34 kg

a) on the surface of the Earth, where $g = 10\,\text{N}\,\text{kg}^{-1}$

b) on the surface of the Moon, where $g = 1.7\,\text{N}\,\text{kg}^{-1}$

c) in deep space, free of gravity?

---

a) $W = mg$
$= 34 \times 10 = 340$ **N on Earth**

b) $W = mg$
$= 34 \times 1.7 = 58$ **N on the Moon**

c) W = zero

Things to do

Hang a few different slotted masses on their hanger, which is hooked on a newton spring balance and note the weight readings.

This table gives some typical readings.

Mass, *m*/kg	Weight, *W*/N
0.1	nearly 1.0
0.5	4.9
1.0	9.8

Key fact

We find that the weight, W, of an object is proportional to its mass, m. In other words, if we double the mass we double the weight and so on. And we find that (on the surface of the Earth) the weight of an object of mass 1 kg is 9.8 N.

$W = mg = m \times 9.8$ newtons

Things to do

Work out the weight of some objects of known mass. Check your answers using a spring balance. Then weigh an unknown mass on a spring balance, and use your reading to find its mass.

Worked example

Weight on Mars

A boy has a mass of 40 kg.
The gravitational field strength on Mars is $3.7\ \text{N kg}^{-1}$.
The gravitational field strength on the Moon is $1.7\ \text{N kg}^{-1}$.

a) Calculate the weight of the boy on Mars.
b) How many times heavier will he be on Mars compared with on the Moon?

---

a) $W = mg$
$= 40 \times 3.7 = 148\ \text{N}$

b) $\dfrac{g \text{ on Mars}}{g \text{ on Moon}} = \dfrac{3.7}{1.7} = 2.18$

He will be 2.18 times heavier on Mars than on the Moon.

Summary questions

1 Give two examples of contact forces.
2 Give two examples of non-contact forces.
3 What is the mass of an object that weighs 20 N on Earth?
4 Calculate the weight of each of the following masses on the Earth.
a 10 g b 3.6 kg c 713 g

Objectives

By the end of this topic you will be able to:

- identify and explain the difference between vectors and scalars
- add vectors such as forces and velocities at any angles using scale drawings and the parallelogram law
- add vectors which are parallel, anti-parallel or at right angles by calculation.

A4.2 Vectors and scalars

Adding forces

We have measured forces in newtons and know that they have a size or magnitude. We have also noticed that all forces act in a particular direction, i.e. they are vectors. For example, weight always pulls towards the Earth and acts downwards. So how do we add two forces that act on the same object taking into account their directions, which may be different?

All vector quantities obey a special rule for addition and subtraction, which takes account of direction as well as magnitude. A vector can be represented by a straight line with an arrow on one end. The length of the line represents the magnitude of the vector quantity (sometimes drawn to scale), and the direction of the line gives the direction and line of action of the vector. The special rule is known as the parallelogram law.

The parallelogram law for adding forces

If two forces, acting at one point on the same object, are represented in magnitude and direction by the sides of a parallelogram drawn from the point, their resultant is represented in both magnitude and direction by the diagonal of the parallelogram drawn from the same point.

This law for adding two forces to find their resultant (single equivalent force) is just one example of how all vector quantities are added. We can also add velocities by this method.

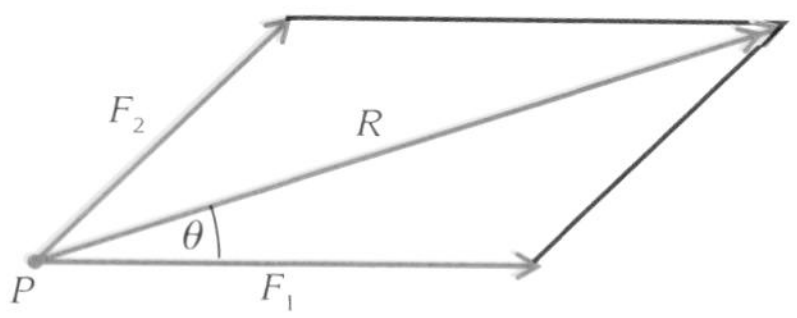

▲ **Figure 4.2.1** Forces F_1 and F_2 (drawn to scale so that their lengths represent their magnitudes) act in the directions shown at point P on an object. Their resultant is given by vector R. The length of R represents its magnitude and θ gives its direction from F_1.

When drawing vectors to scale, choose a simple scale to suit the magnitudes involved. For example a force of 5 N could be represented by a vector 5 cm long or a velocity of 600 m s^{-1} could be represented by a vector 6 cm long.

Key fact

Examples of scalar quantities
- Time, temperature, mass, area, volume, density, frequency, work, energy and power
- (Note: speed and distance are also scalars but when a direction is given we rename these vectors as velocity and displacement respectively.)

Examples of vector quantities
- So far you have met two vector quantities, force and weight. You will meet more.

Adding parallel and anti-parallel forces

Parallel forces that act in the same line on the same object can be added arithmetically taking account of their directions.

Forces acting in opposite directions along the same straight line are called anti-parallel forces and their combined effect is found by subtracting their magnitudes.

Notice how anti-parallel forces acting in opposite directions have opposite signs so that when they are 'added' their magnitudes subtract (examples **b** and **c** in Figure 4.2.2).

To specify the resultant force you must give both its magnitude and direction. For example, the resultant in example **b** is a force of 1 N acting in the same direction as the 3 N force.

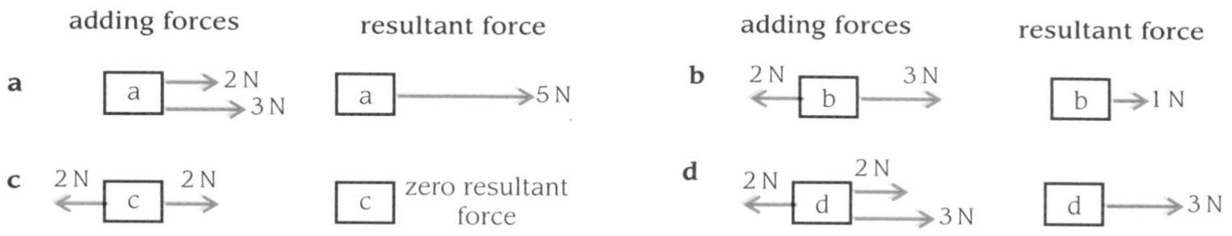

▲ **Figure 4.2.2** Adding parallel forces

Adding forces at right angles

When F_1 and F_2 are perpendicular forces acting at point P on the same object the parallelogram becomes a rectangle PAOB. The triangle PAO is a right-angled triangle with side AO of length equal to F_2.

By Pythagoras' theorem, we have $PO^2 = PA^2 + AO^2$,

So the magnitude of the resultant R (equal to PO) can be calculated:

$$R^2 = F_1^2 + F_2^2$$

The direction of the resultant force can be found either by scale drawing of the forces, or by calculation. Using calculation, the direction of the resultant R can be specified by the angle θ, that is, the angle between the resultant force and one of the original forces. Angle θ is found by trigonometry as follows:

$$\tan\theta = \frac{AO}{AP} \text{ or } \tan\theta = \frac{F_2}{F_1}$$

(The angle θ is found using the inverse or arctan key on a calculator for the value of $\frac{F_2}{F_1}$.)

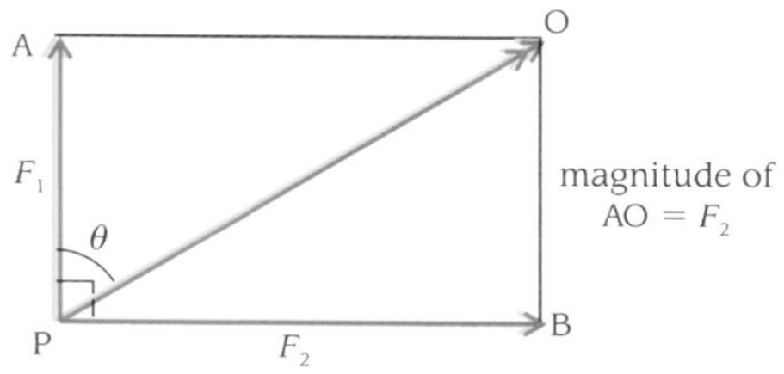

▲ **Figure 4.2.3** Adding forces at right angles

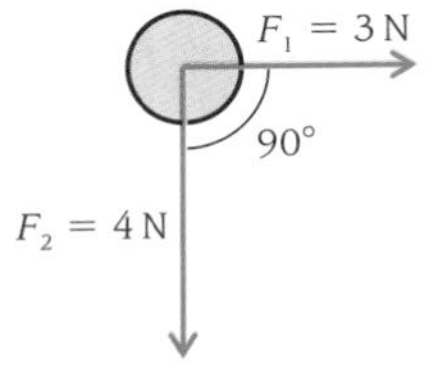

▲ **Figure 4.2.4**

Things to do

Find by both scale drawing and by calculation the resultant of the two forces in this diagram.

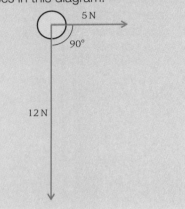

Worked example

Two forces of 3 N and 4 N act at right angles at the same point on an object (Figure 4.2.4). Find by calculation their resultant force.

Using Pythagoras' theorem:

$$R^2 = F_1^2 + F_2^2$$

$$\therefore \quad R^2 = (3\,\text{N})^2 + (4\,\text{N})^2 = 25\,\text{N}^2$$

$$\therefore \quad R = 5\,\text{N}$$

Using the tangent relation we have:

$$\tan\theta = \frac{F_2}{F_1} = \frac{4\,\text{N}}{3\,\text{N}} = 1.33 \text{ and so } \theta = 53°$$

The resultant force has a magnitude of 5 newtons and acts in a direction between the two forces at an angle of 53° from the original 3 newton force.

Summary questions

1 Explain why a force is a vector quantity.

2 Two forces act in opposite directions. How would you find the magnitude of the resultant force?

3 Two forces act at right angles. How would you find the magnitude of the resultant force?

Objectives

By the end of this topic you will be able to:

- define the moment of a force
- state the principle of moments and use it to solve problems
- explain the action of simple tools and devices as levers.

A4.3 Turning forces

Why is it easier to loosen a tight nut using a long spanner? How can a see-saw balance when people of different weights sit on opposite sides? What makes a racing car less likely to turn over than an ordinary car? These are the kinds of questions that we can answer when we understand the effects of turning forces.

The moment of a force

We call the turning effect of a force the **moment** of the force. To find out what factors are involved in the moment of a force try the simple experiment shown in Figure 4.3.1.

- Hang a slotted mass holder from a wire loop attached to a half-metre ruler.
- Hold one end of the ruler in your hand so that you keep the ruler level.
- Try changing: (a) the weight *W* of the slotted masses and (b) the distance *d* of the hanger from the middle of your hand.
- What can you feel?

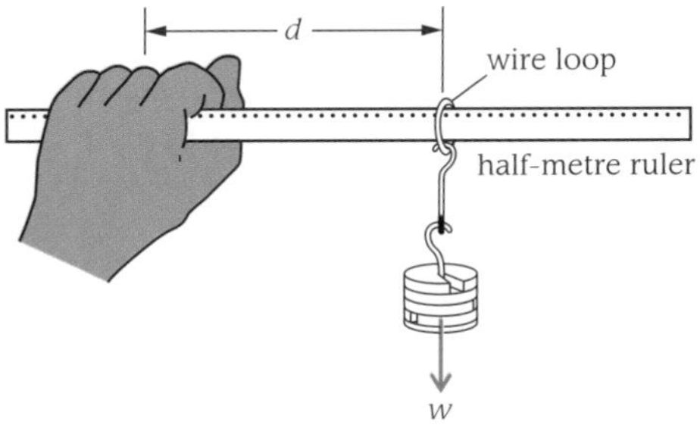

▲ **Figure 4.3.1** Feeling the moment of a force

The twisting or turning effect that your hand feels and has to resist is the moment of the force. The moment of the force depends on both the magnitude of the force and how far away it is from the turning point. The turning point has several names and can be several things. Names that are used include pivot, axis and fulcrum. Knife-edges, axles, hinges and the edges or corners of objects can act as turning points.

The unit of the moment of a force is the newton metre (N m). Note: Although they are both calculated from '$F \times d$', newton metres (N m) are *not equivalent* to joules (J). For calculating work (in J) the force and the distance are in the *same direction*. For calculating moments (N m) the force is *at right angles* to the distance being measured.

The moment T of a force is the product of the magnitude of the force F and the perpendicular distanced d from the pivot to the line of action of the force.

$$T = Fd$$

Things to do

Explain why it is easier to close a door when you push it near the handle rather than near the hinge.

Worked example

The distance from the hinge to handle on a door is 70 cm.
If the handle is pushed with a force of 8.0 N, perpendicular to the door, calculate the moment of the force turning the door.

$T = Fd$
$T = 8.0\ \text{N} \times 0.70\ \text{m} = 5.6\ \text{N m}$

The moment of the force turning the door is 5.6 N m.
Note that the perpendicular distance must be given in metres.

Worked example

The crank of a bicycle pedal is 16 cm long and the downward push of a foot is 400 N. Calculate the moment of the push of the foot when the crank is horizontal.

When the crank is horizontal its length is perpendicular to the downward foot push F. So the perpendicular distance d from the pivot to the line of action of the force is 0.16 m.

Note that distances must be in metres.

Using $T = Fd$

we have $T = 400\ \text{N} \times 0.16\ \text{m} = 64\ \text{N m}$.

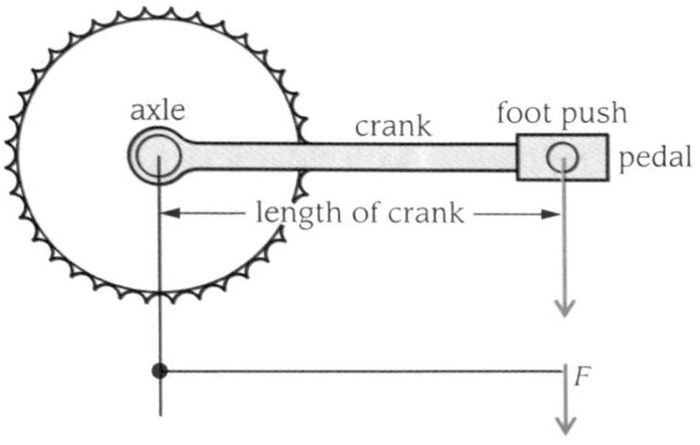

▲ **Figure 4.3.2**

Investigating the principle of moments

The principle of moments is also known as the law of the lever. This law is about objects balancing when the moments of all the forces acting are balanced. A balanced object is said to be in equilibrium. To investigate the law, set up a metre ruler (or half-metre ruler) as shown in Figure 4.3.3.

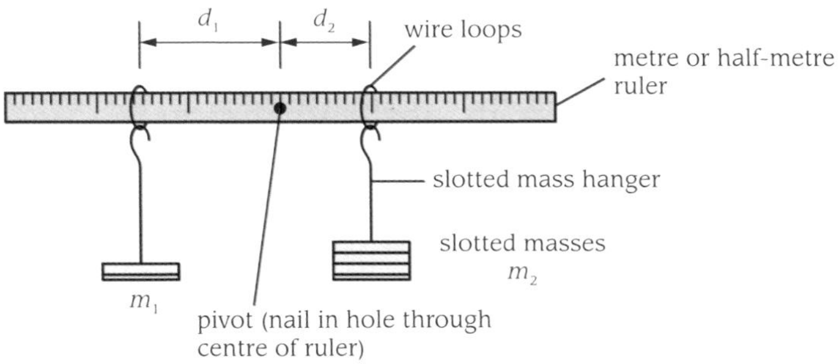

▲ **Figure 4.3.3** When the ruler is balanced, both moments are the same size, but acting to turn the ruler in opposite directions.

Then try the following:

- Hang two slotted mass hangers from small wire loops fitted on the ruler.
- Set mass m_1, at a fixed distance d_1 from the pivot and slide mass m_2 along the ruler until it balances.
- Record the values of m_1, m_2, d_1 and d_2 in a table.
- Repeat the procedure with different values of each of the four quantities.
- Copy and complete the table as shown below.

Mass, m_1/g	Force, F_1/N	Perpendicular distance, d_1/m	Moment of force, M_1/N m	Mass, m_2/g	Force, F_2/N	Perpendicular distance, d_2/m	Moment of force, M_2/N m
200	2.0	0.30	0.60	400	4.0	0.15	0.60

To calculate the forces use $F = mg$.

Example: $F_1 = 0.2\,\text{kg} \times 10\,\text{N/kg} = 2.0\,\text{N}$

To calculate the moment of the forces use $M = Fd$.

Example: $M_1 = 2.0\,\text{N} \times 0.3\,\text{m} = 0.6\,\text{N m}$

The results for the moments of the forces on each side of the ruler show that when the ruler is balanced the moments are always equal: $M_1 = M_2$. It is usually helpful to describe a moment as acting either clockwise or anticlockwise according to which way it tries to turn the object about the pivot.

When there are extra forces on either side we find that the ruler balances when the sum of the moments (not the sum of the weights) are equal.

The principle of moments

When an object is in equilibrium (balanced and not moving), the sum of the clockwise moments about any point (acting as a pivot) equals the sum of the anticlockwise moments about the same point.

Key fact

About moments

- All perpendicular distances are measured from the pivot.
- When two forces produce a moment in the same direction we add the moments of the forces and not the forces themselves.
- An object must be balanced or in equilibrium for the principle of moments to apply.

Worked example

Using the law of moments

A boy of weight 500 N sits on the left side of a see-saw at a distance of 2.4 metres from its pivot (Figure 4.3.4). If a girl can balance the see-saw by sitting 3.0 metres from the pivot on the right side, what is her weight?

Using the law of moments when the see-saw is balanced:

anticlockwise moment of the boy's weight = clockwise moment of the girl's weight

and $W_1 d_1 = W_2 d_2$

$500\,\text{N} \times 2.4\,\text{m} = W_2 \times 3.0\,\text{m}$

The girl's weight, $W_2 = \dfrac{1200\,\text{N m}}{3.0\,\text{m}} = 400\,\text{N}$

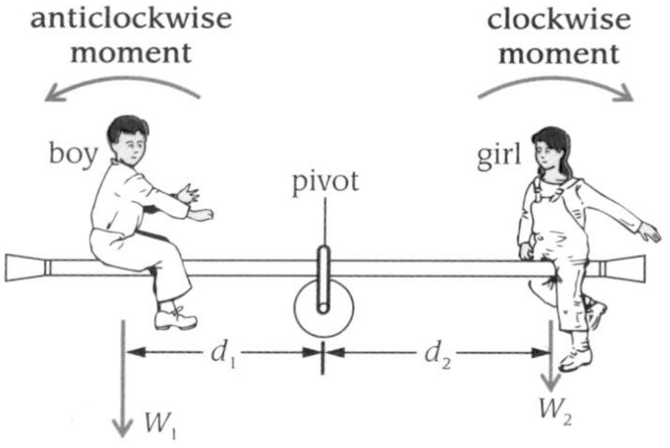

▲ Figure 4.3.4

Equilibrium and parallel forces

When two or more parallel forces act on an object several different things may happen. First we decide whether the object is in equilibrium. If it is neither moving nor turning it is definitely in equilibrium.

For an object to be in equilibrium two conditions must be met:

1 The sum of the forces acting on it in one direction must equal the sum of the forces acting on it in the opposite direction.
2 The sum of the clockwise moments about any point on the object must equal the sum of the anticlockwise moments.

A bridge is supported at both ends by upward contact forces C_1 and C_2 (Figure 4.3.6). Its weight W can be considered to act downwards through its centre. These three forces are in equilibrium and the conditions **1** and **2** above will hold.

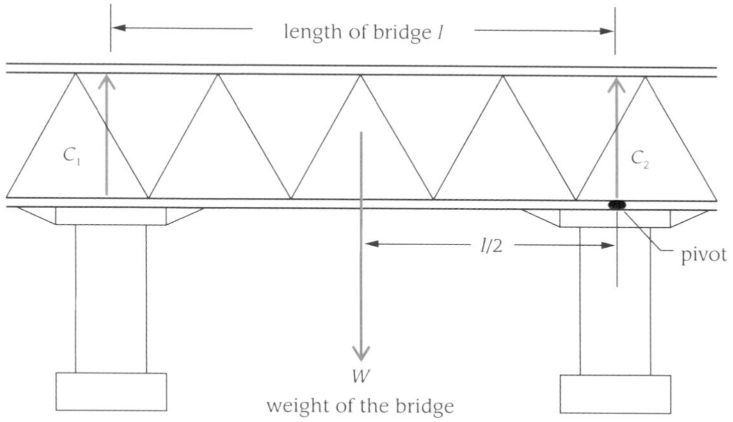

▲ **Figure 4.3.6** Three parallel forces in equilibrium

From **1** we have for the forces acting on the bridge:

$$\text{sum of the upward forces} = \text{sum of the downward forces}$$
$$C_1 + C_2 = W$$

Now we imagine that the bridge might turn or tip up at one end and we choose a suitable pivot. By choosing the point labelled pivot, we make the problem simpler because the force C_2, acting through the pivot, has no moment about it.

Force C_1 gives a clockwise moment $= C_1 \times l$

W gives an anticlockwise moment $= W \times \frac{l}{2}$

Sum of the clockwise moments about pivot = sum of the anticlockwise moments about pivot

which gives us: $C_1 \times l = W \times \frac{l}{2}$

and dividing through by l we get $C_1 = \frac{W}{2}$

and since $C_1 + C_2 = W$, it follows that C_2 also equals $\frac{W}{2}$.

This may seem a complicated way of showing that a bridge with its weight acting in the middle gets equal support from both pillars at its two ends. But the two ideas we have used can be applied to more difficult examples with more than three parallel forces.

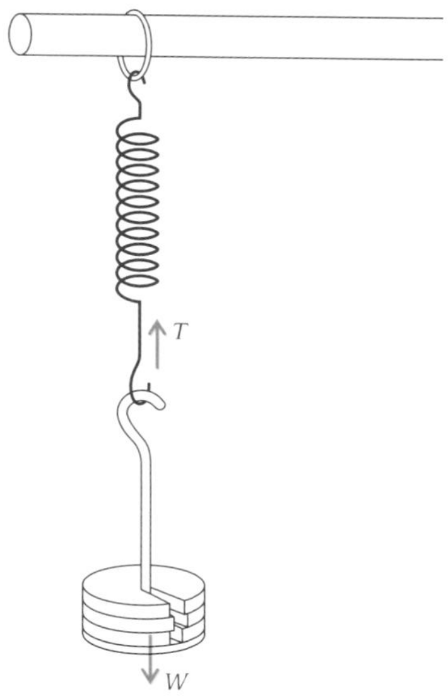

▲ **Figure 4.3.5** Two parallel forces in equilibrium

Forces T and W are equal in magnitude and they are also in equilibrium.

Two parallel forces are in equilibrium when they are equal in magnitude and act on the same object in opposite directions but in the same line.

Things to do

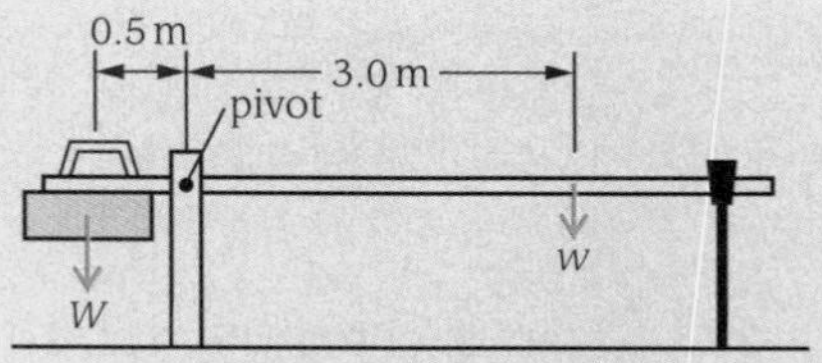

The security boom is counter-balanced by a weight W to make it easier to raise the boom. The weight of the boom, w, is 200 N.

a) What size of counterweight, W, balances the boom?

b) What reaction force is provided by the support?

Answers:

a) W = 1200 N downwards

b) 1400 N upwards

Worked example

Equilibrium

In the worked example on page 34, the weight of the boy was 500 N and we found the weight of the girl to be 400 N. If the see-saw itself weighed 200 N, what is the magnitude and direction of the force acting on the see-saw from the pivot?

The direction of the reaction force acting on the see-saw from the pivot must be upwards to support the see-saw and the children, and to keep them in equilibrium.

Upward reaction force = sum of downward forces

Upward reaction force = (500 + 400 + 200) N = 1100 N

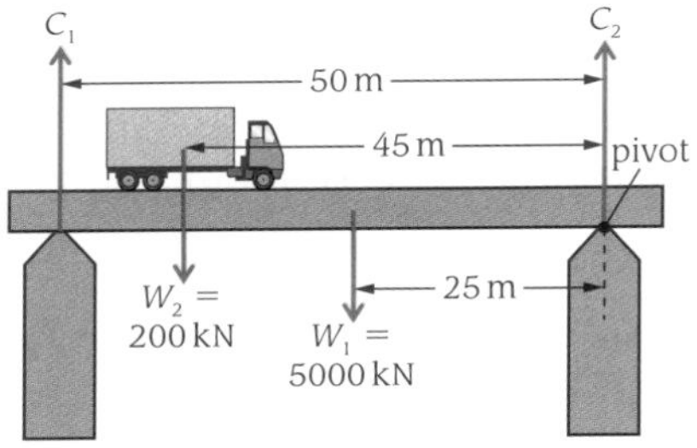

▲ Figure 4.3.8

Worked example

Parallel forces in equilibrium

A truck of weight 200 kN is driving across a steel bridge of weight 5000 kN (Figure 4.3.8). The weight of the bridge can be considered to act at its centre and all the distances are as shown in the figure. Calculate the supporting contact forces C_1 and C_2 provided by the two pillars.

The bridge is in equilibrium, therefore from (1):

The sum of the upward forces = the sum of the downward forces.

$$C_1 + C_2 = W_1 + W_2$$

$$C_1 + C_2 = 5000\,\text{kN} + 200\,\text{kN} = 5200\,\text{kN}$$

Now, using (2), we choose the pivot to eliminate one unknown force, C_2:

the sum of the clockwise moments
= the sum of the anticlockwise moments

$$M_1 = M_2 + M_3$$

$$C_1 \times 50\,\text{m} = (W_2 \times 45\,\text{m}) + (W_1 \times 25\,\text{m})$$

$$C_1 \times 50\,\text{m} = (200\,\text{kN} \times 45\,\text{m}) + (5000\,\text{kN} \times 25\,\text{m})$$

$$C_1 \times 50\,\text{m} = 9000\,\text{kN m} + 125\,000\,\text{kN m}$$

$$\text{C1} = \frac{134\,000\,\text{kN m}}{50\,\text{m}} = 2680\,\text{kN}$$

And since $C_1 + C_2 = 5200\,\text{kN}$

We have $C_2 = 5200\,\text{kN} - C_1 = 5200\,\text{kN} - 2680\,\text{kN} = 2520\,\text{kN}$

Key fact

About equilibrium

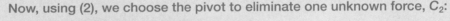

- The principle of moments applies to all objects in equilibrium.
- The sum of the forces in opposite directions are equal.
- Moments can be taken about any point but, when two forces are unknown, choose a point through which one of them acts.

Summary questions

1 Give two things that would decrease the moment of a force.

2 State the principle of moments.

3 What is the unit of the moment of a force?

4 Calculate the moment of a force of 8 N acting 25 cm from a pivot.

5 Which has the larger moment, a force of 15 N acting 60 cm from a pivot, or a force of 20 N acting 40 cm from the pivot?

A4.4 Centre of gravity

When gravity pulls an object towards the Earth it always appears to pull at the same point on the object.

Where is the centre of gravity of an object?

The Earth pulls every molecule of an object in a downward direction, or in other words every molecule in an object has a weight. We can add all these millions of tiny molecule weights together and get a single resultant force for the weight of the whole object.

So an object behaves as if its whole weight was a single force, which acts through a point G called its centre of gravity.

We define the centre of gravity of an object as the point through which its whole weight acts for any orientation of the object.

Finding the centre of gravity of an object with an irregular shape or non-uniform thickness or density

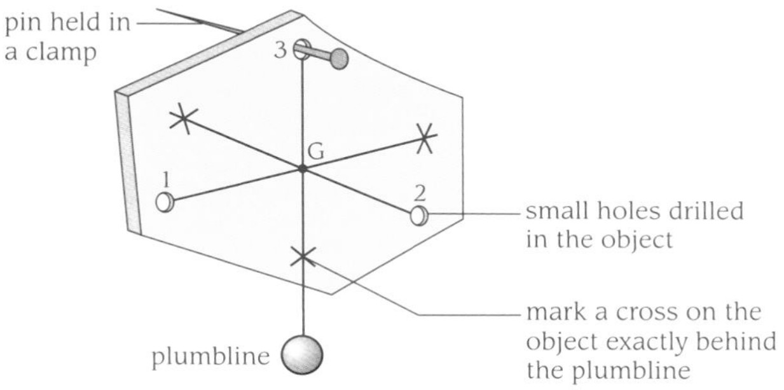

▲ **Figure 4.4.2** Finding the centre of gravity of an object using a plumb line

- A suitable object is an irregular shaped sheet of card or wood. Make three small holes in it near its edges.
- Put a strong pin through one of the holes and fix it in a clamp so that the object can swing freely.
- Attach a plumb line to the pin.
- When the object and the plumb line have both stopped swinging, mark a cross on the object exactly behind the plumb line and near the opposite edge to the hole.
- Repeat this procedure for all three holes.
- Remove the object from the pin and draw straight lines with a ruler from each hole to the opposite cross.

The point where the three lines cross is the centre of gravity of the object. The centre of gravity does not have to be within the object itself. For example the centre of gravity of a uniform ring is nowhere on the ring itself. It is in the gap in the centre of the ring.

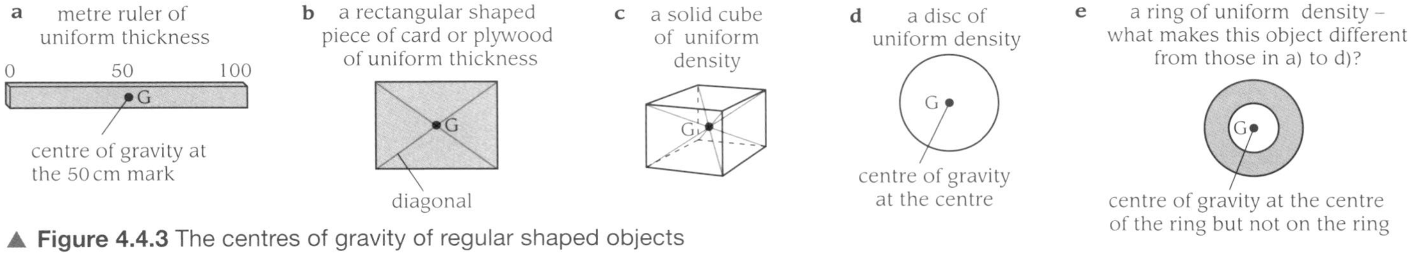

▲ **Figure 4.4.3** The centres of gravity of regular shaped objects

Objectives

By the end of this topic you will be able to:

- find the centre of gravity of a body by drawing or experiment
- explain how the position of its centre of gravity affects the stability of an object.

Key fact

- The centre of gravity, G, stays in the same position on the object.
- The weight of the object always acts through G for all orientations of the object.

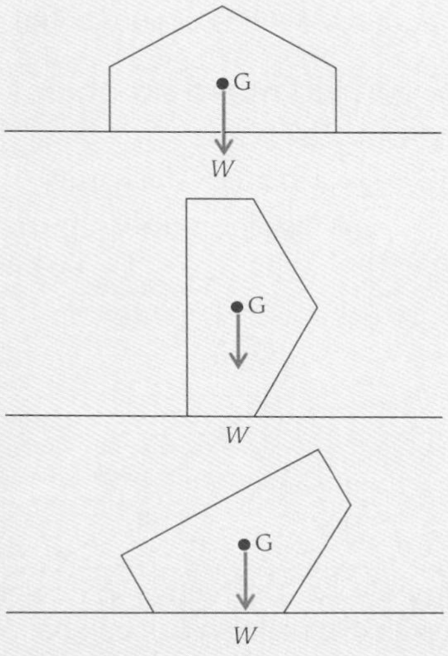

▲ **Figure 4.4.1**

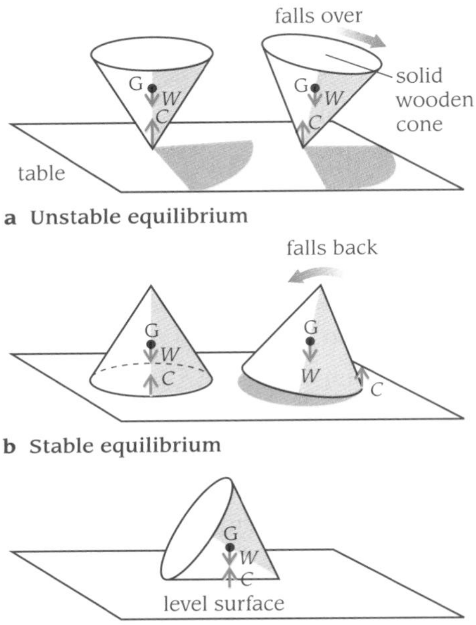

▲ **Figure 4.4.4** Kinds of equilibrium

How can we make an object more stable?

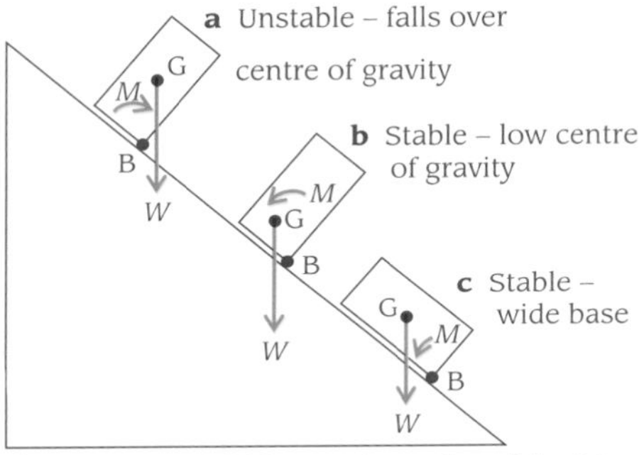

▲ **Figure 4.4.6** The rectangular object is unstable in position **a**. It can be made more stable by either **b** lowering its centre of gravity or **c** giving it a wider base.

Stability

Case a: unstable equilibrium

Here balance is effectively impossible. As soon as the cone has the slightest tilt its weight has a moment about the point of the cone, which makes it fall over. Note that:

- as it tilts, G goes lower and continues to get lower as it falls over
- the line of action of the weight, *W*, passes outside the (very small) area of contact with the table's surface.

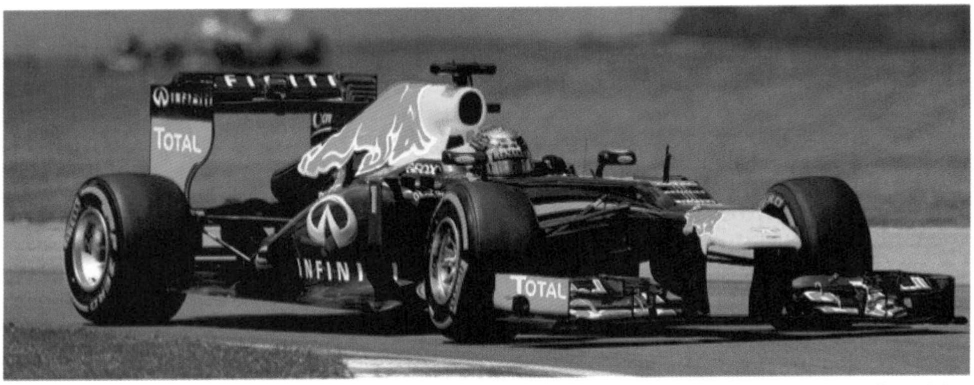

▲ **Figure 4.4.5** The design of a racing car requires both a low centre of gravity and a wide wheel base for improved stability. This makes the car less likely to turn over.

Case b: stable equilibrium

Here the cone rests easily as the two equal forces *W* and the contact reaction force *C* act in opposite directions in the same line. Note that when you slightly tilt the cone:

- its centre of gravity is *raised* and the contact force moves to the edge of its base
- the moment of the weight provides a turning effect, which tries to lower the centre of gravity and makes the cone fall back to its stable position, and
- the line of action of the weight, *W*, passes inside the base area of the cone.

Case c: neutral equilibrium

Now it is possible to roll the cone to many new positions and let it rest there. It will neither roll back to where it came from nor roll on any further. The centre of gravity neither rises nor falls and so cannot gain any greater stability by being lowered. The two forces remain equal, opposite in direction and act along the same line in all positions of the cone. In no position can the weight provide a moment that will turn the cone to a new position.

Things to do

- Explain how the design of a racing car makes it less likely to turn over.
- Explain why filing cabinets are designed so that only one draw can be pulled out at a time.
- In Jamaica, people used to stack all the luggage on the roof of buses. Now it is stored under the bus instead. How does this affect the stability of the bus? Explain why.
- Explain why it is easier to learn to ride a tricycle than to learn to ride a bicycle.

Summary questions

1. Where is the centre of gravity of a uniform sphere?
2. What is meant by 'unstable equilibrium'?
3. Give two ways to make an object more stable.

A4.5 Stretching materials

The attractive forces between the molecules in a solid provide its characteristic elastic or stretchy properties. When we stretch a solid we are very slightly increasing the spacing of its molecules. The tension we can feel in a stretched spring is due to all the forces of attraction between the molecules in the spring.

Objectives

By the end of this topic you will be able to:

- describe experiments to determine extension–force graphs for springs and elastic bands
- state Hooke's law
- identify regions on graphs of extension against force where Hooke's law does and does not apply
- use springs and graphs to find unknown weights of objects.

Stretching a spiral spring

- Arrange a stand to hold a millimetre scale close to a hanging spiral spring.
- Attach a pointer to the end of the spring and take a scale reading of the pointer for an unstretched, unloaded spring.
- Hang a slotted mass hanger on the end of the spring and take a series of scale readings as slotted masses are added to the hanger, increasing the stretching force or load.
- Record your readings in a table.

Mass on hanger, *m*/kg	Stretching force, *mg*/N	Scale reading /mm	Extension of spring/mm	$\frac{\text{Force}}{\text{Extension}}$

- Calculate the stretching force using $F = mg$, where $g = 10\,\text{N kg}^{-1}$.
- Calculate the increase in length or extension of the spring by subtracting the initial length or scale reading for the unloaded spring from all the loaded readings.
- Calculate for all the readings the value of the ratio: stretching force / extension.
- Plot a graph of extension against stretching force.

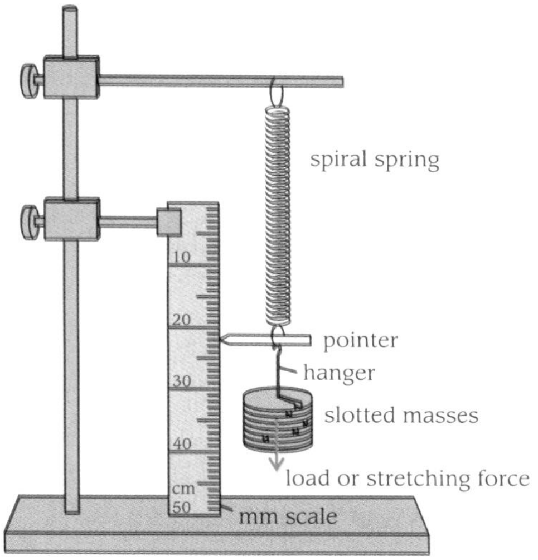

▲ **Figure 4.5.1** Stretching a spring

The graph of extension against the stretching force is a straight line showing that the extension of a spiral spring is directly proportional to the stretching force (Figure 4.5.2). In other words, if the stretching force is doubled the extension is doubled and so on.

$$\text{Extension} \propto \text{stretching force}$$

The same kind of result is obtained if a straight steel wire is stretched. But what happens if we go on stretching a spring or a wire further and further? After a point called the **elastic limit** some of the stretching becomes permanent and the spring or wire will never go back to its original length.

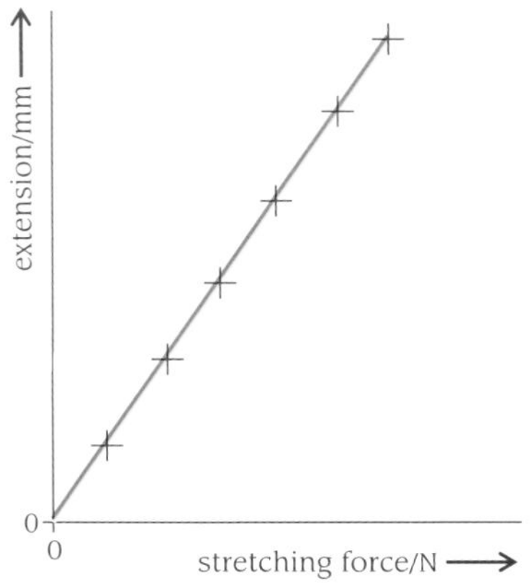

▲ **Figure 4.5.2** Graph of extension against stretching force for a spring

The elastic limit and Hooke's law

The extension against stretching force graph (Figure 4.5.3) is straight from O to a point near E. Over this range of the stretching force the extension is directly proportional to the force. Also, in this region, when the load is removed the spring or wire returns to its original length.

If the stretching force is increased and the spring is taken beyond point E, say to point B, then permanent stretching is produced. When the load is removed, the spring contracts to point P on the graph. OP represents the

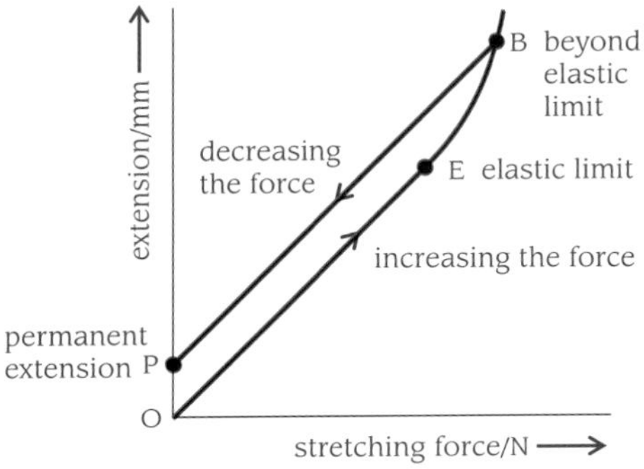

▲ **Figure 4.5.3** A steel spring or wire stretched beyond its elastic limit

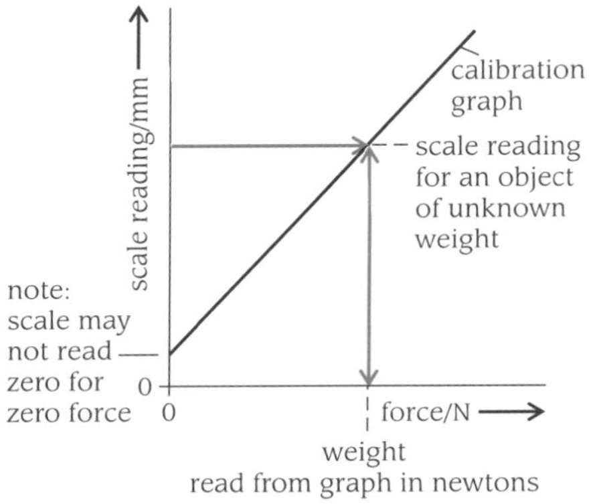

▲ **Figure 4.5.4** Using the calibration graph of a spring balance

! Key fact

The elastic limit, E, is the point beyond which:

- further extension causes some permanent extension
- the extension is not directly proportional to the stretching force and Hooke's law does not apply.

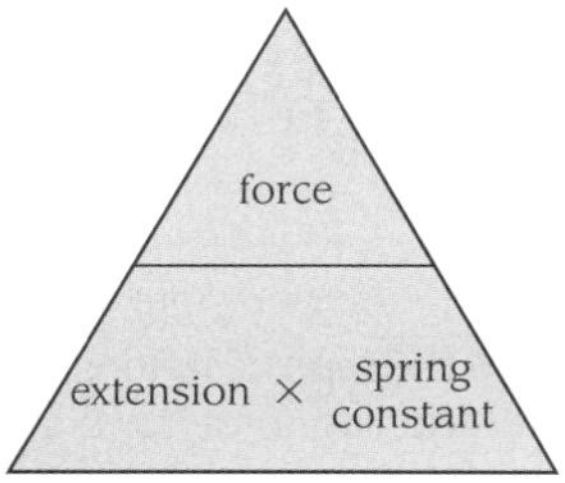

permanent stretching or permanent extension of the spring. As stretching continues beyond the elastic limit, the wire or elastic will eventually snap.

Robert Hooke formulated a law known as Hooke's law:

Provided the stretching force does not extend a spring beyond its elastic limit, the extension of the spring is directly proportional to the stretching force.

Using a spiral spring to find the weight of things

A graph showing how a spiral spring stretches as the load hanging on it is increased can be used to find the weights of objects and is called a calibration graph (Figure 4.5.4). The calibration converts scale readings at the end of the spring into weights in newtons. When a spring balance is manufactured the scale readings in millimetres are converted into the required force units. In a physics laboratory, the scale should be calibrated in newtons but in shops other scales are used. Many weighing machines use the stretching or compressing of springs to give their readings.

The spring constant

The value of the spring constant tells us how strong a spring is.

The ratio: $\dfrac{\text{force}}{\text{extension}}$ = the spring constant in N m^{-1}

The spring constant will be constant only up to the elastic limit. The force can be a compression force or a stretching force.

Worked example

Spring constant

A car has a mass of 1.2 tonne. The suspension springs of the car together have a spring constant of $2.0 \times 10^5\,\text{N m}^{-1}$. How far does the weight of the car compress its springs?

The rearranged formula gives:

$$\text{extension} = \frac{\text{force}}{\text{spring constant}} = \frac{1.2 \times 10^4\,\text{N}}{2.0 \times 10^5\,\text{N m}^{-1}}$$

$$= 6.0 \times 10^{-2}\,\text{m or 6 cm}$$

Worked example

Spring constant

A mass of 500 g is hung from the end of a spring of elastic constant $2.5 \times 10^2\,\text{N m}^{-1}$. Calculate the extension you would expect if the elastic limit is not exceeded and the event happens:

a) on the Earth ($g = 9.8\,\text{N kg}^{-1}$)
b) on the Moon ($g = 1.7\,\text{N kg}^{-1}$)

Using: $\text{extension} = \dfrac{\text{force}}{\text{spring constant}}$

a) $\text{extension} = \dfrac{0.5 \times 9.8}{2.5 \times 10^2} = 1.96 \times 10^{-2}\,\text{m}$ or 19.6 mm on the Earth

b) $\text{extension} = \dfrac{0.5 \times 1.7}{2.5 \times 10^2} = 3.4 \times 10^{-3}\,\text{m}$ or 3.4 mm on the Moon

Worked example

Measuring weight with an elastic spring

When a load of 12 N is applied to a steel spring it produces an extension of 80 mm without exceeding the elastic limit of the spring. Calculate the weight of an object which, when hung from the same spring, produces an extension of 60 mm.

$$\text{Spring constant} = \frac{\text{stretching force}}{\text{extension}} = \frac{12\,\text{N}}{80\,\text{mm}} = \frac{12\,\text{N}}{0.08\,\text{m}} = 150\,\text{Nm}^{-1}$$

This tells us that a force of 150 N would produce an extension of 1 m if the elastic limit was not exceeded. The extension produced by the object of unknown weight is 60 mm = 0.06 m. So the weight of the object W is:

W = spring constant × extension = 150 × 0.06 m = 9.0 N

Stretching elastic bands

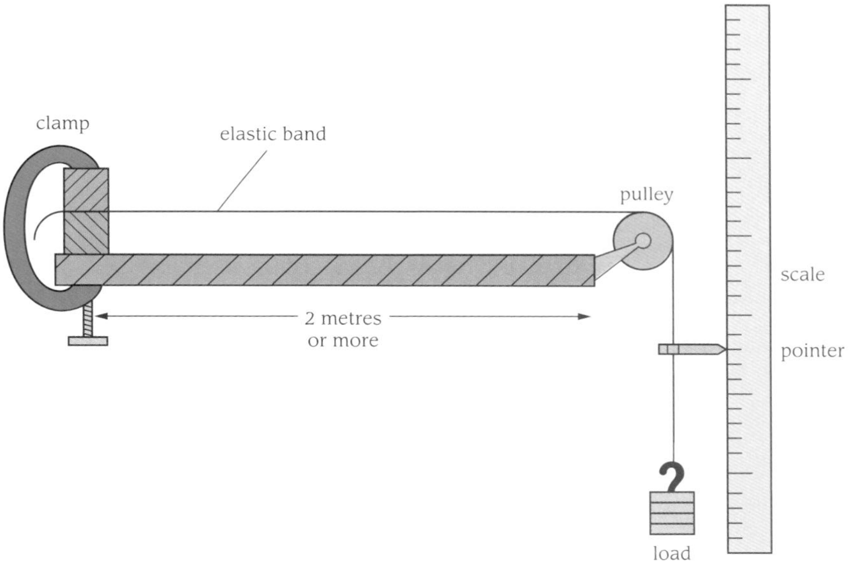

▲ **Figure 4.5.5** Stretching an elastic band

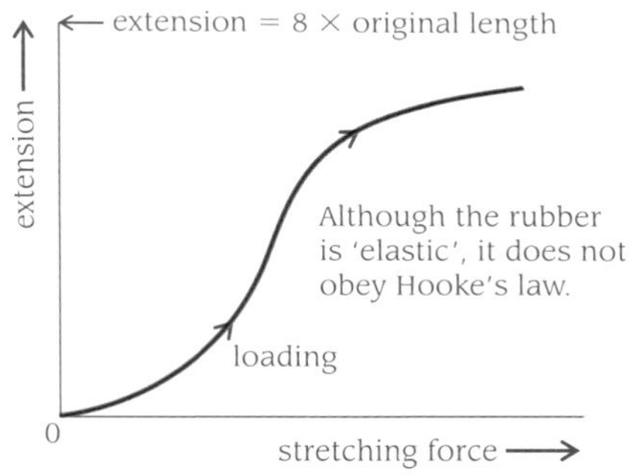

▲ **Figure 4.5.6** Extension graph of rubber

- Clamp the elastic band at one end, attach a slotted mass hanger at the other end and attach a paper pointer where the mm scale is fixed. The mm scale measures the change in length or extension of the elastic band rather than its total length.
- For a range of loads, take a series of scale readings, both as the masses are added and also as they are removed one by one and record your readings in a table.
- Complete the table and plot a graph of extension against stretching force.

Summary questions

1 Sketch a graph of extension against stretching force for a spring that obeys Hooke's law.

2 How does the graph change if the spring exceeds its elastic limit?

3 How can a spring be used to find the value of an unknown mass?

Key fact

About rubber

- At no part of the graph does rubber obey Hooke's law, as no part of it is straight.
- The extension is greater when unloading the masses than when loading. This effect is known as hysteresis and causes energy to be turned into heat in the rubber as it is stretched.

Practice exam-style questions

1 Calculate the weight (in newtons) of:

a) a girl of mass 40 kg

b) a car of mass 1 tonne

c) a pin of mass 300 mg.

2 Find the resultant of a force of 5 N and a force of 12 N acting at the same point on an object if:

a) the forces act in the same direction in the same straight line

b) the forces act in opposite directions but in the same straight line

c) the forces act at right angles to each other. *Remember to give both the magnitude and the direction of the resultant force.*

3 a) Why is force referred to as a vector quantity?

b) Two forces acting at a point have magnitudes 5 N and 8 N. Explain why their resultant may have any magnitude between 3 N and 13 N.

4 A girl uses a spanner of length 20 cm to tighten a nut. If she pulls at right angles to the end of the spanner with a force of 50 N, calculate the moment of her pull.

5 A boy of mass 40 kg and a girl of mass 30 kg play on a see-saw of negligible weight. If the boy sits 270 cm from the pivot of the see-saw, where must the girl sit to make it balance?

6 In the figure below, AC represents a trapdoor of width 100 cm which is hinged at A. The weight of the trapdoor is 30 N and its centre of gravity is 50 cm from A. An object is placed on the trapdoor so that its weight of 40 N acts through B, which is 25 cm from A.

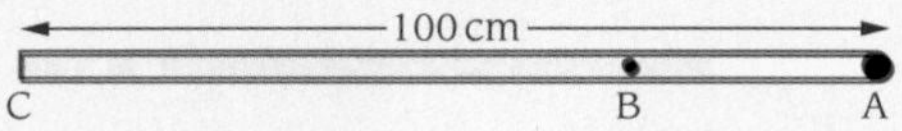

a) Redraw the diagram and show the two forces and add a third force applied vertically at C, which just lifts the door.

b) Calculate the magnitude of this force at C.

7 A workman uses a crowbar to lift a manhole cover. A crowbar is a long lever with its pivot between the load and the effort. An illustration is shown in Figure 6.2.1 on page 59.

The distance from the end of the crowbar where the workman pushes the crowbar downwards to the pivot is 0.90 m.

The distance from the pivot to the end of the crowbar where it lifts the manhole cover is 0.05 m.

The force needed to lift the edge of the manhole cover is 900 N.

a) If all forces act at right angles to the crowbar, calculate the force the workman needs to apply to the crowbar to lift the manhole cover.

b) Calculate the moment of the force applied by the workman.

8 A mechanic uses the spanner shown in the figure below to turn a bolt B into a threaded nut. The force *F* used to do this is applied in a horizontal plane at right angles to the spanner.

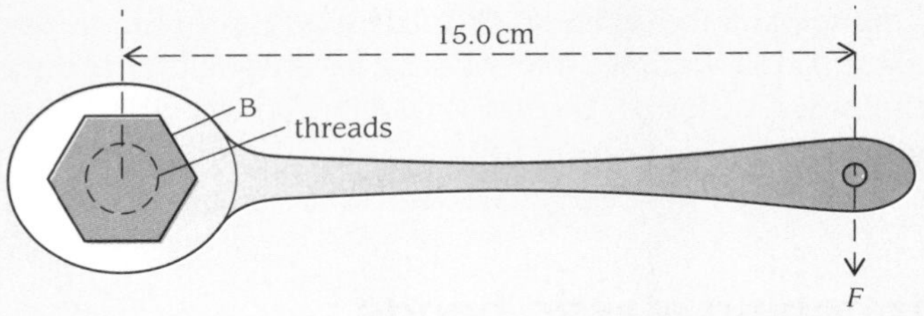

a) Sketch a simple, labelled diagram showing the forces acting in the horizontal plane on the spanner as it begins to turn the bolt.

b) If the effort, *F*, is 80.0 N and is applied 15.0 cm from the axis of the bolt, calculate the moment of the forces opposing *F* as the spanner just begins to turn.

c) Name the principle used in obtaining your result in **b)** above.

d) Explain why, if the mechanic uses a longer spanner, the effort needed will be smaller.

9 a) Describe how you would find, by experiment, the centre of gravity of a thin, irregularly shaped sheet of metal.

b) Explain why a minibus is more likely to topple over when the roof rack is heavily loaded than when the roof rack is empty.

c) A metre ruler is supported on a knife-edge placed at the 40 cm graduation. It is found that the metre ruler balances horizontally when a mass, which has a weight of 0.45 N is suspended at the 15 cm graduation, as shown in the figure below.

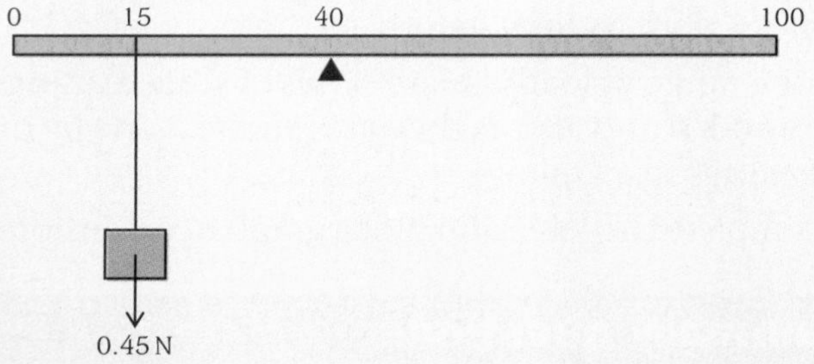

i) Calculate the moment about the knife-edge (in this balanced condition) of the force due to the weight of the ruler.

ii) If the weight of the ruler is 0.90 N, calculate the position of its centre of gravity.

10 The table lamp in the figure below has a circular base of diameter 120 mm and a height of 300 mm. It stands on a rough horizontal surface. The centre of mass of the table lamp is 60 mm above its base.

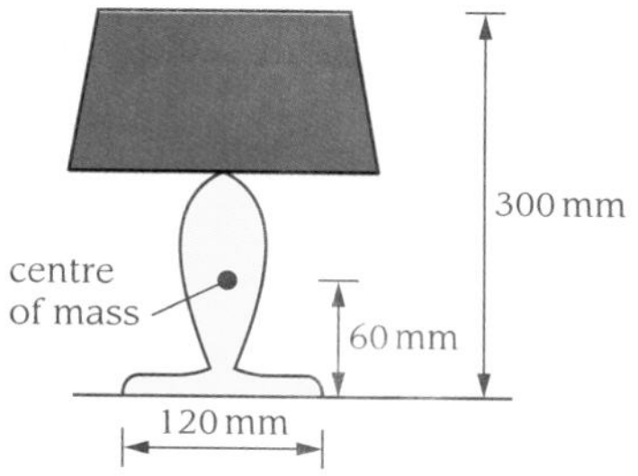

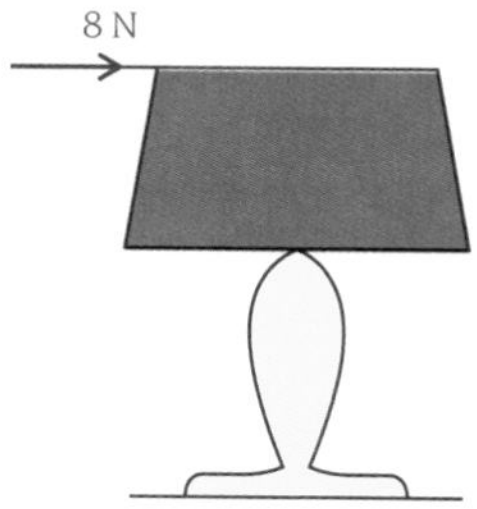

a) With the help of a diagram, explain why the table lamp topples when a certain angle of tilt is exceeded. Find the value of this angle.

b) Explain why it is possible for the centre of mass to be only 60 mm above the base and not midway between the top and base of the lamp.

c) When a horizontal force of 8 N is applied at the top of the table lamp as shown in the lower diagram, the table lamp just begins to pivot about its base. Calculate the weight of the table lamp.

d) Give TWO reasons why fitting a thin but heavy metal disc of diameter 160 mm to the base of the lamp would improve its stability.

11 By giving THREE examples, one for each, of bodies in different states of equilibrium, explain what is meant by

a) stable equilibrium

b) unstable equilibrium

c) neutral equilibrium.

In each case, state what happens to the centre of gravity of the body when the body's equilibrium is disturbed.

12 You are provided with a knife-edge, a uniform metre ruler and a 0.1 N weight. Describe how you would find the weight of the ruler without using any other apparatus. Explain clearly how you would calculate the final result from your measurements.

13 a) Define the moment of a force about a point.

b) State the principle of moments, giving the condition required for the principle to hold true.

c) The figure below shows a tray held horizontally by one hand at its edge.
The tray has a weight of 5.0 N.
The hand supports the tray with a downward force *F* from the thumb and an upward normal reaction force *N* from the fingers.
These two forces are 5.0 cm apart.
A glass of water of weight 2.0 N is supported by the tray at a distance of 30 cm from the normal reaction *N* where the balanced tray is pivoted.
Calculate:

i) the magnitude of the force, *F* provided by the thumb

ii) the magnitude of the reaction force, *N*.

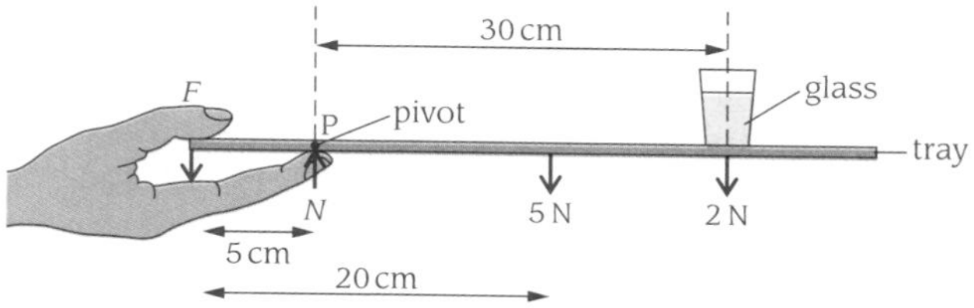

14 The entrance to a private car park is protected by a boom, which closes the entrance as shown in the figure below. The boom can be made to balance by fixing a counterweight *W* a short distance (0.50 m) from the pivot on the main support.

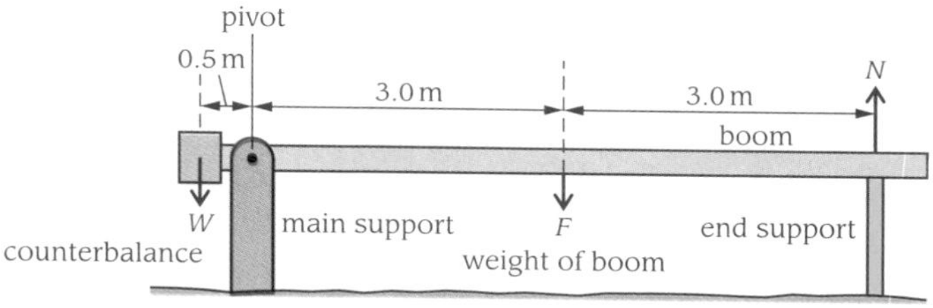

a) If the weight of the boom alone, *F*, is 400 N, and acts 3.0 m from the pivot as shown, calculate the counterweight required for the boom to be balanced.

b) If the actual counterweight fitted to this boom was 2350 N:

i) what additional downward force must be applied by the car park attendant to lift the boom

ii) what will be the normal reaction, *N*, at the end support when the boom is resting on it?

c) Calculate the reaction force at the pivot when the counterweight is 2350 N and the other end of the boom is supported.

d) If the boom is replaced with a stronger one of weight 470 N and the 2350 N counterweight is to be used again, where should the counterweight be fixed to exactly balance the boom?

15 The following results were obtained by a student when a spiral spring was stretched within its elastic limit.

Load/N	2.0	4.0	6.0	8.0	10.0	12.0	14.0	16.0
Length/mm	9.4	10.3	11.2	12.1	13.6	14.0	14.9	15.9

a) Plot a graph of length against load. (You can start the scale on the length axis from a value of 8.0 mm.)

b) Which point on the graph looks as if an error might have been made by the student? You should ignore this point when drawing your 'best fit' line.

c) Find the gradient or slope of the graph, *S*.

d) Find the spring constant. (The spring constant is the *reciprocal* of the slope, i.e. $1/S$.)

e) Use your graph to find the length of the spring when there is no load on the spring.

f) Find the length of the spring when the load is 7.0 N.

g) Calculate the extension of the spring for the same load.

h) What load would produce an extension of 4.0 mm?

i) How would the student know that in his experiment he had not taken the spring past its elastic limit? What additional readings could he take to confirm this?

16 The figure below shows how it is possible to balance a pencil vertically on its point without it falling over. A penknife is firmly attached so that it hangs below the surface on which the pencil point is balanced.

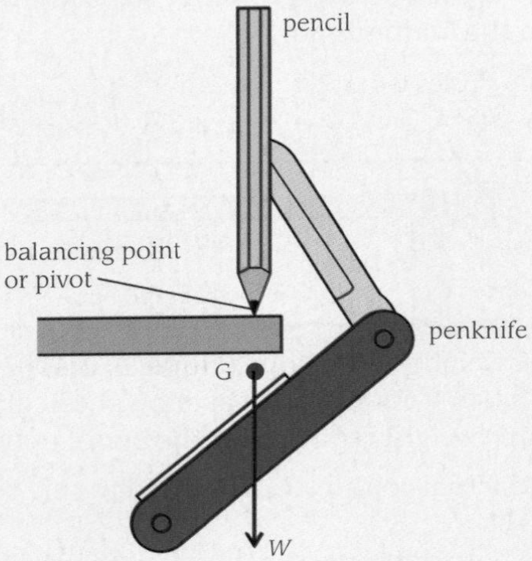

a) Explain:

i) what happens to the centre of gravity, G, of the combined pencil and penknife when they are set swinging

ii) what type of equilibrium this represents

iii) why it is not possible to balance the pencil on its point on its own.

b) Think of another example of an object, which is made to balance in this way by adding extra weight below its pivot, point of suspension or balancing point.

17 The figure below shows how the length of a spring changes when loaded.

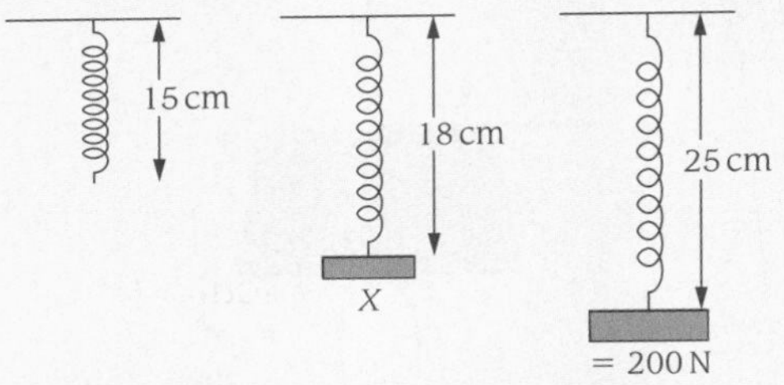

Use the information given in the diagram to calculate:

a) the extension produced by the 200 N load

b) the load that produces an extension of 1 cm

c) the load *X*

d) the length of the spring when a 120 N load is attached to it.

A5 Pressure

▲ **Figure 5.1.1** The pressure of water throws this fountain high in the air.

The pressure under your feet can compress soft ground so that your feet sink in. The pressure of the air can crush an evacuated can. The pressure of water can throw a fountain high in the air. The increased pressure inside a pressure cooker makes the food cook more quickly at a higher temperature and the high air pressure inside a bicycle or car tyre helps it support a heavy load. In these examples the word 'pressure' is being used correctly, but in everyday language it is often used more freely and incorrectly to mean force.

Objectives

By the end of this topic you will be able to:

- use the terms pressure and force correctly
- use the pressure formula
- recall the units of pressure.

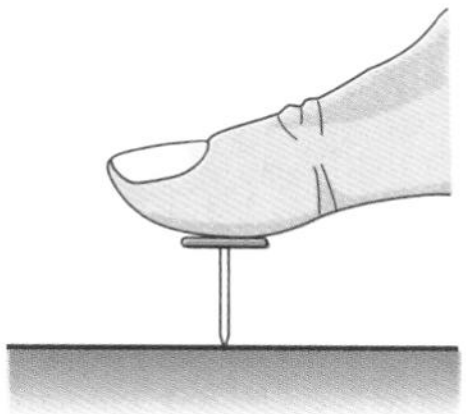

▲ **Figure 5.1.2** The force applied to the head of drawing pin is spread out, compared with applying the same force on the pointed end, which would be very painful.

Key fact

Pressure units: **pascal (Pa)**

1 pascal
= 1 newton per square metre

1 Pa = 1 N m^{-2}

force = pressure × area or $F = pA$

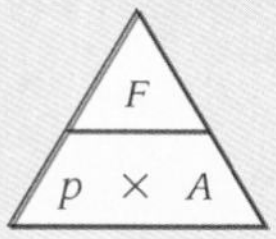

A5.1 Force and pressure

Pressure, force and area

Pressure is a measure of how hard a force pushes against something. The size of the pressure depends on how big the force is, and on the area it pushes against. Sometimes, we can feel whether pressure is high or low. In Figure 5.1.2 you can push hard enough on the head of the drawing pin to push it into the board. The force is spread out over a large area, so the pressure is low. If you pushed equally hard on the tip of the pin, it would hurt a lot! The same force spread over a very small area gives a high pressure – which hurts.

A person wearing high-heeled sandals will sink into soft sand, but the same person wearing flip-flops won't. When they wear high-heeled sandals, the force (their weight) is spread over a small area. The pressure is high and they sink in. With flip-flops the same force is spread over a bigger area. The pressure is less, so they don't sink in.

Calculating pressure

The ratio of normal force (force at right angles to the surface) to area is called pressure.

We calculate the pressure on a surface from the formula:

$$\text{pressure} = \frac{\text{normal force}}{\text{area}} \qquad p = \frac{F}{A}$$

Summary questions

1. State the formula used to calculate pressure.
2. What are the units of pressure?
3. Describe how you could calculate the pressure you exert on the ground.

Objectives

By the end of this topic you will be able to:

- recall key facts about the pressure in a liquid
- calculate the pressure at a depth in a liquid
- measure gas or air pressure.

A5.2 Pressure in liquids and gases

Key facts about the pressure in a liquid

- Pressure in a liquid is not affected by the shape or cross-sectional area of its container.
- All points on the same horizontal level in a liquid at rest have the same pressure.
- Pressure in a liquid acts equally in all directions at the same depth.
- Pressure is directly proportional to the depth below the surface or the height h of liquid above.
- Pressure is directly proportional to the density ρ of the liquid.

Pressure and force in a liquid

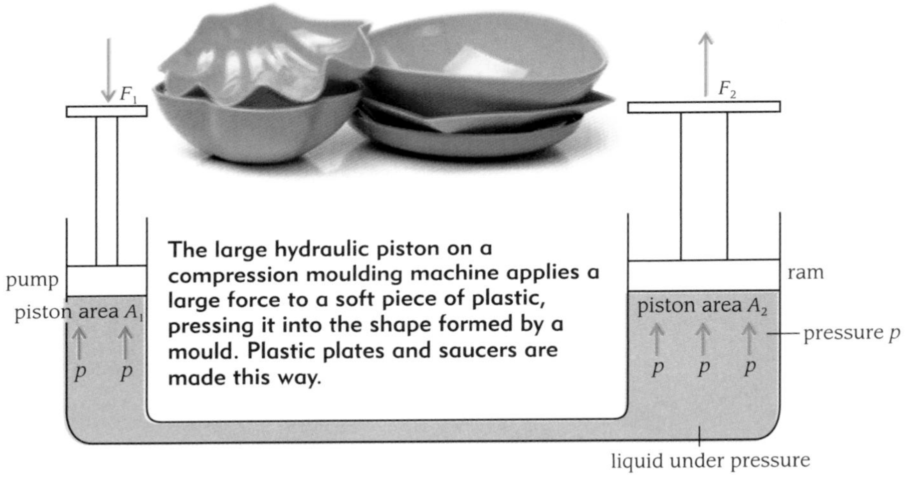

The large hydraulic piston on a compression moulding machine applies a large force to a soft piece of plastic, pressing it into the shape formed by a mould. Plastic plates and saucers are made this way.

▲ **Figure 5.2.1**

The pressure in a liquid can be used to transmit a force because of the following liquid properties:

- Liquids are incompressible.
- Liquid pressure acts equally in all directions (at the same level).
- Changes in liquid pressure are transmitted instantaneously and uniformly to all parts of a liquid.

The force F_1 applied to a piston of small area A_1 produces a pressure p in the liquid given by:

$$\text{pressure} = \frac{\text{force}}{\text{area}} \text{ or } p = \frac{F_1}{A_1}$$

This pressure acts throughout the liquid and pushes the large piston upwards with a force F_2, given by:

$$\text{force} = F_2 = \text{pressure} \times \text{area} = pA_2 = \left(\frac{F}{A_1}\right) A_2$$

Pressure and depth

The demonstration in Figure 5.2.2 is a simple way of showing that the pressure in a liquid increases with depth. The water comes out of the lowest tube in the tank fastest due to the greatest pressure. The pressure is caused by the weight of liquid above the level of the tube, and the weight of liquid is proportional to the height of liquid above that level. The distances reached from the base of the tank by the jets of water are roughly proportional to the heights of water h_1, h_2 and h_3.

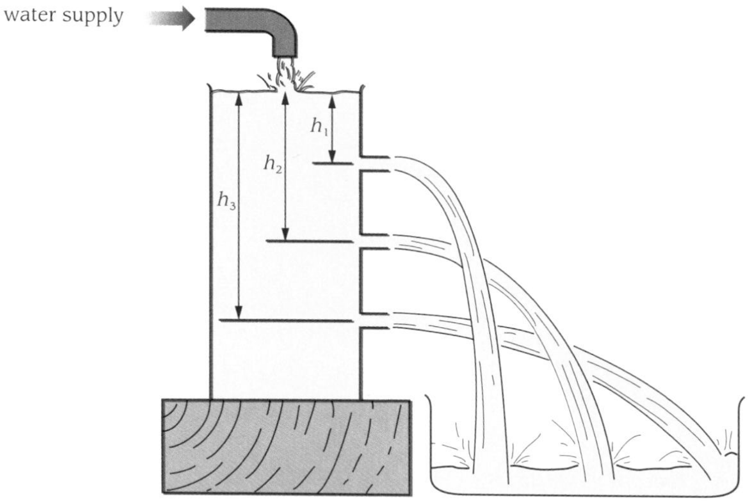

▲ **Figure 5.2.2** Pressure in a liquid increases with depth

Calculating pressure in a liquid

We calculate the pressure, p, in a liquid from the formula:

$p = h\rho g$ where h is the height of liquid above
ρ is the density of the liquid
$g = 9.8\,\text{N kg}^{-1}$

Worked example

Pressure in a liquid

The density of liquid mercury is $14 \times 10^3\,\text{kg m}^{-3}$. Calculate the liquid pressure 0.76 m below the surface of mercury.

$p = h\rho g = 0.76 \times 14 \times 10^3 \times 9.8$

$p = 1.04 \times 10^5\,\text{Pa}$

Worked example

Calculate the pressure under a girl's foot in pascals if her mass is 33.6 kg and the area of her shoe is $168\,\text{cm}^2$.

$A = 168\,\text{cm}^2 = 168 \times 10^{-4}\,\text{m}^2$

$F = mg = 33.6 \times 9.8 = 329\,\text{N}$

$$p = \frac{F}{A} = \frac{329}{168 \times 10^{-4}} = 2.0 \times 10^4\,\text{Pa}$$

Things to do

Calculate the pressure under your own feet:

- Place one shoe on a sheet of graph paper and draw round it.
- Count the number of square centimetres in your footprint.
- Calculate the area of your shoe in square metres.
- Weigh yourself and calculate your weight in newtons.
- Now calculate the pressure under one foot when it supports all your weight using $p = F \div A$.

Things to do

- Explain why it is difficult to remove the lid from a preserving jar, which was closed when the space above the food was full of steam.
- Explain why diving bells used for exploring deep water are built in a spherical shape.

Things to do

The bottle experiment

- Fill a bottle full of water by immersing it in a bowl of water.
- Keeping the top of the bottle below the water surface, lift the rest of the bottle out of the water.

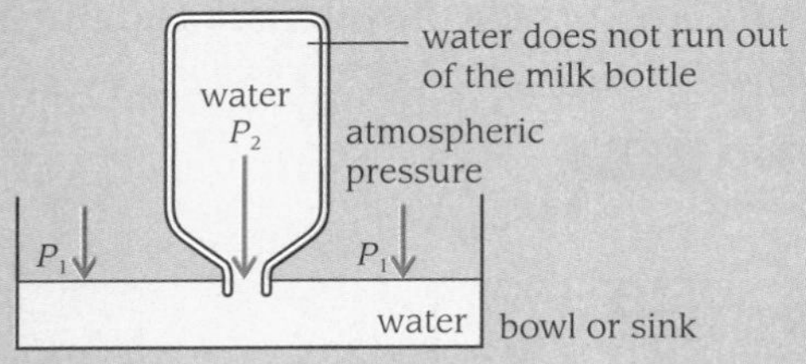

▶ Figure 5.2.3

The water does not run out of the bottle. Why?
The atmospheric pressure P_1 on the surface of the water is more than enough to balance the pressure of the water P_2 inside the bottle.

The can-crushing experiment

- Put a small volume of water in a metal can and boil the water for several minutes to drive out most of the air **a**.
- Stop heating and immediately seal the can with a well-fitting rubber stopper **b**.

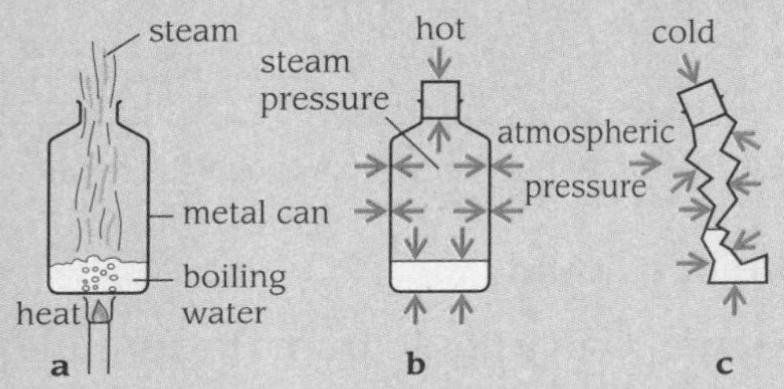

▶ Figure 5.2.4

At the moment you close the can the steam pressure inside exactly balances the atmospheric pressure outside.
As heat is lost from the can the steam inside condenses and the inside pressure falls. The atmospheric pressure is now much greater than the pressure inside the can, so it crushes the can and makes its volume very small **c**.

Air pressure

- Fill a cup or glass to overflowing with water.
- Place a sheet of paper or card over the top and turn upside down.

Air pressure pushes up on the card. Because there is no air pressure pushing down on the other side of the paper/card, it stays in place. Caution: the tiniest bubble of air on the inside of the cup/glass will cause the paper to fall off and the water to spill!

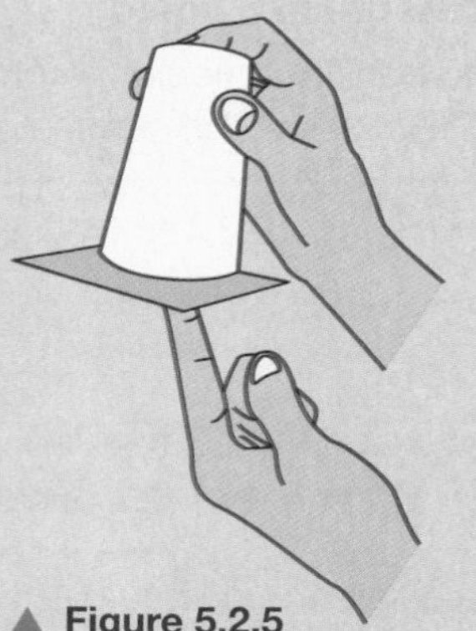

▲ Figure 5.2.5

Egg in a bottle

- Hard boil and shell an egg.
- Take a bottle with a top just smaller than the egg.
- Heat the air in the bottle by placing it in very hot water.
- Place the egg in the neck of the bottle.

As the air cools, it contracts and the pressure falls. The air pressure outside the bottle is greater than that inside, so the egg is 'pushed' into the bottle.

Measuring pressure: U-tube manometers

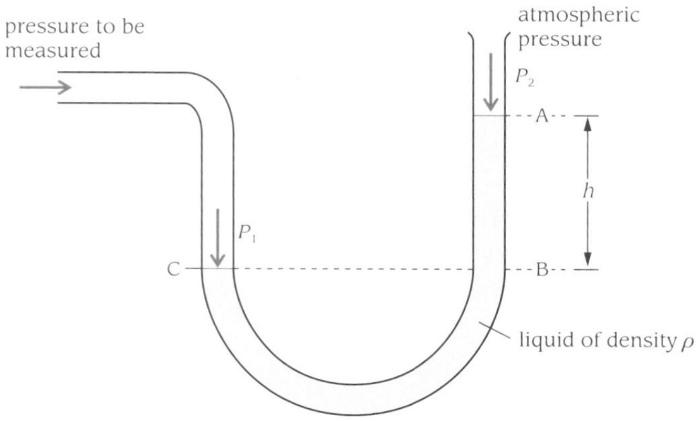

▲ **Figure 5.2.6** Measuring pressure with a U-tube manometer

P_1 is the pressure to be measured (e.g. gas pressure).

The pressure at A is atmospheric pressure, P_2.

The U-tube contains a liquid of density ρ.

The pressure difference between P_1 and P_2 is indicated by the difference between the liquid levels h.

The pressures at C and B are equal because they are at the same level in the liquid and any pressure difference at the same level causes a flow of liquid to equalise that difference: so the pressure at B gives a measure of P_1.

Total pressure at B = atmospheric pressure + liquid pressure

$$P_1 = P_2 + h\rho g$$

$h\rho g$ alone gives the pressure excess of P_1 over atmospheric pressure, P_2.

Measuring pressure: the mercury barometer

A barometer uses the principle of the U-tube manometer.

There is a vacuum above C and zero pressure.

The atmospheric pressure, $P_1 = h\rho g$. (P_2 = zero)

Atmospheric pressure is so large that if we used water in the tube it would need to be over 10 m high. Instead we use mercury which, being 14 times more dense than water, has the same pressure for a height 14 times shorter.

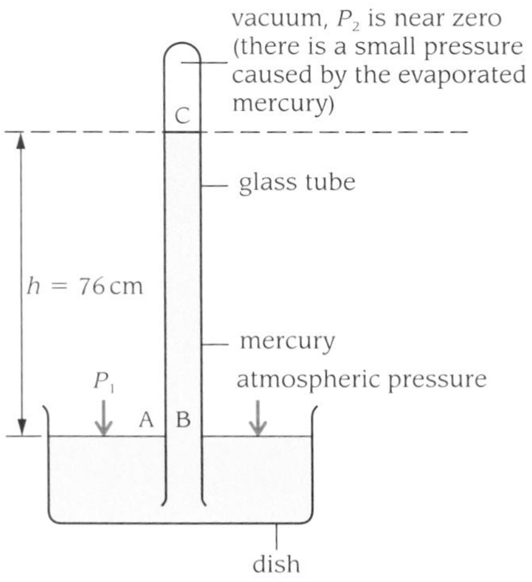

▲ **Figure 5.2.7** The mercury barometer

Atmospheric pressure

Atmospheric or air pressure is caused by the weight of air above us in the Earth's atmosphere. Atmospheric pressure varies around the surface of the Earth and with height above sea level. Atmospheric pressures are quoted in millibars.

1 bar = 100 kPa = normal atmospheric pressure

1 bar = 1000 millibars.

So the atmospheric pressure on an average day near sea level may be quoted as either 100 kPa, 1 bar, 1000 millibars or 76 cm of mercury!

All places on a weather map that have the same atmospheric pressure are joined together by lines called isobars.

Variation of pressure with height above sea level

If the air in the atmosphere was uniformly dense then the pressure of the air would be directly proportional to the height of atmosphere above, in the same way that the pressure in a liquid is proportional to the height of liquid above.

In fact the atmosphere gets gradually less dense with increasing height above sea level. There is no definite upper limit to the atmosphere because it gradually merges into space. At about 80 km above sea level, the pressure has fallen to 1 Pa and at this height radiation from space has ionised the molecules of the air and made them into charged ions. This layer of atmosphere, extending from about 60 km to 600 km above the Earth, is therefore known as the **ionosphere**.

Figure 5.2.8 shows how atmospheric pressure varies with height above sea level. During aircraft take-off and landing your ears may 'pop' or feel uncomfortable. This is because atmospheric pressure is changing rapidly as the aircraft changes height. Aircraft cabins are pressurised to protect us from the changes in atmospheric pressure.

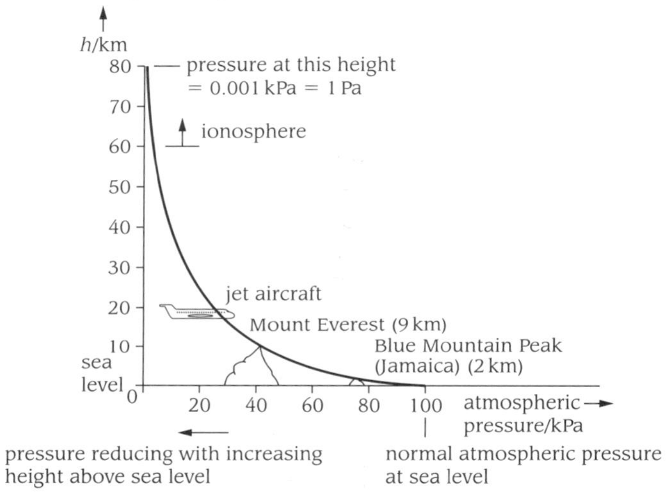

▲ **Figure 5.2.8** Variation of atmospheric pressure with height above sea level

Depressions and hurricanes

Atmospheric pressures at sea level are usually within the range from 960 millibars (96 kPa) to 1040 millibars (104 kPa). Low pressure regions are called **cyclones** or **depressions**. High pressure regions are called **anticyclones**.

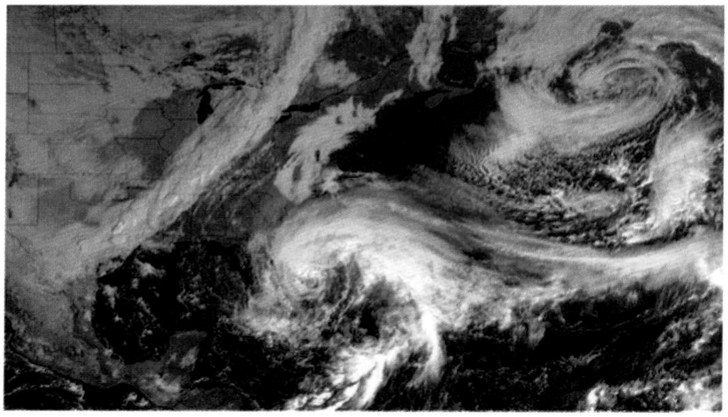

▲ **Figure 5.2.9** Satellite photo of hurricane Sandy as it passes over the Caribbean

Things to do

Explain:

- why high-flying aircraft need to be airtight and have pressurised cabins
- why dams that hold water in reservoirs must be thicker at the base
- how a rubber sucker clings to a wall.

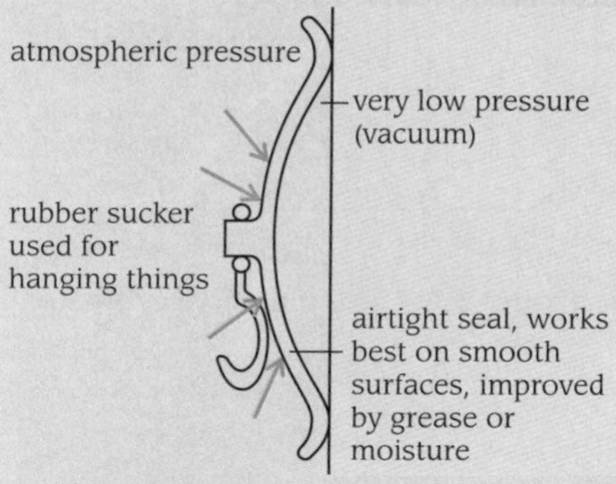

▲ **Figure 5.2.10**

The position and movement of cyclones and anticyclones is used to predict weather. In tropical waters like the Caribbean, clouds and thunderstorms circling a region of falling pressure can build up into hurricanes, with violent seas, torrential rains and wind speeds from 74 mph (category 1 hurricane) to over 155 mph (category 5 hurricane).

Summary questions

1 Give two facts about the pressure in a liquid.

2 Why do bubbles get bigger as they rise to the surface of a liquid?

3 Name an instrument you could use to measure gas pressure. Say how it works.

A5.3 Archimedes' principle and floating

Objectives

By the end of this topic you will be able to:

- recall and apply Archimedes' principle
- predict whether a body will sink or float in a particular liquid.

Key fact

Forces in equilibrium

This diagram shows the forces acting on the block when it is immersed in water.

There is equilibrium between the three vertical forces acting on the block. The downwards weight of 8 N is equal and opposite to the sum of the two upward forces. These are a 5 N tension force measured on the spring balance and a 3 N upthrust force provided by the water and causing the apparent loss of weight of the block.

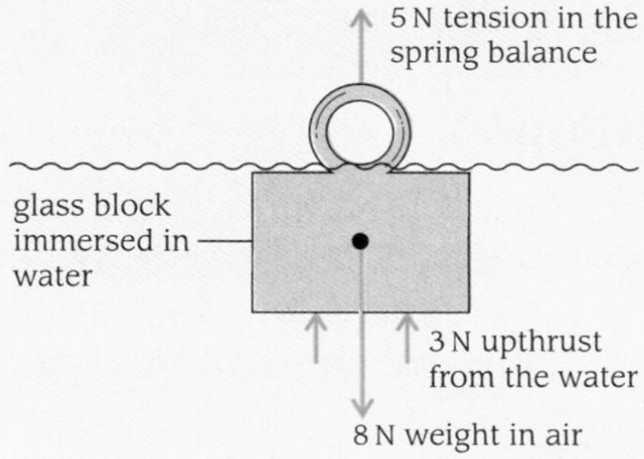

▶ **Figure 5.3.1**

Heavy steel ships can float on water, but as steel is more dense than water we might expect them to sink. If you try to lift a heavy object, which is under water you find it surprisingly light and much easier to lift than when it is out of water.

The Greek scientist Archimedes was the first person to realise that there is an upwards force on an object placed in a liquid, which comes from the liquid itself and makes the object appear to lose weight and sometimes makes it float.

Investigating Archimedes' principle

We need an arrangement for weighing an object in both air and water to find out how much weight it appears to lose when immersed in water. We also need to weigh the water displaced (that is, pushed out of the way) by the immersed object. The apparatus in Figure 5.3.2 allows both these measurements to be made.

The readings on scale A give the weight of the glass block in air (8 N) and then its apparent weight when immersed in a can of water (5 N).

The readings on scale B give first the weight of the empty beaker (2 N) and then the weight of the beaker plus the water displaced from the displacement can by the glass block (5 N).

Scale A shows an apparent loss of weight by the glass block of 8 N − 5 N = 3 N. Although the block has different weights in water and in air, its mass remains constant, at 800 g.

Key fact

The principle of Archimedes

Scale B shows an increase in weight of 5 N − 2 N = 3 N, which is the weight of water displaced by the block.

We can see that the upthrust force (of 3 N) provided by the liquid is equal to the weight of liquid displaced (3 N) by the glass block. This discovery, which is Archimedes' principle, can be demonstrated for all fluids, i.e. for all gases as well as liquids. The same result is produced whether the object is wholly or partially immersed in a fluid and whether it sinks or floats.

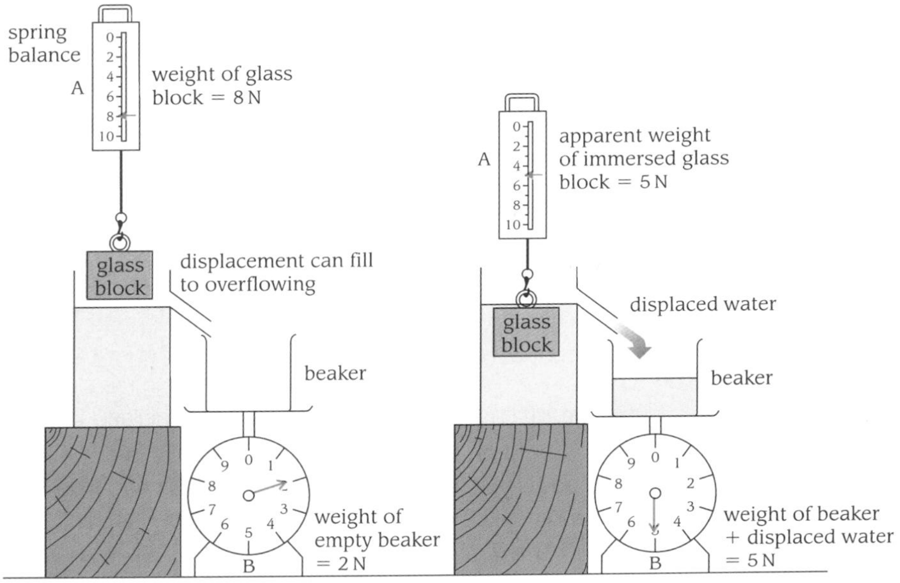

▲ **Figure 5.3.2** Investigating Archimedes' principle

Sinking and floating

The vertical forces acting on an object immersed in a fluid can be represented by the two forces shown in Figure 5.3.3. *W* is the weight of the object and *U* is the upthrust of the fluid. The vertical forces acting on a floating object such as a ship **a** are in equilibrium as the ship neither rises up out of the water nor sinks down into it.

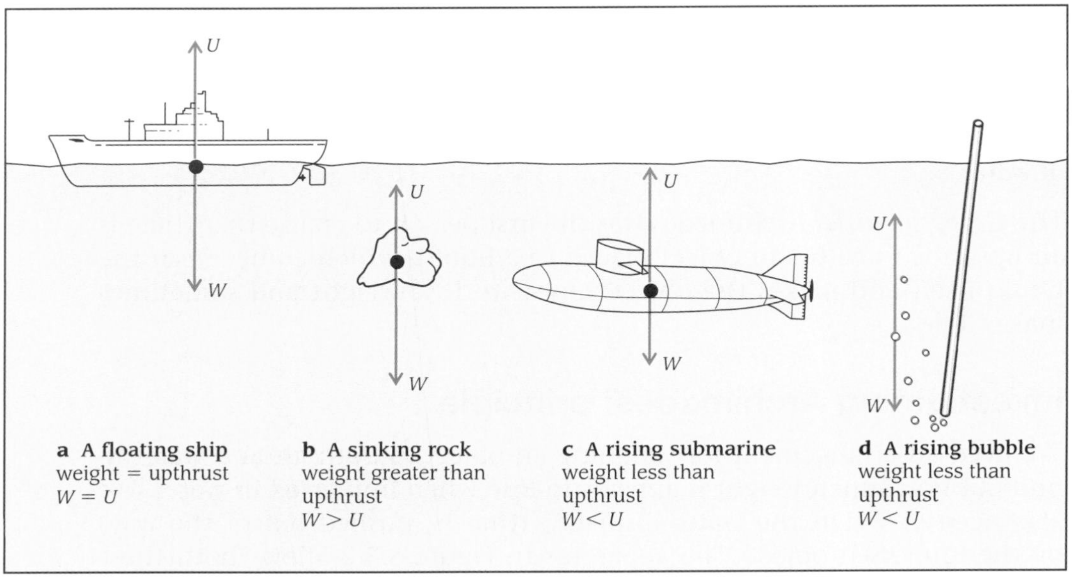

Figure 5.3.3 Sinking and floating

So for a floating object we can say:

The upthrust, U = the weight, W, of the object

Since the upthrust also equals the weight of fluid displaced (Archimedes' principle), we can also say:

The weight of fluid displaced = the weight of the object.

This is the law of flotation:

A floating object displaces its own weight of the fluid in which it floats.

a) This provides the explanation of how a steel ship floats. The hollow steel hull of the ship sinks down into the water and displaces water until the weight of water displaced is as great as the weight of the ship. Then the upthrust equals the ship's weight and it floats.

b) A rock also experiences an upthrust in water and appears to weigh much less in water than in the air. But the weight W of a rock is greater than the upthrust U and so it sinks.

c) An object made of a material less dense than water, such as wood or cork, or a submarine which has filled its flotation tanks with air, will experience an upthrust U, which is greater than its weight W and so will rise to the surface of the water.

Archimedes' principle

The upthrust force on an object wholly or partially immersed in a fluid is equal and opposite to the weight of the fluid displaced by the object.

▲ **Figure 5.3.4** A balloon filled with hot (expanded) air or a gas of low density (hydrogen or helium) will rise in the atmosphere for the same reason as the submarine rises. The weight of the balloon filled with a low-density gas is less than the upthrust on it caused by the displaced denser air.

Worked example

A boat of mass 400 tonnes floats in seawater of density 1030 kg m^{-3}. Calculate the volume of seawater displaced.

The boat will displace a weight of seawater equal to its own weight so the mass of water displaced equals the mass of the boat = 400 × 10^3 kg.

For seawater:

$$\text{volume} = \frac{\text{mass}}{\text{density}} = \frac{400 \times 10^3\,\text{kg}}{1030\,\text{kg m}^{-3}}$$

Volume = 388 m^3

Summary questions

1 What can you say about the forces on a floating object?

2 'A sinking object displaces its own mass of liquid'. Is this statement true or false?

3 Why does a boat settle 'lower' in the water when it is fully laden?

Exam tip

Use of terminology

Be careful to use words precisely. Avoid comments like 'Heavy things sink, light things float'. 'Heavy' and 'light' tell us about an object's mass. Some very heavy things, such as ships, float and some very light things, such as marbles, sink. What determines whether something floats or sinks is its average density; how heavy or light it is for its size.

Practice exam-style questions

1 A stone pillar has a mass of 3.0 tonnes. If the area of its base is 0.3 m^2, calculate the pressure under the pillar. Give your answer in pascals.

2 A block of metal of density 3000 kg m^{-3} is 2 m high and stands on a square base of side 0.5 m, as shown in the figure below.

a) What is the base area of the block?

b) What is the volume of the block?

c) What is the mass of the block?

d) What is the weight of the block?

e) What is the pressure exerted by the weight of the block on the surface on which it stands?

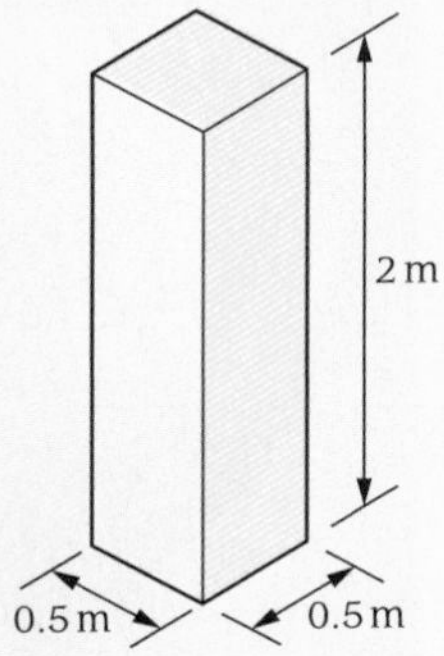

3 a) State TWO factors on which the pressure exerted by a liquid depends.

b) The atmospheric pressure on a particular day was measured as 750 mm of mercury. Convert this pressure measurement into pascals (Pa) (N m^{-2}). Show the units at every stage of your calculations.

(Assume that the density of mercury is 13 600 kg m^{-3} and that the acceleration of free fall (due to gravity) is 10 m s^{-2} (N kg^{-1}).)

4 The pressure at a point below the surface of the sea is caused by both the height of water above that point and the air pressure on the surface. If a diver reaches a depth of 20 m below the surface of the sea, calculate:

a) the additional pressure on him due to the height of seawater alone

b) the total pressure on him.

Density of seawater = 1150 kg m^{-3}.

Air pressure = 1.0×10^5 Pa.

$g = 9.8$ m s^{-2}.

5 a) Explain what is meant by pressure.

b) Describe a simple experiment to show how the pressure exerted by a liquid varies with the depth below the liquid surface. State the result you would expect to obtain.

c) A rectangular block 0.01 m by 0.02 m by 0.04 m has a mass of 0.064 kg. Calculate:

i) the density of the material of the block

ii) the weight of the block

iii) the pressure the block would exert when resting on its smallest side.

Acceleration of free fall is 10 m s^{-2}.

6 The figure below shows a manometer with limbs of area of cross section 0.012 m^2 that contains liquid which weighs 8000 N m^{-3}. The manometer is connected to the laboratory gas supply and the tap turned on. As shown in the diagram, there is a difference in the liquid levels in the two limbs of 0.25 m. Calculate:

a) the volume of liquid between the levels AB and CD in the right-hand tube

b) the weight of this liquid

c) the excess pressure, in N m^{-2}, of the gas supply above atmospheric.

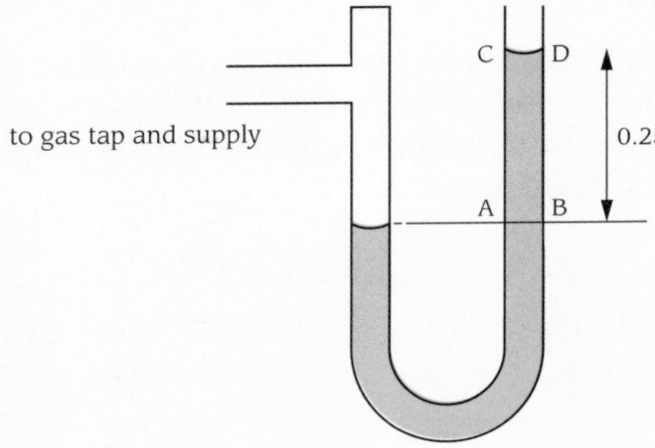

7 The level of water in a measuring cylinder is at the 50 cm^3 mark. A small solid object is put into the cylinder so that it is submerged. The water level is now at the 90 cm^3 mark. Take $g = 10$ N kg^{-1}.

a) What is the volume of the object?

b) If the density of the object is 2.5 g cm^{-3}, find:

i) its mass

ii) its weight.

8 The pressure inside a gas cylinder is to be measured using a U-tube manometer similar to the one shown in the figure in question 6. The U-tube is half-filled with a coloured liquid of density 9.6×10^2 kg m^{-3}.

If the difference in height between the liquid levels in the two arms of the U-tube is 0.16 m, calculate the excess gas pressure (above air pressure) in the cylinder.
($g = 10$ N kg^{-1})

9 A diver reaches a depth in sea water where the pressure on him is five times greater than at the surface. If the air pressure at the surface of the sea is 1.0×10^5 Pa, what depth has the diver reached in the sea? (density of sea water is 1.03×10^3 kg m^{-3}, $g = 9.8$ N kg^{-1})

10 a) State Archimedes' principle.

b) A solid cylinder of wood has a cross-sectional area of $20\,cm^2$ and height 90 cm. It floats upright in water. If two-thirds of the length of the cylinder is submerged, calculate:

i) the weight of water displaced
ii) the weight of the wooden cylinder
iii) the density of the wood.

Acceleration due to gravity, $g = 10\,m\,s^{-2}$
Density of water $= 1000\,kg\,m^{-3}$.

11 a) A rectangular block of wood measures 4 cm × 4 cm × 10 cm and has a mass of 128 g.

i) Calculate its volume in SI units.
ii) Express this volume in standard form.
iii) Express the mass in SI units and standard form.
iv) Calculate the density of the wood.

b) Using Archimedes' principle, explain why this block of wood will float in water of density $1000\,kg\,m^{-3}$.

c) Do you think the same block of wood would float in a liquid of relative density 0.85? Explain.

12 The figure below shows details of an experiment performed by a student and the results obtained. Calculate:

a) the volume of the metal block below water level
b) the mass of water displaced into the beaker
c) the new reading on the compression balance
d) the new reading on the spring balance
e) the reading you would expect to obtain on the spring balance if the metal block were completely immersed in water.

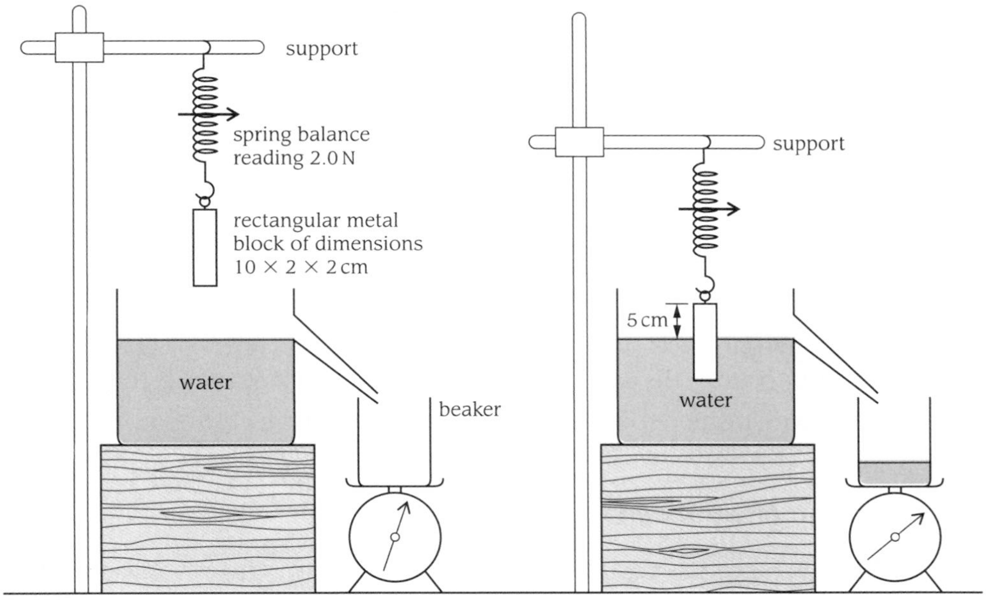

13 a) State the equation that gives the pressure at a depth, h, in a liquid of density ρ.

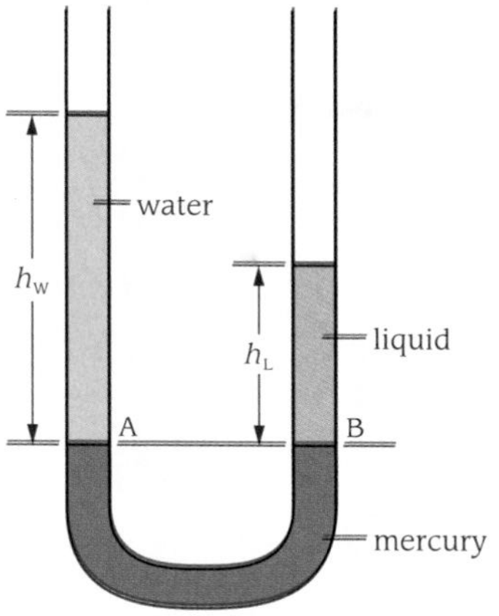

b) The U-tube in the figure can be used to find the density of a liquid by comparison with water. The liquids are level at points A and B where the pressures are also equal.

Calculate the additional pressure at point A below the water column if the height of water, h_W, is 0.20 m.

The density of water is $1000\,kg\,m^{-3}$.

Acceleration due to gravity, $g = 10\,m\,s^{-2}$.

c) If the height of the liquid column, h_L, is 0.16 m, calculate the relative density of the liquid.

A6 Work, energy and power

▲ **Figure 6.1.1** Galileo's pendulum clock was first constructed after his death in 1642 by his son. This sketch shows a simple escapement mechanism, pendulum and gear wheels, which controlled the rotation of the clock hands. However, this machine failed to keep going because it had no energy input. There were no springs or weights to keep the pendulum swinging.

The earliest stone tools ever discovered, thought to have been used by our ape-like ancestor *Homo erectus*, are over two million years old. Since that time long ago, our development and progress have been closely linked with making and using tools and machines.

A6.1 Work, energy and power

All machines, whether simple or complex, allow a force applied at one place to overcome another force at a different place. Overcoming a force involves doing work. Machines in action do work by taking in energy at one end and feeding it out at the other end, perhaps in a different form. So to understand machines we must look carefully at what we mean by work, energy and the power of a machine.

Objectives

By the end of this topic you will be able to:

- define work and power
- define the units: joule and watt
- calculate the work done by, and the power of, a machine.

Work

In science we use the word **work** in a precise way. For example, if you lift a brick from the ground and put it on a wall or if you climb up the stairs you are 'working' in the scientific sense of the word. Similarly if you push a pram or a bicycle and it moves you are also working, but if you push a wall and it remains standing, although you may get tired, you are not working. For work to be done a force must produce motion.

Work is done when a force moves its point of application.

Example **a** in Figure 6.1.2

- Force F is a pushing force that moves the roller.
- The roller moves in the same direction as the force, a distance s.
- The pushing force moves with the roller.
- The weight of the roller (acting downwards) and the normal contact force of the ground (acting upwards) act on the roller but do no work because they act at right angles to the motion.

Example **b** raising the man because it does not move upwards with the man. Internal forces, mainly within the muscles of the man's legs, push his body upwards.

- The internal forces, acting upwards through his centre of gravity, are equal and opposite to his weight and overcome the pull of the Earth (his weight).
- The work done depends on the vertical height h climbed or the distance moved upwards by the pushing force.

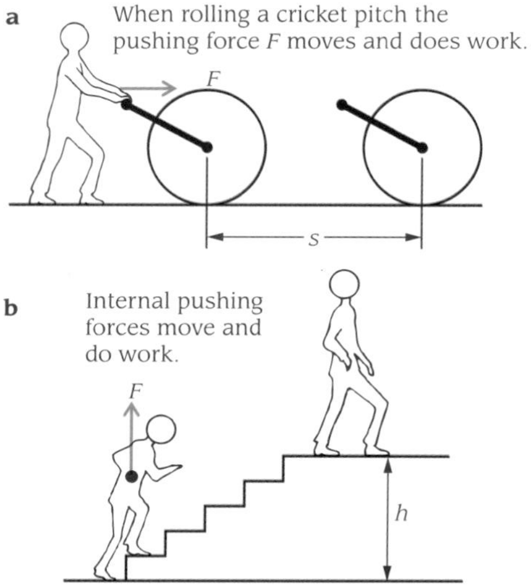
a
When rolling a cricket pitch the pushing force F moves and does work.
F
s
b
Internal pushing forces move and do work.
F
h

▲ **Figure 6.1.2** Measuring work done

Definition of work done

When a force moves its point of application, the work done by the force is given by the magnitude of the force multiplied by the distance moved in the direction of the force.

Work, energy and power

Calculating work done:

work done = force × distance moved in the direction of the force

$$W = Fs$$

The unit of work, given by force × distance, is the newton × metre and is called the joule.

The SI unit of work is called the **joule (J)**.

A joule is the work done when the point of application of a force of 1 newton moves through a distance of 1 metre in the direction of the force.

$$1\ \text{joule} = 1\ \text{newton} \times 1\ \text{metre}$$

$$1\,\text{J} = 1\,\text{N m}$$

Energy and power

The **energy** that something has is a measure of its ability to do work. So, for example, there is more energy stored in a full tank of petrol than in a half-full tank, because it is able to do more work to move the car further.

The unit of energy, the joule (J), is the same as the unit of work.

Machines and energy

Neither people nor machines can do work without a supply of energy. We get our energy supply from the food we eat and machines are 'fed' with energy in many forms. For example, some machines are fed with fuels such as coal, oil and gas. Since the energy stored in these fuels is released by chemical reactions such as burning, we describe them as chemical forms of energy.

Some machines take their energy supply in the form of electricity from power stations. But electrical energy is a form of energy which has first to be produced from another form of energy, such as chemical energy or nuclear energy. A few machines take their energy directly from the Sun or the wind. Can you think of examples of these? All these sources of energy are discussed in more detail in A7.11.

Machines transfer or convert energy

The action of a machine is to convert the energy supplied to it into another form of energy or to transfer the energy to another place. The total energy output from a machine is always equal to the energy input or, in other words, energy is always **conserved** by a machine. In this sense machines do not 'use up' or 'consume' energy even though they need an energy input to be able to do work.

Worked example

If a force of 50 N is used to pull a box along the ground a distance of 8 m and the box moves in the same direction as the force, calculate the work done by the force.

$W = Fs$

$W = 50\,\text{N} \times 8\,\text{m} = 400\,\text{N m}$

Or $W = 400\,\text{J}$

Work, energy and power

Worked example

A man of mass 60 kg walks up a track inclined at an angle of 30° to the horizontal. If he walks 400 m along the track, how much work does he do?
Take $g = 10\,\text{N kg}^{-1}$.

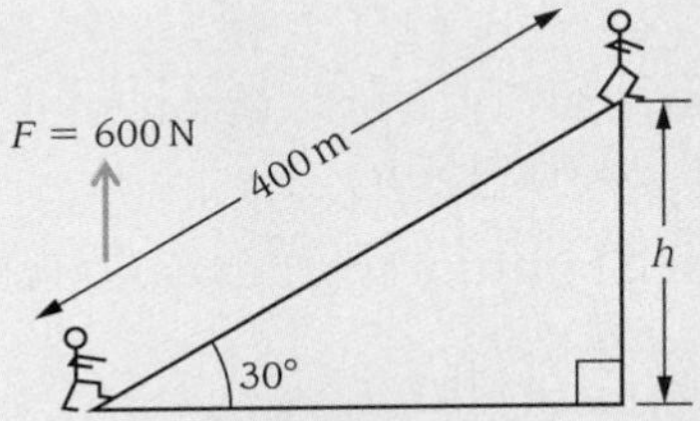

The man must use an upwards force equal and opposite to his weight to climb up the track.

The man's weight = mg

$= 60\,\text{kg} \times 10\,\text{N kg}^{-1} = 600\,\text{N}$,

so the upwards force = 600 N.

The distance moved in the direction of this force is the vertical height h climbed up the track (not the length of the track). In the triangle

$\sin 30° = \dfrac{h}{l}$

$\therefore \quad h = l \sin 30°$

$\therefore \quad h = 400\,\text{m} \times 0.5 = 200\,\text{m}$

Work done = vertical force × vertical distance

Work = 600 N × 200 m
= 120 000 N m
= 120 kJ

Exam tip

Use of terminology

Be careful to use terminology correctly. In everyday language, people often use the words 'work', 'energy' and 'power' and 'force' as though they were the same. Check you can use the words correctly, and explain how they are different.

Power

We all know that a more powerful car can climb hills faster and a more powerful electric saw can cut wood faster. As soon as power is mentioned we are thinking about how quickly work can be done. The **power** of a machine is a measure of how much work it can do (like climbing a hill or cutting wood) in a certain time.

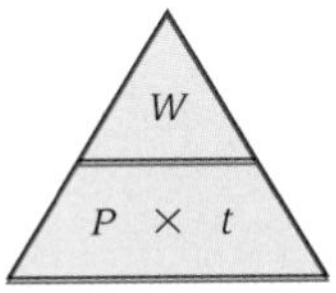

The power of a machine is the rate at which it does work.
Also
The power of a machine is the rate at which it transfers or converts energy from one form to another.

The power of a machine	=	its rate of doing work	=	its rate of conversion of energy
power	=	$\dfrac{\text{work}}{\text{time}}$	=	$\dfrac{\text{energy converted}}{\text{time}}$
P	=	$\dfrac{W}{t}$	=	$\dfrac{E}{t}$

The units of power given by the formula are joule/second or joules per second also called the **watt (W)**, named after James Watt (1735–1819).

A watt is the rate of working or energy conversion of 1 joule per second.
1 watt = 1 joule per second ($1\,\text{W} = 1\,\text{J s}^{-1}$)

Worked example

Calculate the work done in 1 hour by an electric motor in a washing machine which has an output power rated at 1.5 kW.

The time = 1 hour = 3600 s
Power = 1.5 kW = 1500 W
Work done = power × time
Work done = 1500 W × 3600 s
= 5 400 000 J or 5.4 MJ

Measuring your own power output

Your rate of working is probably at its highest when you are running up a hill or up stairs lifting your own weight.

- Get another person to time how long it takes you to run up a long flight of steps.
- Measure the height of one step and count the number of steps you climbed. You also need to know your own weight.

Here are some results for a healthy girl of mass 44 kg.

time to climb the steps = 11 s
height of 1 step = 20 cm
number of steps climbed = 60
vertical height climbed = 60 × 0.20 m = 12 m

The girl's weight = $mg = 44\,\text{kg} \times 10\,\text{N kg}^{-1}$
$= 440\,\text{N}$

and this is equal to the force she uses to lift herself up the stairs.

Work done = Fs = 440 N × 12 m = 5280 N m = 5280 J

$$\text{The power of the girl} = \frac{\text{work done}}{\text{time taken}} = \frac{5280\,\text{J}}{11\,\text{s}} = 480\,\text{W}$$

Things to do

Measure your own power:

a) running up stairs
b) climbing a local hill
c) cycling up a hill (include the weight of the bicycle)
d) lifting a heavy object up and down a measured height for a large number of times.

Summary questions

1 What is the unit of work?
2 Calculate the work done by a force of 15 N moving a distance of 5 m.
3 If it took 10 s for the force to move this distance, calculate the power.
4 Describe how you could measure your own power.

A6.2 Simple machines

Objectives

By the end of this topic you will be able to:

- distinguish between force and distance-multiplying machines
- define MA and VR
- explain the working principles of some simple machines.

Levers

Machines are devices to make work easier to do, or to do work more efficiently. A lever is an example of a simple machine. One force (called the **effort**) is used to move another force (called the **load**). Figure 6.2.1 shows a crowbar being used as a lever. Using what you learned about moments (A4.3), you can see that the effort (the force used) is smaller than the load (the force being overcome).

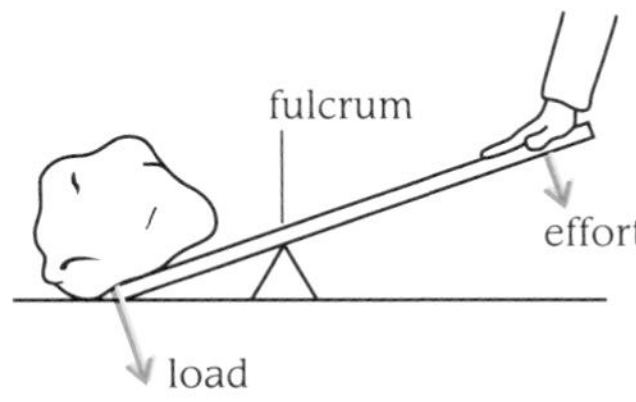

▲ **Figure 6.2.1** Using a crowbar

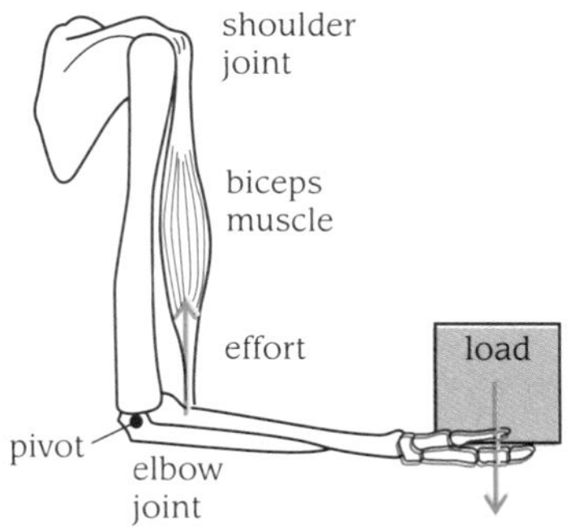

▲ **Figure 6.2.2** Using your forearm

! Key fact

Force multipliers and MA

- The MA of a force multiplier is greater than 1, e.g. a crowbar.
- The VR of a force multiplier is also greater than 1.
- The MA of a machine can only be found by measurement.
- The MA of a machine is reduced by friction.
- MA is a ratio and has no units.

! Key fact

Distance multipliers and VR

- The MA of a distance multiplier is less than 1.
- The VR of a distance multiplier is less than 1, e.g. the human forearm.
- The VR of a machine is not affected by friction.
- The VR of a machine can be calculated from the design of the machine.
- VR is a ratio and has no units.

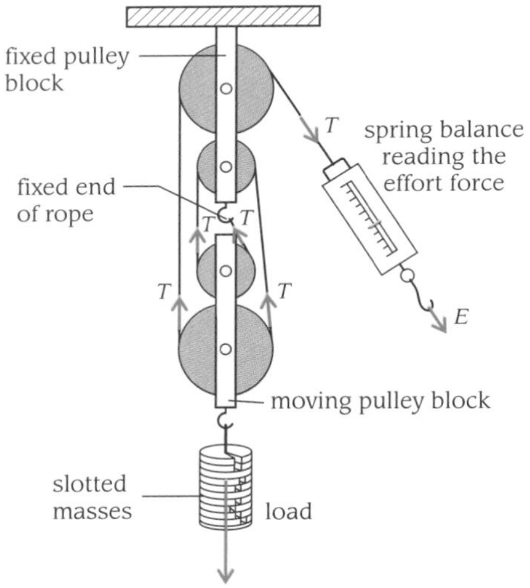

▲ **Figure 6.2.4** A block and tackle with VR = 4

The wheelbarrow and bottle opener in Figure 6.2.3 are both examples of levers. For each one, use moments to decide which force is greater, the load or the effort.

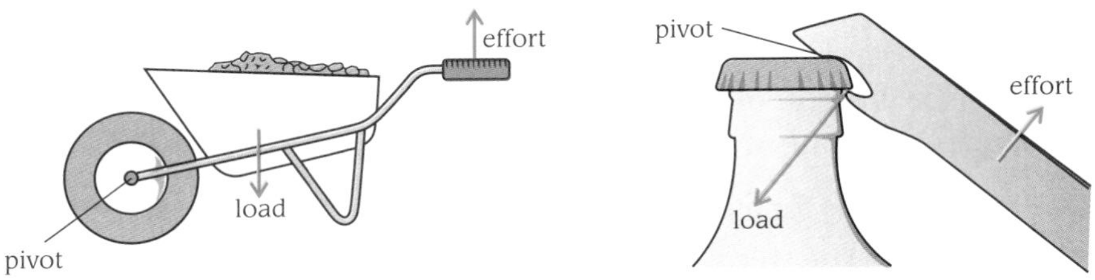

▲ **Figure 6.2.3** Two examples of levers

Mechanical advantage and velocity ratio

Some machines are designed so that a small effort force can overcome a larger load force. These machines are called force multipliers. The crowbar in Figure 6.2.1 is a force multiplier.

The mechanical advantage of a machine is a measure of how great the load force overcome is compared with the effort force.

$$\text{mechanical advantage (MA)} = \frac{\text{load}}{\text{effort}}$$

Some machines are designed so that a small movement of the effort causes a larger movement of the load. These machines are called distance multipliers. The human forearm in Figure 6.2.2 is a distance multiplier.

The velocity ratio of a machine is a measure of how far or how fast the effort moves compared with the load.

$$\text{velocity ratio (VR)} = \frac{\text{distance moved by effort}}{\text{distance moved by load}}$$

The efficiency of a machine

Energy conservation demands that the total energy output of a machine must equal its energy input. However, when we measure the energy output as work done on the load by a machine, we find it is less than the energy input.

The work done by a machine against its load (moving, lifting, cutting it, etc.) is called its **useful work** or **useful energy output**. The machine also does work against frictional forces and sometimes does work in moving itself. For example, in a pulley machine, work is done in lifting the movable pulley block and hook to which the load is attached.

Also the work done against friction converts input energy into wasted heat. The energy equation now looks like this:

$$\text{energy input} = \text{useful work output} + \text{wasted energy output}$$

Efficiency can also be defined by the same ratio but in terms of useful **power output** and **power input**.

We measure the efficiency of a machine by the ratio:

$$\textbf{efficiency} = \frac{\textbf{useful work output}}{\textbf{energy input}} \times 100\%$$

Worked example

A construction worker uses a lever with a velocity ratio of 6 to raise a stone block 15 cm so it can be slid onto a wooden pallet. The block has a weight of 2800 N. If the construction worker pushes down on the lever with an effort of 500 N, calculate:

a) the work done by the construction worker
b) the useful work done by the lever
c) the mechanical advantage of the lever
d) the efficiency of the lever.

---

a) a VR of 6 means the effort moves 6 times the load distance so
distance effort moves = 6 × 15 cm = 90 cm = 0.9 m
work done by worker = force × distance moved = 500 N × 0.9 m = 450 J

b) useful work done = force to overcome load × distance load is raised
useful work done = 2800 N × 0.15 m = 420 J

c) MA = load ÷ effort = 2800 N ÷ 500 N = 5.6

d) efficiency = useful work output ÷ work input × 100%
= 420 J ÷ 450 J × 100% = 93%

Key fact

Efficiency is affected by:

- the weight of moving parts of the machine and, in the case of a vehicle, its whole weight
- friction between all moving parts of a machine (in some machines this is reduced by lubrication).

Worked example

How efficient is a ramp?

A ramp used to raise heavy boxes onto the back of a lorry is 12 m long and the height a box is raised is 2 m. If the weight of the box is 800 N and the force used to push the box up the ramp is 200 N, how efficient is this machine?

---

useful work output = height box is raised × weight of box
= 2 m × 800 N = 1600 N m

work output = distance box is pushed × effort used
= 12 m × 200 N = 2400 N m

$$\text{Efficiency} = \frac{1600}{2400} \times 100\% = 67\%$$

Hydraulic machines

Hydraulic machines use the pressure in a liquid to transfer energy and force from one place to another. (Refer back to A5.2 if you need to.) Hydraulic machines include hydraulic jacks, hydraulic pistons such as those in digger arms, and hydraulic brakes.

MA of a hydraulic machine = the ratio of its pistons' areas.

The effort is applied at the **pump** piston.

The load is pushed by the **ram** piston.

The force multiplication or MA of a hydraulic machine is given by:

$$\text{MA} = \frac{\text{area of ram piston}}{\text{area of pump piston}}$$

Key fact

Advantages of using hydraulic machines:

- the ability to magnify a force simply by using a piston of larger area – most hydraulic machines are force multipliers
- the ability to apply a force in any direction at any point and at any distance by using a flexible pipe
- the ability to apply forces to several points simultaneously (e.g. brakes to all four wheels of a car).

▲ **Figure 6.2.5** This hydraulic jack is being used to lift a car in Kingston, Jamaica.

▲ **Figure 6.2.6** The pistons that operate this hydraulic digger have a large cross-sectional area and so provide a large output force.

Summary questions

1. How is efficiency defined?
2. Give an example of a lever that decreases the effort needed to move a load.
3. How does lubrication increase the efficiency of a machine?

Practice exam-style questions

Assume $g = 10\,\text{N kg}^{-1}$.

1 Calculate the work done when a force of 20 N moves an object a distance of:

a) 5 m in the direction of the force

b) 2 km in the direction of the force.

2 A boy of mass 50 kg runs up a hill of vertical height 300 m in 20 minutes. Calculate:

a) the average vertical force he uses to lift himself up the hillside

b) the work he does climbing the hill

c) his average power.

3 Calculate the power of the following machines:

a) an electric fire, which converts 1.2 MJ of electrical energy into heat in 20 minutes

b) a motor, which raises a lift cage of mass 1000 kg a vertical height of 40 m in 40 s.

4 a) An electric motor is rated at 500 W. How much electrical energy will it require in 1 minute?

b) If the motor can do 24 kJ of useful work in 1 minute, what is its efficiency?

5 In the figure below, an object of weight 1000 N is being pushed up a ramp of length 15 m.

a) Calculate the useful work done, in J, in taking the object from ground level to the platform.

b) If 500 J of energy is wasted in this operation, calculate the effort required.

c) Give a reason for this wasted energy.

d) Calculate the efficiency of pushing the object up the ramp in this way.

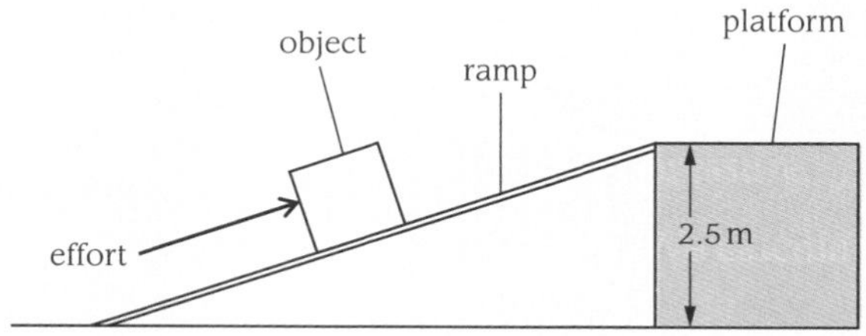

6 A crate, of mass 70 kg, is pulled a distance of 12 m up an inclined plane and in the process its centre of gravity is raised 2.0 m, as shown in the figure below. In order to do this, a force of 150 N is applied to the crate in a direction parallel to the inclined plane.

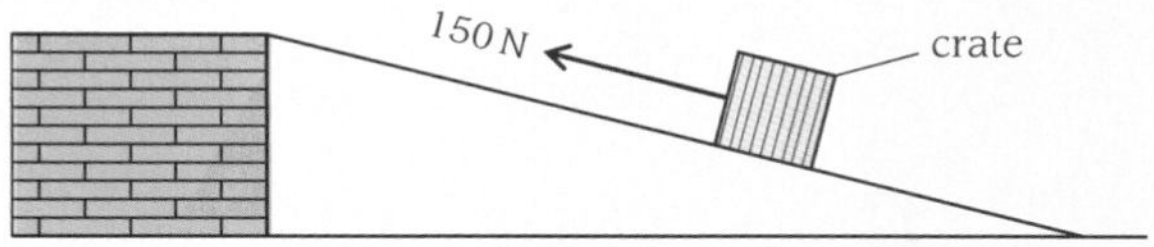

a) What is the increase in the potential energy of the crate?

b) What is the work done by the force?

c) Why do your answers to **a)** and **b)** differ?

7 The figure below represents a hydraulic system in which two cylinders with closely fitting pistons A and B are linked by a tube filled with oil. The area of A is $5.0\,\text{cm}^2$ and the area of B is $50\,\text{cm}^2$. A force of 10 newtons is exerted downwards on A.

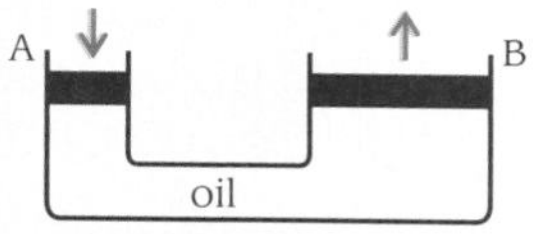

a) What is the pressure exerted on the oil by piston A?

b) What is the pressure exerted by the oil on piston B?

c) What force will B exert upwards if frictional forces between the pistons and cylinders can be neglected?

d) Draw a labelled diagram showing how the same principle can be used to operate the braking system in a car.

8 A hydraulic car jack has a ram piston (the one that lifts the car) of cross-sectional area $30\,\text{cm}^2$. It is used to lift one corner of a car so that a wheel can be removed. The operating lever compresses a pump piston of cross-sectional area $5\,\text{cm}^2$ and applies a compressing force of 600 N to the fluid in the hydraulic system. Calculate:

a) the pressure applied to the fluid by the pump piston,

b) the fluid pressure acting on the ram piston,

c) the lift force applied to the ram piston.

If the ram piston lifts the corner of the car by 50 cm:

d) Calculate the work done by the ram piston.

e) Explain why the work done by the mechanic operating the lever would be greater than this.

9 The figure below shows part of a hydraulic system, which lies horizontally.

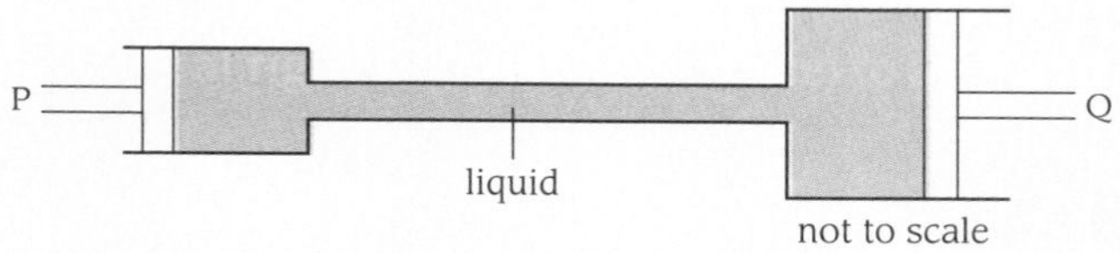

Calculate the thrust that must be applied to piston P, which has an area of $1.25 \times 10^{-4}\,\text{m}^2$, to enable piston Q, which has an area of $6.25 \times 10^{-4}\,\text{m}^2$, to exert a force of 2500 N.

10 The figure below represents part of a hydraulic braking system in which the effort is applied to a pedal at the end of a lever arm, 200 mm from a pivot. On the other side of the pivot, 40 mm away, the lever connects to a piston of area 50 mm^2. The piston transmits pressure through oil to another piston of area 100 mm^2 connected to the brake.

a) When the effort applied is 60 N, what is:

i) the force applied to the first piston

ii) the pressure on the oil?

b) What force is applied to the brake at the end of the system if frictional forces can be ignored?

c) What is the velocity ratio of this system, and what steps could be taken to increase it?

d) With a small amount of air trapped in the oil, why would the system work badly, if at all?

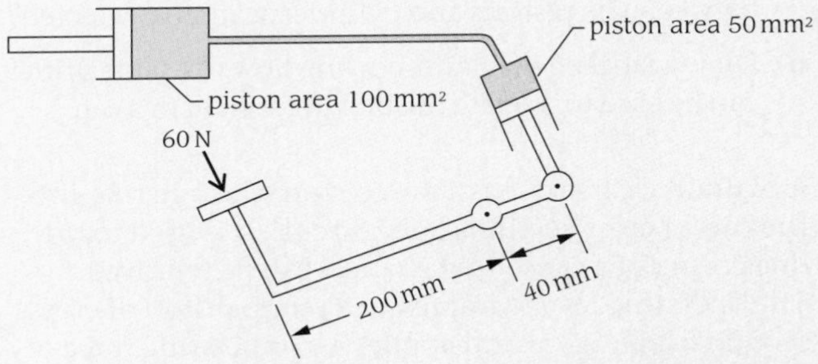

11 A crowbar is used as a force multiplying lever with a mechanical advantage of 4.

a) What effort would it need to move a load of 2000 N?

b) If the load is placed 5 cm from the pivot of the crowbar, what is the minimum length the crowbar needs to be?

A7 Motion

The motion of a satellite in orbit round the Earth and that of a spaceship travelling through deep space are quite different but neither of them needs its engines switched on to keep moving at a constant speed. However, any cyclist knows that he must keep pushing on the pedals to keep his bicycle moving at a steady speed even on a flat road. If a man jumps out of an aeroplane at a great height above the ground his speed increases as he falls, so that when he reaches the ground he will be moving so fast that he is likely to be killed. But if he uses a parachute his speed does not increase and he should land safely. A swimmer swimming across a river finds that she lands some distance downstream on the opposite bank even though she swims in a direction perpendicular to the river banks. Each of these examples of motion is different in some way and in this unit we learn how to describe and explain each kind of motion.

Objectives

By the end of this topic you will be able to:

- define and use equations linking distance, displacement, time, speed and velocity.

! Key fact

Units of speed and velocity

The SI units of distance and time are the metre and the second, so, in SI, speed is measured in metre/second, $m\,s^{-1}$ or m/s.

Useful equivalents are:

1 mile/hour = $0.45\,m\,s^{-1}$

$$1\,\text{km/hour} = \frac{1000\,\text{m}}{60 \times 60\,\text{s}} = 0.28\,\text{m}\,\text{s}^{-1}$$

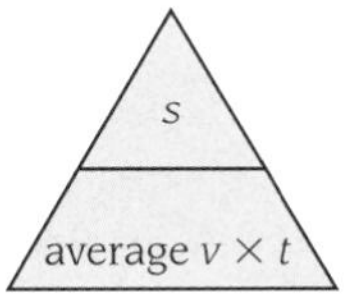

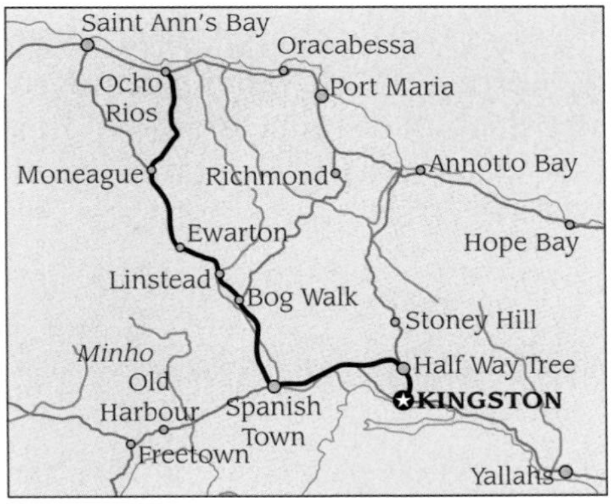

▲ **Figure 7.1.1** The journey from Half Way Tree, Kingston to Ocho Rios via Spanish Town is a distance of about 96 km. However, the displacement of Ocho Rios is only 65 km northwest of Kingston.

A7.1 Speed and velocity

Scalars and vectors

We use both scalar and vector terms to describe the motion of an object. Distance is a scalar quantity, with size only. Displacement is a vector quantity, with both size and direction.

Definition of displacement

The displacement of an object is the distance it has moved in a particular direction.

When we describe how fast an object is moving we are describing its **speed**. Speed is a scalar quantity. When we say which direction it is moving in as well we are stating its **velocity**. Velocity is a vector quantity.

When we say the velocity of the north wind is $90\,km\,h^{-1}$ we are giving a magnitude of $90\,km\,h^{-1}$ and also a direction from north to south.

1 litre of petrol is enough to travel 10 km in a car. The distance of 10 km is a scalar quantity.

The information that the town of Port of Spain in Trinidad is 45 km north of San Fernando gives both the distance and the direction.

The displacement of 45 km north is a vector quantity with a specified direction. However, the distance travelled by road between these two towns will be considerably greater.

Worked example

A racing car completes a 12 km lap of a course in 4 minutes exactly. Calculate its average speed in $km\,s^{-1}$ and $km\,h^{-1}$.

Average speed in $km\,s^{-1}$:

$v = \frac{s}{t} = \frac{12\,km}{240\,s} = 0.05\,km\,s^{-1}$

Average speed in $km\,h^{-1}$:

$v = \frac{s}{t} = \frac{12}{4/60} = \frac{12 \times 60}{4}$

$= 180\,km\,h^{-1}$

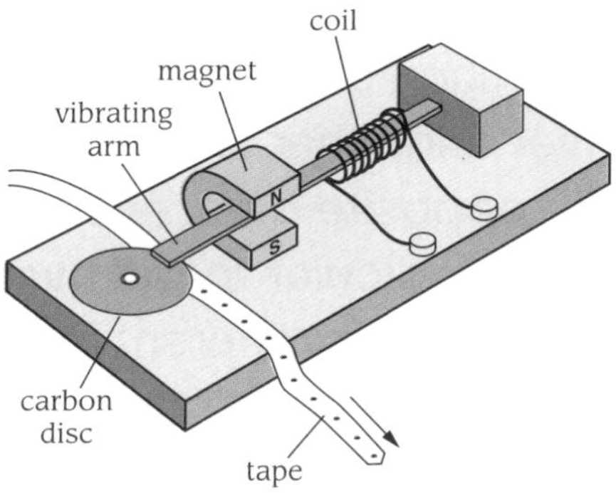

▲ **Figure 7.1.2**

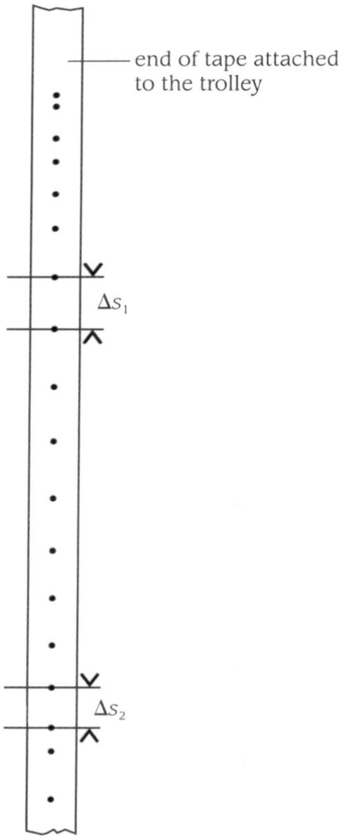

▲ **Figure 7.1.4** Finding the instantaneous speed

Average speed

As a runner completes a lap of a running track we can calculate his average speed from the distance round the track and the time taken to run round. During the lap his speed will vary and our calculation only gives the *average value* of his speed. A cyclist who travels 200 km in 4 hours will, on average, travel 50 km in each hour. So '50 km in each hour' is called his average speed.

The speed of a car calculated from the time taken to travel a full journey or a particular distance is its average speed. However, the speed of a car as indicated by its speedometer at any instant in time is called its instantaneous speed.

$$\text{average speed} = \frac{\text{distance moved}}{\text{time taken}}$$

$$\text{average } v = \frac{s}{t}$$

$$\text{distance moved} = \text{average speed} \times \text{time taken}$$

$$s = \text{average } v \times t$$

Measuring speed using a ticker timer

A ticker timer is connected to an alternating electricity supply and uses the mains electricity frequency of 50 hertz to make 50 ticks a second (Figure 7.1.2). A metal strip is made to vibrate up and down 50 times a second driven by the changes of direction of the electric current in a coil.

The vibrating metal strip strikes a strip of paper tape through a carbon paper disc and so prints a dot on the tape 50 times a second. The time interval Δt between one dot and the next dot is always exactly $\frac{1}{50}$ second or 0.02 s.

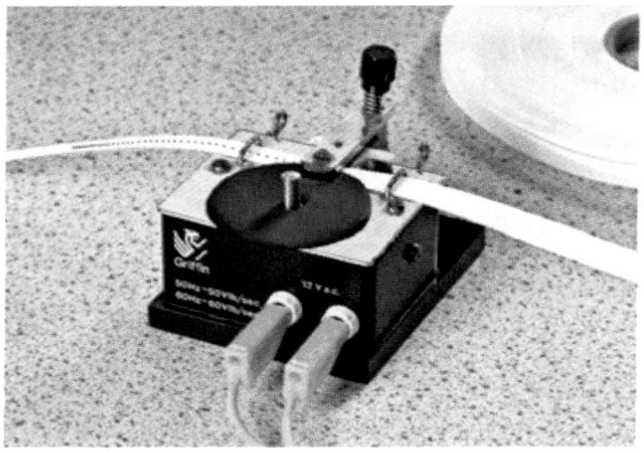

▲ **Figure 7.1.3** This ticker timer is driven by a low voltage alternating supply at the mains frequency of 50 Hz. It produces 50 dots a second on the ticker tape.

The small distance between one dot and the next is the change of distance or difference of distance Δs, which the object (pulling the tape) has moved in the small time interval Δt. By measuring the small distance moved Δs in a small time interval Δt we can find the actual speed or instantaneous speed at that particular moment of time (Figure 7.1.4).

The instantaneous speed $v = \frac{\Delta s}{\Delta t}$

Measuring the average speed

- Attach about 2 m of paper tape to a trolley and thread the tape through a ticker timer (Figure 7.1.5).
- Switch on the ticker timer and give the trolley a push to send it along the bench top.

- Examine the paper tape. What do you notice about the spacing of the dots? Can you explain what you see?
- Measure the total distance, s, covered by dots.
- Calculate the total time, t, given by the number of spaces between dots $\times \frac{1}{50}$ s or 0.02 s.
- Calculate the average speed.

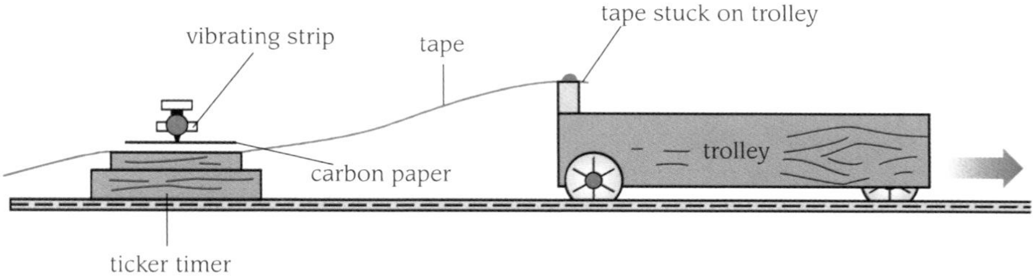

▲ **Figure 7.1.5** Measuring speed with a timer

Example of results obtained from tape:

Total distance $s = 142.5$ cm

Number of spaces between dots = 95

The time taken $t = 95 \times 0.02\ \text{s} = 1.9\ \text{s}$

Average speed, v is given by:

$$v = \frac{s}{t} = \frac{142.5\ \text{cm}}{1.9\ \text{s}} = 75\ \text{cm s}^{-1}$$

Measuring the instantaneous speed

- Measure Δs_1, the distance moved in 0.02 s early on the tape
- Measure Δs_2, the distance moved in 0.02 s later on the tape
- Calculate the instantaneous speeds at both positions using

$$\text{instantaneous speed, } v = \frac{\Delta s}{\Delta t}$$

We can see that the trolley slows down (due to friction) and the average speed, $75\ \text{cm s}^{-1}$, is somewhere in between the early and late instantaneous speeds.

Measuring instantaneous speed, sample data:

$$\Delta s_1 = 1.8\ \text{cm}$$
$$\Delta s_2 = 1.2\ \text{cm}$$

The instantaneous speeds are:

$$v_1 = \frac{\Delta s_1}{\Delta t} = \frac{1.8\ \text{cm}}{0.02\ \text{s}} = 90\ \text{cm s}^{-1}$$
$$v_2 = \frac{\Delta s_2}{\Delta t} = \frac{1.2\ \text{cm}}{0.02\ \text{s}} = 60\ \text{cm s}^{-1}$$

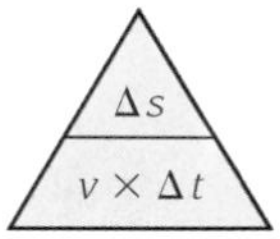

Speed and velocity

In A4.2, we learned about the difference between scalar and vector quantities. Now that we are studying motion we should expect to meet more vector quantities because objects have motions in particular directions.

speed is a *scalar*: speed has only magnitude

For example, the speed of sound is $330\ \text{m s}^{-1}$, but it has no particular direction.

velocity is a *vector*: velocity has magnitude and direction

Definition of velocity

The velocity of an object is the distance it moves in a unit of time, in a particular direction.

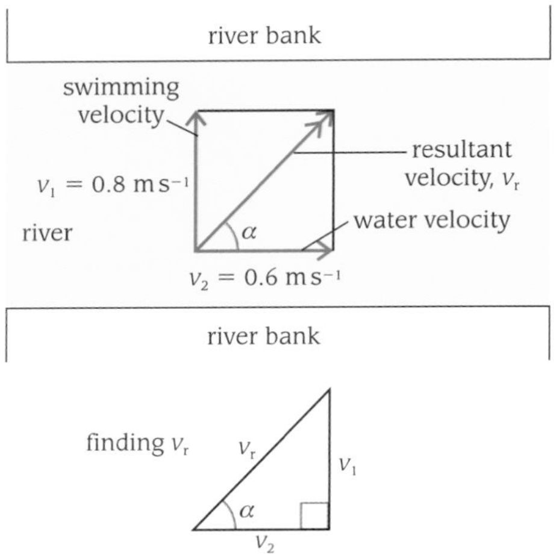

▲ **Figure 7.1.6** Finding the resultant velocity using the parallelogram law

Adding velocities by the parallelogram law

Two velocities can be added by using the same parallelogram law that we used for adding forces in A4.2. We can learn how to use this law by studying the worked example.

Worked example

A swimmer swims across a river at a velocity of $0.8\ m\,s^{-1}$ in a direction perpendicular to the river banks (Figure 7.1.6). The water flows down the river at $0.6\ m\,s^{-1}$. Find the resultant velocity of the swimmer.

The resultant velocity v_r is found using the parallelogram law. The magnitude of the resultant velocity v_r is given by Pythagoras:

$$v_r^2 = v_1^2 + v_2^2$$

$$v_r^2 = (0.8)^2 + (0.6)^2 = 0.64 + 0.36 = 1.00\ (m\,s^{-1})^2$$

So the magnitude of the resultant velocity v_r is $1.0\ m\,s^{-1}$.

The direction of v_r is given by:

$$\tan\alpha = \frac{v_1}{v_2} = \frac{0.8}{0.6} = 1.33$$

Using 'inverse tan' on your calculator, this gives: $\alpha = 53°$

The resultant velocity of the swimmer is $1.0\ m\,s^{-1}$ pointing downstream at an angle of 53° to the river bank.

Adding velocities in a straight line

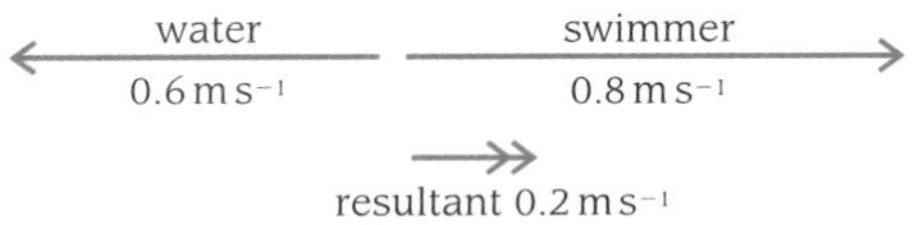

▲ **Figure 7.1.7** Adding velocities in a straight line

If the swimmer in the example above tried to swim upstream against the flow of water his resultant speed would be $0.2\ m\,s^{-1}$. (Figure 7.1.7).

Upstream: $v_r = 0.8 + (-0.6) = 0.2\ m\,s^{-1}$

The two magnitudes are added but direction is also taken into account. So, in the upstream direction, his velocity is positive but the water's velocity is negative.

When adding velocities in a straight line, decide which direction to take as positive and give each velocity an appropriate sign.

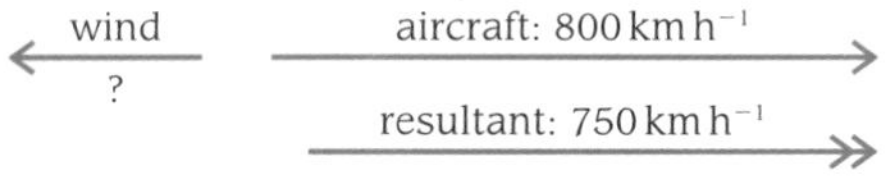

▲ **Figure 7.1.8** Finding the missing velocity

Worked example

An aircraft flies at $800\ km\,h^{-1}$ in stationary air (Figure 7.1.8). The distance to be travelled is 3000 km. What was the wind speed if the journey actually takes 4.0 hours?

Resultant speed $= \frac{\text{displacement}}{\text{time}} = \frac{3\,000\ km}{4.0\ h} = 750\ km\,h^{-1}$

Wind speed = aircraft speed − resultant speed
= 800 − 750
= $50\ km\,h^{-1}$ against the direction of flight.

Summary questions

1. What is displacement?
2. Calculate the average speed of a cyclist who travels 24 km in 1.5 hours.
3. Is velocity a scalar or a vector? Say why.

A7.2 Acceleration and the equations of motion

Making a tape chart

The vibrations of the ticker timer are similar to the ticking of a clock, but the timer makes very rapid ticks: 50 every second. We can call the time from one dot to the next a 'tick' of time. So 1 tick of time $= \frac{1}{50}$ s $= 0.02$ s.

Usually the distance from one dot to the next dot on the tape is quite short, often less than 1 cm. So we find that a useful length of time is ten spaces between dots which we shall call a 'tentick' of time. One tentick of time is the time interval Δt from dot number 0 to dot number 10 on the tape (Figure 7.2.1):

1 tentick of time $= 10 \times 0.02$ s $= 0.2$ s or $\frac{1}{5}$ s.

- Let a trolley run down a sloping runway pulling a tape through a ticker timer as it gains speed (Figure 7.2.2).
- Mark out all the tenticks of time along your tape.
- Number the tenticks strips so that you know their order.

The length of tentick strip is the distance moved in one tentick of time, that is 0.2 s. So the length of a tentick is a measure of instantaneous speed v:

$$\text{instantaneous speed, } v = \frac{\text{length of tentick strip}}{0.2\text{ s}}$$

- Cut up the tentick strips and stick them side by side on a sheet of paper to make a tape chart using six tentick strips.

This chart, known as a speed–time (or velocity–time) graph, shows how the speed of the trolley changed with time.

Objectives

By the end of this topic you will be able to:

- make and interpret motion from tape charts
- define acceleration and uniform acceleration
- use equations linking velocity, displacement, time and acceleration.

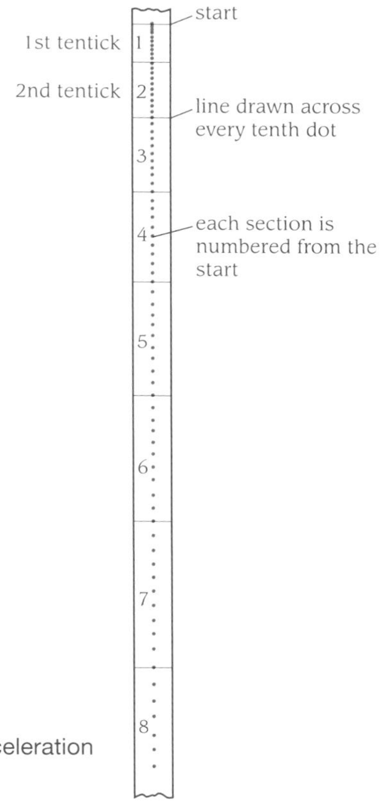

▶ **Figure 7.2.1** Measuring acceleration from a tape chart

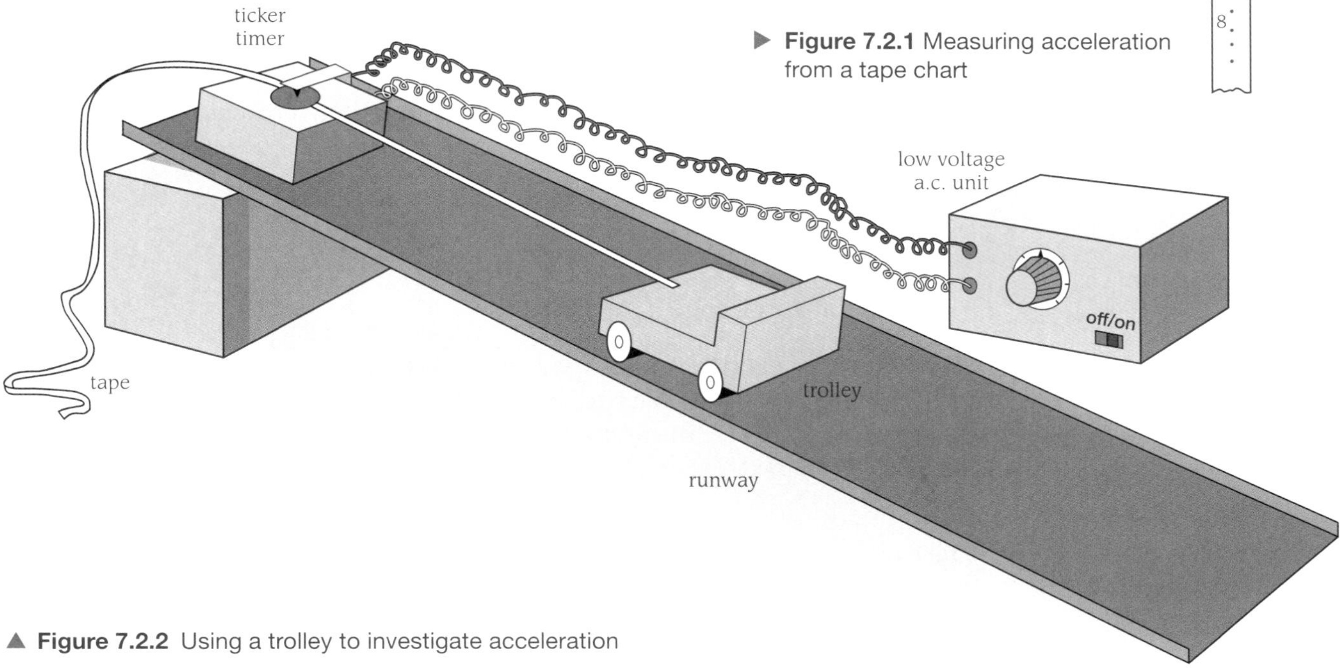

▲ **Figure 7.2.2** Using a trolley to investigate acceleration

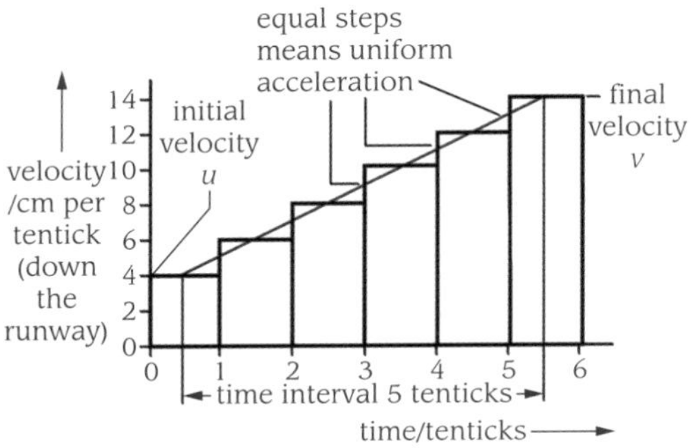

▲ **Figure 7.2.3**

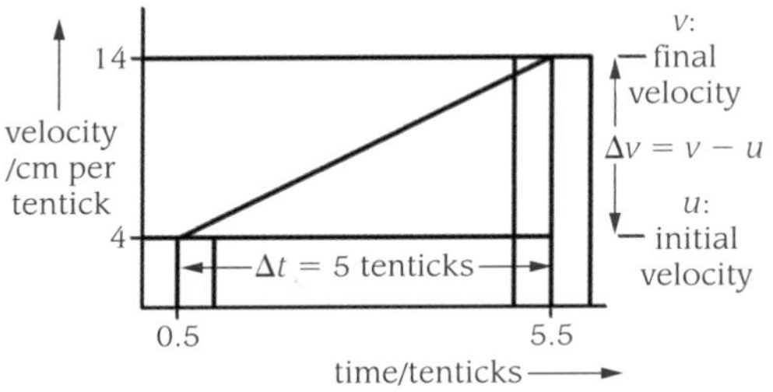

▲ **Figure 7.2.4**

Acceleration is the rate of change of velocity with time.

$$\text{acceleration} = \frac{\text{change of velocity}}{\text{time interval}} \qquad a = \frac{\Delta v}{\Delta t}$$

Acceleration, like velocity, is a vector and has direction.

Uniform acceleration

- Look at the steps on the tape chart (Figure 7.2.3).

If the steps up from the top of one tentick strip to the top of the next are equal, they show equal increases in velocity of the trolley. We call this constant acceleration, or uniform acceleration.

An object has uniform, or constant, acceleration if its velocity changes by equal amounts in equal successive time intervals.

The equal changes in velocity are the equal steps up from the top of one tape strip to the top of the next strip. The equal successive time intervals are the tentick time intervals of the tape strips placed in order along the bottom of the tape chart. The uniform acceleration of the trolley is also shown by the upward sloping straight line that can be drawn through the tops of the tape strips.

Calculating acceleration

The change in velocity, Δv, is given by the difference between the final velocity v and the initial velocity u.

(We usually write u for initial velocity and v for final velocity. Remember that u comes before v in the alphabet and the initial velocity comes before the final velocity.)

$$\Delta v = v - u$$

From the tape chart we have:

$\Delta v = v - u = 14\,\text{cm/tentick} - 4\,\text{cm/tentick} = 10\,\text{cm/tentick}$

Now as one tentick of time $= \frac{1}{5}\,\text{s}$ or 0.2 s,

$\Delta v = 5 \times 10\,\text{cm}$ in each full second

$\Delta v = 50\,\text{cm s}^{-1}$.

The time for the change $= \Delta t$

The length of each tentick tape strip gives the average speed during the tentick of time. So we take the length of a tape strip to represent the speed of the trolley at the moment halfway through the tentick of time. The middle of the sixth tentick is 5 tenticks later than the middle of the first tentick.

The time interval $\Delta t = 5$ tenticks $= 5 \times \frac{1}{5}\,\text{s} = 1\,\text{s}$

$$a = \frac{\Delta v}{\Delta t} = \frac{50\,\text{cm s}^{-1}}{1\,\text{s}} = 50\,\text{cm s}^{-2} \text{ or } 0.5\,\text{m s}^{-2} \text{ in SI units}$$

Exam tip

Caution: Be careful with terminology. Speed is a scalar quantity. When something changes speed it always gets faster or slower. Velocity is a vector quantity. An object does not have to get faster or slower to change velocity. If the direction changes, the velocity changes too.

Key fact

The units of acceleration

At first sight the units of acceleration may seem strange.

We read our result as '50 cm per second per second' or 'per second squared'.

This means that there is a change of velocity or a gain of velocity of 50 cm per second in each second.

The SI unit of acceleration is: 'metre per second squared' or m s^{-2}.

The equations of uniformly accelerated motion

Many motion questions and problems can be solved using graphical methods, but we can also use equations to calculate values we don't know.

These useful equations help us to calculate changes of speed, accelerations and distances moved while accelerating. We can use them only for objects with uniform acceleration. In your future studies, you will need to know how to derive the equations of motion.

Key ideas about motion calculations

- If the motion is at a constant speed or velocity, remember that you need to use only the equations

$$s = vt \text{ and } v = \frac{s}{t}$$

- When you read a question, pick out the key data and make a list as shown in the worked examples. Remember to include zero values for motion that starts at rest or finishes at rest.
- Check that all the units are SI. If there is a mixture of time or distance units, convert them first to SI.
- For a deceleration use a negative value of a in equations ②, ④ and ⑤.
- Your list of data will show which equation of motion links the quantities you have been given.

Worked example

Using equation ①

A cyclist starting from rest with uniform acceleration can reach a velocity of $20\,\mathrm{m\,s^{-1}}$ in 25 seconds. Calculate her acceleration.

Initial velocity $u = 0\,\mathrm{m\,s^{-1}}$,
final velocity $v = 20\,\mathrm{m\,s^{-1}}$,
time taken $t = 25\,\mathrm{s}$.

$$a = \frac{v - u}{t} = \frac{20 - 0}{25} = 0.8\,\mathrm{m\,s^{-2}}$$

Worked example

Using equation ②

A car can accelerate uniformly at $2.5\,\mathrm{m\,s^{-2}}$ and starts from a velocity of 36 km/hour. Find its velocity after 8 seconds.
Note: the units are mixed, so we convert to SI first.

Initial velocity $u = 36\,\text{km/hour} = \dfrac{36 \times 1000\,\mathrm{m}}{60 \times 60\,\mathrm{s}} = 10\,\mathrm{m\,s^{-1}}$
Acceleration $a = 2.5\,\mathrm{m\,s^{-2}}$
Time taken $t = 8\,\mathrm{s}$
Final velocity $v = u + at = 10 + (2.5 \times 8) = 30\,\mathrm{m\,s^{-1}}$

Key fact

In the equations

u = initial velocity or speed
v = final velocity or speed
$v - u = \Delta v$ = change of velocity
t or Δt = time interval
s = displacement or distance
a = acceleration

The equations

We start with the definition of acceleration:

① $a = \dfrac{\Delta v}{\Delta t} = \dfrac{v - u}{t}$

Rearranged this becomes:

② $v = u + at$

Using average velocity $= \dfrac{u + v}{2}$ and $s = vt$, gives:

③ $s = \dfrac{u + v}{2} \times t$

or: $s = \frac{1}{2}(u + v)t$

Two more equations are:

④ $s = ut + \frac{1}{2}at^2$

⑤ $v^2 = u^2 + 2as$

These two equations are derived from equations ①, ②, and ③. You do not need to know how to derive them at this level.

Worked example

Using equation ⑤

A train accelerates uniformly from rest at $0.2\,\text{m}\,\text{s}^{-2}$ over a distance of 1 km. Calculate the final velocity it reaches.

$u = 0$ *(starts from rest)*
$a = 0.2\,\text{m}\,\text{s}^{-2}$
$s = 1\,\text{km} = 1000\,\text{m}$
Note: use equation ⑤ for v when you know s but not t.

$$v^2 = u^2 + 2as$$
$$= 0 + 2(0.2\,\text{m}\,\text{s}^{-2}) \times 1000\,\text{m}$$
$$= 400\,\text{m}^2\,\text{s}^{-2}$$

Final velocity, $v = 20\,\text{m}\,\text{s}^{-1}$

Worked example

Using equations ① to ④

Note: use equation ④ to calculate the distance moved, s, when you know u, a and t, but not v.

A car accelerates uniformly from rest for 20 s with an acceleration of $1.5\,\text{m}\,\text{s}^{-2}$ (Figure 7.2.5). It then travels at a constant speed for 2 minutes before slowing down with a uniform deceleration to come to rest in a further 10 s.

Sketch a velocity–time graph of the motion and find:

a) the maximum speed,
b) the total distance travelled and
c) the acceleration while slowing down.

$u = 0$ (starts from rest),
$a = 1.5\,\text{m}\,\text{s}^{-2}$
$t = 20\,\text{s}$

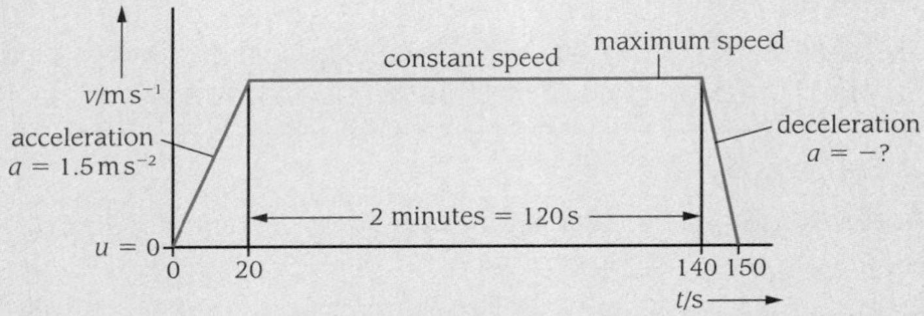

▶ **Figure 7.2.5**

a) $v = u + at = 0 + (1.5\,\text{m}\,\text{s}^{-2} \times 20\,\text{s}) = 30\,\text{m}\,\text{s}^{-1}$

b) The distance is calculated in three parts:

(i) $s = ut + \frac{1}{2}at^2 = 0 + (\frac{1}{2} \times 1.5 \times 20^2) = 300\,\text{m}$

(ii) $s = \text{constant speed} \times t = 30\,\text{m}\,\text{s}^{-1} \times 120\,\text{s} = 3600\,\text{m}$.

(iii) using: $u = 30\,\text{m}\,\text{s}^{-1}$, $v = 0$ (comes to rest) and $t = 10\,\text{s}$

$$s = \left(\frac{u + v}{2}\right)t = \left(\frac{30 + 0}{2}\right)10 = 150\,\text{m}$$

Total distance = 300 + 3600 + 150 = 4050 m.

c) Using: $u = 30\,\text{m}\,\text{s}^{-1}$,
$v = 0$
and $t = 10\,\text{s}$

$$a = \frac{v - u}{t} = \frac{0 - 30}{10} = -3.0\,\text{m}\,\text{s}^{-2}$$

There is a negative acceleration of $-3.0\,\text{m}\,\text{s}^{-2}$, or a deceleration while the car slows down by $3\,\text{m}\,\text{s}^{-1}$ in each second.

▲ **Figure 7.2.6**

To leave orbit and return to Earth, an orbiting spacecraft needs to fire its orbital manoeuvring system (OMS) engines to change its orbital speed. The rear OMS engine can accelerate or decelerate the spacecraft at the rate of $0.6\,\text{m}\,\text{s}^{-2}$.

If the required change of orbital speed is a decrease of $120\,\text{m}\,\text{s}^{-1}$, for how long must the engine be fired?

Rearranging $a = \frac{\Delta v}{\Delta t}$ we have:

$$\Delta t = \frac{\Delta v}{a} = \frac{120}{0.6} = 200\,\text{s}$$

The OMS engine must be fired for 200 seconds to bring the spacecraft out of orbit and into a correct flight path.

Summary questions

1 Sketch a velocity–time graph for an object with uniform acceleration.

2 Write the equation to calculate acceleration.

3 Calculate the acceleration of an object that takes 5 s to speed up from $10\,\text{m s}^{-1}$ to $20\,\text{m s}^{-1}$.

A7.3 Graphs of motion

Objectives

By the end of this topic you will be able to:

- draw, use and interpret graphs of displacement against time and velocity against time
- find and interpret gradients of straight-line graphs
- find by experiment the acceleration due to gravity, *g*.

Velocity–time graphs

Velocity–time graphs or speed–time graphs show us simply how the speed of a moving object changes with time. This is the same information as is obtained by making ticker-tape charts.

The straight lines on the graph in Figure 7.3.1 show uniform velocity, **b** and **d**, or uniform acceleration, **a** and uniform deceleration, **c**. Curved lines would indicate that the acceleration was varying also but understanding such motion is beyond what you need.

Graph a is the same as the tape chart shown in Figure 7.2.3; it shows increasing speed or acceleration.

Graph b with a horizontal line would be obtained if all the tentick strips on a tape chart had the same length. If a moving trolley produces equal length tentick strips then it moves equal distances in each tentick of time and has a constant speed. We can call tenticks taken in order 'equal successive time intervals' and then we have a more formal definition of motion at constant speed:

An object has a constant speed if it moves equal distances in equal successive time intervals.

Graph c shows a decreasing speed as the distances moved in equal successive intervals of time get shorter.

This is deceleration or acceleration with a negative value.

Graph d compared with graph **b** shows an object also moving at a constant speed but the speed of **d** is less than **b**.

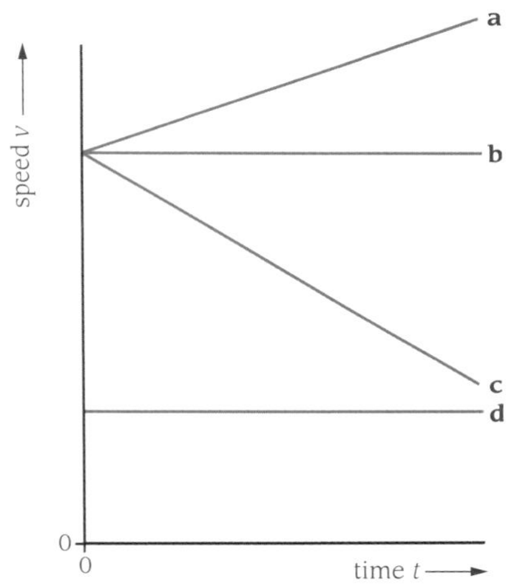

▲ **Figure 7.3.1** Speed–time graphs

Acceleration is the gradient of a velocity–time graph

The gradient of the graph is a:

$$a = \frac{\Delta v}{\Delta t} = \frac{0.5\,\text{m s}^{-1}}{1\,\text{s}} = 0.5\,\text{m s}^{-2}$$

Or using the whole straight-line graph:

$$a = \frac{\Delta v}{\Delta t} = \frac{2.0\,\text{m s}^{-1}}{4\,\text{s}} = 0.5\,\text{m s}^{-2}$$

The straight-line graph in Figure 7.3.2 shows uniform, or constant, acceleration and we can see that the velocity gain Δv is $0.5\,\text{m s}^{-1}$ in each time interval Δt of 1 s. The gradient of the graph is given by $\Delta v/\Delta t$, which is the definition of acceleration.

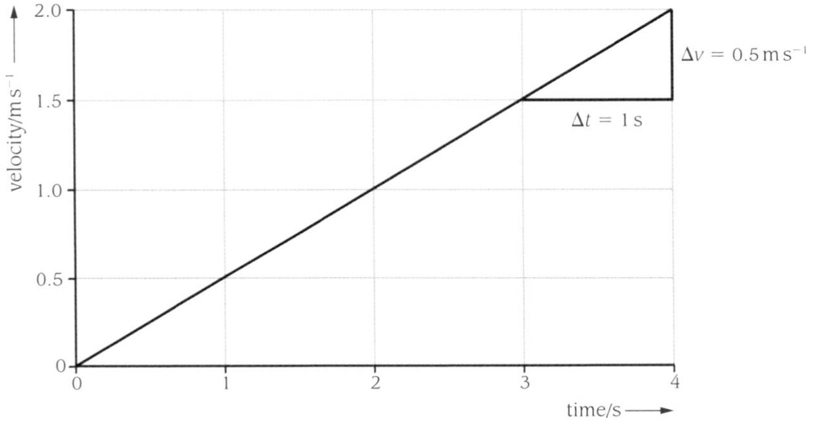

▲ **Figure 7.3.2** A velocity–time graph of uniform acceleration

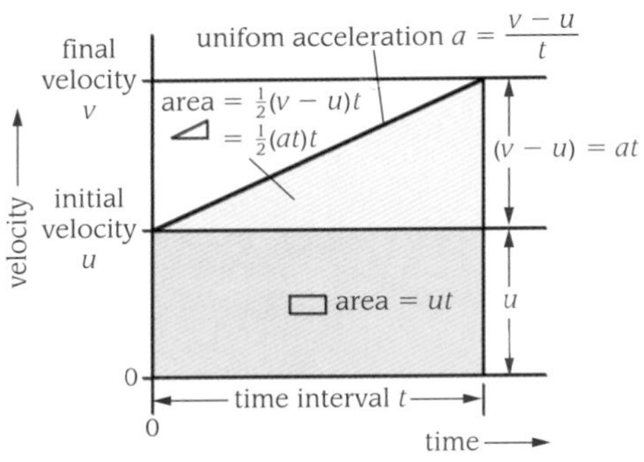

▲ **Figure 7.3.3** The area under a velocity–time graph represents distance moved

Distance is the area under a velocity–time graph

The graph in Figure 7.3.3 shows the motion of an object with uniform acceleration *a*, starting with an initial velocity *u* and accelerating to a final velocity *v* in a time interval *t*.

The area under the graph is made up of a rectangular patch and a triangular patch shaded differently in Figure 7.3.3.

The area of the rectangle = base × height $= u \times t = ut$

The area of the triangle = $\frac{1}{2}$ base × height $= \frac{1}{2} \times t \times (v - u)$

Multiplying out the bracket gives:

area of triangle $= \frac{1}{2}vt - \frac{1}{2}ut$

Adding together the area of the rectangle and the triangle gives:

$$\text{total area under the graph} = ut + \tfrac{1}{2}vt - \tfrac{1}{2}ut$$
$$= \tfrac{1}{2}ut + \tfrac{1}{2}vt$$
$$= \tfrac{1}{2}(u + v)t$$

Distance–time graphs

Distance–time graphs (Figure 7.3.4a) show directly how the distance moved by, or displacement of, an object changes with time. These graphs show us the progress made on a journey and answer directly the question: 'How far has something travelled in a certain time?'

The odometer or milometer on a car gives the total *distance* travelled. The straight-line measurement on a map from one town to another gives the *displacement*, which includes the direction as well. For example: Annotto Bay is 37 km north of Kingston.

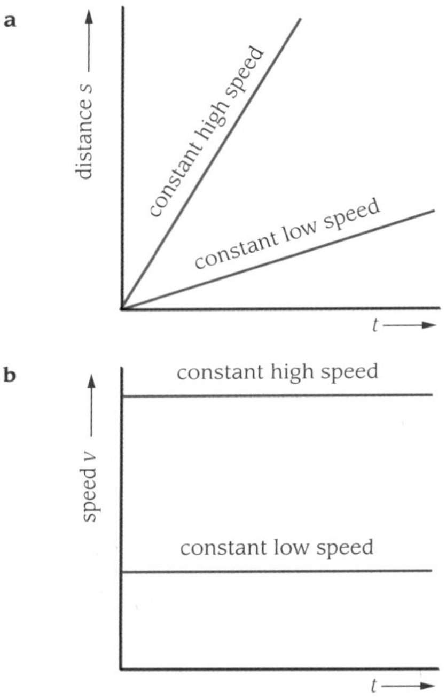

▲ **Figure 7.3.4** Comparing speed–time and distance–time graphs for constant speeds

Comparing speed–time and distance–time graphs

	Speed–time or velocity–time graphs	Distance–time or displacement–time graphs
Gradient	acceleration, $a = \frac{\Delta v}{\Delta t}$	velocity, $v = \frac{\Delta s}{\Delta t}$
Area under graph	distance moved	
Horizontal straight line	constant or uniform speed	object stationary
Straight line with positive gradient	constant or uniform acceleration	constant or uniform speed

Things to do

Try sketching the following as both speed–time and distance–time graphs:

a) a stationary object

b) an object moving at a constant speed that suddenly stops moving

c) an object moving from rest and increasing its speed uniformly.

Summary questions

1. What does the area under a velocity–time graph show?
2. Sketch a distance–time graph and a velocity–time graph for an object travelling at constant speed.
3. Sketch a velocity–time graph for an object travelling with constant acceleration.

A7.4 Aristotle, Galileo and Newton

For nearly 2000 years the scientific ideas of the ancient Greeks, particularly those of Aristotle, were learnt and accepted without question. To appreciate the revolution which the ideas of Newton caused in scientific thinking, we first need to learn about the teaching of Aristotle and the achievements of Galileo.

The teaching of Aristotle

Aristotle was a famous Greek philosopher who lived from 384 to 322 BCE. As a pupil of Plato and tutor of Alexander the Great, he had great influence and authority. Aristotle invented a logical way of presenting an argument. Starting with agreed assumptions, a series of 'if... then...' steps led to a final conclusion that was decisive. The teaching of Aristotle became an essential part of Christian beliefs and people were expected to learn them by heart without question. Many of Aristotle's ideas were wrong because they were based on false assumptions, which had not been tested experimentally. For example, before Galileo most people still believed that the Earth was the centre of the universe with the Sun, Moon and stars moving in spheres around it.

The life and achievements of Galileo

Galileo Galilei was born in Italy in 1564 in the same year as William Shakespeare was born. Galileo died in 1642 in the same year as his famous successor Isaac Newton was born. Galileo was very interested in mathematics and became a professor of mathematics in Padua. He also made several scientific instruments including a telescope, which enabled him to make accurate measurements in support of his theories.

With his mathematical skills and the evidence of measurements made with his telescope, Galileo was able to show that the Earth moved in an orbit around the Sun; therefore the Earth was not the centre of the universe. Galileo's new theory was in direct conflict with the teaching of the Christian Church and he was made to apologise for his 'heresy'. He was sentenced to stay in his house for the rest of his life but, as he publicly withdrew his claim that the Sun was fixed and the Earth moved, he was able to continue his scientific work until he died. Privately Galileo still believed that the Earth moves around the Sun.

The scientific method

Galileo was the first to adopt the scientific approach to the solving of a problem. This achievement changed the way we think and how we investigate the laws of the universe. Galileo realised that facts must be shown to be true by experimental evidence. A theory will lead to certain predictions or consequences, which can be investigated to discover whether they do actually happen. If the observations are different from the predictions the theory is found to be wrong.

Objectives

By the end of this topic you will be able to:

- recall and explain the failings of Aristotle's law of motion
- recall and explain the achievements of Galileo
- describe the scientific method
- recall some of Newton's achievements and his place in the history of science.

Aristotle's law

The arguments:

a) Forces are needed to keep things moving because they stop when the force is taken away. (Evidence: a horse is needed to pull a chariot.)

b) The speed of an object depends on the size of the force. (Evidence: two horses can pull a chariot faster than one horse.)

The speed of an object is directly proportional to the force applied to it.

$$v \propto F$$

Scientific method

The scientific method adopted by Galileo:

1 Make and record precise observations.

2 Seek possible explanations for the observed facts.

3 Test the theory with experiments.

4 Draw conclusions only when all the experimental evidence gathered supports a particular theory.

Galileo's ideas of motion

Galileo used a model to investigate the motion of a falling object.

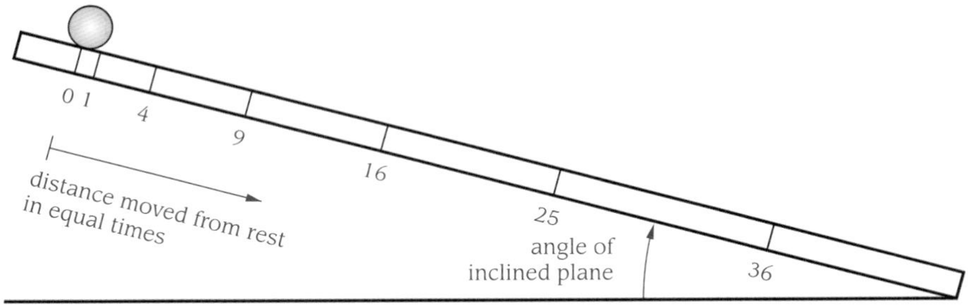

▲ **Figure 7.4.1** By using an inclined plane, Galileo slowed down the motion of a falling object. He showed that the total distance moved was proportional to the total time squared: $s = \frac{1}{2}kt^2$.

Falling objects fell too fast for his timing instruments so Galileo slowed down their motion by rolling them down inclined planes. The angle of the plane controlled the acceleration of the motion. The importance of this step is that Galileo had built a laboratory model, which helped him to study a real event that was otherwise beyond the scope of his instruments.

Galileo laid the foundation of Newton's first law of motion.

▲ **Figure 7.4.2** Galileo noticed that a smooth ball would roll for a very long distance along a smooth horizontal surface. He believed that if all frictional forces could be removed, the ball would keep on moving horizontally for ever.

Newton, architect of the scientific world

▲ **Figure 7.4.3** Isaac Newton 1642–1727

Isaac Newton was born in England in 1642. He was a farmer's son who became professor of mathematics at Cambridge University. By the time of his death in 1727 he had caused a revolution throughout the scientific world.

This shy and quiet man, devoted to his work, produced what is probably the greatest single scientific work of all time: *Philosophiae Naturalis Principia Mathematical* (or the *Principia* for short).

As well as major achievements in mathematics, Newton's influence spread much wider. He became president of England's most famous scientific society, the Royal Society. He also became a member of the British parliament.

Newton's contributions to science and mathematics

- His study of the nature of light showed that sunlight was made up of all colours in the spectrum (see C9.10).
- He invented the first reflecting telescope, which used a large mirror in place of a lens and thus avoided the colour defect of lenses.

- Newton used and invented new mathematics, including calculus, as a tool to handle the data obtained by scientific observations.
- Newton's law of gravitation successfully explained the motion of the planets, the Earth and the Moon.

Summary questions

1 Give one of Aristotle's laws about force. Say why it is wrong.

2 Who first adopted a scientific method, carrying out experiments?

3 What did Galileo conclude about forces?

A7.5 Newton's laws of motion

Objectives

By the end of this topic you will be able to:

- state Newton's laws of motion
- use Newton's laws to explain how everyday moving machines work and behave
- define linear momentum and give its units
- describe events in which momentum is conserved
- understand that centripetal force is an unbalanced force that causes an acceleration towards the centre of orbit
- recall that centripetal force changes the direction of an object's motion but causes no change in speed
- state the law of conservation of linear momentum
- solve problems involving conservation of momentum.

Perhaps the best known of Newton's works are his laws of motion. Here Newton's real achievement lies in his success in showing that all forms of motion, however different, could be described by one system of laws. These laws could describe the parabolic path of a cricket ball hit high in the air, the elliptical orbits of the planets and satellites or the free fall of an apple.

Newton's first law of motion

Newton's first law is about the inertia of an object.

The inertia of matter is the 'laziness' of matter, or the tendency of a mass to resist changes in its motion. Inertia makes an object difficult to start or stop moving, difficult to change its direction of motion or difficult to accelerate.

A spaceship in deep space does not use its engines to keep moving. Away from the influence of gravity, a spaceship moves at a constant speed in a straight line. When it uses its engines, the ejected exhaust gases apply a force to the spaceship to change its speed or direction.

Examples of Newton's first law

A cyclist can freewheel for a very long way without pedalling, if the road is smooth, and the bicycle wheels have good bearings and are well oiled so there is very little friction.

A heavy shopping trolley or wheelbarrow needs a lot of force to start it moving or to stop it, but much less force to keep it moving. To keep it moving it only needs enough force to overcome the force due to friction.

▶ **Figure 7.5.1** A skateboarder, moving with very low friction, will travel at an almost constant speed in a straight line without any effort unless another force is applied to him.

An air track model of first law of motion

We can model motion without friction in the laboratory using a horizontal air track.

- A glider floats with very low friction on a cushion of air along the track. There is no unbalanced or resultant force acting on the glider.
- The glider has a (nearly) constant speed in a straight line along the air track.

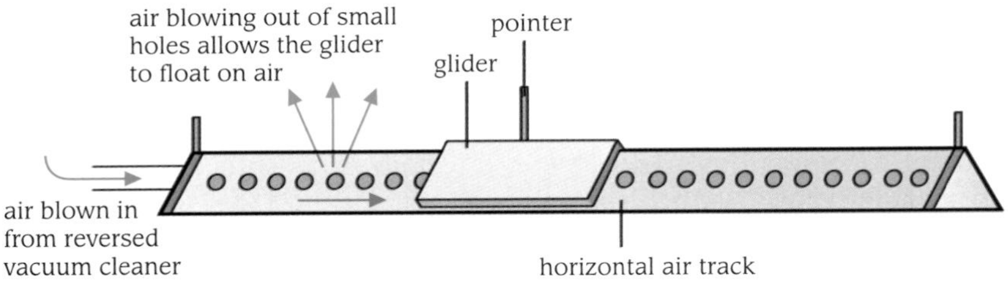

▲ **Figure 7.5.2** A glider on an air track

> **Newton's first law**
> **Stationary objects do not move on their own and moving objects keep on moving at a constant speed in a straight line if you leave them alone.**
> **Or more formally:**
> **An object at rest will stay at rest and a moving object will continue to move with uniform velocity unless an external resultant force acts on it.**
> **(Uniform velocity = constant speed in a straight line.)**

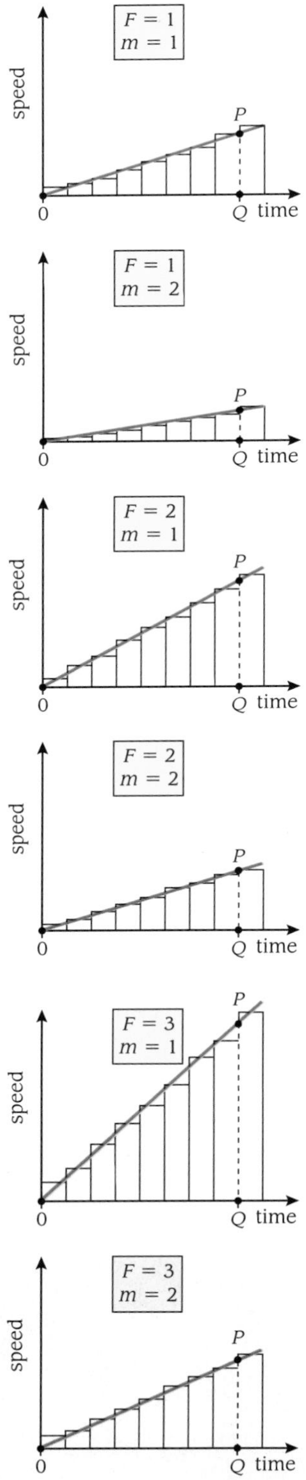

▲ **Figure 7.5.3** Using tape charts to investigate motion

Newton's second law of motion

Investigating how force affects the motion of a trolley

- Set up a trolley and ticker timer on a runway and *adjust the slope of the runway to compensate for friction*, so that the trolley runs down the runway with a constant velocity when given a gentle push.
- Fit a short dowel rod in each of the holes at the ends of the trolley and hook an eyelet of an elastic cord over the rod.
- Walk along the side of a runway pulling the trolley with an elastic cord stretched by a constant amount.
- When you have practised pulling the trolley with a constant force, attach paper tape to it and thread the tape through the ticker timer.
- Use one, two and three elastic cords in parallel to double or triple the pulling force, but remember that they must always have the same constant extension.
- Make a tape chart for the motion of the trolley pulled by 1, 2 and 3 stretched elastic cords.
- Repeat the experiment with two trolleys stacked on top of each other so that the mass of the trolley is doubled.
- Calculate the acceleration from the triangles OPQ on the charts. Because OQ is the same on all the charts, you can use the heights, PQ to compare the accelerations.

Some typical results are shown in the table.

Force (number of elastic cords)	1	2	3	1	2	3
Mass (number of trolleys)	1	1	1	2	2	2
Acceleration (height PQ in mm)	25	48	74	12	24	37
Mass × acceleration	25	48	74	24	48	74

What do these results show?

- Force is directly proportional to mass × acceleration.
- Acceleration is directly proportional to the force for constant mass.
- Acceleration is inversely proportional to the mass for constant force.

Newton's second law

The simplest form of Newton's second law is:

Force is directly proportional to mass × acceleration

$$F \propto ma$$

so $F = kma$, where k is a constant.

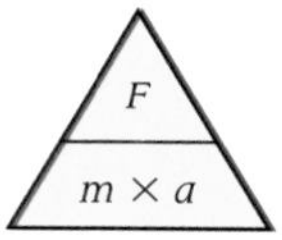

When you use this formula remember:

- all masses must be given in kg (not grams)
- all accelerations must be given in $m\,s^{-2}$ (not $cm\,s^{-2}$)
- all forces must be in newtons
- only an unbalanced or resultant force causes acceleration.

The **newton (N)** is defined as:

1 newton is the unbalanced (or resultant) force that will give a mass of 1 kg an acceleration of $1\,m\,s^{-2}$.

Constant, $k = 1$

Force (N) = mass (kg) × acceleration ($m\,s^{-2}$)

$$F = ma$$

Unbalanced forces

It is important to remember that we have used a friction compensated runway so that all the force provided by the elastic cords was able to produce acceleration. We call this force an unbalanced or resultant force.

Worked example

A car has a mass of 800 kg.

a) What resultant force is necessary to give it an acceleration of $3.0\,m\,s^{-2}$?

b) If the combined air resistance and frictional forces acting against the car equal 1600 N, what is the total driving force required from the car's engine?

Resultant force, $F = ma = 800 \times 3.0 = 2400$ N.

Total driving force = resultant force + frictional forces

= 2400 N + 1600 N = 4000 N

Worked example

A trolley of mass 2 kg is pulled along a horizontal surface by a force of 5 N against an opposing frictional force of 1 N. Calculate the acceleration of the trolley.

The unbalanced or resultant force F acting on the trolley is:

resultant force, F = applied force − frictional force

$$F = 5\,\text{N} - 1\,\text{N} = 4\,\text{N}$$

$$a = \frac{F}{m} = \frac{4\,\text{N}}{2\,\text{kg}} = 2\,\text{m}\,\text{s}^{-2}$$

Key fact

Units of momentum

The units of momentum are those of mass × velocity:

$\text{kg} \times \text{m}\,\text{s}^{-1}$, or $\text{kg}\,\text{m}\,\text{s}^{-1}$.

There is no special name for the units of momentum but the units of momentum and impulse are equivalent.

Units of impulse

Impulse has the units of force × time:

newton × second or N s.

▲ **Figure 7.5.4** The tennis racket delivers a large force to the tennis ball in a short time. This impulse ($F \times t$) changes the momentum ($m \times v$) of the ball.

Linear momentum and impulse

Momentum is a word used mainly in physics. It is a quantity that moving objects have. We could call it 'mass in motion'. The more mass something has, or the faster it is moving, the more momentum it has. When objects move in a straight line, they have linear momentum (often just called 'momentum' in textbooks). When an object moves in a circle it has angular momentum.

The momentum of an object is defined as:

$$\text{momentum} = \text{mass} \times \text{velocity} = mv$$

Momentum is a vector quantity because velocity is a vector quantity. You must always state the direction of the momentum of an object.

Impulse is also a physics term. In everyday language 'impulse' implies doing things suddenly. 'Impulse' in physics is a measure of how the momentum of an object is changing.

The impulse of an object is defined as:

$$\text{impulse} = \text{change of momentum} = mv - mu = m(v - u)$$

Impulse is also a vector quantity because velocity is a vector quantity.

The impulse is greater when:

1 the change of momentum happens very quickly, such as when a ball stops by bouncing on the end of your finger instead of sweeping your hands backwards as you catch it

2 the change of momentum is large, such as when you catch a cricket ball instead of a beach ball, or catch a ball thrown very quickly instead of one tossed slowly.

Using Newton's second law ($F = ma$) and the definition of acceleration $\left(a = \frac{(v-u)}{t}\right)$ gives:

$$F = m\frac{(v-u)}{t}$$

multiplying both sides by t gives:

$$Ft = m(v - u) = \text{impulse}$$

Momentum is a very useful concept in physics because it helps us to understand and calculate what happens in collisions and explosions. For example, we can calculate the motion of a rocket from the mass and velocity of the exhaust gases ejected from its engines.

Explaining momentum using Newton's second law

- When a hammer hits a nail, the change of momentum of the hammer occurs in the very short time during which the nail is driven into the wood. So the hammer has a very rapid loss of momentum. The impulse that drives the nail into the wood is a large force acting for a short time equal to the momentum loss of the hammer.
- Eggs are packed in soft, shock-absorbing boxes so that when they suddenly stop or start moving they do not get cracked. How does this work? A moving egg with a certain amount of momentum requires a force to stop it moving. If the force acts for a short time (as it would in a hard box) then the force on the egg will be large and will crack it. If, however, the force is spread out by the cushioning effect of a soft box and so lasts a longer time, it will be weaker and will not break the egg. The impulse needed to stop an egg moving should be a small force acting for a long time, rather than a large force acting for a short time. Both cause the same change of momentum, but a weak force is needed to avoid cracking the eggs.

▲ **Figure 7.5.5** The egg box stops the eggs moving by delivering a small force in a long time.

Momentum and Newton's second law of motion

For an object of mass m,

with initial velocity, u and

final velocity, v:

mu = its initial momentum and

mv = its final momentum

Its change of momentum $\Delta(mv) = mv - mu$

If this change of momentum is produced by a force F, which acts on the object for a time interval, Δt, then:

$Ft = mv - mu$ becomes: $F\Delta t = \Delta(mv)$

In words this says: impulse = change of momentum

Rearranging the equation we have: $F = \dfrac{\Delta(mv)}{\Delta t}$

In words this says:

the resultant force acting on an object = its rate of change of momentum

This is another way of stating Newton's second law of motion.

Worked example

A boy catches a cricket ball of mass 0.14 kg, which has a velocity of 20 m s^{-1}.

Calculate:

a) the momentum of the ball

b) the average force used by the boy's hands to stop the ball in

i) 0.5 seconds

ii) 0.01 seconds.

Explain why stopping the ball in 0.01 seconds hurts the boy but stopping it in 0.05 seconds does not.

---

a) Momentum $= mv$

$= 0.14\,\text{kg} \times 20\,\text{m s}^{-1}$

$= 2.8\,\text{kg m s}^{-1}$

b) $\Delta(mv = -2.8\,\text{kg m s}^{-1}$

(because its momentum is reduced to zero)

i) $F = \dfrac{\Delta(mv)}{\Delta t} = \dfrac{-2.8}{0.5} = -5.6\,\text{N}$

ii) $F = \dfrac{\Delta(mv)}{\Delta t} = \dfrac{-2.8}{0.01} = -280\,\text{N}$

When the boy applies a force of 280 N to the ball, the ball applies an equal and opposite force to his hands. A force of 280 N acting on the boy's hands hurts him. When he stops the ball more slowly, by allowing his hands to move with the ball, a much smaller force is needed, which hurts less. Note that a small force acting for a long time can cause the same change of momentum as a large force acting for a short time.

Key fact

Examples of centripetal force

- The Moon and satellites are held in orbit around the Earth by gravitational attraction.
- An electron is held in orbit around an atomic nucleus by the attraction between unlike electric charges.
- The washing in a spin-dryer is held in orbit by the inwards push of the rotating drum wall. (The water flies off at a tangent to the orbit when it escapes through holes in the drum wall.)
- When you are whirled round on a roundabout there is a push from your seat that pushes you from behind towards the centre of the orbit.

▲ **Figure 7.5.6** On a fairground wheel, riders experience an inwards pushing force that keeps them turning in a circle.

Circular motion

Force, velocity, acceleration, momentum and impulse are all vector quantities. Imagine an object moving at a constant speed in a circle.

1. Because the direction of motion is changing, the velocity is changing.
2. Newton's first law tells us the object would keep moving in a straight line if there was not a force making it change direction. This force, called centripetal force, acts towards the centre of the circle.
3. The changing velocity tells us there is an acceleration. Because the force acts towards the centre of the circle, the acceleration also acts towards the centre of the circle.
4. The changing velocity tells us the momentum must also be changing.

Conservation of linear momentum

By conservation we mean that we have the same amount of something after an event as we had before it. The useful thing about momentum is that it is conserved in collisions. Knowing this we can calculate the motion of objects before and after collisions.

When two objects collide they apply equal and opposite forces to each other for the same length of time. This causes equal and opposite changes of their individual momenta but their combined momentum does not change.

When two or more objects interact (collide or separate), their total momentum remains constant, providing no external resultant force is acting on them.

As an equation:

total momentum before collision = total momentum after collision

Remember that momentum is a vector quantity, so its direction must be taken into account.

Worked example

A bullet of mass (m_1) 100 g is fired into a stationary target of mass (m_2) 4.0 kg. The target is mounted on low-friction wheels and moves off at a velocity of 5.0 m s^{-1} when the bullet enters it. The bullet stays in the target. Calculate the velocity of the bullet before it strikes the target.

Using the principle of the conservation of momentum and working in kilograms:

total momentum before collision bullet	= total momentum after collision bullet + target
m_1u	$= (m_1 + m_2)v$
$0.1 \times u$	$= (0.1 + 4.0)5.0$
$0.1 \times u$	$= 20.5$
u	$= 205$ m s^{-1}

The velocity of the bullet was 205 m s^{-1} before the collision with the target.

Demonstrating conservation of momentum

A good example of a collision is one in which two trolleys stick together. This is called an inelastic collision. This can be arranged by mounting a pin on one trolley and a cork on the other so that on collision the pin sticks into the cork and holds the trolleys together. A strip of Velcro tape glued on the ends of two trolleys can also be used to hold them together after a collision.

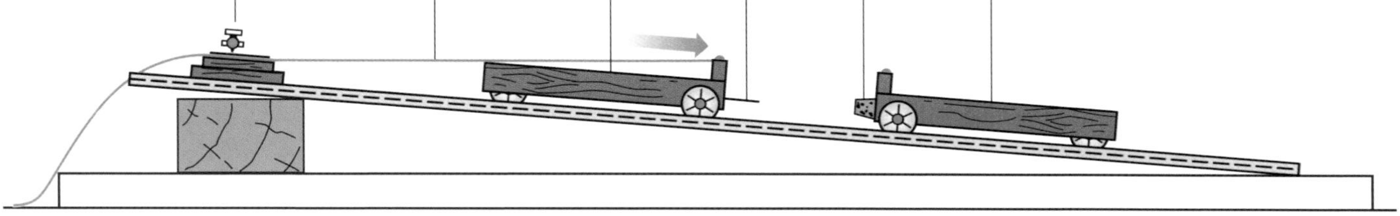

▲ **Figure 7.5.7** An inelastic collision of trolleys

- Use a friction-compensated runway. Set trolley A halfway down it, initially at rest.
- Attach a single length of paper tape to trolley B and, aiming its pin towards the cork in the end of the stationary trolley, give it a quick push.

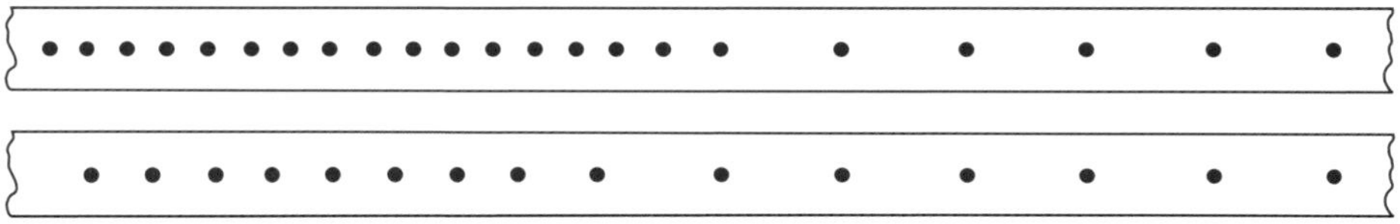

▲ **Figure 7.5.8** Tapes before and after collision

The tapes record the motion of trolley A before the collision and then trolleys A and B joined together after the collision. On tape 1 a single trolley collided with another single stationary trolley. On tape 2 a single trolley collided with a double, stacked stationary trolley of twice the mass m of the single one.

- Mark where the two trolleys collided.
- Measure the spacing of the dots before and after the collision on both tapes.

On tape 1, at collision, the moving mass, m, doubles to $2m$ and the velocity, v, halves to $\frac{1}{2}v$.

On tape 2, at collision, the moving mass, m, triples to $3m$ and the velocity, v, becomes $\frac{v}{3}$.

Momentum is conserved because the momentum before and after the collisions equals mv.

Momentum is conserved in head-on collisions and explosions.

If two cars of equal mass collide head-on at equal speeds and don't bounce back, they will both stop dead. At first sight it appears that momentum is destroyed in this type of collision because both cars stop and thus lose momentum.

To explain this collision in terms of the conservation of the total momentum of the two cars we must remember that momentum is a vector quantity.

If the momentum of the car moving to the right is $+mv$, then the momentum of the car moving to the left is $-mv$. It follows that their total momentum before the collision is $mv + (-mv) = 0$. After the collision both cars are at rest so that their total momentum is again zero and the total momentum is conserved.

Momentum conservation in explosions

- Set up two trolleys with equal mass facing each other. One of them has a spring-loaded piston under compression.
- Release the piston by tapping the release dowel rod in the hole above it.

The trolleys fly apart with equal and opposite momentum so that their combined momentum remains zero after the explosion, as it was before.

You can test whether the trolleys have equal speeds by arranging blocks of wood at equal distances from the two trolleys. Do the trolleys reach the wooden blocks simultaneously?

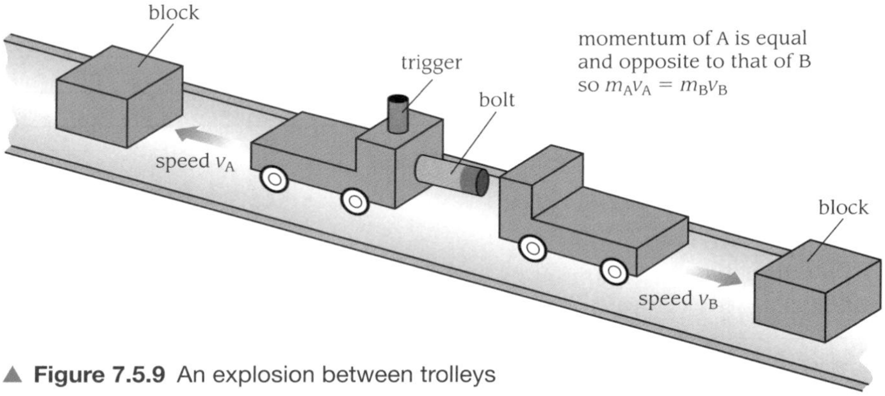

▲ **Figure 7.5.9** An explosion between trolleys

The rocket engine

We can demonstrate the principle of a rocket engine by allowing an inflated balloon to escape from our hands. The action of the air escaping causes the equal and opposite reaction of the movement of the balloon. The momenta of the balloon and air are conserved.

A rocket engine carries its fuel with it and can work in space as well as in the atmosphere. Two fuels, such as liquid hydrogen and liquid oxygen, burn together explosively and force the gases produced out of the rocket nozzle at high speed. The gain of momentum of the rocket is equal and opposite to the momentum of the ejected fuel. Clearly, when the fuel is ejected at high velocity after burning explosively it has a large momentum. Again the total momenta of the rocket and ejected fuel are conserved.

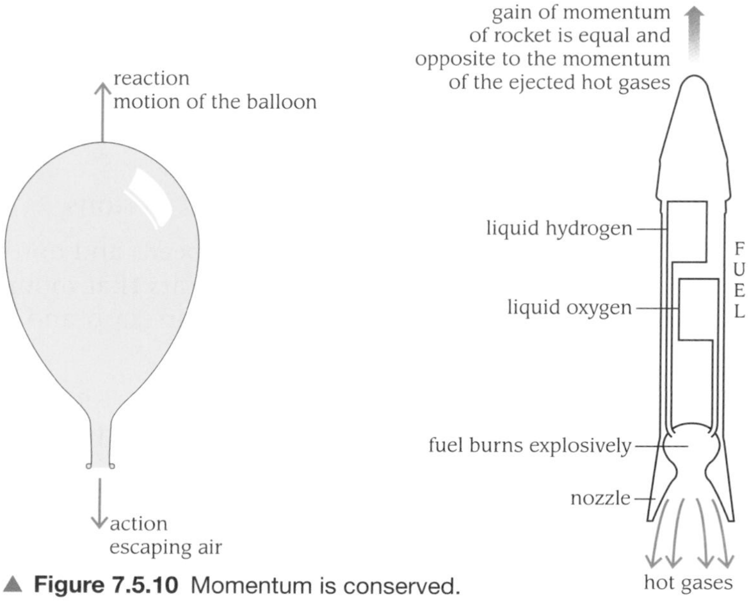

▲ **Figure 7.5.10** Momentum is conserved.

Worked example

Trolley A with mass 300 g and velocity 9 m s^{-1} collides with a stationary trolley B, and both trolleys move off together.

Calculate:

a) the momentum of trolley A before the collision

b) the velocity of both trolleys after the collision.

The trolleys move off together so the collision is inelastic.

a) Momentum of trolley A = mass × velocity = 0.3 kg × 9 m s^{-1}
= 2.7 kg m s^{-1}

b) Momentum is conserved, so momentum of the two trolleys together after collision = 2.7 kg m s^{-1}

So, (0.3 kg + 0.6 kg) × velocity after impact = 2.7 kg m s^{-1}

velocity after impact, v = 2.7 kg m s^{-1} ÷ 0.9 kg = 3 m s^{-1}

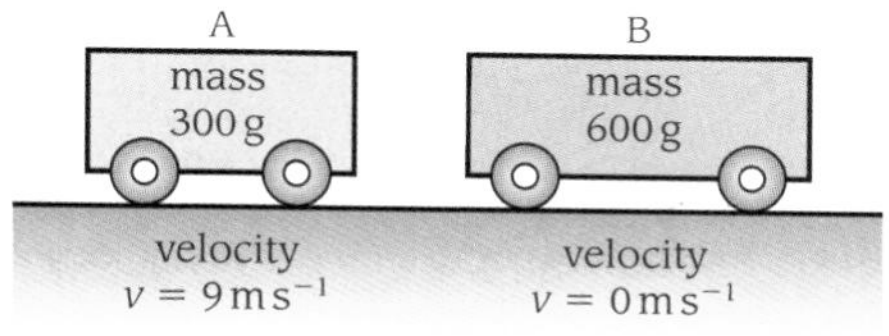

▲ **Figure 7.5.11** Momentum in collisions

Worked example

At an historic re-enactment, a cannon with mass 1000 kg fires a cabbage with a mass of 2 kg at a velocity of 100 m s^{-1}. What is the recoil velocity of the cannon?

Initially the cannon and cabbage are stationary, so initial momentum is zero.

So after the cannon is fired,

momentum of cannon in one direction = momentum of cabbage in opposite direction

1000 kg × v = 2 kg × 100 m s^{-1}

$$v = \frac{200\ \mathrm{kg\,m\,s^{-1}}}{1000\ \mathrm{kg}} = 0.2\ \mathrm{m\,s^{-1}}$$

So velocity of recoil of cannon = 0.2 m s^{-1}

Things to do

1 Trolley A with mass 4 kg and velocity 30 m s^{-1} collides with a stationary trolley B, and both trolleys move off together.

Calculate:

a) the momentum of trolley A before the collision

b) the velocity of both trolleys after the collision.

2 A toy gun fires a plastic pellet with mass 2 g at a velocity of 15 m s^{-1}. If the velocity of recoil of the toy gun is 0.25 m s^{-1}, calculate the mass of the toy gun.

Answers:

1 **a)** 120 kg m s^{-1}

b) 20 m s^{-1}

2 120 g

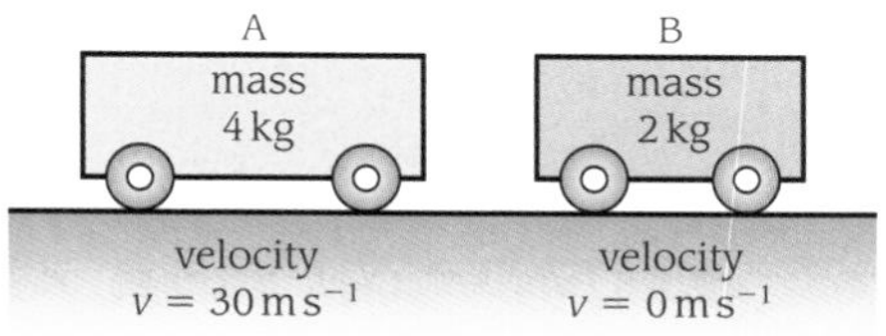

▲ **Figure 7.5.12** Momentum in an inelastic collision

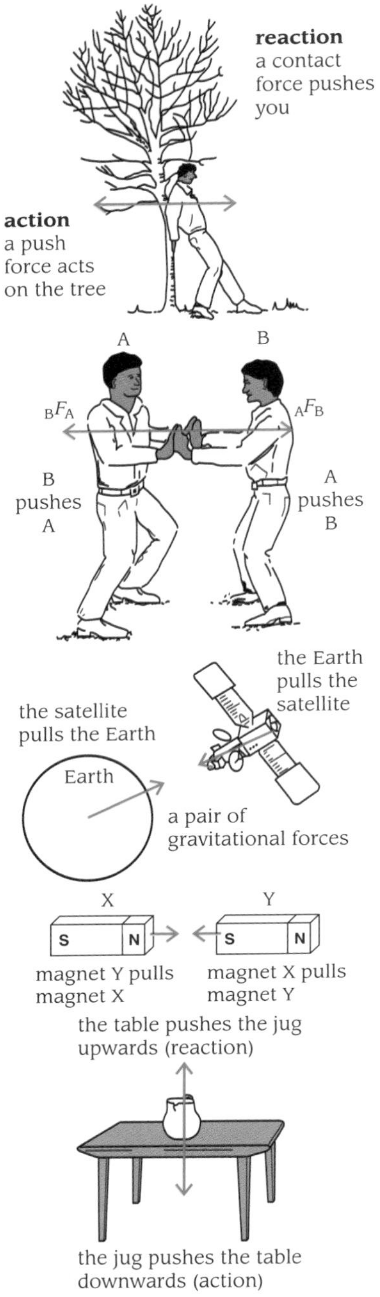

▲ **Figure 7.5.13** Equal and opposite pairs of forces

▲ **Figure 7.5.14** As the wheels spin, mud flies out backwards at a tangent to the wheels. The soft mud fails to provide the forward force required for the wheels to grip and the vehicle to move forwards.

Newton's third law of motion

We have already seen that when a force acts there are always two objects involved. A force can best be described as the action of object A on object B. Newton was the first person to realise that forces always come in pairs and that a single force is an impossibility.

a) When you lean against a tree you are pushing the tree and the tree pushes back at you. The push of the tree is provided by a contact force at its surface. Your push is called the action force and the contact force of the tree is called the reaction force.

It is important to understand why these two equal and opposite forces do not produce a zero resultant force, which would prevent acceleration happening. The reason is that the action and reaction forces always act on two different objects, not on the same one.

b) When one person, A, pushes another person, B, the two pushes, although equal and opposite, do not cancel each other out because they act on different objects. You can test this by pushing someone else when you are both standing on roller skates. The pushes cause both of you to move away in opposite directions.

This is Newton's third law of motion. It can be written as:

If object A exerts a force F on object B,
then object B exerts a force −F
(of equal size but in the opposite direction) on object A.

or:

For every action force acting on one object there is an equal and opposite reaction force acting on another object.

Why does a truck sometimes get stuck in mud?

How does a truck usually move forwards?

The driven wheels of the truck must apply a backwards force to the ground and the reaction frictional force from the ground must apply an equal forwards force to the wheels.

This is an example of Newton's third law in action.

So what goes wrong when a truck gets stuck in mud?

The mud is too soft to be able to react with a strong forwards force. When the driven wheels apply a backwards force to the mud, the mud flies out backwards and the wheels spin. There needs to be a large enough frictional grip to provide the forwards push force that makes the truck move off.

Things to do

Use Newton's third law of motion to explain why the recoil of an empty cannon used to fire a salute is much less than the recoil described by historians when the same cannon was used to fire a cannon ball in battle.

Summary questions

1 Describe how you could use an air track to demonstrate Newton's first law of motion.

2 State Newton's second law of motion.

3 What is impulse? Give the equation to calculate it.

4 Describe what is meant by 'centripetal force'.

5 'If there is a constant acceleration, the speed must keep changing steadily'. Is this statement true or false?

6 Give an example of Newton's third law of motion.

A7.6 Free fall and *g*

Objectives

By the end of this topic you will be able to:

- define gravitational field strength, g
- recall that gravitational field strength is also called acceleration due to gravity, and that the units, $N\,kg^{-1}$ and $m\,s^{-2}$, are equivalent
- describe how the acceleration of a freely falling object can be measured.

The Earth's gravitational field

The Earth's gravitational field is the region around the Earth where there is a force on masses due to the Earth's gravity. In this region, an object not acted on by other forces will accelerate towards the Earth. This acceleration due to the Earth's gravitational force is called 'g'. It is also called the Earth's gravitational field strength. The units of g are usually given as either $m\,s^{-2}$ or $N\,kg^{-1}$. The equation connecting force, mass and acceleration can be used to show that these units are the same; choose whichever unit is most convenient for the calculation you are doing.

Using the equation $F = ma$, you can see that a mass m in the Earth's gravitational field has a downward force on it, called its weight, given by:

$$W = mg$$

When the mass is hung from a spring balance it moves downwards until the downward force due to gravity is balanced by the upward force due to the tension in the spring. The downward force (and downward acceleration) due to gravity are balanced by an upward force (and upward acceleration) due to the stretched spring. If the mass is moved from this equilibrium position, there will be a resultant force and resultant acceleration that moves it back to equilibrium again.

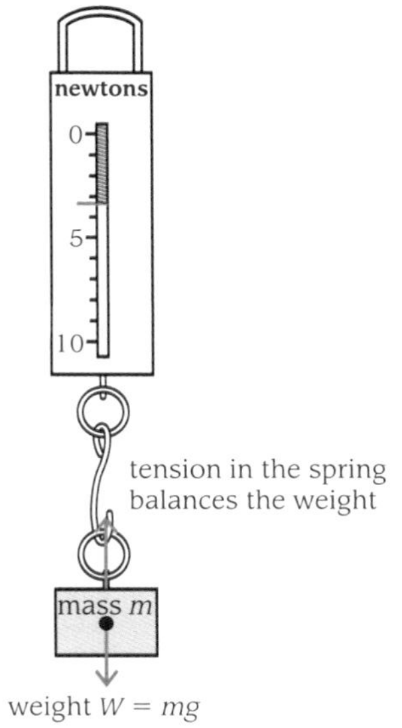

▲ **Figure 7.6.1** An object hanging on a spring balance

Weightlessness

Astronauts in orbit around Earth experience 'weightlessness'. They are still being pulled by the Earth's gravity, so they are not really 'weightless'. However, because they are in orbit and so falling freely towards Earth (their sideways movement as well means they never actually get any closer to Earth) they don't feel any resultant force from their surroundings, so they feel as though they have no weight.

Measuring the acceleration of a falling object

The acceleration of a falling object can be measured using a falling steel ball bearing, held in place above a metal trap door. An electromagnet is used to hold and release the ball bearing and an electronic timer records how long it takes to fall.

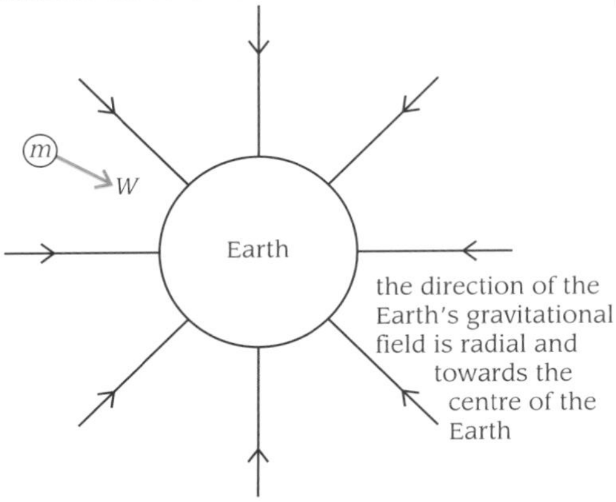
an object of mass m is pulled by a force $W = mg$ towards the centre of the Earth
m
W
Earth
the direction of the Earth's gravitational field is radial and towards the centre of the Earth

▲ **Figure 7.6.2** Object falling towards centre of the Earth

This experiment assumes that the air resistance of the metal ball bearing is very small and can be ignored when measuring g.

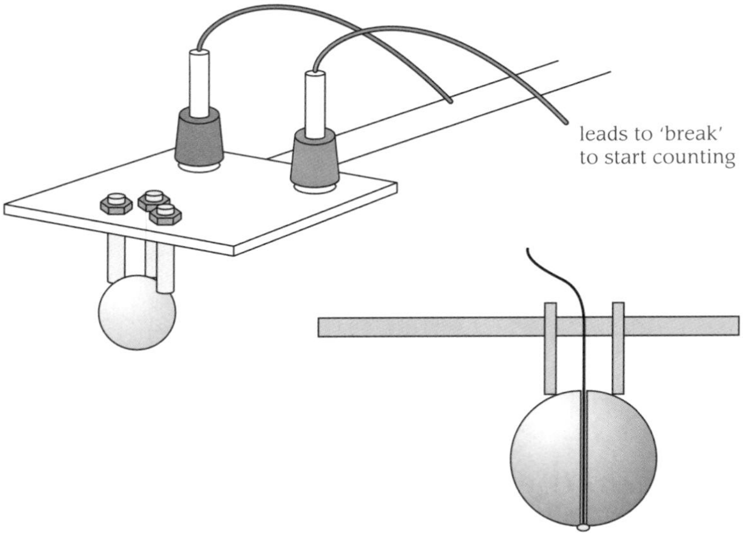
leads to 'break' to start counting

▲ **Figure 7.6.3** Measuring the acceleration of a falling object

An electronic timer is started and stopped by two separate switches. Switching off the electromagnet releases the ball and starts the timer. Opening the trap door stops the timer. Adjust the strength of the electromagnet until it *just* holds the ball, so that the ball is released immediately the electromagnet is switched off.

- Switch on the electromagnet and stick the ball bearing to it
- Measure the height h from the bottom of the ball bearing to the top of the metal trapdoor
- Switch off the electromagnet to release the ball bearing.

Sample results

$h = 925\text{ mm} = 0.925\text{ m}$, $t = 435\text{ ms} = 0.435\text{ s}$, $u = 0$

$s = ut + \frac{1}{2}at^2$ becomes $h = \frac{1}{2}gt^2$ and rearranging:

$$g = \frac{2h}{t^2} = \frac{2 \times 0.925}{(0.435)^2} = 9.78\text{ m s}^{-2}$$

To two significant figures, the acceleration, $g = 9.8\text{ m s}^{-2}$.

Worked example

If a stone is dropped from rest down a well and a splash is heard after 2.5 seconds, how deep is the well? (Assume that sound travels very quickly and $g = 10\text{ m s}^{-2}$.)

$u = 0$ (drops from rest)

$t = 2.5\text{ s}$

$a = g = 10\text{ m s}^{-2}$

$s = ut + \frac{1}{2}at^2 = 0 + \frac{1}{2} \times 10 \times (2.5)^2 = 31.25\text{ m}.$

Worked example

Calculating frictional drag

A man of mass 70 kg jumps out of an aeroplane and, before he opens his parachute, falls with an acceleration of $6.0\,\mathrm{m\,s^{-2}}$. Calculate the frictional drag of the air that is reducing his acceleration if the Earth's gravitational field strength = $10\,\mathrm{N\,kg^{-1}}$.

The resultant force acting on the man is *ma*.

Resultant force = *ma* = 70 × 6.0 = 420 N

The man's weight = *mg* = 70 × 10 = 700 N

The resultant force acting on the man = the man's weight − the frictional drag of the air

420 N = 700 N − frictional drag

So the frictional drag force = 700 N − 420 N = 280 N.

Using multiflash or stroboscopic photography to study motion

A multiflash lamp produces flashes of light at regular time intervals and so can be used to time the motion of a moving object. Each flash lasts for a very short time, perhaps 0.001 s or less. Each flash produces a sharp image of the moving object because the flash is so brief.

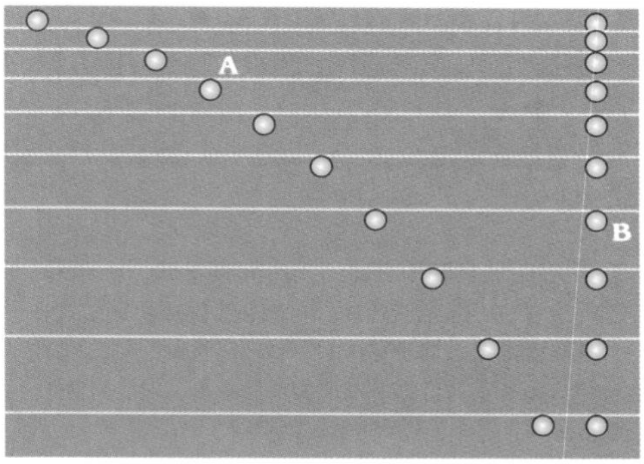

▲ **Figure 7.6.4** Ball A had horizontal motion when it started falling. Ball B fell straight downwards. These paths show that A's horizontal motion has no effect on the rate at which it moves downwards. We say that the horizontal motion and vertical motion are independent.

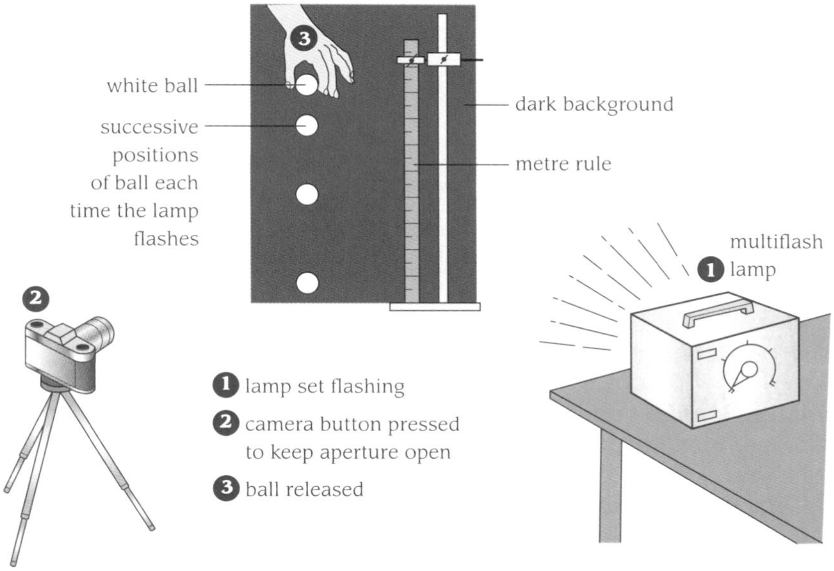

▲ **Figure 7.6.5**

Summary questions

1 What is the size of *g*? Give units.

2 What happens to the weight of an object if *g* increases?

3 Describe briefly an experiment to measure *g*.

Objectives

By the end of this topic you will be able to:

- define and calculate kinetic energies using $E_k = \frac{1}{2}mv^2$
- define potential energy, E_p
- give examples of E_p
- calculate change in gravitational potential energy using $\Delta E_p = mg\Delta h$

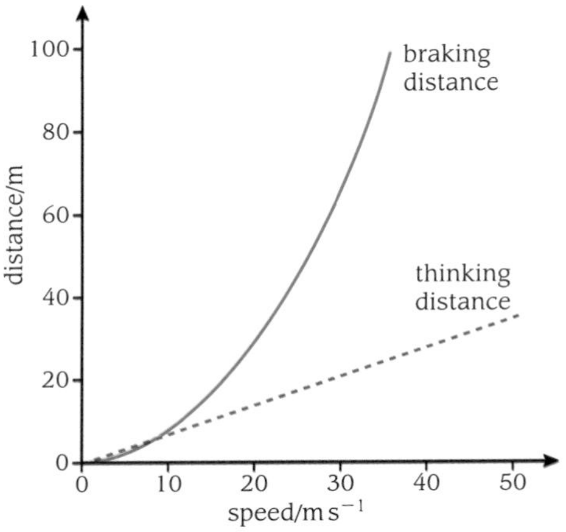

▲ **Figure 7.7.1** The thinking distance is proportional to the speed because the distance travelled for a certain thinking time depends only on the speed. The braking distance is proportional to speed squared.

Comparing the effects of impulses and work

- An impulse ($F \times t$) causes a change of momentum.

$$Ft = mv - mu$$

- Work done by a resultant force ($F \times s$) causes a change of kinetic energy.

$$Fs = \frac{1}{2}mv^2 - \frac{1}{2}mu^2$$

A7.7 Kinetic and potential energy

Kinetic energy and potential energy are two different forms of mechanical energy. Kinetic energy is the energy possessed by an object because it is moving and potential energy is the energy possessed by an object because of its position or condition.

Kinetic energy E_k

Kinetic energy is the energy an object has because it is moving.

A resultant, or unbalanced, force applied to an object makes it accelerate and increases its kinetic energy.

$$\text{Kinetic energy} = \frac{1}{2}\text{mass} \times \text{speed}^2 \qquad E_k = \frac{1}{2}mv^2$$

When the mass, m, is given in kg and the speed, v, is in $m\,s^{-1}$, the kinetic energy, E_k, will always be in joules.

Braking distances

When a car brakes, the kinetic energy of the moving car is transformed into heat by friction in the braking system. Because the kinetic energy of the moving car is proportional to the square of the speed, the braking distance is also proportional to the speed squared. The total distance it takes for the car to stop is the distance the car travels while the driver is reacting to the hazard (the thinking distance) plus the distance the car travels while the car is braking (the braking distance).

Worked example

Calculate the kinetic energy of a sprinter of mass 60 kg running at $10\,m\,s^{-1}$.

$E_k = \frac{1}{2}mv^2 = \frac{1}{2} \times 60 \times 10^2 = 3000$ joules

Worked example

Calculating kinetic energy gained from work

A free-wheeling motorcyclist of mass (including her machine) 100 kg is pushed from rest over a distance of 10 m. If the push of 250 N acts against a frictional force of 70 N, calculate her kinetic energy and speed when the push ends.

Resultant force causing acceleration = push − frictional force

$F = 250\,N - 70\,N = 180\,N$

The work done that causes acceleration is

$F \times s = 180\,N \times 10\,m = 1800\,J$

So the kinetic energy gained E_k is also 1800 J.

By rearranging the kinetic energy formula we have:

$$v^2 = \frac{2E_k}{m} = \frac{2 \times 1800}{100} = 36 \quad \text{so} \quad v = 6\,m\,s^{-1}$$

Potential energy E_p

Potential energy is stored energy that an object has because of its position or condition, or state.

An object can have stored energy if it is held in a position from which it can fall under the influence of gravity. This potential energy, called gravitational potential energy, is possessed by all objects that are raised above the Earth's surface.

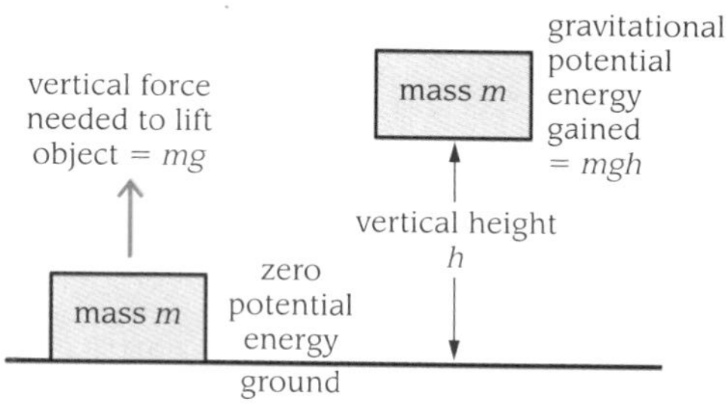

▲ **Figure 7.7.2** The gravitational potential energy of an object due to its position above the ground

Gravitational potential energy

We can calculate the **gravitational potential energy** possessed by an object from the work done in lifting it to a height, h, above the Earth's surface. A force, equal and opposite to the weight of an object, is needed to lift it.

If the object has a mass m, the force needed is mg.

$$E_p = mgh$$

When m is in kg, h is in metres and g is in $\mathrm{N\,kg^{-1}}$, then potential energy is in N m or joules.

So when an object is pulled or pushed up a ramp, the distance used to calculate its gain in gravitational energy is the distance it moves against the force of gravity, that is the vertical height it rises, not the length of the ramp.

Worked example

A grandfather clock uses a mass of 5 kg to drive its mechanism. Calculate the gravitational potential energy stored when the mass is raised to its maximum height of 0.8 m ($g = 10\,\mathrm{N\,kg^{-1}}$).

$E_p = mgh = 5 \times 10 \times 0.8$
$= 40$ joules

Worked example

A force of 200 N is used to slide a mass of 10 kg up a slope to a height of 3 m. Calculate the increase of gravitational potential energy of the mass.

$E_p = mgh = 10 \times 10 \times 3 = 300\,\mathrm{J}$

▲ **Figure 7.7.3** As the bow is bent, elastic potential energy is stored. When the arrow is released this is converted into kinetic energy.

Elastic potential energy

Objects can also possess potential energy called **elastic potential energy** or strain energy because of their condition. For example they can be stretched, compressed, twisted or distorted. A stretched catapult, a bent bow and a wound-up spring all possess elastic potential energy.

Conservation of mechanical energy

In many machines there is a constant interchange between kinetic energy and potential energy. In a frictionless machine the total of the kinetic energy + potential energy would remain constant. This is an example of energy conservation. In real machines frictional forces are always converting some mechanical energy into heat energy.

Key fact

When mechanical energy is conserved:

- gain of E_k = loss of E_p
- loss of E_k = gain of E_p

When mechanical energy is conserved:

$$\text{change of kinetic energy } E_k = -\text{change of potential energy } E_p$$

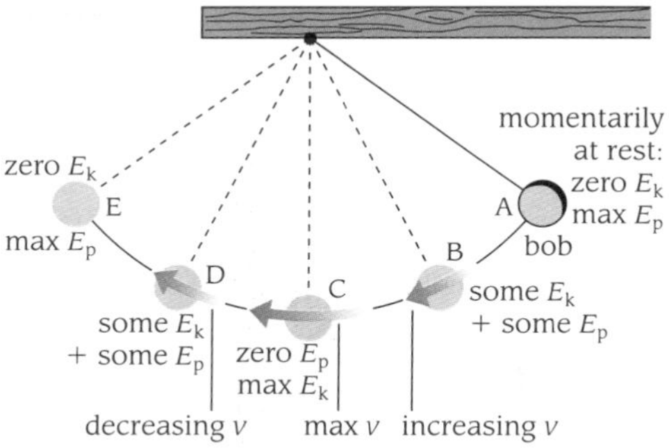

▲ **Figure 7.7.4** Energy changes of a pendulum

Energy changes in a swinging pendulum

- Watch a pendulum swinging from side to side and see how its speed changes.
- What kind of energy has it got at the side of its swing and in the middle of its swing?

The speed v changes from zero at the moment of widest swing and greatest height of the bob (A) to a maximum value at the centre of the swing at the lowest position of the bob (C) (Figure 7.7.4).

At C: the kinetic energy E_k is greatest when v is greatest.

At A and E: the potential energy E_p is greatest when the bob is at its greatest height h.

At B and D: the energy is changing between E_k and E_p, depending on whether v is increasing or decreasing.

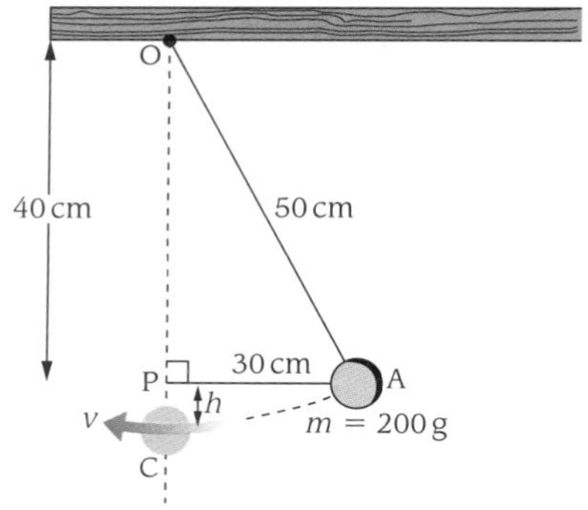

▲ **Figure 7.7.5**

Worked example

The energy of a pendulum bob

A pendulum bob of mass 200 g is pulled sideways a horizontal distance of 30 cm (Figure 7.7.5). If the length of the pendulum is 50 cm, calculate:

a) the potential energy of the bob in this position

b) the maximum speed of the bob.

a) The triangle OPA is right angled with OA = 50 cm and PA = 30 cm. By Pythagoras' we can see that OP = 40 cm. The vertical height h, by which the bob (in position A) is raised above its lowest position C, is:

h = 50 cm − 40 cm

= 10 cm = 0.1 m

The bob in position A has potential energy E_p given by:

$E_p = mgh$

= 0.2 kg × 10 N kg^{-1} × 0.1 m

= 0.2 N m = 0.2 joules

b) When the pendulum swings down to position C all this potential energy is converted into kinetic energy. So we can calculate the maximum speed v of the pendulum bob as it passes position C using:

gain of E_k = loss of E_p

$$\frac{1}{2}mv^2 = mgh$$

$$= 0.2\,\text{J}$$

$$\text{Rearranging: } v^2 = \frac{2 \times 0.2}{\text{m}}$$

$$= \frac{0.4}{0.2} = 2(\text{m s}^{-1})^2$$

$$v = \sqrt{2}\,\text{m s}^{-1} = 1.4\,\text{m s}^{-1}$$

It is interesting to note that we could have found this speed without knowing the mass of the bob. The mass m appears on both sides of the energy equation and cancels out. This explains why the swinging of a pendulum is not changed in either speed or time of swing when the mass of the bob is changed.

Worked example

Using energy equations, find the speed at which a stone hits the ground if it falls from a height of 20 m.

gain of E_k = loss of E_p

$\frac{1}{2}mv^2 = mgh$

The mass cancels from both sides of the equations. Remember objects of all masses fall with the same acceleration.

Cancelling and rearranging:

$v^2 = 2gh = 2 \times 10 \times 20 = 400$

$v = 20\,\text{m s}^{-1}$

Summary questions

1 Calculate the kinetic energy of a mass of 2 kg moving at a speed of $3\,m\,s^{-1}$.
2 Give the formula to calculate gravitational potential energy.
3 What is elastic potential energy?
4 Describe the main energy changes taking place in a child's swing.

A7.8 Energy and people

Energy and our bodies

Food is required by our bodies to provide materials for the repair and replacement of cells and for us to grow. But most of our food is needed to provide energy. As we breathe we absorb oxygen through our lungs. When this oxygen combines with glucose molecules in a process called oxidation, energy is released. Energy can be obtained by this process from carbohydrates, fats and proteins. Any surplus food containing energy is converted to extra fat, which is stored around our bodies. The amount of energy we need varies greatly according to what we are doing but at all times we lose energy as heat. Even the loss of heat energy depends on several factors such as the surrounding temperature, the clothes we are wearing, the surface area of our bodies and the kind of activity we are engaged in.

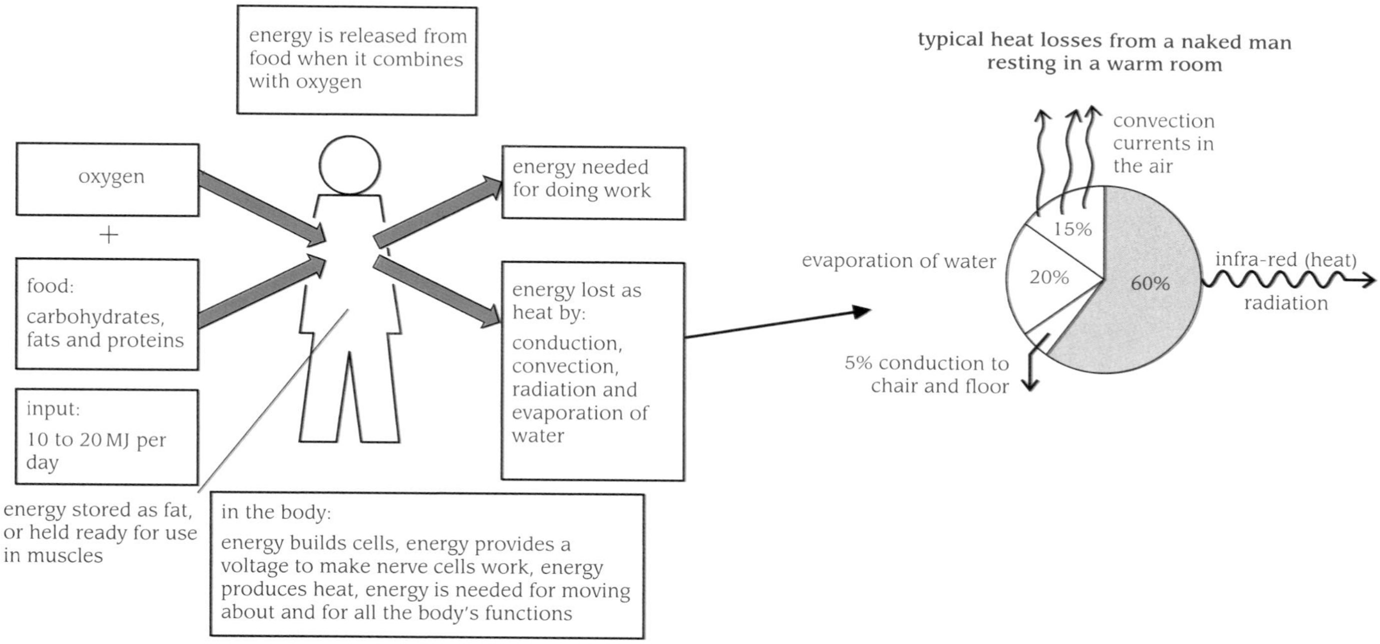

▲ **Figure 7.8.1** Our bodies need energy

▼ Power needed by an adult

Activity of a 70 kg person	Rate of working/W
Sleeping	80
Sitting still	120
Piano-playing	160
Walking slowly	250
Running, swimming or hard physical work	500 to 800
Climbing up stairs	1300

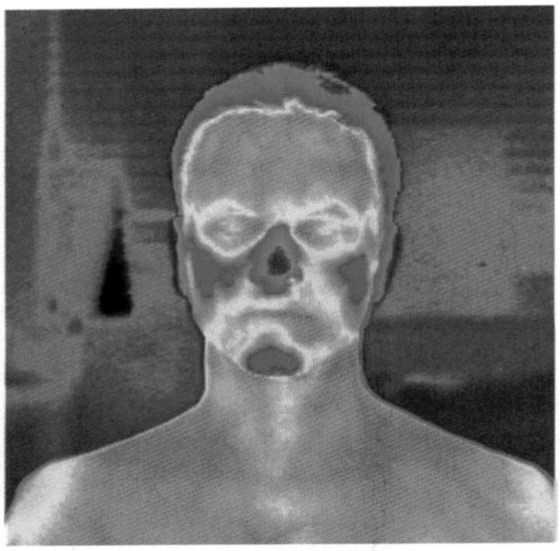

▲ **Figure 7.8.2** Thermogram of a man's head and shoulders. People lose a lot of energy as infra-red (heat) radiation. More infrared radiation is emitted from hot areas of the skin than from cooler areas. In this photograph, taken using an infrared sensor that scans across the body, the hottest areas from which most energy is radiated appear lightest.

How do we lose heat from our bodies?

The pie chart in Figure 7.8.1 shows the percentage of heat lost in each of the four basic ways.

- The total rate of loss of heat from a naked adult in a warm room is about 100 joules per second or 100 watts, which is equivalent to the power of an electric lamp.
- While resting a person loses most heat by radiation. This is really infra-red radiation, which is electromagnetic radiation of longer wavelength than light.
- When people are working very hard or perhaps running in a race, they need to lose much more heat. The greatest increase in heat loss is produced by sweating, which can increase the rate of loss of heat by a factor of 10. As the sweat evaporates, its latent heat of vaporisation is taken from the body surface and helps to keep it cool.
- An average rate of loss of heat of 120 watts would produce a total daily loss of about 10 000 000 joules or 10 MJ of energy. (Energy = power × time, power measured in watts and time in seconds.)

How much energy do we use?

We need energy for many purposes apart from keeping warm. The need for energy can be seen and felt when we are working hard, lifting heavy objects, riding a bicycle or climbing a mountain. In addition, our bodies need energy just to keep them going. The building and repairing of new cells, the pumping of blood round our bodies, the electrical energy that is used for signalling by our nerve cells and all body movements and muscle contractions all need a supply of energy.

So we must eat food to provide enough energy to keep us warm and for all these other needs. The amount of energy needed to do physical work varies greatly according to the kind of work and time spent working. The table gives a few examples of the rate of working of a 70 kg person for various activities. Averaged over 24 hours this person's total energy need is likely to be somewhere between 10 MJ and 20 MJ per day.

Energy can damage our bodies

Your body can be damaged if it receives too much energy too quickly. For example, if you put your hand into a fire you get burnt. This is because heat energy received too quickly damages the cells. Burns treated very quickly with lots of cold water do less damage because the cold water removes the heat energy from the body tissue.

A bullet is a small metal object, which is quite harmless if you hold it in your hand. But when it is fired at high speed by a gun it has kinetic energy that enables it to penetrate your body and do damage. It is the energy of the bullet that is dangerous. Similarly it is the kinetic energy of a fast-moving car and its occupants that causes damage and injury in a collision.

Summary questions

1 Give two things that the energy we take in from food is used for.

2 Explain why a person in a cold climate may need to eat more.

3 Which activity uses energy at a rate of working of 250 W?

A7.9 Forms of energy

The total amount of energy in existence does not change because energy cannot be created or destroyed. We may talk about needing energy and using or consuming it, but in fact we can only convert energy from one form to another. When we have converted some energy to a different form we can show that there is always the same amount of energy after the change as before. We call this idea the conservation of energy.

Objectives

By the end of this topic you will be able to:

- describe the different forms of energy
- understand that energy becomes degraded and converted into heat.

Stored energy: chemical energy

Food

Food in all its variety is our store of chemical energy. So plants and animals are forms of energy that can be converted in our bodies by chemical reactions called oxidation.

Fossil fuels

All the fossil fuels such as coal, oil and gas are stored forms of chemical energy, which are usually converted by burning. (Burning is another chemical reaction involving oxidation.) A car uses stored chemical energy in the form of petrol, which it burns to drive its engine and make it move. The car battery also stores energy in a chemical form and uses a chemical reaction to supply electrical energy to various devices in the car.

▲ **Figure 7.9.1** The workman converts the chemical energy of his food into the kinetic energy of the heavy hammer he swings at the stone block. Some of his food energy will be converted into heat as he works hard.

Stored energy: potential energy

Gravitational potential energy

Potential energy is stored by an object when it is in a particular position or condition. Objects that are able to fall down have stored energy caused by gravity. This form of potential energy is called gravitational potential energy, and depends on the raised position of an object above the ground.

Gravitational potential energy is stored in water at the top of a waterfall, in a high-level reservoir and in the heavy driving weight of a wound-up grandfather clock. A cyclist has gravitational potential energy when she reaches the top of a hill. She has used a lot of stored chemical energy in climbing the hill working against gravity. At the top of the hill, the gravitational potential energy she has gained will drive her down the hill with increasing kinetic energy.

Elastic potential energy

Objects that are elastic in some way can store energy when they are stretched, twisted or bent. The energy stored by such an elastic object can be called elastic potential energy and depends on the strained condition of the object. Some examples include the stretched elastic of a catapult, the wound-up spring of a clockwork motor and the bent condition of a diving board when a diver is about to jump from the end. The springboard briefly stores potential energy while it is bent downwards, and then converts this into kinetic energy for the diver by giving him an upwards push.

▲ **Figure 7.9.2** The diving board stores elastic potential energy when it is bent down. The spring energy of the board allows the diver to gain extra height before his descent into the water.

▲ **Figure 7.9.3** A nuclear explosion occurs as a result of the rapid release of energy from an uncontrolled nuclear reaction. The driving reaction may be nuclear fission, nuclear fusion or a multistage cascading combination of the two. The source of energy in all cases involves the conversion of mass into energy. Atmospheric nuclear explosions produce large amounts of radiation and radioactive debris and the characteristic mushroom-shaped cloud. In 1963, all nuclear and many non-nuclear states signed the Limited Test Ban Treaty, pledging to refrain from testing nuclear weapons in the atmosphere, underwater, or in outer space. The treaty permitted underground tests.

▲ **Figure 7.9.5** Sounds made by musical instruments require an energy input that is converted into sound energy. A drummer hits the drum, converting the kinetic energy of his hands into transverse vibrations of the drum skin. These vibrations cause longitudinal sound waves in the air, which carry sound energy to your ears.

Stored energy: nuclear energy

Energy is released when radioactive decay occurs. The energy radiated when atoms decay has been stored in their nuclei since they were formed, perhaps since the formation of the solar system.

In nuclear power stations, we have found ways of speeding up and controlling the release of the energy stored in the nuclei of atoms. The atomic bomb is the result of an uncontrolled chain reaction of energy released from a very large number of atomic nuclei in a very short space of time.

Kinetic energy: of moving objects

An object has energy if it is moving. The energy of motion is known as kinetic energy. Energy must be supplied to an object to get it moving, and energy must be taken away from an object to make it stop. The process of changing the kinetic energy of an object involves doing work. For example, a car engine does work to get a car moving and give it kinetic energy, and the brakes do work to stop the car and remove its kinetic energy.

▲ **Figure 7.9.4** A fast-moving car has a large amount of kinetic energy provided by the combustion of petroleum or gas. The kinetic energy is proportional to the square of its speed.

Kinetic energy: of atoms and molecules, internal energy

All atoms and molecules have some kinetic energy because they all have some kind of motion. The atoms (or molecules) in a gas or liquid move about randomly with various amounts of kinetic energy according to their speeds. The atoms in a solid also have some kinetic energy as they vibrate about their fixed locations in the solid. When an object is heated, energy is transferred from an external source to the atoms inside the object. To absorb this extra energy, the atoms of the object must increase their kinetic energy. So heating an object makes the atoms (or molecules) of a gas or liquid move faster and the atoms of a solid vibrate more energetically.

The extra kinetic energy possessed by the atoms inside the heated object is actually the heat energy it has absorbed, which now forms part of the total **internal energy** of the object.

The internal energy is all the energy possessed by the atoms and molecules inside a substance or an object. This includes forms of both kinetic and potential energy.

The absorption of heat energy and the resulting increase in internal energy of an object can be detected in a rise in temperature of the object.

Sound energy

Unlike the random motion of molecules associated with heat energy, the motion of molecules through which a sound wave passes has an organised and periodic pattern. A longitudinal wave motion passes sound energy from molecule to molecule in the form of a mechanical vibration with a particular frequency and amplitude.

Electrical energy

▲ **Figure 7.9.6** Electrical energy is carried by a grid of high-voltage power lines.

Electrical energy is produced by a conversion process from another form of energy. For example, electrical energy from a battery comes from a store of chemical energy. The electrical energy from a power station generator is obtained from the store of chemical energy in a fossil fuel, or perhaps from nuclear energy.

Electrical energy is a very convenient form of energy that can easily be carried to the particular place where energy is needed. It is also a very high-grade form and has many specialised applications for which no other energy form would be suitable. Perhaps the best example is the way computers and communication systems depend on electrical energy.

▲ **Figure 7.9.7** Signals arriving at the satellite are very weak and a large collecting surface is needed to detect them. Electrical energy supplied to the satellite is used to amplify the signals before they are re-transmitted.

Electromagnetic radiation

Energy can also exist as radiation without belonging to matter in any form. Electromagnetic radiation can travel in a vacuum. When this radiation interacts with the atoms and molecules of matter it is absorbed and converted into many other forms of energy.

Radio waves

When radio wave energy is absorbed by the metal aerial of a radio or TV receiver it produces a small amount of electrical energy in the form of a small alternating current. Radio transmitters require a lot of electrical energy to generate the radio waves they send out from aerials. All mobile phones and microwave communication systems require energy to transmit microwave radiation, which is also a form of radio wave energy.

Infrared radiation and light

When infrared radiation is absorbed by an object it causes a rise in temperature and a gain of internal energy. Infrared radiation is emitted by all warm or hot objects. Much of the Sun's radiation that we feel as warming is infrared.

When light energy is absorbed by growing plants it is converted into stored chemical energy. Solar cells can convert light energy into electrical energy.

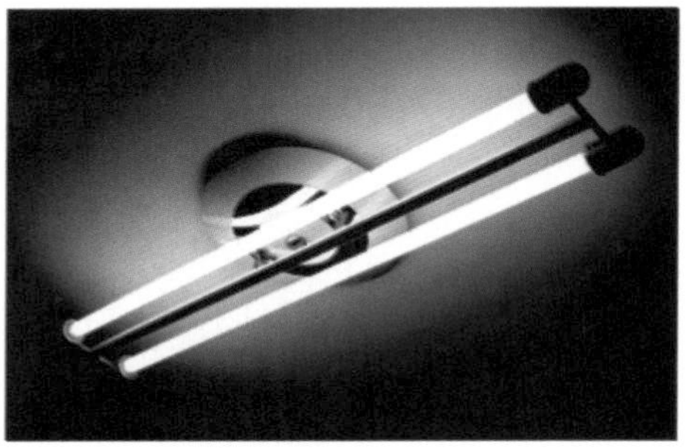

▲ **Figure 7.9.8** A fluorescent lamp provides additional visible white light by converting invisible ultraviolet light into visible light. This is achieved by the phosphor coating on the inside of the glass tube.

Ultraviolet, X-ray and gamma radiation

These radiations are also part of the electromagnetic spectrum. All these radiations exist as energy quanta or photons that can interact with atoms and molecules of matter.

When ultraviolet light is absorbed by atoms it is sometimes converted into visible light energy. This process, called fluorescence, happens inside fluorescent lamps.

When X-ray or gamma-ray energy is absorbed by matter it causes ionisation of atoms and molecules. These processes can turn X-ray film dark or damage living cells.

▲ **Figure 7.9.9** Photovoltaic or solar cells convert light energy directly into electrical energy. Some panels are turned during the day so that they follow the Sun and receive the maximum amount of light. Large panels can generate high voltages if many groups of cells are connected together in series. Larger currents at lower voltages are possible when many cells are connected together in parallel.

▲ **Figure 7.9.10** The mechanism of this grandfather clock is driven by the two heavy weights that are attached to chains inside the clock. Gravitational potential energy is lost as the weights slowly descend inside the clock.

Energy becomes degraded

There is a general drift of energy forms in one direction, from high-grade energy to lower grade. We all expect a wound-up clock spring to run down and not wind itself up. Similarly, when a battery becomes 'flat' we do not expect it to recharge itself. The stored heat energy of a hot drink in a vacuum flask gradually escapes and the drink gets cold. We would not expect it to heat up again by taking heat from the surrounding colder air.

High-grade forms of energy include stored chemical energy and electrical energy. These may be used for a variety of energy needs and can easily be converted to other energy forms as and when required.

Examples of machines in which energy becomes degraded are shown in the photographs. The grandfather clock is driven by weights which, when raised, store gravitational potential energy. We would never expect these weights to rise up on their own, they only run down and the clock stops when they get to the bottom. The spring in the wind-up radio will never wind itself up. That is why we provide a handle on the outside of the radio. The energy stored in the wound up spring becomes degraded as it finally produces the sound output from the radio.

▲ **Figure 7.9.11** Wind-up radio. This radio can be used anywhere in the world and requires neither a mains electricity nor a disposable battery supply. It can be used day and night. In the day time it uses solar cells to keep internal rechargeable batteries topped up and, when there is not enough light, energy can be supplied by winding up a spring that stores potential energy. This stored energy drives a small dynamo to charge up the batteries. In the photo you can see both the solar cells and the handle for winding up the spring.

Heat – the lowest grade of energy

Heat is the lowest grade of energy. While it is very easy to convert electrical energy into heat energy in an electric fire (100% efficiency), it is very difficult to convert the heat energy back into electrical energy and this can only be done at a very low efficiency.

For this reason it is wasteful to deliberately convert electrical energy directly into heat energy since a large amount of energy is lost in generating the electricity in the first place. It would be more efficient to miss out the process of upgrading to electrical energy if the energy is only going to be deliberately downgraded again. In other words, we can get far more heat energy from a certain quantity of coal burnt on a fire at home than we do by first converting the same quantity of coal into electrical energy and then converting it into heat in an electric fire.

Energy conservation

Accurate experiments have shown that when mechanical or electrical energy is converted fully into heat no energy has disappeared. All the energy we appear to 'use up' or lose becomes heat energy. No energy is consumed or destroyed. The total amount is always conserved.

When energy eventually becomes the kinetic energy of the random motion of atoms and molecules it has found the least ordered form of energy possible. This appears to be the eventual fate of all the energy in the universe.

Entropy

Entropy is the word used to describe the degree of degradation or 'running down' of the energy possessed by something. As the energy of an object is degraded to heat energy so its entropy is said to increase.

The idea that all forms of energy are steadily running down into a state of maximum disorder is described by saying that the entropy of the universe is increasing. So our universe appears to be 'unwinding' or 'running down' as its entropy increases. It is thought impossible for the entropy of the universe to decrease; just as a spring will never wind itself up again.

Summary questions

1 Give two sources of stored chemical energy.

2 What is entropy?

3 List all the forms of energy you can.

A7.10 Energy conversions

Energy changes its form

We have already found that energy often changes from one form to another and that machines do work by converting or transferring energy. We can study energy changes by setting up experiments in the laboratory, which are working models of larger scale processes. In all these examples no energy is 'used up' or destroyed; the total amount of energy is conserved.

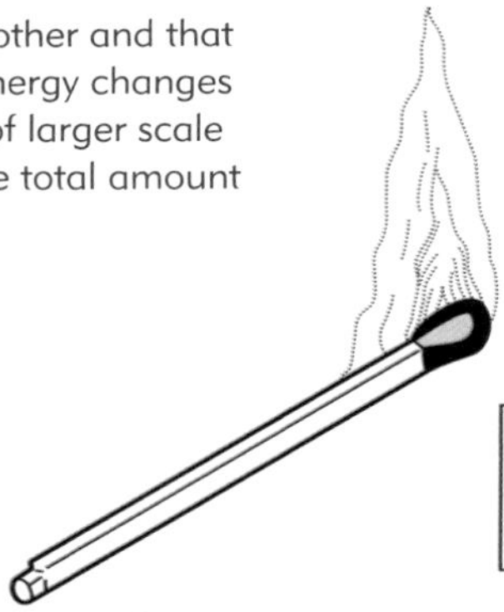

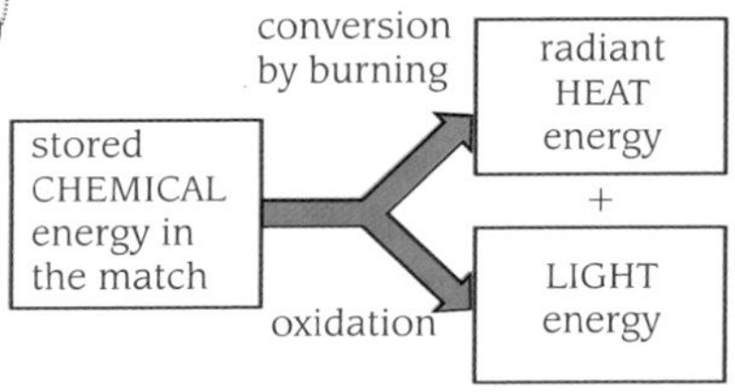

- ***Light a match.***

Before the match burns what kind of energy does it hold?
What else is needed for the match to burn?
What are the final forms of energy?
Is this process reversible?
The forms of energy and changes that occur can be explained by an energy flow diagram. The blocks contain the different forms of energy and the arrows show energy changes or conversion process. The linked forms of energy make an energy chain. Sometimes the flow of energy along this chain can be reversed, sometimes it cannot. Energy often leaks out of the chain.

- ***Connect a battery to a lamp.***

Is this process reversible?
Is energy lost before it reaches the lamp filament?
Feel the lamp as well as looking at it.
What are the final forms of energy?

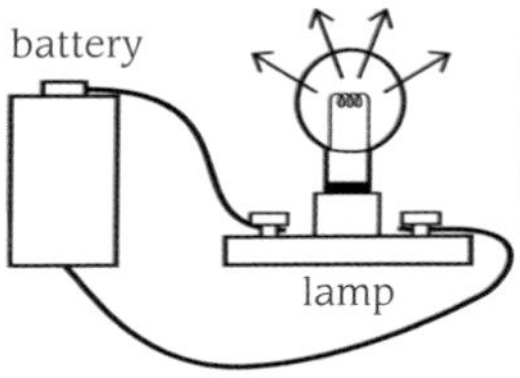

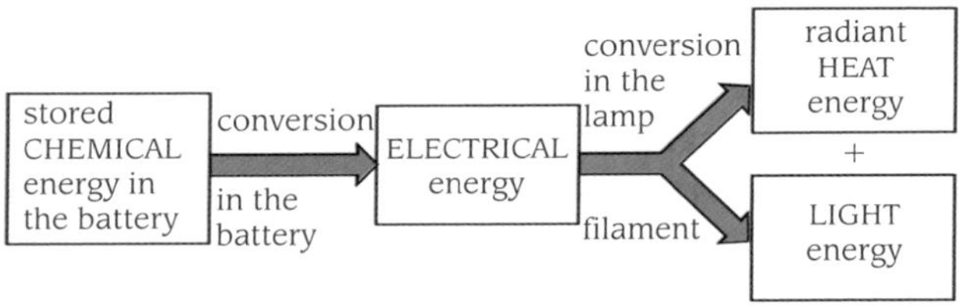

- ***Knock a large nail into a block of wood using a hammer.***

Is this process reversible?
Feel the hammer and the nail after several blows.
What are the final forms of energy in the hammer and nail? What other forms of energy are produced and what happens to some of the stored chemical energy in your body?

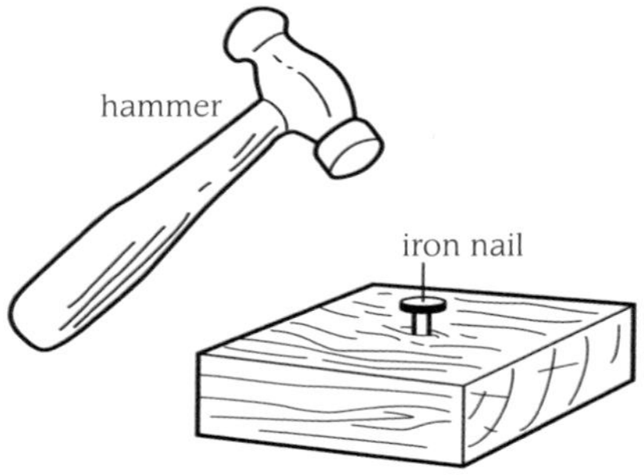

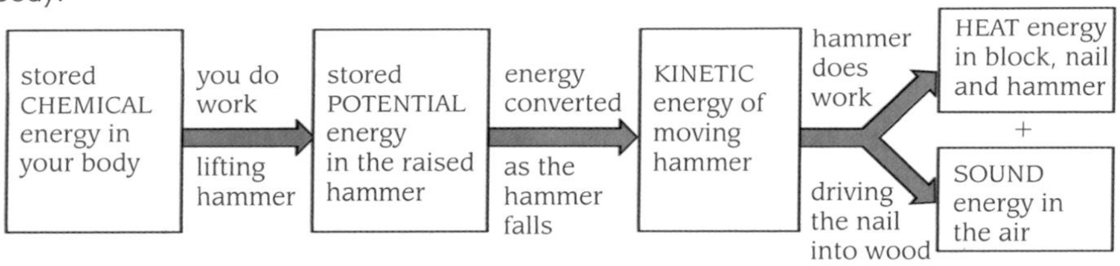

- ***Wind up a steel clock spring. Then let it drive a dynamo, which is connected to a lamp.***

If we tried to use the electrical energy output from the dynamo to drive an electric motor to wind up the spring again, what do you think would happen?
Where, and in what form has energy been lost along the energy chain?
When the brake or ratchet is released on the spring it always unwinds and its stored energy 'runs down'. To reverse this process some more stored energy is needed to wind it up again.

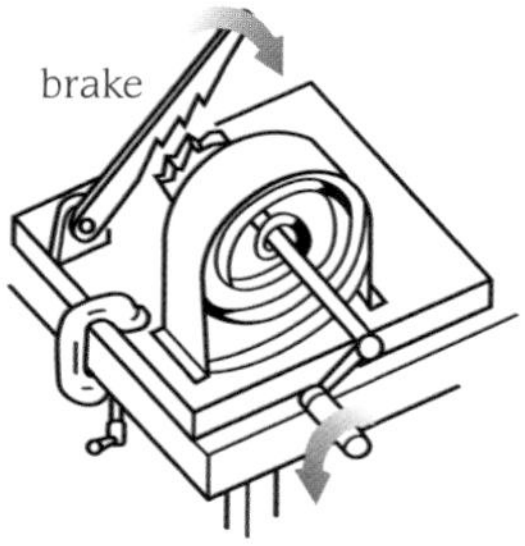

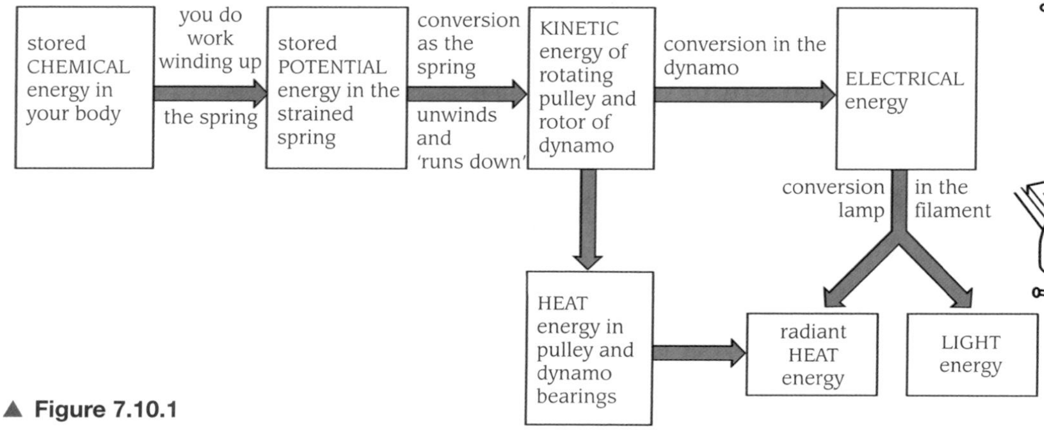

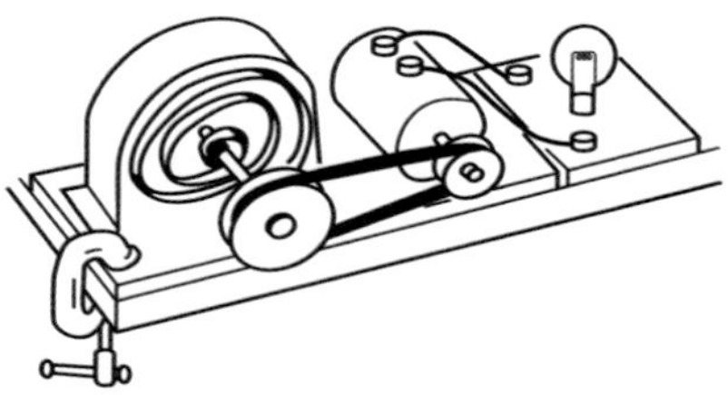

▲ **Figure 7.10.1**

- ***Use a battery-driven electric motor to raise load.***

Try raising different size loads and see what happens.
Where is energy lost in this chain?
Is this chain reversible?

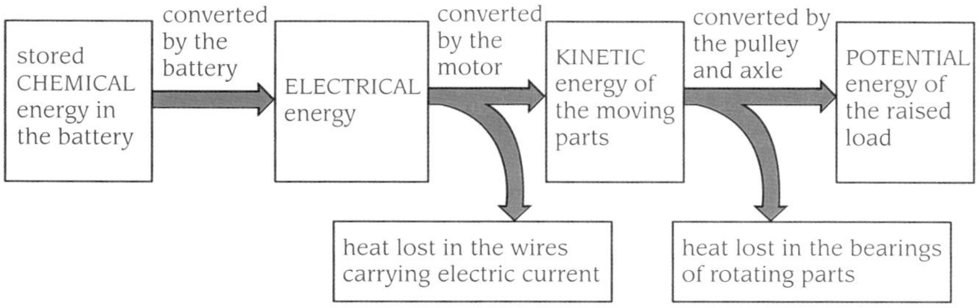

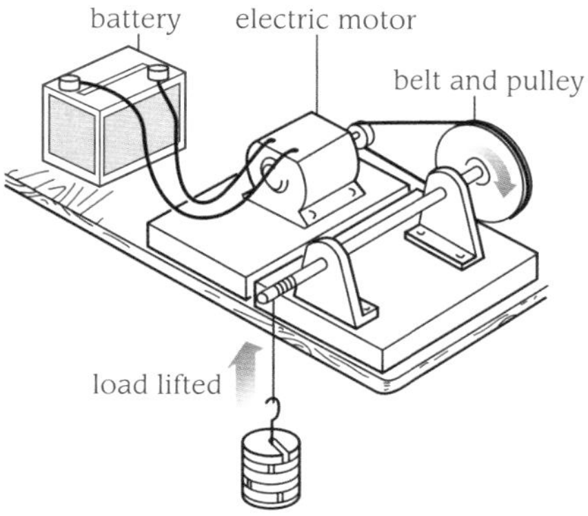

- ***Replace the battery with a lamp and try reversing the energy chain.***

Why do you need a much larger load?

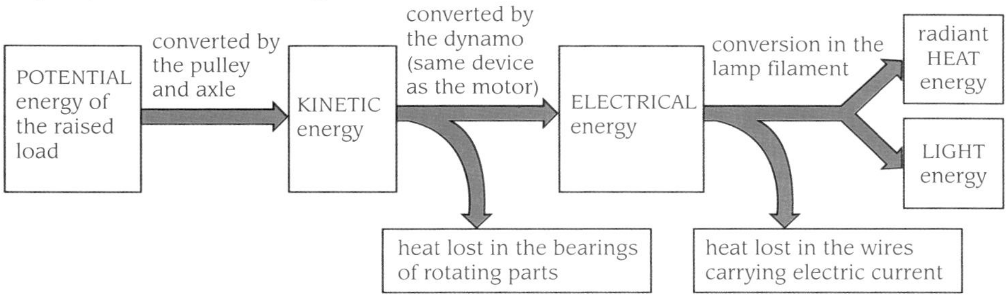

- ***Build a working model of a hydroelectric power station***.

A hydroelectric scheme avoids many of the energy losses found when lighting a lamp using a steam engine, because it uses the running water instead of steam to drive the turbines. Can you explain where some energy is still lost as heat in this scheme? Can you work out a scheme for reversing this energy chain?

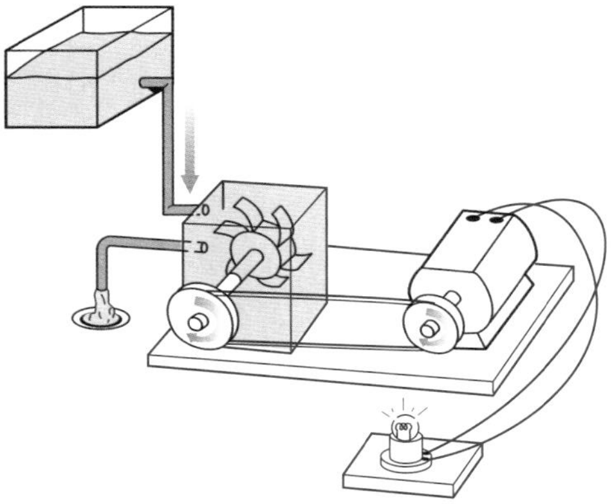

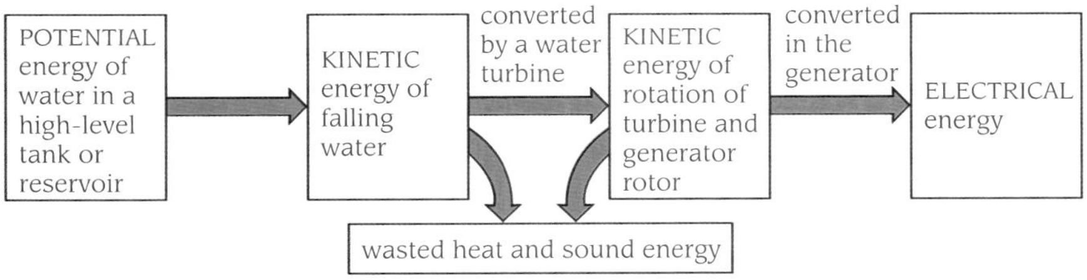

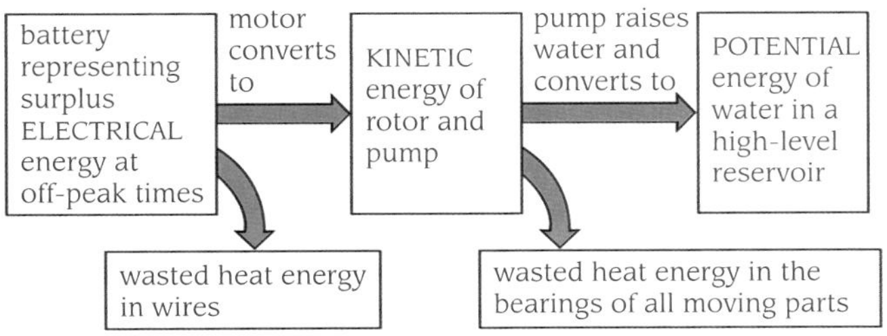

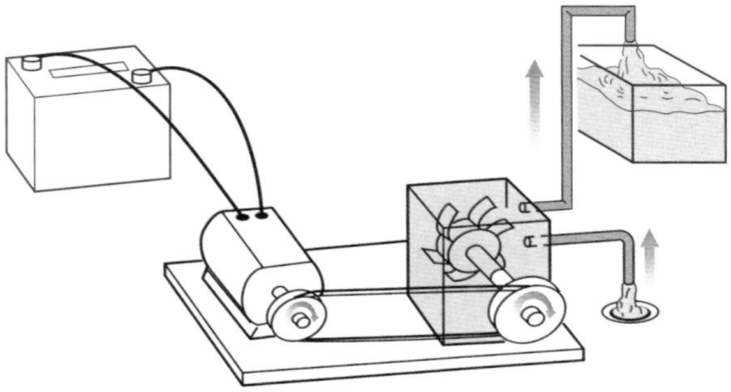

▲ **Figure 7.10.1** (continued)

Energy conversions in a power station

1 Heat energy is produced by burning coal or oil in a furnace or from the fission of uranium nuclei in the core of a nuclear reactor.
2 Water absorbs the heat energy in a boiler or heat-exchanger and is turned into steam at a high pressure. So the steam generator stores the heat energy in the steam. There is now extra internal energy in the steam, which in this case we can think of as a form of potential energy. It is similar to the energy stored in an inflated balloon or in a cylinder of pressurised gas. There is potential energy stored in the gas because of its pressurised condition. Similarly, steam under pressure is capable of doing mechanical work so we shall call it potential energy.
3 Converting heat energy into mechanical energy is the most inefficient of the energy conversion processes. This is because we are reversing the natural tendency of mechanical energy to be degraded by friction into heat energy. Steam turbines extract about 50% of the energy stored in the high-pressure steam and convert it into mechanical energy of rotation, i.e. kinetic energy. For maximum efficiency the steam is expanded to a partial vacuum from its high-pressure state. During this rapid expansion the steam drives the blades of the turbine. Then it is condensed back to water for re-use in the boiler. To condense the steam a large flow of cooling water is needed to absorb its latent heat. The warmed water is exposed to the air in the cooling towers where heat is lost to the atmosphere in the form of warm air and evaporated water. This deliberate loss of heat to the atmosphere as the water is cooled alone accounts for the wastage of about 50% of the total energy input to the power station energy chain. Schemes are being planned for making use of this heat energy to provide heating and hot water for domestic and industrial consumers near to power stations.
4 Generators convert the kinetic energy of the rotating turbine into electrical energy by electromagnetic induction. Here friction converts some mechanical energy into heat and the resistance of the wires in the generator, transformer and transmission lines also produce waste heat.

Energy conversions in a power station

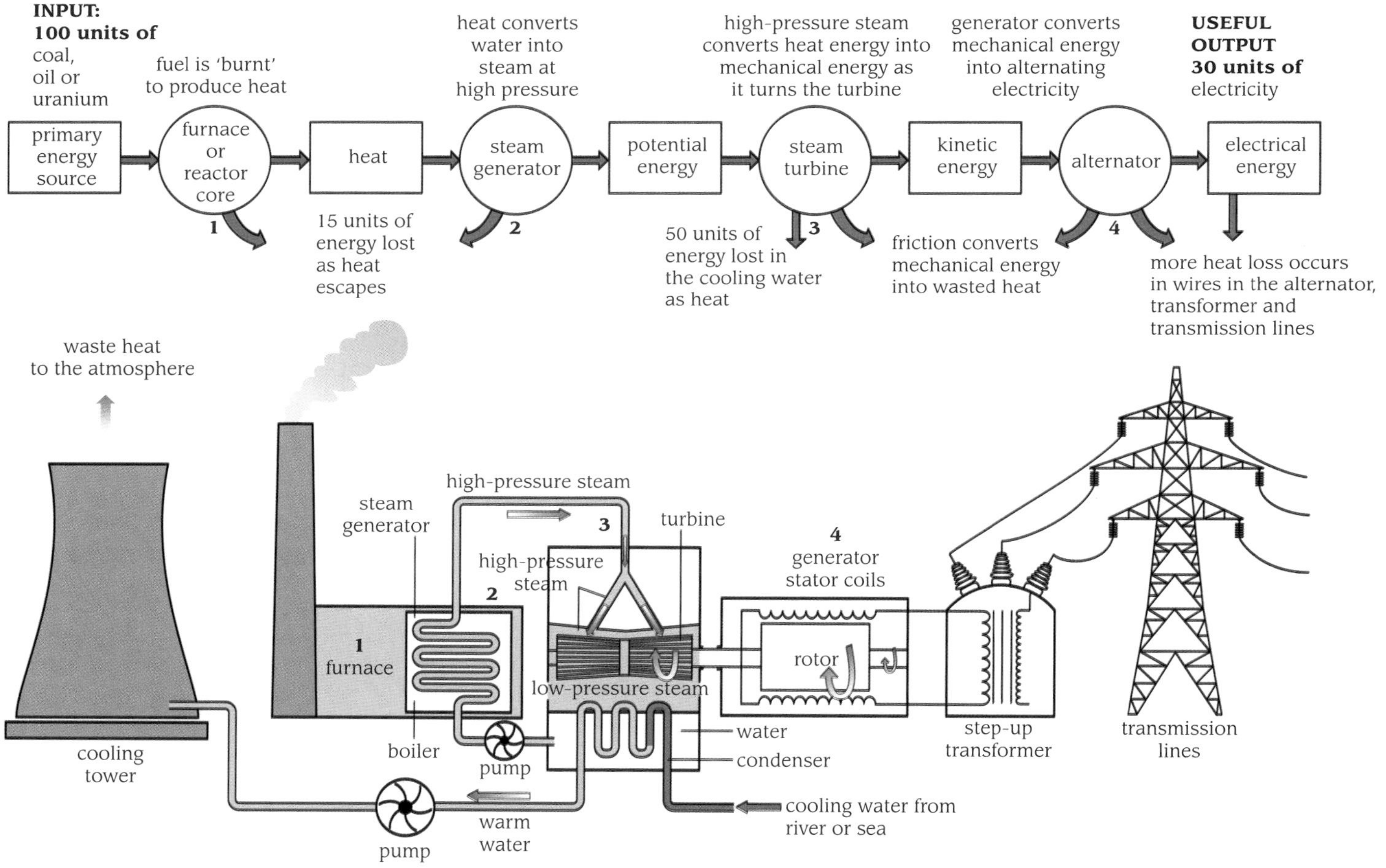

▲ **Figure 7.10.2**

Summary questions

1 Draw a diagram to show the energy changes when a drum is played.
2 Give an example of something that converts sound energy into electrical energy.
3 Give two forms of wasted energy from a motorbike engine.

A7.11 Energy sources

What happens to the solar energy arriving at the Earth?

a) About 30% of the radiation energy is reflected straight back into space. The ice caps and particles in the atmosphere form good reflectors. There is now a real danger that the melting of the ice caps, resulting from global warming, could reduce the amount of reflected radiation causing further warming of the Earth.

b) About 47% of solar radiation is absorbed and converted into heat energy or internal energy. During the day the Earth's surface is warmed up, and during the night this energy is radiated back into space as radiant heat energy, i.e. the long-wave electromagnetic radiation called infrared.

c) About 23% of solar radiation is absorbed causing evaporation of water from the oceans and lakes and from the land and plants. The high latent heat of vaporisation of water means that a lot of absorbed radiant heat energy is used to convert liquid water into water vapour. Convection currents carry the water vapour up into the atmosphere where it forms clouds.

d) A small amount of energy, about 0.2% of the total, drives the convection currents in the oceans and the atmosphere. Some of this energy appears as wind power and wave power, which are forms of kinetic or mechanical energy.

e) An even smaller amount of energy, only 0.02% of the total, is absorbed by growing plants via the chemical process of photosynthesis. This energy is converted into a store of chemical energy. Some will form food for animals, but it will all eventually decay.

Objectives

By the end of this topic you will be able to:

- explain what happens to the solar radiation energy that arrives at the Earth's surface
- describe some key alternative sources of energy available on the planet.

Key fact

Solar energy

- Life is sustained by the energy from the Sun. Without the Sun all plants and animals would die.
- The Sun provides 99.98% of the energy that naturally flows through the surface environment of the Earth.
- The Sun supplies 5000 times more energy than all other energy sources combined.
- Solar energy arrives at the Earth at the rate of 1.7×10^{17} watts, which is 170 thousand million million joules every second!

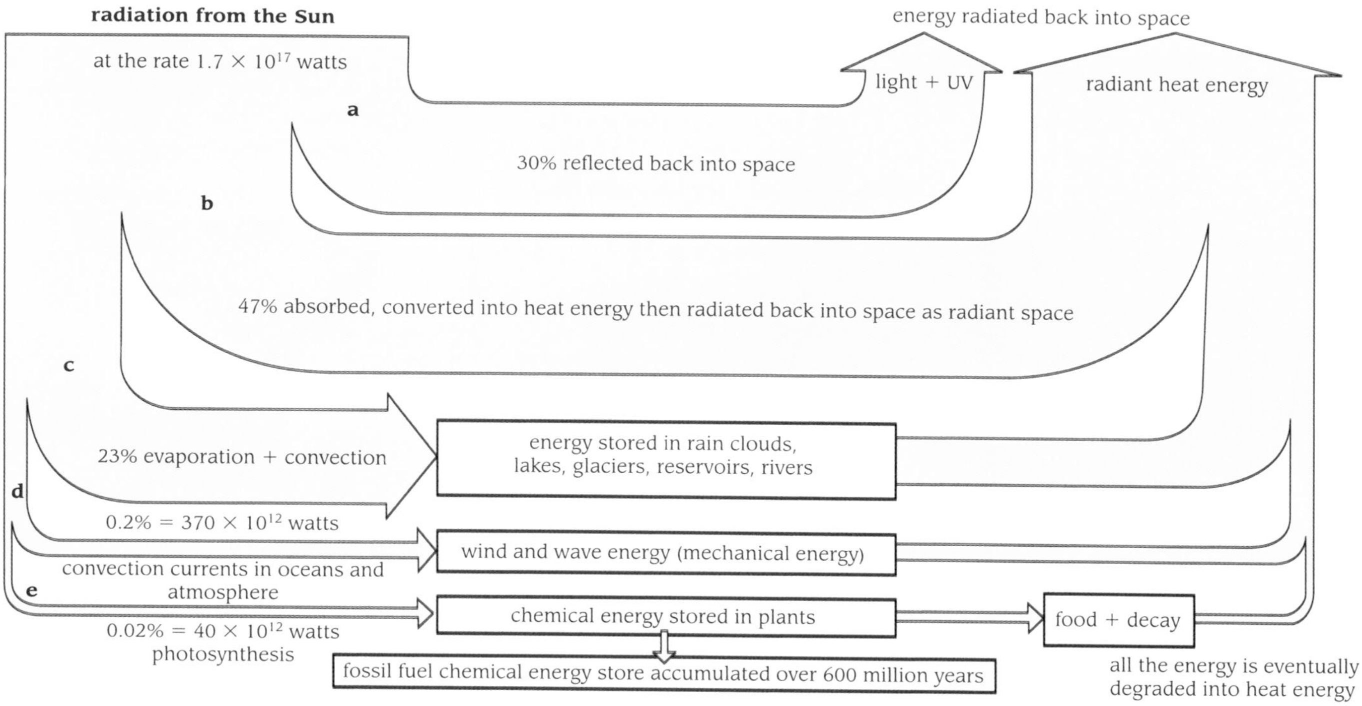

▲ **Figure 7.11.1** What happens to all the energy arriving at the Earth from the Sun?

Solar energy

Photovoltaic cells

▲ **Figure 7.11.2** Photovoltaic cells in a natural reserve park in Curacao

The most common applications of photovoltaic (PV) solar cells are in those appliances that require only a small power output. Examples range from calculators and watches to electrified cattle fences and space satellites. Solar energy arrives at the surface of the Earth in the Caribbean at an average rate of 220 watts per square metre.

PV cells can now be made with a conversion efficiency of 15% so the maximum electrical power that can be generated by the sunlight falling on a square metre of Caribbean earth is $0.15 \times 220 = 33$ watts.

In 2004, the Caribbean region had an electricity-generating capacity of 21 gigawatts and this is produced chiefly from oil-fired power plants. If any significant part of this electrical power was to be generated using PV cells, a vast area of cells would be required and the cost would be prohibitive. 1 gigawatt of power would require 30 million square metres of PV cells.

Solar cells

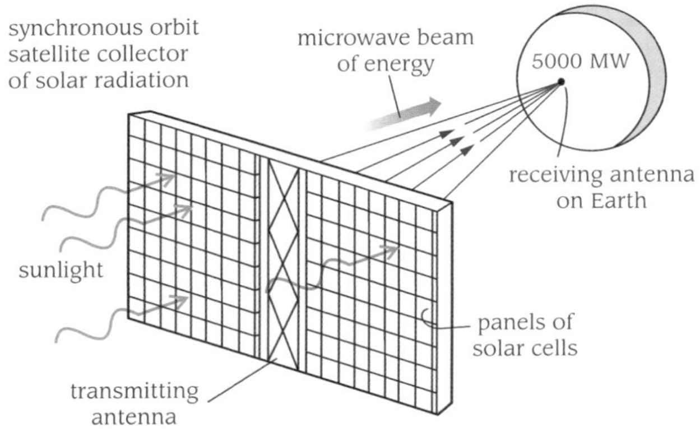

▲ **Figure 7.11.3** Orbiting solar cells

An attractive alternative idea has been suggested for using solar cells to collect energy. A large panel of solar cells perhaps 3 km × 4 km could be assembled in a synchronous orbit around the Earth. The panel would orbit hovering over a fixed receiving antenna 7 km across on the Earth, and the energy would be converted to microwaves for transmission down to Earth. Although solar cells have been used successfully to power satellites and the International Space Station, no scheme for beaming energy down to the surface of the Earth in large quantities has been tried. Such a scheme would be very expensive to build.

Solar furnace

A concave paraboloidal reflector can be used to focus and concentrate the radiant heat energy from the Sun. At the focus the heat energy is as concentrated as that produced by burning fossil fuels. A solar furnace or boiler can be installed at the focus.

▲ **Figure 7.11.4** The French solar furnace in Odielle in the Pyrenees uses over 20 000 electronically controlled mirrors to reflect the Sun's radiation energy into a furnace housed in the building at the focus of the mirrors. The temperature in the furnace can quickly reach over 3000 °C.

Solar panels

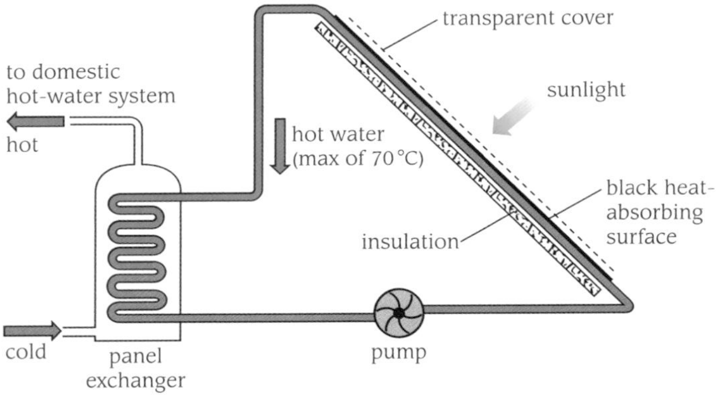

▲ **Figure 7.11.5** Solar panels

A solar water-heating panel is a most successful solar radiant energy absorber. It is so simple and efficient that solar panels are increasingly used by houses and hotels in the Caribbean. The transparent cover traps the solar radiation in the manner of a greenhouse and a black surface improves the rate of absorption of radiation. Water, pumped through a network of pipes in the panel, absorbs the heat energy and carries it to a heat exchanger. Here the heat is passed on to the hot water pipes in the house.

A simple solar water heater for home use needs neither a heat exchanger nor a water pump. The solar panels are connected directly to a storage tank placed on a roof about 0.5 m above the panels. In such a thermo-syphon system natural convection currents carry the heated water up to the tank and cold water down to the solar panels.

Geothermal energy

The temperature of the rocks below the ground increases as the depth increases. Temperatures in certain kinds of rock can reach 200 °C or even 300 °C at depths of several kilometres. Decaying radioactive materials in the rock generate heat from the kinetic energy of the particles emitted. The heat in the rocks below can be used as an economical source of energy providing the amount of energy used to pump the heat up to the surface is less than the heat energy gained.

Cold water is pumped down through a bore hole until it reaches permeable hot rocks at a depth of several kilometres. As the water soaks through these permeable rocks it gets heated and converted to steam which, under pressure, forces its way back up another bore hole to the surface. A heat exchanger then removes the heat. When the heat obtained is used for heating buildings, swimming pools and greenhouses as it is in countries like Iceland, it provides a very cheap, efficient and renewable source of energy.

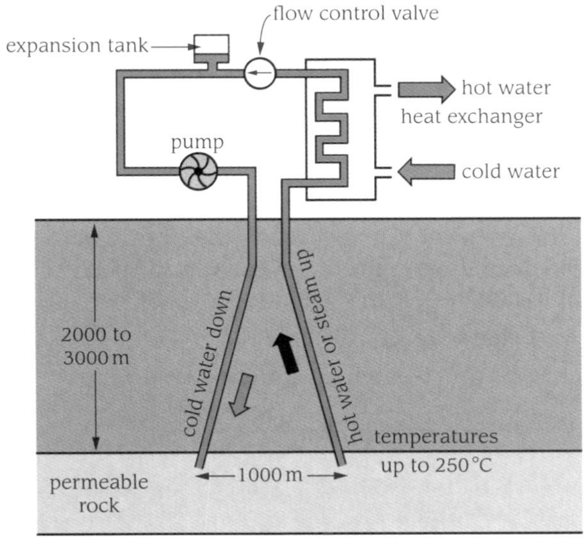

▲ **Figure 7.11.6** Geothermal energy

Wind energy

▲ **Figure 7.11.7** Wind turbines at Wigton windfarm, Jamaica. In 2004 the first wind farm in Jamaica started providing 20.7 MW of power from 23 turbines each rated at 900 kW.

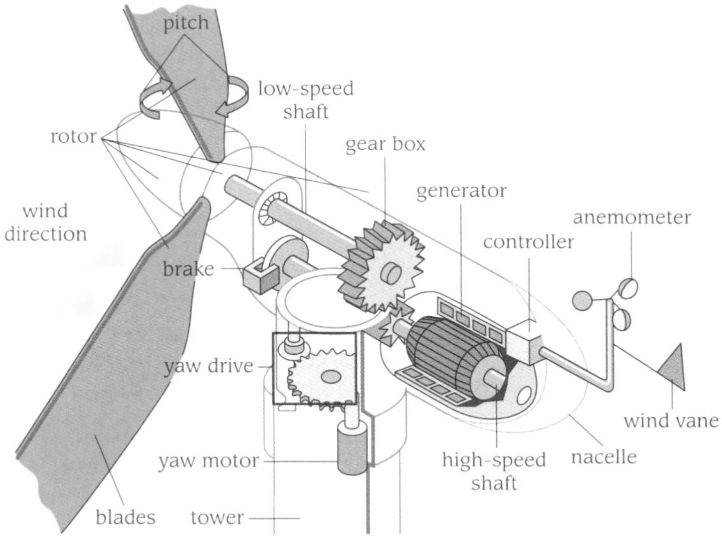

▲ **Figure 7.11.8** Inside a wind turbine

- Wind power produces no waste or greenhouse gases and so does not contribute to global warming.
- Like old-fashioned windmills, today's wind turbines use blades to collect the wind's kinetic energy.
- Wind turbines work because they slow down the speed of the wind. The wind flows over the aerofoil shaped blades causing lift, like the effect on airplane wings, causing them to turn. The blades are connected to a drive shaft that turns an electric generator to produce electricity.
- Wind power is abundant, reliable and safe.

Practice exam-style questions

1 How far will a walker travel if he walks for 6 hours at an average speed of $1.2\,\text{m s}^{-1}$?

2 A girl runs at a constant speed of $5.0\,\text{m s}^{-1}$ round a running track. How long will it take her to run one kilometre?

3 The results of an experiment using a ticker timer and tape to measure the velocity and acceleration of a trolley are shown in the figure in question 6. Every fifth dot from the ticker timer has been marked and labelled A, B, C... to L as shown.

So from A to B is a 'fivetick' strip of tape and ten of these strips are produced every second.

a) What time passes during the motion from:
- **i)** A to B?
- **ii)** A to F?
- **iii)** A to K?

b) Using the cm scale shown in the figure, find:
- **i)** the average speed of the motion between A and K in cm s^{-1}
- **ii)** the instantaneous speed during the short time interval between each of the following pairs of dots: A and B; F and G; K and L. Give the speeds in cm s^{-1}.

c) Mark out 'fivetick' strips of tape on a length of ticker tape using the values indicated by the cm scale against the dots in the figure. Cut the tape into 'fivetick' strips and construct a speed–time tape chart.

d) Describe the motion:
- **i)** between A and F
- **ii)** between F and L.

4 a) Construct a distance–time graph of the motion recorded by the ticker tape shown in the previous question. Measure the distance of each dot from the start of the motion at dot A.

b) Find the gradient of the graph between dots A and F and hence find the speed of the motion in cm s^{-1}. (Note that the time scale will be in time units of 'five ticks' or 0.1 s.)

5 A girl rides a bicycle that records the distance travelled in metres. On a short ride she records the distance every 10 seconds and obtains the following readings:

Time/s	0	10	20	30	40	60	70	80	90	100
Distance/m	0	20	40	60	80	200	260	280	280	280

a) Plot a distance–time graph of her ride.

b) What was her speed during the first 40 s?

c) What was her speed between 40 s and 70 s from starting?

d) What happened after 80 s?

6 Find the acceleration of the motion recorded on the ticker tape shown in the figure, between dots F and K.

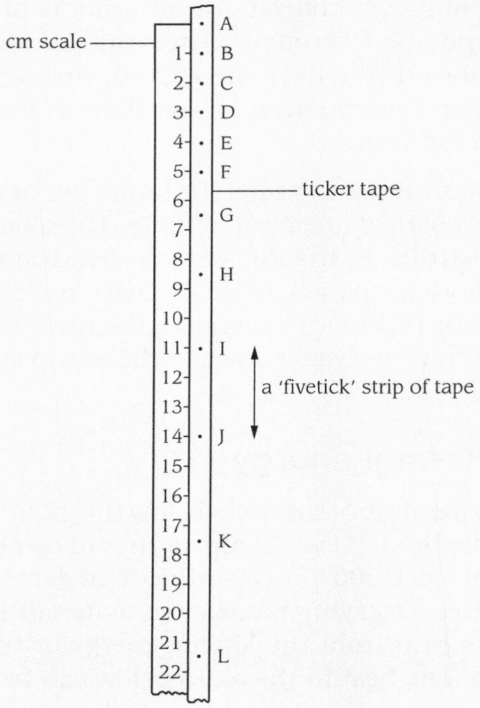

7 A swimmer is 240 m from the beach when he realises that the tide is carrying him out to sea. If the velocity of the tide is $0.5\,\text{m s}^{-1}$ away from the beach and he can swim at a maximum speed of $0.8\,\text{m s}^{-1}$, calculate:

a) his maximum resultant velocity towards the beach

b) the shortest time in which he can reach the beach.

8 A light aircraft is flying horizontally and its engine is pulling it in a due north direction at $80\,\text{m s}^{-1}$. A strong wind is also blowing from the west at $20\,\text{m s}^{-1}$. Calculate:

a) the magnitude of the combined velocity of the aircraft and the wind

b) the direction east of north in which the plane will be moving

c) the distance off-course the plane would be if it flew in this direction for 1 hour, assuming the pilot wanted to fly due north.

9 A river that is 40 m wide flows at $0.40\,\text{m s}^{-1}$ in the direction shown in the figure. A man sets out from A in a rowing boat heading in the direction AB. His speed through the water is $0.80\,\text{m s}^{-1}$. Find:

a) the time taken to reach the far bank

b) the distance from B at which he reaches the bank.

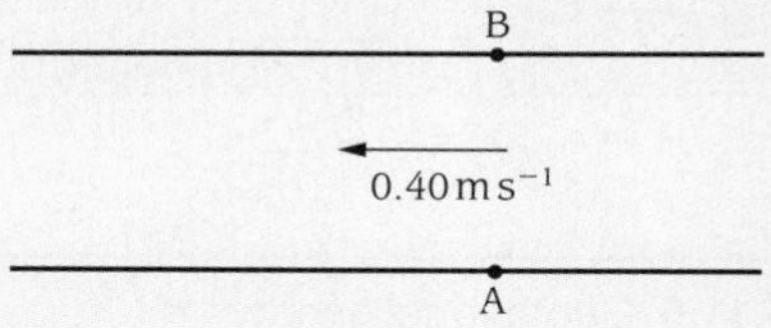

10 The graph represents the velocity–time graph for a lift or elevator in a department store.

a) Briefly describe the motion represented by OA, AB and BC on the graph.

b) Use the graph to calculate:

i) the acceleration of the lift

ii) the total distance travelled by the lift.

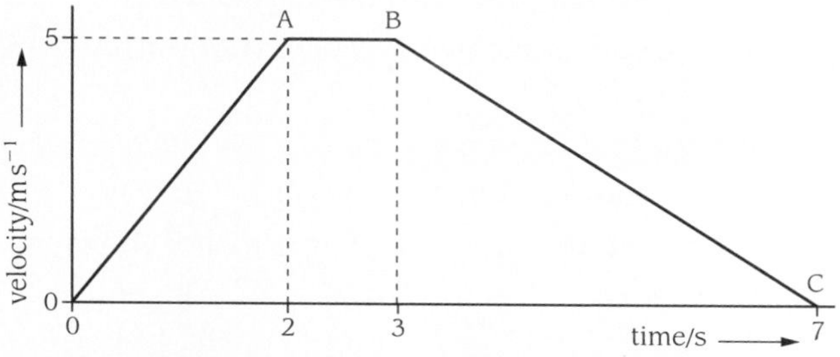

11 The author of a textbook starts to describe the motion of an object thrown horizontally from a cliff in the following way. 'The *horizontal velocity* and the *vertical velocity* of the object's motion are *independent* and ...'

a) Explain the meaning of the three phrases printed in italics.

b) State how the two velocities mentioned would vary as the object fell.

c) If the object described above is thrown horizontally at 15 m s^{-1} and the vertical cliff is 80 m high, calculate:

i) the time taken for the object to reach the ground

ii) the distance from the foot of the cliff to where the object strikes the ground.
Use g = 10 m s^{-2}.

12 a) How is the resultant force acting on a body related to the change in momentum of the body?

b) Which of the physical quantities mentioned in **a)** are vectors?

c) A motorist, driving on a straight level road, suddenly notices a roadblock and nearly has a bad accident. On a sheet of graph paper, draw a speed–time graph for his motion, given the following details:

- At 0 s the motorist, driving at 40 m s^{-1}, notices the roadblock.
- Because his reflexes are slow, after 1.0 s he applies the brakes. These produce a deceleration of 50 m s^{-2}.
- After a further 0.5 s, his brakes fail.
- After another 2.0 s, the car comes to rest.

d) Given that the distance travelled is the area under the speed–time graph, and that the car stopped just at the roadblock, calculate how far away the roadblock was from the motorist when he first noticed it.

e) If the mass of the motorist and his car together is 1000 kg, calculate the value of the resultant force that retarded the car when the brakes were working.

13 If a constant force acts for 5.0 s on an object of mass 20 kg and increases its momentum by 30 N s, calculate:

a) the magnitude of the force

b) the acceleration of the object.

14 A car accelerates from rest. Its speed, recorded every second for 10 s, is given in the table.

Time/s	Speed/m s^{-1}
0	0
1.0	4.2
2.0	8.6
3.0	12.8
4.0	16.8
5.0	21.0
6.0	25.0
7.0	28.0
8.0	30.0
9.0	31.0
10.0	31.2

a) Draw a graph of speed against time for the motion of the car.

b) From the graph find the following:

i) the maximum speed reached by the car

ii) the average initial acceleration over the first 5.0 s

iii) the distance travelled in the first 5 s

iv) the time it takes the car to reach 20.0 m s^{-1}.

15 A 150 g piece of lead falls freely to the ground, taking a metre of paper tape behind it. The tape passes through a ticker timer as it falls, thereby being marked with a dot every $\frac{1}{50}$th second, as shown in the figure.

a) From the figure, find how far the tape fell in the first $\frac{1}{10}$th second and its average speed over that time.

b) From the figure, find the average speed during the second $\frac{1}{10}$th second, and hence the acceleration of the falling lead.

c) If the acceleration of the falling lead were constant, how long would it take to fall 1 metre from rest?

d) What difference, if any, would it make if the experiment were repeated using a 300 g piece of lead? Explain your answer.

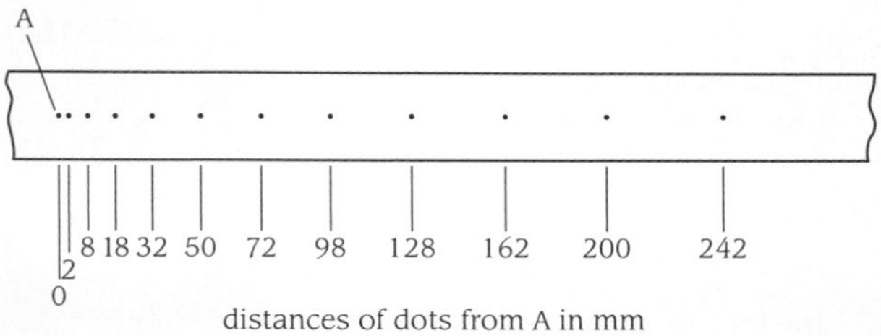

16 **a)** What is meant by acceleration?
An object was thrown vertically upwards and its height above the ground was measured at various times. The results obtained are shown below.

Time/s	0	1	2	3	4	5	6	7	8
Height/m	0	35	60	75		75	60	35	0

b) Plot a graph of height on the *y*-axis against time on the *x*-axis. From your graph, find:
  i) the maximum height reached
  ii) the time taken to reach this height.

c) Using either or both of the answers from part **b)**, calculate the initial velocity with which the object was thrown.
Use $g = 10\,\text{m s}^{-2}$.

17 **a)** If a force of 240 N is applied to an object of mass 8 kg and there are no frictional forces opposing the motion, calculate its acceleration.

b) If the object starts from rest, find its velocity after 4 s.

18 Calculate the force needed to give a mass of 5 kg an acceleration of:

a) $2\,\text{m s}^{-2}$

b) $10\,\text{cm s}^{-2}$

c) $5\,\text{km s}^{-2}$.

19 A sprinter of mass 70 kg accelerates from rest. The speed–time graph of his motion is shown in the figure.

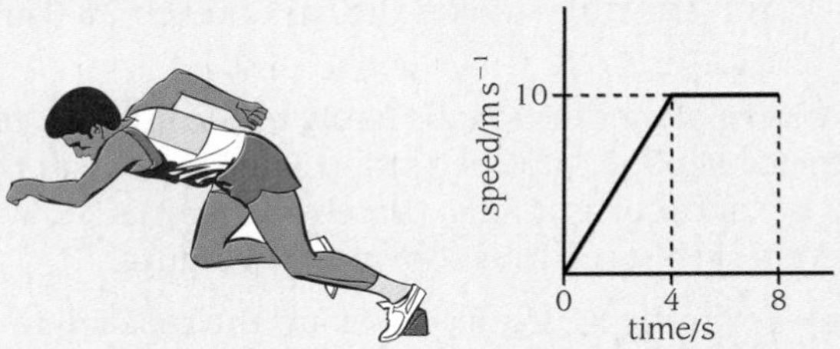

a) Calculate the acceleration of the sprinter at the start of the race.

b) How far did the sprinter travel in 8.0 s?

c) Find the kinetic energy of the sprinter after 4 s.

20 A force of 12 N is used to move a box of mass 20 kg along the ground. If there is a constant frictional force of 4.0 N opposing the motion, what will be the acceleration of the box?

21 A trolley of mass 1.5 kg is pulled by an elastic cord and is given an acceleration of $2.0\,\text{m s}^{-2}$. Find the frictional force acting on the trolley if the tension in the elastic cord is 5 N.

22 Calculate the momentum of an object if:

a) its mass is 4.0 kg and its velocity is $8.0\,\text{m s}^{-1}$

b) its mass is 500 g and its velocity is $3.0\,\text{km s}^{-1}$

c) a force of 20 N is applied to it for 6.0 s and it moves from rest

d) its mass is 2.0 kg and it falls from rest for 10 s (assume $g = 10\,\text{m s}^{-2}$ or $10\,\text{N kg}^{-1}$).

23 A car of mass 1200 kg is pushed along a level road by two men. If they use a force of 800 N and the frictional forces acting against them are 560 N, calculate:

a) the work done by the men if they push the car for 10 m

b) the kinetic energy gained by the car over the 10 m

c) the speed reached by the car

d) the momentum gained by the car if the men push for 10 s.

24 A railway truck travelling along a level track at $9\,\text{m s}^{-1}$ collides with, and becomes coupled to, a stationary truck. Find the velocity of the coupled trucks immediately after the collision if the stationary truck has a mass which is:

a) equal to the mass of the moving truck

b) twice the mass of the moving truck.

25 Two planes of the same mass collide head-on and become tangled so that they move on together. If the engines of both were stopped at the moment of impact and the speeds of the planes at impact were $120\,\text{m s}^{-1}$ and $200\,\text{m s}^{-1}$, find the joint velocity immediately after collision.

26 The kinetic energy of a moving car is transformed during the braking of the car. The distance over which this energy transformation occurs is called the braking distance. The stopping distance is greater than the braking distance because of the additional thinking distance. This is the distance the car travels at constant speed while the driver reacts to the need to stop.

This table gives examples of these distances.

Speed/km h^{-1}	Thinking distance/m	Braking distance/m	Stopping distance/m
50	9	14	23
80	15	38	53
110	21	74	95
160	30	155	185

a) On graph paper, draw a graph of braking distance (*y*-axis) against speed (*x*-axis).

b) Should this graph be extended or extrapolated to the origin? Explain your answer.

c) A graph of thinking distance against speed is a straight line through the origin. What does this tell us about the relationship between the thinking distance and speed?

d) If the car has a mass of 1000 kg, calculate its kinetic energy at $20\,\text{m s}^{-1}$.

e) Convert $20\,\text{m s}^{-1}$ to km h^{-1} (kilometres per hour) and for this speed, read the braking distance from your graph.

f) Calculate the average braking force from this speed if the car is to stop in this distance.

27 An object of mass 4.0 kg is dropped from a height of 1000 m from a helicopter. The air resistance acting against the parachute exerts a steady upward force of 35 N. Calculate the kinetic energy of the object when it reaches the ground and hence find its velocity.
Use $g = 10\,\text{N kg}^{-1}$.

28 Describe an experiment you would perform to determine the acceleration of free fall, g. State the precautions you would take to obtain an accurate result and show how you would calculate a value of g from your results.

29 A spacecraft of total mass 1000 kg is travelling at constant speed round the Earth in a circular orbit of radius 12 000 km. The gravitational field strength at that distance from the Earth's centre is $3\,\text{N kg}^{-1}$.

a) What is meant by 'gravitational field strength'?

b) The astronaut in the spacecraft has weight and yet he feels weightless. Explain.

c) Does the spacecraft need to produce a force from its rockets to keep it moving at constant speed? Explain.

d) How big is the force towards the centre of the Earth acting on the spacecraft?

e) Calculate the speed of the spacecraft.

f) If the spacecraft had been in a circular orbit of twice the radius it would have experienced a gravitational force only $\frac{1}{4}$ as large. How would its speed have compared with its speed in the first orbit? Explain your answer.

g) A part of the spacecraft is fired forward at $50\,\text{m s}^{-1}$ relative to the remainder of the spacecraft. If the mass of this part is 200 kg, what would be the change in the speed of the remainder?

30 Describe an experiment you might devise to measure the power of a student while he is riding a bicycle. Explain why you would not expect your results to be very reliable.

31 How much energy would your body need to provide for the following:

a) climbing a hill 500 m high (use your own mass and $g = 10\,\text{N kg}^{-1}$)

b) sweating and evaporation of 1 kg of water from your skin

c) heat loss by radiation at the rate of 100 watts for 12 hours.
(The specific latent heat of vaporisation of water is $2.3\,\text{MJ kg}^{-1}$.)

32 State the energy changes that occur when:

a) gas is used to boil water in a whistling kettle

b) a child blows up a balloon and then releases it, letting it fly around the room

c) a guitarist plays an electric guitar over a public address system.

33 Water, which flows over a weir at a rate of $800\,\text{kg s}^{-1}$, takes 1.2 s to fall vertically into the stream below.

a) State the energy transformations that occur as the water falls from the weir into the stream below.

b) **i)** At what the speed does the falling water hit the stream?

ii) What is the height through which the water falls?

c) Calculate:

i) the weight of water falling over the weir in 1 minute

ii) the potential energy lost by this water when it reaches the stream below the weir

iii) the power of the falling water at the instant it hits the stream.
(Take the acceleration of free fall to be $10\,\text{m s}^{-2}$.)

34 There are a number of ways in which we can generate electricity on a large scale for the power requirements of a city or country. Some of these are listed below.

i) nuclear power station
ii) coal-fired power station
iii) gas-fired power station
iv) oil-fired power station
v) wind turbine generators
vi) wave-driven generators
vii) tidal barrage
viii) hydroelectric power from dams and reservoirs

Select from this list:

a) those that make a contribution to the global warming of planet Earth by adding greenhouse gases to the atmosphere

b) those that can be described as using a renewable source of energy

c) those for which the required energy source is locally available

d) those that require the importing of the basic energy source or fuel from another country

e) those that may have a significant impact on the local environment and wildlife

f) those being used at this time in your country or on your island

g) those that might be considered for future use in your country or on your island.

35 A solar heating system consists of a panel that may be mounted on the sloping roof of a house to produce warm water, which is stored in a tank. The figure shows a solar panel, which consists of thin-walled copper tube partially embedded in a copper plate. The surface of the copper is blackened. Radiation from the Sun heats the copper through a glass window and water is warmed and stored in the tank. The space behind the plate and tubes is filled with a good thermal insulator.

a) Why is the water tank positioned at a higher level than the solar panel?

b) Which of the two pipes AB or CD carries the warmer water?

c) Why are the tubes and plate made of copper and why is the tube thin-walled?

d) Explain why the solar panel is more effective if the surface of the tubes and plate is blackened rather than shiny.

e) Explain how the glass plate reduces energy loss from the copper tubes and plate to the atmosphere.

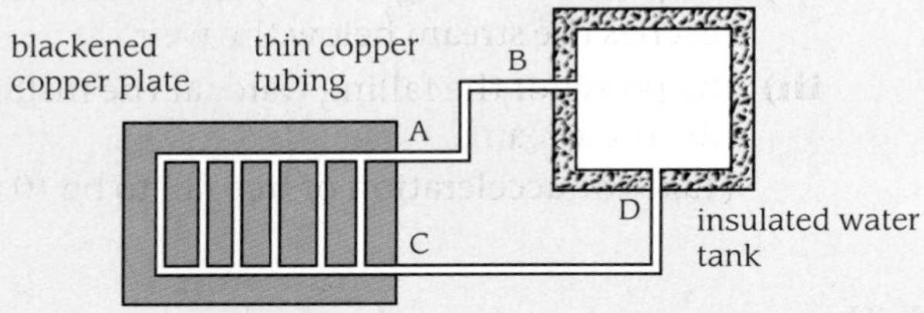

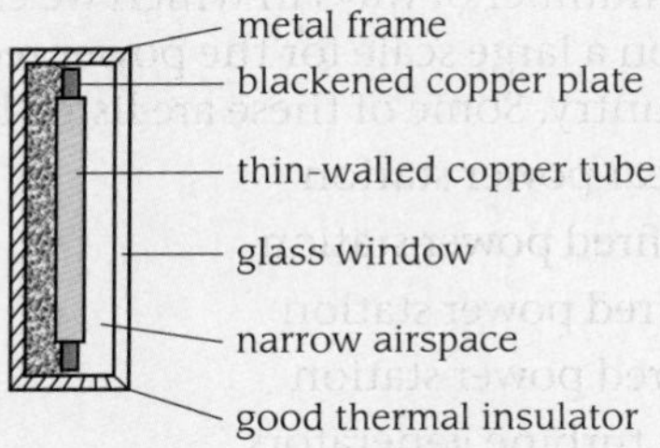

36 Give an account of ONE alternative renewable source of energy that you think could make a significant contribution to the supply of energy in the Caribbean in the 21st century. Suggest some possible disadvantages of this alternative as well as its obvious advantages.

37 People who are concerned about the safety and environmental impact of a planned power station may ask some of the following questions:

a) Can the operators of the power station work safely with no threat to their health even in the long term?

b) Are there any hazards for the public living in the vicinity of the power station, in the surrounding area or even in another country, either resulting from pollution or from the possibility of a major accident at the station?

c) Will there be any long-term environmental effects or environmental pollution caused by the power station or by its waste products?

Select a new type of power station that might be built in the Caribbean and try to answer these questions. You should understand that even experts do not always agree about what is the correct answer to some of these questions.

B8 Heat and matter

We feel heat when the Sun shines and when we sit near a fire. A hot drink or hot food contains heat. Heat flows along the metal handle of a pan placed on a fire or a hot stove and will burn our hands unless the handle is insulated. Heat causes ice to melt, water to boil and many things to expand. Matter exists in many forms and phases that are changed by heat.

Objectives

By the end of this topic you will be able to:

- discuss Rumford's contribution to our understanding of the nature of heat
- explain how Joule's experiments led to the principle of conservation of energy
- describe the development of the kinetic theory of matter and the failures of the caloric theory
- describe what is seen in Brownian motion and explain what inferences can be made.

! Key fact

Rumford showed that:

- the longer the boring took place, the greater was the amount of heat produced
- when the barrel was bored in a tank of water, the water could be made to boil even though no flame was used.

Rumford concluded that:

- heat was created when mechanical work was done against friction (as it is when a metal is bored) and that therefore heat is related to mechanical energy
- therefore, as heat could be created, it could not be a material substance.

B8.1 The nature of heat

Until the beginning of the nineteenth century heat was considered to be an invisible material substance called 'caloric'. When an object was heated and got hotter it was thought to have gained some caloric. However, there was no experimental evidence to show that a hot object was any heavier than a colder one as it should have been if caloric was a real substance with weight.

The caloric theory

- Heat is a fluid called caloric.
- Caloric flows from a hot object to a cold object when they are in contact. Evidence: the hot object gets cooler and the cold object gets hotter.
- Friction creates small particles caused by the rubbing process and these particles produce more caloric.

The kinetic theory

- All atoms have some form of motion.
- Heat is the kinetic energy of moving atoms.
- The heat produced by friction is explained as the energy supplied when mechanical work is done.

Count Rumford

Benjamin Thompson was born in North America and fled to Europe where, in recognition of his scientific work, he was made Count Rumford by the Bavarians. In 1798, he made an observation that could not be explained by the caloric theory. Rumford was supervising the boring of a gun barrel at a factory in Bavaria when he noticed that a lot of heat was generated while only a small quantity of brass chips were removed from the barrel. He thought it unlikely that all the heat (or caloric) could have been stored in such a small mass of brass chips.

Count Rumford founded the Royal Institution in London.

▲ **Figure 8.1.1** Sir Humphry Davy 1778–1829. Sir Humphry Davy was born in Penzance, Cornwall, England. He is famous for his work on electrochemistry and for inventing the Davy safety lamp used by miners.

Sir Humphry Davy

In 1799, Sir Humphry Davy showed that when two pieces of ice below freezing point were rubbed together, they melted and produced water at +2 °C. This could only be explained by saying that the work of rubbing had produced the heat. This evidence strongly supported the kinetic theory of heat.

James Prescott Joule

In 1842, James Joule of Manchester, England began a series of important experiments, which proved that heat was not a material substance. He converted different forms of energy, such as mechanical and electrical energy, into heat. He measured the amount of energy expended or converted and the quantity of heat produced and found that they were always in a constant ratio. Joule realised that friction converted the energy required for work into energy in the form of heat and that the whole process neither gained nor lost energy, in fact the total energy was always **conserved**.

Today the unit of energy, the joule, is named after him. The joule is the universal unit used for all forms of energy including heat. We now believe that when heat energy is gained by an object its molecules gain more kinetic energy and so move faster or vibrate faster.

▲ **Figure 8.1.2** James Prescott Joule 1818–1889. James Prescott Joule was born in Sale, Manchester, England. He is most famous for his study of the nature of heat. He measured the amount of mechanical work that produced a certain amount of heat and realised that heat and work had equivalent energy values. The unit of work and energy, the joule, is named after him.

Key fact

Joule concluded that:

heat is a form of energy

Evidence for the kinetic theory of matter

Watching Brownian motion

We cannot see molecules moving because they are too small, but we can look for motion of larger particles, which may be caused by the movement of molecules. Some evidence that air molecules move around randomly with kinetic energy is provided by the effect called Brownian motion. This effect is seen in both liquids and gases. It is easily demonstrated with small smoke particles in air (Figure 8.1.3).

- Remove the lid from a smoke cell apparatus and hold a drinking straw upright in the glass smoke cell.
- Light the top end of the straw so that smoke passes down the inside of the straw into the smoke cell.
- Quickly replace the lid to trap the smoke inside the cell.
- Place the apparatus under a microscope and adjust the microscope to focus on the smoke particles inside the glass smoke cell.

It is best to start with the microscope objective lens (the one at the bottom) very close to the smoke cell and then to raise the microscope slowly until the smoke particles come into focus.

- Watch the smoke particles carefully and describe their motion.

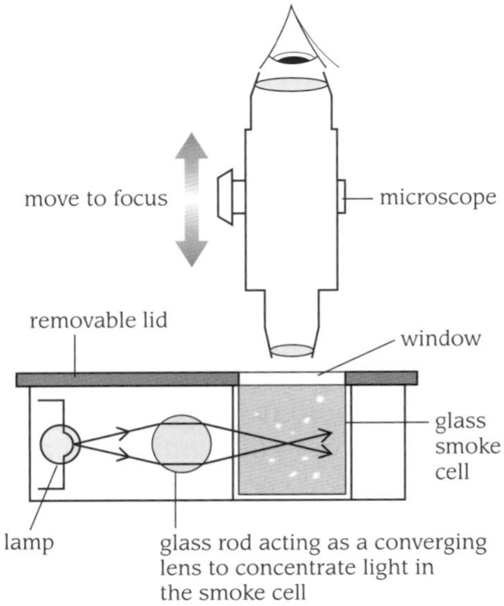

▲ **Figure 8.1.3** Brownian motion in a smoke cell

The bright specks seen dancing about in a jerky, erratic or random way are the smoke particles brightly illuminated by the concentrated light. They do not often collide with each other, but rather appear to be knocked about by some other invisible particles in the smoke cell.

The significance of Brownian motion

We believe that the motion of the smoke particles is evidence that air molecules also are moving. The smoke particles, which are large enough to be seen under the microscope, are also small enough to be knocked about by the fast moving air molecules. The jerky, erratic movement of the smoke particles, known as Brownian motion, shows that air molecules move in all directions with a range of speeds and kinetic energies. We describe the motion of the air molecules as random motion.

The same effect can be seen with pollen grains or sulfur particles suspended in a liquid. So we also have evidence that the molecules of a liquid have random motion within the liquid. The theory that molecules all have some kind of motion and kinetic energy is called the kinetic theory of matter.

Observing diffusion in a liquid

- Half-fill a gas jar or tall beaker with water.
- Using a funnel with a long tube reaching to the bottom of the gas jar, slowly pour saturated copper sulfate solution down the tube to form a separate layer of deep blue solution below the water (Figure 8.1.4).
- Slowly and carefully remove the funnel and tube so that the water and copper sulfate solution are not mixed together. Do not disturb the jar.
- Observe the liquids several times over a period of 2 or 3 days.

The blue copper sulfate and colourless water gradually become mixed. We call this process diffusion. Diffusion can be explained in terms of the random motion of molecules in the liquids. Molecules of each liquid, moving about randomly, cross the boundary between the two liquids. The molecules do this accidentally, because of their random motion, without the liquid being stirred, shaken or heated.

Diffusion into air

- Close all the windows and doors in your classroom to cut down the draughts.
- Open a bottle of scent in one corner of the room.
- Put your hands up when the scent first reaches you.
- Watch the spread of the scent across the room.
- How long does it take for the scent to reach the far corner of the room?

The molecules of scent spread around the room by diffusion, and we can detect them by our sense of smell. We cannot see the molecules because they are too small. This demonstration provides more evidence that in the air all the molecules are moving about randomly all the time. Eventually, by random motion, all the molecules of air and scent get completely mixed up.

Summary questions

1 Describe the caloric theory.
2 What does Brownian motion give evidence for?
3 Will diffusion happen faster in warmer or cooler water?

Key fact

In Brownian motion:

- you cannot see the molecules
- the dancing specks of light are small smoke, pollen or sulfur particles
- the motion is random, which means jerky, irregular and unpredictable
- the motion is caused by lots of fast-moving molecules hitting the small particles from all directions at different speeds.

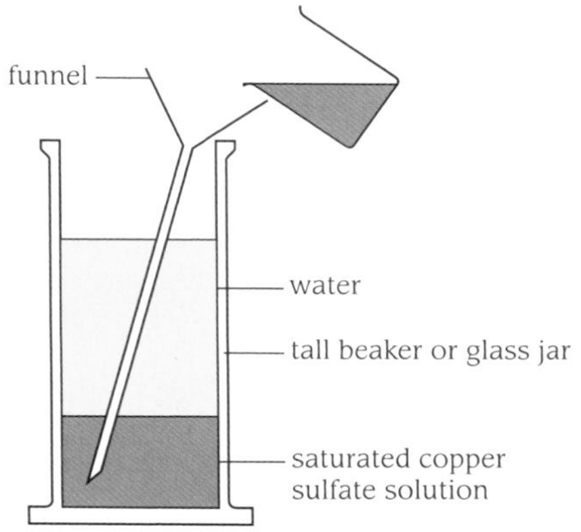

▲ **Figure 8.1.4** Diffusion in a liquid

Things to do

- Think of some everyday examples of diffusion.
- Draw what you think is a typical path of a smoke particle in a smoke cell. It helps if you watch one particle for a minute or two.
- Explain the difference between the motion of smoke particles you observed in a smoke cell and the motion that you would expect to see if it was caused by a draught or by convection.

Objectives

By the end of this topic you will be able to:

- describe the properties of, and differences between, solids, liquids and gases
- describe models that demonstrate some of these properties and differences
- explain the properties of each phase in terms of the kinetic theory of matter.

▲ **Figure 8.2.1** Water forms drops as it falls through the air. The mutual attraction of molecules of water form a surface tension effect like a skin around each water drop and hold it together. The spherical shape of a drop gives the smallest surface area for its stretched 'skin' that can contain the volume of water inside.

B8.2 The phases of matter

Gases are 'springy', solids are 'stretchy' and liquids form drops. These simple ideas give us clues about the different nature of the three phases or states of matter. If you put your finger over the end of a bicycle pump you can feel the 'spring' in the gas as you try to compress it. Watch the water slowly dripping from a tap or running down a window pane and you can see how water likes to form drops. Stretch a spring and you can feel the forces in the solid pulling against you. To help us explain and understand these properties we shall look at some models of a gas, a liquid and a solid.

A model of a gas

- Put about 20 marbles in a tray with vertical sides (Figure 8.2.2).
- Shake the tray in an erratic way, keeping the tray flat on the bench top.
- Watch the path of one particular marble. (It helps to have one marble a different colour from the rest.)
- Describe its motion over a period of a minute or two. You should notice changes of speed as well as direction.
- Listen to the sounds of collisions. Note the difference in sound when marble collides with marble and marble collides with the walls of the tray.
- What changes do you see and hear when:
  - you shake the tray more violently or more gently
  - you change the number of marbles in the tray to half as many or twice as many?

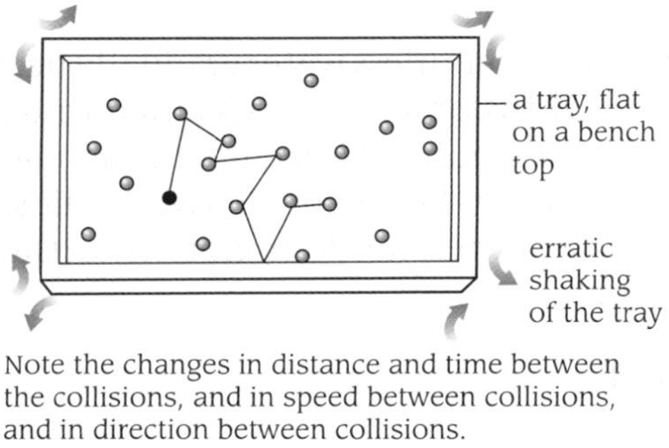
a tray, flat on a bench top
erratic shaking of the tray
Note the changes in distance and time between the collisions, and in speed between collisions, and in direction between collisions.

▲ **Figure 8.2.2** The random path of a marble

Faster moving marbles with more kinetic energy represent molecules of a gas at a higher temperature. They collide with each other and with the walls of the tray more often and, having more energy, make more noise.

Adding more marbles to the tray is like putting more air in a car or bicycle tyre. Now marbles collide with the walls of the tray more often. This is why more air in a tyre increases the pressure.

A model of a liquid

- Cover about a quarter of the tray with marbles (Figure 8.2.3).
- Slightly tilt the tray and again agitate it with erratic movements.
- Observe the movement of the marbles, particularly in the space above those which are jostling each other.
- Notice how the marbles become thinned out near the 'liquid' surface.
- Notice how the 'liquid' marbles occupy much less space that the 'gas' marbles.

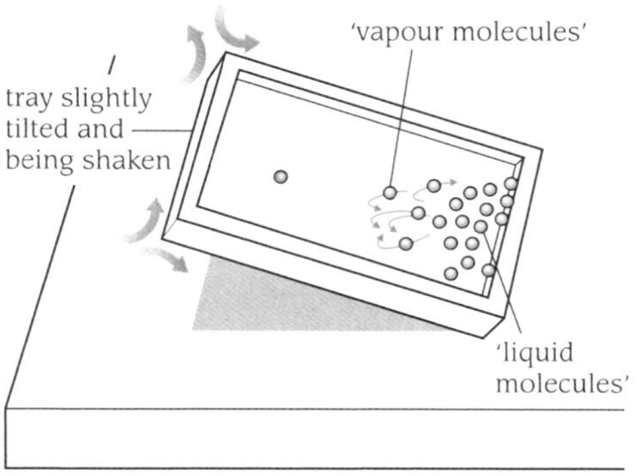

▲ **Figure 8.2.3** A model of a liquid

The marbles that are close together represent the *liquid* phase. These marbles are able to move around, but are mostly confined to the lower section of the tray.

A few energetic marbles get thrown out of the 'liquid' region into the space above. These marbles represent molecules that have 'evaporated' and entered the 'vapour' or 'gas' region. They return to the 'liquid' region and are replaced by other fast moving marbles.

Models of a solid

1 A model crystal

- Try to pack a large number of marbles in a single layer into the smallest possible space in a tray.
- What do you notice about their arrangement?

The marbles arrange themselves in rows and form a regular pattern. The outside edges of the rows of marbles tend to be straight and set at particular angles to each other (Figure 8.2.4). This is a two-dimensional model showing how regular crystalline shapes are formed in solids. The molecules in crystalline solids are arranged in a regular pattern in three dimensions. The marbles are packed close together and take up a minimum of space. There are in fact several different regular patterns in which molecules can be arranged in three dimensions, with slightly differing packing densities. These different patterns give rise to crystals of different characteristic shapes.

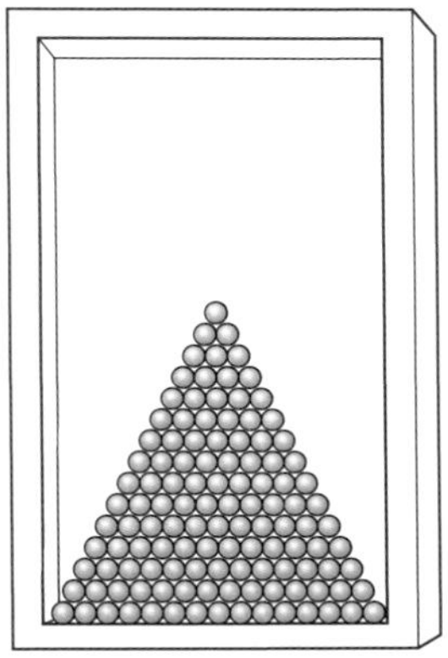

▲ **Figure 8.2.4** Model of a crystalline solid

This marble model shows how a crystalline solid can be formed, but does not give us any idea of the kind of movement that molecules have in a solid.

2 A vibration model

Another model of a solid, which uses springs to link balls together can give us an idea of the way molecules move in a solid (Figure 8.2.5). Each ball, representing an atom or group of atoms, is joined to its neighbours by springs, which allow it to vibrate in many directions.

- Shake the model and watch the movements of the spheres.

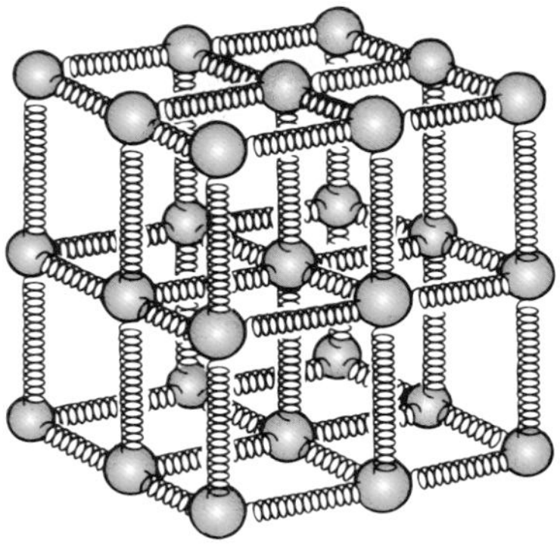

▲ **Figure 8.2.5** Vibration model of a solid

As the spheres vibrate they continually exchange their kinetic energy of motion with elastic potential energy stored in the connecting springs.

We can see that it is possible for a solid to keep its overall regular shape while the individual atoms vibrate about fixed positions. The springs represent the forces of attraction and repulsion between the atoms due to the electric charges of their nuclei and electrons.

How molecules produce gas pressure

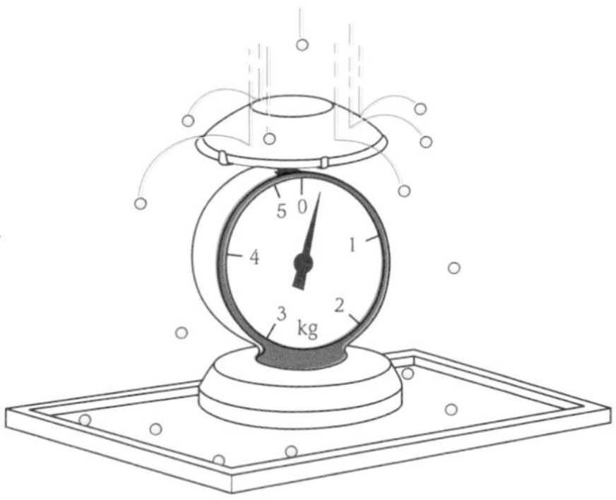

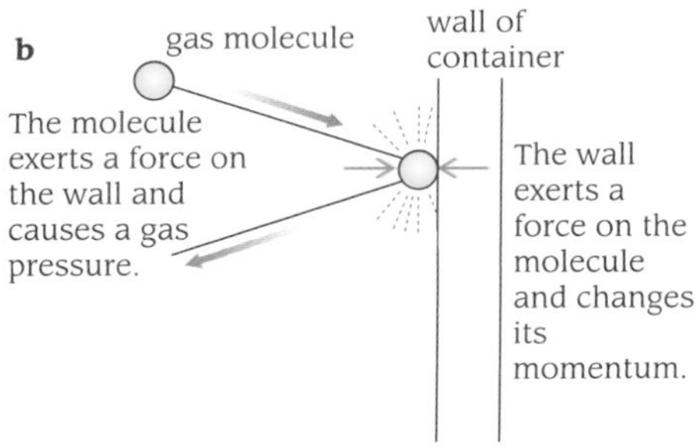

▲ **Figure 8.2.6** Moving molecules produce gas pressure.

The demonstration shows how gas pressure can be understood in terms of moving molecules. The model shows a spring weighing machine with its scale pan inverted.

- Watch the pointer on the scale as a stream of marbles, or ball bearings, is poured over the inverted scale pan (Figure 8.2.6).

The irregular impacts of a large number of marbles produce a fairly constant average force on the scale pan, shown by the reading on the scale. The irregular impacts of the marbles simulate elastic gas molecules bouncing off the walls of their container. As the molecules bounce off the container walls they exert an average force on the walls, which is the gas pressure.

From Newton's third law of motion we know that the force exerted by the molecules hitting the wall is equal and opposite to the force exerted by the wall on the molecules. From Newton's second law of motion we know that the force exerted is equal to the rate of change of momentum of the molecules. So when the gas molecules bounce off the walls of their container and their direction is reversed they also have a change of momentum. This change of momentum of the gas molecules is the cause of the force on the container walls and is what we describe as the gas pressure.

The forces on molecules in a liquid

Inside a liquid the molecules space themselves out so that there is a balance between attractive and repulsive forces. If the molecules come too close together the repulsive forces get much stronger and push them apart again. This strong repulsive force makes liquids almost incompressible. If, however, the molecules get any further apart, there is a strong attractive force that pulls them together again and keeps the liquid volume very nearly constant. This is the cohesive force that keeps liquid molecules bound together.

At the surface of a liquid the molecules are found to be in a state of attraction and tension. There is an increased force of attraction between the molecules at the surface of a liquid and their near neighbours. These increased attractive forces make the surface of a liquid more difficult to break and produce the effect of an elastic skin over the surface. This effect is known as **surface tension**. Insects can rest on the surface of a liquid supported by its surface tension.

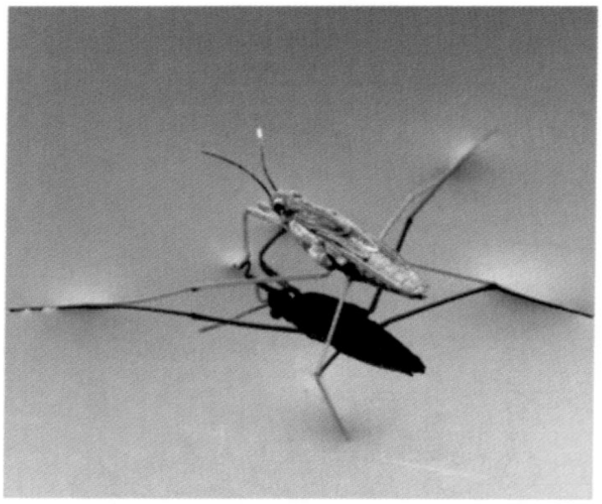

▲ **Figure 8.2.7** A pond skater can rest on the surface of water without breaking the surface. You can see the dimples where the water surface has been 'stretched' by the insect's feet. Pond skaters 'row' themselves, or skate, across the surface of water at high speed using their long middle legs. Because they do not break the surface of the water, their weight is supported by the stretched bonds between the water molecules where their feet rest.

Summary questions

1. How do molecules move in a liquid?
2. Explain how the movement of molecules produces gas pressure.
3. Explain what causes surface tension.

B8.3 Heat and temperature

Heat is a form of energy, which when absorbed by an object makes it hotter and when lost by an object leaves it colder. Words such as hot, warm, tepid, cool and cold tell us about the 'hotness', or temperature, of an object. These words are not very precise, so when we need to be more exact about the temperature of an object we use scales of temperature with graduations called degrees.

Objectives

By the end of this topic you will be able to:

- name physical properties that can be used to measure temperature
- select thermometers that are most suitable for a task
- draw and explain the design of some common thermometers
- define the lower and upper fixed points on the Celsius scale
- convert temperatures between the Celsius and Kelvin scales
- relate temperature of an object to the kinetic energy of its molecules.

What is temperature?

Heat is not the same as temperature. Heat is a form of energy, temperature is a measure of how concentrated that energy is in an object. Heat tells us about the total energy in an object, temperature tells us about the kinetic energy of the individual particles in that object. A bath of cool water has a lot of heat energy but a low temperature, because each water molecule does not move very fast. In a mug of boiling water, the molecules have a lot of kinetic energy and move very quickly, so the temperature is high, but the heat is much less than in the cool bath because there are many fewer molecules in a mug.

Temperature also tells us which way thermal energy is being transferred. When thermal energy is transferred to an object, its temperature increases. When thermal energy is transferred away from an object, its temperature decreases.

! Key fact

- Absolute zero = 0 K or −273 °C
- The ice point = 273 K or 0 °C
- The steam point = 373 K or 100 °C
- We write 273 K without a ° (degree) sign.
- Capital K is the symbol for kelvin whereas small k is the symbol for kilo (= ×1000).

Temperature scales

Temperature is measured with an instrument called a thermometer. To fix a temperature scale on a thermometer we choose two easily obtainable temperatures, such as the temperatures of boiling and freezing water, and give them numbers. These two temperatures are called the upper fixed points and lower fixed points of the temperature scale. We then divide the temperature range between the two fixed points into a number of equal parts called **degrees**.

On a **centigrade scale** there are 100 equal graduations or 100 degrees between the upper and lower fixed points.

The Celsius scale

On the Celsius scale the lower fixed point is the temperature of melting pure ice, known as the ice point. The ice point is fixed at zero degrees, written 0 °C.

The upper fixed point is the temperature of steam just above boiling water, known as the steam point. The steam point is fixed at 100 °C. So, as there are 100 degrees between the two fixed points on the Celsius scale, this is a centigrade scale.

The absolute, or Kelvin, scale

Temperatures exist that are much colder than the freezing point of ice, 0 °C on the Celsius scale. Experiments suggest that there is a limit to how cold things can get.

At a temperature of −273 °C all the heat energy has been removed from any substance. We call this lowest possible temperature **absolute zero**.

A new temperature scale is now used, which has the zero of its scale at this absolute zero of temperature. This scale is called the absolute scale or Kelvin scale, after Lord Kelvin who devised it.

One division on the Kelvin temperature scale is called a **kelvin (K)** and is exactly equal to one division or degree on the Celsius scale. It follows that there are 100 kelvins between the ice point and steam point of water.

As the scale divisions on the two scales are equal, 1 kelvin = 1 Celsius degree.

Key fact

Converting temperatures

If T is the temperature on the Kelvin or absolute scale and θ is the temperature on the Celsius scale, then:

$$T \text{ in K} = \theta \text{ in °C} + 273$$

or more simply

$$T = \theta + 273$$

- To convert from a Celsius temperature to a Kelvin temperature, add 273.
- To convert from a Kelvin temperature to a Celsius temperature, subtract 273.

Worked example

Convert:

a) 37 °C to a temperature on the Kelvin scale

b) 200 K to a temperature on the Celsius scale.

a) $T = \theta + 273 = 37 + 273 = 310\,\text{K}$

b) $\theta = T - 273 = 200 - 273 = -73\,°\text{C}$

Finding the fixed points on a mercury thermometer

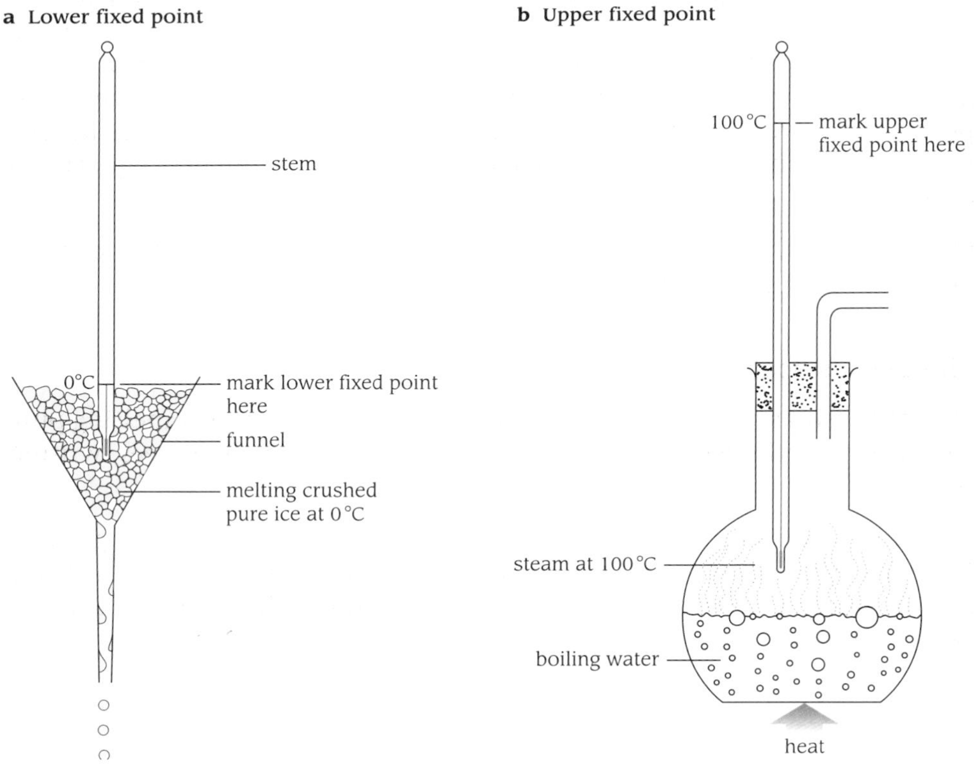

▲ **Figure 8.3.1** Finding the fixed points of a thermometer

The lower fixed point

- Freeze some pure (distilled) water.
- Crush the ice into small, roughly pea-sized pieces and fill a funnel with them.
- When the ice begins to melt (and has warmed up to 0 °C) insert the bulb of a thermometer so that it is covered with ice (Figure 8.3.1a). This should cool all the mercury to 0 °C.
- When the mercury stops shrinking, mark the stem of the thermometer at the mercury level.

This is 0 °C, the lower fixed point or ice point, on the Celsius scale.

The upper fixed point

- Arrange the thermometer inside a flask so that its bulb is just above the surface of boiling water (Figure 8.3.1b).
- When the mercury stops expanding, mark its level on the thermometer stem.

This is 100 °C, the upper fixed point or steam point, on the Celsius scale.

- If you are making a thermometer, divide the distance between these two fixed points into 100 equal parts, marked as a scale along the stem.

Special conditions for accurate fixed points

1. The ice must be pure, because impurities lower the freezing point of water. There are some everyday applications of this effect. For example, in cold countries salt is used on the roads in winter to lower the freezing point of rainwater or melted snow, making it less likely to freeze. Antifreeze is added to car radiators to prevent water freezing.
2. The thermometer bulb is not immersed in boiling water because the temperature at which water boils is also affected by impurities. In this case, a dissolved impurity such as salt raises the boiling point.
3. The steam above boiling water does not contain molecules of any dissolved impurities, although its temperature is affected by pressure. To find the steam point accurately the pressure above the water must be standard atmospheric pressure, which is 760 mm of mercury.

Choosing a thermometer

- Does the thermometer work over the range of temperatures required?
- Is the thermometer sensitive enough? (This means can it detect small enough changes of temperature?)
- How quickly does the thermometer respond?
- How small, portable and convenient is the thermometer?
- Can the thermometer give continuous readings and be connected to a digital display or an electrically operated recording device or warning device?
- How expensive is it?

Some important temperatures

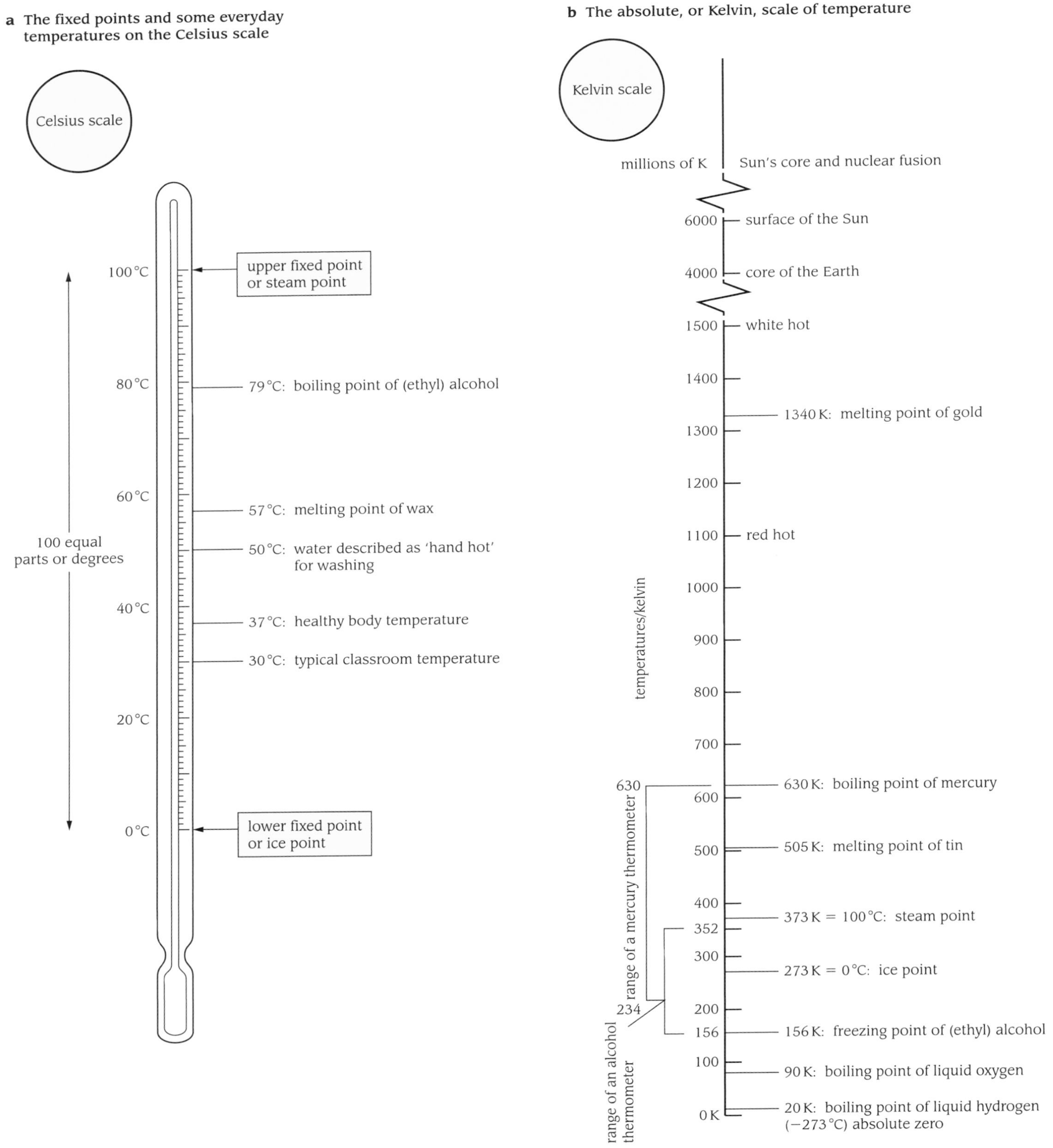

▲ **Figure 8.3.2** As well as being familiar with the relation between the Celsius and Kelvin scales it is useful to have some idea of where some important temperatures fit on these scales. **Figure 8.3.2a** shows some everyday temperatures between the fixed points. There are so many important temperatures outside the 0°C to 100°C range. Some of these are shown in **Figure 8.3.2b**.

Liquid-in-glass thermometers

Liquid-in-glass thermometers use the cubical expansion of alcohol or mercury to measure temperature.

- Mercury thermometers can measure temperatures in the range −39 °C to 357 °C. Alcohol thermometers can measure temperatures in the range −117 °C to 79 °C.
- The bulb of the thermometer has very thin walls so heat is conducted quickly to the liquid.
- The small volume of liquid heats up quickly and does not take much heat from the object.
- The narrower the tube, the more the liquid level changes for a given temperature change.
- The space above the liquid is evacuated to reduce the effect of pressure from the trapped air.

The clinical thermometer

The clinical thermometer is a liquid-in-glass thermometer with these features:

- A range from 35 °C to 42 °C and a very narrow bore to give $\frac{1}{5}$ or $\frac{1}{10}$ degree accuracy in this range.
- A pear-shaped cross-section acts as a magnifying glass in one direction, making the thermometer easier to read.
- A narrow constriction in the bore means the thermometer must be shaken or flicked to return the mercury to the bulb, so the temperature can be read after the thermometer is removed from the patient.

Many clinical thermometers are now digital. They measure the heat energy radiating from the eardrum. They are more accurate than mercury-in-glass thermometers and do not release harmful mercury if broken.

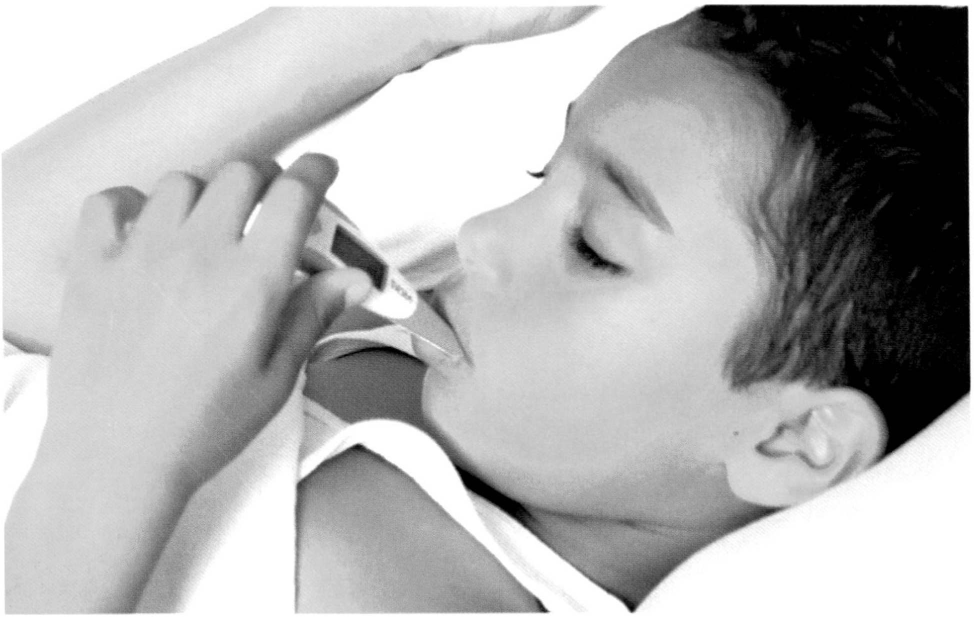

▲ **Figure 8.3.4** Clinical thermometers are placed where they give an internal body temperature reading, usually under the arm or in the mouth. They must be left there for a minute or two before reading.

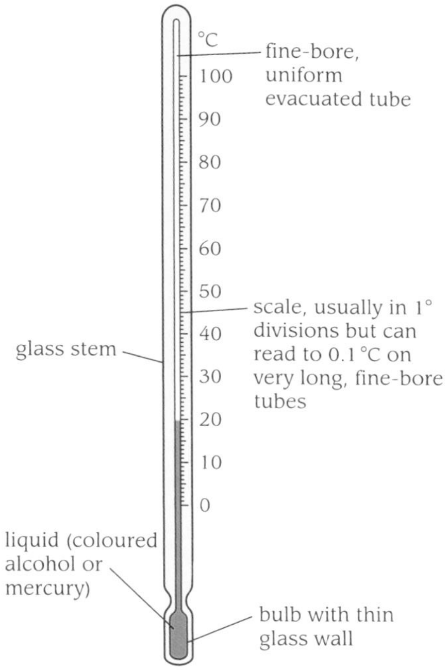

a A standard liquid-in-glass thermometer

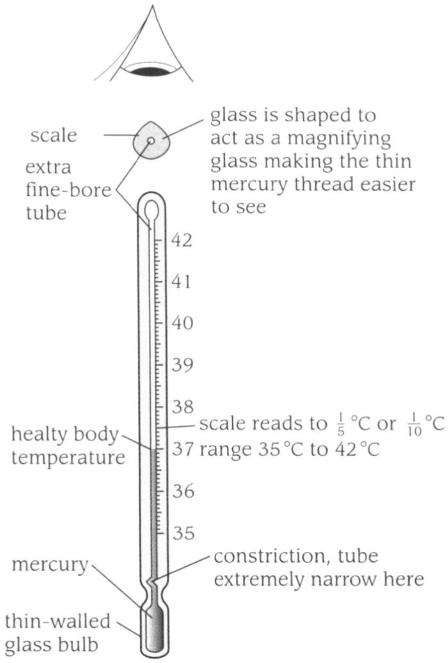

b A clinical thermometer

▲ **Figure 8.3.3** Some liquid-in-glass thermometers

Things to do

- Liquid-in-glass thermometers are cheap to manufacture. List other advantages and disadvantages that they have.
- Think about what things might lead to a liquid-in-glass thermometer giving an inaccurate reading.

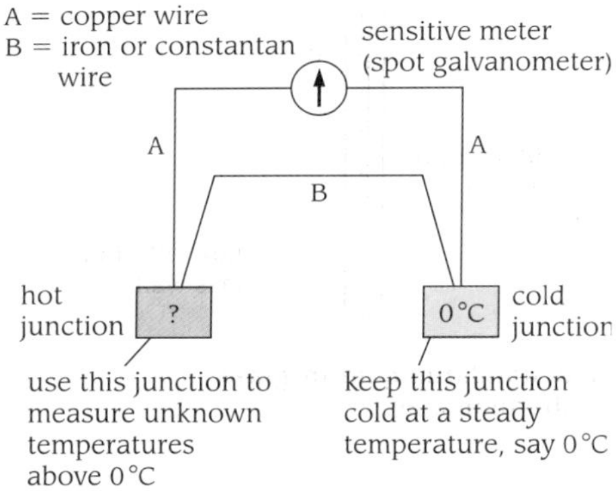

▲ **Figure 8.3.5** A thermocouple thermometer

Thermocouple thermometers

If two different metals are joined in an electric circuit and one wire junction is cold and the other is hot, a small electric current is generated in the circuit (Figure 8.3.5). The voltage increases as the temperature difference between the two junctions increases. So if one junction is kept at a fixed cold temperature such as 0 °C, then the other junction can be used as a small probe to measure temperatures above 0 °C.

The main advantages of thermocouple thermometers are:

- The wire junction can be *very small* and absorbs *very little heat*. So it responds very quickly to changing temperatures and can be used in small or precise locations, such as in industrial or scientific research.
- The electrical output signal means the thermocouple can be linked easily to equipment, giving warning of unexpected or large temperature changes. This is useful in many industrial processes needing carefully controlled temperatures.
- Different pairs of metals give different temperature ranges.
- Thermocouples can measure temperatures of up to 1500 °C, making them useful in furnaces, such as in steel, glass or ceramic manufacturing.

Summary questions

1. Describe the difference between heat and temperature.
2. What is the upper fixed point for water?
3. Give a circumstance where a liquid-in-glass thermometer would be unsuitable. What would you use instead?

Objectives

By the end of this topic you will be able to:

- compare how well different solids conduct heat
- show that water is a poor conductor of heat
- explain the importance of air as a bad conductor of heat in insulating materials
- explain conduction of heat in terms of the kinetic theory
- explain heat transfer by convection
- explain land and sea breezes in terms of convection currents
- explain the transfer of heat by radiation and that it does not require a medium
- describe experiments to investigate the absorption and emission of radiation
- describe how devices are designed to reduce or enhance the transfer of heat energy.

B8.4 Heat transfer

Conduction

The conduction of heat through solids

Heat is a form of energy. We also call it **thermal energy**.

We can demonstrate that heat flows at different rates through different materials.

- Rest some rods of various materials across the top of a tripod (Figure 8.4.1).

The rods should be of similar length and thickness to make a fair comparison of the different materials.

- Attach a small nail or matchstick to one end of each rod with Vaseline or wax.
- Now heat the other end of all the rods at the same time and watch what happens.

Heat flows along the rods at different rates and the matchsticks drop off after varying lengths of time.

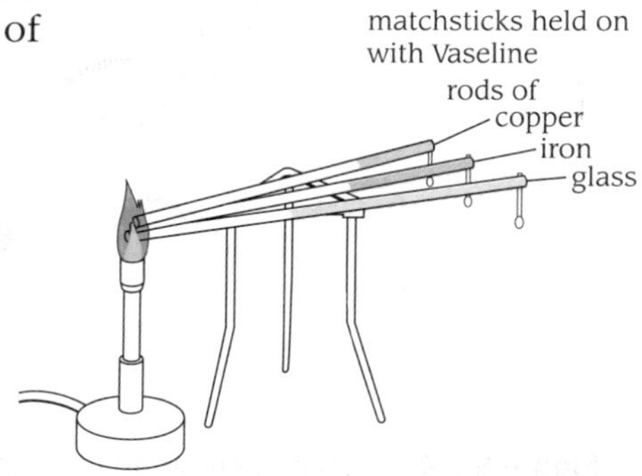

▲ **Figure 8.4.1** Comparing rates of heat conduction of different materials

Heat flows through the material of the rods without any flow of the materials themselves. The flow of heat through a material without any flow of the material is called conduction of heat.

In conduction of heat (thermal conduction), kinetic energy is passed from one vibrating particle to the next. Materials that conduct heat easily, such as metals, are called thermal conductors. Materials that don't conduct heat easily, such as glass, wood, plastics, are called thermal insulators.

Solids generally conduct heat better than liquids and much better than gases. The more rigid structure of solids makes it easier for vibrations to pass from one particle to the next. Metals are very good thermal conductors. They contain 'free' electrons, which transfer readily from one atom to another and so can 'flow' through the metal structure, transferring energy. This makes metals good at conducting both heat and electricity. Copper, silver and aluminium are particularly good thermal conductors.

Water is a poor conductor of heat

- Wedge a piece of ice at the bottom of a test tube so that it cannot float (Figure 8.4.2).
- Almost fill the tube with cold water and then heat it near its upper end.
- Note the order in which things happen.

The water at the top of the tube boils, while the ice remains unmelted at the bottom. Eventually slow conduction of heat through the water and the walls of the glass test tube will melt the ice. Liquids (except molten metals such as mercury) and all gases, including air, are bad conductors of heat.

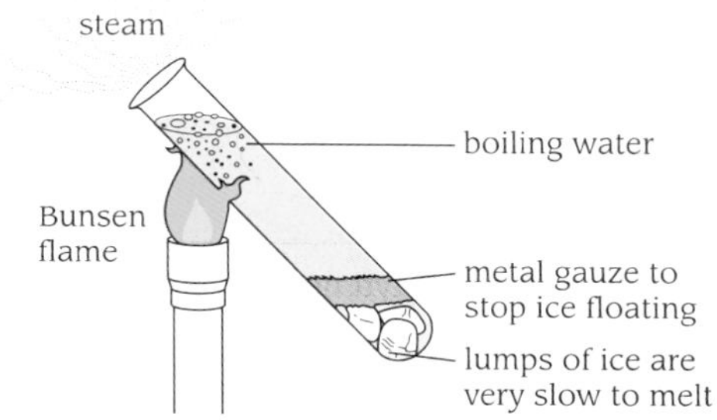

▲ **Figure 8.4.2** Water is a bad conductor of heat

Convection

Convection currents in water

- Fill a beaker with cold water almost to the top. When the water is still, drop in a few small crystals of potassium permanganate (potassium manganate(VII)) near one side (Figure 8.4.3).
- Using a small flame, gently heat the beaker just below the crystals and watch what happens.

Purple streaks can be seen rising with the water above the crystals (a) which are then carried down the far side of the beaker away from the heat (b). The whole body of the water is circulating in the beaker. This flow of water is called a convection current.

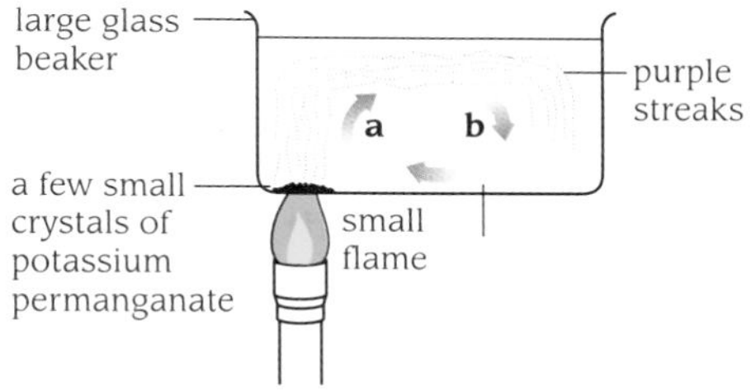

▲ **Figure 8.4.3** Convection currents in water

Convection currents in air

- Using a glass-fronted box as shown in Figure 8.4.4, position a lighted candle under one chimney and then place a smouldering rag or piece of cardboard into the top of the other chimney.
- Compare what happens when the candle is alight with what happens when it is not.

Although we cannot see the air moving we can feel a draught of warm air rising out of the candle chimney and we can see smoke being carried down the first chimney **b** and up the candle chimney **a**. This flow of air is also called a convection current.

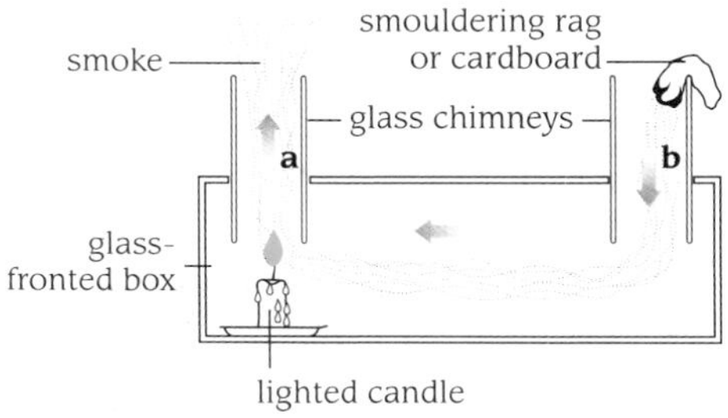

▲ **Figure 8.4.4** Convection currents in air

What causes a convection current?

Convection currents occur when a liquid or gas rises above a source of heat. When the water, which is at the bottom of the beaker and in close contact with the heat source receives some heat energy it expands. This expansion is caused by the molecules, now moving faster with more kinetic energy, pushing each other further apart. The expanded water is less dense than the surrounding water and so rises above the cooler and denser water around it.

Convection currents are a flow of liquid or gas caused by a change in density, in which the whole medium moves and carries heat energy with it.

Natural convection in the air

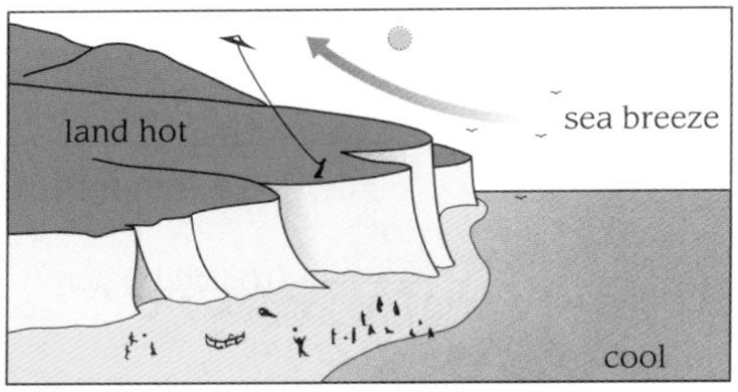

▲ **Figure 8.4.5** Daytime sea breeze

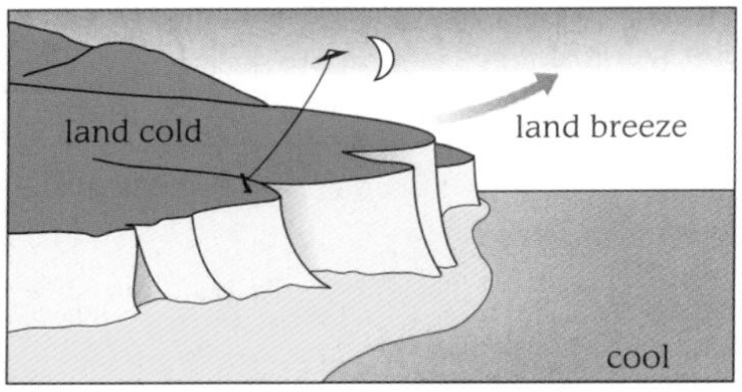

▲ **Figure 8.4.6** Night-time land breeze

Breezes and winds are often caused by one region of air being heated while a neighbouring region remains cool. For example, heated air rises above large towns and industrial estates, which are hotter than the countryside.

At the coast there is often a temperature difference between the land and the sea. The water in the sea hardly changes its temperature between night and day. During the day the land becomes much hotter than the sea. As air is heated by the hot land, it rises and is replaced by sea breezes (Figure 8.4.5). During the night the air above the sea is warmer and rises, drawing cooler air off the land forming land breezes (Figure 8.4.6).

When forest fires become well established they are very hard to put out. The heat of the fire causes hot air to rise upwards, so drawing cooler air in towards the base of the fire. The winds blowing towards the forest fire supply oxygen, which helps keep the fire burning.

Air conditioning units are placed high on one side of a room. Cooler, denser air from the unit sinks down to the floor, so drawing more warm air towards the air conditioning unit and creating a current of air that flows around the room.

Gliders and large birds often circle round and round, rising as they go. They are using thermals, currents of warm air flowing upwards, to gain height.

Radiant heat

What is radiation?

Radiation, more correctly called 'thermal radiation' to distinguish it from 'nuclear radiation', is the transfer of thermal energy as electromagnetic, infrared radiation. It travels at the speed of light and does not need particles to transmit the energy; it can travel through a vacuum. Thermal radiation can be detected by observing the rise in temperature it causes when it falls on objects, and by infrared cameras. All objects give out thermal radiation, but hotter objects give out more thermal radiation than cooler objects.

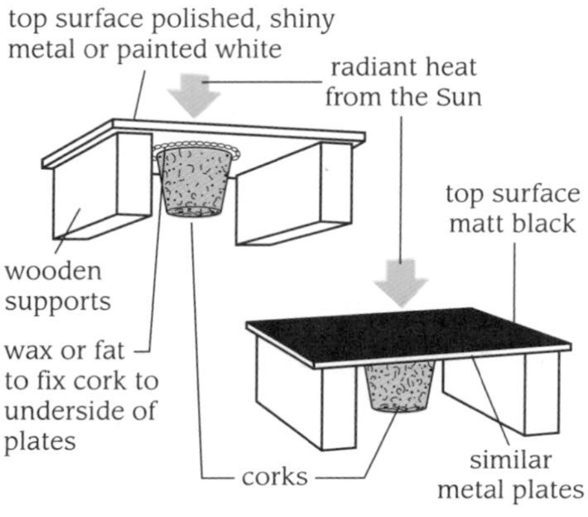

▲ **Figure 8.4.7** Absorption of radiant heat

Absorption of radiant heat

The absorption of radiant heat can be investigated using two similar metal plates, one painted matt black and the other polished to a shiny mirror-like surface or painted with white gloss paint.

- In a cool, shady place, fix a cork to the underside of each plate using wax or fat, which will melt in direct sunlight (Figure 8.4.7).
- Put the two plates out into the direct radiant heat of the Sun and observe.

The cork on the black surface falls off first. This demonstration shows that the black surface absorbs radiant heat more quickly than the shiny or white surface. You feel cooler if you wear light-coloured or shiny clothes in the hot summer. These clothes are poor absorbers of radiant heat energy from the Sun. If you wear black or dull and dark coloured clothes, or sit inside a dark coloured car, the greater absorption of radiant heat energy will make you much hotter.

Emission of radiant heat

- Mount a thick sheet of copper with one surface painted dull black and the other highly polished in a metal clamp and stand.
- Heat it with several Bunsen burners to make it very hot.
- Remove the burners.

The whole sheet should be at about the same temperature because copper is a good conductor of heat.

- Carefully bring the backs of your hands up near the two surfaces of the plate (Figure 8.4.9). (The backs of your hands are very heat-sensitive.)

The dull black surface feels hotter even though it is at the same temperature as the shiny surface. This shows that the dull black surface is emitting more radiant heat than the shiny one.

Many machines need to lose heat and are often fitted with cooling fins to help radiate the heat away. For example, a car radiator, a motorbike engine and a large transformer have cooling fins for this purpose. Heat is radiated more quickly if:

a) the fins are painted a dull black colour and

b) the fins have the largest surface area possible.

▲ **Figure 8.4.10** It is important to cool a motor cycle engine efficiently. Attaching metal fins greatly increases the surface area and allows more cooling air to come into contact with the hot engine. A black surface radiates heat most efficiently.

Reflecting radiant heat

A concave metal reflector or mirror can be used to concentrate radiant heat from the Sun. This can be tested by directing the focused radiation onto the bulb of a thermometer or even by using it to heat food. It is important to realise that although light is also focused at the same spot, it is not the light that produces most of the heating effect but rather it is the invisible radiant heat from the Sun.

▲ **Figure 8.4.8** Solar water heater on the roof of a building in Barbados. It comprises two rectangular plate collectors and, above those, a cylindrical water storage tank. Inside each collector are a series of small tubes that pass over a black absorber plate. The plates absorb sunlight and warm the water passing through the tubes. Warmed water rises to the storage tanks by convection as it is heated. Colder water sinks down into the collector. This system, known as a thermosiphon solar water heater, is cheap to install and maintain, and produces no waste products.

Key fact

Solar water heaters

Solar panels and solar water heaters use matt black surfaces to absorb the radiant heat energy from the Sun.

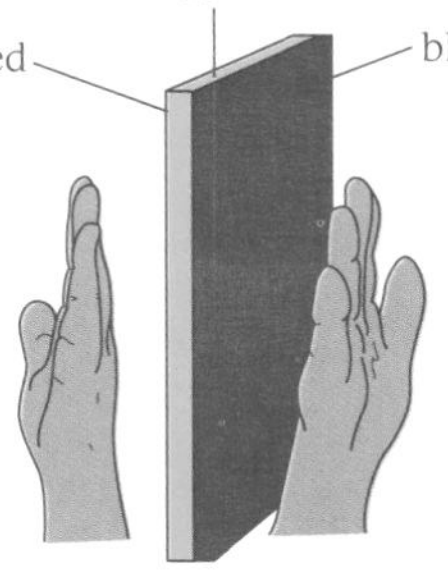

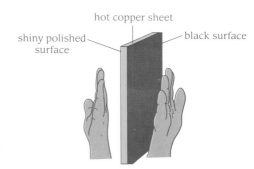

▲ **Figure 8.4.9** Emission of radiant heat

Exam tip

Remember that objects that are good emitters of thermal radiation are also good absorbers of thermal radiation.

▲ **Figure 8.4.11** Buildings in hot countries are often painted white because this helps them keep cool. White is best at reflecting visible and infrared radiation from the Sun.

▲ **Figure 8.4.12** A fire-fighting suit needs to be covered in shiny, reflective material to reflect the heat radiation and help keep the fighter cool.

Buildings are often painted white in hot countries because the white surface reflects most of the radiant heat from the Sun as well as the light. A fire-fighting suit and a space suit are sometimes covered in a shiny metallic surface. Sensitive electronic equipment in space probes is protected from radiant heat from the Sun by shiny metal foil. The shiny surface reflects the invisible radiant heat energy and so prevents the radiation reaching and being absorbed by the person or equipment behind it.

Evidence of the nature of radiant heat

- Radiant heat is absorbed by all objects and surfaces causing a temperature rise, but dull black or matt surfaces absorb it most quickly.
- Radiant heat is also radiated by all objects and surfaces causing a temperature fall and dull black surfaces are the best radiators.
- When someone walks between you and a warm fire the sensation of heating on your skin is immediately stopped at the moment the fire is hidden and just as quickly returns when the person has passed by. This tells us that the radiant heat travels very quickly, in fact almost instantaneously.
- The radiant heat energy coming from the Sun must have travelled through space to reach us, so this form of heat does not need a medium to travel in or molecules to carry the heat energy.
- Radiant heat energy can also be reflected in the same way that light can, and is often emitted by sources, such as the Sun and fires, which also emit light radiation at the same time.
- Radiant heat energy is part of the electromagnetic spectrum of radiation. This is a family of many kinds of radiation, all of which have certain common properties that link them together. Radiant heat energy is called **infrared radiation** and belongs next to red light in the electromagnetic spectrum.
- Infrared radiation is itself invisible to the human eye but can be detected by its heating effect and thermal images can be recorded on infrared sensitive film. The thermal images obtained from buried bodies in disaster areas are formed from the infrared radiation emitted by the warm bodies.

The greenhouse effect

The greenhouse effect in glass houses

Greenhouses are used to help certain plants grow better by providing a warmer air temperature. This is particularly helpful in countries where the weather is cold in winter and cooler in the spring. Most greenhouses do not need an internal source of heat because they are able to trap enough solar radiation by the **greenhouse effect**, keeping them very warm inside.

Sunshine (or solar radiation) contains radiation of many different kinds. Some of that radiation is the light that we can see, but much of it is invisible infrared radiation, or radiant heat energy. The Sun is very hot and sends most of this infrared radiation in a form that can easily pass through the glass of a greenhouse. (This is short wavelength infrared radiation.)

Things to do

Find out and explain:

- What are the bases and handles of your cooking pans at home made of? Why do you think these materials were chosen?
- Why do people use fans to keep cool?
- Why does a hot-air balloon rise up in the air?
- Why, when you open the door of a refrigerator, does the cold air come out at the bottom?
- Why is it a good idea to paint houses white in hot countries?
- What colour were the heat shield tiles on a space shuttle and why?

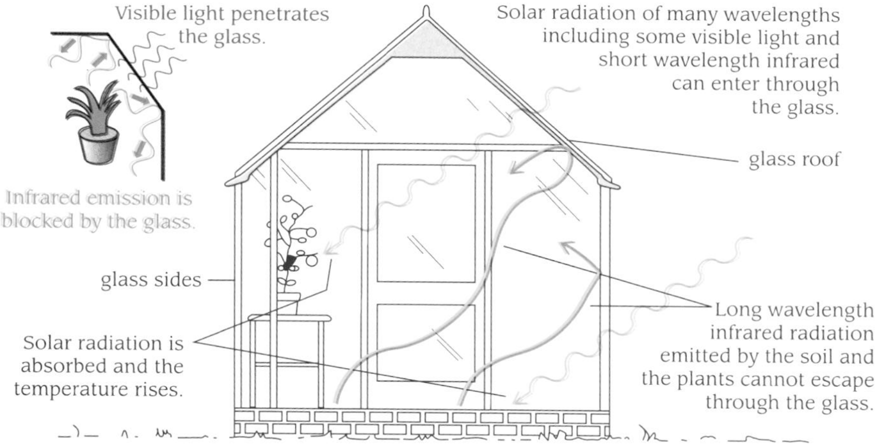

▲ **Figure 8.4.13** The greenhouse effect

Once inside the greenhouse this infrared radiation is absorbed by the plants and the soil, making them warmer. The warm soil and plants now also emit infrared radiation, but, since the soil is cool compared with the Sun, this radiation is different (it has a much longer wavelength) and cannot pass through the greenhouse glass. In this way, solar radiation becomes trapped inside the greenhouse and causes its temperature to rise.

Another application of the greenhouse effect and the absorption of solar radiation is the solar panel, used in some houses to heat water.

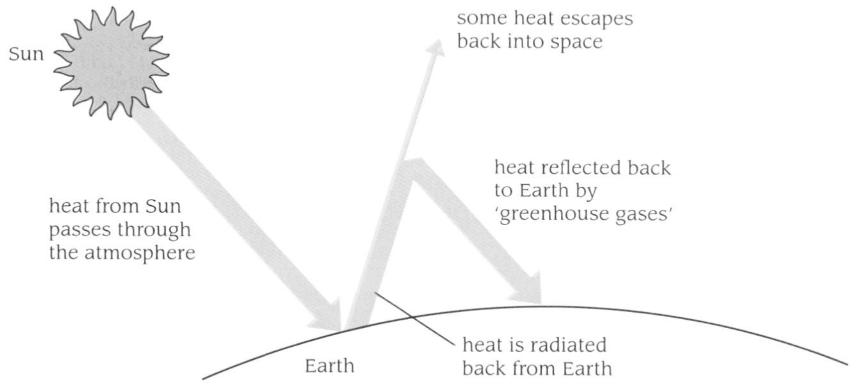

▲ **Figure 8.4.14** The greenhouse effect on planet Earth

Key fact

The greenhouse effect on planet Earth

The increasing use of fossil fuels across the planet has increased the amount of the gas carbon dioxide in the Earth's atmosphere.

Carbon dioxide and other gases such as methane and nitrous oxide are now known as 'greenhouse gases'. This is because the increasing amounts of these gases in the Earth's atmosphere are acting like the glass of a greenhouse.

Radiant heat from the Sun (short wavelength infrared) is allowed in through the atmosphere and is absorbed by the surface of the planet.

The infrared radiation re-emitted from the surface of the Earth has a longer wavelength and most of it cannot penetrate the Earth's atmosphere, being reflected back to the Earth. In this way, the Sun's radiant heat energy becomes trapped on the Earth and cannot escape.

The long-term consequences of this effect are likely to be:

- global warming and climate change
- melting of the ice caps and glaciers, causing the sea level to rise.

Using conduction, convection and radiation

Keeping warm and keeping cool

In cold countries, people wear thick clothes to keep warm. Warm clothes contain a lot of trapped air. Trapped air that cannot be blown away or carried upwards by convection currents forms a very good insulator. Materials such as fibreglass and expanded polystyrene contain lots of trapped air and so make excellent insulators.

In hot climates, things often need to be kept cool. Today there are many ways of keeping things cool.

- Refrigerators and freezers are really heat pumps, which take heat energy from inside and release it outside an insulated chamber. Heat pumps like these use the cooling effect of an evaporating liquid to remove the heat from inside.

- 'Coolers', which are insulated boxes made from expanded polystyrene, are used to keep drinks cold and picnics fresh. Ice placed inside the cooler helps to keep the contents cool.
- Plastic jugs and food containers are made with a double wall so that air trapped between them acts as an insulator.
- Earthenware pottery used to store food is kept wet so that the evaporation of water produces a cooling effect.
- People keep cool by blowing air past them, which causes moisture on the skin to evaporate and produce cooling. Hand-held fans have been used for thousands of years. Electric cooling fans help to keep people cool by moving the air and causing evaporation of moisture from the skin.
- Shiny metallic reflecting surfaces are used to reflect radiant heat. Fire fighters and space vehicles use this method of keeping cool.

Home heating

In colder countries people build houses with cavity walls around the outside. The outside wall of the house is made from two layers of brick a few centimetres apart with air between them. The air acts as a good insulator to stop heat energy escaping from the house. Often the gap is filled with foam, which is an even better insulator. A layer of loft insulation, made from thick, fluffy, fibreglass padding, is put above the ceiling to reduce the heat energy escaping upwards. Double-glazed windows have two sealed layers of glass with air or a partial vacuum between them. Very cold countries may even have triple-glazed windows, with three layers of glass and two layers of air.

All these ways of keeping houses warm in colder countries could be used to help keep houses cool in hotter countries, but they are expensive.

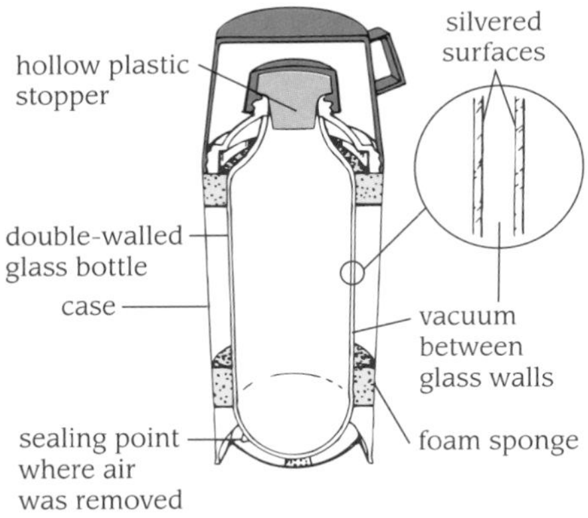

▲ **Figure 8.4.15** The vacuum flask

The vacuum flask

To keep a drink hot or cold inside a flask, heat flow by all three heat transfer processes must be reduced to a minimum (Figure 8.4.15).

Conduction is totally prevented through the sides of the flask by the vacuum between the double glass walls of the bottle. The cork or plastic stopper contains a lot of trapped air, which is also a bad conductor of heat.

Convection too is totally prevented by the vacuum.

Radiant heat loss is more difficult to prevent because it can travel through the vacuum. This loss is greatly reduced by the two silver coatings on the glass walls of the bottle. Radiant heat travelling either into or out of the flask is reflected by one of the shiny surfaces back the way it came.

Summary questions

1 Describe an experiment to demonstrate conduction in different materials.

2 Explain a natural example of a convection current.

3 Which surfaces are the best emitters of thermal radiation?

4 Describe one method used to keep things cool.

B8.5 Expansion of solids and liquids

The increase in size of objects when they get hotter is called expansion. This expansion can be a cause of problems in the construction of machines and buildings, but design engineers have often found ingenious ways of allowing for the expansion of materials and sometimes of making positive use of it.

Objectives

By the end of this topic you will be able to:

- explain everyday observations of the effects of thermal expansion
- describe some applications of thermal expansion, including the bimetallic strip
- describe demonstrations that show expansion of solids and liquids and the forces of expansion and contraction.

Demonstrating expansion of a solid

In Figure 8.5.1 the metal bar will just fit into the gap in the gauge when both the bar and the gauge are cold. Similarly the metal ball will just pass through the ring when both are cold.

- Heat the bar and the ball over a Bunsen burner flame and then test the fit again.

With the rise in temperature of the bar and the ball comes an increase in size: an expansion. This gauge shows that the bar has increased in length, which is called linear expansion.

The ring shows that the diameter of the ball has increased in all directions. The expansion in area of a solid is known as superficial expansion and the expansion in volume is called cubical expansion.

We need the gauge and the ring to show that there has been any expansion, because the change in size is so very small.

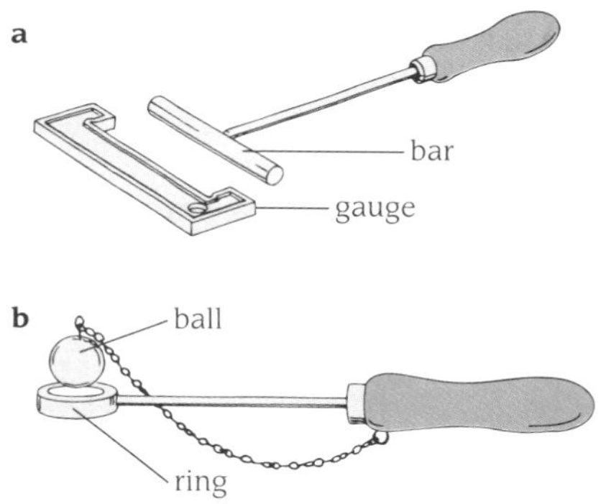

▲ **Figure 8.5.1** Demonstrating expansion of a solid

Testing the force of expansion and contraction

- To test the force of expansion, fit the tensioning nut and cast-iron bar in the inside positions in the bar-breaking apparatus as shown in positions E (Figure 8.5.2).
- Before heating the steel rod, turn the tensioning nut hand tight so that there is no room for expansion.
- Now heat the steel rod with one or more Bunsen burners and watch the cast-iron bar.
- To test the force of contraction fit the tensioning nut and cast-iron bar in the outside positions C.
- Heat the steel rod first and tighten the tensioning nut while the flames are still on the rod.
- Now when there is no room for contraction, remove the heat and again watch the cast-iron bar.

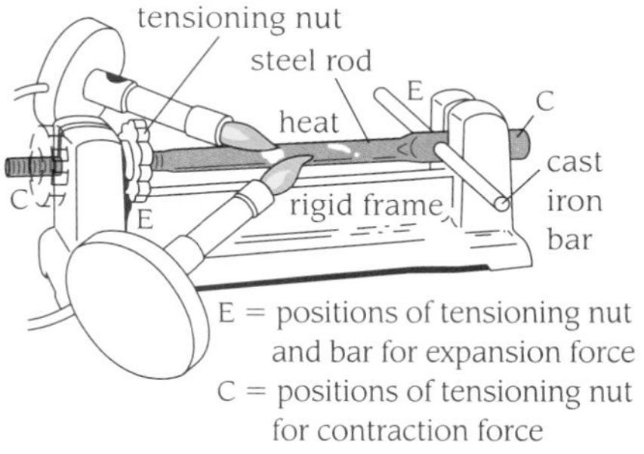

▲ **Figure 8.5.2** The forces of both expansion and contraction are very strong in metals.

Molecules provide the forces

Although the cast-iron bar is brittle, it requires a large force to break it. When a solid is heated, its molecules gain extra energy and vibrate more violently and need more room for movement. The molecules try to push their neighbours slightly further away, against their mutual attraction. So heating a solid slightly increases the distance between the molecules and causes expansion in all directions. When a solid has no room to expand, its molecules, in trying to make more space between themselves, produce the force of expansion.

When a hot solid cools down, but is not allowed to shrink, its molecules are held too far apart so that they pull on their neighbours, producing a tension in the material that we observe as the force of contraction.

Expansion and contraction, precautions and use

Although the expansion of a short length of metal is too small to see without magnification, the expansion of a steel or concrete bridge in hot weather is too great to be ignored. For example, a 100 m span of steel will increase in length by as much as 5 cm due to temperature changes.

To allow room for expansion in a bridge, an expanding joint must be made in the road surface. The concrete or steel span is usually mounted on rollers or rockers, which allow it to move without straining the vertical support pillars.

When you cross a bridge you will see an expansion joint at both ends of each main span. The joint usually takes the form of interlocking triangular points, which move closer together as the bridge span expands and open up as it contracts. In the photograph the two sides of the joint are quite well separated so the photograph must have been taken on a cold day.

Have a look at the expansion joints in a bridge near you. Try to visit it when the Sun is at its hottest and also at night time when it is much cooler. Note how the joint closes up in the heat of the Sun but moves apart at night in the cool.

▲ **Figure 8.5.3** Expansion joint of a bridge

Pipelines in the chemical industry that carry liquids and gases over long distances must have flexible expansion joints built in them at regular intervals.

▲ **Figure 8.5.4** Pipelines expand and contract as the temperature of their contents vary and the surrounding air temperature varies. The expansion of long lengths of pipeline can be considerable and would cause the pipes to buckle if arrangements were not made to allow for the expansion. Large loops built into the pipeline at regular intervals allow movement of the pipes.

High speed aircraft expand in flight because of the heating effect of friction at high speed. (An aircraft flying at twice the speed of sound may expand almost 5% in length.) Different parts of the aircraft expand different amounts because there is most heating effect at the nose and on the leading edge of the wings where the friction is greatest. The aircraft has to be designed so it can expand and contract regularly without damage, and special paints are used that don't crack as they are heated and stretched.

▲ **Figure 8.5.5** Aircraft are designed so they can expand and contract without damage.

A bimetallic strip is made of two strips of different metals, e.g. brass and iron, welded or riveted together. When cold the double strip is straight (a). As it is heated the brass expands more than the iron and so the brass forms the outside of a curve and the iron the inside (b).

Bimetallic strips are used in thermostats and many other mechanical switching circuits, but increasingly these are being replaced by electronic circuits with no moving parts. Can you work out how the bimetallic strip in (c) works as a thermostat? It should switch a heater on when the temperature falls.

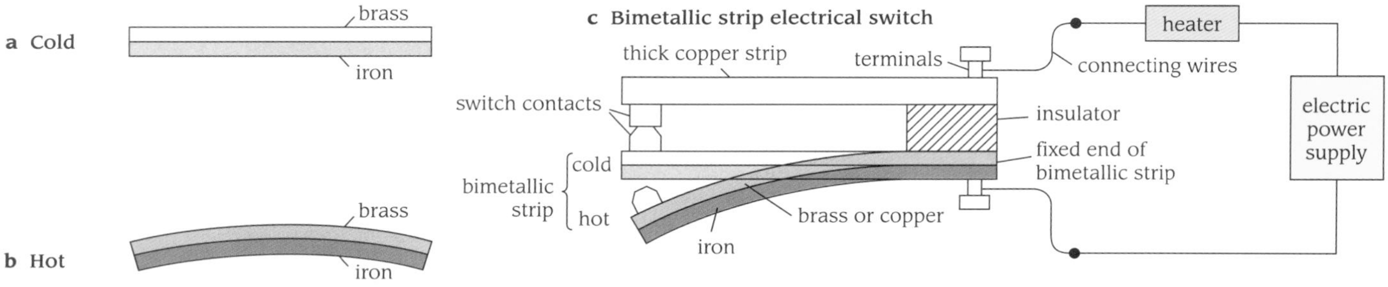

▲ **Figure 8.5.6** Bi-metallic strip

Demonstrating the expansion of liquids

- Fill a glass flask with coloured water and fit a stopper with a long glass tube so that there is no air in the flask and the water rises a short way up the tube (Figure 8.5.7).
- (The glass tube should not extend below the stopper.)
- Heat the flask and watch the level of the water in the tube. What happens in the first few seconds of heating? Can you explain this?
- To compare the expansion of water with the expansion of other liquids such as alcohol or ether, arrange identical flasks in a water bath so that the different liquids are heated equally and there is less risk of fire with any flammable liquids.

We find that in the first few seconds of heating the liquid level drops. Glass is a bad conductor of heat, so at first the glass flask expands and its volume inside increases. The liquid, which has not started to expand yet, drops to fill the extra volume inside the flask. Once heat reaches the liquid it expands rapidly up the tube and over the top. This shows that the cubical or volume expansion of a liquid is very large. Liquids expand much more (in volume) than solids do.

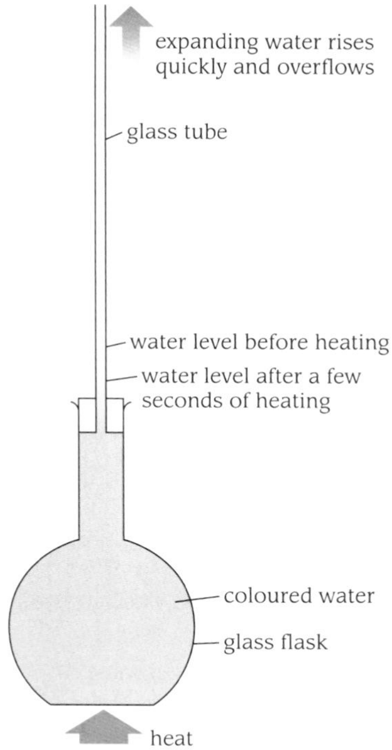

▲ **Figure 8.5.7** Demonstrating the expansion of water

The expansion of water

Most liquids contract steadily as they cool, and contract further on reaching their freezing point. Water contracts as it cools down from 100 °C to 4 °C. However, between 4 °C and 0 °C water behaves unusually in that it expands as it gets colder.

When water freezes its volume increases by about 8%, which is a much larger increase in volume than occurs between 4 °C and 0 °C. The maximum density and minimum volume of water occurs at +4 °C.

When a pond is freezing over, the densest water at 4 °C remains at the bottom of the pond. The less dense (but lower temperature) water, between 3 °C and 0 °C, floats in layers above it. The water on the surface freezes first and floats because it is less dense than the water below it.

Ice is a bad conductor of heat so that the layer of ice on the top of a pond acts like an insulating blanket and slows down further loss of heat from the water below.

Aquatic animals and plants make use of this phenomenon, by living in the liquid layers when the water freezes over in the winter.

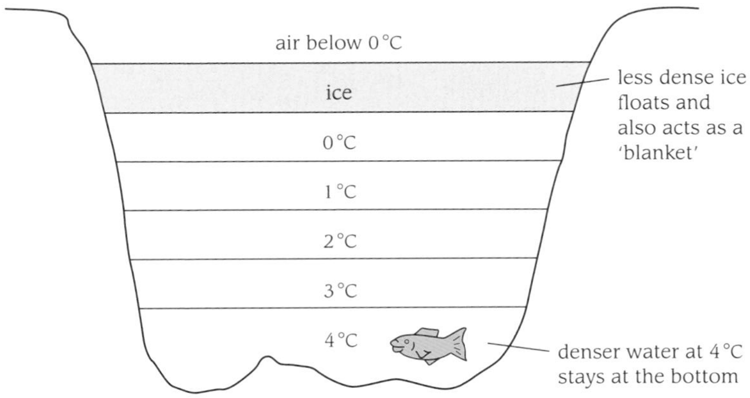

▲ **Figure 8.5.8** Water temperatures in a frozen pond

Things to do

Find out and explain:

- What method is used to allow for the expansion of a local bridge near your home or school?
- Why are the joints between slabs of concrete on a road surface filled with pitch?
- Why is it easier to remove a tight metal lid from a glass jar after running hot water over it?
- Why do some glass bottles crack when boiling hot water is suddenly poured inside them?
- Why do telephone wires and power cables hang lower on hot days and become tighter at night?

Summary questions

1 Use kinetic theory to explain why solids expand when they are heated.

2 Explain why ice floats.

3 How does a bimetallic strip work?

Objectives

By the end of this topic you will be able to:

- define specific heat capacity and specific latent heat and use them in heat calculations
- describe how to measure specific heat capacities of solids and liquids, the latent heat of vaporisation of water and the latent heat of fusion of ice
- obtain a cooling curve and find a melting point from it
- distinguish between evaporation and boiling and use the kinetic theory to explain these processes
- explain the importance of evaporation to refrigeration, earthenware vessels and perspiration.

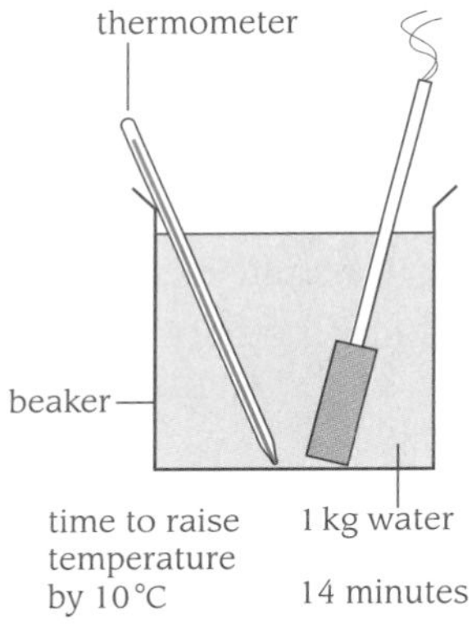

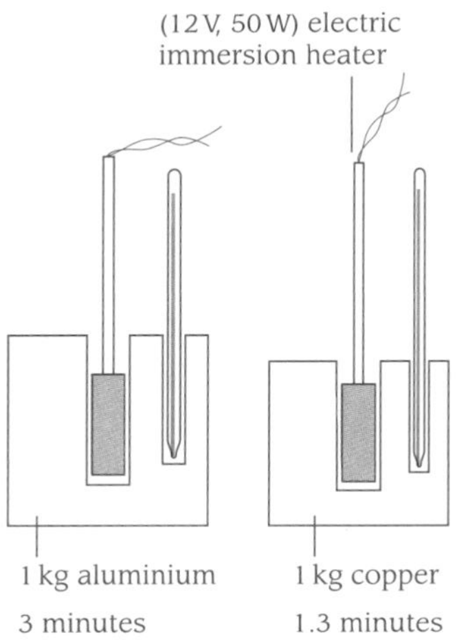

▲ **Figure 8.6.1** Different substances have different heat capacities.

B8.6 Specific heat capacity

Heat capacity and specific heat capacity

1 The heat capacity of an object depends on its mass

Compare an electric kettle with an immersion heater in a hot water tank. An electric kettle holds about 1.6 kg of water and a hot water tank could hold about 160 kg of water, that is about 100 times as much. The power of the kettle is 2.5 kW and the power of the immersion heater in the water tank is 5 kW.

As the 5 kW immersion heater heats twice as quickly as the 2.5 kW kettle, it will take only half as long to produce the same amount of heat. So if the kettle takes 2 minutes to heat 1.6 kg of water, the immersion heater would take only 1 minute to heat 1.6 kg. But in fact the immersion heater takes 100 minutes to heat 160 kg of water. We find that the amount of heat needed is directly proportional to the mass of water.

These figures agree with our experience of waiting for kettles to boil and hot water tanks to be heated for baths. We know that it takes much longer to heat up the water in the tank than it does to boil a kettle. This is because the water in the tank has a much larger heat capacity. In other words, it requires much more heat energy to raise its temperature.

The heat capacity of an object is directly proportional to its mass.

2 The heat capacity of an object depends on its material

We can compare the heat required by different materials by heating equal, 1 kg masses of them with the same electric heater.

- Connect a 12 volt, 50 watt immersion heater to a low voltage power supply set at 12 volt.
- Fit the heater in the hole drilled in the top of a 1 kg block and add a few drops of lubricating oil to improve the heat transfer from the heater to the block.
- Fit a thermometer in the smaller hole in the block and again add a few drops of oil for good thermal contact.
- Read the initial temperature of the block.
- Switch on the heater and measure the time taken for a temperature rise of 10 °C, or 10 K.
- Repeat the experiment for similar 1 kg blocks of different materials and for beakers containing 1 kg of a liquid.

We find that different materials take different times to warm up by 10 K, which shows that they need different amounts of heat and therefore have different heat capacities. Aluminium needs more than twice as much heat as copper, and water needs about 11 times as much heat as copper, to produce the same temperature rise in the same mass of substance.

The heat capacity of an object depends on what it is made of.

Heat capacity

Heat capacity refers to a *whole object* and we define it as follows:

The heat capacity, *C*, of an object is the heat energy needed to raise its temperature by 1 kelvin (1 degree Celsius).

$$\text{heat capacity} = \frac{\text{heat energy}}{\text{temperature rise}}$$

$$C = \frac{E_H}{\Delta T} \text{ (in J K}^{-1}\text{)}$$

Rearranged, the heat energy needed to warm up an object is:

$$E_H = C\Delta T$$

Specific heat capacity

Specific heat capacity refers to 1 kg of a substance. We use the word specific in physics to mean per unit mass which, in SI units, is per kilogram, or for each kilogram.

The specific heat capacity, *c*, of a substance is the heat energy needed to raise the temperature of 1 kg of the substance by 1 kelvin (1 degree Celsius).

We use the symbol E_H to stand for a quantity of heat energy to distinguish it from mechanical work W.

- Both E_H and W are measured in joules.
- The units of heat capacity, C are: J K^{-1}
- The units of specific heat capacity, c are: J kg^{-1} K^{-1}

$$\text{specific heat capacity} = \frac{\text{heat energy}}{\text{mass} \times \text{temperature rise}}$$

$$c = \frac{E_H}{m \times \Delta T} \text{ (in J kg}^{-1}\text{ K}^{-1}\text{)}$$

Rearranged: the heat needed to warm up an object is:

$$E_H = mc\Delta T$$

The relation between heat capacity, *C* and specific heat capacity, *c*

$$E_H = C\Delta T = mc\Delta T$$

So: $$C = mc$$

The heat capacity of an object depends on both its mass and the material it is made of.

Worked example

A hot water tank contains 160 kg of cold water at 20 °C. Calculate the quantity of heat energy required to raise the temperature of the water to 60 °C.

---

specific heat capacity of water = 4200 J kg^{-1} K^{-1}

The temperature rise

$$\Delta T = 60\,°\text{C} - 20\,°\text{C} = 40\text{ K}$$

$$E_H = cm\Delta T$$

$$= 4200 \times 160 \times 40$$

$$= 26\,880\,000\text{ J or } 27\text{ MJ}$$

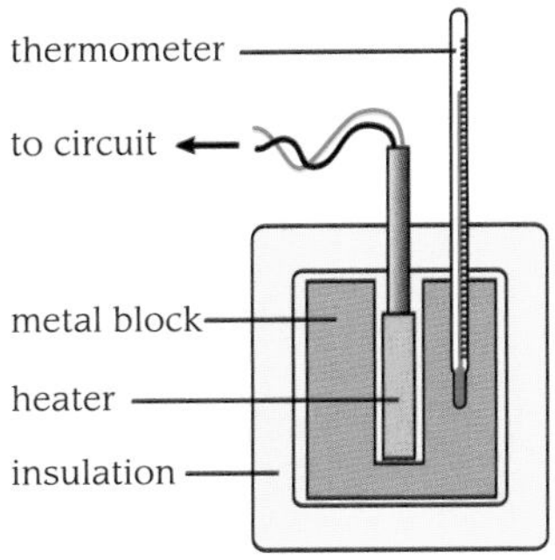

▲ **Figure 8.6.2** Electric immersion heater used to find the specific heat capacity. Why must the block or beaker be well insulated?

Things to do

Think about how you could change this experiment to decrease the loss of heat energy to the surroundings.

Key fact

- A joule meter gives the energy supplied.
- If you use an ammeter, voltmeter and timer, the energy supplied can be calculated using the formula:

  energy = $I \times V \times T$

Measuring specific heat capacity – electrically

The specific heat capacity of a solid in the form of a block (or a liquid) can be measured by using a heater, as shown in Figure 8.6.2.

- Connect a 12 volt heater to a 12 volt DC power supply.
- Find the mass m of the block by weighing.
- Wrap the metal block in heat insulating material, called lagging.
- Record the initial temperature T_1 before switching on the heater.
- Use a joulemeter or an ammeter, voltmeter and timer to find the electrical energy supplied to the heater.
- When the temperature has risen by about 10 °C, switch off the heater. (If the temperature rise is too large then too much heat will be lost.)
- Note the highest temperature reached T_2 after switching off the heater. (Stir a liquid before reading T_2.)
- Calculate the temperature rise $\Delta T = T_2 - T_1$ and the energy supply from heater E_H.
- Calculate the specific heat capacity using: $c = \dfrac{E_H}{m \times \Delta T}$

The heat capacity of an electric kettle full of water

The heat energy, E_H supplied by the kettle is given by:

energy = power × time

the power of the kettle is 2.5 kW = 2500 W

the time of heating is 2 minutes = 120 seconds

temperature rise, ΔT from 20 °C to 60 °C = 40 °C or 40 K

the mass of water = 1.6 kg

$$E_H = 2500\,\text{W} \times 120\,\text{s} = 300\,000\,\text{J}$$

The heat capacity, C of the kettle full of water is given by:

$$C = \frac{E_H}{\Delta T} = \frac{300\,000}{40} = 7500\,\text{J K}^{-1}$$

The specific heat capacity, c of water is given by:

$$c = \frac{E_H}{m \times \Delta T} = \frac{300\,000}{1.6 \times 40} = 4700\,\text{J kg}^{-1}\,\text{K}^{-1}$$

What do these two answers mean?

- $C = 7500\,\text{J K}^{-1}$ means that 7500 joules of heat energy are needed to warm up the kettle full of water by 1 kelvin or 1 degree Celsius.
- $c = 4700\,\text{J kg}^{-1}\,\text{K}^{-1}$ means that 4700 joules of heat energy are needed to warm up each 1 kg of water by 1 K.
- The relationship between heat capacity and specific heat capacity is: $C = mc$.

Errors

The value of c for water found in this experiment is not correct. The correct value for c for water is 4200 J kg^{-1} K^{-1}. The heat energy being supplied to the kettle does not just heat up the water. Some is used to heat the material of the kettle itself, and some will be lost to the surroundings as heat is radiated, conducted and convected away from the hot kettle. An accurate calculation of c would have to take account of this.

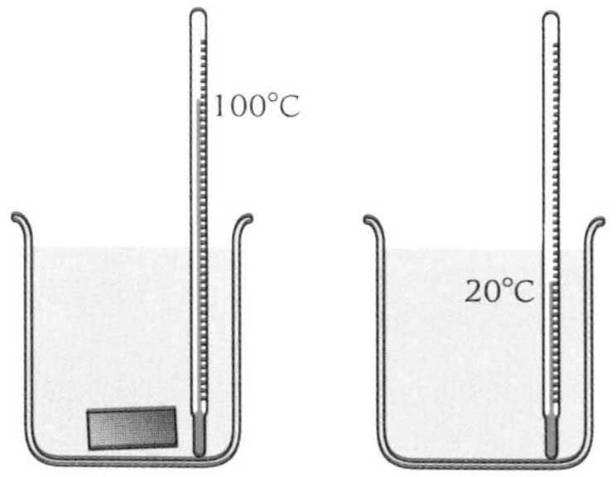

▲ **Figure 8.6.3** Measuring specific heat capacity – by method of mixtures

Measuring specific heat capacity – by method of mixtures

The specific heat capacity of a solid or a liquid can also be measured by a method that involves mixing something hot with something cold. In the mixing process, if no heat escapes to the surroundings:

heat lost by hot object = heat gained by cold object

To find the specific heat capacity of aluminium

- Heat a 0.5 kg mass of aluminium in water boiling at 100 °C.
- Put 1.0 kg of cold water into an insulated container and measure its temperature.
- Quickly transfer the hot aluminium block to the cold water.
- Stir and note the final temperature of the mixture.

Key fact

Precautions to take:

- Avoid splashing water to avoid inaccuracies in the mass of the water.
- Transfer quickly to minimise heat energy lost to the surroundings.
- Stir well before reading to ensure a uniform water temperature.
- Ensure container is well insulated to minimise heat energy lost to the surroundings.

Worked example

The method of mixtures is used to calculate the specific heat capacity of aluminium. The mass of the block is 0.5 kg, the initial temperature of the cold water is 20 °C and its final temperature is 28 °C. The mass of water is 1.0 kg. Calculate the specific heat capacity of aluminium.

Temperature rise of cold water = 28 − 20 = 8 °C.

Temperature fall of hot aluminium = 100 − 28 = 72 °C.

Specific heat capacity of water = 4200 J kg^{-1} K^{-1}.

Heat lost by hot aluminium block = heat gained by cold water

Using $E_H = mc\Delta T$:

$0.5 \times c \times 72 = 1.0 \times 4200 \times 8$

The specific heat capacity of aluminium, c = 930 J kg^{-1} K^{-1}.

Things to do

Find out and explain how the enormous heat capacity of the water in the sea affects:

- the temperature of the sea between day and night
- the temperature of the land near the sea in summer and winter.

Latent heat

An iceberg can survive many weeks floating on the sea before it all finally melts. It takes much longer to turn a kettle full of boiling water into steam than it does to bring cold water to the boil in a kettle. These examples show that a lot of heat energy is needed to change ice into water and water into steam. This heat energy, which changes the phase or state of a substance, is called latent heat.

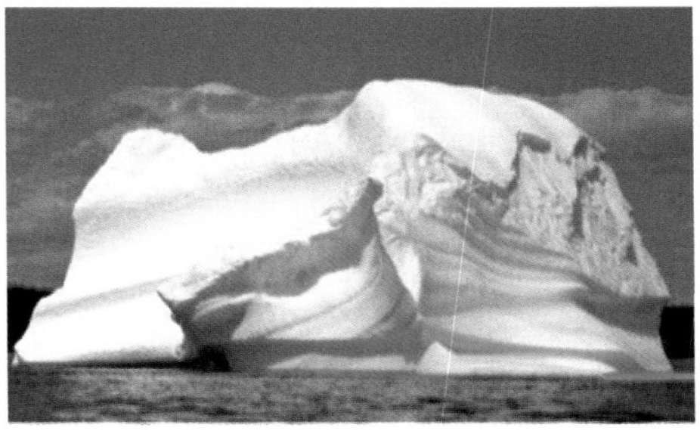

▲ **Figure 8.6.4** An iceberg can float on the sea for weeks before it melts.

Change of phase or change of state

Latent heat means *hidden* heat. The heat that changes ice into water is hidden in the sense that when the ice melts it is no hotter than before it received the heat. The latent heat turns ice at 0 °C into water at 0 °C. So latent heat changes the phase of an object without causing any rise in temperature.

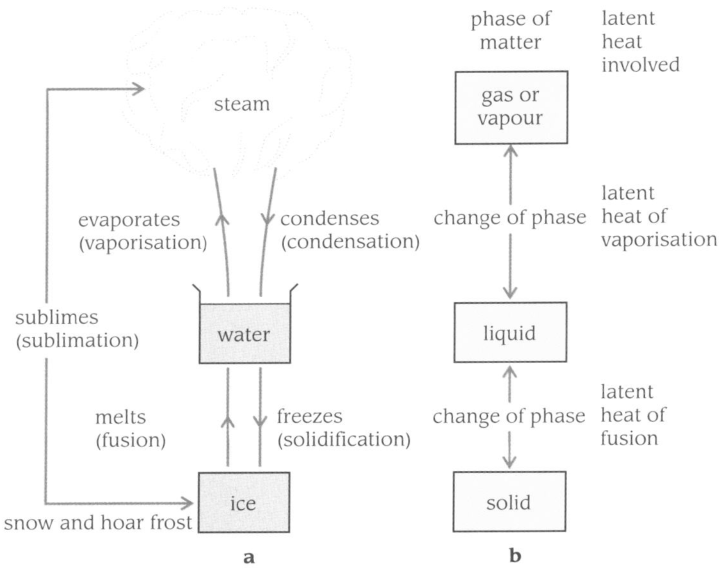

▲ **Figure 8.6.5** Changes of phase

It is also possible for a change to occur directly from water vapour to ice, or from ice to water vapour. This change of phase that misses out the liquid phase is called **sublimation**. White hoar frost, which forms on plants and on the ground, is water vapour from the air turned directly into ice crystals without becoming drops of dew first. Sometimes the hoar frost can turn back into water vapour in the air without melting first.

Sublimation is a change of phase direct from solid to vapour or vapour to solid.

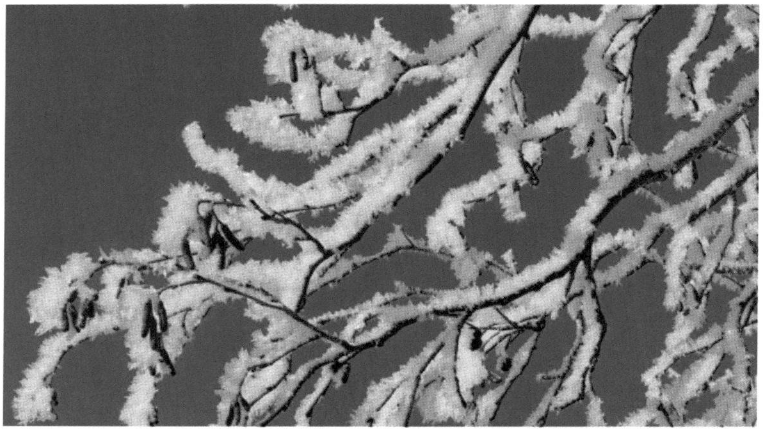

▶ **Figure 8.6.6** Hoar frost on the branches of a tree

Key fact

Some key words

- A change of phase is also called a change of state.
- **Melting** or **fusion** is the phase change from solid to liquid.
- **Freezing** or **solidification** is the phase change from liquid to solid.
- The **latent heat of fusion** is the latent heat required for melting or lost when freezing occurs.
- **Evaporation** or **vaporisation** is the phase change from liquid to vapour or gas.
- **Condensation** is the phase change from vapour to liquid.
- The **latent heat of vaporisation** is the latent heat required for vaporisation and lost when condensation occurs.

Evaporation requires heat energy and causes cooling

- Set up a small beaker containing some ether as shown in Figure 8.6.7a.
- Draw a stream of air through the ether, using a pump to increase the rate of evaporation. (Do not suck by mouth.)
- Watch the glass beaker and feel it from time to time.

Ether is very volatile, i.e. it evaporates rapidly. Water vapour condenses from the air on the outside of the beaker showing how cold the glass has become. Eventually the water freezes on the sides of the beaker and on the sheet of wood.

- Try lifting the beaker.

This experiment shows that as ether evaporates it needs heat energy for its latent heat of vaporisation. This heat is removed from the remaining liquid ether and from everything around it, which causes cooling. If the surrounding water is cooled to 0 °C then further removal of heat takes away its latent heat of fusion and freezes it.

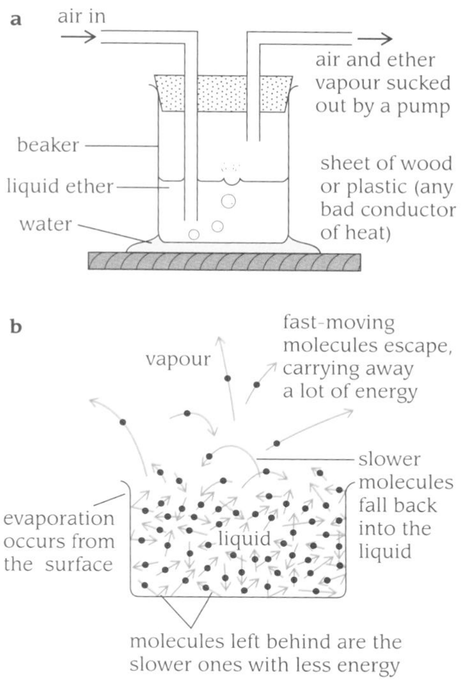

▲ **Figure 8.6.7** Evaporation causes cooling

In evaporation the faster molecules escape

Figure 8.6.7b shows how evaporation occurs at the surface of a liquid. Molecules reaching the surface may either escape or fall back into the liquid. Only the faster molecules actually get away, because only they have enough energy to escape from the attraction of the liquid molecules.

The general effect of the faster molecules being able to escape and the slower molecules remaining in the liquid is the lowering of the average energy of the molecules in the liquid. A liquid with slower molecules having less kinetic energy is a cooler liquid. So evaporating molecules leave a cooler liquid behind. That is why using an alcohol hand gel makes your hands feel cold. The alcohol evaporates from your skin readily, gaining its latent heat of vaporisation from your skin.

When heat energy is given to a liquid to help it evaporate, more molecules in the liquid are given enough kinetic energy to escape. So the latent heat of vaporisation of a liquid is the extra energy required by the molecules of the liquid to enable them to escape from the liquid surface.

The refrigerator

A refrigerator makes food cold by removing heat energy from it. Heat is a form of energy, so it cannot be destroyed, but it can be transferred or pumped from one place to another. So the basic idea is to pump heat energy from food inside the refrigerator and give it to the air outside. A machine that pumps heat is called a **heat pump**.

Once it is cold inside a refrigerator, heat tends to conduct back in through the cabinet to warm the inside up again so the refrigerator needs to be well insulated. Inside a refrigerator, within closed pipes, an evaporating liquid is used to remove heat in the same way as the evaporating ether removed heat from its surroundings. A volatile liquid is circulated inside a refrigerator, through a closed circuit of pipes, by a pump. The pump aids evaporation by pumping vapour out of the evaporator pipes and reducing the pressure. The latent heat required for the evaporation is removed from the air and food inside the refrigerator making them cold.

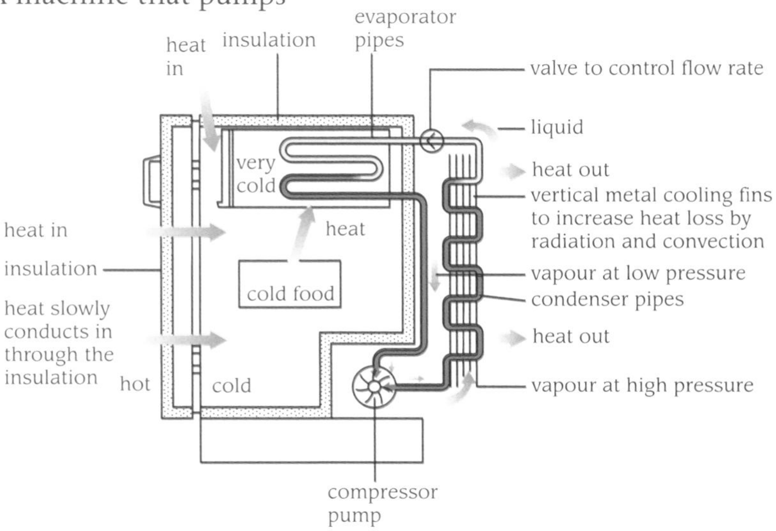

▲ **Figure 8.6.8** A refrigerator

Specific latent heat of fusion

The latent heat of fusion of an iceberg is the heat energy needed to melt all of it. None of this heat causes any temperature rise of the water formed from the ice.

The latent heat of fusion, L, of a solid object is the heat energy required to change it from solid to liquid without any temperature change.

Again using specific to mean per unit mass or for each kilogram of mass, the specific latent heat of fusion of the ice in an iceberg is the heat energy needed to melt each kilogram mass of it without raising its temperature.

The specific latent heat of fusion, l, of a solid substance is the heat energy required to change 1 kg of it from solid to liquid without any temperature change.

$$\text{The specific latent heat of fusion of a substance} = \frac{\text{heat energy}}{\text{mass}}$$

$l = \frac{E_H}{m}$ The units of l are joule per kilogram or J kg^{-1}.

Specific latent heat of vaporisation

The latent heat of vaporisation of a kettle full of boiling water is the heat energy needed to turn all the water at 100 °C into steam at 100 °C. Similarly the specific latent heat of vaporisation of water is the heat energy needed to turn 1 kg of boiling water into steam without any temperature rise.

The definitions and formulae for vaporisation are very similar to those for fusion. In symbols, the formulae are identical.

The specific latent heat of vaporisation, l, of a liquid substance is the heat energy required to change 1 kg of it from liquid to vapour without any temperature change.

Key fact

How big are specific latent heats?

Experiments show that the specific latent heat of fusion of a substance and its specific latent heat of vaporisation are quite different amounts of heat energy. For water:

- it takes 340 000 J to melt 1 kg of ice at 0 °C, and
- it takes 2 300 000 J to convert 1 kg of boiling water into steam.

Calculating the heat required to warm up, melt or evaporate things

We have two formulae for heat energy:

1 This heat energy causes a temperature change, ΔT.

$$E_H = cm\Delta T$$

2 This heat energy causes a change of phase, but no temperature change.

$$E_H = lm$$

Worked example

An ice lolly has a mass of 100 g. If the specific latent heat of fusion of ice is 340 000 J kg^{-1}, calculate the heat energy needed to melt the ice lolly. (Assume the ice is at 0 °C and no temperature rise occurs.)

Note: the mass in kg = 0.1 kg.

$E_H = lm = 340\,000 \times 0.1$ J
$= 34\,000$ J

Worked example

A kettle containing 1.6 kg of water is left switched on. After starting to boil, how much heat energy will be used in turning all the water to steam, and how long will it take for the 2.5 kW kettle to boil dry?

Specific latent heat of vaporisation of water = 2.3×10^6 J kg^{-1}

$E_H = 2.3 \times 10^6 \times 1.6$
$= 3.7 \times 10^6$ J

$$t = \frac{E_H}{P} = \frac{3.7 \times 10^6}{2.5 \times 10^3} = 1.5 \times 10^3 \text{ s}$$

= 25 minutes to boil dry

Measuring the specific latent heat of vaporisation of water

- Connect an electric immersion heater to its power supply and measuring circuit (Figure 8.6.9)
- Nearly fill a beaker with hot water and weigh it, m_1. Fit the beaker into a lagged jacket.
- Insert the heater and heat the water until it just begins to boil.
- At the same moment, start the clock and read the joulemeter (circuit **a**) or read the ammeter and voltmeter (circuit **b**).
- After 15 minutes switch off the heater and stop the clock.
- Read the joulemeter again (circuit **a**) and record the time of heating.
- Remove the heater and lagging.
- Weigh the beaker again, m_2.

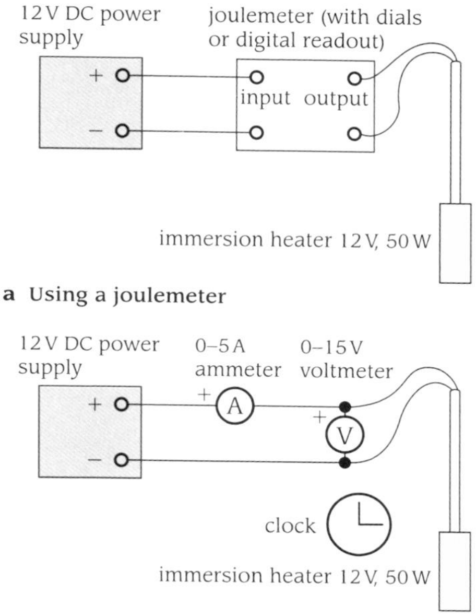

a Using a joulemeter

b Using an ammeter and voltmeter

▲ **Figure 8.6.9** Circuits for measuring the energy supplied to an electric heater

Specimen results:

$m_1 = 312\text{ g} = 0.312\text{ kg}$

$m_2 = 294\text{ g} = 0.294\text{ kg}$

mass of water converted into steam, $m = m_1 - m_2 = 0.018\text{ kg}$

time of heating, $t = 15$ minutes $= 900\text{ s}$

current, $I = 4.0\text{ A}$

voltage, $V = 12.0\text{ V}$

Heat energy supplied, $E_H = IVt = 4.0 \times 12.0 \times 900 = 43\,200\text{ J}$

The specific latent heat of steam is given by:

$$l = \frac{E_H}{m} = \frac{43\,200}{0.018} = 2\,400\,000\text{ J kg}^{-1}$$

or

$$2.4 \times 10^6\text{ J kg}^{-1}$$

Cooling curves

A cooling curve is a graph of temperature against time for a substance or an object that is losing heat to its surroundings. Such a graph can be used for the following purposes:

a) to compare the heat capacities of different objects (an object with a larger heat capacity cools more slowly)

b) to compare the insulation properties of different materials or thicknesses of material (the better the insulation around a hot object, the slower the cooling)

c) to find the melting or freezing point of a substance.

Finding a freezing point using a cooling curve

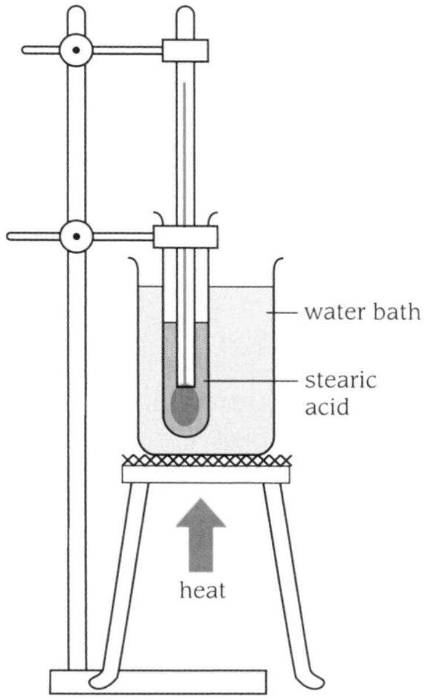

▲ **Figure 8.6.10** Finding the freezing point of a substance – heating the substance

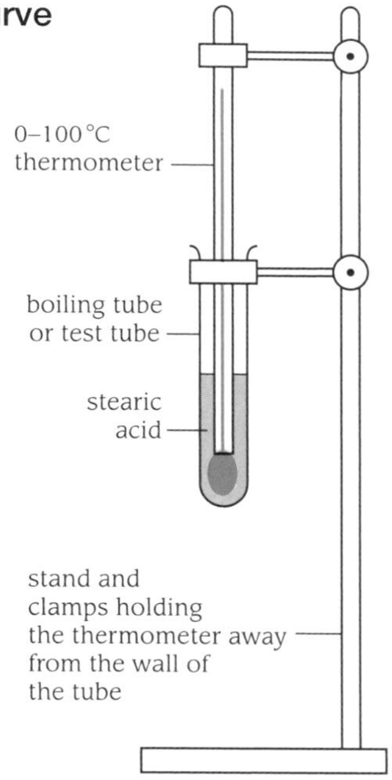

▲ **Figure 8.6.11** Finding the freezing point of a substance – cooling the substance

It is convenient to use a substance that has a melting or freezing point somewhere between room temperature and the boiling point of water. A suitable substance is stearic acid or naphthalene (melting point 80 °C).

- Put some of the substance in a test tube and heat the test tube in a water bath (Figure 8.6.10).
- When all the substance has melted and reached 100 °C carefully lift the test tube from the water bath (Figure 8.6.11).
- Using a clock, record the temperature of the substance every minute until all of it has solidified and cooled below its freezing point.
- Draw a graph of temperature against time and join the points following the curve (Figure 8.6.12).

Note:

i) Having a test tube ready mounted in a stand while it is being heated allows it to be lifted safely from the boiling water and also allows temperature readings to be taken immediately.

ii) Clamping the thermometer separately so that the thermometer bulb does not rest on the wall of the test tube gives a better graph because the glass wall of the tube cools below the temperature of the substance inside.

iii) Before removing the thermometer, first re-melt the substance.

Interpreting the cooling curve

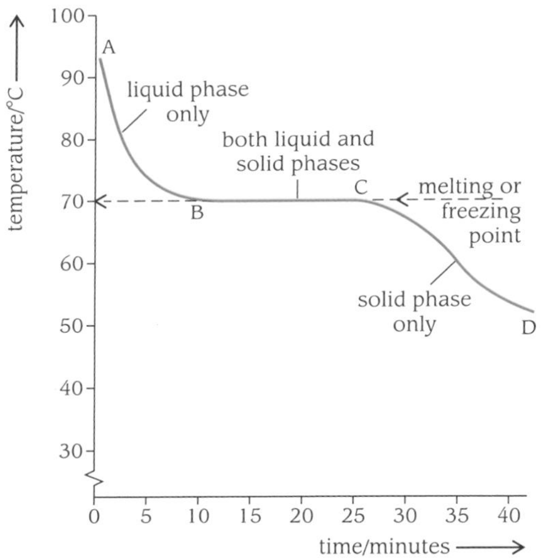

▲ **Figure 8.6.12** A cooling curve for stearic acid

- From A to B on the graph the substance is all in its liquid phase. Loss of heat to the surrounding air results in a fall in temperature.
- At B freezing begins.
- From B to C on the graph both solid and liquid phases exist together at the freezing point temperature. Loss of heat results in more liquid freezing but no fall in temperature until all the substance is frozen.
- *Latent heat is being lost during part B to C.*
- From C to D on the graph the substance is all in its solid phase. Loss of heat results in a further fall in temperature towards room temperature.

Note that the temperature falls more gradually as it gets nearer to the surrounding air temperature. This is because the rate of loss of heat from an object depends upon how much hotter it is than its surroundings.

Exam tip

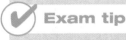

Make sure you can identify the source of heat energy whenever there is a change of state.

Evaporation and boiling

Evaporation

There is always some vapour above the surface of a liquid because liquid molecules are continually escaping from the liquid surface. Experiments show that the rate of evaporation is increased by:

- an increase in the temperature of the liquid
- an increase in the surface area of the liquid
- a draught or wind that blows over the surface.

Things to do

Find out and explain:

- Why does wearing wet clothes make you feel cold?
- How does sweating help keep you cool?
- How do earthenware vessels help keep things cool?
- How does a dog keep cool?

Hint: all these processes involve the cooling effect of the evaporation of a liquid.

Boiling

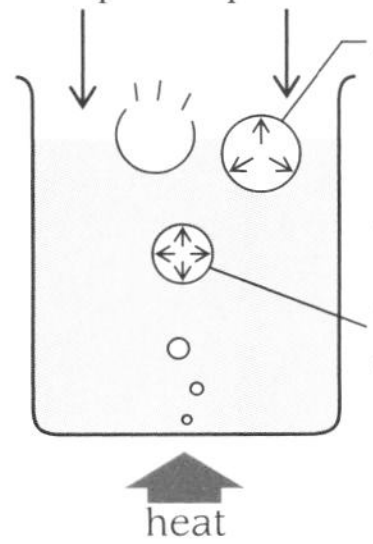

▲ **Figure 8.6.13** Boiling water

We can tell the difference between **boiling** and **evaporation** by looking for bubbles forming inside the liquid, which indicate that the liquid is boiling (Figure 8.6.13). Another important difference is that boiling occurs only when a certain definite temperature, called the boiling point, is reached.

Evaporation	Boiling
occurs only at the surface of liquids where the fastest molecules escape	bubbles of vapour form within the liquid as fast molecules escape into the bubbles
occurs at all temperatures	occurs only at the boiling point

Can you think of any other similarities or differences?

Pressure and boiling

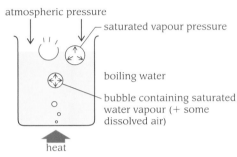

When water boils, the fastest moving molecules with the highest kinetic energy are able to escape from the surface of the liquid. When the atmospheric pressure pushing on the surface of the liquid is higher, the molecules need more energy before they are able to escape. So at higher pressures, water boils at a higher temperature. Pressure cookers work by increasing the pressure inside the cooker so that the water boils at a higher temperature and so food cooks faster. At the top of tall mountains, where the atmospheric pressure is lower, water boils at a lower temperature. On top of Everest, water boils at 71 °C.

Summary questions

1. Give the definition of specific heat capacity.
2. How are heat capacity and specific heat capacity related?
3. Name the two types of latent heat. When does a material give out latent heat of fusion?
4. Explain the difference between evaporation and boiling.

B8.7 The gas laws

Objectives

By the end of this topic you will be able to:

- state the gas laws
- explain the gas laws in terms of the kinetic theory of gases
- use the gas laws to solve problems
- describe experiments to investigate the relationships between the pressure, volume and temperature of a gas
- draw and interpret graphs of *p* and *v* against temperature including sub-zero °C
- use the relationship: T in $K = \theta$ in °C + 27

Key fact

Extrapolation

The process of extending a graph beyond the range of the experimental results is called extrapolation. This process should always be used with caution because the information it provides is not fully supported by experimental evidence. On the volume against temperature graph our experiment tells us nothing about what happens below 0 °C, and we are assuming that gases expand and contract the same way at temperatures below 0 °C as they do above 0 °C.

Accurate measurements predict that the volume of all gases should contract to zero at −273 °C. This is the temperature known as **absolute zero** on the Kelvin, or absolute, temperature scale.

Gases do in fact follow the extrapolated graph quite closely down to very low temperatures, near absolute zero. Eventually they liquefy and the volume of the molecules themselves prevents further reduction in volume of the gas and zero volume is never reached.

When a gas is heated, its molecules gain extra kinetic energy and move about at greater speeds. We detect this change as a rise in temperature of the gas. The increase in energy of the gas molecules may cause both the volume and the pressure of the gas to increase. The gas laws describe the experimental evidence about the ways in which the temperature, pressure and volume of a gas are related to each other.

Temperature in kelvin

Temperatures can be measured on the Kelvin temperature scale. In the 19th century, Lord Kelvin realised that molecules move more slowly at lower temperatures. He designed the Kelvin temperature scale so that 0 degrees kelvin (0 K) is the temperature at which molecules stop moving. The divisions on the Kelvin temperature scale are the same size as the divisions on the centigrade scale. 0°C is 273 K, and 100 °C is 373 K. 0 K is called absolute zero, and it is −273 °C.

Charles' law

The expansion law at constant pressure

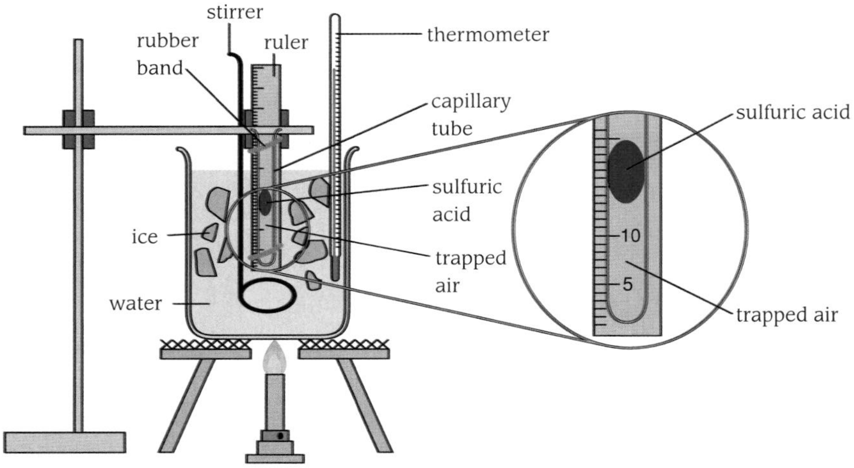

▲ **Figure 8.7.1** Investigating Charles' law

Charles' law, like the other gas laws, applies to a *fixed mass of gas*. The relations between the temperature, pressure and volume of a gas describe the behaviour of a constant number of gas molecules. When the gas is heated or compressed no molecules must be added or allowed to escape.

We can investigate Charles' law using a fixed mass of air, which is trapped in a capillary tube by a drop of acid.

- Fit the capillary tube on a 30 cm ruler using rubber bands so that its sealed end lines up with the zero on the scale and support it in a tall beaker of water (Figure 8.7.1).
- Heat the water slowly. The air must have time to expand slowly, so that the pressure remains constant.
- Stir the water so the temperature of the air column is the same as the temperature measured by the thermometer.

- Record your readings of temperature and the corresponding lengths of the air column in a table.
- Plot a graph of volume against temperature.
- When you have marked your results on the graph for temperatures between 0 °C and 100 °C they will appear to be in a straight line. Draw a straight line through the plotted points (Figure 8.7.2).

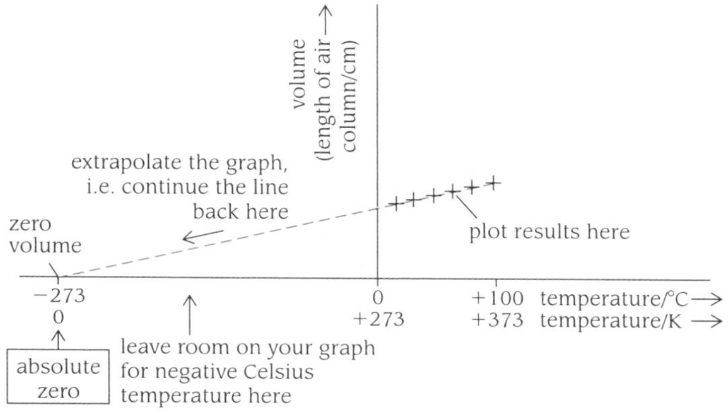

▲ **Figure 8.7.2** A graph for Charles' law

You can see that at 0 °C the volume of your sample of air is not zero, but as the temperature falls the volume decreases so that perhaps there is a temperature at which its volume would contract to zero.

- Extend your graph backwards by continuing the straight line to find out the temperature at which the volume becomes zero.

This is the temperature where the line touches the horizontal temperature axis.

The straight-line graph through the origin on the Kelvin temperature scale gives us:

Charles' law

The volume of a fixed mass of gas is directly proportional to its absolute temperature (on the Kelvin scale) if the pressure is constant.

$$V \propto T$$

$$V = \text{constant} \times T$$

$$\frac{V}{T} = \text{constant}$$

***T* must be given in kelvin.**

Boyle's law

Compressing a gas at constant temperature

The apparatus shown in Figure 8.7.3 gives a direct reading for both the volume and pressure of a fixed mass of gas.

A sample of air is trapped in a strong glass tube by a column of oil. The oil is supplied from a reservoir where it can be pressurised using air from a tyre pump. The pressure above the oil in the reservoir is read directly on a Bourdon pressure gauge. The pressure above the oil in the reservoir is transmitted through the oil to the trapped air in the glass tube. The Bourdon gauge reads

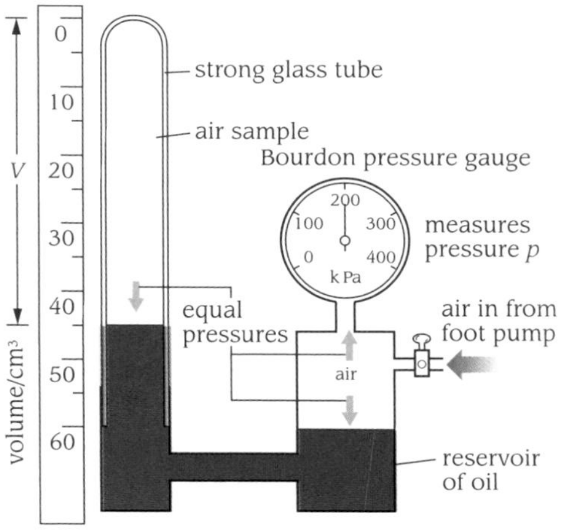

▲ **Figure 8.7.3** Investigating Boyle's law

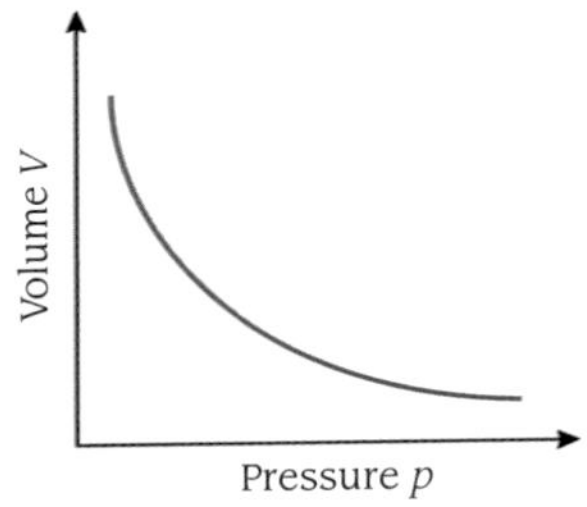

▲ **Figure 8.7.4** A graph of volume V against pressure p

the actual pressure of the air including the atmospheric pressure. So when no air has been pumped into the reservoir the gauge reads about 100 kPa, which is normal atmospheric pressure at sea level.

- Gradually increase the pressure p of the air sample and record several readings for p and the volume V, read from the vertical volume scale. Put your readings in a 4-column table.
- Calculate $p \times V$ and put the values in the third column of your table of results.

We see that as the pressure p increases, the volume V decreases. The values of $p \times V$ are almost constant. These figures suggest that the volume V is *inversely proportional* to the pressure p. If you plot volume against pressure you would get a reciprocal curve (Figure 8.7.4) showing this.

A graph for Boyle's law

- Calculate values of $1/p$ for each of your readings and put these in column 4 of your table.
- Plot a graph of V/cm^3 against $1/p$ (Figure 8.7.5). (Converting p to MPa gives easier values of $1/p$ to plot on the x-axis.)

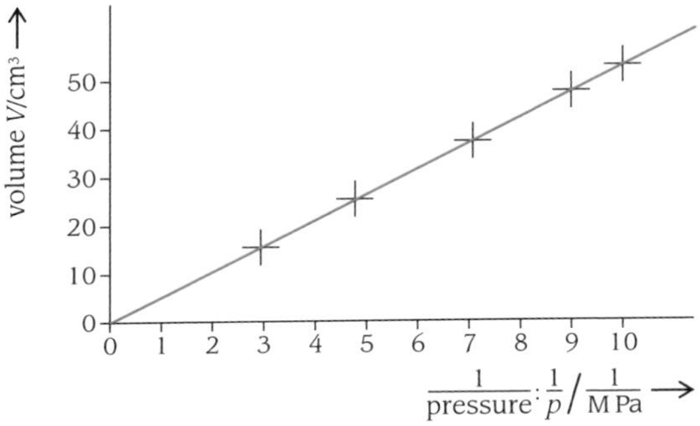

▲ **Figure 8.7.5** A graph for Boyle's law

How do we know that the temperature is kept constant?

Why is the pressure increased gradually and *slowly*?

The straight-line graph through the origin gives us the relationship between V and p.

We see that the volume doubles when $1/p$ doubles, etc. It follows that:

if V is proportional to $1/p$,

V is *inversely* proportional to p.

This relationship is stated as:

Boyle's law

The volume of a fixed mass of gas is inversely proportional to its pressure if the temperature is constant.

$$V \propto \frac{1}{p}$$

$$V = \text{constant} \times \frac{1}{p}$$

$$pV = \text{constant}$$

The pressure law

Heating a gas at constant volume

A third gas law can be investigated by keeping the volume of a fixed mass of gas constant. A gas is heated but not allowed to expand. As a result of the gas molecules hitting the walls of their container with higher speeds, the pressure of the gas increases.

Another apparatus with a Bourdon gauge gives direct readings for both the pressure and temperature of a fixed mass of gas (Figure 8.7.6).

A sample of air (or other gas) is trapped inside a round-bottomed flask, which is connected to a Bourdon pressure gauge. The volume of the gas remains constant at the point where it reaches the gauge, assuming that the volume of the flask itself does not change significantly when the gas is heated.

- Starting with ice-cold water, record the temperature t and the pressure p for a number of temperatures up to the boiling point of the water bath. Tabulate your readings in a table.

Precautions to take to obtain good results:

1 To get accurate values for the temperature of the gas inside the flask, hold the thermometer so that it does not rest on the base of the water bath. Stir the water after heating it a little and allow time for the gas inside the flask to reach the temperature of the surrounding water.

2 Heat the water slowly, as temperatures and pressures that are changing rapidly are less likely to give accurate values.

3 As the volume of gas under test includes all the flask and the connecting tube, the flask should be almost completely immersed in the water bath and the connecting tube should be as short as possible.

4 The flask must be supported to keep its bottom off the heated base of the water bath.

- Plot a graph of pressure p (from the Bourdon gauge) against temperature t (in °C), leaving room for temperatures down to −300 °C (Figure 8.7.7).
- Draw the 'best fit' straight line through the points on the graph and extend the line down to negative Celsius temperatures until the pressure of the gas would have dropped to zero.
- Read from the temperature scale the temperature at which your results predict that the pressure would be zero.

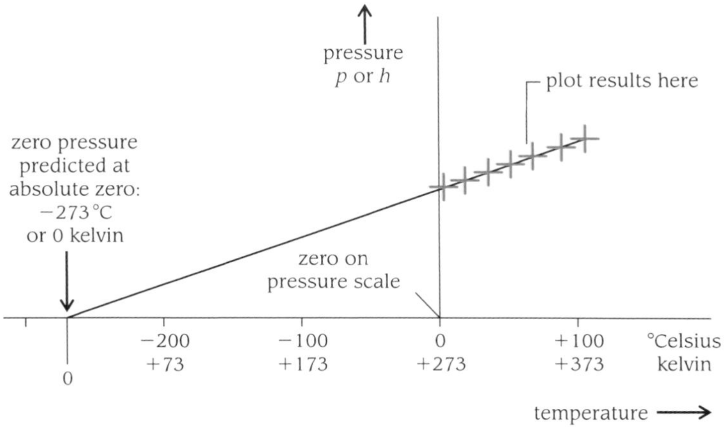

▲ **Figure 8.7.7** A graph for the pressure law

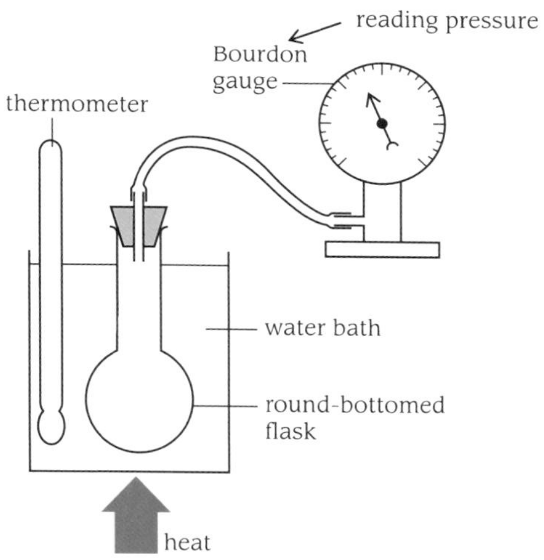

▲ **Figure 8.7.6** Investigating the pressure law

Key fact

The temperature of −273 °C is absolute zero, the lowest temperature that can be reached.

You can think of absolute zero as the temperature at which the gas molecules have stopped moving.

At absolute zero the molecules would no longer hit the walls of their container and therefore give no pressure.

This leads to the definition of the pressure law:

The pressure law

The pressure of a fixed mass of gas is directly proportional to its absolute temperature if its volume is constant.

$$p \propto T$$

$$p = \text{constant} \times T$$

$$\frac{p}{T} = \text{constant}$$

***T* must be given in kelvin.**

The gas equation

We can combine the three relations between p, V and T from the three gas laws into one gas equation. We have:

$$\frac{V}{T} = \text{constant}$$

$$pV = \text{constant}$$

and $\frac{p}{T} = \text{constant}$

Putting these equations together we get:

$$\frac{pV}{T} = \text{constant}$$

which is known as the *gas equation* or *general gas law*.

This equation can be used to solve problems about gas pressures and volumes when all three of the quantities p, V and T change at the same time.

If the initial values are p_1, V_1 and T_1 and after a change in the gas they become p_2, V_2 and T_2, providing the mass of the gas is constant we can write:

$$\frac{p_1 V_1}{T_1} = \frac{p_2 V_2}{T_2}$$

Worked example

Compression of a gas reduces volume and raises temperature.
A bicycle pump holds 60 cm^3 of air when the piston is drawn out. The air is initially at 17 °C and 1.0 atmospheres pressure.
Calculate the pressure of the air as it is forced into the tyre if compression reduces its volume to 15 cm^3 and raises its temperature to 27 °C.

$p_1 = 1.0$ atmospheres
$V_1 = 60\ \text{cm}^3$
$T_1 = 17 + 273 = 290\ \text{K}$

$p_2 = ?$
$V_2 = 15\ \text{cm}^3$
$T_2 = 27 + 273 = 300\ \text{K}$

Rearranging the gas equation gives:

$$p_2 = \frac{p_1 \times V_1 \times T_2}{V_2 \times T_1}$$

$$= \frac{1.0 \times 60 \times 300}{15 \times 290}$$

$$p_2 = 4.1 \text{ atmospheres}$$

Rules for using this formula

a) The mass of gas must be constant.

b) The temperatures T_1 and T_2 must be given in kelvin.

c) The units in which p and V are calculated must be the same on both sides of the equation (but any convenient units such as mm of mercury and cm^3 may be used).

Worked example

In a chemistry experiment, 240 cm^3 of oxygen gas are collected. The temperature of the room is 20 °C and the atmospheric pressure, read on a barometer, is 770 mm of mercury. Calculate the volume of gas at standard temperature and pressure. (Standard temperature is 0 °C = 273 K and standard atmospheric pressure is 760 mm of mercury.)

Listing the data given we have:

$p_1 = 770$ mm of mercury

$p_2 = 760$ mm of mercury

$T_1 = 20 + 273 = 293$ K

$T_2 = 0 + 273 = 273$ K

$V_1 = 240\ cm^3$

$V_2 = ?$

Rearranging the gas equation:

$$V_2 = \frac{V_1 \times p_1 \times T_2}{p_2 \times T_1}$$

$$= \frac{240 \times 770 \times 273}{760 \times 293}$$

$$= 227\ cm^3$$

If you find rearranging this equation difficult you can use it in the form

$$\frac{p_1V_1}{T_1} = \frac{p_2V_2}{T_2}$$

and substitute values first. Then find the unknown quantity, in this example, V_2.

Summary questions

1 Sketch a graph of volume against temperature, showing Charles' law.

2 What does Boyle's law show?

3 Write the gas equation.

4 What units are used for temperature in all the gas laws?

Things to do

Explain:

- When you pump air into a tyre to blow it up, why does the air inside the tyre not obey the gas laws during pumping?
- Why does water vapour sometimes condense on the bathroom windows when you have a shower or a bath?

Practice exam-style questions

1 a) Convert the following temperatures on the Kelvin scale into degrees Celsius:

i) 300 K
ii) 100 K
iii) 473 K?
iv) 263 K

b) Convert the following temperatures on the Celsius scale into kelvin:

i) 1000 °C
ii) 1273 °C
iii) −50 °C
iv) 110 °C

2 a) 'There had for a long time been two theories of heat. The usual one was that it was a sort of matter – tiny material particles that could penetrate through and into bodies: it was in fact listed as a chemical element by Lavoisier and named "caloric"....'
Discuss briefly the chief difficulty with the caloric theory mentioned above.

b) The figure below illustrates the classic experiment carried out by Rumford. Describe this experiment and, from the results of the experiment, present arguments to show that the caloric theory could not be supported.

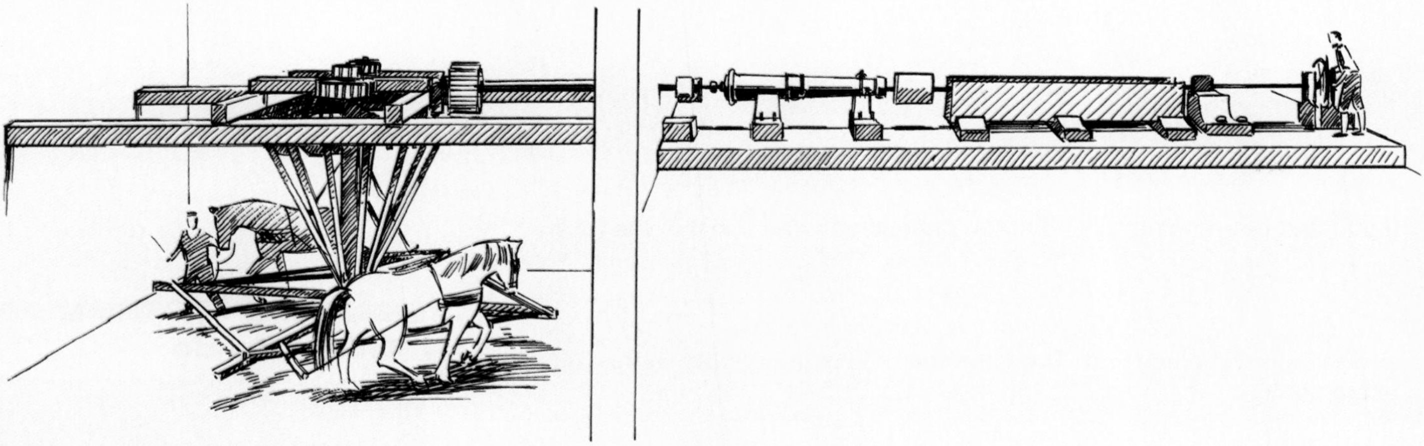

3 a) What are the TWO principal ideas of the kinetic theory of matter?

b) Use the kinetic theory to describe and distinguish between the three phases of matter.

c) The specific latent heat of vaporisation is greater than the specific latent heat of fusion for most substances. Use kinetic theory to explain this in terms of the separation of the particles in each phase.

d) If steam from a kettle is captured in a closed container at 100 °C and then heated, the pressure in the container would be observed to increase. Use kinetic theory to explain this effect.

e) If some copper sulfate crystals are added to a beaker of water, it is found that after some time the entire contents of the beaker become a uniform blue colour.
What is this phenomenon called?
Use the kinetic theory to explain what happens.

4 Explain in terms of the kinetic theory of gases:

a) how the air inside a bicycle tyre keeps the tyre inflated and hard, and is able to support the weight of a cyclist

b) how the pressure in a car tyre increases and the tyres get hot when the car is driven fast.

5 The figure below, which is drawn to scale, shows a mercury-in-glass thermometer with only 0 °C and 100 °C markings shown on it. The capillary tube can be assumed to be uniform.

a) What temperature is the thermometer recording?

b) State ONE advantage of making the bulb of the thermometer of thin glass.

c) State ONE advantage of making the capillary tube very narrow and the thermometer longer.

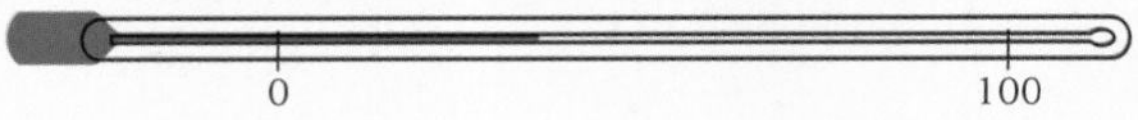

6 Explain why:

a) the glass surrounding the bulb of a thermometer is thin even though this makes it fragile

b) the mercury level inside the capillary tube will not immediately rise to its final steady level when a thermometer is first placed in a warm liquid

c) an alcohol-filled thermometer might be preferred to a mercury-filled one by an Arctic explorer

d) in a clinical thermometer the bulb is not quite full of mercury at room temperature.

7 Two similar cans are partly filled with equal quantities of oil. Each holds a thermometer, is covered by a lid, and stands on a wooden bench at the same distance from a radiant heater. One can has a dull black surface, the other a bright silver surface.

The table shows how the temperature of the oil in each can changed over a 5-minute period.

Time/minutes	0	1	2	3	4	5
Temperature dull black can/°C	20	22	24	26	28	30
Temperature bright silver can/°C	20	21	22	23	24	25

a) Why can we say that the cans are not heated by conduction?

b) Why can we say that the cans are not heated by convection?

c) By what process are the cans heated?

d) Explain the different rates of temperature rise of the two cans.

e) Explain why it was better to use oil rather than water in the cans.

8 The figure below shows the metal shade and bulb of an electric table lamp.

Redraw the diagram and add arrows to indicate the convection currents in the air inside the shade when the bulb of the lamp is hot.

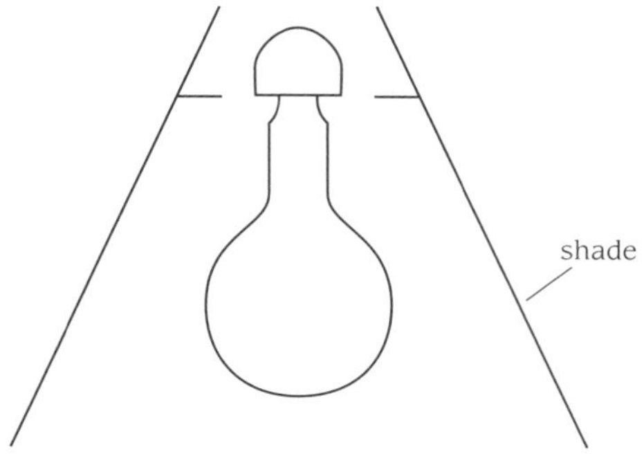

9 Describe an experiment that you would carry out to compare how the nature of TWO different surfaces affects the rate at which heat is radiated from them.

How would you show that the surface that was the better emitter of radiation was also the better absorber?

10 A lump of ice, wrapped in a piece of copper gauze, is weighted down in a test tube of water (see figure below).

Explain how it is possible for the water to be heated to boiling point at the top of the tube without the ice melting.

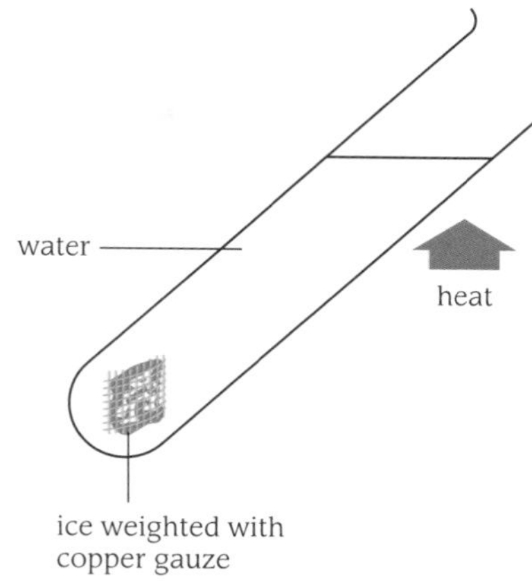

11 The figure below shows an electric hotplate used to heat a saucepan containing water.

a) By what process is heat transferred through the saucepan to the water?

b) Describe how a convection current is set up in the water.

c) Explain any advantages or disadvantages of keeping the saucepan highly polished.

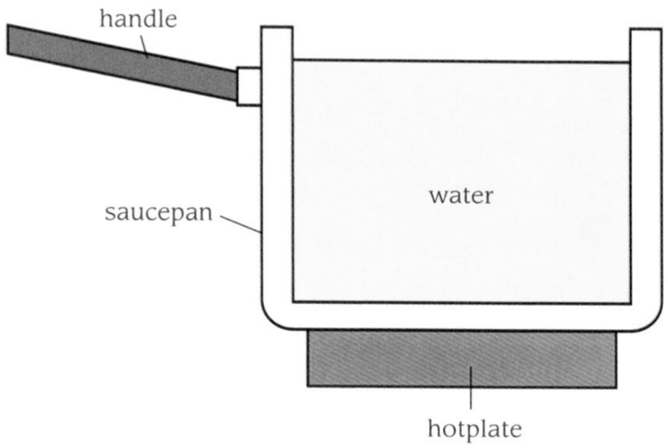

12 Explain why:

a) the cooling pipes inside a refrigerator are placed near the top of the cabinet

b) the handles on cooking pans are usually made of wood or plastic

c) heat energy from the Sun can reach us only as infrared radiation and not by conduction or convection.

13 The figure below shows a cross-section of a vacuum flask with an enlarged view of part of the side wall shown in the circle.

a) What is the material of items A and C?

b) What types of transfer of heat energy are reduced or prevented by the items B, C and D?

c) How does surface A reduce heat transfer?

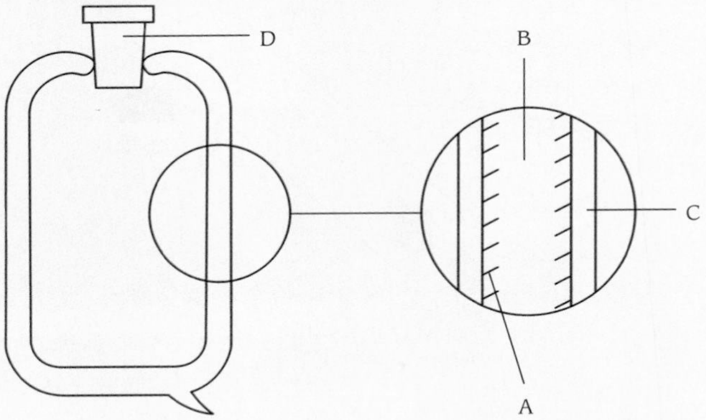

14 a) A glass stopper is jammed inside the glass neck of a bottle. Explain why running hot water over the bottle neck may help to loosen the stopper.

b) Explain why a glass bottle is likely to crack if very hot water is poured inside it when the glass is cold.

15 The figure below shows a device that switches off a domestic appliance when it reaches a desired temperature.

a) What is this device called?

b) Name TWO domestic appliances that make use of this device.

c) What electrical property must material Z possess?

d) What materials could be used for X and Y?

e) Explain why bending occurs when the device is heated.

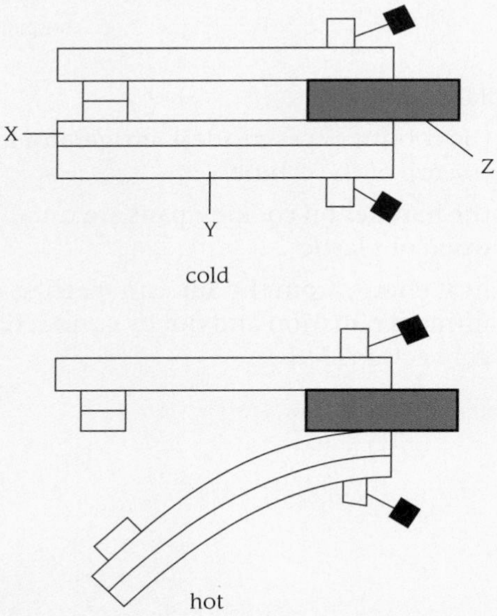

16 The figure below illustrates an experiment in which a measured quantity of electrical energy is used to produce a measured rise in temperature of a liquid.

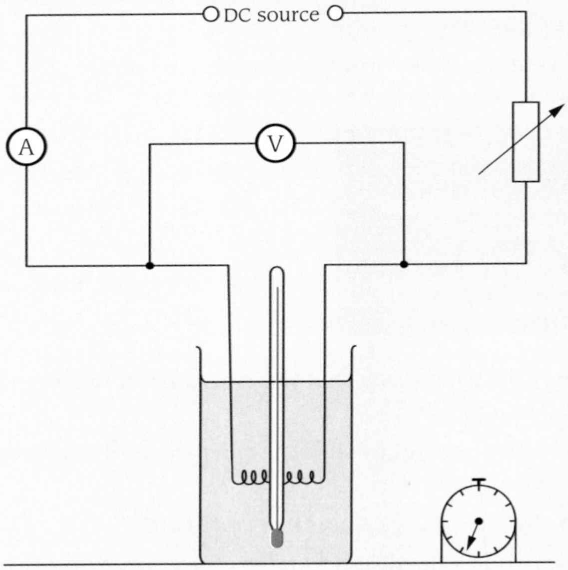

a) The liquid will tend to be warmer at the top of the container than at the bottom. Explain why and state what action should be taken to prevent this happening.

b) Explain why the rate of rise of temperature would be increased if the container were:

i) lagged with glass fibre

ii) covered with a lid.

c) When this apparatus is used to determine the specific heat capacity of the liquid, the accuracy of the experiment can be increased if the liquid is first cooled to about 5 K below room temperature and the current passed until the temperature is about 5 K above room temperature. Explain why.

d) In the apparatus shown above, the heater supplies $40\,J\,s^{-1}$ to a liquid of mass 0.6 kg and specific heat capacity $4200\,J\,kg^{-1}\,K^{-1}$. Calculate the rate of rise of temperature:

i) in kelvin per second

ii) in kelvin per minute.

17 A 12 W electric heater, working at its stated power, is found to heat 0.02 kg of water from 15 °C to 30 °C in 2 minutes.

a) Calculate:

i) the heat energy produced by the heater in 2 minutes

ii) the heat energy absorbed by the water in 2 minutes.

b) Account for the difference in the answers to part **i** and part **ii**.
(Assume that the specific heat capacity of water is $4200\,J\,kg^{-1}\,K^{-1}$.)

18 A waterfall is 210 m high. The temperature of the water at the top is 10.0 °C and the temperature of the water at the bottom is 10.5 °C.

Calculate the specific heat capacity of water.

State any assumption you have made regarding energy in your calculation.
($g = 10\,\text{N kg}^{-1}$)

19 A heater supplying energy at a constant rate of 500 W is completely immersed in a large block of ice at 0 °C. In 22 minutes, 2.0 kg of water at 0 °C is produced.

Calculate a value for the specific latent heat of fusion of ice.

20 A 100 W heating coil is totally immersed in 200 g of water contained in an insulated flask of negligible heat capacity.

a) If the temperature of the water is 20 °C when the heater is switched on, how long would it take for the water to boil?

b) After the water has been boiling for 7.5 minutes, it is found that the mass of water in the flask has decreased to 180 g. Assuming no external heat losses, calculate a value for the specific latent heat of vaporisation of water.
(Assume that the specific heat capacity of water = $4200\,\text{J kg}^{-1}\,\text{K}^{-1}$.)

21 A pressure cooker with a weight on the needle valve is heated until the water boils.

a) Is the temperature of the water greater than, less than or equal to 100 °C?

b) If the needle valve sticks, what will happen?

c) A climbing expedition to Mount Everest finds that a pressure cooker is essential to cook its food effectively. Explain why this is so.

22 Explain why a bubble of air increases in volume as it rises from the bottom of a pond to the surface. If the volume as it just reaches the surface is double that at the bottom of the pond, estimate the depth of the pond. Assume that the water temperature is uniform.
The pressure at the water surface = 10^5 Pa.
The density of water = $1000\,\text{kg m}^{-3}$.

23 A vessel of fixed volume contains gas at a temperature of 300 K.

a) What would happen to the pressure if the temperature were increased to 600 K?

b) How would you account for this change in pressure in terms of the kinetic theory?

24 The results shown in the table below were obtained in an experiment to verify Boyle's law.

Presuure/kN m^{-2}	800	640	320	160
Volume/mm^3	2.0	2.5	5.0	10.0
$\frac{1}{\text{volume}}$/mm^{-3}	0.5			

a) Copy the table and complete it.

b) Plot a graph of pressure on the y-axis against 1/volume on the x-axis.

c) State the relationship that this graph shows between pressure and volume.

d) From your graph, calculate the volume when the pressure was $480\,\text{kN m}^{-2}$.

e) State which TWO physical properties of the gas were kept constant.

25 a) Explain what is meant by the absolute zero of temperature. Describe a simple experiment that you could perform in your school laboratory, which would allow you to estimate the value of absolute zero on the Celsius scale of temperature. Sketch the apparatus that you would use, list the observations you would make and show how these observations would be used to arrive at the final result. What result would you expect?

b) A car tyre contains a fixed mass of air. The pressure of the air was measured as $200\,\text{kN m}^{-2}$ above atmospheric pressure when the air temperature was 17 °C. After a high-speed run, the air pressure in the tyre was measured again and was found to be $230\,\text{kN m}^{-2}$ above atmospheric pressure. What was the new temperature of the air in the tyre if its volume remained constant?
(Atmospheric pressure = $100\,\text{kN m}^{-2}$.)

C9 Light rays

Objectives

By the end of topics C9.1–C9.5 you will be able to:

- recall evidence and demonstrate that light travels in straight lines
- describe, using ray diagrams, how shadows and eclipses are formed
- state the laws of reflection and use them to solve problems
- perform experiments to show that the angles of incidence and reflection are equal
- describe images seen in a plane mirror and construct ray diagrams to explain the formation of virtual images
- locate virtual images using both ray plotting and no parallax methods.

Key fact

Shadow properties, using a point source

- The shadow is uniformly and totally dark all over. It is called the umbra, a Latin word meaning shade.
- The shadow has a sharp outline, supporting the idea that light travels only in straight lines.

Shadow properties, using an extended source

- The centre of the shadow remains uniformly dark as before but is somewhat smaller in size. This part of the shadow, the umbra, still receives no light at all from the source.
- The edge of the shadow is now blurred and graded, getting gradually lighter further out from the umbra.

Early in the day when the Sun is low on the horizon and shadows are long, the sunlight streaming through a group of trees is broken into straight beams or rays of light. When sunlight breaks through the clouds after a storm the light rays can be seen clearly against the dark background of the clouds. The beams of light from the headlamps of a car can be seen as they shine out through a heavy rainstorm or fog. Many natural effects of light have not only inspired us by their beauty but have also helped us to understand light.

C9.1 Light rays travel in straight lines

Rays and shadows

A ray of light is a narrow beam of parallel light which can be drawn as a single line on a diagram. In diagrams, rays are drawn with an arrow on them showing the direction of travel of the light. Rays are produced when light shines through a small hole, which we call a point source of light. A beam of light containing many rays is produced by a larger aperture or large lamp, which we call an **extended source** of light.

Demonstrating that light travels in straight lines

- Make a single small hole in each of three screens at exactly the same height above the bench.
- Set the three holes exactly in line by threading a length of cotton or string through the holes and pulling it tight.
- Carefully remove the thread without disturbing the screens and position a lamp so that it can be seen through the three holes.

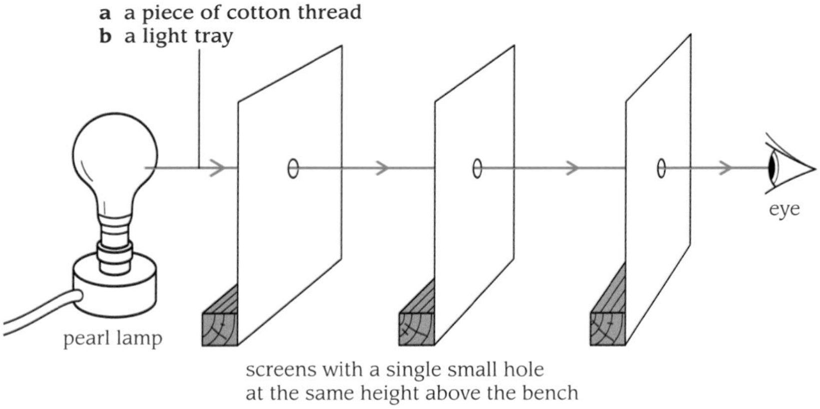

▲ **Figure 9.1.1** Light travels in straight lines

If any one of the screens is moved very slightly then the eye cannot see the lamp. This shows that light can only travel in a straight line. The property of light travelling in straight lines is called **rectilinear propagation** (literally, 'straight-line travel'). Note that the ray of light travels from the lamp to the eye as indicated by the arrows; rays do not come out of the eye.

Pin-hole cameras

The simplest type of camera is a pin-hole camera, with no lens, just a very small pin-hole and a screen. Light travels in a straight line from each point on the object, through the pin-hole to the corresponding point on the image. The smaller the pin-hole the sharper the image will be.

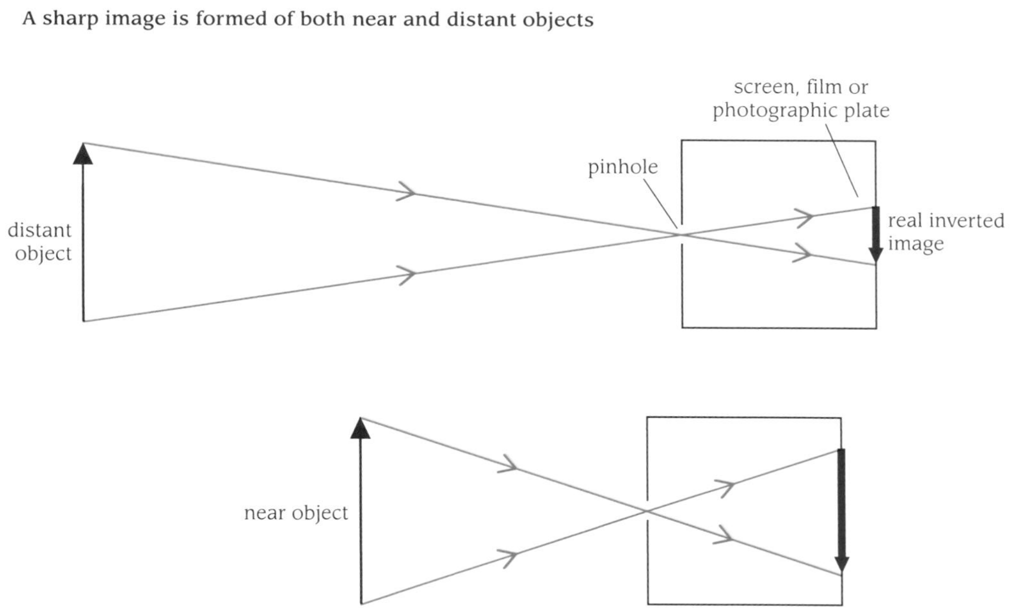

▲ **Figure 9.1.2** The pin-hole camera

Shadows

One direct effect of light travelling in straight lines is the casting of shadows by opaque objects.

The shadow formed by a point source of light

A point source of light is one that is small enough for all the rays of light to come effectively from a single point. A small hole in a screen placed in front of a lamp acts as a point source.

- Hold a circular opaque object like a small ball fairly close to a white screen as shown in Figure 9.1.3a and describe its shadow.

The shadow formed by an extended source of light

An extended source of light is large enough for rays to be seen to come from many points. The large pearl lamp shown in Figure 9.1.3b provides a suitable extended source.

- Using the arrangement shown in Figure 9.1.3b, describe the shadow and note the differences between it and the one cast by a point source of light.

! Key fact

The penumbra

Penumbra means partial shade.

- With an extended source of light we get a penumbra. This is the fading grey region between the totally dark umbra and the fully bright screen.
- In the penumbra, light from some parts of the extended source reaches the screen, but light from other parts is cut off by the opaque object.
- Shadows formed by extended light sources are much softer without sharp edges.

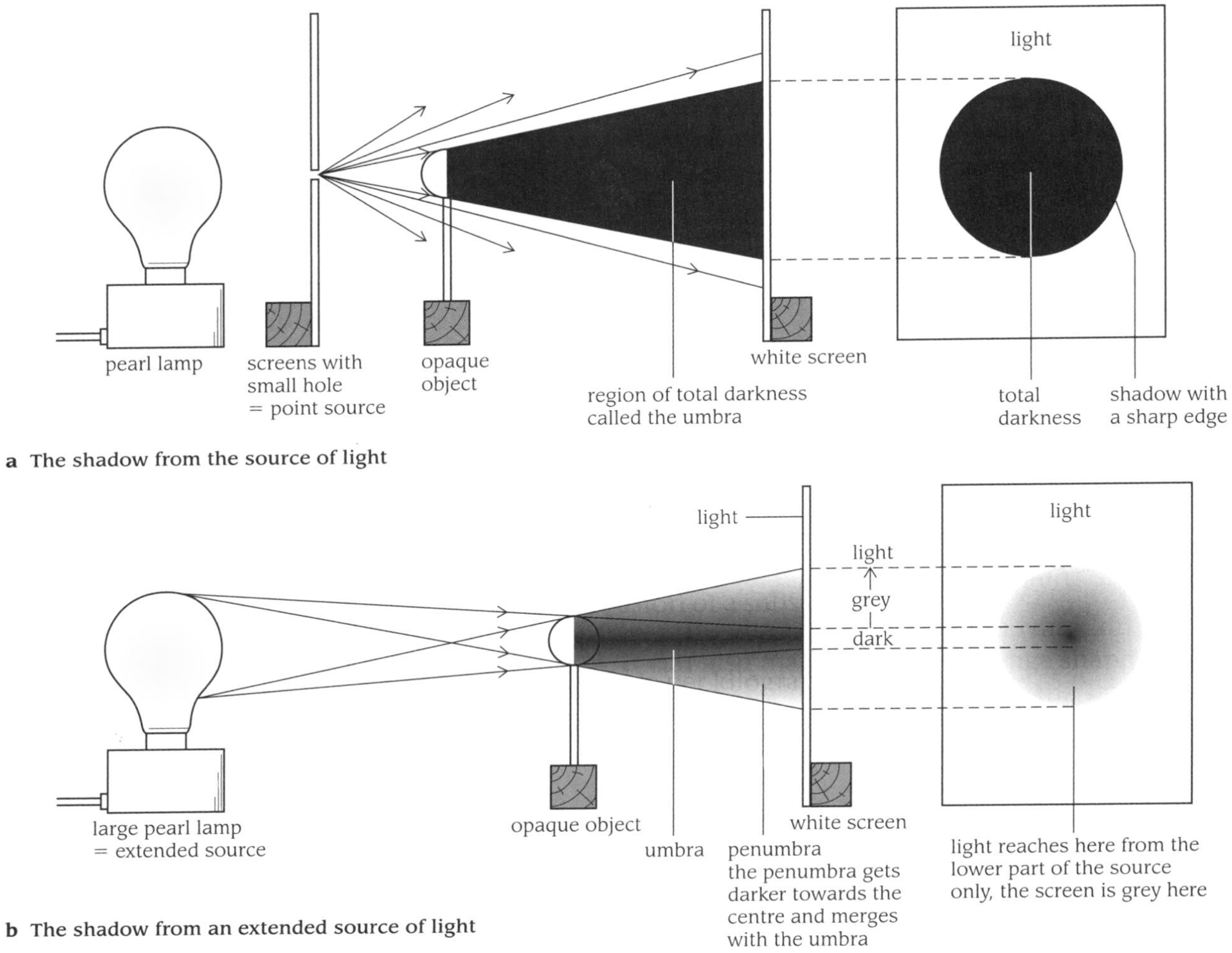

▲ **Figure 9.1.3** Shadows

Summary questions

1. How do shadows demonstrate that light travels in straight lines?
2. What are the properties of a shadow formed by a point source of light?
3. What are the properties of a shadow formed by an extended source?

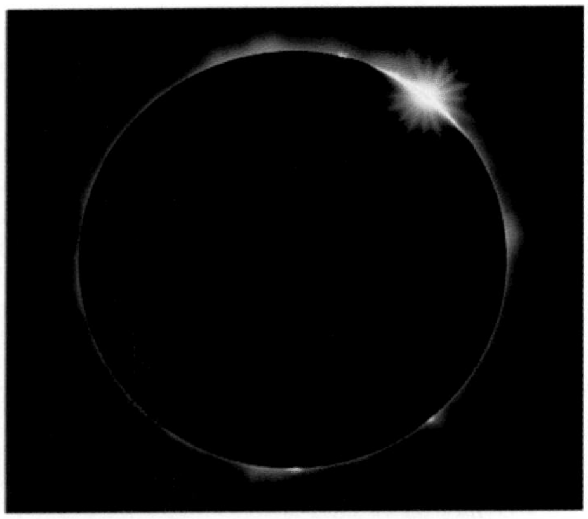

▲ **Figure 9.2.1** In this photograph of a total eclipse of the Sun, the Moon's dark disc just covers the Sun's full bright disc leaving a ring of light from the Sun's corona.

C9.2 Eclipses

An eclipse is the total or partial disappearance of the Sun or Moon as seen from the Earth. Eclipses are explained in terms of the motions of the Earth and Moon and the shadow that one casts on the other.

The solar eclipse or eclipse of the Sun

Records of solar eclipses have been kept since the time of the ancient Chinese who were afraid of them, thinking that a dragon was trying to devour the Sun. The philosophers of ancient Greece understood that the Moon was responsible for eclipses of the Sun and were even able to predict a solar eclipse. In 1543, Copernicus started a revolution of thought and understanding when he published a book in which he suggested that only the Moon went round the Earth and that the Earth, like all the other planets, went round the

Sun. Until this idea of the motion of the Earth and Moon was accepted it was impossible to explain fully how the different types of eclipses happened.

Key fact

Why are solar eclipses rare?

- A solar eclipse can happen only at new moon (when the Moon is totally dark). If the orbit of the Moon lay in the same plane as that of the Earth there would be an eclipse every month. The Moon's orbit is, however, inclined at an angle of about 5° to the Earth's orbit so that only rarely does the new moon pass exactly through the line joining the Earth and the Sun, producing a solar eclipse.
- When a solar eclipse does occur, the path of the Moon's umbra across the surface of the Earth is very narrow, (never wider than 272 km) so that most people on the Earth see only a partial eclipse.

We now know that the Sun is eclipsed when the Moon passes between the Sun and the Earth. When it happens it causes unexpected darkness during the daytime (Figure 9.2.2a).

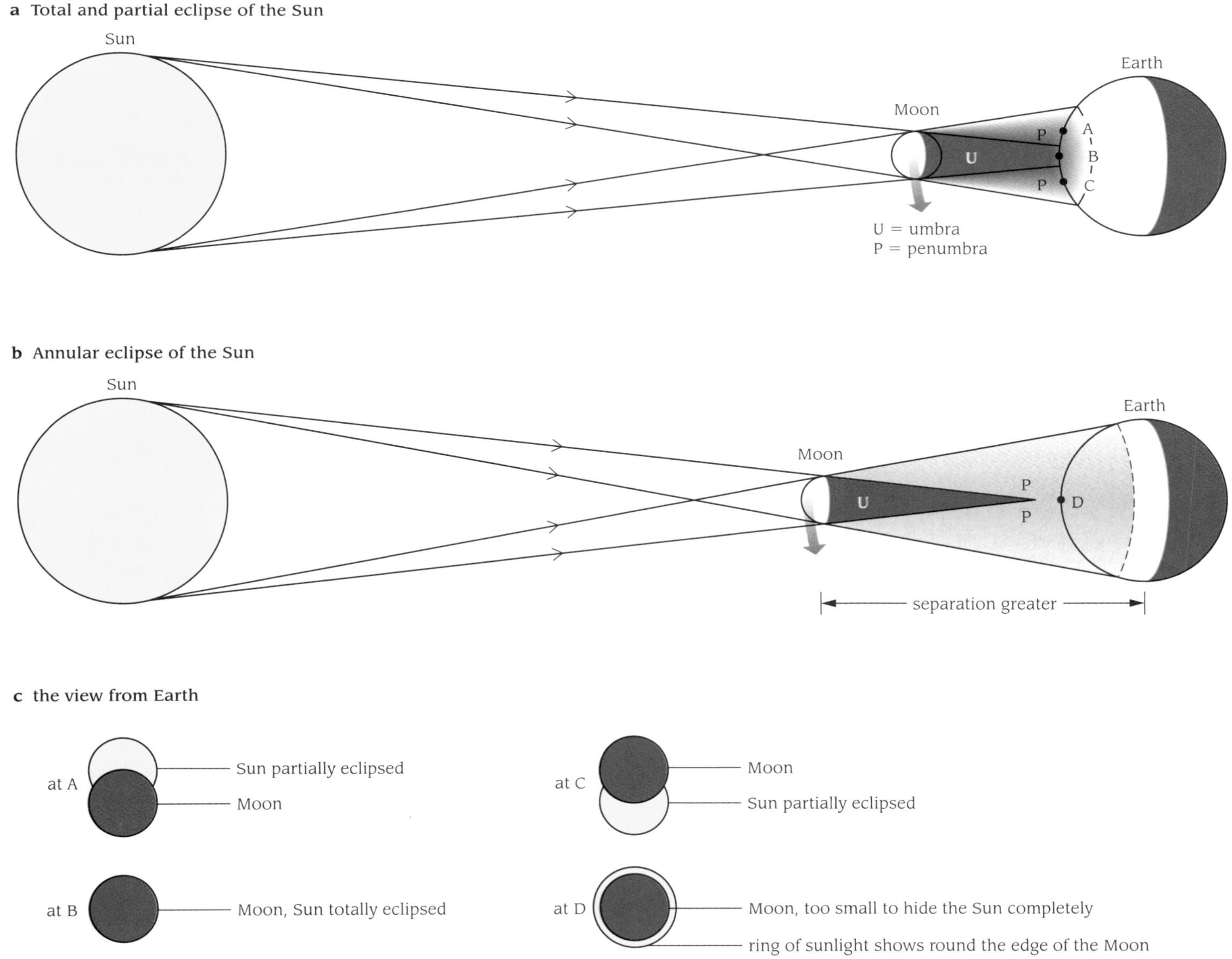

▲ **Figure 9.2.2** Eclipses of the Sun (diagrams not to scale)

The photograph in Figure 9.2.1 shows the view from position B in a total eclipse. This magnificent sight, which can never last for more than about 8 minutes, allows us to see the Sun's atmosphere, which is normally not visible because of the brightness of the Sun's disc itself. Red prominences and the pearly corona, which rings the circumference of the Moon, can be seen at the same time as stars in the sky.

An annular eclipse of the Sun

Sometimes the umbra of the Moon is not quite long enough to reach the Earth because the distance between the Moon and the Earth varies (the Moon's orbit is elliptical). When the Moon is further from the Earth its disc is very slightly smaller than the Sun's disc, so when a solar eclipse occurs the Moon is not large enough to totally cover the Sun. A bright ring of sunlight can be seen around the edge of the dark disc of the Moon. An annular or ring eclipse is a solar eclipse in which this bright ring can be seen around the Moon's disc, as shown in Figure 9.2.2b.

The lunar eclipse or eclipse of the Moon

The Moon does not emit light itself, but only reflects light from the Sun; thus when it passes into the Earth's shadow its supply of direct sunlight is cut off. A lunar eclipse occurs when the Moon passes through the Earth's umbra, but it only happens occasionally when the Moon is full. Lunar eclipses can last as long as $1\frac{3}{4}$ hours because the Moon is much smaller than the Earth and takes some time to pass through the Earth's umbra. During a total lunar eclipse it is still just possible to see the Moon because a small amount of sunlight reaches it by way of the Earth's atmosphere. This sunlight, bent or refracted by the Earth's atmosphere, reaches the Moon, turning it a dim coppery colour.

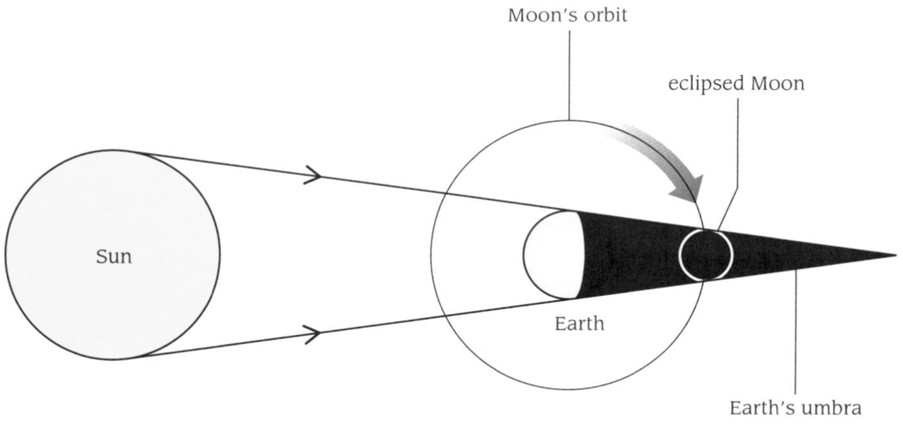

▲ **Figure 9.2.3** Eclipse of the Moon (not to scale)

Things to do

Find out:

- When was a total eclipse of the Sun last visible in the Caribbean?
- When is the next total eclipse of the Sun expected in the Caribbean?
- How long does it take the Moon to orbit the Earth once?
- Why does a lunar eclipse not occur every month?
- Why are the lunar eclipses more common than solar eclipses?
- If the ray diagrams of the solar eclipses were drawn to scale and the Sun was drawn the same size, how far away should the Earth be drawn?

Summary questions

1 Draw the positions of Sun, Earth and Moon in a lunar eclipse.

2 Draw the positions of Sun, Earth and Moon in a solar eclipse.

3 During a solar eclipse, what would people in the penumbra see?

C9.3 Reflection

Specular and diffuse reflection of light

Most things can only be seen when light bounces off the surface of the object and reaches our eyes. We call this bouncing of light **reflection**. An object that reflects no light appears a dull black colour and is difficult to see. An object that reflects all light appears the same colour as the light it is reflecting, so when white sunlight shines on it, its colour is white.

A white sheet of paper and a highly polished silvery metal surface as on a mirror both reflect all the light that falls on them; why then do they appear so different?

The difference is due to the nature of the surfaces of the materials.

- The surface of a polished sheet of metal or a mirror is very smooth and reflects all the parallel rays of light from a particular source in one direction only; this is called regular or **specular** reflection (Figure 9.3.1).
- The irregular scattering of the light rays in different directions by a rough surface such as a sheet of paper is called **diffuse** reflection (Figure 9.3.2).

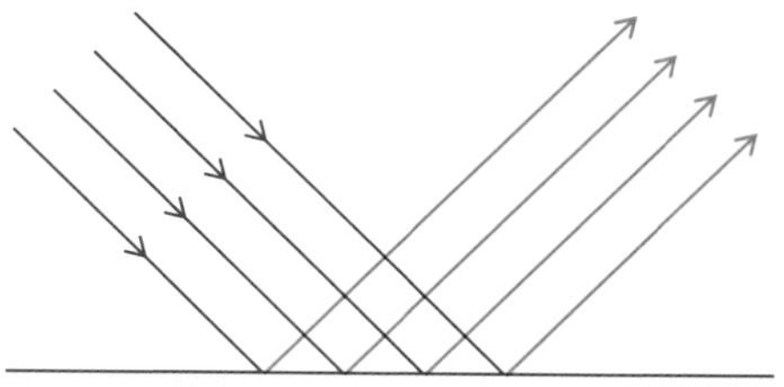
parallel rays from a light source
mirror or polished surface
• regular reflection or specular reflection
• all parallel rays are reflected in the same direction
• mirror-like surfaces form images

▲ **Figure 9.3.1** Regular or specular reflection

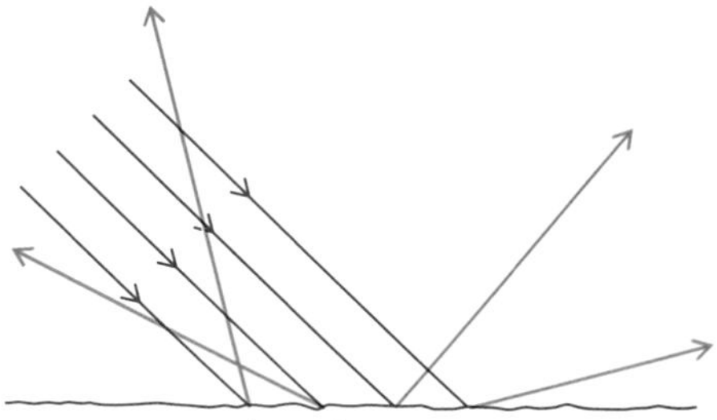
rough surface like paper
• irregular reflection or diffuse reflection
• all parallel rays are randomly reflected in different directions
• matt or rough surfaces scatter or diffuse light

▲ **Figure 9.3.2** Diffuse reflection

Reflection by a plane mirror

A plane mirror is a flat smooth reflecting surface which, by regular reflection, is used to form images. It is often made by bonding a thin polished metal surface to the back of a flat sheet of glass. In diagrams, the silvered side of a mirror is shown by the shading behind the reflecting surface. When using a glass plane mirror in an experiment the silvered surface should be placed on the reflecting line drawn for the experiment. In many ray diagrams, the glass of a mirror is not shown.

Investigating the laws of reflection using light rays

The laws of reflection are true for all reflecting surfaces, for curved mirrors as well as plane mirrors. If a darkened room is available the reflection of light is most easily studied using a ray box and plane mirror arranged on a sheet of paper as shown in Figure 9.3.3. (A ray box is an arrangement of a lamp and a single slit and usually a cylindrical converging lens. By adjusting the distance between the lamp and the lens a thin parallel ray of light may be produced.)

- First draw a reflecting line XMY on the paper and then, using a protractor, another line MN at right angles to the first.
- Using a protractor, measure and mark several angles of incidence on the paper.
- Stand a plane mirror upright with its reflecting surface on the line XMY and then shine the ray of light along each of the directions in turn, being careful to see that each time the ray strikes the mirror at M.
- Mark the direction of each of the reflected rays.
- Draw in the reflected rays and measure the angles of reflection, recording these in a table. Typical results are shown in the table.

The normal, MN is drawn at right angles to the mirror where the incident ray strikes it.

The incident ray is the ray striking the mirror. It must be carefully directed at the point M. We say that the line MN is the normal *at the point of incidence.*

The angle of incidence, *i*, is the angle between the incident ray and the normal.

The angle of reflection, *r*, is the angle between the normal and the reflected ray.

▼ Investigating the laws of reflection using light rays

Angle of incidence *i*/degree	Angle of reflection *r*/degree
0	0
15	14
30	32
45	44
60	60
75	72

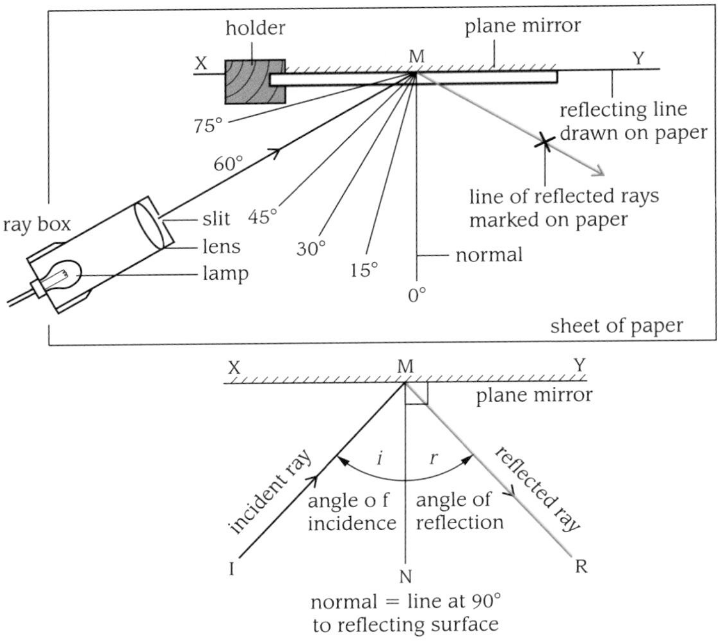

▲ **Figure 9.3.3** Experiment to measure the angles of incidence and reflection

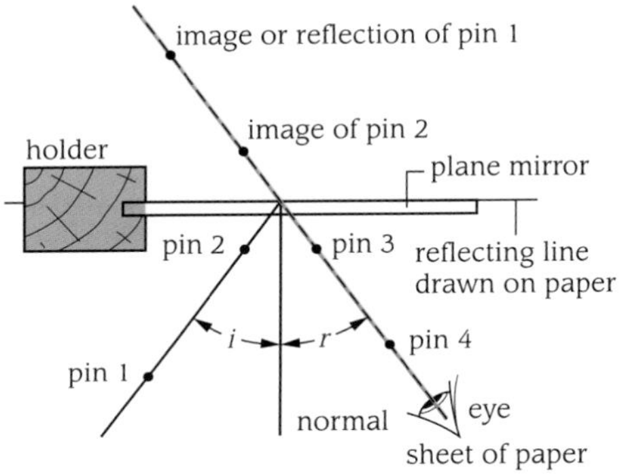

▲ **Figure 9.3.4** Using the pin method

Investigating the laws of reflection using pins

- Fasten a sheet of paper to a drawing board or flat surface into which pins can be pressed easily.
- Mark the reflecting line and normal on the paper.
- Draw an incident ray at 30° to the normal, (i = 30°).
- Press pins 1 and 2 into the paper at the positions shown.
- Stand the mirror upright on the reflecting line.
- With your eye at bench level, look into the mirror and find a position where the image of pin 2 covers the image of pin 1. Now press in first pin 3 and then pin 4 so that they each in turn cover the images of pins 1 and 2.

Now pins 3 and 4 will be in line with the images of pins 1 and 2.

- Draw the reflected ray through pins 3 and 4.
- Measure the angle of reflection r.
- Repeat the experiment for other angles of incidence.

The laws of reflection

- **The angle of incidence equals the angle of reflection.**
- **The incident ray, the reflected ray and the normal at the point of incidence all lie in the same plane.**

The second law means in effect that the rays can all be drawn on a flat sheet of paper.

! Key fact

The incident ray, the reflected ray and the normal at the point of incidence all lie in the same plane.

A plane is a flat sheet, like an uncreased or uncurved sheet of paper. Because the incident ray, the reflected ray and the normal are in the same plane, they can all be drawn on the same sheet of paper. In your experiments, replace the sheet of paper on the bench with a sheet of white card. Try moving the card, the incident ray and the mirror to see for yourself how the rays stay in the same plane as each other.

Summary questions

1 State the laws of reflection.

2 What is diffuse reflection?

3 Describe briefly an experiment to investigate reflection from a plane mirror.

C9.4 Images

Finding the image in a plane mirror

A fairly accurate method of finding the position of an image in a plane mirror is to use pins to mark the direction of two or more rays of light from an object, which reach the eye after reflection by the mirror. Figure 9.4.1 shows an arrangement that can be used to find the image I of the object pin O.

- Fasten a sheet of paper on a drawing board into which pins can easily be pressed.
- Mark the reflecting line on the paper, and stand the reflecting surface of a plane mirror upright on the line.
- Press an object pin O into the board and mark its position.
- With one eye, view the image I of this pin, then place a sighting pin P_1 exactly in line with the image I and your eye so that the image is covered up.
- With your eye in the same position place a second sighting pin P_2 so that it covers up both the object pin's image I and P_1.

The image I is now known to lie in line with P_1 and P_2.

- Mark these pin positions and remove the pins.
- Now view the image I from a different position and repeat the process using sighting pins P_3 and P_4.

As the image also lies on a line drawn through P_3 and P_4, it will always be found where the two lines cross.

- Remove the pins and mirror, draw the lines through P_1P_2 and P_3P_4 and also the line joining the object O and image I.
- What do you notice about the positions of the object and image?

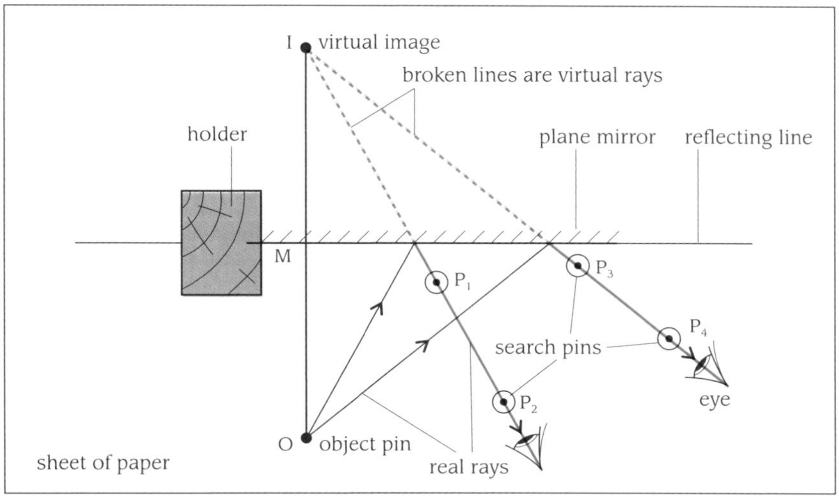

▲ **Figure 9.4.1** Finding the position of the image formed by a plane mirror

Measurements from this experiment show that

- OM = IM The object and image are the same distance from the mirror.
- IMO is at right angles to the mirror.

Virtual images are those from which rays of light only appear to come but no real rays ever reach.

Real images are formed when all the rays coming from a point on an object are brought together again at another single point and can be formed on a screen or photographic film/image sensor.

Real and virtual

Light actually travels from the object pin O to the eye via the mirror, so this is called a **real** ray of light and it is shown as a solid line with an arrow.

Our eyes are easily fooled and cling to the belief that light travels in straight lines. In this case, the eye believes that light has come from the image I, but in fact we know that there is nothing behind the mirror at all and light cannot pass through the reflecting surface of the mirror.

The imaginary rays behind the mirror are called virtual rays and to distinguish them from real rays we shall always draw them as broken lines.

Virtual images

The image formed by a plane mirror is called a **virtual image** because it is formed where the virtual rays appear to come from when the real rays are reflected by the mirror.

Just as the virtual rays are not there, the virtual image does not exist either; it is an illusion.

No light ever reaches a virtual image so it cannot be formed on a screen and it cannot affect photographic film/image sensor placed at its apparent position.

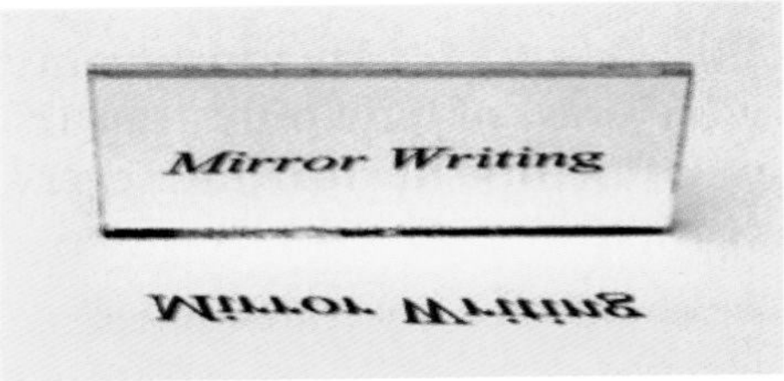

▲ **Figure 9.4.2** The image in this plane mirror shows laterally inverted writing.

Lateral inversion

You may have noticed that sometimes the writing on the front of a police car or ambulance is written backwards. This is so that when it is seen through the rear-view mirror of a vehicle in front, the writing will appear normal. The image formed by a plane mirror has left and right reversed as shown in the photograph; this is called lateral inversion. The image you see of yourself in a plane mirror is always different from the way everyone else sees you. A parting in your hair, which you see on one side of your head is seen by everyone else on the other side. Compare a photograph of yourself with your image in a mirror.

Key fact

Describing images

To describe an image answer the following questions:

1. Is it real or virtual?
2. Is it inverted in any way?
3. How does its size compare with the object?
4. Where is it?

The image formed by a plane mirror is:

1. virtual (meaning imaginary)
2. erect (meaning the right way up) but laterally inverted
3. the same size as the object
4. as far behind the mirror as the object is in front, and the line joining the object and image is normal to the mirror.

Worked example

The angle between an incident ray and a plane mirror is 25°. Calculate:

a) the angle of incidence, **b)** the angle of reflection, **c)** the angle turned through by the ray of light.

Referring to Figure 9.4.3 we can see that:

a) the angle of incidence $i = 90° - 25° = 65°$

b) the angle of reflection = the angle of incidence = 65°

c) the angle the ray is turned through = $180° - (65° + 65°) = 50°$.

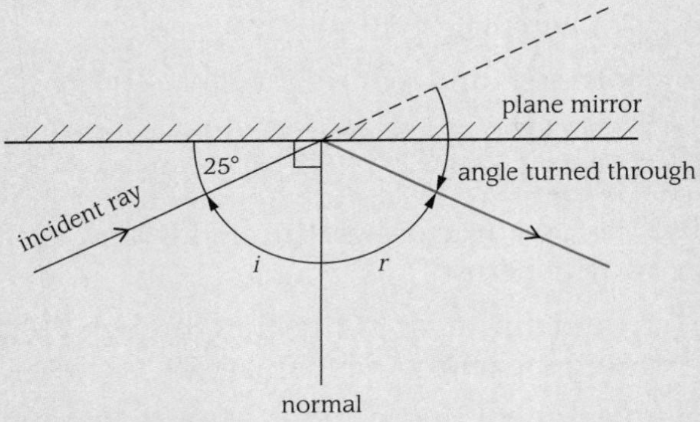

▲ **Figure 9.4.3**

The periscope

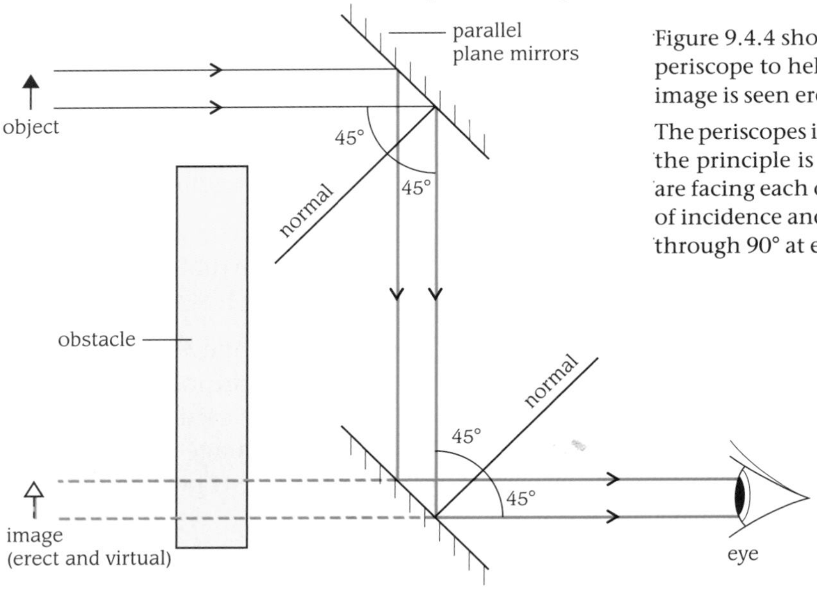

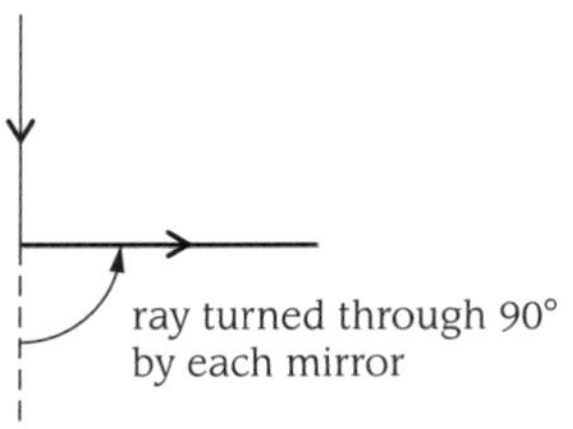

▲ **Figure 9.4.4** Ray diagram for a periscope

Figure 9.4.4 shows how two plane mirrors are used in a simple periscope to help a person see over an obstacle. Note that the image is seen erect, but will it be laterally inverted?

The periscopes in submarines use prisms instead of mirrors but the principle is the same. In each case the reflecting surfaces are facing each other and are parallel but set so that the angles of incidence and reflection will be 45°, turning the ray of light through 90° at each mirror.

Summary questions

1 Describe the image formed by a plane mirror.
2 What is lateral inversion?
3 Draw a diagram of a periscope.

C9.5 Uses of mirrors

Uses of plane mirrors

The laser

LASER is an acronym for Light Amplification by the Stimulated Emission of Radiation.

Light reflects backwards and forwards through a crystal or gas that amplifies the light each time it passes. A laser gives a narrow beam of very intense light that is very useful, but can also be dangerous. Lasers are used in surgery because they can be used to make very small, very accurate cuts.

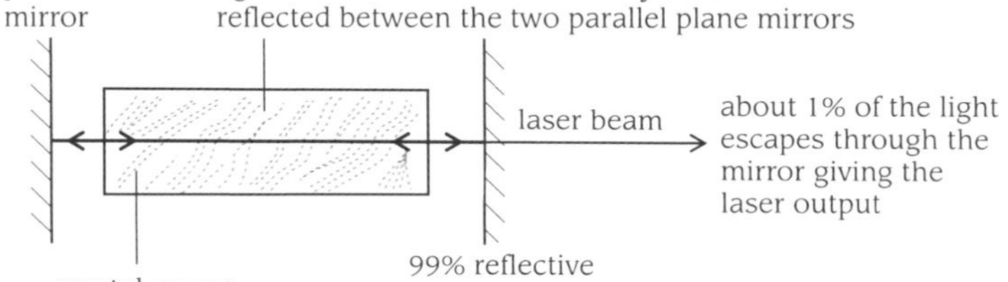

▲ **Figure 9.5.1** How a laser works

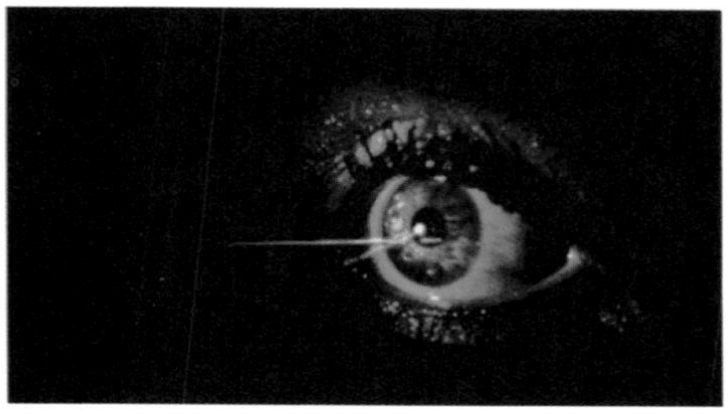

▲ **Figure 9.5.2** This photograph shows a red laser being used for an eye operation. The laser light is fed along a flexible optical fibre and is directed with great precision at exact positions in the eye. This procedure can be used to join the retina to the back of the eye when it has become detached. The process effectively 'welds' the retina to the tissue behind by burning it. As the injury heals, the tissues remain joined together.

The kaleidoscope

Two plane mirrors placed at an angle of less than 180° will produce multiple images. The smaller the angle the more images there will be. A kaleidoscope usually has mirrors at 60° to produce a symmetrical pattern of six views of an object.

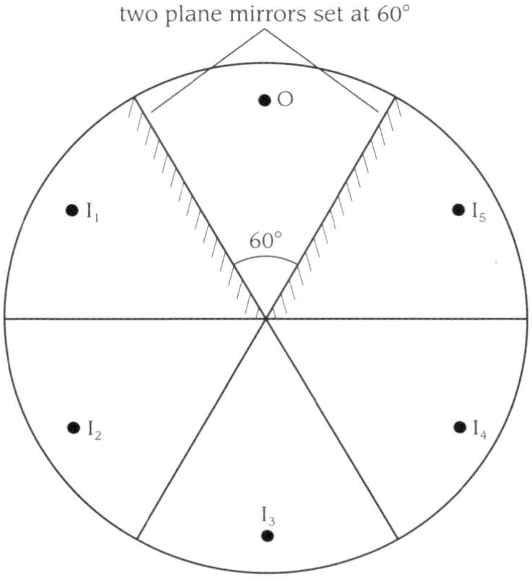

▲ **Figure 9.5.3** How a kaleidoscope works

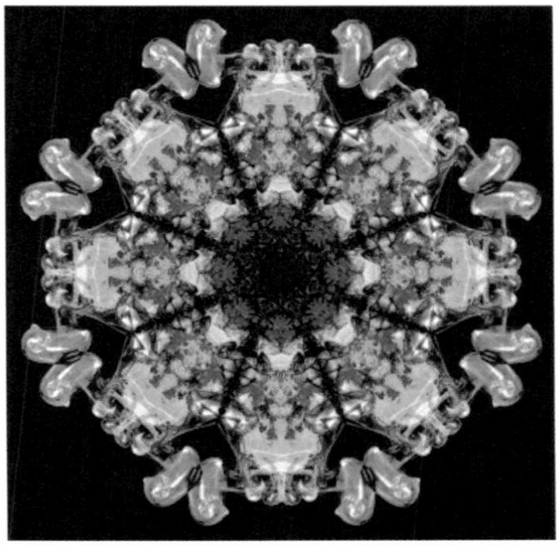

▲ **Figure 9.5.4** The image formed in a kaleidoscope is produced by multiple reflections from two plane mirrors usually set at 60° to each other.

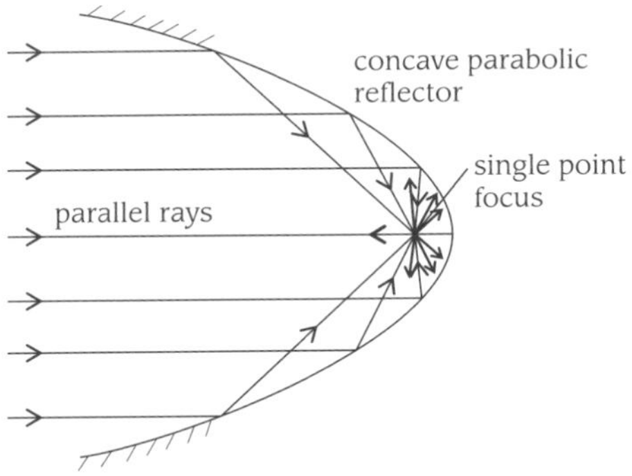

▲ **Figure 9.5.5** A concave parabolic mirror has a true point focus for all rays parallel to its principal axis.

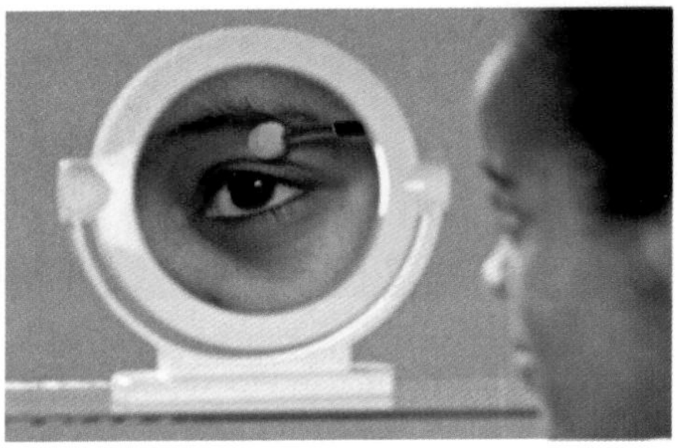

▲ **Figure 9.5.7** The mirror used for shaving or make-up, which gives a magnified effect and virtual image of your face is also a concave mirror.

Uses of curved mirrors

Concave mirrors are converging mirrors

Concave mirrors are used in reflecting telescopes to concentrate dim light from great distances, in torches and lamps to give a bright, narrow beam, and in dentists' and make-up mirrors to give a magnified view of close objects.

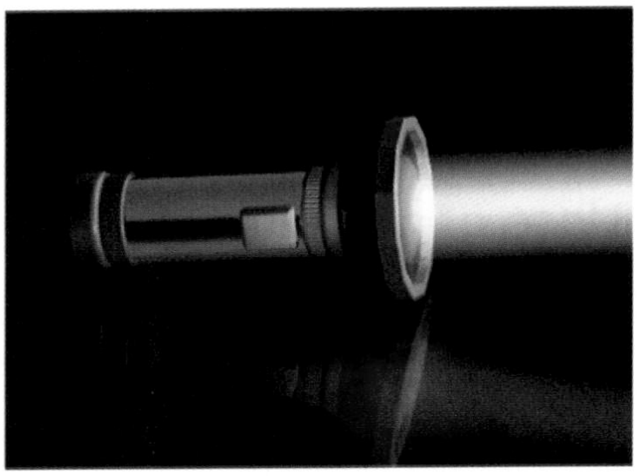

▲ **Figure 9.5.6** The mirrors fitted behind a torch bulb or car head lamp are concave and are shaped to produce a near parallel beam of light. The best shape for this is a concave parabolic mirror.

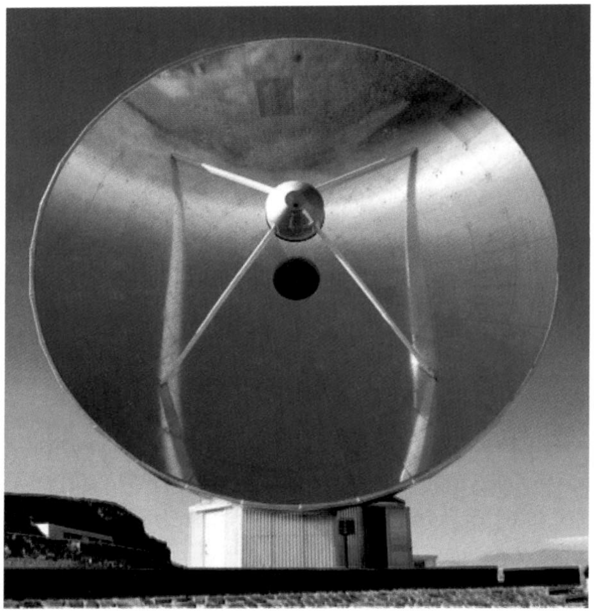

▲ **Figure 9.5.8** The optical telescope at La Silla, on a mountain top in Chile, uses a large concave parabolic reflecting mirror of diameter 3.5 m as its objective.

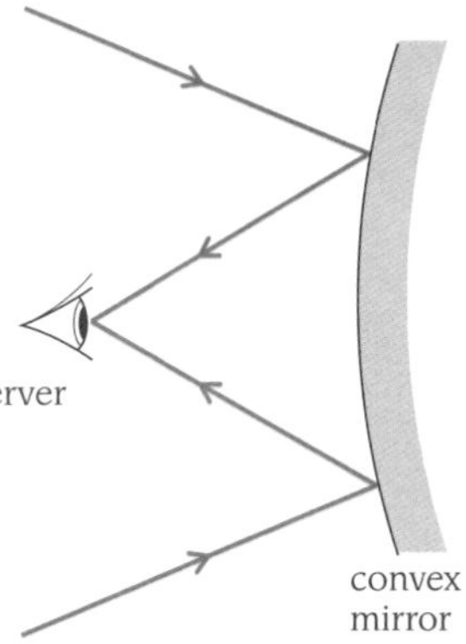

▲ **Figure 9.5.9** A convex mirror can be used to give a wide field of view. This application is useful when we want to see round a blind corner on a road and is even used on some car wing-mirrors. The image seen in a convex mirror is smaller or diminished.

Convex mirrors are diverging mirrors

Convex mirrors are used to give a wide field of view: in car wing-mirrors to increase the amount of the road behind that can be seen; in security mirrors in shops and safety mirrors at road junctions to enable a view around corners (Figure 9.5.9).

Summary questions

1 What happens to light hitting a concave mirror?

2 Give one use of lasers.

3 Give one use of a convex mirror.

C9.6 Refraction

Light rays change direction

Investigating rays passing through a glass block

- In a darkened room, arrange a ray box with a single slit to send a narrow ray of light into a rectangular block of glass or Perspex (Figure 9.6.1).

The block should be placed with its largest face on a sheet of white paper so that the ray enters at an angle through a long side, near one end.

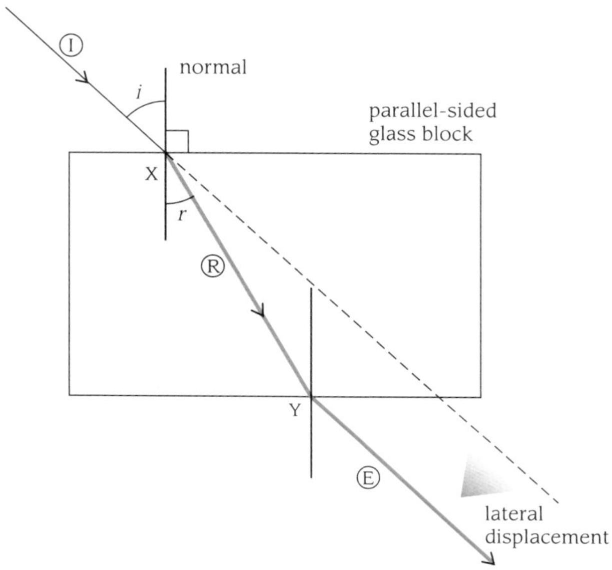

▲ **Figure 9.6.1** A light ray passing through a glass block

- Look for a ray emerging at the opposite side. Notice what happens to this emergent ray as the angle of incidence *i* is changed.
- Draw round the block of glass.
- Using a protractor, draw a normal, in a position as shown and measure from it several angles of incidence *i*.
- Accurately aim the incident ray at X, and for each angle of incidence mark the direction of the emergent ray.
- Remove the glass block, draw in the emergent and refracted rays and measure the angles of refraction *r*.
- As the ray enters the block at X and leaves at Y, which way is it bent, towards or away from the normal? Which angles are equal? What do you notice about the directions of rays Ⓘ and Ⓔ?
- Tabulate the values of the angles *i* and *r* and also, using a calculator, the values of sin *i* and sin *r*.

Observations

- At X the incident ray Ⓘ is bent or refracted as it enters the glass.
- At X, as the ray enters the glass, angle *r* is smaller than angle *i* and we say that the ray is bent towards the normal.
- At Y, as the ray leaves the glass, it is bent back to its original direction. The angle of refraction, now in the air, is larger than the incident angle.
- When a ray of light enters an optically denser medium it is bent *towards the normal.*
- Conversely, when it enters a less dense medium it is bent *away from the normal.*
- If the block of glass has parallel sides, the emergent ray Ⓔ is parallel to the incident ray Ⓘ, but it is laterally displaced.

Objectives

By the end of this topic you will be able to:

- recall the laws of refraction
- describe how to investigate Snell's Law experimentally
- explain what is meant by lateral displacement
- understand the term 'refractive index' and what its value tells us for a medium.

Refraction

Refraction is the bending of light that occurs when it passes at an angle to the normal from one transparent material to another.

Refraction happens because light slows down as it enters a transparent material like water or glass. If the light ray enters at an angle, one side slows down first, so the light ray changes direction. If the ray enters along the normal, both sides slow down at the same time so the ray does not change direction.

! Key fact

Lateral displacement

This means the ray is travelling in the same direction but it has been shifted sideways when it emerges. This happens to light whenever it passes through a plane glass window at an angle to the normal.

▼ Typical results

i/degree	r/degree	$\sin i$	$\sin r$	$\frac{\sin i}{\sin r}$
15	10	0.26	0.17	1.53
30	20	0.50	0.34	1.47
45	28	0.71	0.47	1.51
60	35	0.87	0.57	1.53

The laws of refraction

In 1621, a Dutch mathematics professor called Snell discovered that the ratio of the sines of the angles gave a constant value.

The mean value of the ratio for light passing from air to glass is about 1.5. This ratio is called the refractive index.

Law 1

The incident ray, refracted ray and the normal at the point of incidence all lie in the same plane.

Law 2: Snell's law

For light rays passing from one transparent medium to another, the sine of the angle of incidence and the sine of the angle of refraction are in a constant ratio called the refractive index.

Refractive index

▼ The refractive indices of some transparent materials

Medium	Refracive index, n
glass	1.5
Perspex	1.5
water	1.33
ice	1.3
diamond	2.4

The refractive index of a material is a measure of how much light slows down as it enters that material. So the refractive index of a material tells us how much the light will change direction. The larger the refractive index the more a ray changes direction. The values in the table are for light entering from air or from a vacuum.

- The value of the refractive index for a medium indicates how much refraction or bending will occur when a ray enters it from air.
- The refractive index, n, of air is given as 1. The refractive index of other materials is always given compared with the value for air. Because the refractive index is a ratio, it has no units.

The reversibility of light

The principle of reversibility of light simply states that the paths of light rays are reversible. This means that if a ray of light is sent in the exact opposite direction it will follow the same path.

When a ray of light passes from medium 1 to medium 2 this is indicated by using the symbol ${}_1n_2$ for the refractive index (Figure 9.6.2).

$${}_1n_2 = \frac{\sin i}{\sin r}$$

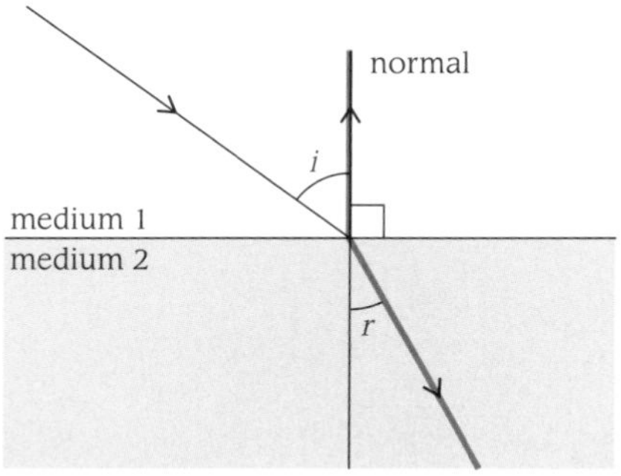

▲ **Figure 9.6.2** The ray entering along the normal does not change direction.

For a ray travelling in the opposite direction, from medium 2 into medium 1, the symbol used is ${}_2n_1$. Using the same labels for the angles we get:

$${}_2n_1 = \frac{\sin r}{\sin i}$$

From these relations we see that:

$$ {}_2n_1 = \frac{1}{{}_1n_2} $$

Thus the refractive indices for a ray of light passing in opposite directions between two media are reciprocals.

For example: if the refractive index from air to glass, symbol ${}_an_g$, is about 1.5 or $\frac{3}{2}$, then the refractive index from glass to air, ${}_gn_a$ can be found as follows:

$$ {}_gn_a = \frac{1}{{}_an_g} = \frac{1}{1.5} = 0.67 $$

The ray is bent the opposite way.

Summary questions

1 Which way does light bend on entering a more dense medium?

2 What does the refractive index of a material indicate?

3 For light refracted through a rectangular block, what can you say about the rays into and out of the block?

C9.7 Total internal reflection

Objectives

By the end of this topic you will be able to:

- explain what is meant by the critical angle and total internal reflection and recall the conditions required
- calculate critical angles
- measure the critical angle for a glass to air surface
- draw diagrams showing how total internal reflection is used in:
  - prisms
  - periscopes
  - prism binoculars
  - fibre optic cables
  - endoscopes.

Total internal reflection sometimes happens when a ray meets a surface going from glass to air or water to air.

In Figure 9.7.1a, a ray meets the surface at a small angle of incidence *i* and a weak internally reflected ray is produced as well as the refracted ray. The angle of refraction *r* is greater than the angle of incidence *i*.

In Figure 9.7.1b, the angle of incidence has increased up to a critical value where the angle of refraction is just 90° and the refracted ray grazes along the surface of the glass. This value of the angle of incidence is called the critical angle:

The critical angle between two media is the angle of incidence in the optically denser medium for which the angle of refraction is 90°.

In Figure 9.7.1c, the angle of incidence *i* has further increased, becoming greater than the critical angle. As it is impossible for the angle of refraction to exceed 90°, no light emerges and all the light is totally internally reflected. The inside surface of the glass behaves like a perfect mirror.

Total internal reflection occurs when

- **a ray of light is inside the optically denser of two media**
- **the angle of incidence at the surface is greater than the critical angle for the pair of media, that is when i > c.**

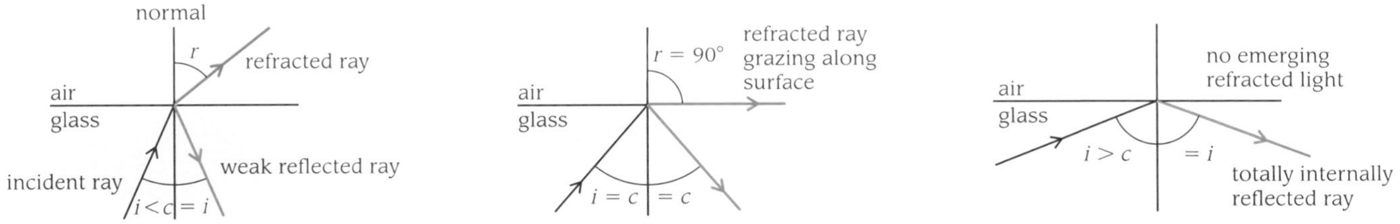

a Angle of incidence *i* less than the critical angle *c*

b When the angle of refraction *r* = 90°, the angle of incidence *i* = the critical angle *c*

c When the angle of incidence is greater than the critical angle *c*, total internal reflection occurs

▲ **Figure 9.7.1** Internal reflection and critical angle

Measuring the critical angle for glass

A semicircular block of glass or Perspex is suitable for this experiment because it allows a ray of light to enter the glass through the curved edge without being refracted. This happens when a ray is directed at the centre of the flat edge along a radius so that it enters the curved surface at 90°, as shown in Figure 9.7.2.

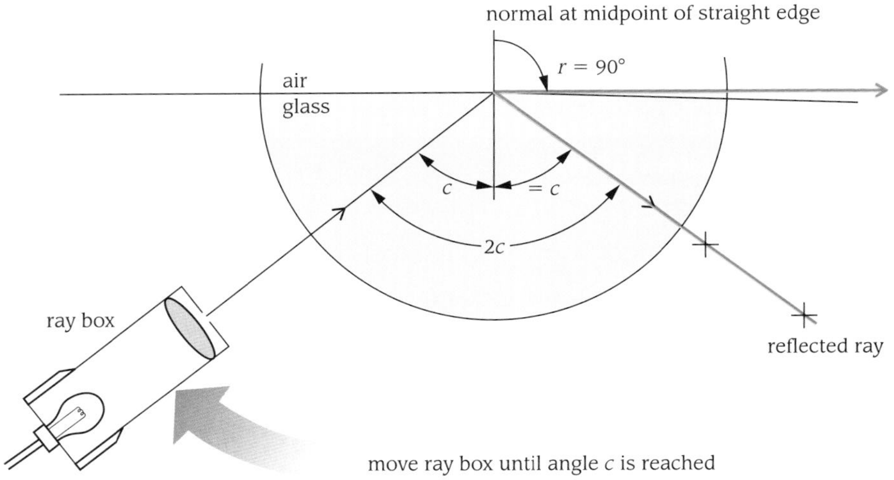

▲ **Figure 9.7.2** Measuring the critical angle

- Draw round the semicircular block on a sheet of paper and by measurement draw a normal at the midpoint of the straight side.
- Direct a ray of light through the glass to be internally reflected exactly at the midpoint of the straight side.
- Move the ray box round until the critical condition is found.

It should be possible to see a refracted ray grazing just along the surface so that $r = 90°$.

- Mark the direction of the incident ray and reflected ray.
- Remove the block and draw in the rays.
- Measure the angle between the incident and reflected rays with a protractor.

The angle is twice the critical angle since the angle of reflection equals the critical angle of incidence. Thus half this angle gives the critical angle c.

Key fact

The critical angle c between a medium of refractive index n and the air is given by:

$$\sin c = \frac{1}{n}$$

Worked example

If the refractive index of glass, ${}_a n_g = 1.5$, calculate the critical angle from glass to air.

$$\sin c = \frac{1}{n} = \frac{1}{1.5} = 0.67$$

Using $\sin^{-1}$ on your calculator, the critical angle, $c = 42°$.

Calculating the critical angle

For a ray of light going from glass to air, the angle of incidence i equals the critical angle c when the angle of refraction r is just 90°:

$i = c$ when $r = 90°$

and the refractive index from glass to air ${}_g n_a$ is given by:

$${}_g n_a = \frac{\sin i}{\sin r} = \frac{\sin c}{\sin 90°} = \frac{\sin c}{1}$$

$$\sin c = {}_g n_a = \frac{1}{{}_a n_g} \text{ or } \sin c = \frac{1}{\text{refractive index of glass}}$$

How a thick glass mirror forms multiple images

Internal reflection will also occur when the angle of incidence is less than the critical angle but in such cases only a proportion of the light is internally reflected (Figure 9.7.3). These partial reflections can spoil the image formed in a mirror.

All glass mirrors silvered at the back surface produce faint ghost-like images which blur the main clear image. To avoid these problems, mirrors used in accurate instruments are made with a polished aluminium film on the front surface of the glass.

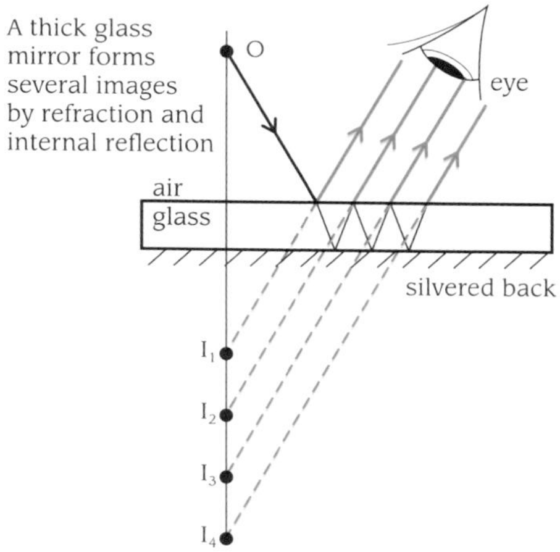

▲ **Figure 9.7.3** How a thick glass mirror forms multiple images

I_2 is the clear image formed by a single reflection of light at the silvered back surface of the mirror.

The faint image, I_1, is formed by a small amount of light being reflected from the front surface of the glass.

Images I_3, I_4 and so on, get fainter as less light remains.

Each time the light reaches the inside of the front surface of the glass some of it escapes and is refracted, while the rest is internally reflected.

Applications of total internal reflection

Prisms at work

Prisms are triangular blocks of glass or other transparent material. Figure 9.7.4a shows a right-angled prism used to reflect light through 90°. Figure 9.7.4b shows a right-angled prism used to reflect light through 180°. The diagram shows that this produces an inverted image. In the prism binoculars in Figure 9.7.4c an upright image is produced by using two prisms. This also makes the binoculars shorter and so lighter to carry.

Two advantages of using prisms instead of mirrors to reflect light are that the prisms do not produce multiple images, and there is not a silvered surface to get scratched.

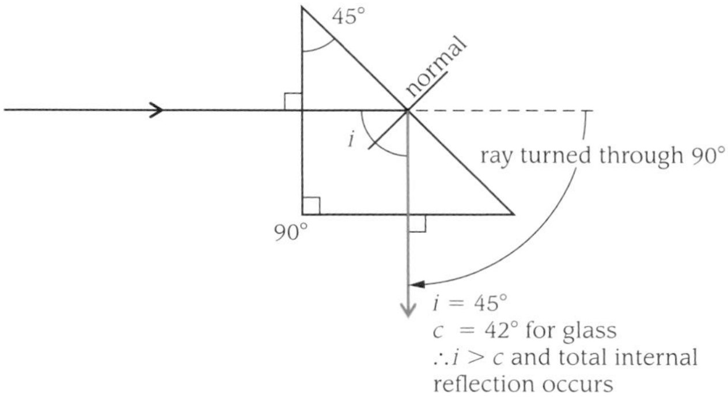

a A right-angled prism to deviate a ray by 90°

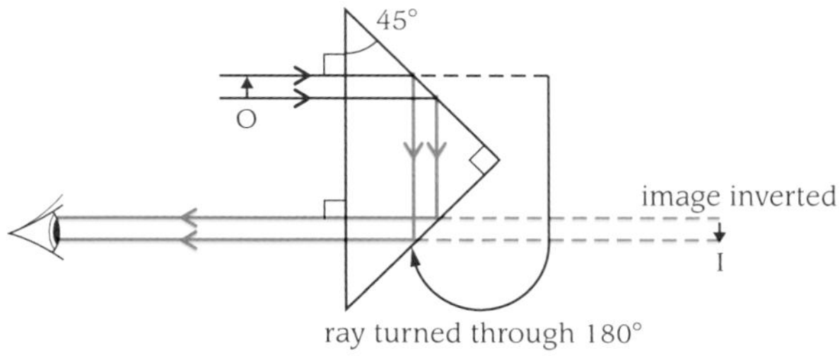

b A right-angled prism used to turn rays of light through 180°

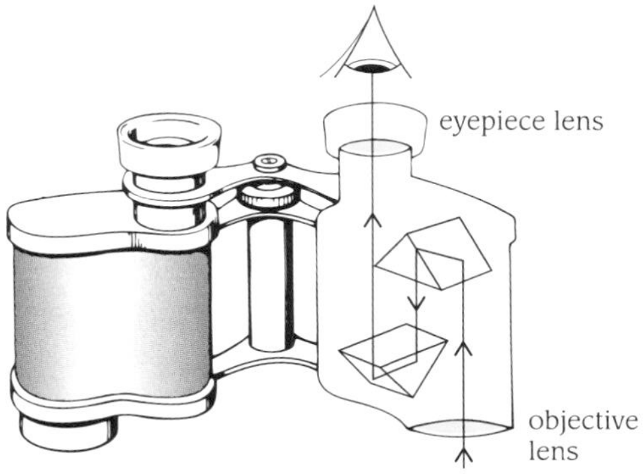

c Prism binoculars

▲ **Figure 9.7.4** Prisms at work

Things to do

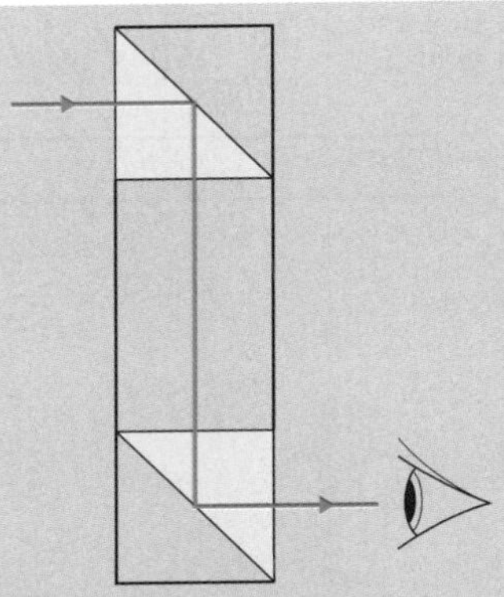

▲ **Figure 9.7.5** Two prisms are used in a periscope

Look at Figure 9.7.5 then copy this diagram and show a second ray of light passing through the periscope. Use your diagram to decide if the image is upright or inverted.

Optical fibres

An optical fibre is a very thin, flexible glass rod. Most 'optical fibres' are actually a bundle of individual optical fibres. When a ray of light strikes the inside of the surface of an individual fibre, if the angle of incidence i inside the glass is greater than the critical angle, then total internal reflection traps the light inside the fibre. Figure 9.7.6a shows how light can travel along the fibre in this way.

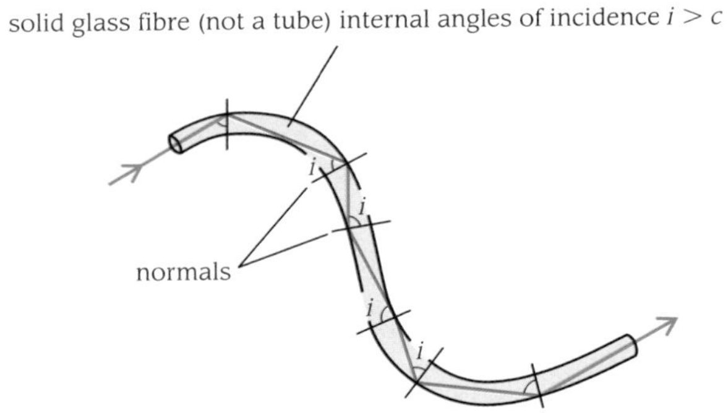
solid glass fibre (not a tube) internal angles of incidence $i > c$
normals
i
i
i
i

a **Single optical fibre or light pipe, contains light ray by multiple total internal reflections**

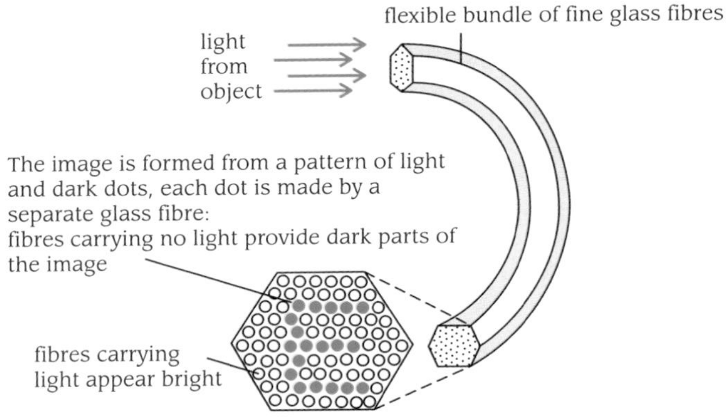
flexible bundle of fine glass fibres
light from object
The image is formed from a pattern of light and dark dots, each dot is made by a separate glass fibre:
fibres carrying no light provide dark parts of the image
fibres carrying light appear bright

b **A bundle of glass fibres used to transmit an image**

▲ **Figure 9.7.6**

Optical fibres are used in the communications industry. Optical fibres transmit laser light, which pulses on and off to transmit telephone conversations, computer data or television pictures as a digital signal. Optical fibres can carry more information than the older copper cables, and they are thinner, lighter and are becoming cheaper.

The endoscope

An endoscope is an optical fibre used to carry light into places it would be difficult to reach otherwise, such as inside the body. A tiny camera at the end of the endoscope can be used to take images to assist a doctor in making a diagnosis, for example.

Summary questions

1 Explain what the critical angle is.

2 When does total internal reflection occur?

3 Write the equation relating critical angle and refractive index.

4 Give an example where total internal reflection is used.

C9.8 Real and apparent depth

If you look into a clear pool of water it appears to be shallower than it really is. A swimming pool, for example, which is really 4 metres deep will appear to be only about 3 metres deep.

An object O, seen through a transparent medium like water, appears closer than it really is (Figure 9.8.1). Rays of light coming from the object O are bent away from the normal as they leave the water, so that they appear to come from a virtual image I which is above the object O.

Light is passing from water to air with a refractive index, ${}_wn_a$:

$${}_wn_a = \frac{\sin i}{\sin r}$$

also angle XOY = angle *i* (alternate angles)

and angle XIY = angle *r* (corresponding angles)

$${}_wn_a = \frac{\sin \text{angle XOY}}{\sin \text{angle XIY}}$$

$$= \frac{\text{XY/OY}}{\text{XY/IY}} = \frac{\text{IY}}{\text{OY}}$$

Now when the eye is vertically above the object, Y and X are together, then OY = OX and IY = IX, therefore

$${}_wn_a = \frac{\text{IX}}{\text{OX}} = \frac{\text{apparent depth}}{\text{real depth}}$$

Now by reversing the light direction we get the refractive index from air to water.

$${}_an_w = \frac{\text{real depth}}{\text{apparent depth}}$$

This relation is only accurate when an object is seen vertically through a surface.

Measuring refractive index by real and apparent depth

- Stand a glass block on end across a straight line drawn on a sheet of paper (Figure 9.8.2).
- Support a search pin in a movable holder so that it can be moved up and down and then held steady while measurements are made.

Looking from above, the line under the glass block will appear to be nearer when seen through the glass than when seen through the air.

- To find the apparent position of the line as seen through the glass, move the search pin up and down the side of the block until it is at the same level as the apparent position of the line inside the glass. Find this position by looking for no-parallax.
- Fix the search pin and measure the apparent depth of the block, measuring down from the top of the block to the pin.
- From the measured values of the real and apparent depths of the block, calculate the refractive index of glass.

Objectives

By the end of this topic you will be able to:

- explain why the depth of a swimming pool appears less than it really is
- describe how to measure refractive index using real and apparent depth
- understand and use the condition known as 'no parallax' to locate a virtual image
- use a refractive index to calculate a real or apparent depth
- explain why straight objects can appear to bend as they enter water.

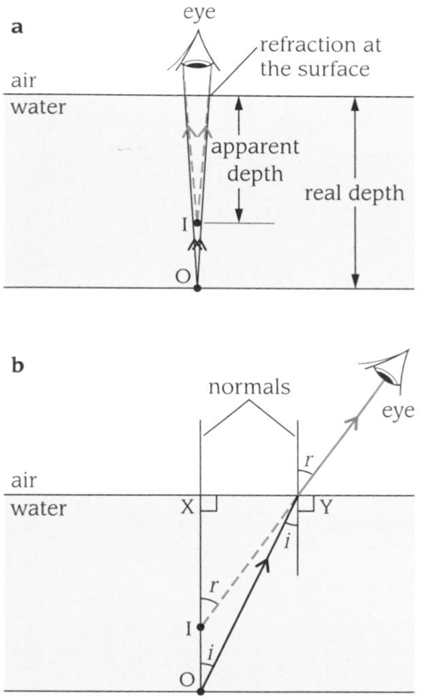

▲ **Figure 9.8.1** Real and apparent depth

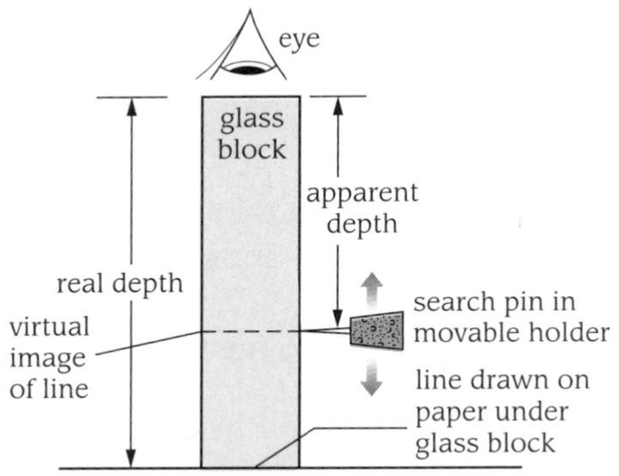

▲ **Figure 9.8.2** Measuring refractive index by the real and apparent depth

No-parallax

A virtual image can be located by looking for no-parallax between the line and the search pin. Move your eye across the top of the block at right angles to the line. When no-parallax is found the search pin and line, seen through the glass, should move together and stay in line. If, however, they separate as your eye moves across, then raise or lower the search pin by a small amount and look again for no-parallax.

When the position of no-parallax is found, the search pin indicates the apparent depth of the block.

Worked example

A swimming pool appears to be only 1.5 metres deep. If the refractive index of water is $\frac{4}{3}$, calculate the real depth of water in the pool.

$$_{a}n_{w} = \frac{\text{real depth}}{\text{apparent depth}}$$

$$\frac{4}{3} = \frac{\text{real depth}}{1.5\,\text{m}}$$

The real depth of water = $\frac{4}{3} \times 1.5\,\text{m} = 2.0$ metres.

How water appears to bend a ruler

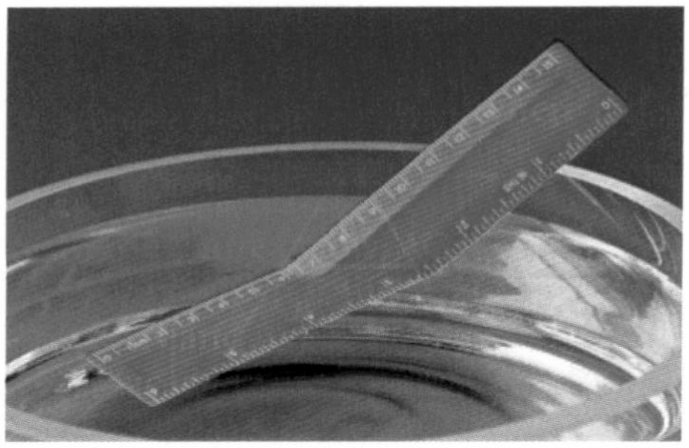

▲ **Figure 9.8.3** The effect of half immersing a ruler in a bowl of water

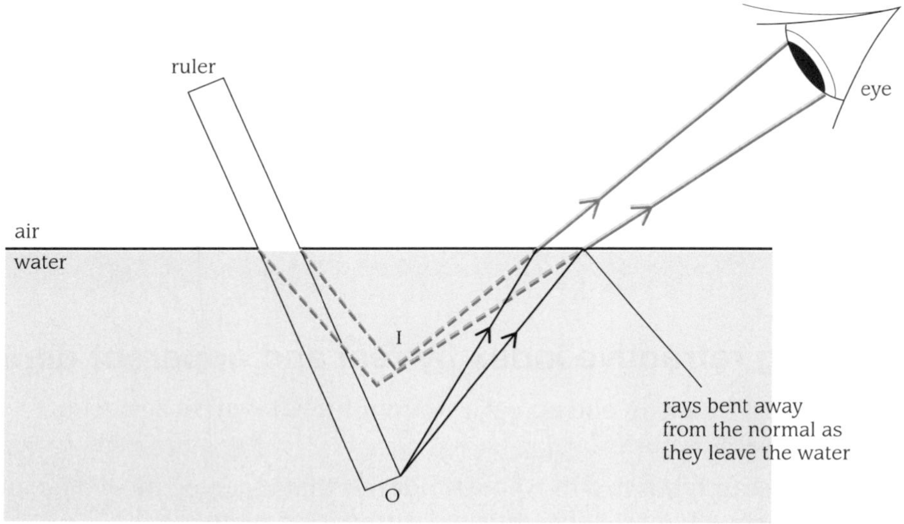

▲ **Figure 9.8.4** The refraction of light as it passes from water to air causes the ruler to appear bent. The slower speed of light in water also makes the water appear more shallow and the graduations on the ruler to appear closer together.

This effect can be seen by half immersing a ruler in a sink or bowl full of water, as shown in Figure 9.8.4. The rays of light from the end of the ruler at O are refracted at the surface of the water (away from the normal, entering an optically less dense medium) so that they appear to come from the virtual image I. The real ruler is not bent, and is drawn straight. The virtual image is, as usual, drawn with broken lines.

What appears to happen to the length of the ruler and the size of its graduation below the water surface?

Things to do

- Have a careful look at the rear reflector on a bicycle or car and explain how it works.
- Sit at a table and place a coin in the bottom of a cup. Move the cup so that you just cannot see the coin inside. Ask a friend to pour water into the cup without moving the cup. Draw a ray diagram to explain how the coin becomes visible to you.

Summary questions

1. Does water appear deeper or shallower than it really is?
2. Sketch a diagram to show why.
3. Give the equation relating real and apparent depth to refractive index.

C9.9 Refraction and the speed of light

Objectives

By the end of this topic you will be able to:

- explain refraction and apparent depth as consequences of changes in the speed of light
- solve problems involving the speed of light and refractive indices.

The speed of light in a vacuum has been very accurately measured; in calculations you can use $3.0 \times 10^8\,\mathrm{m\,s^{-1}}$ or 300 million metres per second. Light travels more slowly in transparent materials and it is thought that the bending or refraction of light is due to this change of speed. An explanation of this is given in terms of the wave theory of light (C12.1).

For light passing from a vacuum or air into a medium:

$$\text{the refractive index of a medium, } n = \frac{\text{speed of light in air}}{\text{speed of light in medium}}$$

And for light passing from medium 1 to medium 2:

$${}_1n_2 = \frac{\text{speed of light in medium 1}}{\text{speed of light in medium 2}} = \frac{v_1}{v_2}$$

For example: for light passing from air to glass the speed of light in air is $3 \times 10^8\,\mathrm{m\,s^{-1}}$, and the refractive index, ${}_an_g = \frac{3}{2}$. This means that light travels $\frac{3}{2}$ times as fast in the air as it does in glass. The above relationship shows that the speed in glass is therefore $2 \times 10^8\,\mathrm{m\,s^{-1}}$.

$${}_an_g = \frac{3}{2} = \frac{3 \times 10^8 \text{ (speed of light in air)}}{2 \times 10^8 \text{ (speed of light in glass)}}$$

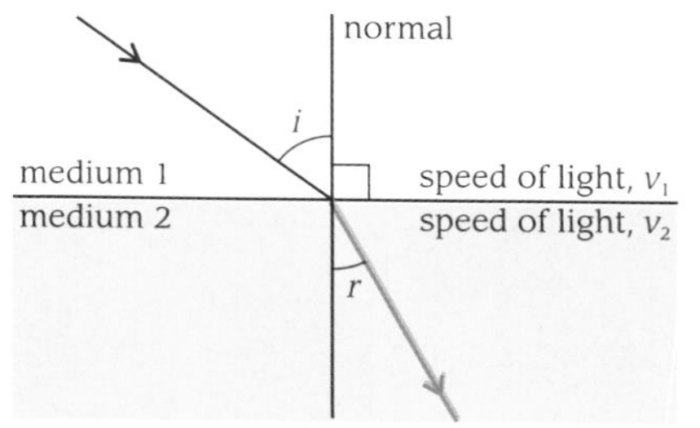

▲ **Figure 9.9.1** The relation between refraction and the speed of light, *c*

Linking the three equations for refractive index

$${}_1n_2 = \frac{\sin i}{\sin r} = \frac{v_1}{v_2} = \frac{\text{real depth}}{\text{apparent depth}}$$

Key fact

Your eyes are easily fooled

Our eyes and brains are easily fooled. They make no allowance for any change in the speed or direction of a light ray.

The apparent depth of a swimming pool is easily explained in terms of the reduced speed of light in water.

Compared with light travelling in air, the distance travelled by light in water in the same time is reduced by the refractive index. So a real depth of water of 4.0 m is reduced by a factor of 1.33 to an apparent depth of 3.0 m. The real depth is how far the light travels in air and the apparent depth is how far it travels in the same time in water.

Worked example

The speed of light in water is $2.25 \times 10^8\,\mathrm{m\,s^{-1}}$ and in air is $3.00 \times 10^8\,\mathrm{m\,s^{-1}}$.

a) Calculate the refractive index from air to water.

b) If a ray of light passing from air to water is incident at the surface at an angle of 30°, calculate the angle of refraction in the water.

---

a) The refractive index, $_an_w = \frac{\text{speed lf light in air}}{\text{speed of light in water}}$

$${}_an_w = \frac{3.00 \times 10^8}{2.25 \times 10^8} = 1.33 \text{ (no units)}$$

b) $_1n_2 = 1.33 = \frac{\sin i}{\sin r} = \frac{\sin 30°}{\sin r}$

$$\sin r = \frac{\sin 30°}{1.33} = \frac{0.5}{1.33} = 0.376$$

The angle of refraction, $r = 22°$

Mirages

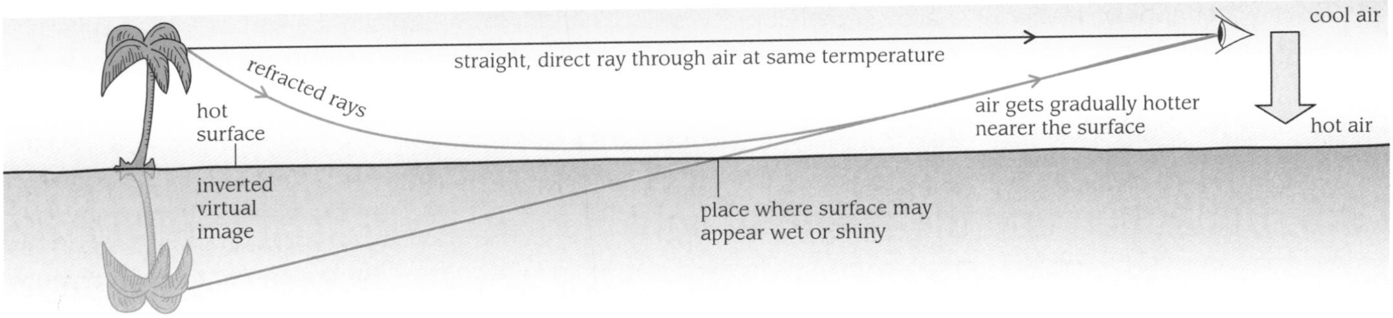

▲ **Figure 9.9.2** How a mirage is produced

▲ **Figure 9.9.3** A heat mirage is caused by refraction of light near to the hot ground where the heated air expands and has a lower refractive index than the colder air above. The mirage is a virtual image of a distant object, often inverted, which appears in the hazy region close to the ground and may appear much closer than the real object actually is.

The mirage is produced by refraction in the air, as shown in Figure 9.9.2. A mirage can happen when the air nearer the surface of the ground is less dense than that above. When the Sun has been shining on a desert or a road and has made the surface very hot, the air next to it is heated and expands, becoming less dense. The optical density and refractive index of the air gradually increases with height above the surface as the air gets cooler.

Light from a distant object may reach an observer's eye by the two paths shown in the figure, with the result that the object is seen in its true position and also as an inverted image below it. The inverted image is virtual and is called a mirage.

The most likely explanation of the curved ray path is that it is gradually refracted as the light passes through air of gradually changing density. Approaching the surface, as the air gets hotter and less dense, the decreasing refractive index bends the ray away from the normal. After skimming along the surface the ray is gradually bent back towards the normal as it rises through air of increasing density and refractive index.

There is a hazy region on the ground between the object and the observer where the surface seems shiny or reflective and a hot dry road may appear to be wet.

Summary questions

1 What happens to the speed of light as it enters a less dense medium?

2 What conditions are needed for mirages to be seen?

C9.10 Dispersion and colour

Newton's experiment

Newton observed that a ray of white sunlight was split into a spectrum of colours as it passed through a glass prism. We can reproduce that original experiment using a ray box as the source of a white light ray as shown in Figure 9.10.1.

- Direct the light ray through the prism onto a white screen some distance away in a darkened room.
- Where do you find the spectrum?
- Which colours can you see in the spectrum?
- Which colour has been deviated most and which least?

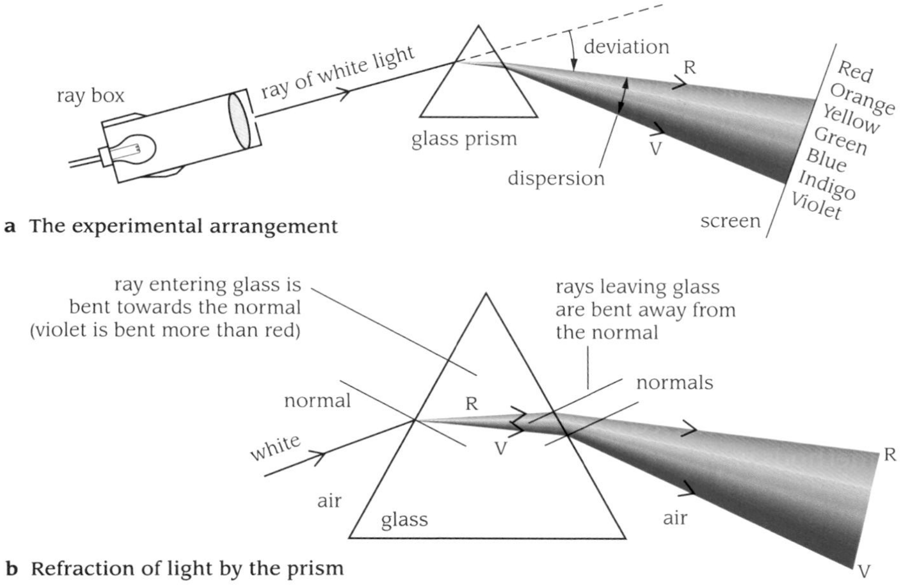

▲ **Figure 9.10.1** Newton's experiment

The colours of the spectrum of white light

The colours of the spectrum of white light are those seen in a rainbow. They are usually named in order as: red, orange, yellow, green, blue, indigo and violet. These colours gradually change from one to the next and there are no boundaries between the colours. We describe the spectrum of white light as continuous, which means that there is a complete range of colours from the red end to the violet end of the spectrum with no gaps or breaks. Each colour of light has a different frequency and wavelength and the light spectrum is only a small part of a much larger spectrum of radiation called the electromagnetic spectrum.

Testing a hypothesis

When Newton discovered that white light, passed through a prism, was turned into a spectrum of coloured light, he made a hypothesis (guess). He guessed that white light contained all the colours and that the action of the prism was to split them up. However the true explanation might have been different, for example, the colours might have been added by the glass of the prism. To test his hypothesis Newton carried out two further experiments shown in Figure 9.10.2.

Objectives

By the end of this topic you will be able to:

- describe how a prism produces a spectrum from white light
- explain and distinguish between the deviation of a light ray caused by refraction and the dispersion of a light ray
- discuss the significance of Newton's prisms experiment for scientific methodology
- describe the addition of colours in light and explain that the colour of objects is a result of the absorption of certain colours of light
- name the three primary colours of light
- name and explain what is meant by a secondary colour and complementary colours
- demonstrate colour addition with light beams on a white screen.

Exam tip

The phrase 'Blue bends best' may help you remember which colour of the spectrum is deviated most.

Key fact

Deviation is the angle between a ray's original direction and its new direction after refraction. The prism causes a spectrum because each colour has a different deviation. The refractive index of glass is slightly different for each colour.

Dispersion is the separation of white light into the colours of the spectrum. White light is made up of a range of different colours. The prism enables us to see these different colours.

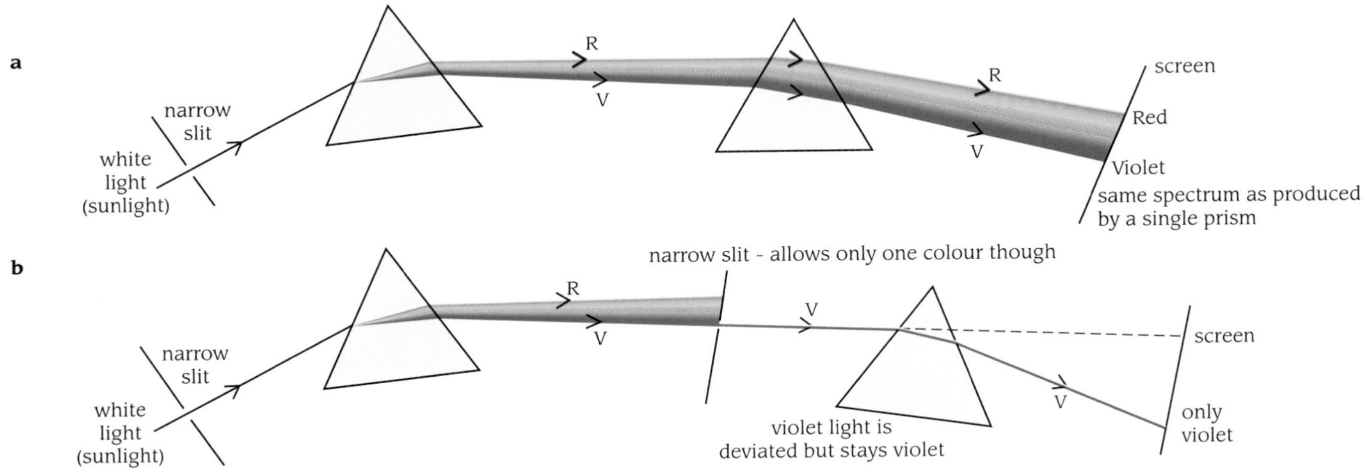

▲ **Figure 9.10.2** Newton testing his hypothesis

In the first experiment (Figure 9.10.2a), a second prism added no extra colours, suggesting that the prism did not produce the colours. In the second experiment (Figure 9.10.2b), a single colour was selected by placing a narrow slit in the spectrum from the first prism. The single colour (monochromatic light) was deviated by the second prism but it stayed the same colour. These two experiments are important because they show how Newton tested his hypothesis by showing that other possible explanations were not true.

Recombining the spectrum

White light can be separated into a spectrum of different colours of light; it can also be synthesised (meaning put together) from the separate colours. Two methods may be tried. These are shown in Figure 9.10.3.

a) The second prism reverses the deviation and dispersion of the first prism so that the colours of the spectrum recombine where the colours overlap. The edges of the emerging beam may be tinged with violet and red.

b) Newton's disc is a card coloured with all the colours of the spectrum in equal areas. If the disc is spun round rapidly the persistence of vision of the human eye remembers all the colours it sees as the colours change places. The colours of the spectrum are added together and appear as nearly white. The off-white colour is due to the imperfect reflection of colours from the disc.

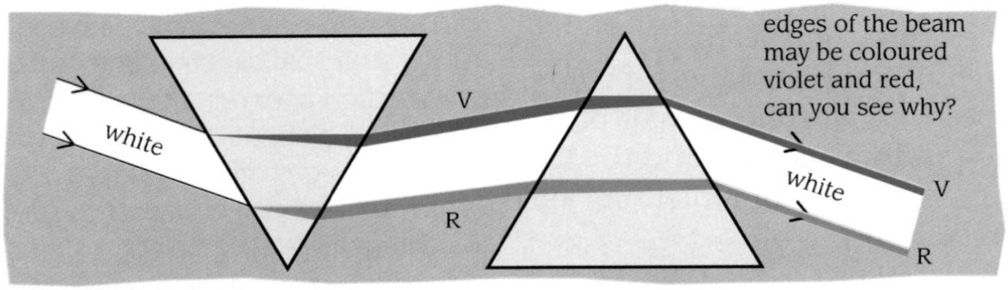

a Using two prisms

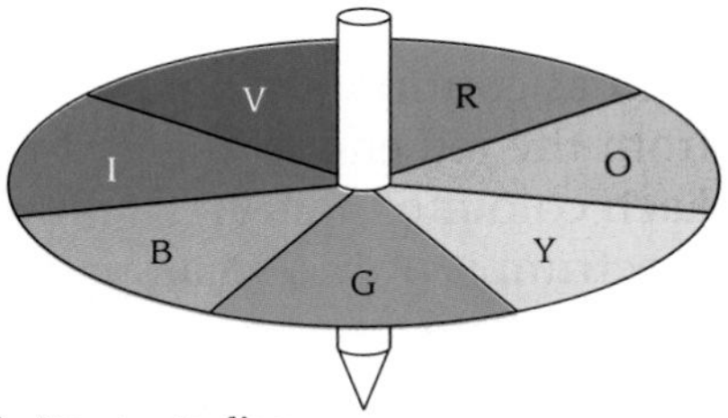

b Newton's disc

▲ **Figure 9.10.3** Recombining the colours of the spectrum

Summary questions

1 Give the colours of the spectrum in order, from most refracted to least.

2 What did Newton's experiment with a prism show?

3 What is deviation?

Practice exam-style questions

1 Describe the shadow produced by:

a) a small filament lamp

b) sunlight on a sunny day

c) a fluorescent tube

d) a spot lamp

e) a candle.

2 Explain why sharp shadows support the theory that light travels in straight lines.

3 The figure below shows a very small source of light producing a shadow of the object X on a screen S. What is the size of the shadow, in metres?

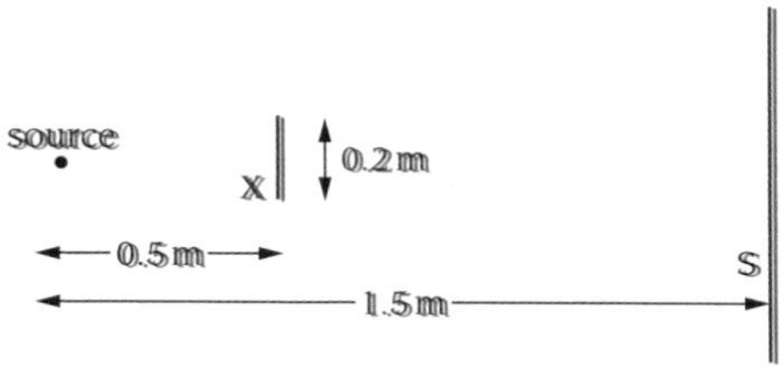

4 a) Draw a diagram to show how a solar eclipse is formed. On your diagram, mark the positions of:

i) an observer, P, who sees a partial eclipse

ii) a second observer, T, who sees a total eclipse.

b) Draw a diagram to show what the observer, P sees as he looks (through a protective filter) towards the Sun.

c) What property of light must you assume to explain how eclipses are formed?

5 With the aid of diagrams, explain the differences between the reflection of light which occurs:

a) from a flat sheet of white cloth

b) from a flat sheet of shiny aluminium foil.

6 a) Draw a vertical line down the centre of a sheet of paper to represent a plane mirror. The mirror is viewed from the left side of your diagram, looking to the right.

b) Draw a large, upright letter L to the left of the mirror some distance away from it, so that the base line of the letter points towards the mirror.

c) Draw two light rays from each corner of the letter reflected at different angles from the mirror.

d) Draw a broken line backwards behind the mirror in line with each reflected ray to locate the position of each corner of the virtual image.

e) Draw the shape of the virtual image of the letter behind the mirror.

f) What does your diagram show about this virtual image?

7 a) Describe an experiment that you could use to locate the position of the image of a pin in a plane mirror.

b) Name FOUR properties of this image.

c) A plane mirror is sometimes seen below the scale of pointer instruments such as ammeters. With the aid of diagrams, explain why this is an advantage and describe how the mirror must be used to obtain accurate pointer readings.

8 Draw a ray diagram showing a plane mirror, a normal to it, and a light ray incident at 30° to the normal. Draw the reflected ray and label the value of the angle of reflection. Now, if the incident ray stays in the same direction, show what happens to the reflected ray when the mirror is turned so that the angle of incidence increases by 10°. What angle has the reflected ray been turned through?

9 Explain why you might see the following word painted on the front of an ambulance.

10 The figure below shows two plane mirrors set at an angle 100° to each other. A ray strikes one of the mirrors, as shown, at an angle of incidence of 45°. Redraw and complete the diagram showing the path of the ray and calculate the angle of reflection at which it leaves the second mirror.

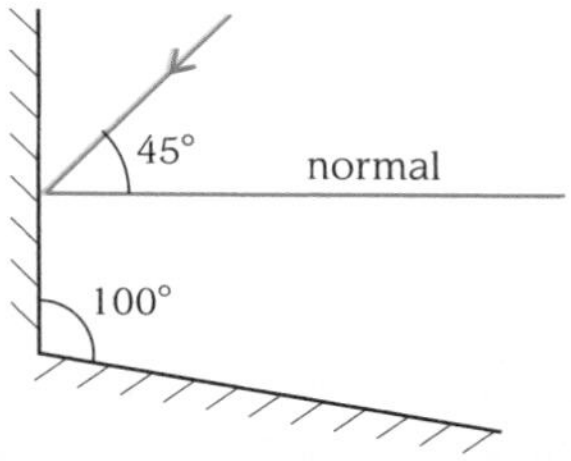

11 When an object is placed in front of a single plane mirror, there is only one virtual image visible.

a) Draw a diagram to explain how images can be seen in three positions when a single object is placed in front of two plane mirrors set exactly at right angles to each other.

b) With the help of another diagram, predict how many images would be visible when looking into two mirrors set at exactly 60° to each other.

12 Glass mirrors are usually made by bonding a reflecting or silvered surface to the back of a flat sheet of glass.

a) Draw a simple diagram to show how multiple images can be formed as a result of reflection from both the front and the back surface of the sheet of glass.

b) Explain how this problem is overcome by manufacturers of large reflecting telescopes.

13 A narrow beam of monochromatic light in air is incident on a plane boundary between air and glass, such that the angle between the beam and the normal is 60°. If the refractive index of the glass is 1.5, through what angle will the beam be bent or deviated on refraction?

14 a) Draw a clearly labelled ray diagram to show why a tank of water viewed vertically downwards appears less deep than it really is.

b) Describe in detail an experiment to measure the apparent depth of a glass block. State how you would expect this depth to relate to the real value.

c) To a person underwater, looking upwards, all objects above and outside the water appear to be within a certain cone of vision.

i) Use a clear diagram to explain this.

ii) If the refractive index of water is 1.33, calculate the vertical angle of the cone.

15 How is the refractive index of a material related to the velocity of light in the material?

If the velocity of light in air is $3 \times 10^8\,\text{m s}^{-1}$ and the refractive index of glass is 1.5, calculate the velocity of light in the glass.

16 Copy the diagram below and complete the paths of the two narrow beams of monochromatic light XY. (The critical angle of the glass of both prisms is 42°.)

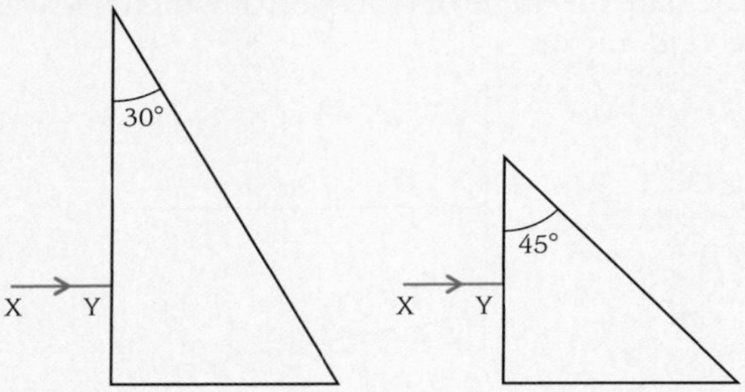

17 The speed of light in air is $3.0 \times 10^8\,\text{m s}^{-1}$.

The speed of light in a sample of glass is $2.2 \times 10^8\,\text{m s}^{-1}$.

a) Calculate the refractive index of the glass.

b) If a light ray enters the glass from air at an angle of 40°, calculate the angle of refraction in the glass.

18 A ray of light passes through a block of glass that is 40 mm thick. The ray enters the block at an angle of incidence of 60° and the refractive index of the glass is 1.5. The ray emerges from the far side of the block, travelling in the same direction as the incident ray but laterally displaced.

a) Explain what is meant by 'lateral displacement'. You may draw a diagram to help your explanation.

b) Calculate:

i) the angle of refraction inside the glass

ii) the lateral displacement of the light ray.

19 a) Draw ray diagrams to illustrate the meaning of:

i) critical angle

ii) total internal reflection.

b) Describe an experiment by which the refractive index of glass could be measured.

c) How would you use the refractive index to calculate the critical angle for a glass/air boundary?

d) Draw a diagram showing how a glass prism can deviate a narrow beam of light through a right angle. Show how this forms the basis for the design of a simple periscope.

20 The figure below shows a waterproof torch being held under water in such a way that a ray of light is produced that can strike the surface of the water at different angles *i*.

a) Calculate a value for the critical angle. (The refractive index of water is $\frac{4}{3}$.)

b) Draw sketches to show what will happen to the ray of light after it has struck the water–air boundary when *i* is about 20° and when *i* is about 60°. Account for the different behaviour of the ray in the two cases.

c) Why in one case does the resulting ray have coloured edges whereas in the other case it has not?

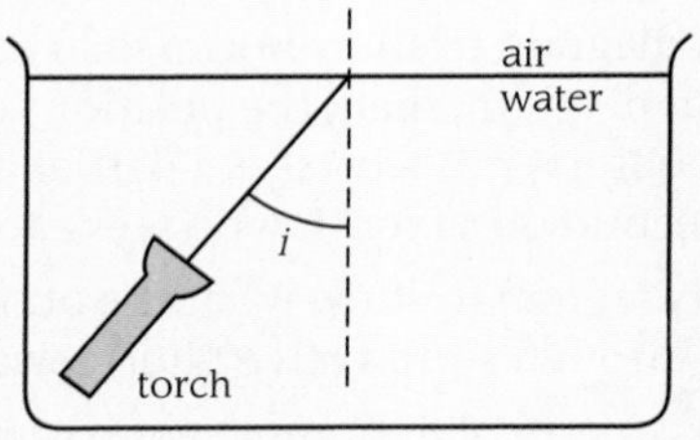

21 a) Draw ray diagrams to show how a glass prism may be used to deviate a light ray:

i) by exactly 90° **ii)** by exactly 180°.

b) Explain why using a prism to reflect rays of light can be preferable to using a plane glass mirror for the same purpose.

22 A swimming pool is 4.0 m deep. When a diver looks vertically downwards into the water, it appears to be less deep than it really is.

a) Explain what causes this effect.

b) If the refractive index of water is $\frac{4}{3}$, what depth of water will the diver appear to see below him?

23 Measurements of the real depth and apparent depth of a transparent liquid, viewed from vertically above in air, gave the following results:

Real depth = 0.72 m

Apparent depth = 0.60 m

Calculate:

a) the refractive index of the liquid

b) the speed of light in the liquid if the speed of light in air is $3.0 \times 10^8\,\text{m s}^{-1}$.

24 In an experiment to determine the refractive index of water, a black line is painted on the bottom of a tall glass container, which is then partially filled with water. On looking vertically down into the water the black line appears to be closer than it really is.

a) Explain, with the help of a ray diagram, why this is so.

b) The following results were obtained in such an experiment.

Real depth/cm	8.1	12.0	16.0	20.0
Apparent depth/cm	5.9	9.1	12.0	15.1

Plot a graph of real depth (*y*-axis) against apparent depth (*x*-axis) and hence determine a value for the refractive index of water.

25 Figure **a)** below represents a ray of light falling normally on the curved face of a semicircular plastic block at X, meeting the opposite face at an angle of incidence of 30° at O, and emerging into the air at an angle of 40°.

a)

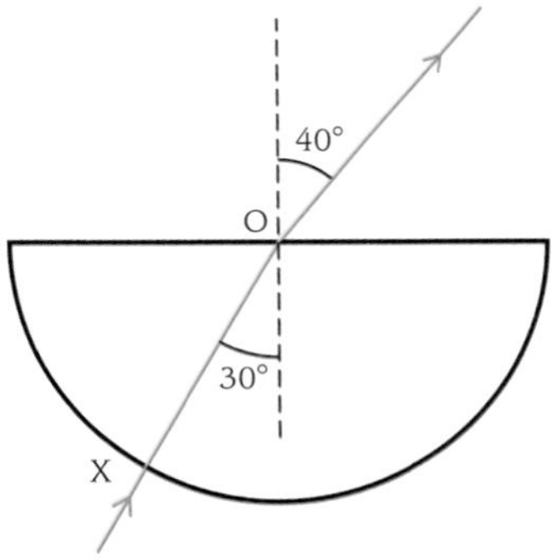

b)

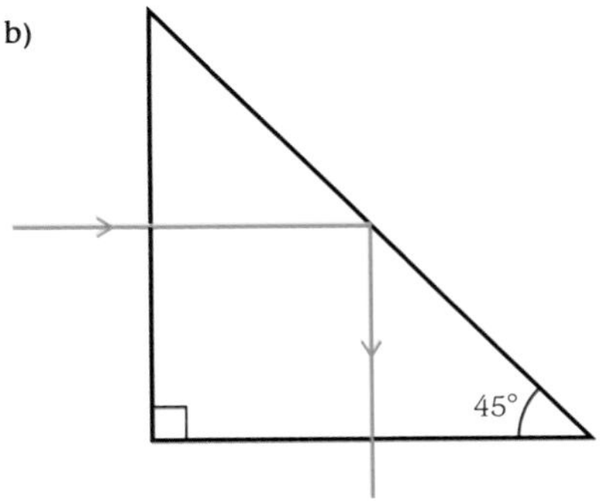

a) Explain what happens to the ray at X, between X and O, and at O. Why has the emerging ray been refracted?

b) Calculate the refractive index of the plastic.

c) Describe how the apparatus could be used to find the critical angle experimentally. Calculate the value of the critical angle for this plastic.

d) Glass prisms are sometimes used to turn light through 90° as shown in figure **b)** above. Would prisms of this plastic be able to do the same?

26 The figure below shows a ray of light, PQ, passing normally through the face, AB, of a 90°–60°–30° glass prism.

a) On a copy of this diagram:

i) sketch the path of the ray emerging into the air at R. *Label this ray 'Ray 1'*

ii) show where the eye could be placed to view the image of a pin placed at P.

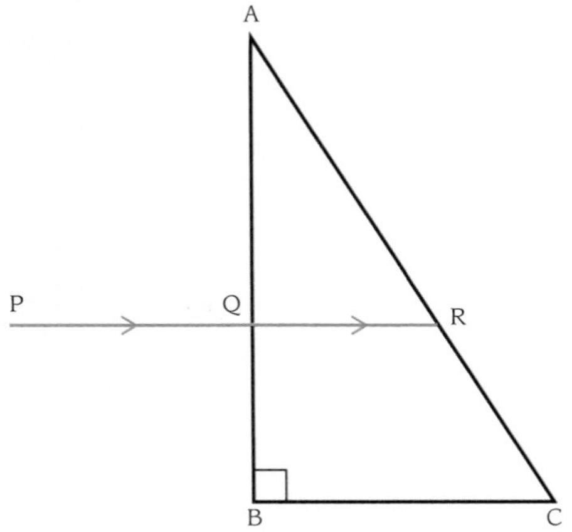

b) It is possible for some of the light travelling along QR to be reflected at R and then emerge from the prism.

i) On the same diagram, sketch the path of such a ray. *Label this 'Ray 2'*.

ii) Explain whether the image produced by rays such as 'Ray 1' above is real.

27 Sketch a ray diagram illustrating how a single ray of white light is refracted and dispersed as it passes through a 60° triangular glass prism.

28 A ray of light enters a prism as shown in the diagram below.

a) Calculate the refractive index of the glass.

b) On a copy of this diagram, draw the path the light ray will take before it leaves the prism and re-enters the air.

c) On your diagram, mark the value of all the angles where the ray changes direction.

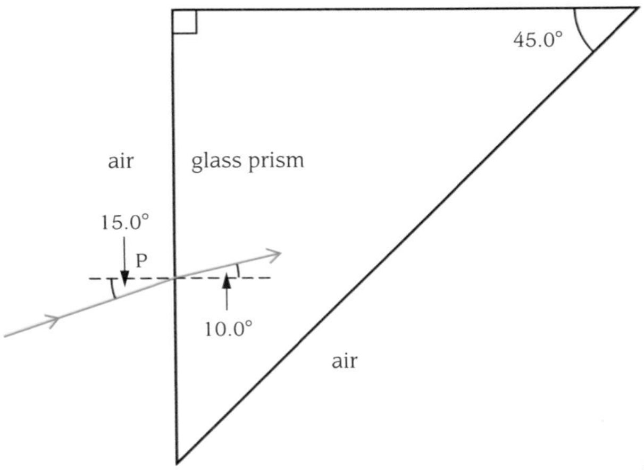

29 The figure below shows a light ray entering a glass prism from the air. The ray is refracted at the first surface and emerges along the outside edge of the second surface.

The refractive index of the glass is 1.5.

a) Calculate the angle of incidence, θ_1.

b) Calculate the critical angle for glass to air.

c) On a copy of this diagram, mark the critical angle.

d) Calculate the angle of the prism at corner B.

e) Another ray enters the prism at the same point but at a smaller angle of incidence. On your copy of the diagram, draw the path of this second ray as it passes through the prism and emerges into the air.

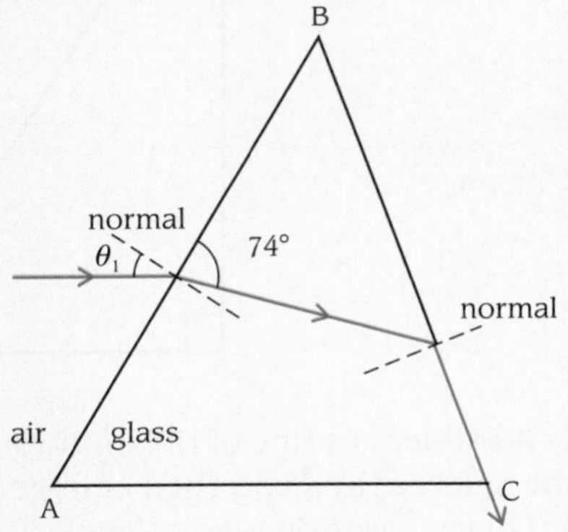

30 The figure below shows a light ray passing from air, through two parallel-sided transparent media and back into air.

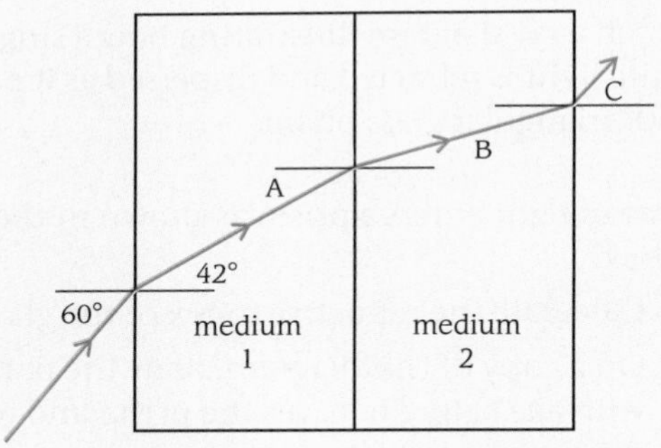

a) Calculate the refractive index from air to medium 1.

b) What is the value of angle A?

c) If the refractive index from medium 1 to medium 2 is 1.20, calculate angle B.

d) State a value for the angle of refraction at C.

31 A light ray strikes the end of an optical fibre from air at an angle of incidence of 30° as shown in the figure below.

a) If the refractive index of the glass is 1.60, calculate the angle of refraction of the ray as it enters the optical fibre.

b) Calculate the critical angle for this glass.

c) Copy the diagram carefully, ideally by tracing or photocopying it. Using a ruler, carefully draw the path of the light ray inside the optical fibre.

d) If all of the glass fibre, except the end where the ray enters, was immersed in water, do you think this would make any difference to what happened to the light ray?

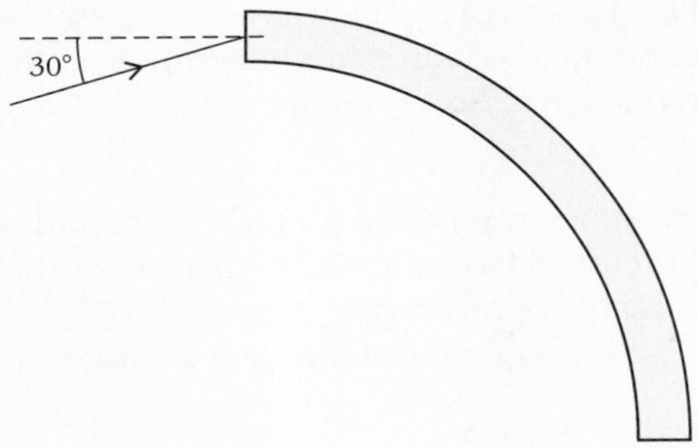

32 A prism is used to produce a spectrum of white light by refracting each colour through a slightly different angle. Which colour is deviated most and which is deviated least?

C10 Lenses

Objectives

By the end of this topic you will be able to:

- draw diagrams to show the effect of converging and diverging lenses on a beam of parallel rays of light and investigate the properties of these types of lenses.

The action of lenses, like prisms, depends on the refraction of light. To understand how lenses work we learn how to construct the paths of rays as they are refracted by a lens. We discover how lenses form images and magnify. We will appreciate how lenses are vital to all optical instruments including our own eyes.

More information about lens types

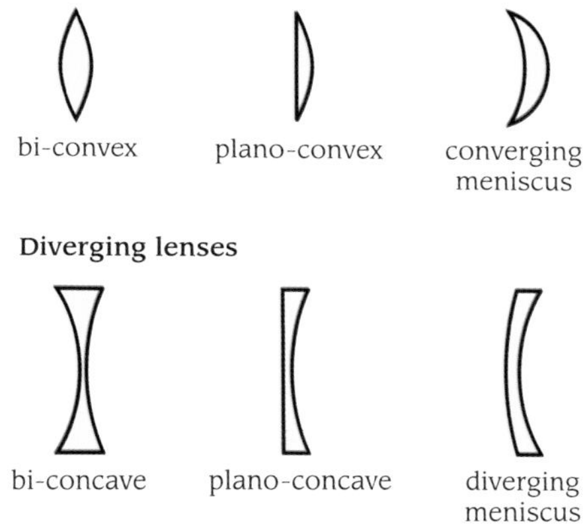

▲ **Figure 10.1.1** Lens shapes

C10.1 Lenses bend light rays

Comparing the converging and diverging properties of lenses

- Use a light box or lamp in a holder to produce multiple rays by passing a broad beam of light through a multiple slit.
- Using convex and concave cylindrical lenses, stand them with their flat edges on a sheet of paper.
- Mark on the paper the paths of the rays before and after passing through each lens.
- Compare the ray paths you have obtained for each lens.

A lens can be thought of as a series of prisms. At the centre of the lens, the 'prism' is like a rectangular block of glass that does not make a light ray change direction. At the edges of the lens, the angles of 'prism' mean it makes light deviate more.

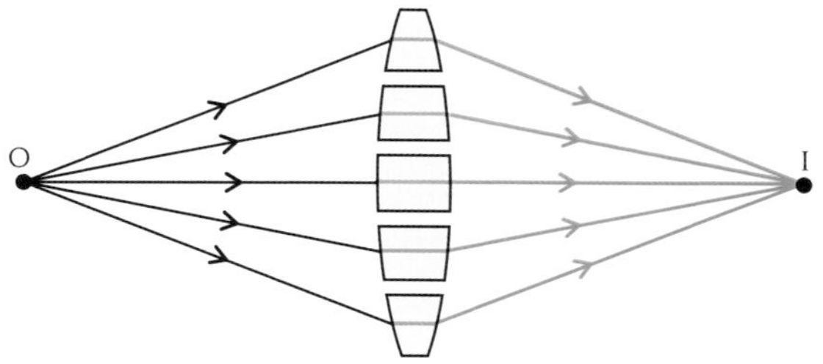

◀ **Figure 10.1.2** A lens works like a set of prisms joined together. Each part of a lens refracts and deviates light like a prism.

How does a lens form an image?

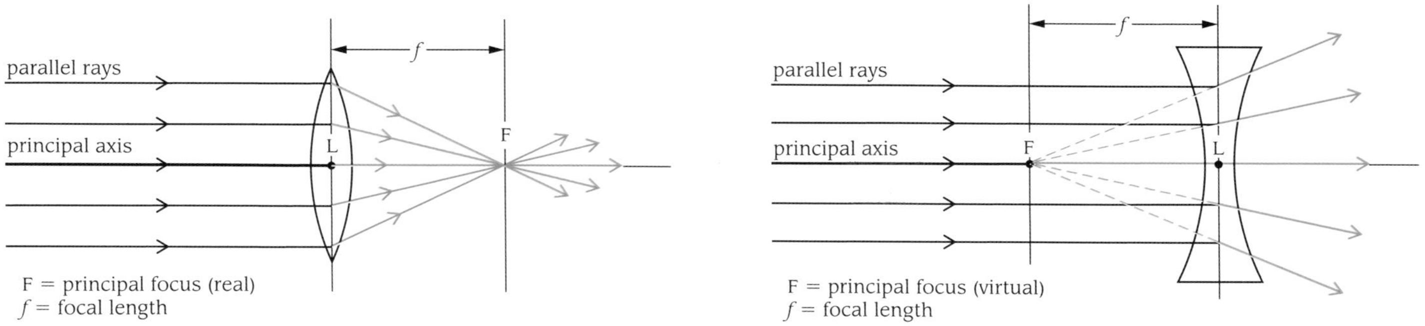

a The principal focus, F, and focal length, *f*, of a converging lens

b The principal focus, F, and focal length, *f*, of a diverging lens

▲ **Figure 10.1.3**

The action of a lens on parallel rays

A converging lens converges or brings together all the parallel rays to pass through a single point called its principal focus, F (Figure 10.1.3a).

A diverging lens diverges or spreads out all the parallel rays so that they appear to come from a single point which is a virtual principal focus, F (Figure 10.1.3b).

The principal focus of a lens lies on the focal plane. The focal plane is the plane that is at right angles to the principal axis of the lens, and has a distance from the lens that is the focal length of the lens.

Rays of light pass through a lens from every point on an object, but it would be very confusing to draw all the rays of light. So to find out what an image is like, we only draw rays from the top and the bottom of an object. You will learn how to find out about images by drawing ray diagrams in C10.3.

Summary questions

1 Sketch how parallel rays of light are refracted by a convex lens.

2 What is a diverging lens?

3 What is the focal length of a lens?

Key fact

Lens definitions

The principal axis of a lens is the line joining the centres of curvature, C_1 and C_2 of its surfaces.

The optical centre of a lens L is the point midway between the surfaces of the lens on its principal axis. Rays passing through the optical centre are not deviated.

The principal focus F of a converging lens is the point to which all rays incident parallel to the principal axis converge after refraction by the lens.

The principal focus F of a diverging lens is the point from which all rays incident parallel to the principal axis appear to diverge after refraction by the lens. This focus is virtual. It is given a negative value in calculations.

The focal length f of a lens is the distance between its optical centre and principal focus.

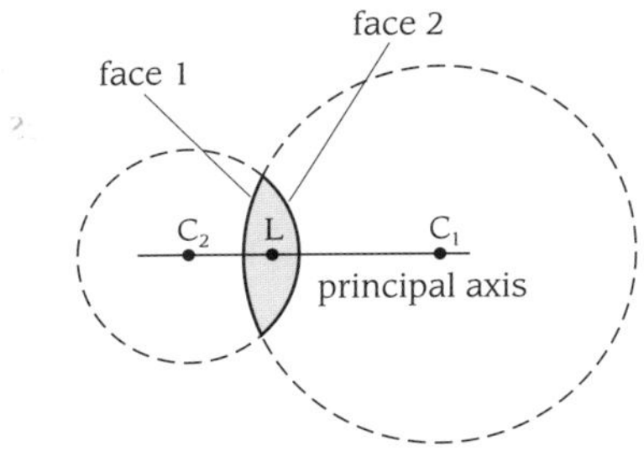

C_1 = centre of curvature of face 1
C_2 = centre of curvature of face 2
L = optical centre

▲ **Figure 10.2.1** The principal axis and optical centre, L

C10.2 Focal lengths and magnification

Objectives

By the end of this topic you will be able to:

- recall the meaning of the terms: principal axis, principal focus, focal length, focal plane, magnification
- describe an experiment to measure the focal length of a converging lens
- calculate magnification using size and distance equations.

Measuring the focal length of a converging lens

A rough method

As an object is moved away from a lens the light rays collected from the object become almost parallel to each other. So the image of a distant object formed by a converging lens will be roughly at the principal focus of the lens.

- Using the window frame at the far end of a room (or better still something like a building visible through the window) as a distant object, obtain a sharp image on the wall (Figure 10.2.2).
- Measure the distance from the lens to the image to obtain a rough value of the focal length of the lens.

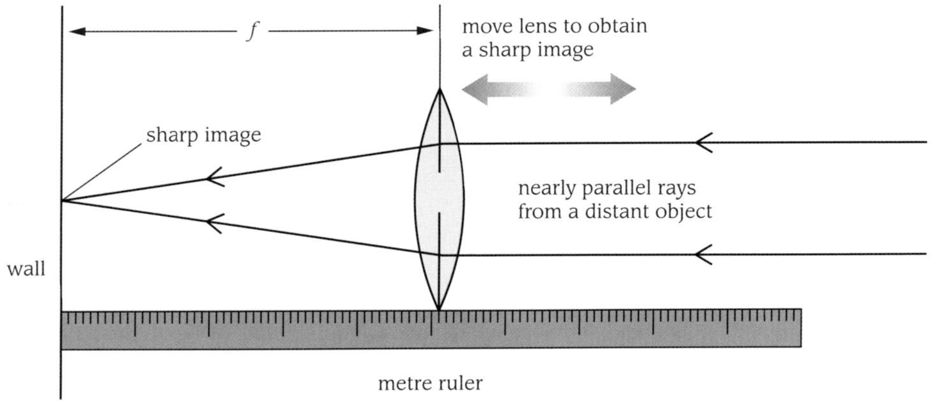

▲ **Figure 10.2.2** A rough method of measuring the focal length of a converging lens

An accurate method

- Draw an object (such as an arrow) on a piece of translucent paper and fit it over a circular hole in a white screen (Figure 10.2.3).
- Mount a converging lens and plane mirror in holders so that light passing through the lens will be sent back by the mirror along the same path. Arrange the lens and mirror facing the illuminated object.
- Move the lens until a sharp image of the object is formed alongside the illuminated object. The image will be sharpest when it is exactly the same size as the object.
- Measure the distance between the optical centre of the lens and the front of the light box. This is the focal length.

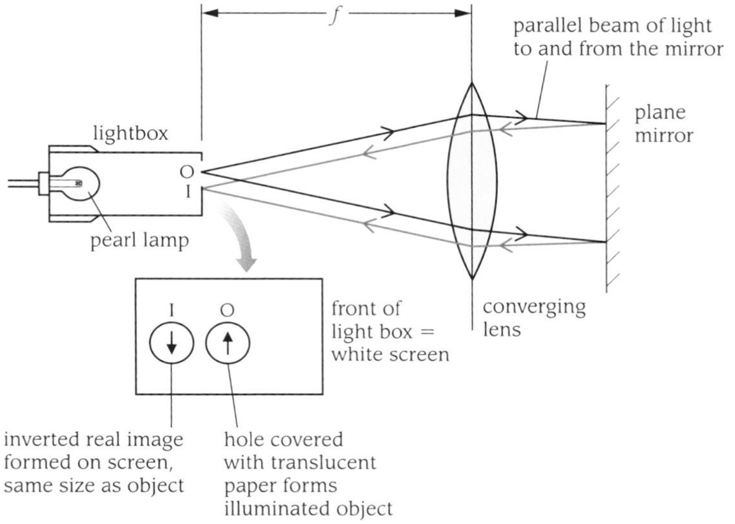

▲ **Figure 10.2.3** Measuring the focal length of a converging lens using a plane mirror and an illuminated object

The magnification equations

The linear magnification, *m*, of a lens is defined by the equation:

$$\text{linear magnification, } m = \frac{\text{image size}}{\text{object size}}$$

In the similar triangles XOL and YIL, the sides OX and IY are the sizes of the object and image respectively (Figure 10.2.4).

The side OL is the object distance from the lens, symbol *u*.

The side IL is the image distance from the lens, symbol *v*.

The corresponding pairs of sides of the triangles are in the same ratio:

$$\frac{IY}{OX} = \frac{IL}{OL}$$

or

$$\frac{\text{image size}}{\text{object size}} = \frac{\text{image distance}}{\text{object distance}} = \frac{v}{u} = m$$

which gives us another magnification formula:

$$m = \frac{v}{u}$$

Key fact

Magnification, *m*

- An image is magnified when the linear magnification *m* is greater than 1 ($m > 1$).
- An image is diminished when the linear magnification *m* is less than 1 ($m < 1$).
- Note that *m* is a number and has no units.

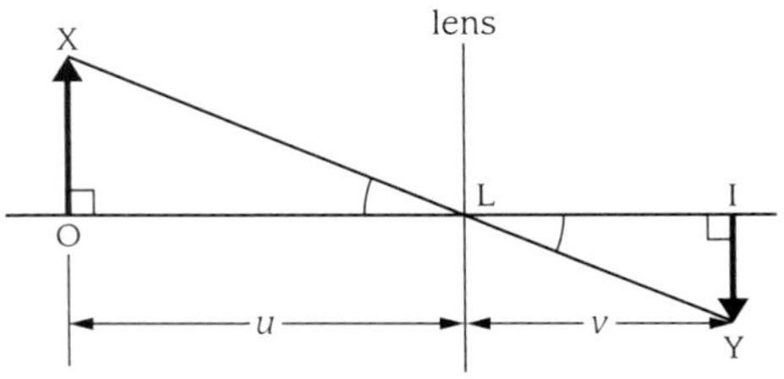

▲ **Figure 10.2.4** Linear magnification $m = v/u$

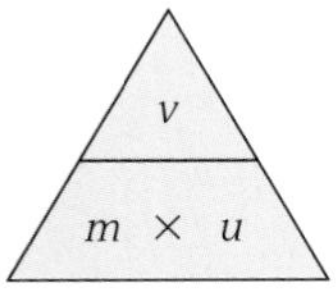

Worked example

A building is 6.0 m high and 80 m from a converging camera lens. The camera forms an image, which is 6.0 mm high.

a) What is the magnification?

b) How far must the image sensor be behind the lens for a focused image to be formed?

---

a) $m = \frac{\text{image size}}{\text{object size}} = \frac{6\text{ mm}}{6000\text{ mm}} = \frac{1}{1000} = 0.001$ so diminished

b) $m = \frac{v}{u}$

Rearranged, this gives: $v = m \times u = 0.001 \times 80\text{ m}$
Image distance behind the lens, $v = 0.08$ m or 8.0 cm.

Summary questions

1. Describe a method to find the approximate focal length of a lens.
2. Write down the equation for magnification.
3. A lens has a magnification of 4. If the image is 8 cm high, how high is the object?

Objectives

By the end of this topic you will be able to:

- draw ray diagrams to explain the formation of real and virtual images
- distinguish between real and virtual images
- perform experiments to locate real and virtual images
- use the lens formula to find the focal length of a lens and solve problems.

C10.3 Ray diagrams and the lens formula

There are three particular rays which can be drawn accurately in lens ray diagrams. We use these to find the position of the image formed by a lens.

The distance of the object from the lens is critical in deciding the nature, size and position of the image and for this reason it is vital to mark clearly the position of the principal focus of a lens. When the object is nearer to a converging lens than its principal focus it can only form a virtual image.

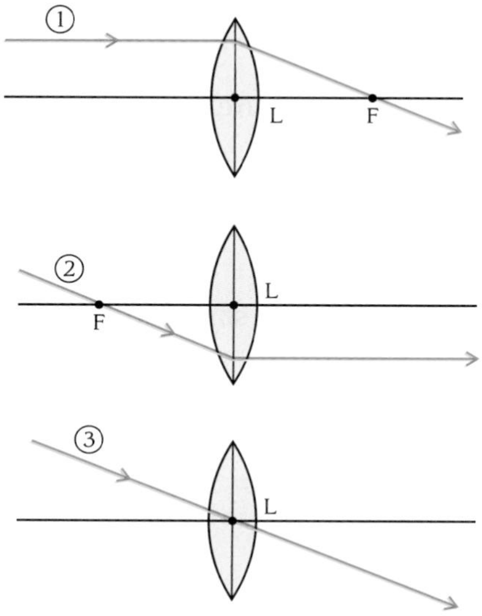

① A ray parallel to the principal axis is refracted (by the lens) to pass through F.

② A ray arriving through F is refracted parallel to the principal axis (ray ① reversed).

③ A ray through the optical centre L is undeviated.

▲ **Figure 10.3.1** Three special rays used in lens ray diagrams

a) Object between F and L
Image
- **i)** virtual
- **ii)** erect
- **iii)** magnified
- **iv)** on the same side of lens as O and further away

Uses:
- **i)** magnifying glass
- **ii)** instrument eyepieces
- **iii)** spectacles correction for long-sightedness

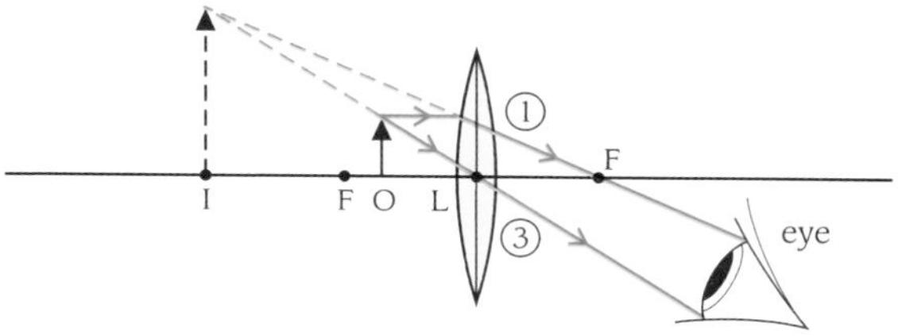

b) Object at F
Image at infinity

Uses: produces a parallel beam of light as in a spotlight with lamp at O

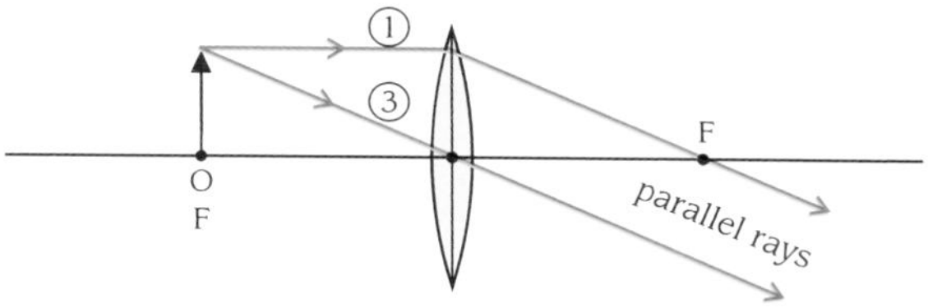

c) Object between F and 2F
Image:
- **i)** real
- **ii)** inverted
- **iii)** magnified
- **iv)** on opposite side of lens to O, beyond 2F

Uses:
- **i)** projector
- **ii)** microscope objective lens

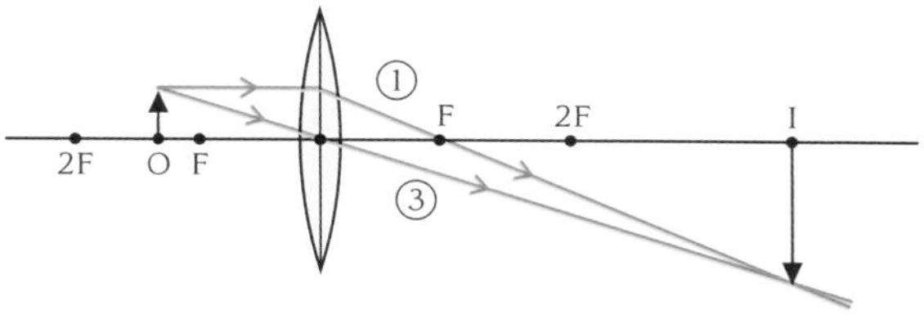

d) Object beyond 2F
Image:
- **i)** real
- **ii)** inverted
- **iii)** diminished
- **iv)** on opposite side of lens, between F and 2F

this is diagram **c)** reversed

Uses:
- **i)** camera
- **ii)** the eye

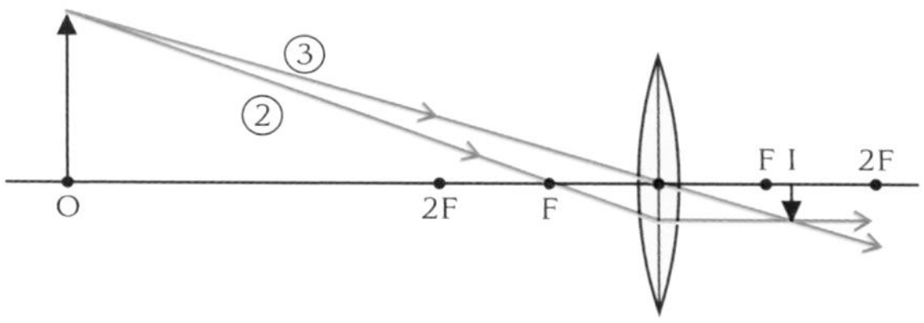

e) Object at infinity
Image:
- **i)** real
- **ii)** inverted
- **iii)** diminished
- **iv)** on opposite side of lens, at F

this is diagram **b)** reversed

Use:
objective lens of a telescope

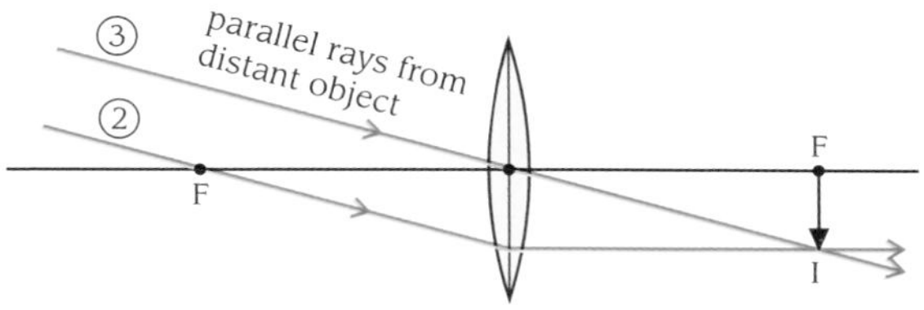

▲ **Figure 10.3.2** Images formed by converging lenses

! Key fact

Real images

- Real images can be formed on a screen or inside a camera.
- Light rays travel to a real image from the object.
- Real images are inverted, i.e. an upside-down version of the object.

Virtual images

- Virtual images are not really there and no light reaches them.
- Virtual images occur where rays of light appear to come from after changing direction.
- Virtual images are erect, i.e. the same way up as the object.
- Virtual images can be seen only by looking through a lens or into a mirror.

Things to remember when drawing ray diagrams

- Draw rays as solid lines with arrows indicating their direction.
- Draw virtual rays and images as broken lines.
- Draw rays from the tip of an object at a point off the axis so that you can find the size of the image and which way up it is.
- Draw rays bending only once, halfway through the lens, and nowhere else.
- Images on the same side of a lens as the object are always virtual and erect.

The lens formula

Experimental results show that the relation between the focal length, *f*, the object distance (from the lens), *u*, and the image distance, *v*, for all lenses is given by the formula:

$$\frac{1}{u}+\frac{1}{v}=\frac{1}{f}$$

The real-is-positive sign convention

When using the lens formula, distances to real objects and images are given positive values and distances to virtual images are given negative values. So, if your answer to a calculation of an image distance, *v* is negative, you know that the image is virtual.

Measuring the focal length of a converging lens using the lens formula

Use an illuminated object in a darkened room to form a real image on a screen as shown in Figure 10.3.3. The arrangement is the same as in a projector. The illuminated object takes the place of the film or slide in the projector. The image on the screen is real and inverted but its size depends on the distances *u* and *v*.

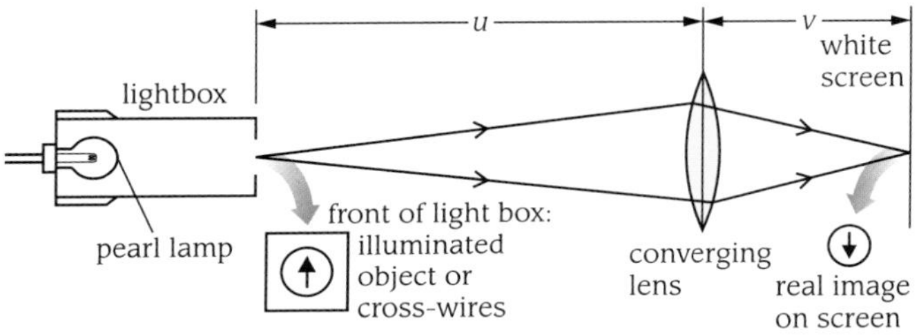

▲ **Figure 10.3.3** Measuring the focal length of a converging lens using the lens formula

- Keep the illuminated object in a fixed position at one end of a bench or table and then, for various positions of the screen, move the lens until the image is sharp on the screen.
- Decide on the best position for the lens by finding the point midway between the positions where you can tell that the image is just going out of focus.

There are two lens positions for each screen position. Do you notice anything about the values of *u* and *v* for these two positions?

- Find values of $1/u$, $1/v$. Then calculate $1/u + 1/v$ to two significant figures using a calculator. The reciprocal of this value gives *f*.

Sample results

u/cm	*v*/cm	$\frac{1}{u}/\frac{1}{\text{cm}}$	$\frac{1}{v}/\frac{1}{\text{cm}}$	$\frac{1}{u}+\frac{1}{v}=\frac{1}{f}/\frac{1}{\text{cm}}$	*f*/cm
60	40	0.017	0.025	0.042	24

Worked example: converging lens

An object is placed in front of a converging lens of focal length 12 cm. Find the nature, position and magnification of the image when the object is 16 cm from the lens.

$u = +16$ cm (real object)

$f = +12$ cm

Rearranging the lens formula:

we have: $\frac{1}{u} + \frac{1}{v} = \frac{1}{f}$

$$\frac{1}{v} = \frac{1}{f} - \frac{1}{u} = \frac{1}{12} - \frac{1}{16}$$

$$= \frac{4-3}{48} = \frac{1}{48}$$

$v = 48$ cm

Using: $m = \frac{v}{u} = \frac{48}{16} = 3$

The image is real (v is positive) and inverted, 48 cm from the lens on the opposite side to the object and magnified 3×.

Worked example: diverging lens

An object is placed in front of a diverging lens of focal length 4 cm. Find the nature, position and magnification of the image when the object is 12 cm from the lens.

$u = +12$ cm (real object)

$f = -4$ cm (diverging lens)

Rearranging the lens formula, and substituting in values we have:

$$\frac{1}{v} = -\frac{1}{4} - \frac{1}{12} = -\frac{4}{12}$$

$v = -3$ cm

Using $m = \frac{v}{u}$ gives $m = \frac{3}{12} = 0.25$

So the image is virtual (negative value for v), and smaller than the object (value of m is less than 1). Because it is a diverging lens, the image will be upright and on the same side of the lens as the object.

Summary questions

1. When does a convex lens act as a magnifying glass?
2. What does a negative image distance mean?
3. Calculate the image distance if the focal length is 2 cm and the object distance is 6 cm.

Objectives

By the end of this topic you will be able to:

- draw a diagram of the eye
- explain how the eye forms an image and focuses on near and distant objects
- explain how the eye copes with different amounts of light.

C10.4 The eye

When we look at an object our eyes form an image of it at the back of the eye as a camera does, but our eyes are much more than an optical instrument. They are our window on the world, and what we see and do not see through them affects our whole view of life. With our eyes we send and receive messages; in them we see love and hatred, hope and fear. By learning about the eye we realise even more what an amazing instrument it is.

The structure and action of the eye

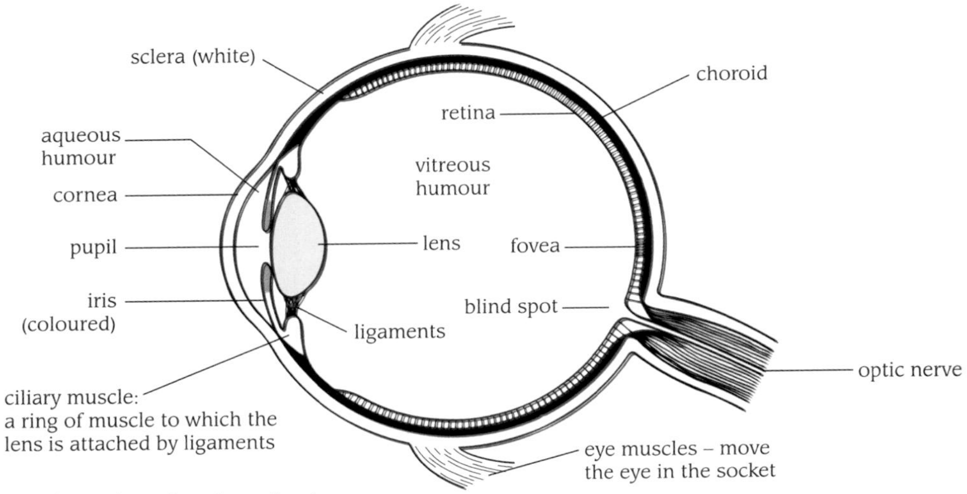

a A horizontal section through a human eye

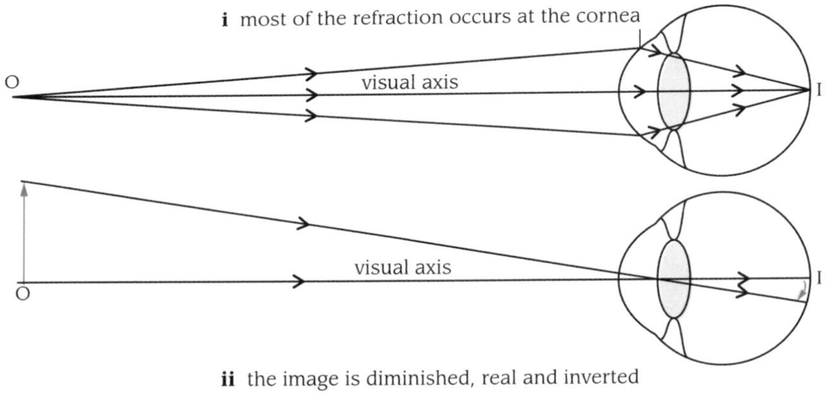

b Ray diagrams for a human eye

▲ **Figure 10.4.1** The human eye

Figure 10.4.1 shows the structure of the human eye. Light entering the eye is refracted by the **cornea**. This does most of the focusing of the eye. Some visual defects can be corrected by laser surgery to reshape the cornea to adjust the way it refracts light onto the back of the eye. Further focusing is done by the lens. Muscles pull the edges of the lens to change its shape and so enable the eye to focus on near or distant objects. The cornea and the lens together act like the lens of a camera. Both the eye and the camera form an image that is inverted. Our brain adjusts this automatically so we see things 'the right way up.'

Light entering the eye falls on light-sensitive cells in the **retina**, which sends electrical signals to the brain along the **optic nerve**. The retina acts like the film in an old-fashioned camera and like the light-sensitive photoelectric surface in a digital camera.

The pupil is the black hole in the centre of the eye that lets light into the eye. The iris is the coloured part of the eye. The iris makes the pupil larger in dim light and smaller in bright light. Too little light entering the eye would mean the retina could not form an image; too much light would damage the retina. This is similar to adjusting the exposure time for an old-fashioned camera (Figure 10.4.2). Digital cameras adjust the exposure time automatically.

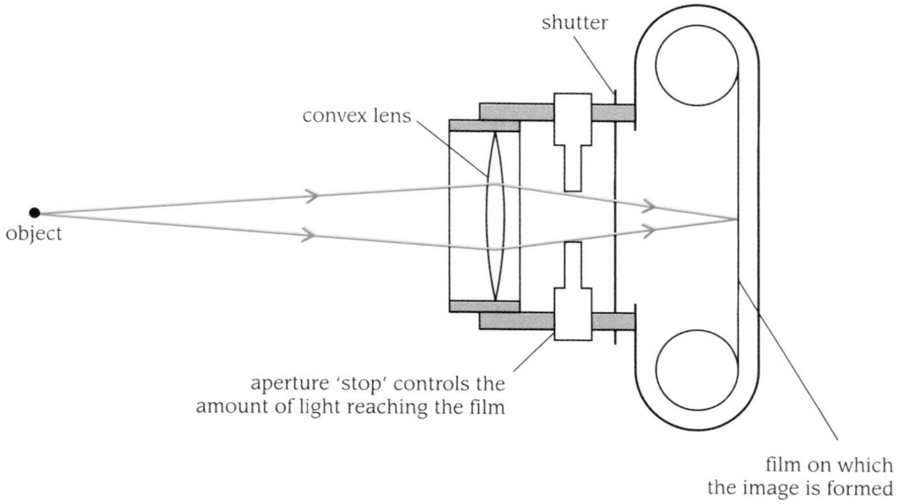

▲ **Figure 10.4.2** An old-fashioned camera

Finding your own blind spots (you do not need to remember this)

Look at the cross and dot in Figure 10.4.3 with your left eye and close your right eye. Starting with the book about 30 cm from your eye, concentrate on the dot and slowly bring the book towards you. When the image of the cross falls on your blind spot what happens?

▲ **Figure 10.4.3** Find your blind spot

Focusing the eye

The lens is a converging lens of a jelly-like, flexible and transparent material. It is suspended inside the eye by a circular band of ligaments.

The ligaments are attached to a circular ring of muscle called the **ciliary muscle**, which controls the shape of the lens.

When the ciliary muscle is relaxed it becomes a larger ring and the lens is stretched into a flatter shape. The flatter lens has its longest focal length and focuses rays from distant objects onto the retina.

Contraction of the ciliary muscle reduces its diameter and allows the lens to become fatter and more powerful. This shorter focal length lens now focuses images of near objects on the retina.

Accommodation

Accommodation is the name given to the ability of the lens of the eye to change its focal length and produce focused images of both distant and near objects on the retina.

The eye lens changes its focusing distance by changing its shape. The lens becomes fatter and more powerful when we focus on near objects.

As we get older the accommodation of our eyes becomes limited and we may need to use glasses to read.

Summary questions

1 How does the human eye focus light?

2 Which bit of the human eye functions like the photosensitive surface in a digital camera?

3 What is the function of the pupil?

Practice exam-style questions

1 The figure below shows two rays from the top of an object OA, which pass through the lens L to the image IB.

a) On a sheet of graph paper, redraw the ray diagram and draw two rays from the top of the object O_1A_1, which pass through the lens; hence find the image of O_1A_1 and label it I_1B_1.

b) State the difference between the image IB and the image I_1B_1.

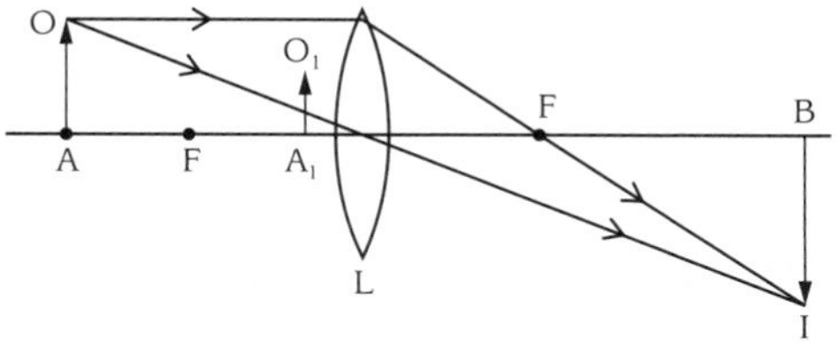

2 A projector is used to produce a magnified image of an object that is 1 cm tall on a colour slide. If the focal length of the projector lens is 20 cm and the colour slide is placed 25 cm from the lens, find the position and size of the image formed on a screen.

3 An object 2 cm tall is placed on the axis of a converging lens of focal length 5 cm at a distance of 3 cm from the optical centre of the lens.

a) Draw a ray diagram to show how the image is formed and observed.

b) Find the position and size of the image.

c) Without drawing further ray diagrams, state the nature and position of the image, saying also whether it is large or small, when the object is at a distance from the lens of:

i) 6.0 cm

ii) 20 m.

d) State a practical application of the use of such a lens with the object in each of positions **i)** and **ii)**.

4 A film projector is used to produce a magnified real image on a screen. The screen is 30 m away from the lens of the projector and the film is 3.0 cm from the lens. Calculate:

a) the magnification produced by this arrangement

b) the size of an image on the screen if the object on the film was 5 mm high.

5 A camera takes a close-up photograph of a ruler with a millimetre scale. If the focal length of the camera lens is 8.0 cm and the ruler is 24 cm away from the camera lens, calculate:

a) the distance the lens should be in front of the image sensor in the camera to give a sharp image

b) the distance apart of the images of the millimetre graduations on the sensor.

6 The figure below shows scale drawings of a window frame and the image of the frame produced on a screen by a converging lens.

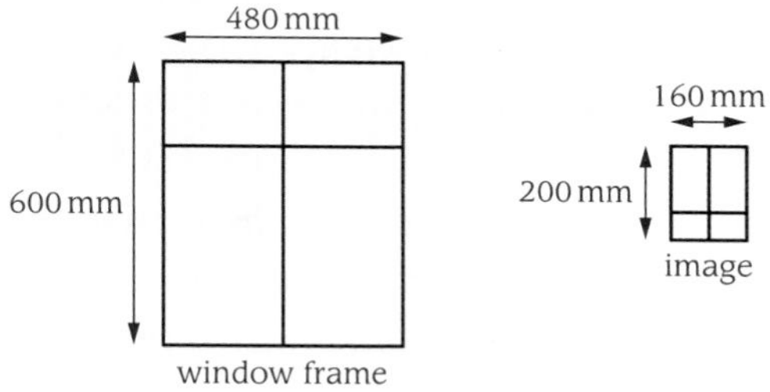

a) Calculate the linear magnification of the image.

b) If the image of the frame was produced 500 mm from the lens. Find:

i) the distance of the actual frame from the lens

ii) the focal length of the lens.

7 The figure below shows parallel rays of light from a small distant object arriving at a converging lens.

a) Which of the labelled positions represents the principal focus of the lens? Give your reasons for rejecting each of the other positions.

b) At which position is the image of the small distant object formed? Describe the image.

c) Which distance is the focal length of the lens?

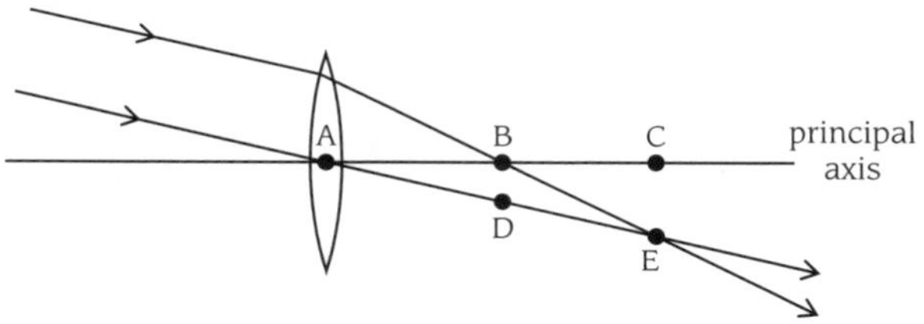

8 A camera is used to take a close-up picture of an object 3 cm tall. The object is positioned 24 cm in front of the lens and a focused image is formed on the sensor 12 cm behind the lens. Using graph paper, find the focal length of the camera lens and the size of the image formed on the sensor.

9 a) An object 2 cm high is placed 6 cm in front of a converging lens with focal length 3 cm. Use graph paper to find the position of the image, and describe its nature. Draw the lens in the centre of the page.

b) The same object is moved closer to the lens so that the new object distance is 2 cm. Using graph paper, find the position and nature of the new image.

c) A diverging lens of focal length 3 cm forms an upright, virtual image 2 cm from the lens, and 1 cm high. Use graph paper to find out how far the object must have been placed from the lens and what size the object must be.

10 For each of the images described below, state the type of lens used to produce the image, and where the object must be placed.

a) Image is always upright and virtual.

b) Image is formed at a distance of $2f$ from the lens, is inverted, real and the same size as the object.

c) Image is inverted, real and formed at infinity.

d) Image is virtual, upright and larger than the object.

e) Image is real, inverted and larger than the object.

f) Image is real, inverted and smaller than the object.

11 A lens is used as a magnifying lens. What type of lens must be used and where must the object be placed?

a) How can the lens be changed to give a larger magnification?

b) How can the position of the object be changed to give a larger image with the same lens?

C11 Vibrations and waves

Objectives

By the end of this topic you will be able to:

- describe vibrations in terms of their frequency, period and amplitude
- recall the units of these physical quantities
- distinguish between displacement and amplitude
- recall and use the relationship:

$$T = \frac{1}{f}$$

▲ **Figure 11.1.1** Bob Marley's son, Stephen Marley, performing on stage. The strings on a musical instrument vibrate.

Key fact

A complete to-and-fro movement is usually called an oscillation or cycle (Figure 11.1.3). One complete oscillation involves both a forwards and backwards swing of the pendulum or, starting at the mid-point of its swing, an oscillation is completed when the bob passes through the midpoint again moving in the same direction.

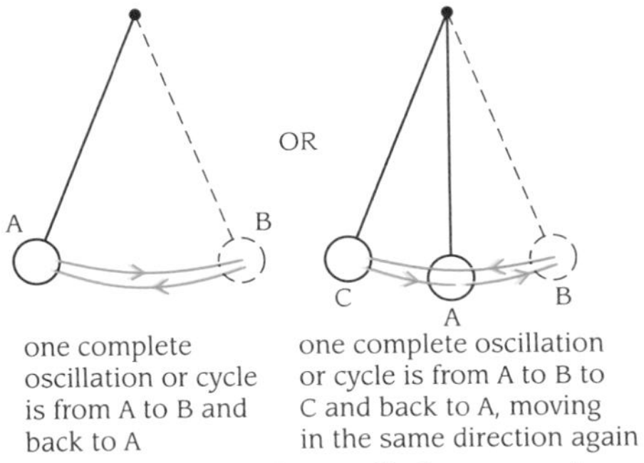

▲ **Figure 11.1.3** An oscillation or cycle

We hear the vibrations of musical instruments and feel the vibrations made by heavy vehicles. We see light and feel the warmth of a fire. Surprisingly, all these sensations have something in common; they all involve the transfer of energy in the form of a wave motion.

C11.1 Vibrations and oscillations

Observing oscillations

Lots of things that move with a regular to-and-fro motion are said to vibrate or oscillate. Many things vibrate slowly enough for us to study their properties while watching them.

- Set up some of the oscillators shown in Figure 11.1.2.

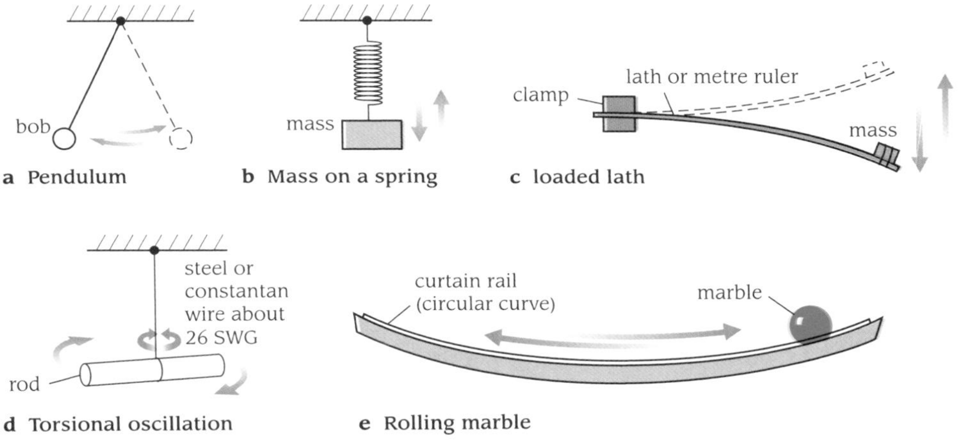

▲ **Figure 11.1.2** Vibrations (the arrows indicate motion, not forces)

There are others that may be added, like the oscillations of a compass needle or a liquid in a U-tube set oscillating by blowing down one side of the tube. Each example is set vibrating by displacing it from its rest position and letting it go; each then vibrates or oscillates naturally in a way that depends on the forces acting on it. Make the following observations:

- What happens to the size of the vibration after letting go?
- In what position do they stop vibrating?
- How long does each swing or oscillation take? Are the time intervals equal or do they get smaller as the vibrations get smaller?
- Can any of them be made to vibrate freely at a different rate?

Describing oscillations

Damping

All the vibrations die away, some more quickly than others. The vibrations are said to be **damped**. They gradually lose their energy as frictional forces, such as air resistance, converting it into heat energy.

Worked example

If a vibrating string makes 10 complete oscillations in 1 second, it has a frequency f of 10 hertz. What is its period?

The time it takes for 1 complete oscillation is its period T:

$$T = \frac{1}{f} = \frac{1}{10} = 0.1 \text{ Hz}$$

Equilibrium position

In these examples, the oscillator always comes to rest at the same position or level, which is usually the central position in the vibration called the **equilibrium position**. Here the various forces acting are in equilibrium, i.e. balanced.

Period, *T*

Usually the time taken for an oscillation stays the same even as the movement gets smaller. Not only does the time for each oscillation remain the same from one to the next, but it is also the same every time we start if off. For example, the timing of a pendulum swing is so precisely constant that it is often used to control the speed of clocks. The constant time taken for one complete oscillation is called the **period**.

The period, T, is the time a vibrating object takes to make one complete oscillation.

The period, T, like all time intervals, is measured in seconds.

Frequency, *f*

The frequency, f, is the number of complete oscillations (or cycles) made in 1 second.

Frequency is measured in hertz, symbol Hz. One hertz is defined as one oscillation per second. If in 1 second there are f complete oscillations, then each oscillation takes $1/f$ of a second, which is its period T.

$$\text{period} = \frac{1}{\text{frequency}} \qquad T = \frac{1}{f}$$

Displacement, *s*

The displacement, s, of a vibrating object is its distance, in either direction, from the equilibrium or central position.

Amplitude, *a*

The amplitude, a, is the maximum displacement, in either direction, from the equilibrium or central position.

The vibrations we have looked at that have a constant period T, whether the amplitude is large or small, are called **isochronous vibrations** ('isochronous' means of equal period). However, not all vibrations are isochronous.

- Try dropping a ball and listen to its bouncing. What do you notice about the time intervals between bounces?

Summary questions

1 Describe what is meant by one complete oscillation.

2 What is the relationship between frequency and time for one oscillation?

3 What is the amplitude of a vibration?

C11.2 Waves on a spring

Observing waves

- Stretch out a slinky spring along a smooth floor or bench top allowing plenty of room on either side for movement of the spring.
- Holding one end fixed, generate waves by shaking the other end. Try to produce the different kinds of waves shown in Figure 11.2.1.

Pulses

A pulse is a short-lived or single wave motion.

a) A single **transverse pulse** is produced by a quick flick of the hand, a to-and-fro sideways movement at right angles to the slinky spring.

b) A single **longitudinal pulse** is produced by a quick jerk of the hand forwards and backwards along the line of the slinky.

Wavetrains

A wavetrain is a continuous group of waves with features that repeat regularly.

c) A **transverse wavetrain** is produced by swinging the hand to-and-fro sideways (at right angles to the line of the slinky) at a constant frequency of about 4 hertz. If the slinky is long enough the waves can be seen to travel continuously in one direction.

d) A **longitudinal wavetrain** can be seen to travel along the slinky if the hand is oscillated backwards and forwards (in line with the spring) several times at a constant rate.

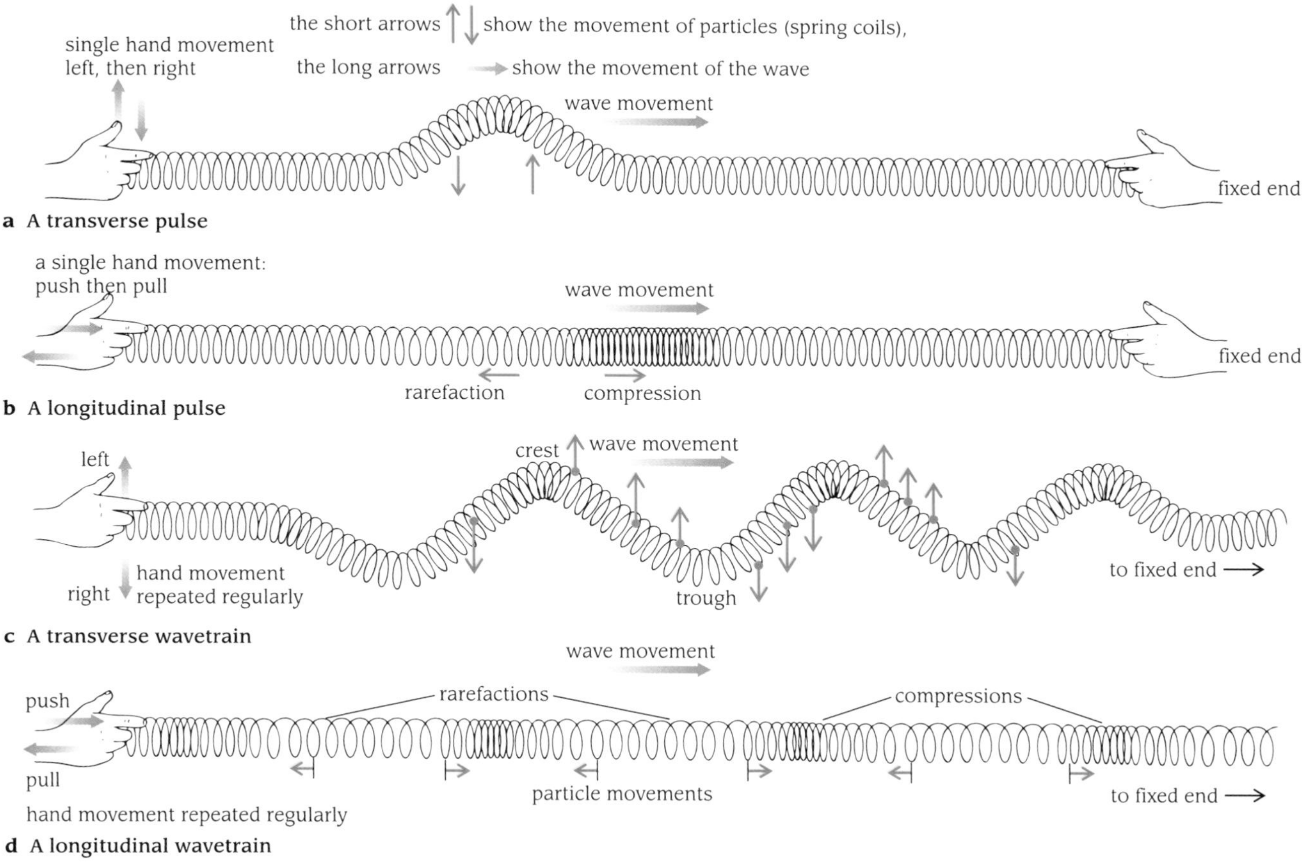

▲ **Figure 11.2.1** Wave motions on a slinky

Objectives

By the end of this topic you will be able to:

- differentiate between pulses and wavetrains of progressive waves and between transverse and longitudinal waves
- draw diagrams of transverse and longitudinal waves
- explain the meanings of wavelength and phase
- use the wave equation: $v = f\lambda$
- represent transverse and longitudinal waves in displacement–position and displacement–time graphs and extract information about waves from these graphs.

Things to do

- Describe what happens to the amplitude of the pulses and waves as they travel along a slinky and why.
- Describe what happens to the speed of the pulses and waves as they travel along a slinky, and whether the speed is affected by how much the spring is stretched.
- For each type of wave motion describe the motion of a single coil in the slinky. (This can be made easier by attaching a light pointer like a drinking straw to one of the coils.)
- Describe what happens when pulses reach the fixed end.
- Explain what actually travels along the slinky.

Describing waves

The wave motions seen on a slinky are made up of vibrations of its individual coils; this is a mechanical wave. All mechanical waves require a medium or material to travel through and they cause the individual particles of that medium to vibrate or oscillate. We can begin to describe a wave motion by noting what happens to the particles that it causes to vibrate.

There are two main kinds of wave motion called **transverse** and **longitudinal**.

Transverse waves are ones in which the displacement of the particles is at right angles to the direction of travel of the wave motion.

Transverse waves can easily be recognised by their crests and troughs.

Longitudinal waves are ones in which the displacement of the particles is in line with, or parallel to, the direction of travel of the wave motion.

Longitudinal waves can be recognised by their compressions and rarefactions. (In compressions, the particles are pushed together and in rarefactions they are pulled apart.)

The Slinky spring

Richard James, a mechanical engineer, was employed by Philadelphia's Cramp Shipyard in 1943 when he accidentally invented the Slinky. As James tested hundreds of springs of varying sizes, metals and tensions, he piled the discards onto his desk. One day, an experimental torsion spring fell off the desk and 'walked' down a pile of books, tumbling end-over-end. James designed and engineered machines to transform 80 feet of wire into a two-and one-half-inch stack of 98 coils, and he and his wife, Betty, cofounded James Industries. Today the company manufactures some 3 million to 4 million Slinkys annually.

▲ **Figure 11.2.1** A Slinky spring

The first Slinkys were manufactured from a dark steel from Sweden. Then the Jameses switched to a more silver-looking steel. Since 1978, the Slinky is also made of the plastic, K-Resin® styrene-butadiene copolymer. Using this plastic a larger diameter Slinky, which is easier for small hands to manage, can be manufactured. Since 1947, sales have topped more than 250 million.

Progressive or travelling waves

In all the examples of wave motions so far described, both transverse and longitudinal, there appears to be something moving or travelling with the waves; but what is actually moving? We can say the following about these waves:

A progressive or travelling wave is the movement of a disturbance that carries energy away from a source.

These waves have the following important features:

- A progressive or travelling wave carries energy.
- The medium or material through which a wave travels does not usually travel with the wave.
- The particles of the medium, which are displaced by the wave motion, vibrate about their rest positions, but do not travel with the wave.
- Each particle in the wave motion vibrates in the same way, but the vibrations have a time lag in the direction of travel of the wave.
- The shape of the wavetrain or pulse stays the same as it travels through a medium, but its amplitude gets smaller as the energy is lost or the waves spread out.
- The speed of a wave is not affected by the shape of the waves or their amplitude, but it *is* affected by the nature of the medium it travels through.

Graphs of waves: displacement–position graphs

A displacement–position graph (Figure 11.2.3) shows how the position of particles on a progressive wave varies when time is kept constant. It is like a snapshot or photograph of the whole wave at a moment in time. Although this graph looks like a transverse wavetrain it can be used to show the displacement of particles in both transverse and longitudinal waves. The displacement can be the distance the particles are moved from their rest positions either at right angles to, or parallel to, the direction of travel of the wave motion.

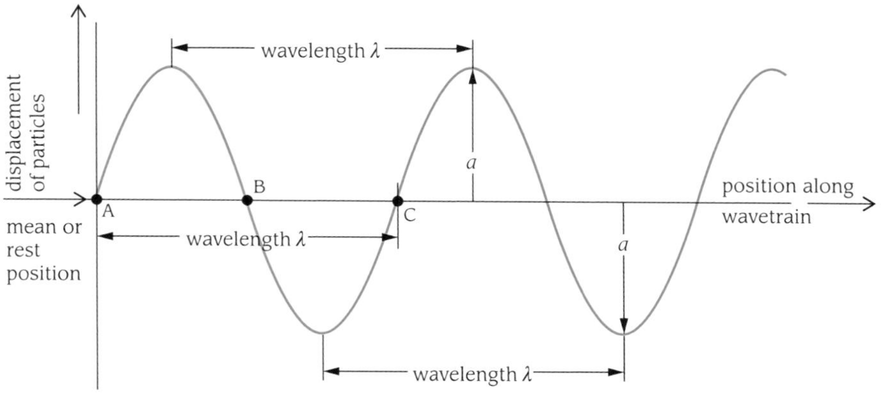

▲ **Figure 11.2.3** Displacement–position graph (at a single moment in time, like a photograph)

Wavelength, λ

The wavelength, λ of a transverse wave is most easily understood as the distance between two successive crests or between two successive troughs (successive crests follow next to each other). Similarly the wavelength of a longitudinal wave is seen as the distance between two successive compressions or two successive rarefactions. The symbol for wavelength is a Greek letter 'ℓ', written λ and called lambda.

Graphs of waves: displacement–time graphs

A displacement–time graph shows how the displacement of a particle in a particular position on a progressive wave (position kept constant) varies with time as the wavetrain passes. The motion of a particle in a wavetrain is exactly the same as the motion of a single oscillating object such as a pendulum. In particular, the motion is repeated regularly with a constant period T, and a graph of the displacement has the same characteristic sine-wave shape (Figure 11.2.4).

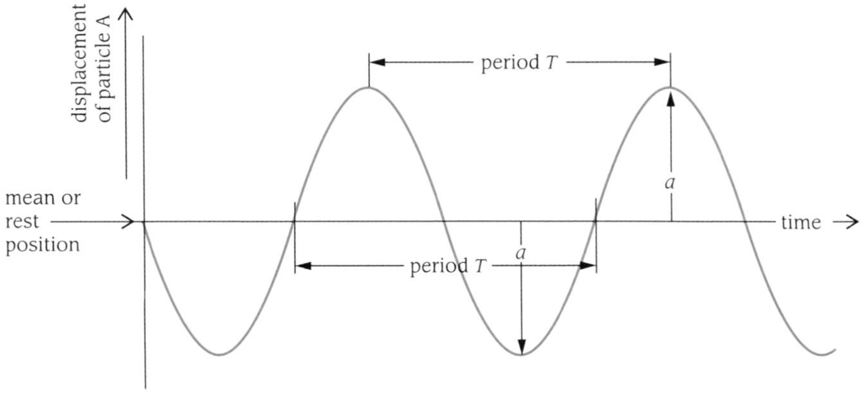

▲ **Figure 11.2.4** Displacement–time graph (of a single particle in the wave)

! Key fact

FOR A PROGRESSIVE OR TRAVELLING WAVE

Wavelength, λ

In the wave diagram (Figure 11.2.3), particles at points A, B and C are at the midpoints in their paths, but only the particles at A and C are moving in the same direction.

The wavelength = AC.

The wavelength, λ of a wavetrain is: the distance between two successive particles that are at exactly the same point in their paths at the same time and are moving in the same direction.

Amplitude, a

The amplitude, a is the maximum displacement of the particles in the wavetrain from their rest positions.

The amplitude of the wave is marked as a. Note that the height of the wave from trough to crest is $2a$.

Phase

The particles in a wavetrain, which are one wavelength apart, move in step with each other and are said to be in phase with each other.

Period, T

The period, T is the time a particle in the wavetrain takes to make one complete oscillation.

Frequency, f

The frequency, f is the number of complete oscillations made in 1 second by a particle in the wavetrain.

(f is measured in hertz.)

Key fact

The speed of a wave:

- is independent of the shape or amplitude of the wave
- is independent of its frequency or wavelength
- is dependent on the nature of the material it travels through.

Worked example

A hand displaces a slinky to-and-fro at a frequency of 3 hertz. If the distance between successive crests of the wavetrain is 0.8 metres, calculate the speed of the waves along the slinky.

$f = 3\,\text{Hz}$
$\lambda = 0.8\,\text{m}$

Using $v = f\lambda = 3\,\text{Hz} \times 0.8\,\text{m} = 2.4\,\text{m Hz} = 2.4\,\text{m s}^{-1}$

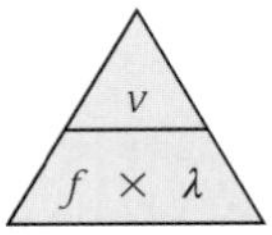

Worked example

A wave is sent along a wire at a speed of $80\,\text{m s}^{-1}$. If its frequency is 20 Hz, find its wavelength.

Rearranging the wave equation

$$\lambda = \frac{v}{f} = \frac{80}{20} = 4\,\text{m}$$

Wave speed, *v*

Observations of pulses and wavetrains travelling along a slinky suggest that the shape and amplitude of a wave do not affect its speed. When we listen to an orchestra the waves of high frequency sounds and low frequency sounds arrive at the listener together, having travelled at the same speed. But waves that travel through different materials are found to travel at different speeds. For example, both sound and light waves are found to travel through water and air at different speeds.

The wave equation

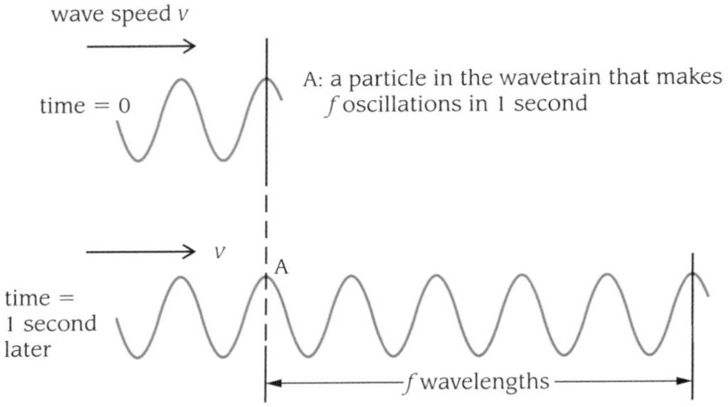

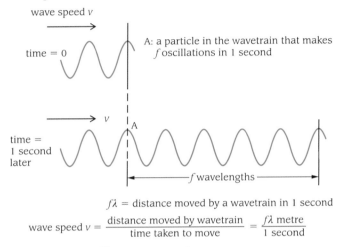

$f\lambda$ = distance moved by a wavetrain in 1 second

$$\text{wave speed } v = \frac{\text{distance moved by wavetrain}}{\text{time taken to move}} = \frac{f\lambda \text{ metre}}{1 \text{ second}}$$

▲ **Figure 11.2.5** The wave equation

In 1 second, the particle at A in the wavetrain makes f complete oscillations. The wavetrain moves forward f wavelengths, a distance of $f\lambda$.

The distance moved by the wavetrain in 1 second is also the wave speed v:

$$\text{wave speed} = \text{frequency} \times \text{wavelength} \qquad \text{or } v = f\lambda.$$

The SI units of the three quantities are: v in metres per second (m s^{-1}), f in hertz (Hz) and λ in metres (m).

Things to do

1 Using a stopwatch and a slinky (or 4 metres or more of flexible rubber or plastic tubing or rope), estimate:
- the frequency of the oscillations of your hand
- the wavelength of the waves generated
- the wave speed.

Check whether your results agree with the wave equation.

2 Name some more types of wave and find out:
- whether they involve single pulses or wavetrains
- whether the displacement is transverse or longitudinal
- whether it is mechanical (requiring a medium) or electromagnetic (requiring no medium and able to travel through space).

3 Name a musical instrument and find out:
- the name of the part of it that vibrates
- how it is made to vibrate
- how the frequency of the vibration is changed for different notes
- whether the vibration is transverse or longitudinal.

Summary questions

1 Sketch a diagram of a longitudinal wave on a slinky spring.

2 Sketch a diagram of a transverse wave on a string.

3 Give one thing that affects the speed of a wave, and one thing that does not.

C11.3 Waves on water

Some of the properties of water waves can be seen on a pond, a lake or a river; but accurate observations are more easily made in a ripple tank. What we discover about water waves helps to explain the nature of other types of wave like sound waves and light waves.

Setting up a ripple tank

One type of ripple tank is like a glass table on legs with an edge round the glass top so that it can hold a shallow layer of water (Figure 11.3.1). A lamp positioned above the table casts shadows of the water waves through the glass onto a white sheet of paper or board on the floor below. We look at the wave shadows on the floor, rather than the actual water waves in the tank. These shadows show the shapes of the wavefronts.

- Fill the tank with water to a depth of about 5 mm.
- Connect the lamp to a suitable power supply.
- To level the tank, look at the two reflections of the lamp, one from the water surface and one from the glass surface, and put wedges under the feet of the tank until the two images of the lamp coincide.
- Adjust the height and position of the lamp to centre the wave picture on the white sheet on the floor. (A suitable height is about 50 cm above the tank, but lowering the lamp will enlarge the picture if this is necessary.)
- Fit pieces of metal gauze or sponge around the edges of the tank. (These act as a 'beach' to scatter or absorb the waves at the edges of the tank, which reduces unwanted reflections from the sides.)

Investigating single wave pulses

The simplest experiments with water waves can be done by making single circular or straight wave pulses.

- To make circular wave pulses, dip a pencil into the water but avoid touching the glass bottom and shaking the tank.
- To make straight waves, lay a length of thick dowel rod in the water and give it a quick forwards roll.

Generating continuous wavetrains

- Hang a small electric motor mounted on a wooden beam by rubber bands from the support above the ripple tank.

An eccentric (off-centre) metal disc on the axle of the motor causes the beam to vibrate at the same frequency as the revolutions of the motor. The speed of the motor is controlled by a rheostat in series with a low-voltage DC supply or battery.

Objectives

By the end of this topic you will be able to:

- describe how to use a ripple tank to demonstrate wave behaviour and properties
- use water waves to demonstrate and draw diagrams to explain:
  - reflection
  - refraction
  - diffraction
  - interference of waves
- relate refraction to change of wave speed across a boundary
- predict and observe the effects of changing the gap width or the wavelength on the pattern of waves diffracted through a single slit
- draw and explain interference patterns in terms of superposition of crests or troughs of waves
- demonstrate double slit interference and predict changes of the pattern caused by changing the slit spacing or the wavelength of the waves
- use the following equations to solve problems on refraction:

$$\frac{\sin\theta_1}{\sin\theta_2} = \frac{v_1}{v_2} = \frac{\lambda_1}{\lambda_2}$$

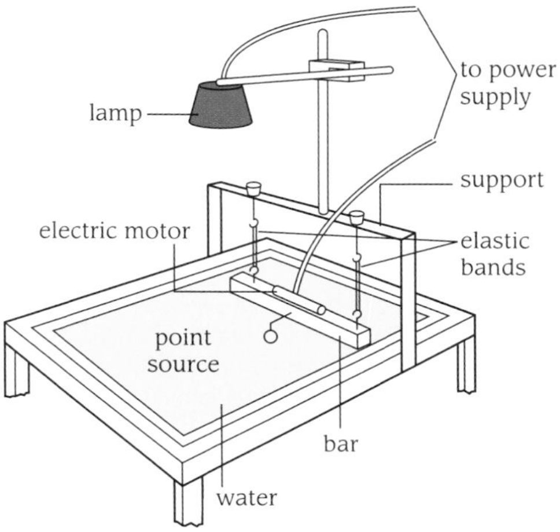

▲ **Figure 11.3.1** A ripple tank

- To generate continuous straight waves, adjust the height of the vibrating beam so that it just touches the water surface.

Smoother waves are produced if the surface of the wooden beam is rubbed in the water so as to wet it thoroughly.

- To generate continuous circular waves, fit a small spherical dipper to the beam and raise it so that the dipper just touches the water surface.
- Adjust the speed of the motor to vary the frequency and wavelength of the continuous wavetrains.

Using a stroboscope to freeze the movement of the waves

- Use a handheld stroboscope, or an electronic stroboscope if available, to view the wave patterns.
- Adjust the frequency of the stroboscope so that it is the same as the frequency of the vibrator producing the waves. This produces a stationary wave pattern on the screen.

Wave diagrams and wavefronts

Wave diagrams show the positions of wavefronts at a particular instant. Wave diagrams are like a photograph of the wave shadows seen on the screen of the ripple tank. The shadow patterns can represent the positions of wave fronts.

A wavefront is an imaginary line that joins a set of particles which are in phase (in step) in a wave motion.

All the particles along a crest of a wave are in phase and can be considered as a wavefront. In effect, when we draw a wavefront we draw the shape of the wave as seen from above, i.e. a plan view. The shape of the wave seen from the side would be a wave profile.

Wavefronts and wave velocities

When you draw a wave diagram it is important to distinguish between wavefronts and the direction of travel of the waves. Mark the direction of travel or velocity of the waves with an arrow. The wave velocity vector follows the same path as a light ray would when reflected by a mirror or refracted by a medium.

The stroboscope principle

When we use a stroboscope to view something that has a regular repetitive motion, if the frequency of the glimpses matches the frequency of the repetitive motion then the motion will appear to stop.

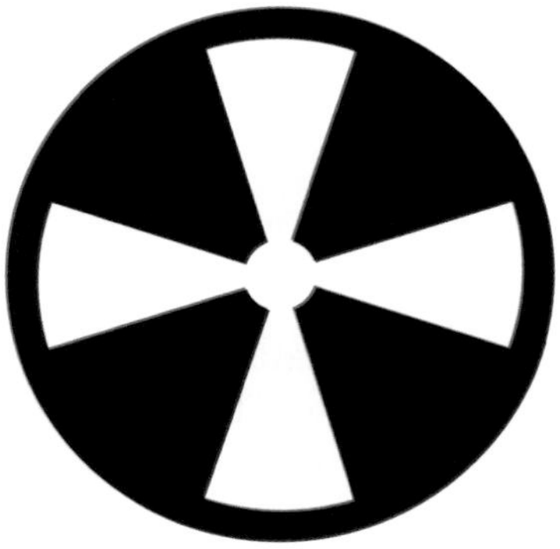

Figure 11.3.2 A disc with cut out sectors can be used to create a stroboscopic effect. The disc can be turned by hand or driven by an electric motor. The disc should be mounted under the light source if motor driven. When handheld, the wave patterns can be 'frozen' by viewing them through the rotating disc.

Key fact

- In water of a constant depth, the waves travel at a constant speed, therefore we draw the wavefronts equally spaced and parallel.
- The direction of travel of the waves, which should be shown, is always at right angles to the wavefronts.
- When drawing wave diagrams of reflection or refraction it helps to bear in mind the equivalent light-ray diagrams. The direction of travel of the waves obeys the same laws as the direction of light rays. (See C9.3.)
- Sources of circular waves and their images formed by reflection should be labelled.

Reflection of straight and circular wavefronts

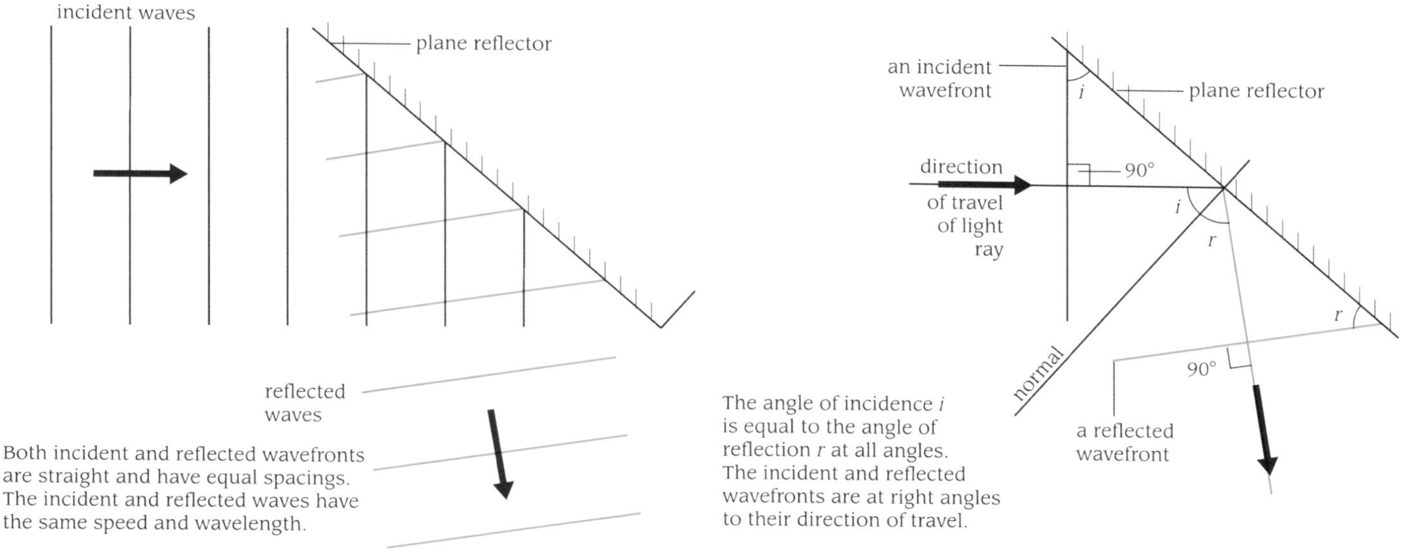
incident waves
plane reflector
reflected waves
Both incident and reflected wavefronts are straight and have equal spacings. The incident and reflected waves have the same speed and wavelength.
an incident wavefront
i
plane reflector
direction of travel of light ray
90°
i
r
r
normal
90°
a reflected wavefront
The angle of incidence i is equal to the angle of reflection r at all angles. The incident and reflected wavefronts are at right angles to their direction of travel.

▲ **Figure 11.3.3** Reflection of straight waves by a plane reflector compared with reflection of a light ray

- Using first the straight beam to produce parallel straight waves, then a single dipper to produce circular waves, investigate reflection by a straight metal strip acting as a plane reflector or mirror.
- Note the shape, spacing, speed and direction of travel of the reflected wavefronts and draw wave diagrams.
- Using a stroboscope, measure roughly the wavelengths and distances of sources from the reflectors.

In all the results, the incident and reflected waves can be seen to travel at the same speed and to obey the laws of reflection. The similarities between the reflection of light rays and the reflection of waves are pointed out in the caption to each diagram in Figure 11.3.3. Bold arrows are used to represent the speed of the waves and all have the same length when the speed does not change.

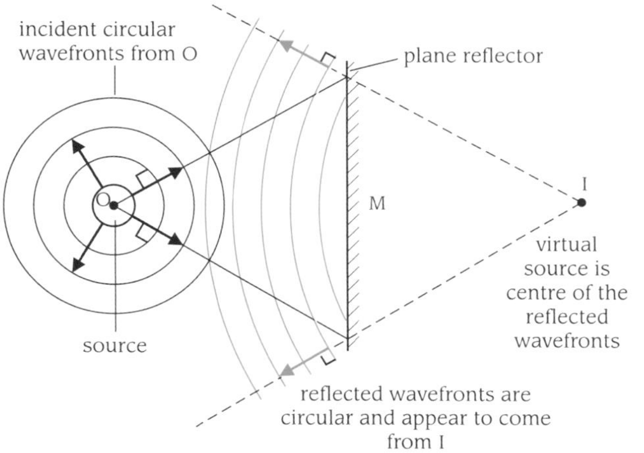
incident circular wavefronts from O
plane reflector
O
M
I
virtual source is centre of the reflected wavefronts
source
reflected wavefronts are circular and appear to come from I

The source O corresponds to the object and the virtual source I of the reflected waves corresponds to the virtual image formed by a plane mirror, OM = MI and OI is at right angles to the reflector

▲ **Figure 11.3.4** Circular waves reflected by a plane reflector (some wavefronts are omitted for clarity)

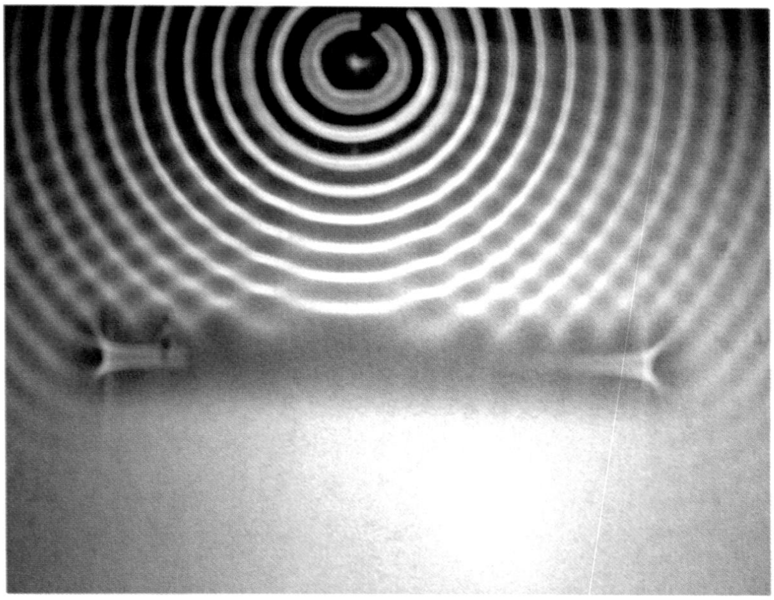

▲ **Figure 11.3.5** Circular waves reflected by a plane reflector

! Key fact

Experimental notes

- Washers are used to make it easier to remove the wet glass plate and to give the glass more thickness.
- A drop of detergent added to the water will reduce unwanted surface tension effects.
- The plate can be arranged so that straight wavefronts arrive parallel to the edge of the glass plate, or at an angle of incidence *i*.
- A stroboscope is particularly useful in these experiments because by freezing the waves it is possible to make wavelength measurements.

Observations

- The waves can be seen to travel more slowly in the shallow water.
- The waves in both the deep and the shallow water are 'frozen' at the same time by the same stroboscope frequency. This shows that the wave frequency *f* does not change with the wave speed.
- The ratio of the wave speeds is the same as the ratio of their wavelengths or the separations of their wavefronts.

Refraction of waves by a plane boundary

▲ **Figure 11.3.6** Waves in a ripple tank being deflected by a straight barrier

- Lay a thick glass plate flat in the ripple tank, separated from the glass base by metal washers.
- Add more water to the tank until it just covers the glass plate.
- Measure the wavelength in shallow water λ_1 and in deep water λ_2 (measure over several wavelengths).
- Measure the angles of incidence *i* and refraction *r*.
- From each of these two measurements calculate the refractive index and compare the values.

Using the wave equation $v = f\lambda$ we can write:

Wave speed in medium 1 (deep water), $v_1 = f \times$ wavelength in medium 1, λ_1

Wave speed in medium 2 (shallow water), $v_2 = f \times$ wavelength in medium 2, λ_2

By dividing and cancelling *f* we get:

$$\frac{v_1}{v_2} = \frac{\lambda_1}{\lambda_2}$$

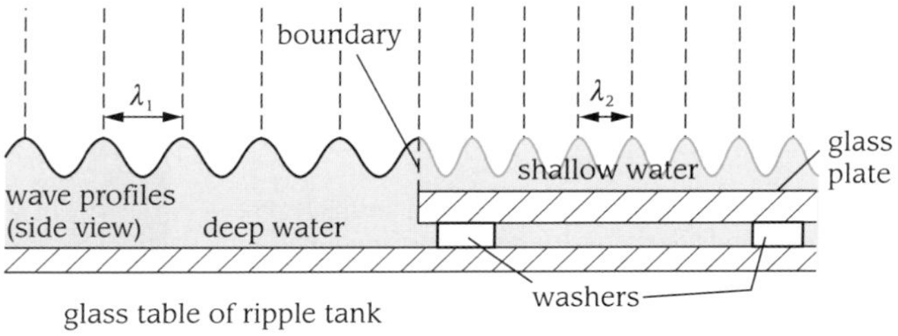

▲ **Figure 11.3.7** Straight wavefronts passing from deep water to shallow water

Refractive index

The **refractive index** is an indicator of how much the speed of a wave changes at a boundary between two media. It also indicates how much the direction of travel of a wave will change at the boundary. It turns out that the change of wave speed is the cause of the change of direction, known as refraction.

Finding the refractive index from the wavelengths

As we have shown above, by measuring the wavelengths in deep water (medium 1) and shallow water (medium 2), we can calculate the ratio of the wave speeds. This is useful because it gives us an alternative method of measuring the refractive index, ${}_1n_2$ at a boundary. ${}_1n_2$ is a shorthand way of indicating that this is the index when the wave is going from medium 1 to medium 2.

Refractive index from medium 1 to medium 2,

$$ {}_1n_2 = \frac{v_1}{v_2} = \frac{\lambda_1}{\lambda_2} $$

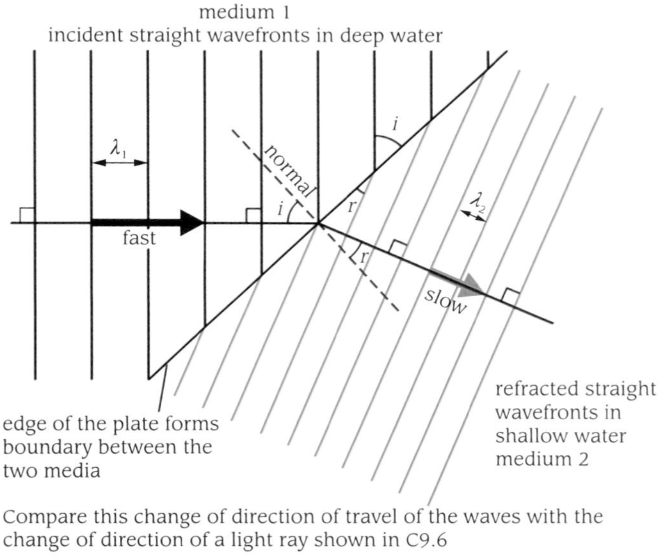

▲ **Figure 11.3.8** Refraction of straight wavefronts at a plane boundary

Finding the refractive index from the angles

The angles labelled *i* and *r* are the same angles of incidence and refraction as are used when studying the refraction of light rays. In this case, the angles are those between the directions of travel of the waves and the normal at the boundary between the two media, 1 and 2.

- Measure the angles *i* and *r*.
- Calculate the refractive index ${}_1n_2$ for the two media using:

$$ \text{Refractive index, } {}_1n_2 = \frac{\sin i \text{ (in medium 1)}}{\sin r \text{ (in medium 2)}} $$

The value for the refractive index calculated from the wavelengths should agree with the value obtained from the sines of the angles.

Key fact

Observations

- No refraction occurs for waves incident normally at a boundary (wavefronts parallel to the boundary), so to investigate the relation between refraction and wave speed, turn the glass plate to give an oblique boundary as shown in Figure 11.3.8.
  i is the angle of incidence.
  r is angle of refraction.
- When the wavefronts arrive at an angle *i* to the boundary, the change in wave speed can be seen to cause a change of direction as well.

Worked example

A wavefront travelling at 20 m s^{-1} arrives at a boundary between deep and shallow water at an angle of incidence of 40°. If the wave speed drops to 12 m s^{-1}, calculate:

a) the direction of the refracted waves in the shallow water

b) the refractive index at this boundary.

a) combining the two equations that give the refractive index, we have:

$$ \frac{\sin i \text{ (in medium 1}}{\sin r \text{ (in medium 2)}} = \frac{v_1}{v_2} $$

$$ \frac{\sin 40}{\sin r} = \frac{20}{12} $$

$\sin r = 0.6 \times 0.64 = 0.38$
angle of refraction, $r = 22°$.

b) The refractive index can be found using either equation.

$$ {}_1n_2 = \frac{v_1}{v_2} = \frac{20}{12} = 1.67 $$

Refractive index is a ratio and has no units.

Diffraction of waves

Diffraction is a property that belongs only to waves. The diffraction effects demonstrated with water waves can also be observed with sound waves and light waves.

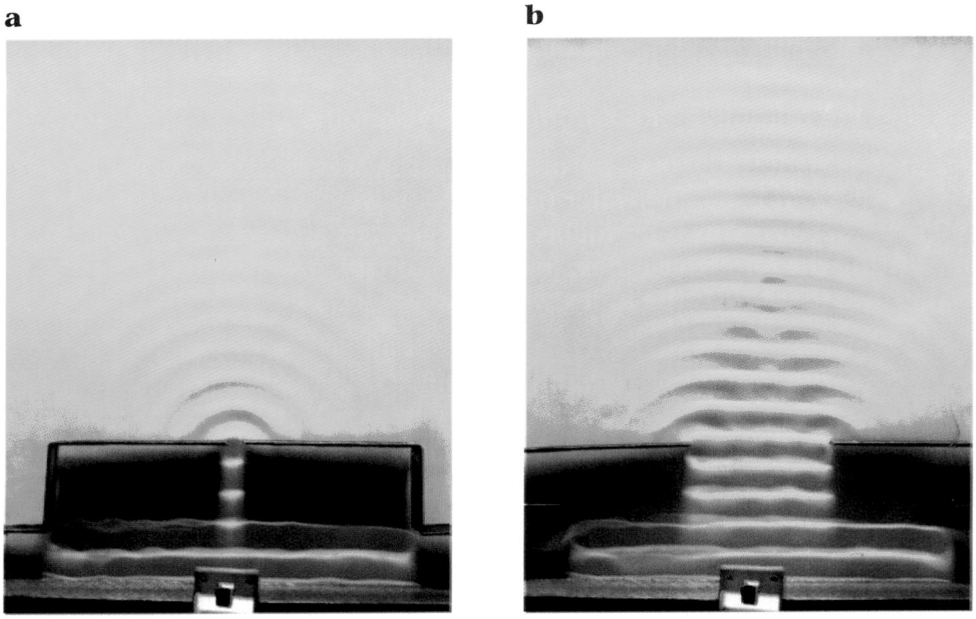

▲ **Figure 11.3.9** Diffraction of waves through **a** a narrow gap **b** a wide gap

! Key fact

Observations

- When the gap is wide the wavefronts emerge almost straight, apart from a slight curvature and spreading at the edges.
- When the gap is narrow the straight wavefronts are converted into circular wavefronts, which appear to be produced by a new point source of waves in the gap.
- The circular wavefronts spread out around the edges of the gap in all directions.
- The amount of spreading or diffraction of the waves is greatest *when the gap width is similar to the wavelength of the waves*. The diffraction effect is most obvious with the water waves when the gap in the barrier is quite narrow.

Observing the diffraction of water waves

- Set up a ripple tank to produce continuous straight waves.
- Place two straight metal barriers in the tank parallel to the wavefronts.
- Try varying the gap or aperture between the two barriers and compare the shape and amount of spreading of the waves for different widths.
- Try varying the wavelength of the waves by adjusting the motor speed on the vibrating beam and compare the amount of spreading of the waves at different wavelengths.

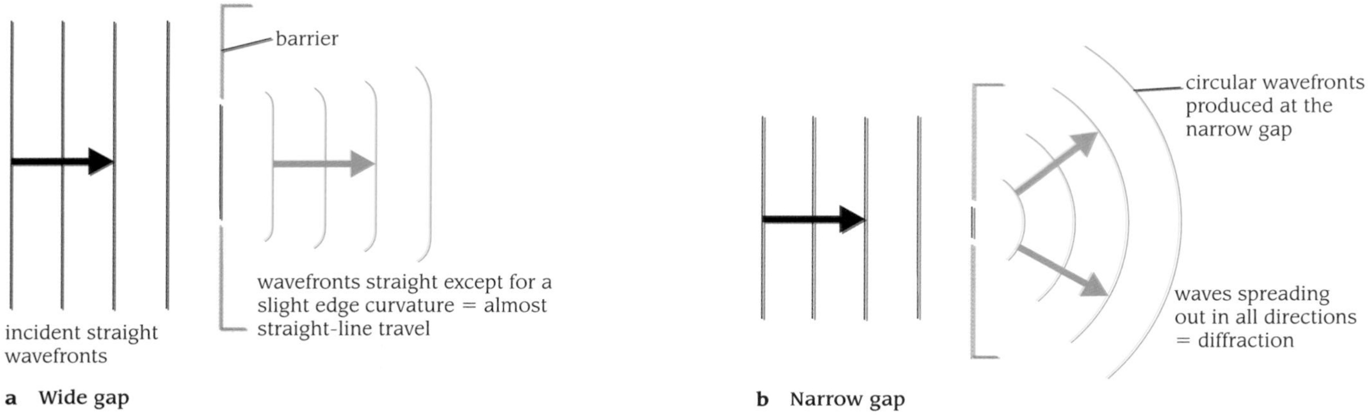

▲ **Figure 11.3.10** Diffraction of straight wavefronts

The spreading of waves round corners and edges of barriers or through openings or apertures is called diffraction.

Interference of waves

Interference is the name given to the effects that occur when two separate wavetrains overlap. It is interesting that waves usually do not seem to bump into one another, rather they pass through each other and merge or combine their effects. For example, the different sounds from a group of instruments played together can be heard combined and merged; the various sound waves do not collide.

Observing interference

To investigate the effects known as interference of waves we superpose (overlap) two separate wavetrains produced by two sources of circular waves.

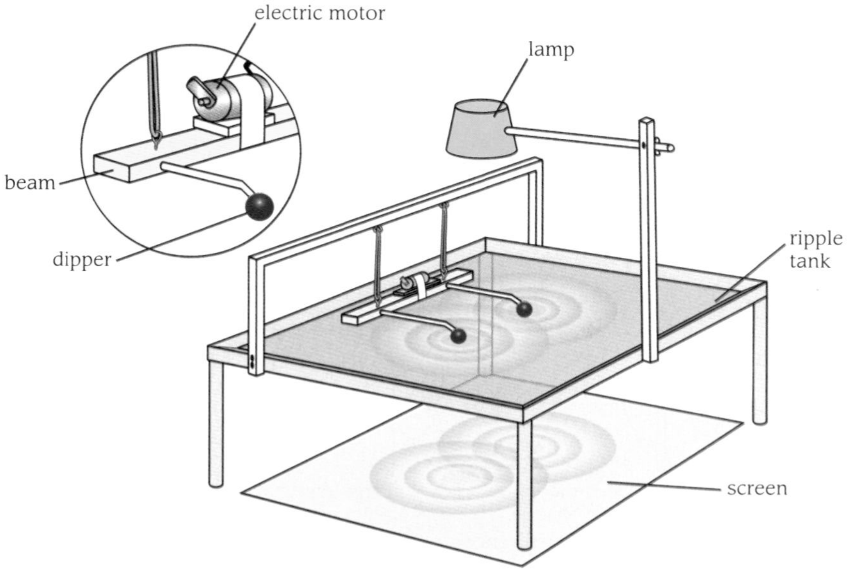

▲ **Figure 11.3.11** Ripple tank with two dippers

- Fit two dippers, about 3 cm apart, to the wooden beam and raise it so that the dippers just touch the surface of the water (Figure 11.3.11).
- Run the motor slowly and observe what happens where the two sets of circular waves overlap.
- Increase the speed of the motor and note the effect.
- What happens where the crest of one wave overlaps the crest of another wave? (The waves are in phase or in step.)
- What happens where the crest of one wave overlaps the trough of another wave? (The waves are in antiphase, or out of step by half an oscillation.)

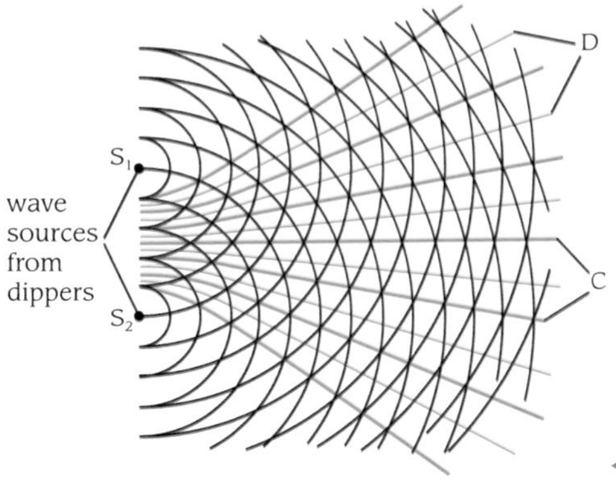

◀ **Figure 11.3.13** Interference of waves

Key fact

Superposition of waves

- The ability of wave motions to combine together, when they occur together in the same place at the same time, is known as the superposition of waves.
- Interference is what happens when two sets of wavetrains are superposed.
- The displacement of any particle caused by overlapping waves is the sum of the separate displacements caused by each wave at a particular moment.

The principle of superposition

At high speeds the use of a stroboscope is helpful in studying the interference patterns by keeping the wave positions steady.

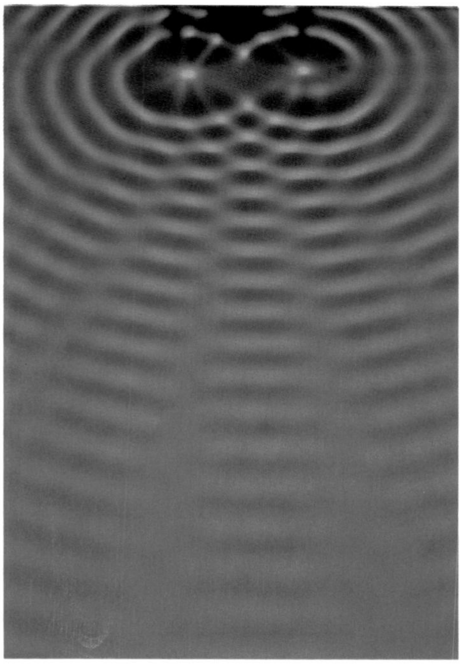

▲ **Figure 11.3.12** Two dippers making circular waves that interfere

Key fact

What affects the spacing of the interference bands?

- Moving the sources closer together moves the interference bands further apart.
- Using a longer wavelength moves the interference bands further apart. Longer wavelengths are produced by a lower frequency vibration.

Coherent sources of waves

- Interference effects can be seen only when the two sources of waves are coherent.
- For two sources to be coherent they must have:
  - the same frequency
  - a constant phase relationship.

This means that the two sets of waves must set off together in step (in phase) or with some other constant phase difference.
This is achieved by fitting the two dippers to the same vibrating beam so that their vibrations are kept in step at all times.

Lines of constructive interference

The amplitude of the disturbance has increased along the lines, marked C in Figure 11.3.13, where the waves are in phase. Here the displacement at the crest of one wave has been added to the displacement at the crest of the other wave to produce a larger displacement.

This effect is called constructive interference.

The two wave motions have *constructed* a larger amplitude wave along the lines marked C.

Lines of destructive interference

The water is quite still along several lines, marked D in Figure 11.3.13. These are where the waves are in antiphase. In effect, the crest of one wave has filled in the trough of the other to produce no displacement of the water.

This effect is called destructive interference.

The two wave motions have *destroyed* each other along the lines marked D.

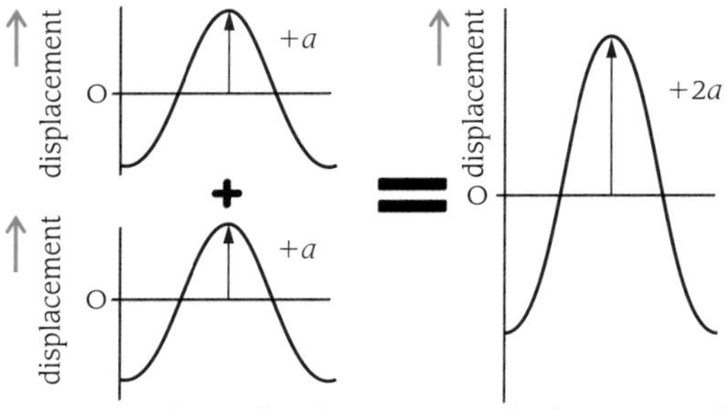

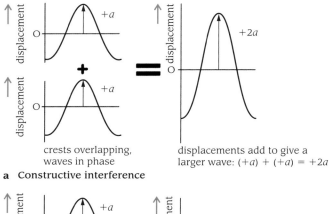

a Constructive interference

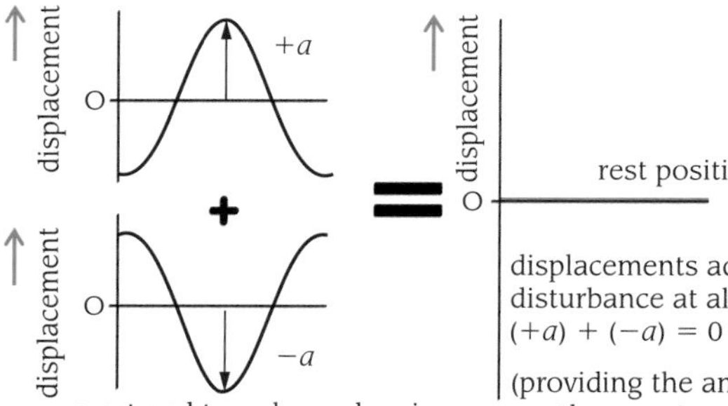

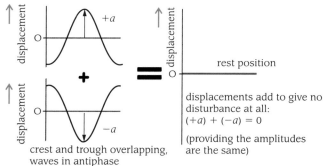

b Destructive interference

▲ **Figure 11.3.14** Superposition of waves

Double-slit interference

The two dippers may be replaced by two gaps or slits about 1 cm wide and 3 cm apart in a plane barrier. When straight wavefronts reach the two gaps, circular waves emerge on the other side. Where these two sets of waves are superposed the same interference effects are produced as occurred with the two dippers.

With this arrangement it is more difficult to produce good results but it is important because it provides a water wave model of the double-slit experiment in light, known as 'Young's slits'.

Summary questions

1. What causes the pattern of light and dark seen when a ripple tank is used to demonstrate water waves?
2. Sketch a diagram to show the reflection of straight water waves from a plane surface.
3. Sketch a diagram to show diffraction of straight water waves through a narrow gap.
4. After refraction, straight water waves have a shorter wavelength. If the frequency is unchanged, what has happened to the speed?

C11.4 Sound waves

Objectives

By the end of this topic you will be able to:

- explain how we know that sound requires a medium
- describe a travelling sound wave as a longitudinal wave
- explain pitch and loudness as wave properties
- describe how to measure the speed of sound
- describe the properties of sound waves: reflection, refraction, diffraction and interference.

We live in a world filled with a great variety of sounds that affect us in many ways. Many kinds of vibrations send out waves, which carry sound energy to our ears. What are these waves like?

Travelling sound waves

We know that sound can travel through solids, liquids and gases. There is plenty of evidence of this, for example, sounds from distant sources reach our ears through the air and sounds can be heard through solid walls. Whales communicate by sound over great distances through the sea. So can sound travel through space or through a vacuum the way light does?

Vibrations in a vacuum

We can investigate this by mounting an electric bell or an alarm clock inside a large glass jar, called a bell jar (Figure 11.4.1). The bell should have a hammer, which can be seen vibrating inside the jar, so that we can check whether the bell is working even if we cannot hear it. We can hear the bell very clearly when the bell jar is full of air, but as we pump the air out the sound fades away until, at a very low air pressure called a vacuum, we can no longer hear it at all. We can see the hammer still vibrating but it fails to send waves out through the vacuum.

Sound cannot travel through a vacuum.

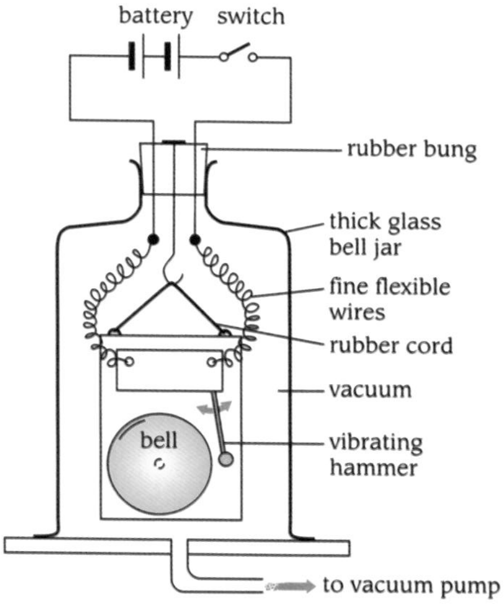

▲ **Figure 11.4.1** Vibrations in a vacuum can be seen – but not heard

Sound travels as a longitudinal mechanical wave motion

We cannot hear the bell in a vacuum because there is no medium for a sound wave to disturb. Similarly we cannot hear the nuclear explosions on the Sun because there is no medium in space. Astronauts cannot speak to each other on the Moon without using radio waves, because there is no air on the Moon through which sound waves can travel.

When a vibrating object disturbs the surrounding medium the particles of the medium are displaced in the same direction as the resulting sound wave will travel. The particles of the medium are first pushed away by the vibration and then bounce back after collision with more particles further from the source; thus a longitudinal wave motion is established through the medium.

Sound is a longitudinal wave motion and, being mechanical, requires a medium to travel through.

Key fact

Practical notes

- The bell jar is sealed with grease to a flat metal plate, which has an outlet connected to a vacuum pump.
- The vacuum pump is used to remove the air from inside.
- If the bell assembly rested on the metal plate at the base of the jar, sound could escape through the plate to the air outside. So the whole bell assembly must be hung on a rubber cord and supplied with electricity through fine coiled flexible wires.

> **Key fact**
>
> **Practical notes**
>
> - Sound waves in air are **travelling pressure waves**.
> - Sound waves from a loudspeaker produce compressions and rarefactions of the (invisible) air molecules.
> - When molecules pushed forwards (to the right in Figure 11.4.2) meet molecules bouncing backwards (to the left), after collisions with other molecules in front, a region of compression is produced where the air pressure is higher.
> - In between the compressions are rarefactions, where the number of molecules is reduced and the air pressure is lower.
> - A sound wave in air is a travelling pressure wave in which regions of increased air pressure travel along where the air molecules are compressed together, separated by regions of reduced air pressure at the rarefactions.
> - The travelling sound wave carries energy through the air without carrying the air molecules along with it.
>
> **Hearing and 'seeing' sound**
>
> - An audio frequency generator is connected to both a loudspeaker and an oscilloscope (Figure 11.4.3).
> - The loudspeaker cone vibrates in and out, producing longitudinal sound waves.
> - The oscilloscope displays the same electrical signal as a waveform. It appears as a transverse waveform matching the pressure variations produced by the sound wave.

The medium is simply whatever form of matter the vibrating source of sound is surrounded by or immersed in; it is usually air, but can be any gas, liquid or solid.

Evidently sound waves can travel and are therefore travelling or progressive waves, but, as we shall see in the next section, sound waves can also form another type of wave, called a stationary wave, which appears to stand still and not travel.

Sound waves in air

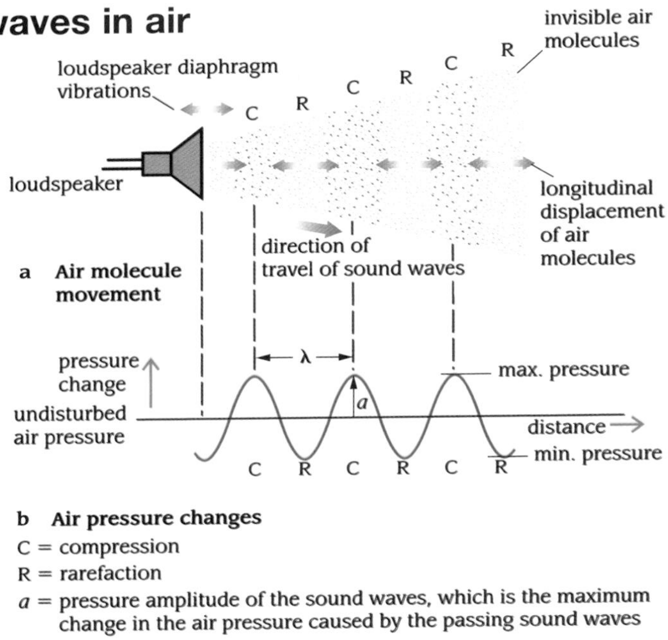

▲ **Figure 11.4.2** Longitudinal sound waves travelling through air

Wavelength, λ

> **The distance between two successive compressions or two pressure maxima is the wavelength λ of the longitudinal sound wave.**

Sound waves displayed on an oscilloscope

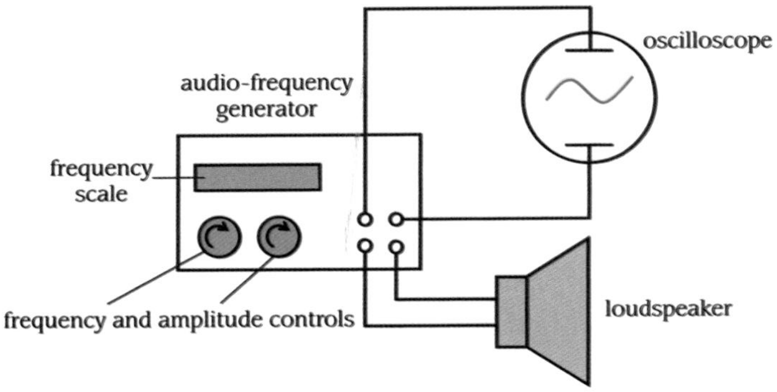

▲ **Figure 11.4.3** Hearing and 'seeing' sound waves

To spread the waveform out on the screen, the oscilloscope time-base must be switched to a suitable speed to produce a time scale in the *x*-direction, in which several up and down oscillations of the electron beam are traced out on the screen. The trace produced is a displacement against time graph of the electrical oscillations. Any change in the vibrations producing the sound can be seen and heard simultaneously.

Frequency and pitch

Increasing the frequency of the sound has two effects:

- The number of waves produced in a certain time increases and the number of waves displayed on the oscilloscope screen increases – compare trace **b** with trace **a**.
- The pitch of the sound rises.

The pitch of a sound depends on frequency.

Amplitude and loudness

Changing the amplitude of the sound also has two effects:

- a smaller amplitude wave **c** sounds quieter and
- a larger amplitude wave **d** sounds louder.

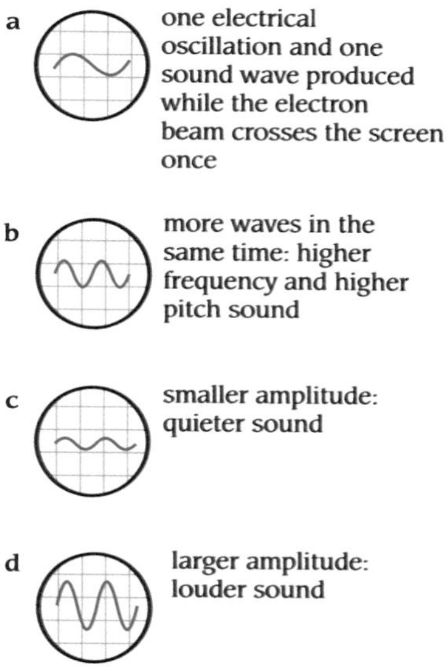

a
one electrical oscillation and one sound wave produced while the electron beam crosses the screen once
b
more waves in the same time: higher frequency and higher pitch sound
c
smaller amplitude: quieter sound
d
larger amplitude: louder sound

▲ **Figure 11.4.4** Oscilloscope traces

The loudness of a sound depends on the wave amplitude.

We also observe that changing the amplitude has no effect on the frequency or pitch of the sound.

An oscilloscope

An oscilloscope is a device that displays a varying voltage as a trace on a screen. A receiver can be used to detect a sound wave and send it to an oscilloscope as an electrical signal. The *y*-axis of the oscilloscope trace shows the amplitude (the loudness) of the sound wave, and the *x*-axis of the oscilloscope trace shows the frequency (the pitch) of the sound. So the oscilloscope trace can be used to convert a longitudinal wave that we hear into a transverse wave that we can 'see' on the oscilloscope.

The speed of sound waves

The delay between a flash of lightning and the sound wave it produces, thunder, is caused by the sound travelling much slower than light. Light travels so fast, at 300 000 000 or $3 \times 10^8\,\mathrm{m\,s^{-1}}$, that over a short distance it is almost instantaneous. Sound travelling at about $330\,\mathrm{m\,s^{-1}}$ in air often takes several seconds to reach us from the location of the lightning. For example, a 3 second delay would mean that the sound had travelled 3×330 metres or about 1 kilometre, which is quite close in a thunder storm. Light travels 1 kilometre in about 3.3 microseconds (3.3×10^{-6} s), which is almost a million times quicker than sound.

Measuring the speed of sound by timing echoes

Using an echo method doubles the time and better still, using multiples of the echo travel time can greatly increase the total time measured. This will increase the accuracy of the measurement of the speed of sound.

- Measure a distance of 100 m at right angles to a large wall. (There should be no other large reflecting surfaces nearby.)
- Make a sharp clapping sound by banging two blocks of wood together. Repeat the sound at regular time intervals to coincide exactly with the echoes.
- Starting at zero as a stopwatch is started, count the number of claps and stop the stopwatch at 50 or 100 claps.
- Calculate the speed of sound using the formula:

$$\text{speed} = \frac{\text{distance travelled}}{\text{time taken}}$$

Remember that the distance is doubled, there and back, and the stopwatch reading must be divided by the number of claps.

! Key fact

Accuracy

- The accuracy with which the speed of sound can be measured depends mainly upon the timing accuracy, since the distance travelled can be measured easily with much greater precision.
- A distance of 100 metres can be measured by a tape measure to a precision of 1 centimetre, which gives an accuracy of 1 part in 10 000.
- The time for sound to travel the same distance (about 0.3 seconds) can at best be measured by stopwatch to a precision of $\frac{1}{100}$ second, which could only give an accuracy of 1 part in 30.
- Stopwatch readings are unreliable due to human reaction times and only become more accurate when measuring relatively long times.

Some typical results for the speed of sound:

distance from wall = 100 m

distance sound travels = 200 m

time taken for 50 claps = 30.3 s

time between claps = 0.606 s

$$\text{speed} = \frac{\text{distance travelled}}{\text{time taken}}$$

$$\text{speed} = \frac{200\text{ m}}{0.606\text{ s}} = 330\text{ m s}^{-1}$$

Reflection of sound waves

Do sound waves obey the same laws of reflection as light rays and water waves?

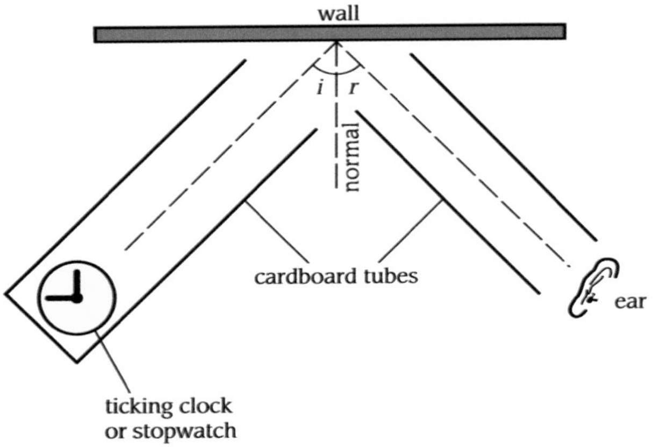

▲ **Figure 11.4.5** Sound waves obey the laws of reflection.

- Place a ticking clock or stopwatch inside a long cardboard tube at its closed end (Figure 11.4.5).
- Point the open end of the tube towards a wall at an angle of incidence *i*. (The reflecting surface needs to be hard to reduce absorption of the sound.)
- With your ear close to the end of an open cardboard tube, listen to reflections of the sound from the board at different angles of reflection *r*.

It is found that the reflected sound is loudest when:

a) the angle of reflection *r* is equal to the angle of incidence *i*, and

b) both tubes lie in a plane that is normal to (at right angles to) the reflecting surface.

It is found that sound waves do obey the laws of reflection.

Refraction of sound waves

Refraction occurs when the speed of the waves changes. The speed of sound waves in air is affected by the air temperature, so if sound waves pass through layers of air at different temperatures they will be refracted (Figure 11.4.6). On a summer's evening when the air near the ground becomes cool, refraction makes it easier to hear distant sounds across the countryside. The sound waves are bent or refracted down towards the ground. The wavefronts are further apart in the warm air (higher up) where the sound travels faster, and they are closer together nearer the ground where the sound travels slower in cooler air.

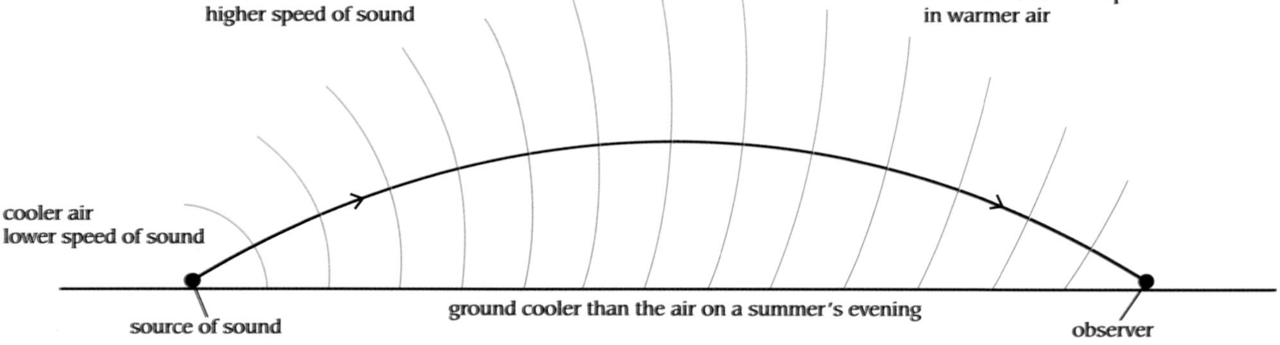

▲ **Figure 11.4.6** Refraction of sound waves in the air

Sound travels faster in water than in air, so a sound wave passing from air to water will speed up, and refract away from the normal. The wavelength of the sound also changes as the speed changes. This, together with temperature changes in the air above the water, can mean that sounds heard underwater appear very muffled or distorted.

Reverberation

In a cathedral or large hall there are many reflecting walls and surfaces, which form multiple reflections and create the impression that a sound lasts for a long time. A sound produced in a brief moment may linger for several seconds, only gradually fading away. At each reflection some of the sound energy is absorbed and the reflected sound becomes a little quieter. When many echoes merge into one prolonged sound the effect is known as **reverberation**. Too much reverberation causes sounds to become confused and indistinct, making it necessary to speak very slowly. The sound reflecting and absorbing properties of a room are called its **acoustics**.

Diffraction of sound waves

As well as reflection and refraction we find that sound waves also show diffraction effects. Sound waves may have wavelengths as short as 20 cm or as long as 10 m. Which wavelengths are diffracted most?

- Waves that have wavelengths similar to the size of the gap they are passing through are diffracted most.
- A doorway may be about 1 metre wide, which is very similar to the wavelength of many sounds in the lower part of the audible frequency range. So low pitch, low frequency sounds are diffracted a lot and spread round corners and through openings well.

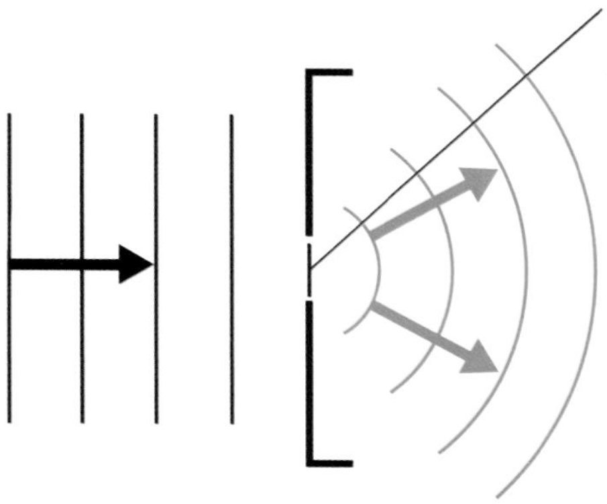
Note: doorway is similar in width to the wavelength of the sound.

▲ **Figure 11.4.7** Diffraction is greatest when the width of the gap is the same as the wavelength of the wave

- Short-wavelength, high-pitched sounds are diffracted less around corners and obstacles than longer wavelength, lower pitched sounds. The high-pitched sounds are more directional. As you approach a room where music is being played, you hear the low notes before you hear the higher notes, because the lower notes are refracted more around walls and corners. That is also why men's voices tend to 'carry' better than women's voices, even if the volume is the same.

Interference of sound waves

Overlapping sound waves produce regions of louder sound by constructive interference and regions of quiet by destructive interference.

> **Key fact**
>
> **Examples of diffracted sound**
>
> - Sound spreads round corners. You can hear a vehicle approaching from around a blind corner.
> - Sounds can be heard coming round a building from the far side.
> - Sound does not come through an open door in a narrow beam, but fans out so that it can be heard in any direction.
> - Sound made outside a house comes in through a window and can be heard anywhere inside the room.

When two similar loudspeakers are connected to the same audio frequency generator they will produce sound waves of identical frequency and very similar amplitude. If the coils in the loudspeakers are connected to the generator the same way round, when a current flows through them their sound-producing cones or diaphragms will move forwards together, sending out sound waves that are in step, or in phase.

- Set two speakers, facing the same way, about 0.5 to 1.0 m apart and select sound frequencies in the range 500 Hz to 2 kHz on the generator (Figure 11.4.8).
- Walk slowly across the room parallel to the two loudspeakers and a few metres in front of them.
- Estimate the distance between places where you hear a loud sound with a quiet place in between.

The listener hears variations in the loudness of the sound as he moves across the room. A loud sound is produced where the waves from the two speakers arrive in phase and so interfere constructively. A quiet sound is heard where destructive interference occurs, which is where a wave crest from one speaker is cancelled out by a wave trough from the other speaker.

Note that it is essential to use two sources of sound that are of identical frequency, similar amplitude and that set off from the loudspeakers together in phase. These conditions are provided by connecting the two speakers to the same generator.

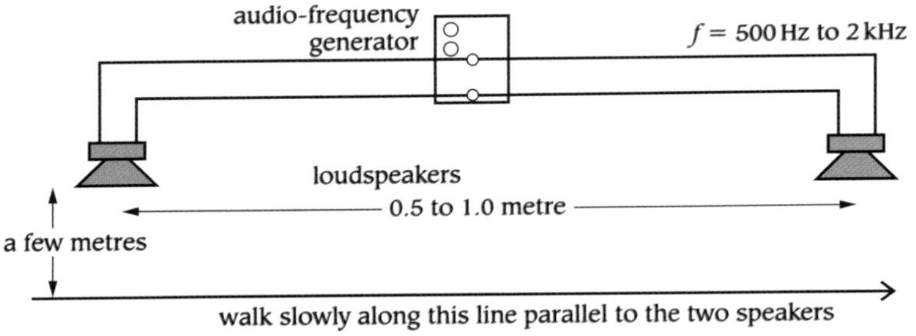

▲ **Figure 11.4.8** Demonstrating interference with sound waves

Things to do

What affects the spacing of the loud and quiet positions:

- the separation of the speakers
- the wavelength of the sound
- the distance of the listener from the speakers?

Find out how each of these affects the spacing.

Summary questions

1. Name an experiment, which could be used to show that sound does not travel through a vacuum.
2. Is sound a transverse wave or a longitudinal wave?
3. What is meant by the pitch of a sound wave?
4. Give an example of how you could demonstrate interference of sound waves.

C11.5 Hearing and using sounds

Objectives

By the end of this topic you will be able to:

- recall the human hearing range of frequencies
- describe how the ear detects sound waves
- explain the difference between music and noise
- recall what is meant by ultrasound and describe some of its applications.

The frequency spectrum of sound waves

At the low-frequency end of the hearing range it is difficult to say when sound becomes just a sensation of vibration.

- Below about 20 hertz the vibrations are felt rather than heard and are called subsonic (below sound).

At the high-frequency end of the audible range the limit is also difficult to find exactly because the ear gradually becomes less sensitive as the frequency rises above about 10 kHz. Also, as we get older, the range of high frequency sounds that we can hear gradually reduces. Very few people can hear a frequency of 20 kHz and this is a convenient upper limit to choose.

- The full human hearing range is about 20 Hz to 20 kHz.
- Above 20 kHz the waves are known as ultrasound (beyond sound).

Some animals can hear ultrasonic frequencies and bats use ultrasound in the same way as radar to 'see' with. Many uses have been found for ultrasound where it has several advantages over audible sound.

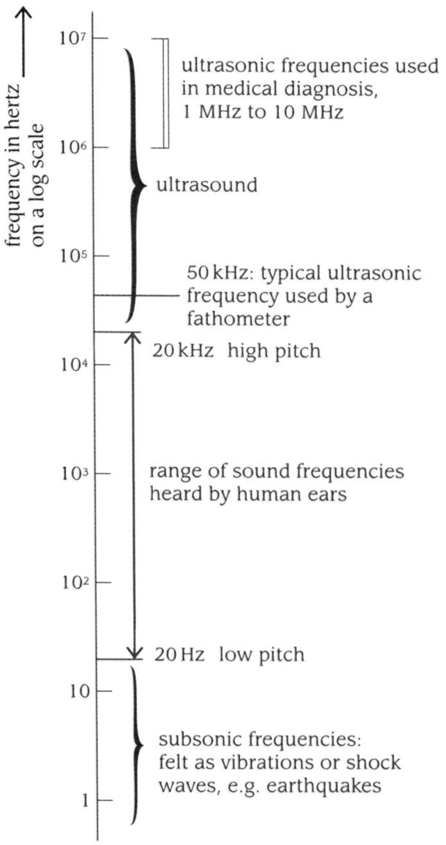

▲ **Figure 11.5.1** The frequency spectrum of sound waves

The problem of noise

An interesting sound to one person may be described as a noise by another person. One person's work may disturb another's rest, and one person's leisure music may cause others to complain. Noise generally is an unwanted sound that a person would rather not hear. Noise can be so loud that it becomes dangerous. The effects of exposure to loud noise get more serious as the level and time of exposure increase. Some people are regularly exposed to sound with an intensity level above 90 dB (relative to the threshold of human hearing). This may happen in a factory, when driving a large vehicle, or when listening to very loud music at close range. Their hearing may be only temporarily impaired, but it can become permanently damaged with a serious loss of hearing ability. The symptom of 'ringing in the ears' after exposure is a warning sign to avoid frequent repetition of the experience. Temporary blindness and nausea can also be caused by very loud noise. However, even comparatively short exposures to loud noises can have undesirable effects. A person may become less alert and less capable of carrying out a skilled job accurately. Persistent noise causes many people to become irritable, short-tempered, tired and distressed.

So serious is the problem of noise pollution that much is now being done to reduce noise at its source and to protect people who are regularly exposed to it.

Some particular sources of noise make a major contribution to the noise around us. These include road traffic, aircraft and heavy industrial machinery. It is wise for tractor drivers, pneumatic drill operators and machine operators in factories to wear ear protection.

◀ **Figure 11.5.2** When using noisy machinery, it is important to protect your ears. Sustained exposure to loud noise can permanently damage your hearing.

Music and noise

Some combinations of sounds we describe as music, while others we treat as a noise. What is the difference between musical sounds and noise? How are these different kinds of sounds produced and how do we detect and measure them? How can we prevent or reduce a noise that is a nuisance?

Quality of sound

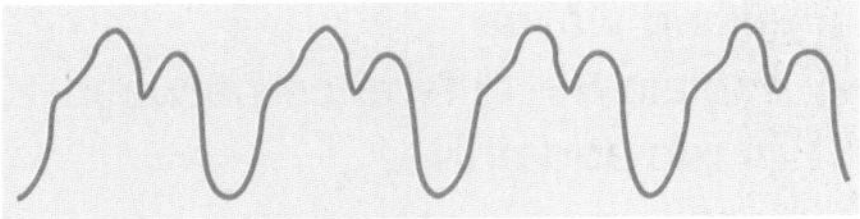

▲ **Figure 11.5.3** Sound pattern produced by a flute

What makes a sound musical? People enjoy, and dislike, very different kinds of music, but despite its great variety, all music usually contains recognisable common features. Most music uses sounds of particular and constant frequencies, combined together in various ways. Certain combinations of frequencies produce sounds with interesting musical qualities or character. Music also usually has a pattern or rhythm of sounds, which are used according to a theme or plan.

Noise, however, is usually random in frequency, constantly varying without plan or purpose.

Ultrasound

Sound vibrations and waves above the highest frequencies that humans can hear are called ultrasound.

All vibration frequencies above 20 kHz are described as ultrasonic.

- A typical ultrasound frequency used by fishing boats to find fish in the sea below them might be 50 kHz.
- Medical applications typically use frequencies of several megahertz (MHz).

Uses of ultrasound

Ultrasound at sea

Ultrasound is used at sea to measure the distance to reflecting surfaces such as the seabed or shoals of fish. Brief pulses of sound are sent out from a transmitter, and the time is measured between the pulse of sound and when its echo is detected by a receiver. Provided the speed of ultrasound in seawater is known, the distance can be calculated from:

distance (there and back) = speed × time

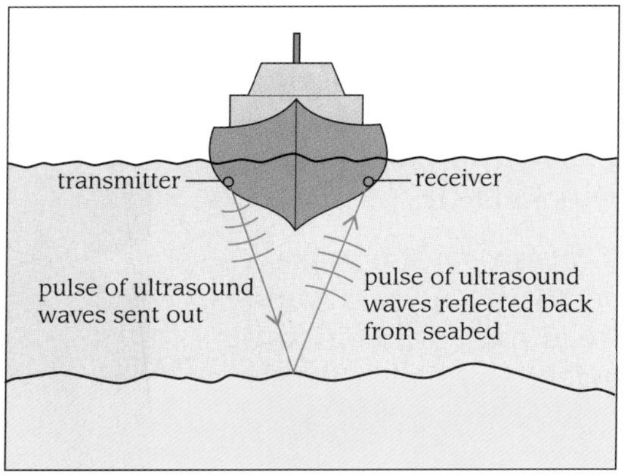

▲ **Figure 11.5.4** Measuring the depth of the sea using a fathometer

Key fact

A fathometer

- A fathometer is an instrument used to measure the depth of water below a ship.
- By measuring the time interval between the sending out of a pulse of ultrasound and its echo arriving back from the seabed, the depth of water can be calculated.

Worked example

If the time interval is 0.8 s and the speed of ultrasound in water is $1500\,m\,s^{-1}$, calculate the depth of water.

distance = speed × time
distance = 1500 × 0.8 = 1200 m
This is the distance there and back, so the depth of the water is 600 metres.

The advantages of using ultrasound rather than audible sound are:

- Ultrasound waves have a shorter wavelength so are diffracted less than audible sound waves. Less energy is lost by the waves spreading out, so the ultrasound can penetrate deeper than sound could.
- The short wavelength means small objects and greater detail can be detected. This improves the **resolution** of the image.

A disadvantage is that ultrasound has been shown to harm wildlife that depends on ultrasound for communication, such as whales and dolphins.

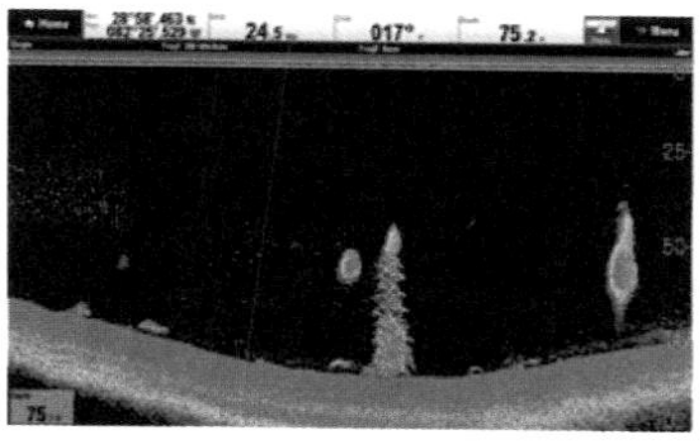

▲ **Figure 11.5.5** Ultrasound echo techniques used to locate fish below a ship

Ultrasound in medicine

Ultrasound pulses reflect from boundaries between tissues of different densities. A computer measures the time, and so calculates the distance, to different boundaries. In this way a three-dimensional image of internal organs can be built up. This is safer than X-rays as it does not cause ionisation or tissue damage. It can also reveal details that don't show up in X-rays or other techniques.

Examples of where ultrasound is used include:

- checking the development of unborn babies
- observing blood flow to monitor the heart and circulatory system
- scanning for tumours.

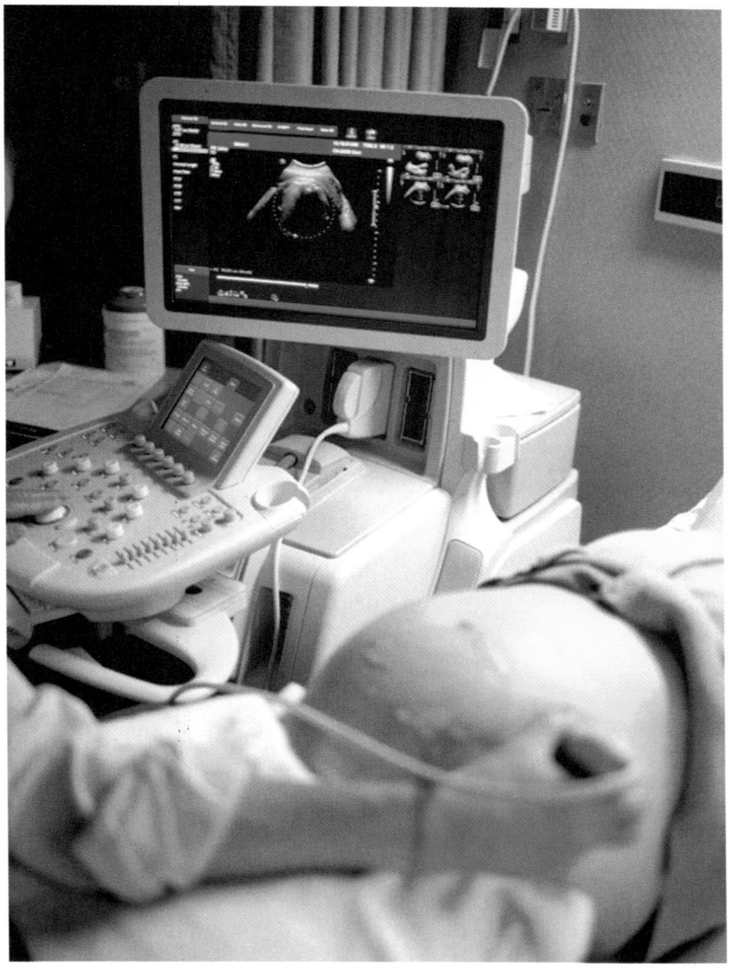

▲ **Figure 11.5.6** An ultrasound scan in progress

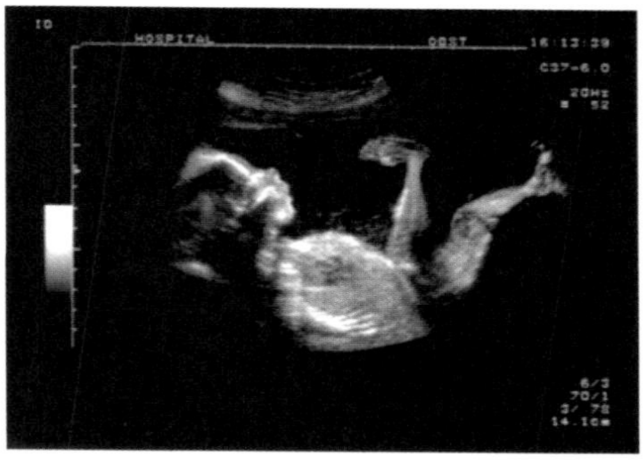

▲ **Figure 11.5.7** An ultrasound image of a foetus produced by ultrasound scanning

Ultrasound in industry

▲ **Figure 11.5.8** Ultrasonic testing of the walls of high-pressure gas cylinders. An ultrasound narrow beam transducer is held against the wall of a cylinder and passes a high-frequency sound column wave through the metal walls. Echoes will be produced by any defects in the metal and the thickness of the wall can also be measured.

Ultrasound is also useful in industry. It can be used to:

- check metal containers, aircraft and inaccessible machinery parts for cracks or damage
- monitor the thickness of paint, sheets of paper and so on
- clean delicate or inaccessible equipment, by causing vibrations that shake off dirt particles.

Summary questions

1 What is noise?

2 What is the frequency range of human hearing?

3 Describe one example of the use of ultrasound.

Practice exam-style questions

1 The figure below shows the wavefronts seen on the surface of the water in a ripple tank reproduced here full scale.

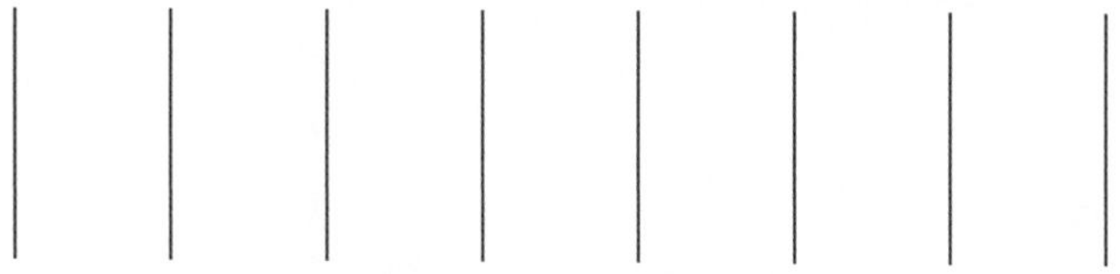

a) Measure the wavelength of the water wave.
The figure below shows the vertical displacement of a cork floating on the water in the ripple tank as the water wave passes by.

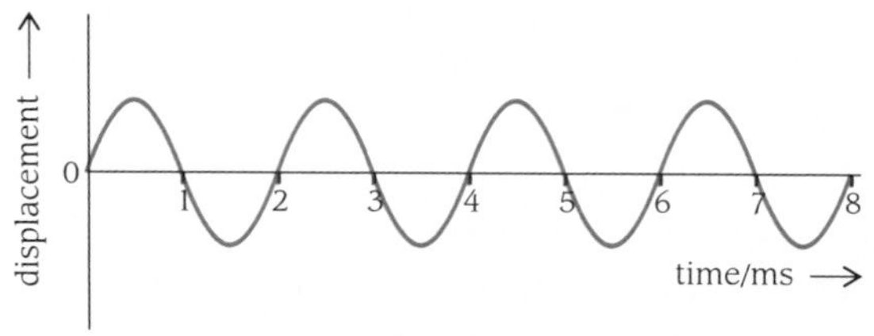

b) What is the time period of the water wave?

c) Calculate the frequency of the water wave.

d) Calculate the speed of the water wave.

2 The figure below shows water waves in a ripple tank at one moment in time.

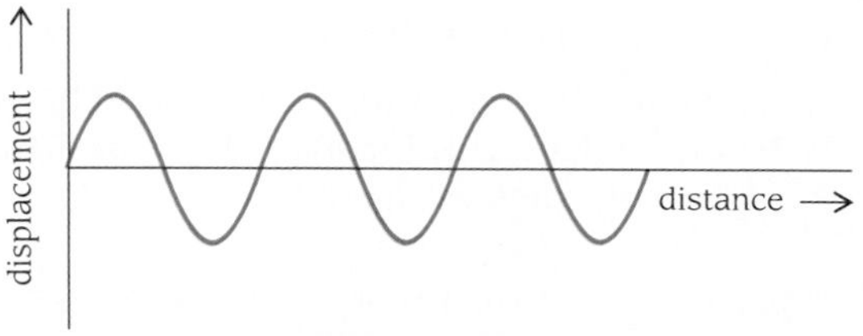

a) Redraw the figure and on it label clearly:
- **i)** the amplitude of the wave
- **ii)** the wavelength of the wave.

b) Calculate the frequency of the wave if its velocity is 30 cm s^{-1} and the wavelength is 0.5 cm.

3 A fisherman sits in his boat and sees a fast motorboat pass by. A little later, waves created by the motorboat make his boat rise and fall with a frequency of 0.5 Hz. If the waves are 3.0 m apart:

a) calculate the speed of the waves across the water

b) calculate the time period of the oscillations of the boat

c) sketch a graph of displacement against time for 6.0 s of the vertical motion of the fisherman's boat. Label your time axis with suitable values.

4 a) Frequency, velocity and wavelength are physical properties of a wave. Which of these three properties depends for its value:
- **i)** only on the behaviour of the wave source
- **ii)** only on the medium through which the waves travel?

b) When a water wave is reflected, which, if any, of the three properties change in value?

c) When a water wave is refracted, which, if any, of the three properties change in value?

5 a) Sketch the waveform of a pure note or simple sine-wave signal, and label its amplitude, *a*, and wavelength, λ.

b) Sketch the waveform of a pure note of twice the frequency and double the intensity of *a*.

6 In a simple experiment to determine the speed of sound, an observer with a stopwatch stands on a flat sports field and an assistant standing at a measured distance of 800 m fires a starting pistol. The observer starts his stopwatch when he sees the flash of the pistol and stops it when he hears the sound of the shot. The time intervals obtained for six experiments are: 2.2, 2.3, 2.2, 2.1, 2.3 and 2.1 s.
Calculate a value for the speed of sound in air.

7 A person claps his hands at approximately $\frac{1}{2}$ second intervals in front of a wall 90 m away. He notices that each echo produced by the wall coincides with the next clap.

a) Calculate an approximate value for the speed of sound.

b) If you were using the above as a basis for an experimental method to determine the speed of sound, what procedure would you adopt to obtain higher accuracy in the timing part of the experiment?

8 A fishing boat uses ultrasound of frequency 6.0×10^4 Hz to detect fish directly below. Two echoes of the ultrasound are received, one after 0.09 s coming from a shoal of fish and the other after 0.12 s coming from the seabed. If the seabed is 84 m below the ultrasound transmitter and receiver, calculate:

a) the speed of the ultrasound in water

b) the wavelength of the ultrasound waves in water

c) the depth of the shoal of fish below the boat.

9 Ultrasound waves are used to measure the size of an unborn baby's head. Echoes are received from the front and back of the skull bone. The reflected sound pulses are detected and displayed on an oscilloscope screen, which shows that the echoes are 0.15 m s apart. If the speed of ultrasound waves through the baby's head is 1400 m s^{-1}, calculate the diameter of the baby's head. Remember that reflected waves travel twice the distance.

10 a) Describe an experiment to show that sound waves cannot pass through a vacuum.

b) Explain why in the experiment you have described, the sound volume never quite falls to zero.

11 A student standing between two walls, as shown in the figure below, shouts once and finds that the time interval between hearing the first and second echo is 2.0 seconds. What value would the student obtain for the speed of sound in air?

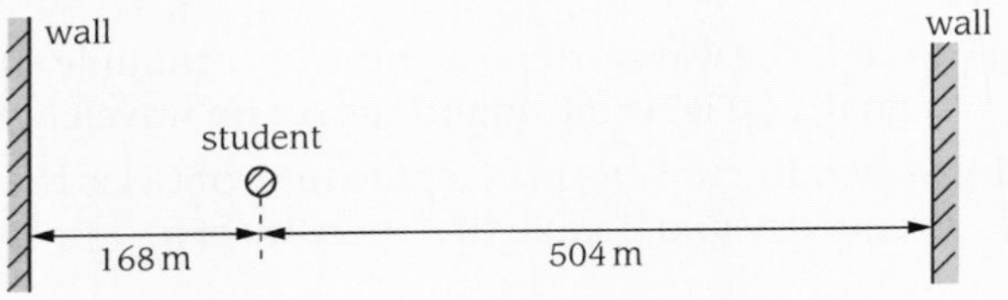

12 a) State the range of frequencies that can be heard by a normal human ear.

b) What names are given to sounds with frequencies above and below this range?

c) Give examples of sound sources that produce sounds with the following characteristics:

i) frequency below the human hearing range
ii) frequency above the human hearing range
iii) with a high audible pitch
iv) with a single pure frequency
v) with a number of frequencies that give the sound a special character.

13 a) A student places a loudspeaker, which is producing a musical note, on a metal water pipe. To his amusement, the sound passes along the pipes to other parts of the school.

i) Describe the movement of the metal 'particles' of the pipe caused by sound waves passing along the pipe.
ii) State the name of this type of wave.

b) The speed of the waves along the pipe is greater than the speed of the waves in air.

i) How does the wavelength of the waves in the air differ from the wavelength of the waves in the pipe?
ii) How does the frequency differ in each situation?

14 Two small loudspeakers, P and Q, emit sounds of the same frequency and intensity as shown in the figure below An observer walks along the line XY and when he is at A he hears a loud sound from the speakers while he hears no sound from them when he is at C.

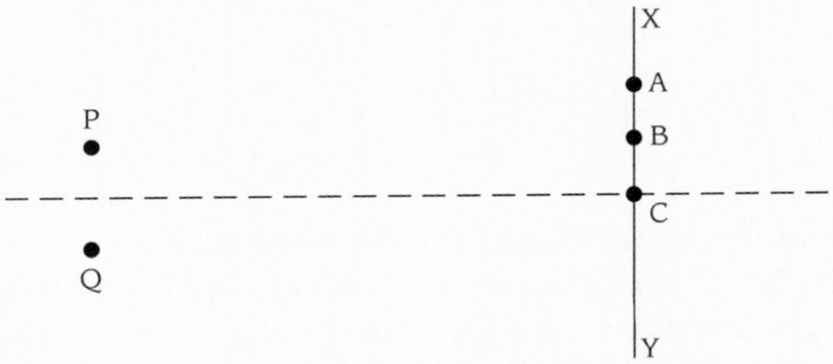

a) By considering the fact that there is silence at C, state, without explanation, the phase difference between the two sources of sound.

b) Explain why no sound is heard at C.

c) Explain why a loud sound is heard at A.

d) If the observer stood at C while P was switched off, what change in sound would be heard?

e) How will the sound heard at B, which is halfway between A and C, differ from that heard at A?

f) Describe the position of one other point where the observer could hear a loud sound similar to that heard at A.

g) Describe the position of one other point where the observer could hear no sound.

h) State, without explanation, what would be heard at A, B and C if the sounds leaving the two speakers were in phase with each other.

15 a) If you lived in a street that carried heavy traffic, suggest three ways, other than altering the traffic flow, by which you could reduce the noise entering your home.

b) Explain how each of the methods you gave in part **a)** works, and where appropriate suggest suitable materials you would use.

C12 Wave phenomena

Objectives

By the end of this topic you will be able to:

- compare the rival theories of light held by Huygens, Young, Newton, Planck and Einstein
- describe the nature of light
- recall the properties of light
- explain how polarisation confirms that light waves are transverse waves.

! Key fact

Facts about light waves

- Light waves are part of the electromagnetic spectrum of travelling waves.
- Light waves are transverse and can be polarised.
- Light waves carry energy.
- Light waves are emitted and absorbed by matter.
- Light waves can travel through both a vacuum and some matter, but involve no movement of that matter along with the wave motion.
- In a vacuum light waves travel at $3.0 \times 10^8\,m\,s^{-1}$.
- Light waves can be reflected, obeying the laws of reflection.
- Light waves are refracted as their speed changes in different media. The change of speed causes a change of wavelength but no change of frequency.
- Light waves show diffraction and interference effects under certain circumstances.
- Light also shows particle-like properties under different circumstances.
- Planck and Einstein proposed that particles of light energy, called quanta or photons, could exist at the same time as light demonstrated a wave-like nature.

Light from the Sun is the source of all life on planet Earth. The Sun and sunlight have given inspiration to us all throughout our history. It is very important that we understand the nature of light and its properties, which make it so vital and so fascinating.

C12.1 The nature of light

Scientists have long sought an explanation of the nature of light. The experimental evidence has often appeared to be conflicting and has led to rival theories.

Thomas Young and Huygens

In 1801, Thomas Young was the first person to produce evidence of the wave nature of light when he produced interference fringes in the light that passed through two narrow slits. Young was not the first person to imagine that light might have a wave nature; as early as 1690 Huygens suggested that light could travel as a wave motion.

Isaac Newton

An alternative theory, proposed by Newton, suggested that light travelled as small particles called corpuscles. The particle theory could apparently account for reflection and refraction of light by applying Newton's laws of motion to the small corpuscles. However, the particle theory of light failed to account for the properties of light that we call interference and diffraction. Here the wave theory triumphed!

Einstein

The physicist, Max Planck, suggested that radiation came in tiny 'packets' called 'quanta'. Albert Einstein developed this idea and used it to describe light as both a wave *and* a particle. This is called the **wave–particle duality** of light.

Detecting light

Our eyes detect light by having special cells in the retina at the back of our eyes. Light falling on a cell causes an electrical signal to be sent from the cell to our brain. Photo sensors (from 'photo', the Greek word for light) detect light in a similar way. Photo sensors contain photosensitive materials that give an electrical signal when light falls on them. A digital camera has a sheet of photosensitive material at the back, made up of millions of photosensitive **pixels**. A computer converts the electrical signals from the all the pixels into a picture that can be displayed on a screen or printed out.

Wave properties

All waves can demonstrate reflection, refraction, interference and diffraction. You learned about reflection and refraction of light in units C9 and C10. In unit C11 you learned about diffraction and interference for water waves and sound waves. Light can also show interference and diffraction; scientists use these to demonstrate that light is a wave. The very short wavelength of light (less than one millionth of a metre) makes interference and diffraction of light much more difficult to observe than interference or diffraction of water waves.

Summary questions

1 What theory about light was proposed by Isaac Newton?

2 List as many facts as you can about light.

3 What is the speed of light in a vacuum?

C12.2 Interference and diffraction of light waves

Objectives

By the end of this topic you will be able to:

- describe a Young's slits experiment demonstrating interference of light waves and confirming the wave nature of light
- describe the interference pattern produced by the double-slit experiment
- state that light is diffracted through very narrow slits
- describe what a diffraction grating is.

Practical details for viewing Young's fringes

- Use a colour filter in front of a white light source.
- Do not look directly at a laser source.
- Set the lamp filament parallel to the double slits.
- Use the adjustable single slit to adjust the brightness and clarity of the patterns.
- The interference pattern will be seen more easily if the double slits are surrounded by a black screen so that light reaches the eye only through the slits.
- The pattern can be viewed on a translucent screen or through an eyepiece with a measuring scale.
- The experiment requires a good blackout and often it is necessary to cut out stray light reflections, but the most usual cause of not seeing the pattern is misalignment of the apparatus.

The most striking feature of **interference** between light waves is that in some places where they overlap we find that light added to light produces darkness. This unexpected result, which seems to conflict with our ordinary experiences, can be explained as destructive interference of waves.

Double-slit interference, Young's experiment

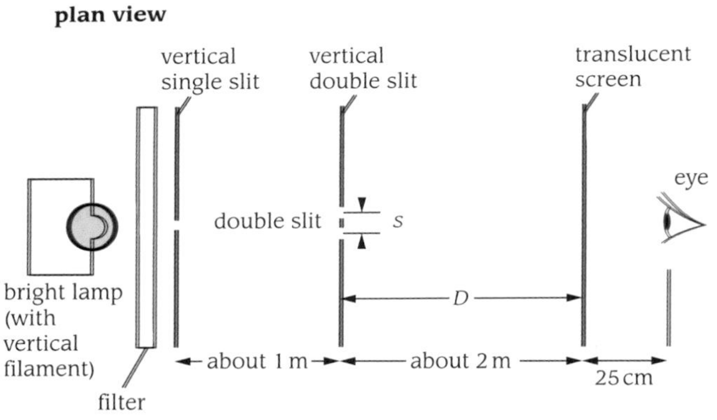

▲ **Figure 12.2.1** A practical arrangement for observing Young's double-slit interference fringes

Figure 12.2.1 shows how equipment may be set up to demonstrate interference of light. This is similar to the experiment in C11.3, using two dippers and a ripple tank to show interference of water waves, but the small wavelength of light means the slits must be very close together for interference to be seen. Each slit must be about the same width as the wavelength of the light.

Although it is possible to show interference of light with a filament lamp, it is much easier to show with a laser lamp, but great care must be taken to follow the correct safety rules otherwise eyes may be damaged by the intense light of the laser beam.

A laser mounted firmly above a bench, pointing away from the viewers towards a screen or wall, will produce a single bright spot of light. When a narrow double slit is placed in front of the laser a pattern of dots can be seen on either side of the original central spot.

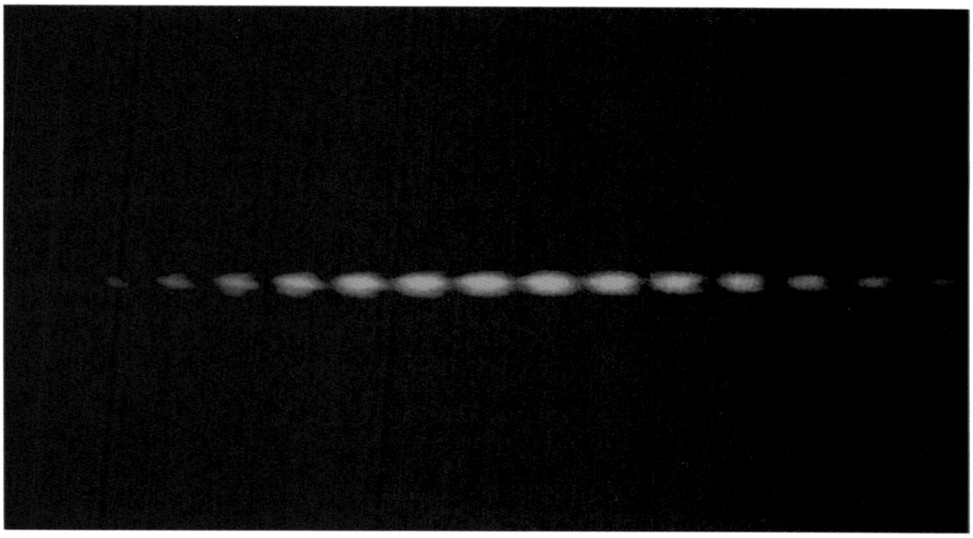

▲ **Figure 12.2.2** The narrow beam of laser light, after passing through a pair of narrow slits 0.25 mm apart, produces this pattern of bright spots that are equally spaced and symmetrical on either side of a central spot. The central spot has the same size and spacing as its neighbours.

- What do you notice about the spacing of the dots?
- What is the effect of using double slits that are closer together or further apart?

Interference occurs with ordinary light as well as laser light. We can produce a similar pattern using a small laboratory light source such as a 12 V lamp with a straight or vertical 'line' filament (Figure 12.2.1).

The fringe pattern is brightest in the centre, with fringes getting fainter as they are further from the centre. The distance between the fringes depends on the wavelength of the light. Blue fringes are closer together than red fringes because their wavelength is less.

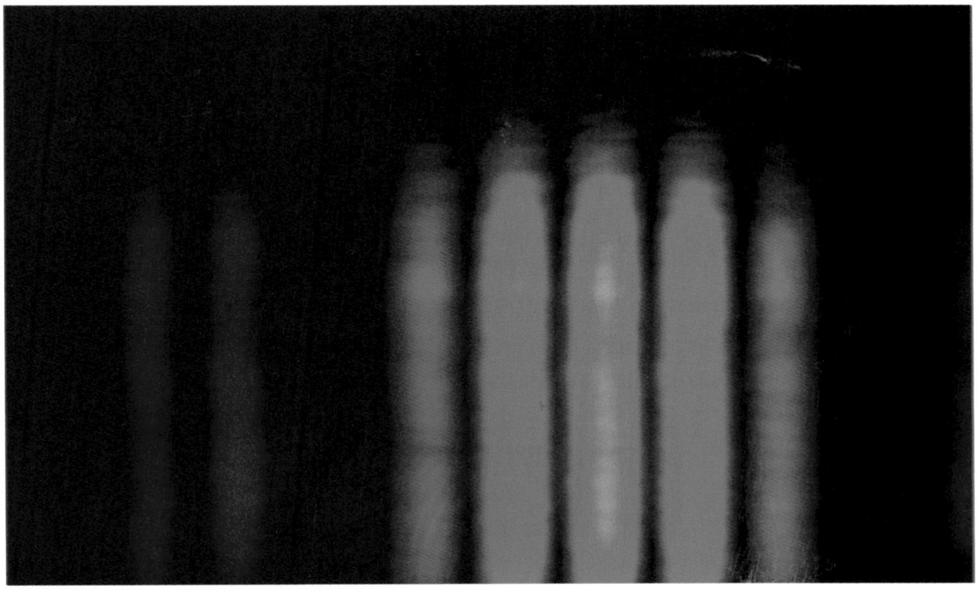

▲ **Figure 12.2.3a** Interference fringes

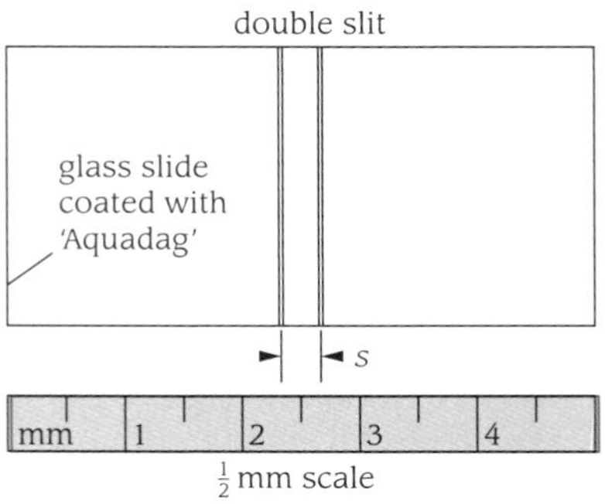

▲ **Figure 12.2.3b** A double slit to produce interference

Key fact

- The central fringes are brighter.
- The fringes are evenly spaced.
- For shorter wavelengths the fringes are closer together and the blue fringes have about half the spacing of the red ones.
- The slit separation has an inverse effect, i.e. for slits closer together the fringes are further apart.
- **Bright fringes** occur where crests overlap and cause constructive interference. Here the waves are in phase. light + light = brighter light
- **Dark fringes** occur where a crest and a trough overlap. Here the waves are out of phase and cause destructive interference. light + light = darkness

Coherent sources of waves

- When the double slit is illuminated by a single lamp, each wavetrain passes through both slits at the same time.
- Any change in the phase of the waves, as different wavetrains reach the two slits, happens at both slits.
- The wavetrains that emerge from the two slits bear the same phase relation to each other at all times and are therefore coherent waves.
- The wavetrains from two separate sources of light would each change in phase independently and randomly with each new wavetrain emitted from the sources. No constant phase relationship can exist between two sets of waves emitted randomly. Such waves are said to be incoherent and do not produce interference fringes in fixed positions.

Observing the interference patterns

The vertical bright and dark lines seen on the screen or through the eyepiece are called interference fringes.

- How many bright fringes can you see?
- Are the fringes sharp or blurred?
- Are the fringes equally spaced and equally bright?
- Insert red, green and blue filters in front of the lamp. For each colour answer the previous questions and note any differences.
- Try using double slits with a different slit separation and repeat the observations, again noting any differences.

A wave explanation of double-slit interference

The wavefronts from the single slit arrive at the double slits, S_1 and S_2, in phase (Figure 12.2.4). We can think of this as a wave crest arriving at both slits at the same moment. Each slit diffracts the light waves, spreading them out, so that in the space between the double slits and the screen there is a region where the two beams of waves overlap. Where waves overlap, superposition results in constructive and destructive interference.

Note that these interference effects occur throughout the region of overlap of the waves from the two slits.

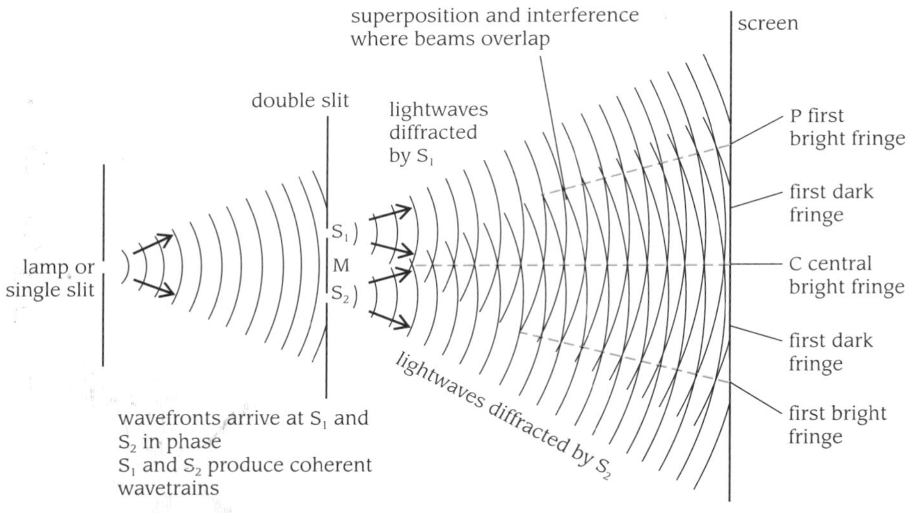

▲ **Figure 12.2.4** Double-slit interference

The conditions for interference fringes

- The two light sources must be coherent, that is they must have exactly the same frequency. This is achieved by having a single light source of only one colour, and allowing the light to pass through a double slit.
- The two sets of waves must have roughly equal amplitude, otherwise the larger one will swamp the smaller one and fringes will not be seen.

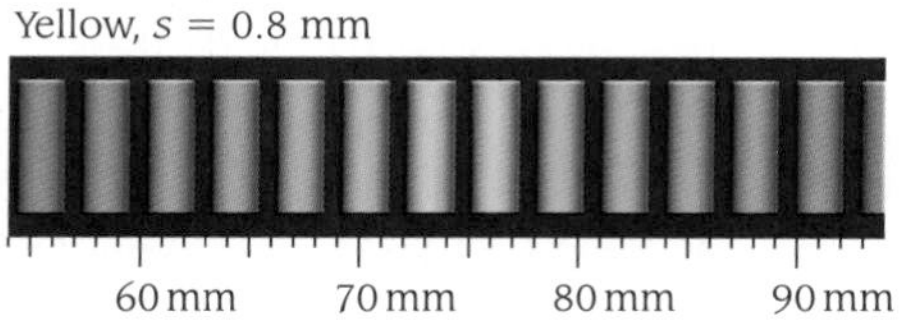

▲ **Figure 12.2.5** Double-slit interference pattern using yellow light

Diffraction of light waves

Diffraction by a single slit or a diffraction grating

Now we shall see that light can spread around corners where rays, travelling in straight lines, should not go. This effect, which is due to the **diffraction** of light waves, gives support to the theory that light has a wave-like nature.

Light can be diffracted by a single, very narrow slit, in a similar way to water waves being diffracted by a narrow gap. If it is diffracted through lots of parallel slits, called a diffraction grating, a spectrum is produced.

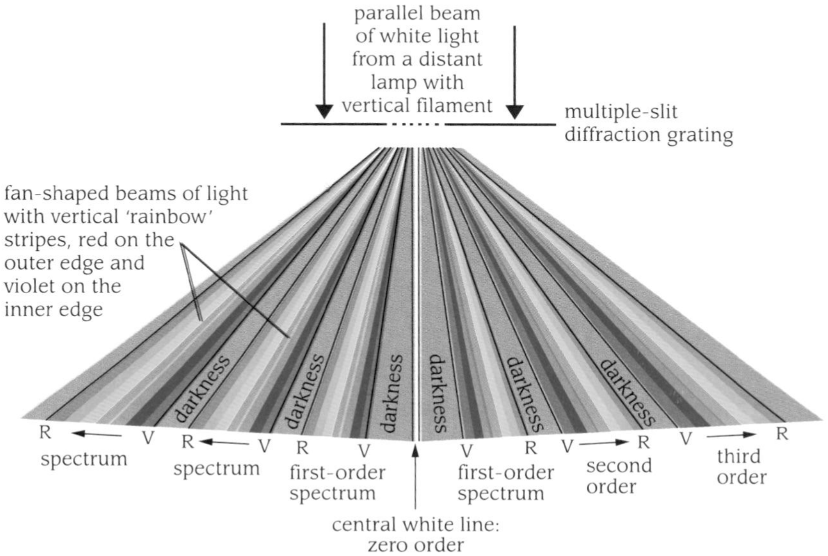

▲ **Figure 12.2.6** The diffraction grating produces a spectrum

CDs have very narrow grooves on their surface that can behave as a diffraction grating for light falling on the CD. When this happens, you see multi-coloured reflections from the CD.

◄ **Figure 12.2.7** This compact disc shows coloured fringes produced by the diffraction of white light from the fine grooves on its surface. The colours are produced by constructive interference between rays of light of particular wavelengths.

Summary questions

1 Give two conditions for observing interference fringes.

2 If the wavelength decreases, what happens to the spacing of bright fringes?

Making a single slit

If two razor blades or knife edges are mounted in a frame so that one is fixed and the other can be moved towards it, a narrow and adjustable single slit is formed between the two blade edges.

Key fact

Key features of the single slit diffraction pattern

- a bright central band situated where the light is expected to arrive by straight-line travel and wider than the straight-through band should be
- narrow fringes of light in the region where there should be totally dark shadow
- at the outside edges, fringes gradually getting fainter and closer together.

Things to do

A CD has very fine, equally spaced, rings on its surface. Diffraction grating effects can be produced by reflection from these regular rings. Tilt a CD at an angle nearly level with your line of vision, so that the rings appear much closer together. Now observe the reflection of light from a distant small source of light. Describe what you see.

C12.3 An electromagnetic family

Objectives

By the end of this topic you will be able to:

- recall the common properties of all electromagnetic waves
- distinguish between the members of the family in terms of their wavelengths and distinctive properties
- identify a source of each type of electromagnetic wave
- describe an application of each type of electromagnetic wave.

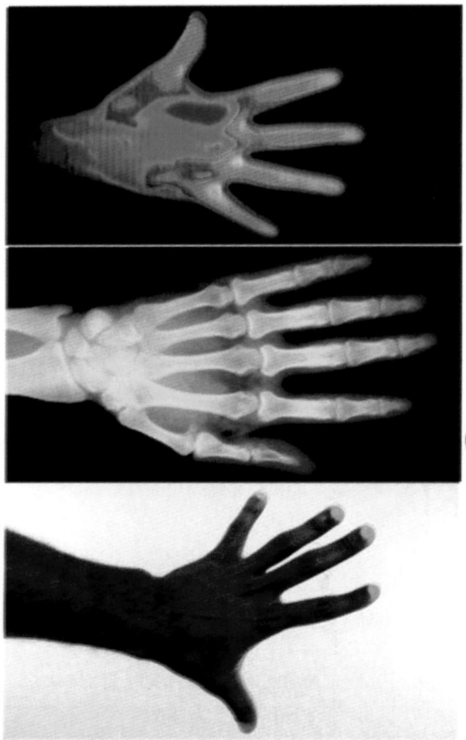

▲ **Figure 12.3.1** These three images of a human hand show how different it appears when the image is formed using different parts of the electromagnetic spectrum.

- The top image is a thermogram taken using infrared radiation. The false colours, converted by a computer from infrared wavelengths to visible wavelengths, show the coldest areas in blue and the hottest areas in yellow.
- The middle image is obtained by passing X-radiation through the hand onto a photographic plate.
- The bottom image is the view of a hand we see when reflected visible light reaches our eyes.

Which radiations belong to this family?

What are the common family features?

What makes each member of the family distinctive and different?

The images of the human hand in Figure 12.3.1 are formed by radiation from three different parts of the electromagnetic spectrum: emitted infrared (heat), transmitted X-rays and reflected light.

Figure 12.3.2 shows the members of the electromagnetic radiation family and how they fit together in a continuous spectrum. The spectrum is arranged with the highest frequency of radiation at the top and the lowest frequency at the bottom. Note that the scale is a logarithmic or constant ratio 'ladder' with each rung of the ladder representing an increase in frequency of $\times 10$. The frequency scale increases upwards but has no definite beginning or end.

Frequency and wavelength

All electromagnetic radiation has the same speed: $3 \times 10^8\,\mathrm{m\,s^{-1}}$ in a vacuum.

From the wave equation $v = f\lambda$ (page 196), we can calculate the wavelength λ for any frequency f of electromagnetic radiation. Note that in Figure 12.3.2 the shortest wavelengths are at the top of the spectrum ladder and the longest wavelengths are at the bottom.

Worked example

Calculate the wavelength in a vacuum of green light of frequency 5.0×10^{14} Hz. The speed of electromagnetic radiation in a vacuum is $3.0 \times 10^8\,\mathrm{m\,s^{-1}}$.

Using $\lambda = \frac{v}{f}$ we have

$$\lambda = \frac{3.0 \times 10^8\,\mathrm{m\,s^{-1}}}{5.0 \times 10^{14}\,\mathrm{s^{-1}}} = 0.6 \times 10^{8-14}\,\mathrm{m} = 0.6 \times 10^{-6}\,\mathrm{m} = 0.6\,\mu\mathrm{m}$$

The wavelength of green light in a vacuum is 0.6 micrometres.

A continuous spectrum

In the spectrum of white light produced by a hot filament lamp there is a range of colours that gradually change from a deep red through orange to yellow and so on to deep violet. There are no sudden changes of colour and no gaps. We describe such a spectrum as **continuous**.

The electromagnetic spectrum is also continuous. There are no gaps in it and no frequencies anywhere in the range that do not exist. Like the colours of light, the different kinds of radiation gradually change from one to another as their properties gradually change. So there is no sharp boundary between one type of radiation and the next. The dividing lines are given only in order to help us give a name to particular wavelengths in the spectrum. There is often a large overlap at the boundaries.

The electromagnetic spectrum

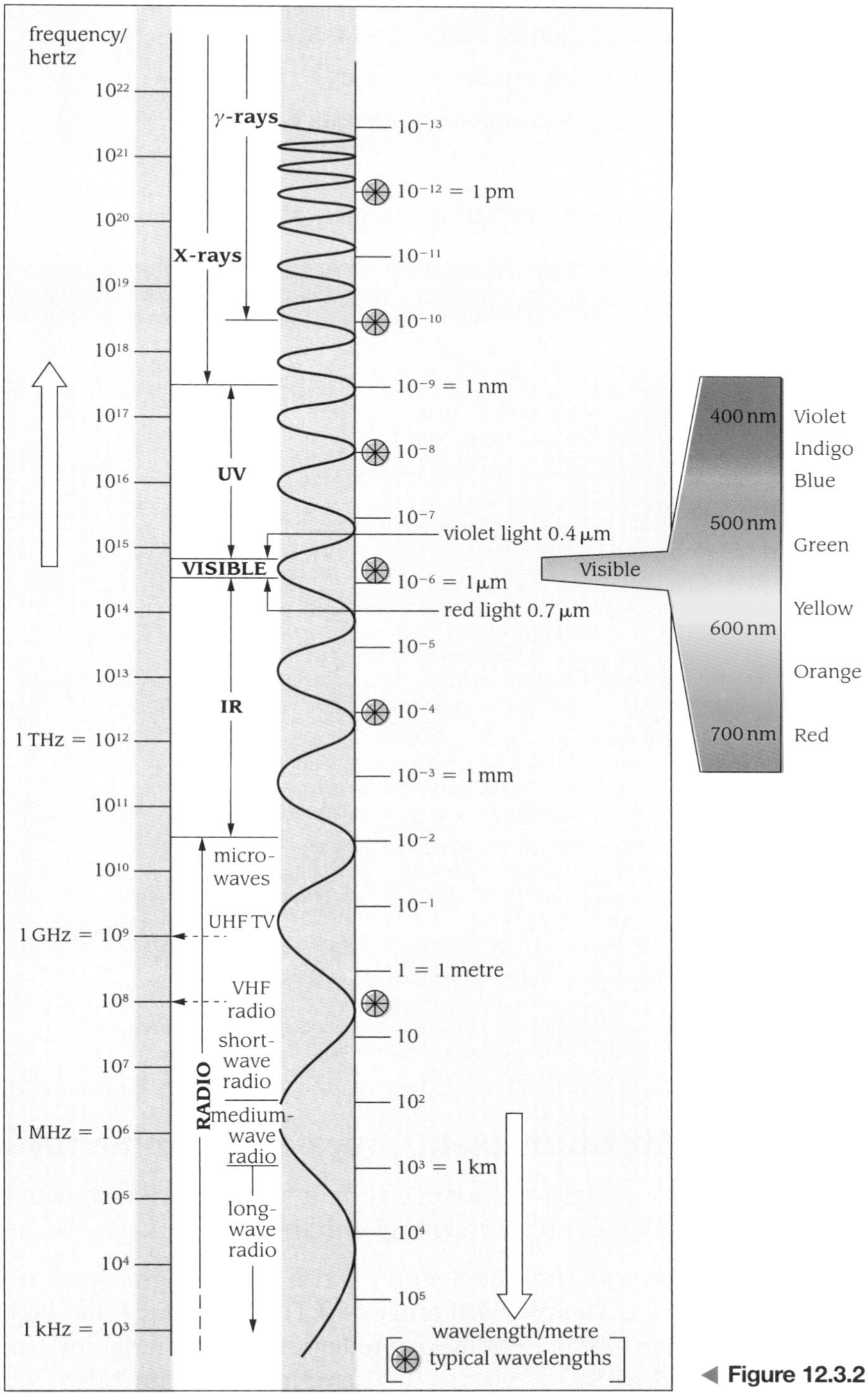

◀ **Figure 12.3.2**

Key fact

The range of wavelengths

- The shortest wavelengths are gammas and X-rays in the range from 1 nanometre (10^{-9} m) to 1 picometre (10^{-12} m), and even shorter. These wavelengths are similar to the dimensions of molecules (10^{-9} m), atoms (10^{-10} m) and atomic nuclei (10^{-14} m).
- Light waves, in the middle of the spectrum have wavelengths of a few tenths of a micrometre (0.4 to 0.7 μm).
- The longest wavelengths in the spectrum belong to the radio waves.

You will find it helpful in recognising where a particular wavelength belongs in the spectrum to think of something with similar dimensions.

- For example, you can say that a radio wavelength of a few metres is similar in length to a radio aerial thus suggesting a radio wave.
- A wavelength of 10 nm, 10^{-8} m, is too short for a light wave and too long for an X-ray. Between light waves and X-rays we can label the wavelength as ultraviolet.

Examples of typical wavelengths are given in Figure 12.3.2. Note how these wavelengths can be remembered in a series:

- gamma rays 10^{-12} m
- X-rays 10^{-10} m
- ultraviolet 10^{-8} m
- light is near 10^{-6} m
- infrared 10^{-4} m
- radio waves are 10^{-2} m upwards.

Things to do

Carry out some research using books or the internet. For each of the sections of the electromagnetic spectrum listed below, name an object that has similar size or dimensions as the wavelength of the radiation.

a) radio waves used for the medium or long wave wavebands

b) radio waves used for mobile phone communication

c) microwaves used for microwave cooking

d) infrared light

e) visible light

f) ultraviolet light

g) X-rays

Summary questions

1 List the types of waves in the electromagnetic spectrum.
2 Which type of wave has the highest frequency?
3 Which type of wave has the longest wavelength?

C12.4 Sources and applications of electromagnetic waves

Name and typical wavelength	Sources	Detectors	Special properties and uses
γ-rays, gamma rays 1 pm = 10^{-12} m	nuclei of radioactive atoms and cosmic rays	photographic film Geiger–Müller tube	very penetrating } high-energy photons very dangerous } used to kill cancerous growths used to find flaws in metals used to sterilise equipment
X-rays 100 pm = 10^{-10} m	X-ray tubes	photographic film fluorescent screen	same radiation as γ-rays, only the source is different very penetrating and dangerous used to take X-ray pictures: radiography used to treat skin disorders used to study crystal structures: X-ray crystallography
UV, ultraviolet light 10 nm = 10^{-8} m	the Sun very hot objects arcs and sparks mercury vapour lamps	photographic film photo cells fluorescent chemicals	absorbed by ordinary (not UVB or UVC) glass causes many chemical reactions damages and kills living cells, causes sunburn UV lamps used in medicine for skin treatment but dangerous to eyes fluorescence used in washing powders and to detect forgeries
visible light 0.6 μm = 0.6 × 10^{-6} m (green)	the Sun hot objects lamps lasers	eye photographic film photo cells	refracted by glass and focused by the eye essential for photosynthesis and plant growth used for communication systems: laser and optical fibres used to identify elements in chemistry flame tests
IR, infrared light 100 μm = 10^{-4} m	the Sun warm and hot objects such as fires and people	special photographic film semiconductor devices such as LDR and photodiode skin	causes heating when absorbed, makes skin feel warm used for heating: radiators and fires emit IR used for photography through haze and fog, IR is not scattered as much as visible light IR photographs taken by satellite provide special information, see text
radio 3 m (VHF)	microwave ovens TV and radio transmitters using electric circuits and aerials	aerials connected to tuned electric circuits in radio and TV sets	spread around hills and buildings by diffraction microwaves used for cooking used for radio, TV, telephone and satellite communications used for radar detection of ships, aircraft and missiles used in radio astronomy

! Key fact

All electromagnetic waves:

- transfer energy from one place to another
- can be emitted and absorbed by matter
- do not need a medium to travel through
- travel at $3.0 \times 10^8\,m\,s^{-1}$ in a vacuum
- are transverse waves (page 218)
- can be superposed (page 220) and produce interference effects
- obey the laws of reflection and refraction discovered for light
- can be diffracted (page 221)
- carry no charge.

Above visible light: ultraviolet, X-rays and gamma rays

These radiations are above light in the spectrum in the sense that they have higher frequencies and higher photon energies than light.

Ultraviolet light is beyond the violet end of the visible light spectrum. Ultraviolet light or UV has a wavelength range of 0.4 μm to about 1 nm. Being next to visible light, UV is also present in solar radiation and the radiation from other very hot objects. Sparks and electric arcs used in welding metals at very high temperatures emit UV light. Because of this UV light, welders must wear protective goggles that filter out the UV, which would be harmful to the eyes.

The higher frequency and energy of UV light also causes fluorescence in a number of chemicals. When the atoms of a fluorescent material absorb UV light they re-emit the energy as visible light, which makes the material appear to glow. A document may have a signature written in invisible ink containing a fluorescent substance that will show up in UV light. Some soap powders contain a fluorescent chemical that will absorb the UV in sunlight and release it as extra visible light, making the washing appear 'whiter than white'.

X-rays and gamma rays have higher frequencies than UV light, higher photon energies, greater penetration of matter and greater danger to living cells in plants and animals. Gamma rays come from the nuclei of atoms. We discuss gamma rays in unit E20. The effects of X-rays and gamma radiation on people are discussed in E20.4.

Below visible light

Infrared radiation has a wavelength range of 0.7 μm to about 1 cm. All warm or hot objects lose heat energy by emitting infrared or IR radiation. When objects absorb IR radiation they gain energy and become hotter. Infrared radiation is invisible radiant heat energy. When an object is red-hot it emits red visible light as well as infrared radiation. At a lower temperature there is less heat energy available in an object and so it emits radiation photons of lower energy and lower frequency. In this sense infrared radiation is *below* red visible light.

When we warm ourselves near a fire the red glow is attractive to see, but it is the invisible IR radiation not the red light that warms our skin. IR lamps are used to provide heat treatment for various illnesses. Everyday objects and people are sources of infrared radiation and they emit this radiation at night as well as during the day. Special photographic films that are sensitive to IR can take pictures in the dark without a flashlight. A satellite IR photograph can show where crops are infected by a disease by revealing differences in surface temperature.

Radio waves have a wide range of wavelengths, extending from about 1 cm to hundreds of kilometres. There is considerable overlap with the infrared part of the spectrum in the region also known as microwaves. Various parts of the radio wave spectrum have distinctive uses and well-known names, such as microwaves and VHF radio.

Microwaves have the shortest wavelengths in the radio wave family, being typically a few centimetres. The microwaves used in microwave ovens, of frequency 2450 MHz and wavelength 12 cm, produce a heating effect by exciting water and fat molecules in the food.

Microwaves are used particularly for communication. Radio links between satellites and ground stations usually use microwaves. Some telephone links also use microwaves transmitted between small dish-shaped aerials often mounted on hilltops and the roofs of high buildings.

Radar systems use microwaves to find the direction and distance of objects, which reflect the microwaves back to a large receiving aerial mounted near the transmitter.

Ultra-high frequency radio waves, (UHF) have frequencies of about 10^9 Hz or 1 GHz. Television pictures are tra nsmitted as modulated radio waves of this frequency.

Very high frequency radio waves, (VHF) have a typical wavelength of about 3 metres and a typical frequency of about 10^8 Hz or 100 MHz. Radio broadcasts using FM (frequency modulation) use this range of radio frequencies.

Summary questions

1 Give one source of UV radiation.

2 Give one use of gamma rays.

3 List the common characteristics of all electromagnetic radiation.

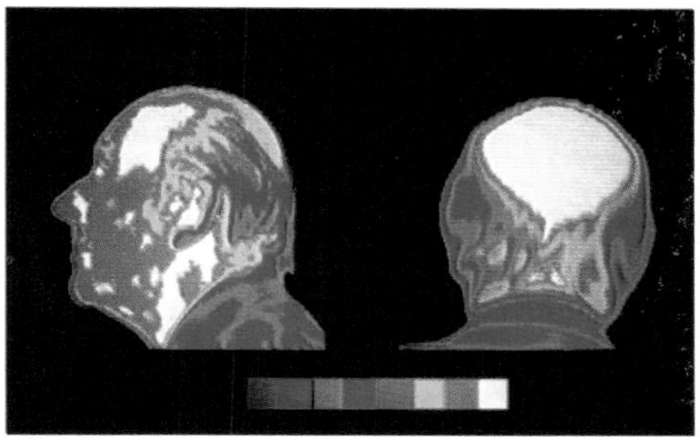

▲ **Figure 12.4.1** The thermographs or infrared images show the temperature variations over the head of a bald man. White areas are hottest and dark blue/black areas are coldest.

▲ **Figure 12.4.2** The metal mirrors focus microwaves onto a small aerial at the focus of the parabolic dish and transmit or receive digital information such as telephone calls.

▲ **Figure 12.4.3** The welder must wear a protective mask to provide protection from the ultraviolet light as well as physical protection against sparks. The high temperature of the welding flame produces a lot of ultraviolet light.

Practice exam-style questions

1 At the end of the 19th century there were two rival theories about the nature of light. For each theory, list the following information:

a) Which famous scientists supported it?

b) How was it thought that light energy was transmitted?

c) Which experimental evidence appeared to support the theory?

d) Which experimental evidence could not be explained by the theory?

2 Interference fringes are formed on a screen when monochromatic light is passed through two narrow slits that are close together.
State how, if at all, and explain why the separation of these fringes increases if:

a) the screen is moved towards the slits

b) the slits are made narrower but the separation is unchanged

c) a more intense light source is used

d) light of a longer wavelength is used

e) the separation of the slits is increased.

3 The figure below shows rays of red light passing through two narrow slits and reaching a screen. A series of bright and dark bands is produced on the screen.

a) Explain why the first dark band is formed.

b) Explain why the first dark band is followed by the first bright band.

c) If the red light is now replaced by green light, how will the pattern on the screen change?

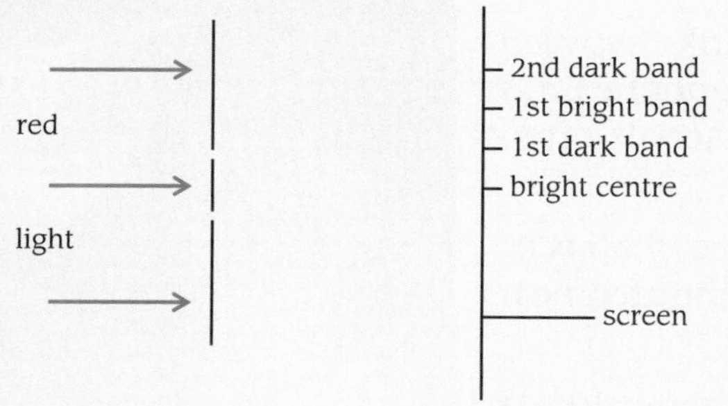

4 Groups of students are each using a narrow source of white light, a red filter and double slits to form interference fringes on a screen as shown in the figure below.

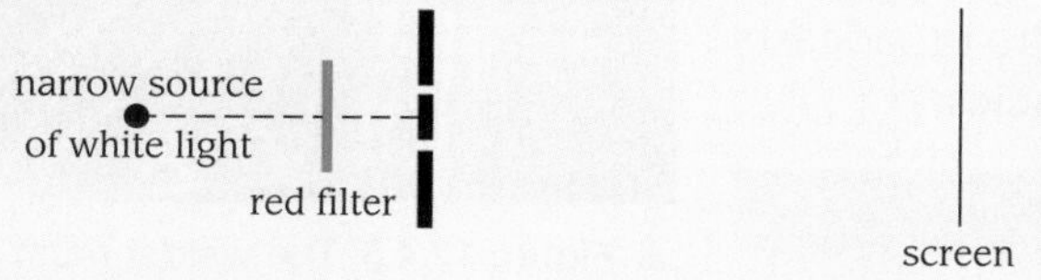

Four comments are made by some of the students. For each comment write a paragraph that will explain to the student the answer to his question. It may help to include diagrams in your explanation.

a) 'There are only two slits, but there is a series of bright and dark fringes. Why is this?'

b) 'When I move the screen away from the slits the fringes get further apart. Why should they do this?'

c) 'My neighbour has the same distance between the screen and the slits as I have, but his fringes are closer together than mine. Why?'

d) 'When I remove the red filter I can see colour in the fringes, although the light source is white. Why?'

5 Two filament lamps are connected to the same power supply and are equally bright. Also, two loudspeakers are connected to the same signal generator and are producing the same sound at equal volumes.

a) State whether it is possible to observe interference effects either between the two light sources or between the two sound sources.

b) Explain your answers in terms of the coherence of TWO sets of waves.

6 a) The figure below represents the fringe pattern obtained in a double-slit experiment when monochromatic red light was used.

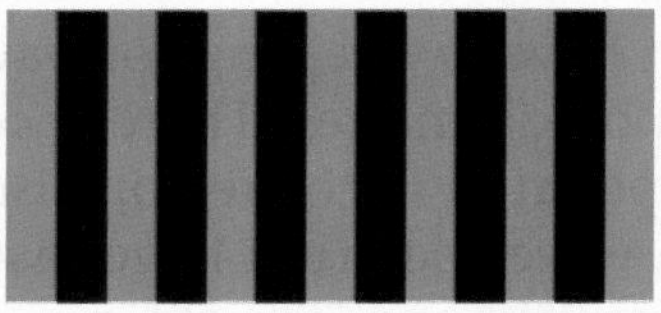

b) Explain clearly, using the wave theory of light, why dark and red fringes occur.

c) State clearly how the pattern would change if monochromatic blue light were used, the rest of the apparatus remaining unchanged.

d) What deduction could be made about the difference between red and blue light from the two fringe patterns?

7 Diffraction of light waves is not normally seen under ordinary lighting conditions.

a) Describe a simple way of demonstrating diffraction of light waves using a single slit and explain how the special conditions make the effect observable.

b) What would be the effect on the diffraction pattern of changing the wavelength of the light from a red colour to a blue colour?

c) What effect does the width of the gap in the slit have on the diffraction pattern?

8 Using the equation, $v = f\lambda$ for each of the following electromagnetic waves, calculate the frequency of the radiation. Speed of all electromagnetic waves is $3.0 \times 10^8\ \mathrm{m\,s^{-1}}$.

a) gamma rays of wavelength 3.0×10^{-12} m

b) ultraviolet light of wavelength 60 nm

c) visible light of wavelength 600 nm

d) infrared light of wavelength 1000 nm

e) radio waves of wavelength 1500 m

9 Copy and complete the following paragraph.

'In a vacuum, electromagnetic waves all have the same .... Light waves have a greater .... than radio waves. Another type of electromagnetic radiation is .... and this can be detected by .... An example of a non-electromagnetic wave is ....'

10 a) How would you show that there is invisible radiation beyond the red end of the visible spectrum?

b) Name ONE region of the electromagnetic spectrum that has a wavelength greater than visible light. State how this radiation may be produced and may be detected.

c) Visible light and X-rays are both types of an electromagnetic wave. State:

i) FOUR similarities and

ii) ONE difference between the two types of wave.

11 Consider the following types of wave: infrared, ultraviolet, sound, X-rays and radio.

a) Which of these is not part of the electromagnetic spectrum?

b) Of those that are electromagnetic:

i) which has the shortest wavelengths

ii) which has the lowest frequencies

iii) which is unlikely to be detected by a photographic method

iv) what is significant about their speed?

12 a) Orange light has a wavelength in air of 6.0×10^{-7} m. Calculate the frequency of this light. (The speed of light in air is $3.0 \times 10^{8}\ \mathrm{m\,s^{-1}}$.)

b) Which of the following characteristics of light does not change when light passes from air into water: speed, wavelength and frequency?

13 a) Explain the following terms:

i) superposition

ii) constructive interference

iii) destructive interference.

b) Describe what you would see or hear for all of the above, using sound waves OR water waves OR light waves.

D13 Static electricity

Objectives

By the end of this topic you will be able to:

- explain and demonstrate the charging of objects in terms of the transfer of negatively charged electrons from one surface to another
- demonstrate and understand how like charges repel and unlike charges attract.

Practical note

The air in tropical countries is often very humid. The moisture that covers the surfaces of objects allows charge to leak away. Experiments on static electricity need dry equipment to work. Dry all apparatus with a hair drier or in the sunshine.

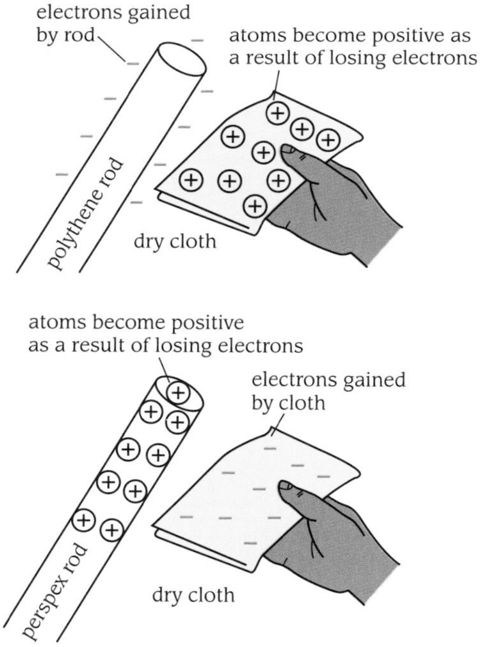

A positively charged object has lost electrons. A negatively charged object has gained electrons.

▲ **Figure 13.1.1** Charging by friction

All matter contains vast numbers of electrons. When a few of them get transferred from the surface of one object to the surface of another, they produce what is known as static electricity.

D13.1 Charge

Friction and charge

The Ancient Greeks made spindles for spinning silk threads out of amber, a material known to them as 'electron'. They found that when these spindles were rubbed, the silk was attracted and the clinging threads were easier to manage. If we rub a plastic comb on fabric, the comb can pick up small pieces of paper. We imagine that friction produces something invisible called **charge** on the surface of the comb, which makes it attractive to the small bits of paper or particles of dust.

Attraction and repulsion

- Rub a strip of polythene on your sleeve or with a woollen duster then hold it near some small pieces of paper on the bench top and notice what happens.
- Repeat the test with small pieces of aluminium cooking foil, or small metallised polystyrene balls (expanded polystyrene balls coated with metal paint).

The charged strips of polythene attract the bits of paper and these may cling on to the strips for some time. The metallised polystyrene balls jump rapidly up and down between the bench top and the charged strips, being first **attracted** to the strips and then thrown off or **repelled**.

Two kinds of charge

- After rubbing it, support a polythene strip A in a stirrup as shown in Figure 13.1.2.
- Charge another polythene strip B by rubbing it and then slowly bring it close to one end of strip A without touching.
- Test the other end of A and notice what happens.
- Now charge two strips of glass C and D, by rubbing them with a duster and repeat the test with C in a stirrup and D brought near it.
- Finally, investigate what happens when the charged glass strip D is brought near to the suspended charged polythene strip A, and similarly when the charged strip B is brought near to suspended strip C.

When the two charged strips are made of the same material they repel each other but when the two different materials are charged and brought near they attract each other. We conclude that *two different kinds of charge are produced by friction* on these two different materials.

When the glass strip is rubbed with the cloth, friction causes electrons to move from the strip to the cloth. The cloth gains negatively charged electrons, so becomes negatively charged. The glass strip loses negatively charged electrons, so is left with a positive charge.

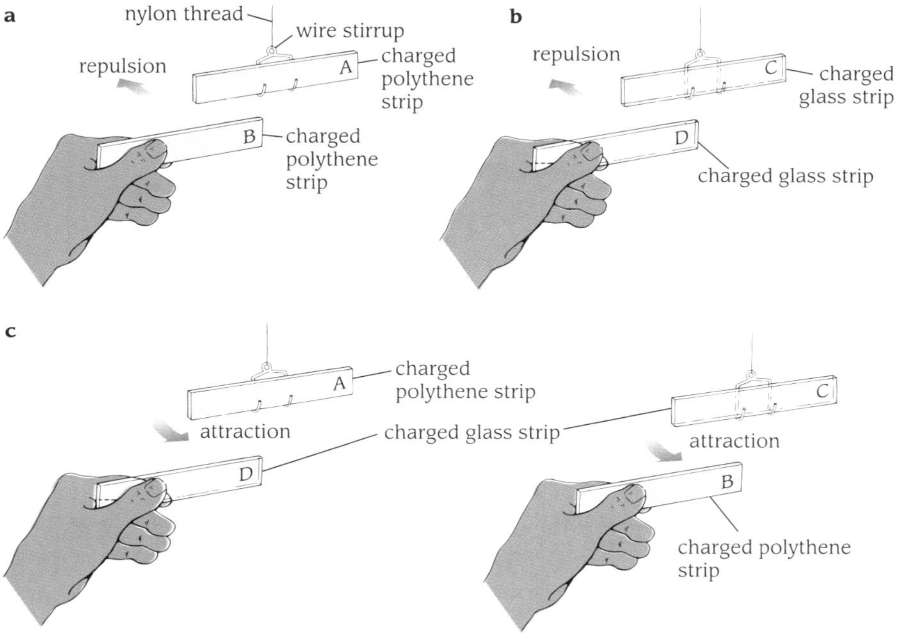

▲ **Figure 13.1.2** Two kinds of charge

Experimental results

Rubbed polythene gains a negative charge and rubbed glass (or Perspex) gains a positive charge.

Since both the polythene strips have a negative charge and both glass strips have a positive charge, the tests give the following results:

- Two negatively charged strips repelled each other.
- Two positively charged strips repelled each other.
- One negatively charged strip and one positively charged strip attracted each other.

! Key fact

- *Like* charges *repel*.
- *Opposite* charges *attract*.
- Only two types of charge exist.

Only repulsion confirms that an object is charged

- Hang a metallised polystyrene ball on a nylon thread and make no attempt to charge it.
- First bring a negatively charged polythene strip near to the ball but do not let it touch (Figure 13.1.3a).
- Now bring a positively charged glass strip near to the ball, again without touching it (Figure 13.1.3b).

In both **a** and **b** the uncharged ball is attracted to the strip whether the attracting charge is positive or negative.

- Allow the metallised ball to touch the negatively charged polythene strip and repeat the tests **a** and **b**.

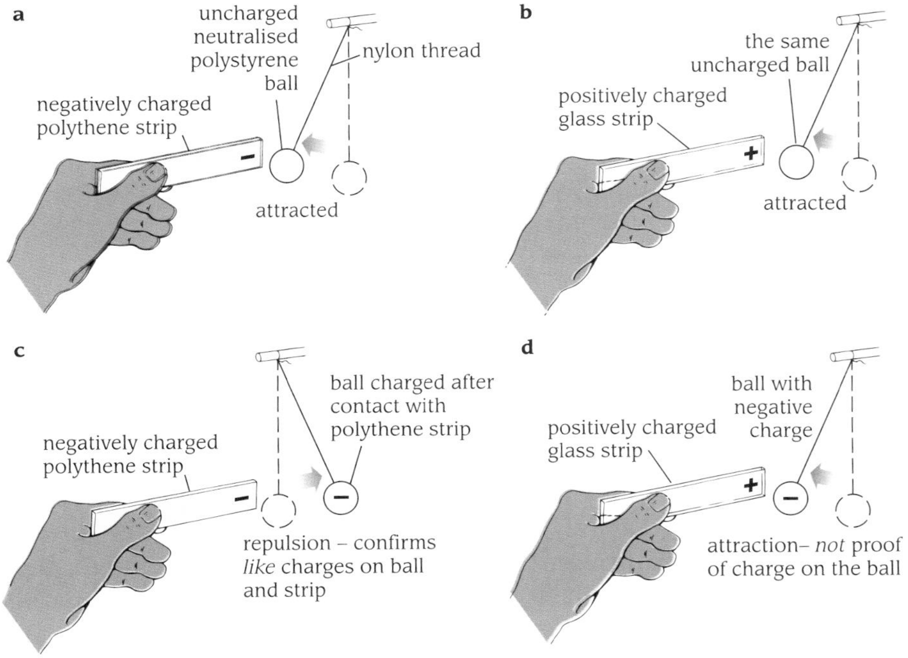

▲ **Figure 13.1.3** Repulsion confirms that an object is charged

In Figure 13.1.3d, attraction occurs because opposite charges attract. But in **a** and **b** attraction also occurs even though the ball has no net charge. So when attraction occurs we cannot confirm that an object is charged.

In Figure 13.1.3c, the ball is repelled by the polythene strip because it has the same negative charge as the strip. When the ball touched the strip it picked up some of its negative charge. Only if repulsion occurs do we have reliable evidence that the repelled object has the same charge as the one repelling it.

! Key fact

Only repulsion can confirm that an object is charged.

Summary questions

1 Why does friction cause some objects to become electrically charged?

2 How many types of electric charge are there?

3 What test confirms that an object is electrically charged?

Objectives

By the end of this topic you will be able to:

- explain charging by induction and how a charged object can attract an uncharged object.

Key fact

- When conductors share a charge by contact they have charge of the *same* sign.
- When a conductor is charged by induction and earthed during the process, it always receives the *opposite* charge to the one used to induce it.

Things to do

Charge a plastic comb or ruler by rubbing it on fabric. Turn on a tap to give a smooth slow stream of water. Explain what happens when you bring the comb or ruler near to the water stream. Hint: induction.

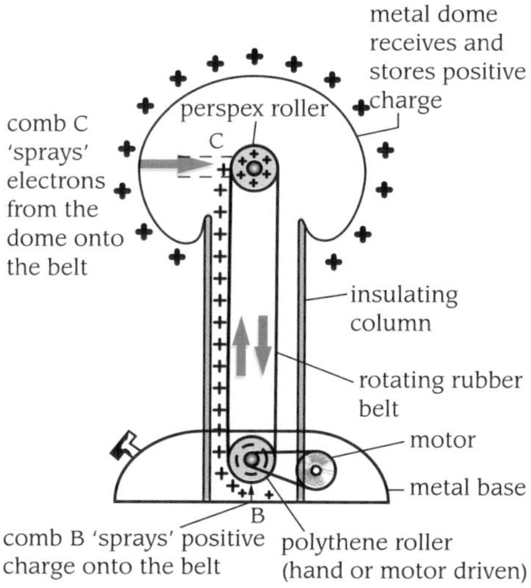

◀ **Figure 13.2.2** The Van de Graaff generator

D13.2 Induction

Charging by induction

Initially the insulated conductor A has no net charge.

- Bring a charged strip S up to, but not touching, the conductor A (Figure 13.2.1a).

Repulsion between the negative charge on strip S and the negative electrons in the conductor A causes the conductor's electrons to flow away from S. The deficiency of electrons produces a positive charge on the near side of A. The excess of electrons produces an equal, negative charge on the far side of A.

- Earth conductor A by touching with a finger (Figure 13.2.1b). This allows the excess electrons on the far side of the conductor to flow further away to Earth.
- Remove the finger so that the escaped electrons cannot return, leaving conductor A with a permanent deficiency of electrons, or a positive charge.
- Remove the charging strip S so that the positive charge spreads over the surface of conductor A (Figure 13.2.1c).

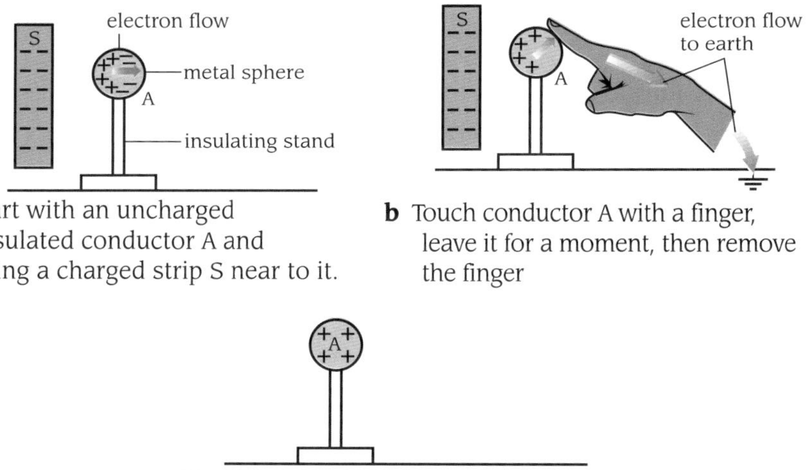

a Start with an uncharged insulated conductor A and bring a charged strip S near to it.

b Touch conductor A with a finger, leave it for a moment, then remove the finger

c Finally remove the charged strip S

▲ **Figure 13.2.1** Charging by induction

Why a charged object can attract an uncharged one

A charged plastic strip or comb will attract small, uncharged objects to it. If the plastic strip is negatively charged it will repel negative electrons in the uncharged object. Although the object still has zero net charge, the side facing the charged strip will be depleted of electrons and so have an induced positive charge. The negatively charged strip attracts the object because it sees the opposite positive charge on its near side.

In 1929, Robert Van de Graaff demonstrated his first generator.

A Van de Graaff generator collects a large static electric charge on a dome. A positively charged 'comb', sprays positive charge onto a moving, insulating belt, which carries it up to the dome. Negative charges from the dome are attracted to the belt and carried away, leaving the dome with a high positive charge.

▲ **Figure 13.2.3** The positive charge on the Van de Graaff generator flows onto the person. Because all their hairs have a positive charge, they all repel each other, so stand on end.

The action of points

Electric charge concentrates at points. The more pointed something is, the higher the concentration of charge. A lightning conductor uses this fact. A negatively charged thundercloud induces a positive charge on buildings and the ground below. This positive charge is concentrated at the tip of the lightning conductor. The high positive charge attracts electrons from the thundercloud and repels positive ions in the air. This causes a steady flow of negative charge away from the cloud, discharging it. It also means that if the cloud discharges suddenly, in a lightning strike, it is much more likely to discharge down the lightning conductor than through the building, so the building is protected from damage.

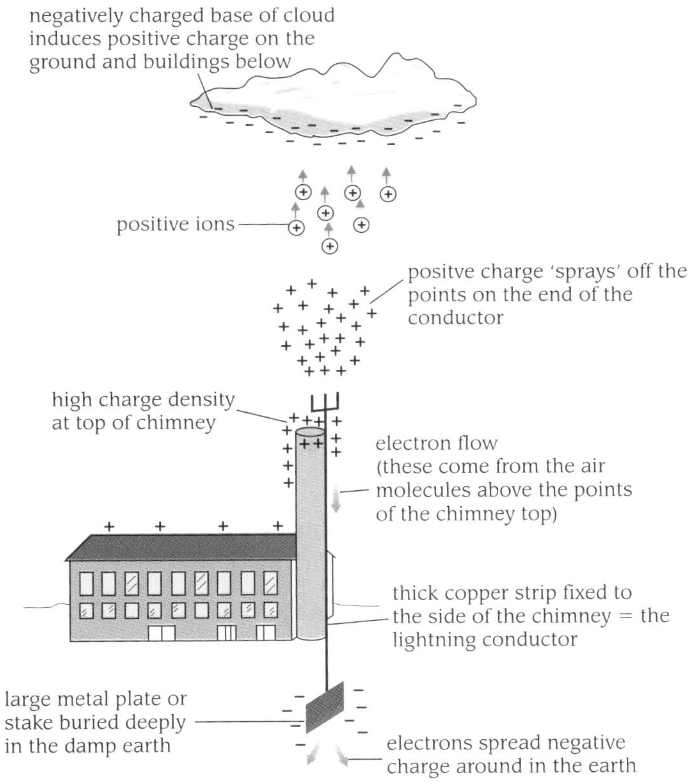

▲ **Figure 13.2.4** A lightning conductor

Summary questions

1 Sketch diagrams to demonstrate charging by induction.

2 Use induction to explain how a rubbed balloon can stick to an insulating surface.

3 Describe how a lightning conductor works.

Objectives

By the end of this topic you will be able to:

- define an electric field and describe its properties
- draw the electric fields around point charges and between charged parallel plates
- compare electric fields with gravitational and magnetic fields.

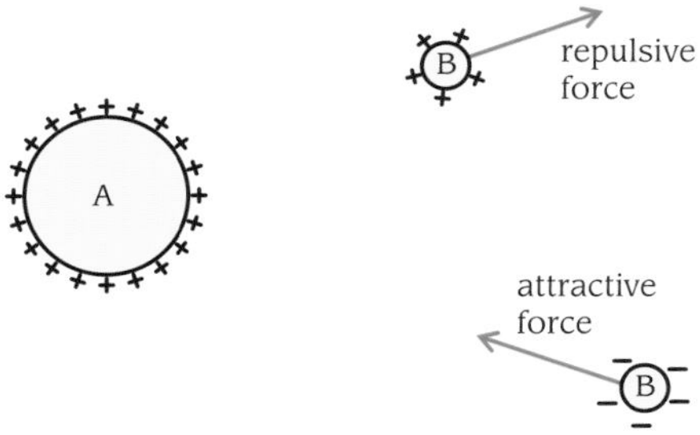

▲ **Figure 13.3.1** A force acts on charges in the space around charged object A

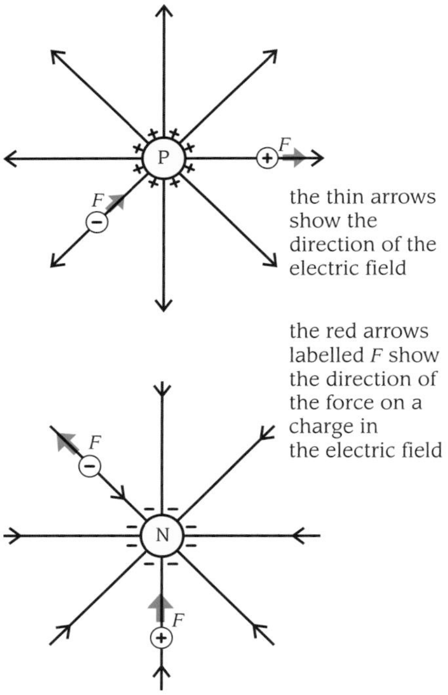

▲ **Figure 13.3.2** The electric field in the space around a charged spherical or point object

D13.3 Electric fields

We have seen that a charged object can affect other objects nearby without touching them. This action at a distance can be explained by what is called the **electric field** of the charged object.

The idea of an electric field

In the space around a charged object A we can detect various effects. For example another charged object B may move away from or towards A. Such effects are the result of a force that acts on any charge which comes into the region of influence of the charged object. We call this influence around a charged object its electric field.

Any charge entering an electric field has a force acting on it and that action reveals both the existence of the electric field and its nature. Since it causes a force to act, we can say that an electric field has a vector nature with both a magnitude and a direction.

The direction of an electric field

As Figure 13.3.1 shows, the direction of the force acting on the charged object B in the electric field of object A is either away from or towards A, according to the sign of the charge.

The direction of the electric field at a particular place is the direction of the force it produces on a positively charged object.

Making the shape of an electric field visible

An electric field exists between any two charged objects. We can make suitable objects from various shapes of metal wire and plates, which when charged are called **electrodes**. Some simple shapes of electrode that can be used are shown in Figure 13.3.3 and Figure 13.3.4. Your teacher may demonstrate the shape of electric fields using electrodes connected to a high voltage power supply or a Van de Graaff generator. **Caution**: do not use a high voltage power supply without qualified supervision.

- Assemble a pair of these metal electrodes in a shallow glass dish so that they are just covered by a layer of an insulating liquid such as castor oil.
- Connect the electrodes to the terminals of the power supply.
- Lightly sprinkle tiny grains or needles of an insulating material onto the surface of the oil. (Grass seed or semolina powder work quite well.)

The needles receive induced opposite charges at their ends and as the electric field between the electrodes causes forces to act on these charges, the needles become aligned in the direction of the electric field. The lines of force and shape of the electric field are made visible as the needles link together forming lines between the two electrodes. The direction of the electric field is, in each case, from the positive electrode to the negative electrode along the lines formed by the needles.

- Compare the shape of the electric fields around different charged particles with the shape of magnetic and gravitational fields you have met.

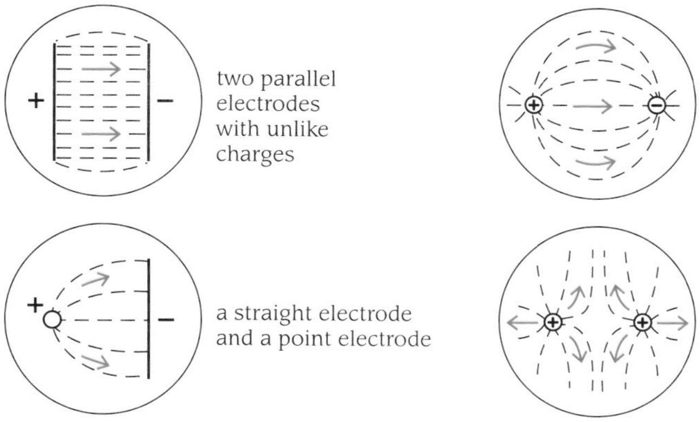

▲ **Figure 13.3.3** The shapes of some electric fields (the arrows show the direction of the electric fields)

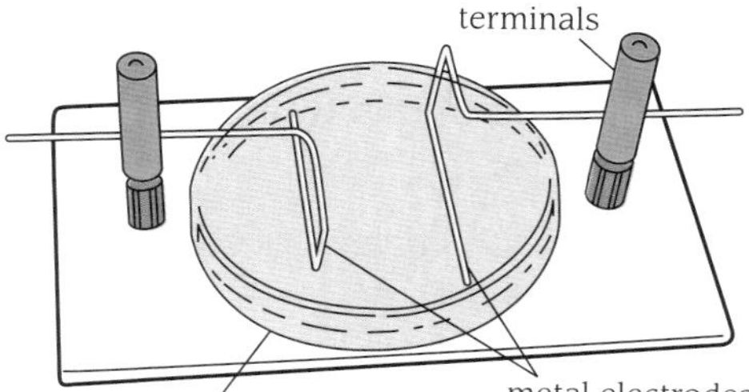

▲ **Figure 13.3.4** Demonstrating electric fields

Investigating the force between charged objects

Figure 13.3.5 shows how we can investigate how the force between two charged objects depends on their separation. A charged metal ball B is suspended so that it can be deflected when repelled by a like charge on another ball A. The deflection of ball B indicates the size of the force acting on it. A larger deflection indicates a stronger force of repulsion.

- Charge both balls.
- Bring ball A gradually closer to ball B and notice how the deflection of B changes.

We find that the force of repulsion increases as the separation decreases, which is an inverse relation. Accurate measurements show that *the force varies inversely with the square of the distance between two charged objects.* This relation, first discovered by Coulomb in 1785, is known as the **inverse-square law** of the force between two charged objects.

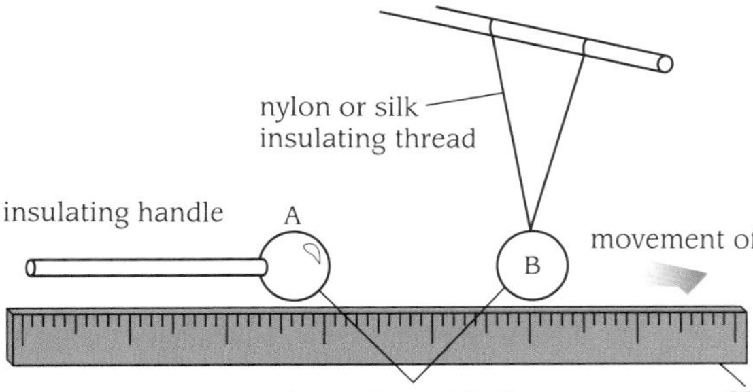

▲ **Figure 13.3.5** The force between charged objects

Summary questions

1. What does the direction of an electric field tell you?
2. Sketch the shape of the electric field around two oppositely charged point sources.
3. What happens to the strength of an electric field if the distance from the charge is doubled?

Key fact

Properties of an electric field

- An electric field is a region around a charged object in which a force acts on other charged objects.
- The electric field at a point is a vector quantity with a magnitude and direction.
- The direction of the field is the same as the direction of the force on a positively charged object.
- The force on a negatively charged object is in the reverse direction to the field.
- The electric fields around point or spherical objects are symmetrical in three dimensions.
- The lines representing the electric field are usually called **field lines**, or **lines of force**.
- Electric field lines always start at a positive charge and end at a negative charge.
- Newton's third law of motion tells us that there will always be an equal and opposite (reaction) force acting on the charged object producing the electric field.

The inverse-square law

This law means that if we double the distance between two charged objects, the force of attraction or repulsion (caused by the electric field of one object acting on the other) becomes four times weaker.

Objectives

By the end of this topic you will be able to:

- describe hazards of static electric charge
- describe useful applications of static electric charge.

▲ **Figure 13.4.1** Trailing strip behind a car

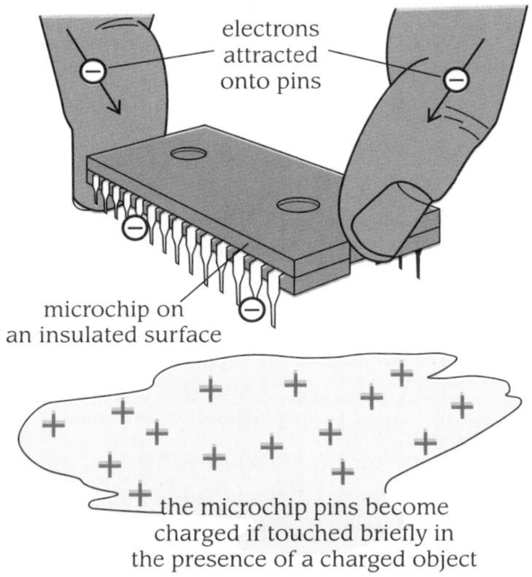

▲ **Figure 13.4.2** How a microchip becomes damaged

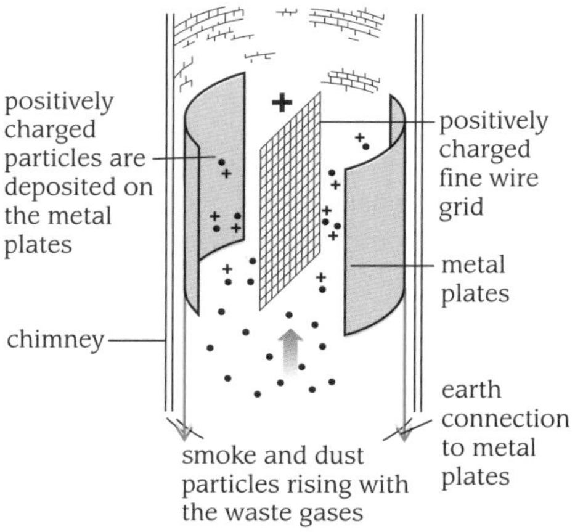

▲ **Figure 13.4.3** An electrostatic precipitator

D13.4 Hazards and applications of static electricity

Preventing electric shocks from vehicles

In hot dry weather friction between moving plastic and fabric parts of a vehicle can charge it up. The charge cannot escape to ground because the rubber tyres act as good insulators. If you walk up to a charged vehicle and touch the metal handle you can get an electric shock.

To prevent this happening, vehicles can be fitted with a flexible conducting strip that trails behind. This connects the metal chassis to the ground and discharges the vehicle continuously (Figure 13.4.1).

Protecting microchips from damage by static electricity

Static electricity from handling, or induced static electricity from charged objects nearby, can be enough to damage miniature components on microchips. To prevent this:

- microchips are always stored in anti-static packets
- microchips should be handled only with special insulating tools
- people working with microchips should wear anti-static clothing, avoiding fabrics like nylon
- rooms where equipment using microchips is made should have anti-static floors.

Storage of flammable liquids and dry powders

Some fine powders, and the vapour above flammable liquids such as petrol, can explode if ignited by a spark. To prevent sparks caused by static electricity:

- powders and flammable liquids should be stored in earthed metal tanks
- explosive vapours can remain in tanks after the liquid has been removed so care must be taken to avoid sparks being produced by any equipment
- electronic devices such as mobile phones, which can generate static electricity should not be used where flammable vapours can escape, such as at petrol stations and when aircraft are being fuelled.

Dust extraction by electrostatic precipitation

An electrostatic precipitator removes smoke and dust from the waste gases going up the chimneys of factories and power stations. Figure 13.4.3 shows how the precipitator works. The wire grid is kept highly charged so that a continuous electrical discharge occurs between the grid and the earthed metal plates. This discharge involves a stream of ions, which attach themselves to the dust particles in the gas going up the chimney. The charged dust particles are now repelled from the wire grid and attracted to the earthed plates where they become deposited. These plates are tapped from time to time so that the dust and smoke particles fall down the chimney and can be removed at the bottom.

Making photocopies by xerography

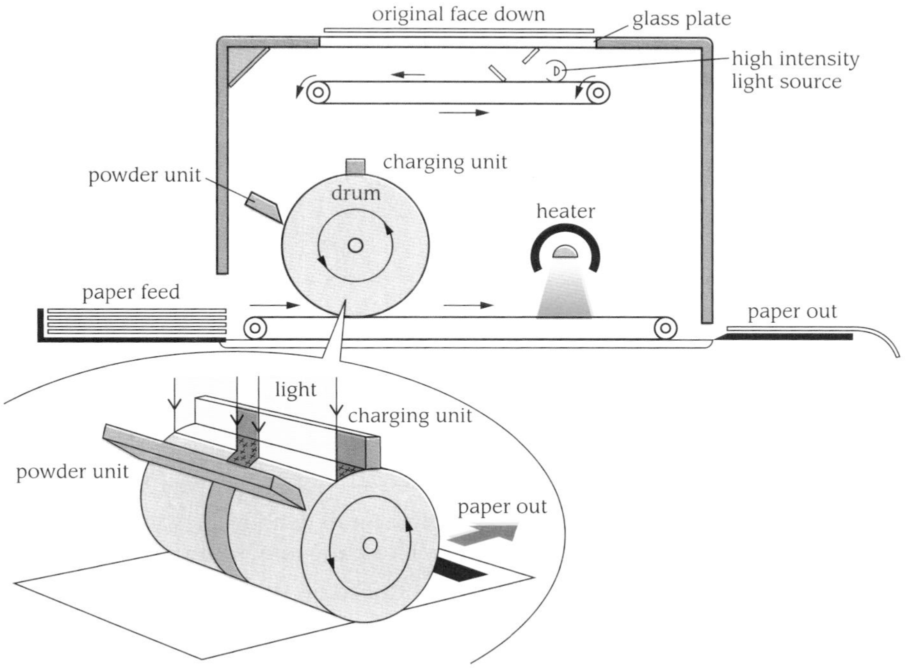

▲ **Figure 13.4.4** A photocopier

The surface of a photocopier drum is made from a photoconductive material, which is an insulator when dark but conducts when light shines on it.

1 The dark drum is charged with static electricity.

2 Light reflecting from the sheet to be copied, shines onto the drum, so the static electricity only remains where the original copy is dark.

3 Tiny toner powder particles stick to the charged parts of the drum, and are transferred to a new sheet of paper.

4 A heater melts the toner onto the new paper to make a copy.

Summary questions

1 State two precautions you would take when handling microchips.

2 Why is the risk of an explosion caused by static electricity greater in dry conditions?

3 Describe briefly how a photocopier works.

Using electrostatics when spraying paint

▲ **Figure 13.4.5** Paint spraying equipment required to give an even coating of fine paint particles on a car body often uses electrostatic charges to control and direct the distribution of paint. Paint particles pick up charges from the spray gun nozzles and are attracted to the oppositely charged metal bodywork of the car. The paint particles, following the electric field lines, end up on the car body and not on the floor or wall behind.

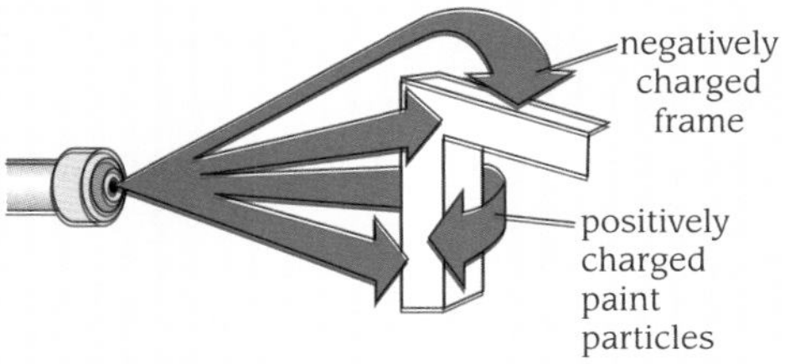

▲ **Figure 13.4.6**

Practice exam-style questions

1 In dry weather, when a driver touches the door before getting out of her car, she sometimes gets an electric shock as soon as her foot touches the ground.

a) Explain why this happens.

b) Why does it not happen in wet weather?

c) Some people fix a piece of fine chain to the car, which drags on the road. How does this prevent a shock taking place?

2 Describe an experiment to investigate whether lightly rubbing a dry polythene rod produces only a small charge, whereas rubbing it more often and more quickly produces a greater charge.

3 A polythene rod may be charged negatively by rubbing it with a cloth but a brass rod held in the hand cannot be charged in this way.

a) State clearly what happens when the polythene is being charged.

b) Explain why the brass cannot be charged by rubbing.

4 A manufacturer of nylon thread put heavy rubber mats under his spinning machines (which were made of metal) to deaden the noise. The following effects were subsequently noticed:

i) The workers sometimes received an electric shock when touching the machines. (There was no leak from the mains cable.)

ii) Small bits of nylon fluff stuck to the thread but this could be overcome by keeping the air in the workshop moist.

State and explain the physical reasons for **i)** and **ii)**, and say how you could overcome **i)**.

5 Explain why a dressing table mirror or computer screen may become more dusty if wiped with a dry cloth on a warm day.

6 Write a few sentences to explain each of the following in terms of the behaviour of electrostatic charges. You may find that drawing a simple diagram showing where electrostatic charges occur, or go, helps to explain what happens.

a) When a charged plastic comb is held near to a stream of water drops, the drops are deflected towards the comb.

b) When a wire 'windmill' is connected to a supply of electric charge it rotates.

c) When a long metal spike, fixed on the very top of a tall building, is connected to the ground by a thick metal conductor, the building will be protected from lightning strikes.

d) When you touch the metal door handle on a car that has been driven around in dry weather, you may experience an electric shock.

7 Figure **a** below shows two conductors, A and B. A is a metal plate mounted on an insulating stand. B is a very light metal sphere suspended from P by an insulating thread. Initially there are no charges on A or B. A is then charged positively.

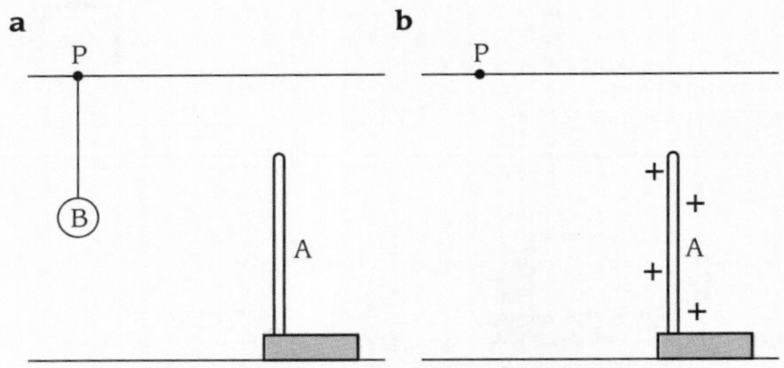

a) Redraw and complete figure **b** above to show how you would now expect B to hang in equilibrium.

b) Show the charges induced on the conductor B.

c) A free positive charge, carried on a very small, and very light sphere, is placed between A and the new position of B.

i) In which direction will the very light sphere move?

ii) Give a reason for your answer.

8 Copy and complete the following statements:

a) An electric field line starts on a .... charge and ends on a .... charge.

b) The force on a negatively charged object placed in an electric field is in the .... direction .... the field.

c) The electric field at a point is a .... quantity because it has direction as well as magnitude.

d) The strength of the force between two charged objects will be .... times .... if their separation doubles.

e) The strength of the force between two charged objects will be .... times .... if their separation halves.

f) Two objects with like charges will always .... each other.

g) An uncharged object will always be .... a charged object.

h) The electric field lines point towards a .... charged object.

9 Suppose you are supplied with a negatively charged rod and two identical and uncharged metal spheres, A and B, on insulating stands.

a) Describe how, using the negatively charged rod, you would charge the two spheres equally so that A became negatively charged and B became positively charged.

b) Account for the production of the two equal charges in terms of the movement of charged particles.

10 a) Describe how microchips used in computers are stored, transported and handled so that they do not suffer damage by static electricity.

b) Describe an application in which the properties of static electric charge are a key component and vital to the process. State what component in the process is charged with static electricity and what effect this has.

11 Draw electric field or force lines for the following configurations of charged objects. Mark with arrows the directions of the electric fields in each case.

a) an isolated positively charged object

b) a positively charged sphere close to another positively charged sphere

c) two parallel metal plates, one positively charged, the other negatively charged

d) one positively charged sphere near a negatively charged plate

12 a) Explain why tall buildings are most likely to be hit by lightning.

b) What precautions or protection can be used to reduce the risk of a lightning strike and to minimise damage?

13 a) Explain why it is not a good idea to shelter under a tall tree during a thunderstorm.

b) Make a list of FOUR precautions you would take during a lightning storm.

14 An aircraft flies just below a negatively charged thundercloud. Movement of free electrons causes electrostatic charges to be induced in the aircraft.

a) Copy the figure below and mark on it the positions and signs of the charges induced on the aircraft.

b) Explain what will happen when the aircraft flies away from the cloud.

15 If you rub a balloon on your clothes you can charge it with static electricity.

a) Explain how it is then possible to get the balloon to stick to the ceiling.

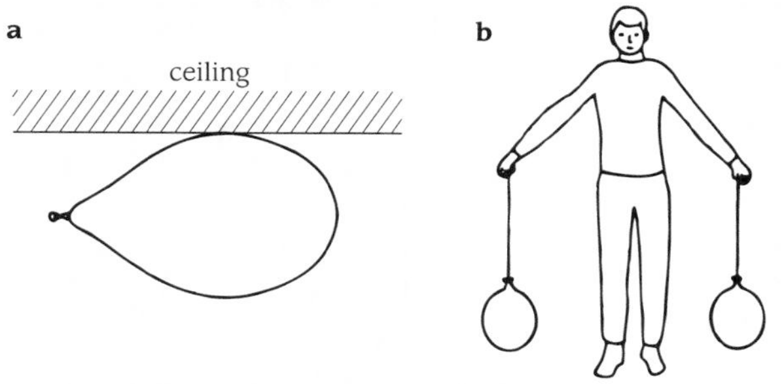

b) On a copy of figure **a** above showing the balloon on the ceiling, draw negative charges. Add suitable charges to the ceiling also. Where do all these charges come from?

c) Figure **b** above shows two negatively charged balloons hanging from insulating threads. What would happen as the balloons were brought closer together? Explain why.

16 The forces between static electric charges on two bodies obey an **inverse-square law** if bodies are spheres or point charges.

a) Explain what is meant by an 'inverse-square law'.

b) Give an example of another kind of force in physics which obeys a similar inverse-square law.

c) Are there any differences between the forces in your example and those between charged bodies?

D14 Electrical circuits

The charge that produces attraction and repulsion between charged objects also produces electric currents when it flows in conductors. To sustain an electric current, charge needs a continuous path or circuit to flow around. Charge, however, does not exist on its own. It is a property of certain charged particles.

Objectives

By the end of this topic you will be able to:

- explain how electric currents flow only in closed circuits
- differentiate between electron flow and conventional current.

D14.1 Circuits

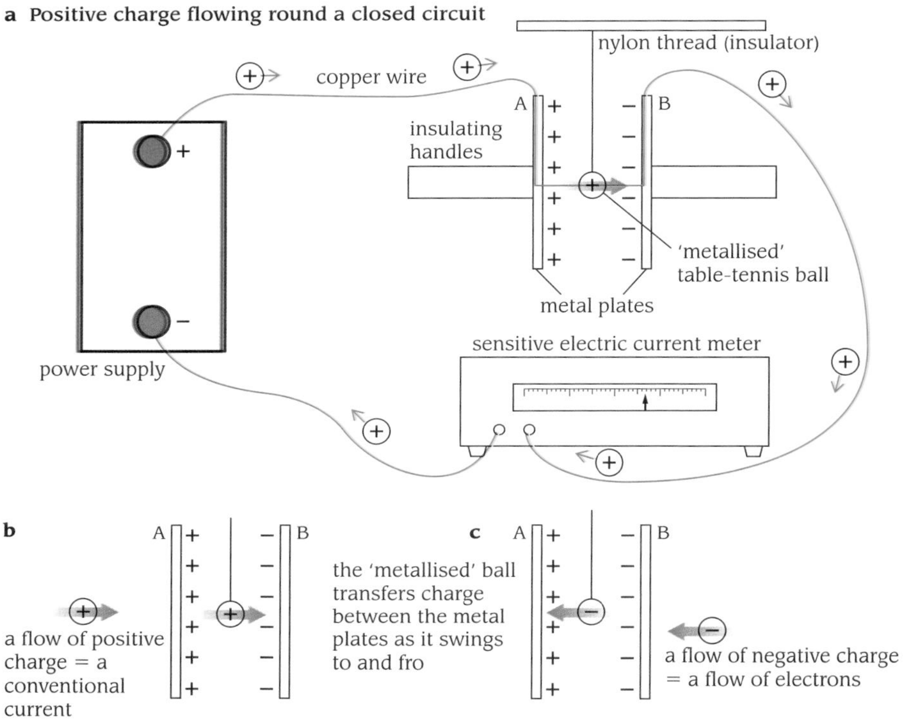

▲ **Figure 14.1.1** Charge flows round a circuit

Key fact

- This demonstration confirms that the static charge carried by the ball is the same charge that flows through the meter as an electric current. We believe that static charge and the charge that flows in an electric current have the same origin – the electron.
- Electric charge can flow continuously only round unbroken conducting paths called closed circuits.

When the metallised ball is touched onto one of the metal plates, it will swing quickly to and fro between the plates. As it swings, the ammeter shows that an electric current is flowing. Plate A has a positive charge because it is connected to the positive terminal of the power supply. Plate B is connected to the negative terminal of the power supply and has a negative charge.

When the metallised ball touches plate B, electrons flow onto the metallised ball, giving it a negative charge. It is then repelled by plate B and attracted by plate A. It swings until it touches plate A. Electrons flow from the ball onto plate A, until the resulting positive charge on the ball repels it back towards plate B again. Each swing of the ball transfers electric charge between the plates.

We say the swinging ball completes an electric circuit, allowing a flow of electric charge around the circuit. This flow of electric charge is measured by the ammeter and is called an electric current.

Key fact

- Conventional electric current flows from a positively charged point to a negatively charged point in a circuit.
- In wires, negative electrons flow in the opposite direction to the conventional current.
- Current arrows on wires point in the direction of conventional positive charge flow.

Conventional current and electron flow

Early experiments with electricity were done long before electrons were discovered. Scientists knew that something flowed around an electric circuit, but they didn't know what. They called it 'electric current' and said it went from positive to negative. Many years later they discovered that an electric current is actually a flow of electrically charged electrons moving from negative to positive.

Metallic conductors, such as copper wires, contain many free, negatively charged, electrons that are able to move through the conductor. Thus electrons drifting through a conductor produce a flow of negative charge in their direction of travel. Negative charge flows from negatively charged points towards positively charged points. This is the opposite direction to the conventional current.

Not all currents are just a flow of negatively charged electrons. In the electrolyte liquids inside batteries, and in semiconductor materials such as silicon and germanium, the electric current is caused by a flow of both negatively and positively charged particles. You will learn more about these later.

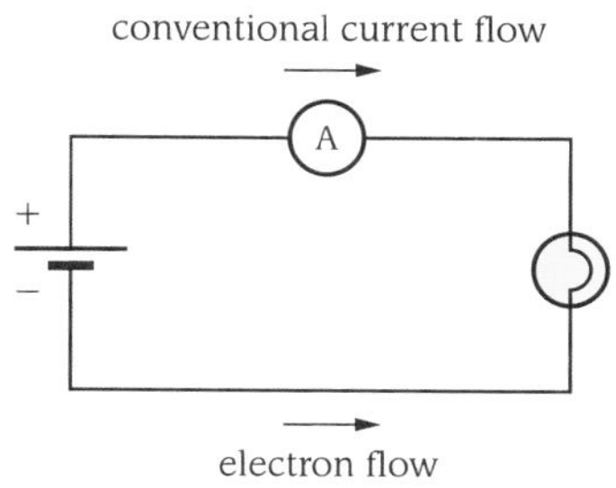

▲ **Figure 14.1.2** Conventional current and electron flow

Conductors and insulators

The simple circuit in Figure 14.1.3 can be used to test materials. The lamp lights for materials that are electrical conductors, but not for materials that are electrical insulators.

- All metals are good conductors of electricity, allowing large electric currents through them. Silver and copper are very good conductors. These materials have large numbers of electrons in them that are free to move through them.
- Some materials conduct electricity, but rather less well than metals. These include graphite (used in pencils), certain solutions called electrolytes and water and the materials used in electronic devices, which include germanium and silicon. Electrolytes and semiconductors use both electrons and positive charge-carriers to allow current to flow, but these are not as plentiful or mobile as the electrons in metals.
- It is very difficult to pass any current through some materials. The best insulators are polythene, PVC (used to insulate electric cables), nylon and plastics in general, glass, rubber, and natural materials such as quartz (a crystalline mineral), resins and wax. These materials have no mobile and free charge-carriers.
- Materials form a spectrum from the best conductors to the best insulators and there is no clear division between them.

▼ A range of conductors and insulators

Material	Class	
silver, copper, aluminium	good conductors	Increasing current, better conduction ↑
alloys, Manganin, constantan	conductors	
graphite	poor conductor	
electrolytes including water	poor conductor	
germanium	semiconductor	
silicon	semiconductor	
plastic and rubber	insulator	
quartz	excellent insulator	

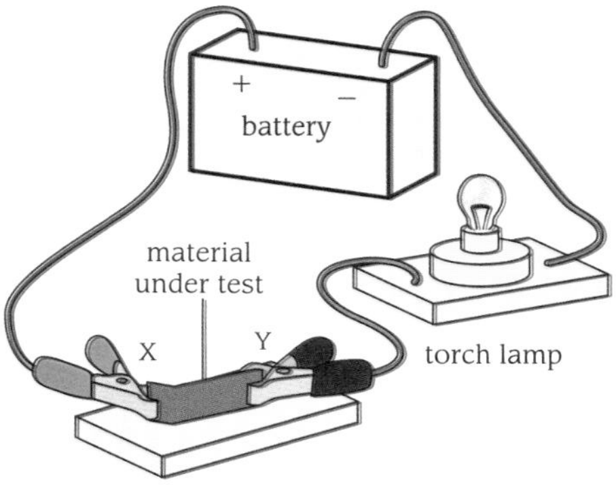

▲ **Figure 14.1.3** Conductors and insulators

▲ **Figure 14.1.4** High-voltage insulators used for high-voltage power transmission are made from glass, porcelain or composite polymer materials. Porcelain insulators are made from clay, quartz or alumina and feldspar, and are covered with a smooth glaze to shed dirt.

Summary questions

1 Which way does conventional current flow?

2 Why are metals good conductors of electricity?

Objectives

By the end of this topic you will be able to:

- recognise circuit symbols
- recognise series and parallel connected circuits
- explain what happens to the other lamps when one lamp fails in each kind of circuit.

D14.2 Circuit diagrams

Common devices in electric circuits

▼ Some common devices and their symbols

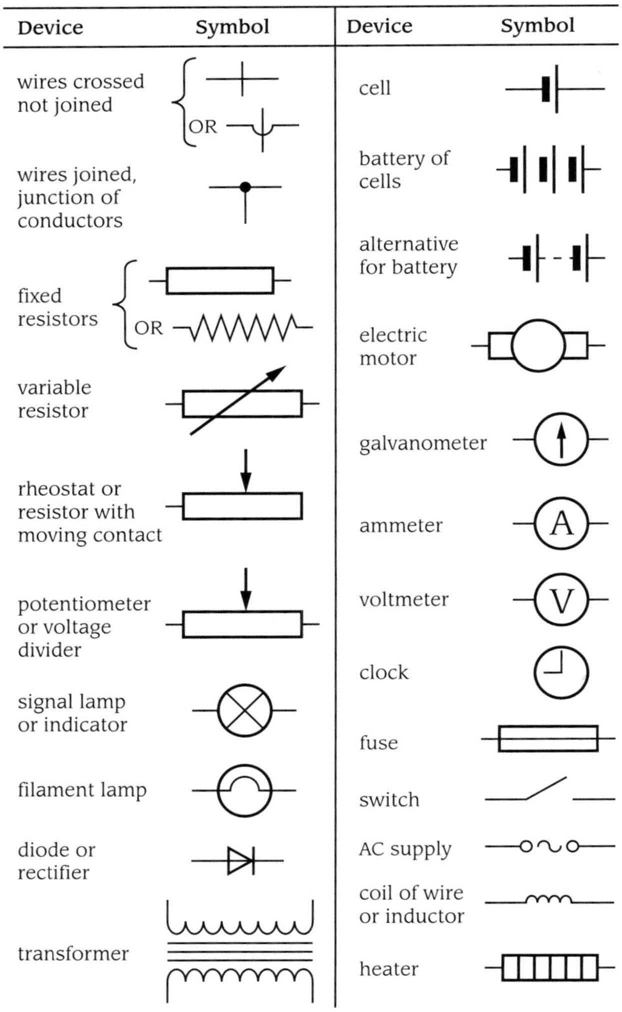
Device
Symbol
Device
Symbol
wires crossed not joined
OR
wires joined, junction of conductors
fixed resistors
OR
variable resistor
rheostat or resistor with moving contact
potentiometer or voltage divider
signal lamp or indicator
filament lamp
diode or rectifier
transformer
cell
battery of cells
alternative for battery
electric motor
galvanometer
ammeter
A
voltmeter
V
clock
fuse
switch
AC supply
coil of wire or inductor
heater

The components in a circuit are joined together by wires and these are usually drawn in a particular way:

- Although wires are usually flexible and bent they are drawn as straight lines with right-angled corners for clarity and neatness.
- Where wires cross they are shown as lines crossing at right angles. When they are joined a round blob is used, which looks rather like a soldered joint.
- When the current direction needs to be shown, the arrow drawn represents the conventional current direction, i.e. positive to negative.

Making circuits work

For a circuit to work it must have:

- something to supply an electric current, usually cells or a power supply
- a complete circuit, that is one or more complete 'paths' for the electric current to flow along from one side of the power supply to the other. Current won't flow along 'dead ends'

- good connections between the components. Twist bare wires tightly round terminals, rather than just touching them. Make sure connecting plugs fit tightly. Make sure crocodile clips and wires are clean, not dirty or corroded.

Series and parallel connection of conductors

The circuits in Figure 14.2.1 show some possible arrangements of conductors.

In a series circuit there is only one possible 'path' through the lamps for the current to flow along (Figure 14.2.1a). In a parallel circuit, there are several possible 'paths' through the lamps for the current to flow (Figure 14.2.1b). Figure 14.2.1c has a mixture of series and parallel. There are some places where there is only one possible 'path' through the lamps, and some places where there is more than one 'path'.

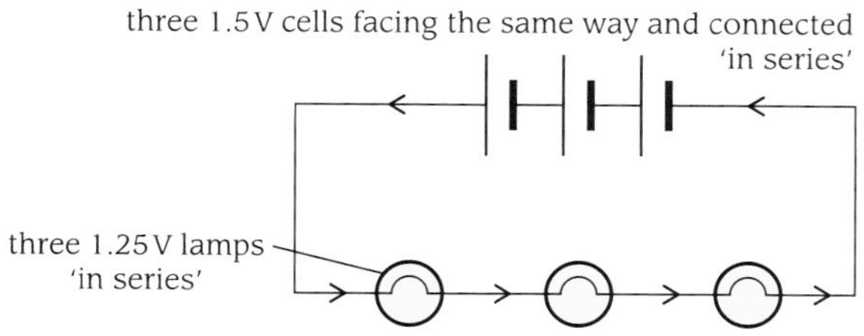

a Lamps connected in series

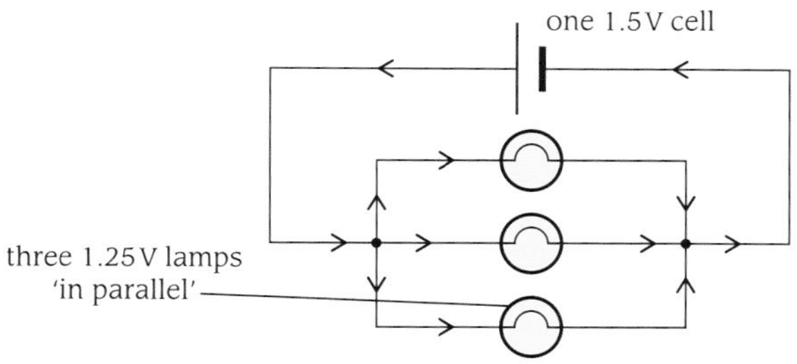

b Lamps connected in parallel

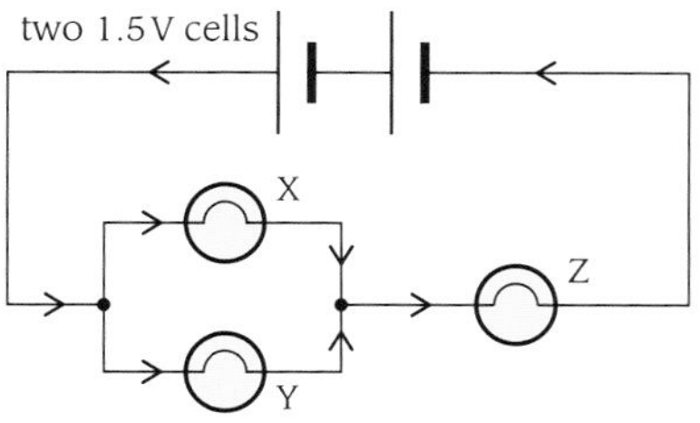

c The parallel pair of lamps, X and Y, are in series with lamp Z

▲ **Figure14.2.1** Connecting in series and parallel

Things to do

Find out what kind of circuit connections are used in the following examples:

- Christmas tree lights
- street lights
- two toy electric trains running on the same track
- an electric bell with a battery and push-button switch
- the two headlights, main beam switch and the battery of a car.

Draw the following circuit diagrams using the correct circuit symbols:

- a torch lamp with two cells and an on-off switch
- a car battery connected with on-off switches to its four side lamps and to its windscreen wiper motor.

Explain how the following circuit works. The two switches allow you to switch a lamp on or off from two different places such as opposite ends of a staircase.

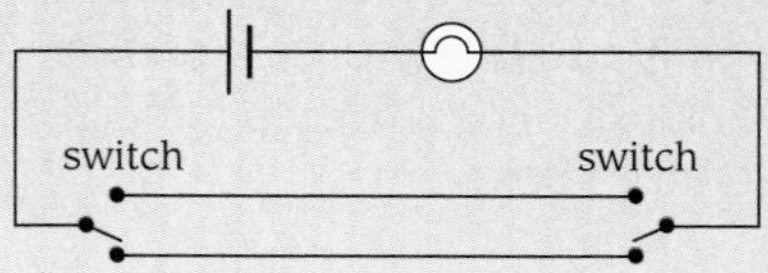

▲ **Figure 14.2.2**

Summary questions

1. Sketch a circuit showing three bulbs connected in parallel.
2. Sketch the circuit symbols for a resistor, a filament lamp and a cell.
3. Would you connect Christmas tree lights in series or in parallel? Why?

Objectives

By the end of this topic you will be able to:

- describe an electric current as a rate of flow of electric charge
- recall and use the equation connecting current and charge
- understand that the current in a series circuit is the same all the way round
- recall and use Kirchhoff's first law about currents at a junction.

Key fact

How large is a coulomb?

- Each electron has a tiny charge of only 1.6×10^{-19} coulomb.
- About 6×10^{18} electrons are needed to make up just 1 coulomb of charge, i.e. 6 million million million electrons!
- A coulomb is a large quantity of charge and is difficult to store. We more often use millicoulombs (1 mC = 1/1000 C or 10^{-3} C) and microcoulombs (1 μC = 10^{-6} C).

How large is an ampere?

In practical terms the ampere has a convenient size since the currents found in most domestic machines vary from about $\frac{1}{4}$ A in a light bulb to about 10 A in a heater. However, very small currents of milliamperes and microamperes are common in electronic circuits, while a car battery can briefly pass a current as high as 400 amperes through a starter motor.

D14.3 Measuring electric currents

Measuring current in a series circuit

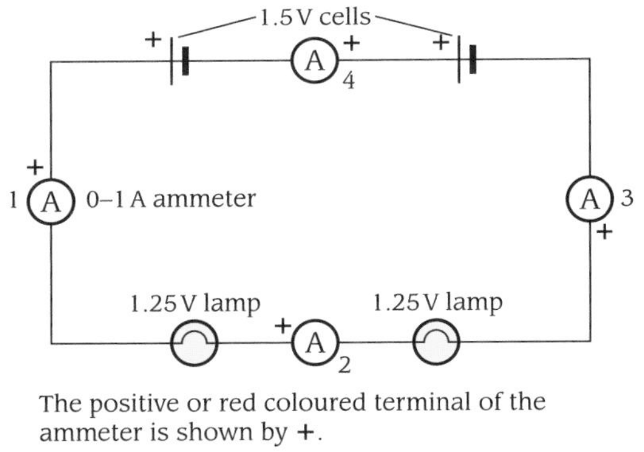

▲ **Figure 14.3.1** Measuring current in a series circuit

Note that for its pointer to move the correct way across the scale, the positive (or red coloured) terminal of the ammeter should be connected to the positive terminal of the battery. (This is shown by the + sign in the circuit.)

Ammeters, as their name suggests, are 'amp meters' and measure electric current in amperes.

- Wire up the circuit shown in Figure 14.3.1, in turn connecting the ammeter in each of the positions shown.
- Note the reading of the ammeter when connected in each position.

In all four positions the ammeter gives the same reading showing that the current is the same all round a series circuit. It is even the same through the battery! In this series circuit of a single closed loop there is only one conducting path for the current. So, wherever the ammeter is connected in the circuit, all the current must flow through it, and it will give the correct reading.

- The ammeter can be connected anywhere in the series circuit.

For a series circuit

- The lamps have equal brightness.
- This shows that the same current flows through all the lamps when they are connected in series.
- If any one lamp fails or comes loose in its holder the whole circuit is broken and, with no current anywhere in the circuit, all the lamps go off.

The current at a junction in a circuit

- Connect two lamps together in parallel in a circuit as shown in Figure 14.3.2 so that ammeter 1 reads the current through one lamp, ammeter 2 reads the current through the other lamp and ammeter 3 reads the current returning to the cell.

- Note the readings on the ammeters when all three switches are closed and when, in turn, each switch is opened.
- More readings can be obtained by using different lamps and more cells in the circuit.

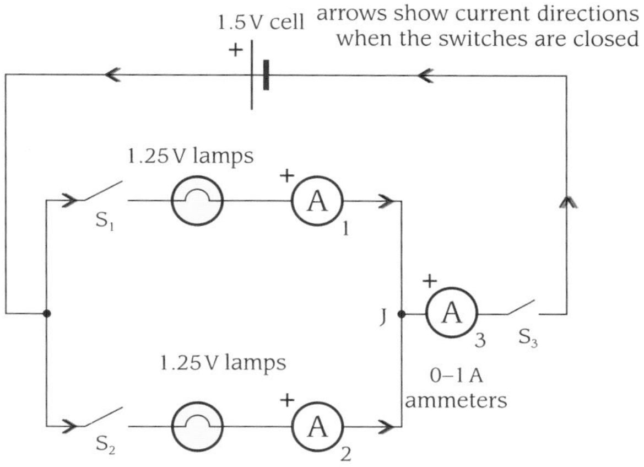

▲ **Figure 14.3.2** Currents at a junction in a circuit

J is a junction in the circuit. The current entering the junction is measured by ammeters 1 and 2. Ammeter 3 measures the current leaving the junction. The results show that the readings of ammeters 1 and 2 always add up to equal the reading of ammeter 3.

Parallel connections

In parallel connection the current in a circuit divides up and only part of it flows in each conductor.

- When lamps are connected in parallel, if one fails it does not affect the other lamps; less current flows in the circuit as a whole.
- The lights in a house are connected in parallel with each other so that each one can be switched on independently. When any one switch is closed there is a complete circuit from the fuse box, through the switch and lamp, back to the fuse box.
- Parallel connection of electrical equipment is most usual.

Mixed series and parallel connections

- Connect the same three lamps together as shown in Figure 14.3.3, using two 1.5 volt cells.
- Again compare the brightness of the lamps, then unscrew each one of them in turn and note what happens.
- Lamps X and Y are connected in parallel and are equally bright, sharing the circuit current equally.

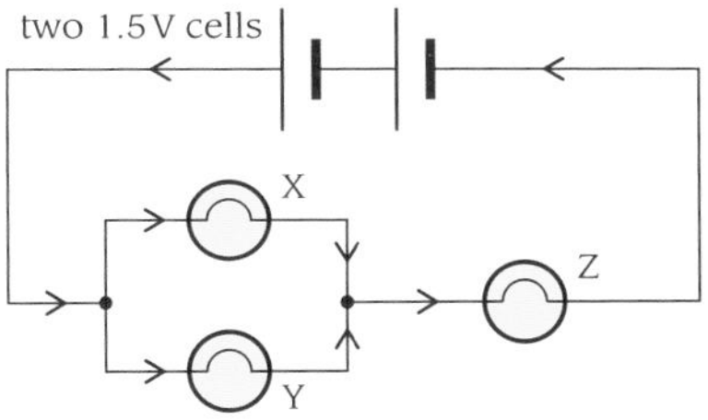

▲ **Figure 14.3.3**

- Lamp Z is in series with the other two, conducts all the circuit current and is much brighter.
- If Z is unscrewed, the whole circuit is broken and all lamps go off, but if either X or Y are unscrewed a series circuit remains and the other two lamps become equally bright.

Electric current and charge

To get an idea of the 'strength' or size of an electric current we can compare the flow of electric charge with the flow of water in a river.

We would say that the current was strong if a large quantity of water was flowing quickly down a river. The strength or size of this current could be measured in litres of water flowing past a point in the river in a certain time. We would in fact be measuring the rate of flow of the water.

Similarly the 'strength' or size of an electric current is a measure of the rate of flow of electric charge past a point in an electric circuit or through a conductor.

> **! Key fact**
>
> Current is never lost around a circuit. The total current flowing out of the power supply is always equal to the total current flowing into the power supply.

Worked example

If a charge of 180 C flows through a lamp every 2 minutes, what is the electric current in the lamp?

$Q = 180\,\text{C}$
$t = 2 \text{ minutes} = 2 \times 60\,\text{s}$
$I = \dfrac{Q}{t} = \dfrac{180\,\text{C}}{2 \times 60\,\text{s}} = 1.5 \text{ ampere}$

Worked example

A battery circulates charge round a circuit for 30 s. If the current in the circuit is 5 A, what quantity of charge passes through the battery?

$Q = It = 5\,\text{A} \times 30\,\text{s}$
$= 150\,\text{A s}$ or 150 coulomb
(ampere × second = coulomb)

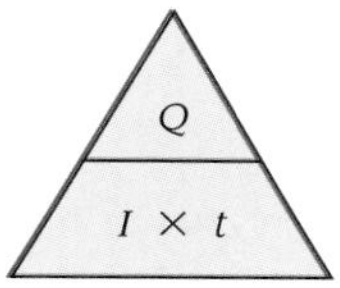

Things to do

Copy the table and complete it by calculating the missing values.

Charge, Q/C	Current, I/A	Time, t/s
400	5.0	
	2.5	100
360		60

The quantity of electric charge Q is measured in coulomb (C).

The strength of an electric current I is measured in ampere (A).

An electric current is defined as a flow of electric charge through a conductor.

The relationship between current I and charge Q

$$\text{current} = \frac{\text{charge}}{\text{time}} \qquad I = \frac{Q}{t}$$

A current of 1 ampere is a flow of charge at the rate of 1 coulomb per second.

Another way of saying this is that 1 coulomb = 1 amp second. This idea of the ampere being 'a coulomb per second' is the one to understand and remember.

Kirchhoff's first law

The total current entering a junction in a circuit must equal the total current leaving it.

Worked example

In Figure 14.3.4, currents of 5 A and 3 A are entering a junction in a circuit and a current of 2 A is leaving. Find the size and direction of the unknown current x.

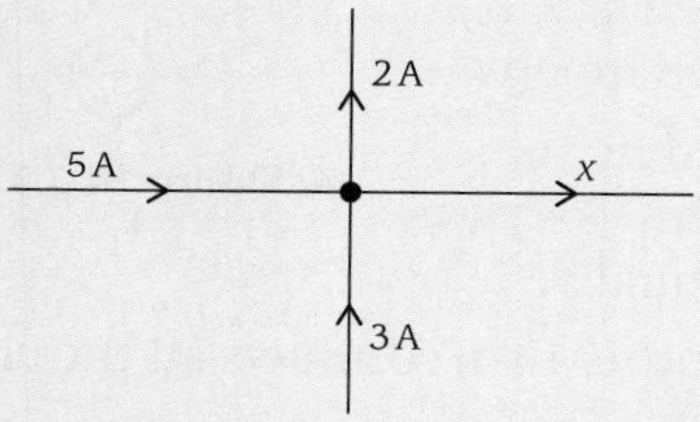

◀ **Figure 14.3.4**

Using Kirchhoff's first law:
total current entering junction = 5 A + 3 A = 8 A
total current leaving junction = 2 A + x
As these must be equal we have: 2 A + x = 8 A
Answer: x is a current of 6 amperes leaving the junction.

Summary questions

1 What happens to current at a junction in a circuit?

2 What is the equation relating charge, current and time?

3 Use this equation to calculate how much charge is transferred by a current of 3 A in 25 s.

D14.4 Potential difference and the volt

We have seen that charge flows round electric circuits; but what makes it flow and what energy changes take place when it does so? To answer these questions it helps if we first consider what makes water flow.

- Why does a stream flow downhill?
- What effect on the flow of water has the height or steepness of the hill down which it flows?
- What energy changes occur as the water descends?

Of course water flows downhill; it is pulled down by gravity like everything else. We also expect water to flow faster down steeper hills. Water has potential energy at the top of a hill, which is mostly converted into heat by the time it reaches the bottom of the hill.

Charge flows 'downhill'

As shown in Figure 14.4.1, there are high and low levels in electric circuits and charge flows 'downhill' like water. The electrical level or 'height' is called the voltage or the potential. Using the conventional current direction (i.e. a flow of positive charge) 'downhill' is towards the negative terminal of the battery. The battery does the job of pumping charge up to the 'top of the hill' so that it can then flow 'downhill' as a current through the conductors in the circuit. The higher the voltage to which the battery raises the charge, the steeper will be the downward slope and the faster the charge will flow, thus increasing the electric current. At the top of the 'hill' the charge has electrical potential energy, which is converted into other forms of energy as it flows round the circuit.

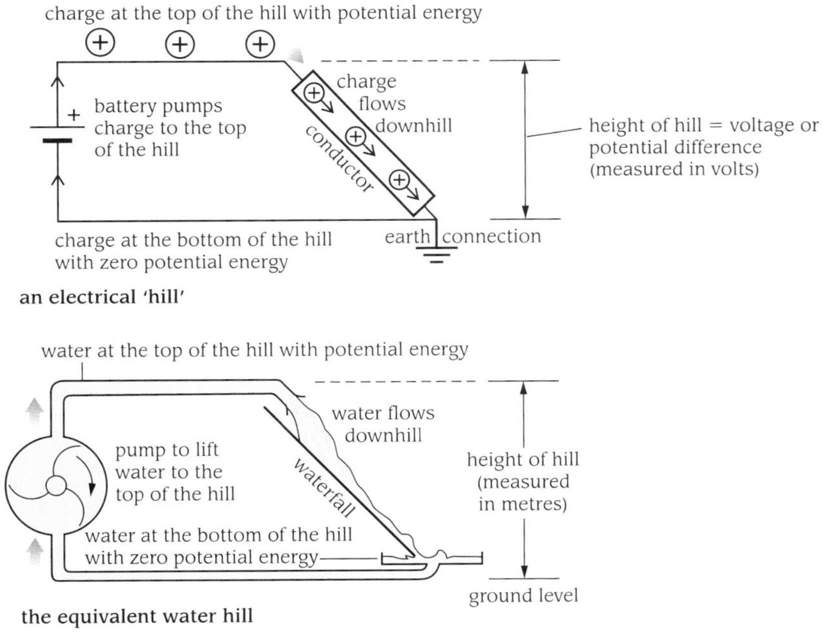

▲ **Figure 14.4.1** Comparison of electrical and water 'hills'

Potential difference, p.d. or voltage

A potential difference in an electric circuit causes charge to flow 'downhill', and the current depends upon the size of the potential difference.

Objectives

By the end of this topic you will be able to:

- define the potential difference between the ends of a conductor
- define the volt as 1 joule per coulomb
- use the relationship $V = E/Q$ to solve problems in which E is the electrical energy transformed by a conductor in a circuit.

Key fact

Earth potential

- Sometimes a point in a circuit is connected to the earth or ground, which fixes it at earth potential or zero volts. This is equivalent to using sea level as a reference for heights, sea level being zero height.
- Earth connections are often made to metal water pipes or metal stakes that go deep into the ground.
- The symbol ⏚ in a circuit indicates connection to earth or ground.

Key fact

Use electrical terms correctly

- *charge* flows
- current *in* or *through* a conductor
- current *in* or *round* a circuit
- the p.d. or voltage *between* two points (in a circuit)
- the p.d. or voltage *across* a conductor

Never talk about:

- a p.d. or voltage 'flowing' or 'going through' a conductor.

The words 'potential difference' are often abbreviated to p.d., but the symbol used in equations is V.

The unit of potential difference is the volt and its symbol is also V (not printed in italics).

We often talk about 'voltage' because it is easier than 'potential difference'.

Voltage and energy

The electrical energy E converted or transformed by a conductor depends on the quantity of charge flowing through it and also on the potential difference or voltage across it. As the charge Q flows 'downhill' from a 'height' measured as a number of volts V, it loses the potential energy E given to it by the battery or power supply.

$$\text{energy transformed} = \text{charge} \times \text{potential difference}$$

$$E = QV$$

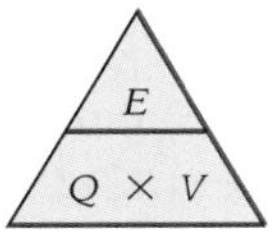

Definition of voltage or potential difference

The voltage or p.d. between the ends of a conductor is equal to the energy converted in it from electrical to other forms per coulomb of electric charge flowing through it.

Definition of the volt

The p.d. between the ends of a conductor is 1 volt if 1 joule of energy is converted when 1 coulomb of charge flows through it.

1 volt = 1 joule per coulomb

Worked example

A battery circulates 60 C of charge round a circuit. If the p.d. across a lamp in the circuit is 12 V, how much energy is converted into heat and light by the lamp?

$E = QV = 60\,\text{C} \times 12\,\text{V} = 720\,\text{J}$
(coulombs × volts = joules)

Battery voltage

A single dry cell or battery has a voltage of 1.5 volts. This is sometimes called the electromotive force of the battery, usually shortened to e.m.f. This voltage is a measure of the ability of the battery to pump charge round a circuit. A 1.5 volt battery can do 1.5 joules of work pumping 1 coulomb of charge round a circuit. 1.5 joules of energy will be transformed in the circuit for every coulomb circulated.

Worked example

A current of 10 A flowing through an electric heater for 1 hour converts 8.64 MJ of electrical energy into heat energy.
Calculate:
a) the total charge circulated through the heater
b) the voltage across the heater.

$I = 10\,\text{A}$
$t = 1\,\text{h} = 60 \times 60 \times 1\,\text{s} = 3600\,\text{s}$,
$E = 8.64 \times 10^6\,\text{J}$

a) $Q = It$ gives
$Q = 10\,\text{A} \times 3600\,\text{s} = 36\,000\,\text{C} = 3.60 \times 10^4\,\text{C}$

b) $V = \dfrac{E}{Q} = \dfrac{8.64 \times 10^6}{3.60 \times 10^4} = 240\,\text{V}$

Summary questions

1 Give the definition of potential difference.

2 Give the equation relating V, E and Q. What do these letters stand for?

3 Calculate the charge circulating when a p.d. of 9 V transfers 45 J of energy.

D14.5 Measuring voltage

Voltmeters measure potential difference in volts, i.e. they measure 'voltage'. Because they do not measure currents in circuits, voltmeters are not connected in series. Instead, voltmeters should be connected in *parallel* with the voltage to be measured, or as we often say, they are connected *across* something in a circuit. But like an ammeter, the positive terminal of a voltmeter must be connected to the point nearer to the positive terminal of the battery so that the pointer moves the right way across the scale.

Objectives

By the end of this topic you will be able to:

- draw circuit diagrams with voltmeters connected correctly
- use a voltmeter as a cell counter.

Using a voltmeter as a cell counter

- Connect three similar cells together in series and facing the same way.
- Connect a voltmeter across first one cell, then two and three and so on.

The voltmeter readings increase in equal steps (of 1.5 V for dry cells) for each additional cell, thus indicating the number of cells.

We find that when cells are connected in series, their voltages add up.

It is helpful to compare this use of the voltmeter with measuring heights. A scale placed alongside a wall could measure its height either in centimetres or in 'rows of bricks'. In Figure 14.5.1, the wall is 40 cm or 5 rows of bricks high. In the same way a voltmeter could measure the electrical 'height' or voltage between two terminals of a battery either by a reading in volts or in terms of the number of cells. For example, in the figure, the voltage across the whole battery is either 4.5 volts or it is 3 cells 'high'. Note that in both cases the scale is placed alongside or parallel to the object to be measured.

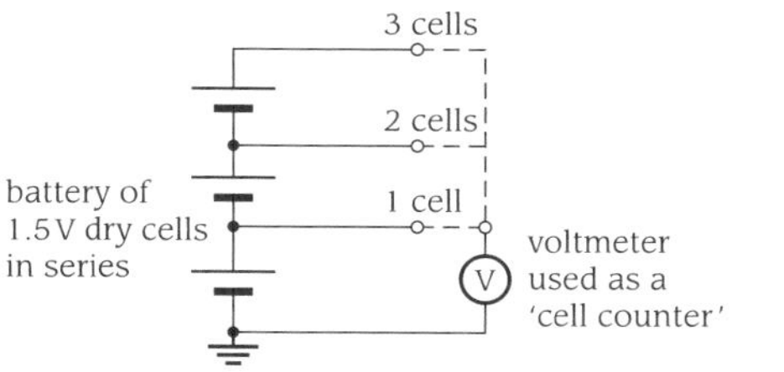

a The voltmeter is connected across or in parallel with the battery to be measured. The battery is a total of 3 cells or 4.5 volts 'high'.

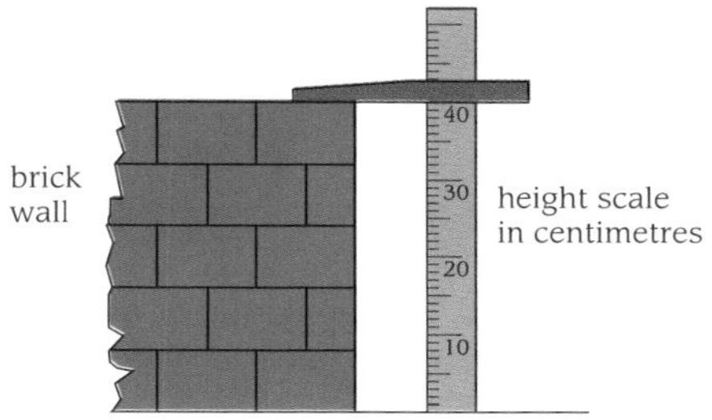

b The scale is placed alongside or parallel with the height of the wall to be measured. The wall is 5 rows of bricks or 40 cm high.

▲ **Figure 14.5.1** Comparing a voltmeter with a height scale

Using a voltmeter in a series circuit

When a voltmeter is used to measure the voltage across a conductor in a circuit or any part of a circuit, it is connected in parallel with it. Figure 14.5.2 shows the correct positions for a voltmeter when connected to measure the voltage across conductors in a series circuit. The arrows show the current round the series circuit. Note that it does not flow through the voltmeters.

- Connect up the circuit shown in Figure 14.5.2 using three 1.5 V cells in series with three similar lamps as the conductors (lamps rated at 1.25 V are suitable).
- Connect a voltmeter (0–5 V range) across each lamp in turn and then across all three lamps and record its readings, V_1, V_2, V_3 and V_T (V_{total}).
- Change two of the lamps for others of different ratings, say 2.5 V, and repeat the voltmeter readings.

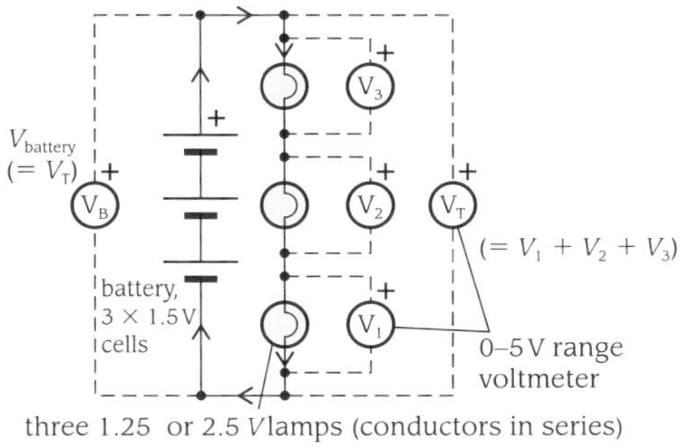

▲ **Figure 14.5.2** Connecting a voltmeter to a series circuit

The voltmeter readings show that in both cases:

$$V_1 + V_2 + V_3 = V_T$$

The voltages across each of the three lamps connected in series add up to the total voltage across all three of them, V_T.

- Now connect the voltmeter across the terminals of the battery and note its reading, V_B.

We find that $V_B = V_T$, i.e. the voltage across the battery terminals is always equal to the total voltage across the conductors in series with it.

These two positions of the voltmeter are measuring the p.d. or voltage between the same two points in the circuit and must give the same reading. Notice that one terminal of each voltmeter (reading V_B and V_T) is connected to the 'top' of the circuit with only a connecting wire between their joining places, and the other terminal of each voltmeter is connected to the 'bottom' of the circuit, again with only a wire between their joining places. When there is only a piece of wire between two places in a circuit they are at the same potential or voltage and can be considered to be the same place in the circuit.

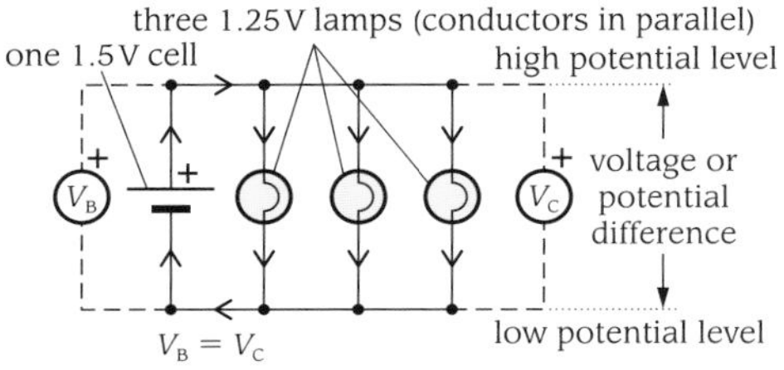

▲ **Figure 14.5.3** Connecting a voltmeter to parallel conductors

Using a voltmeter in a parallel circuit

- Reduce the battery to only one 1.5 V cell as shown in Figure 14.5.3. (This is to avoid burning out the lamps.)
- Connect three lamps in parallel to the battery.
- Connect the voltmeter in each of the positions shown and note its readings: V_B across the battery and V_C across the conductors, i.e. the lamps.

We find that $V_B = V_C$, i.e. the voltmeter reads the same in both positions again. One end of each lamp is connected to the same low potential level in the circuit and the other end of each lamp is connected to another common, but higher, potential level. Thus the p.d. or voltage between these levels is the same for all the lamps and equals the voltage between the terminals of the battery.

▲ **Figure 14.5.4** An analogue or digital multimeter can be used to measure current or voltage.

Making measurements safely

Range

If an ammeter or a voltmeter has more than one range, always use the highest range first. This is to prevent the meter being overloaded and possibly damaged.

If the reading is too small to be accurate on the highest range, change to a lower, more sensitive range.

Choosing ammeters and voltmeters

1. Do you want to measure current or voltage?
   Select an ammeter or a voltmeter or the correct range on a multimeter.
2. Is the supply DC (direct current) or AC (alternating current)?
   Select a suitable instrument or range.
   Note batteries are DC sources and the mains electricity is AC.
3. Do you want an analogue meter (with a pointer and a scale) or a digital meter?
   Digital meters are easier to read but if the current or voltage is changing it can be easier to see what is happening with an analogue meter, e.g. recording studios use analogue voltmeters to show the signal level of the sound.

Key fact

- Ammeters have a low resistance, so they don't have much effect on the size of the current flowing.
- Voltmeters have a very high resistance, so they don't change the circuit by 'diverting' current though the voltmeter.

Key fact

- The voltages across conductors connected in series in a circuit add up.
- The voltage across the terminals of a battery always equals the total voltage across the components in its circuit.
- The p.d.s or voltages across conductors connected in parallel are equal.

Summary questions

1. What can you say about the total voltage across identical cells connected in series?
2. What can you say about the total voltage across identical cells connected in parallel?

D14.6 Resistance

Definitions

The resistance of a conductor is the ratio of the voltage across it to the current through it.

The ohm is the resistance of a conductor through which the current is 1 ampere when the p.d. between its ends is 1 volt.

Objectives

By the end of this topic you will be able to:

- explain the concept of resistance
- calculate resistance using

$$R = \frac{V}{I}$$

Measuring resistance by a simple method

Resistance arises in all components of a circuit, but while the wires that connect components should have as little resistance as possible, the resistance in a lamp plays a vital role. The resistance is where the electrons give up the potential energy they carry from the battery. If a lamp filament had no resistance, no energy change could occur in it and it would not light up.

The resistance of a conductor opposes the current in a circuit, so to investigate its resistance we must measure the current through it. We must also measure the voltage that causes charge to flow through the conductor. (A length of thin wire made of a high-resistance alloy called constantan is suitable as the conductor; use a length of 1 m of insulated wire of diameter 0.4 mm, or standard wire gauge 28 or 30. Alternatively use any standard resistor of value between 5 and 10 ohms.)

- Connect the conductor to one cell (Figure 14.6.1).
- Measure the current through the conductor and the voltage across it.
- Increase the number of cells connected in the battery so that the current in the circuit increases.
- Record readings of both meters as each extra cell is added.
- You should be able to see a pattern of regular increases for both current and voltage.
- Divide the voltage by the current for each pair of readings giving a value for V/I.

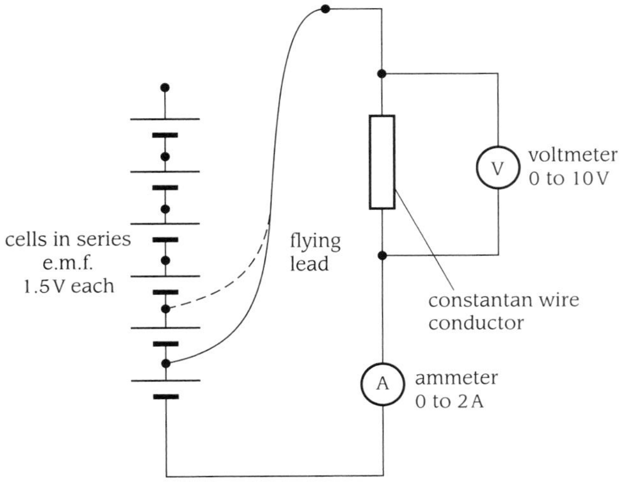

▲ **Figure 14.6.1** A simple circuit to measure resistance using an ammeter and voltmeter

The table shows an ideal set of readings.

Voltage *V*/volts	0	1.5	3.0	4.5	6.0	7.5	9.0
Current *I*/amperes	0	0.2	0.4	0.6	0.8	1.0	1.2
$\frac{V}{I}$ **= *R*/ohms**	–	7.5	7.5	7.5	7.5	7.5	7.5

The constant value obtained for V/I is called the resistance of the conductor.

The symbol for the ohm is Ω, called ‘omega’. This is the last letter of the Greek alphabet.

$$\text{resistance} = \frac{\text{voltage}}{\text{current}} \qquad R = \frac{V}{I} \qquad \left(\text{ohms} = \frac{\text{volts}}{\text{amperes}}\right)$$

Worked example

If a current of 4 A flows through a car headlamp when it is connected to a 12 V car battery, what is its resistance?

$$R = \frac{V}{I} = \frac{12\,\text{V}}{4\,\text{A}} = 3\,\text{V}$$

(volts/amperes = ohms)

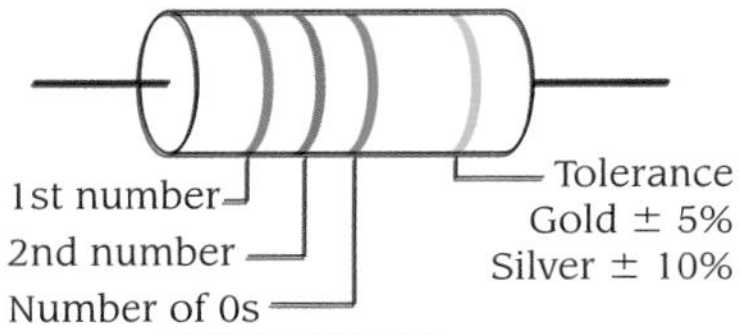

0	black
1	brown
2	red
3	orange
4	yellow
5	green
6	blue
7	violet
8	grey
9	white

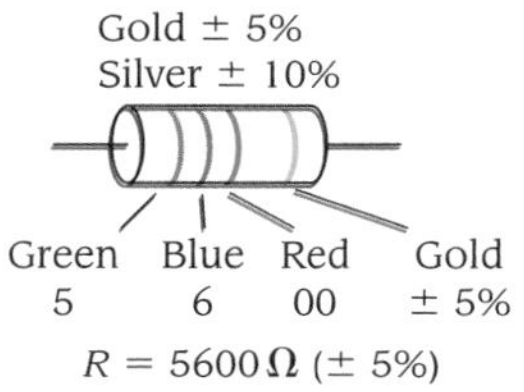

▲ **Figure 14.6.2** Resistor values. You don’t need to remember the resistor colour code.

The resistance of a conductor depends on two things:

- its dimensions
- the material of which it is made.

A thin wire has a higher resistance than a thick wire; a long wire has a greater resistance than a short one. Thinking of water flowing through a pipe, we would expect more resistance when it flows through a long, thin pipe than through a wide, short one.

The material the conductor is made of affects its resistance. A good conducting material has more ‘free’ electrons than a poorer one, and if these electrons can flow easily through the material its resistance is lower.

Fixed resistors

Resistors are manufactured with specific values for use in many electronic circuits. Their resistance values are given by four coloured bands painted round them (Figure 14.6.2).

High-power resistors are usually wire-wound. The wire usually used is an enamelled nichrome alloy, which has a very high resistance. Apart from increased accuracy and stability, wire-wound resistors can be made to conduct large currents without being damaged by the heat produced in them.

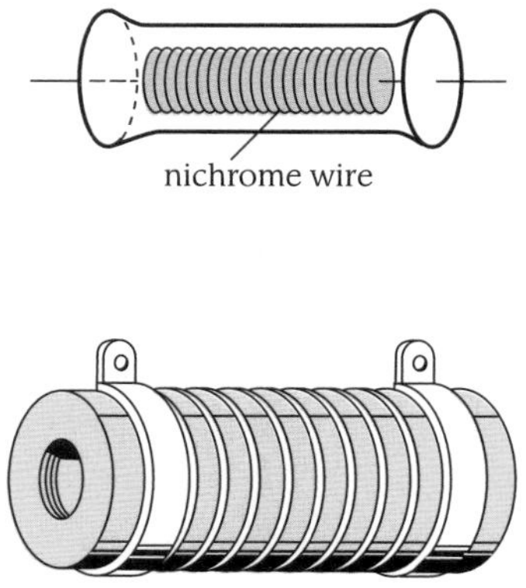

▲ **Figure 14.6.3** Wire-wound resistors

Variable resistors

The current that flows in a circuit is determined by two factors, the e.m.f. or voltage of the battery and the total resistance of the circuit. The current can be increased by reducing the circuit resistance, or reduced by increasing the resistance. By including a variable resistor in a circuit we can vary or control the current in the circuit.

Rheostats

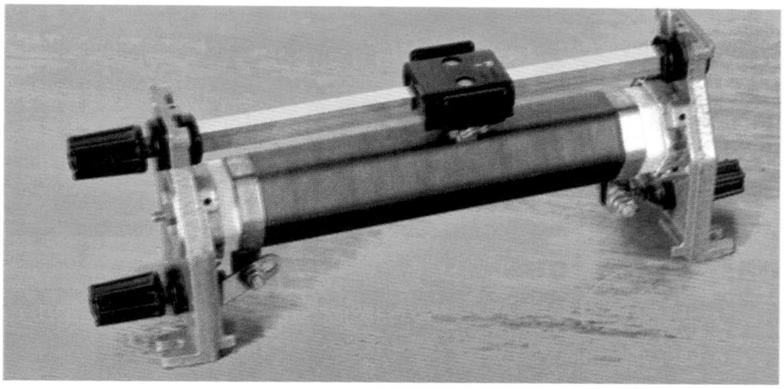

▲ **Figure 14.6.5** The much larger laboratory rheostat can conduct currents of several amperes without being damaged.

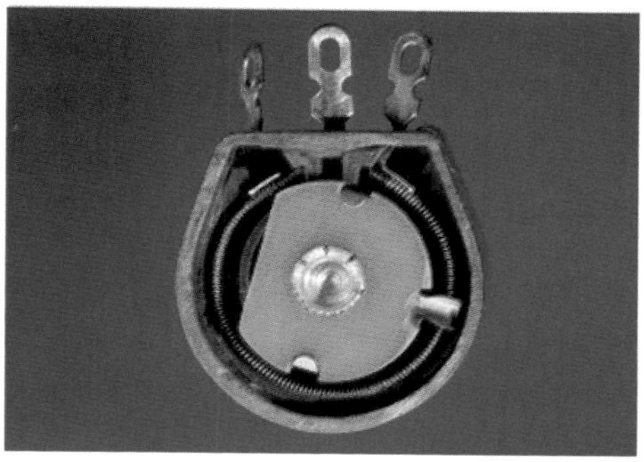

▲ **Figure 14.6.4** The circular type of variable resistor shown here with its back removed has a curved, wire-wound track, which may be from about 2 cm to 4 cm in diameter. A knob is fitted to the other end of the central shaft. This device is often used as a volume control on hi-fi equipment and radios.

The length of the track through which the current flows determines the amount of resistance in the circuit. Although these devices (Figure 14.6.6) have three terminals, A, B and C, when they are used as rheostats, only two terminals are needed. If terminals A and B are used, then the minimum resistance is when the slider is at A and the maximum when it is at C. Note that the resistance between terminals A and C is fixed and cannot be varied.

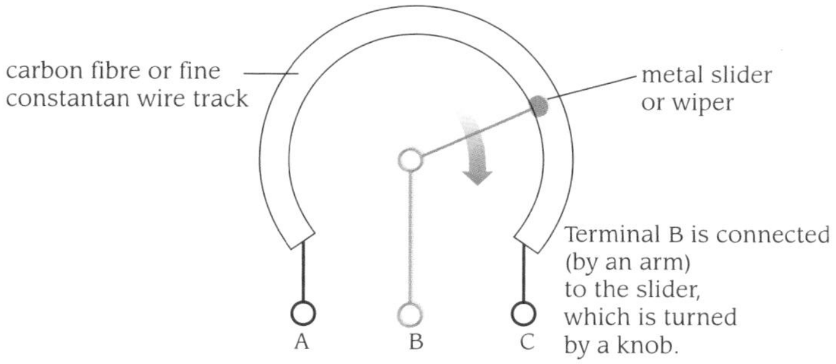

a A rotary type of rheostat. For a variable resistor use terminal B and either A or C. For a voltage divider (also known as a potentiometer or 'pot') use all three terminals.

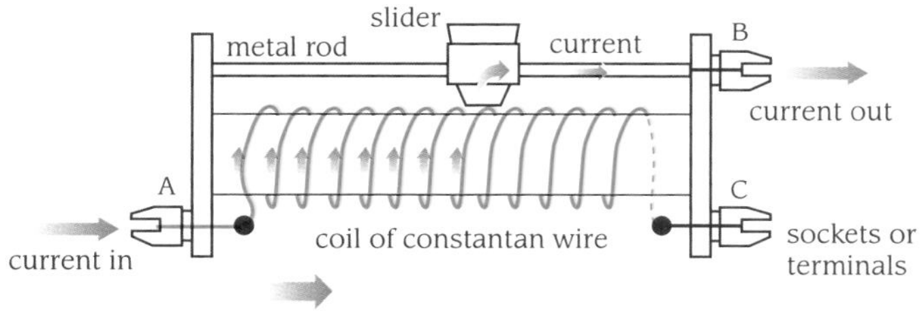

b A laboratory rheostat, which can be used to control currents of several amperes. The slider has a spring contact with the wire coil.

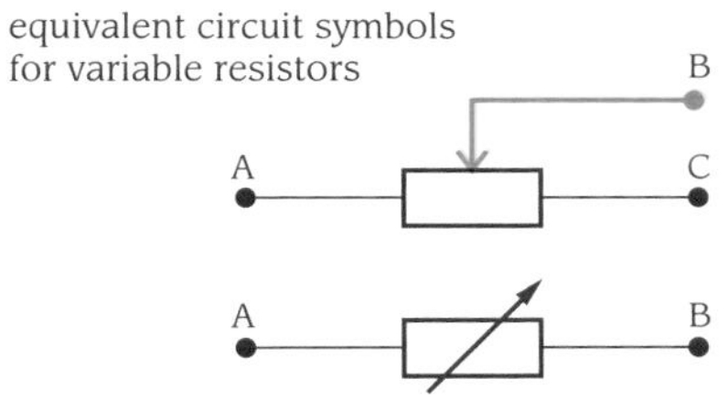

▲ **Figure 14.6.6** Variable resistors or rheostats

Key fact

- The rheostat is connected in *series* with the circuit and the current to be varied or controlled.
- The rheostat cannot reduce the current in the circuit to zero (to do that it would require an infinitely high resistance).
- When the rheostat is set at its maximum resistance, the ammeter still indicates some current even though the lamp is not lit.

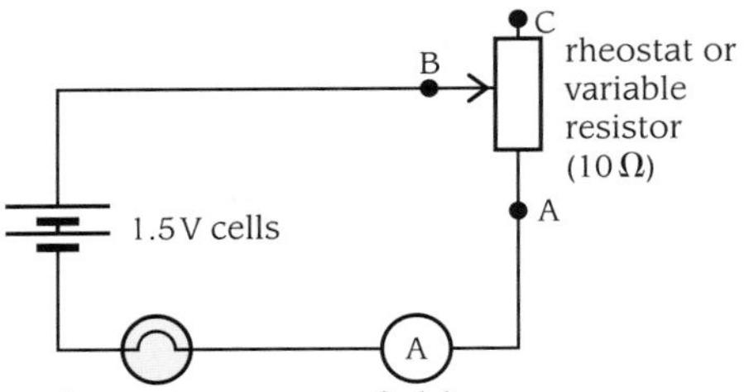

▲ **Figure 14.6.7** Circuit using a rheostat to vary brightness of a lamp. Variation of circuit resistance controls current. There is zero resistance from the rheostat, and therefore maximum current, when B slides to A.

Things to do

Using a rheostat to vary the current in a circuit

Wire up the circuit shown in Figure 14.6.7 and see how the rheostat varies the current in the circuit. This is shown by both the brightness of the lamp and the reading of the ammeter.

Summary questions

1 Give the equation that shows the relationship between voltage, current and resistance of a conductor.

2 Draw the circuit symbol for a variable resistor.

3 Calculate the resistance of a conductor if a voltage of 12 V produces a current of 1.5 A.

Objectives

By the end of this topic you will be able to:

- describe experiments using an ammeter and a voltmeter to investigate the characteristics of:
  - **a)** metallic conductors at constant temperature
  - **b)** filament lamps
  - **c)** semiconductor diodes
  - **d)** copper sulphate solution using copper electrodes
- draw *I*–*V* graphs for these conductors and draw conclusions from them.

D14.7 Characteristics

Things to do

- Draw the characteristic obtained for a filament lamp using the results in the table.
- Draw a smooth curve through the plotted points.
- Comment on the shape of the characteristic.
- Explain why you would expect the characteristic of a filament lamp to be symmetrical for both directions of the current.

V/volts	*I*/ampere
0	0
0.5	0.04
1.0	0.08
1.5	0.12
2.0	0.15
2.5	0.175
3.0	0.19
3.5	0.20

The characteristic of a circuit component or device tells us about the way it conducts electric current and shows how it may be used in an electric circuit.

Ohm's law

The 19th-century scientist, Georg Ohm, made measurements of current and voltage for wires, and he discovered that provided wires did not get warm the resistance, the ratio of V/I, remained constant. In 1826 he published Ohm's law.

Conductors with a constant value for the ratio V/I are said to obey Ohm's law and are described as ohmic conductors.

The current through a metallic conductor, maintained at constant temperature, is directly proportional to the potential difference between its ends.

$$I \propto V$$

Ohm's law and the characteristic of a conductor

If we measure the current I through a conductor for various values of the p.d. or voltage V across it and calculate the value of its resistance R, we usually find that each pair of values for V and I gives a slightly different value for the resistance R.

The most common reason for this change in the resistance of a conductor is the change in temperature produced by the heating effect of the electric current in it. Because of the variation of resistance with temperature, conductors are unlikely to obey Ohm's law unless their temperatures are kept constant. For metals, R increases at higher temperatures while for semiconductors, R usually decreases at higher temperatures.

When we plot a graph of the current I through a conductor, against the voltage V between its ends, the shape of the curve obtained is known as the **characteristic** of the conductor.

A straight-line graph (of positive gradient, through the origin) would show that the current was directly proportional to the voltage for a particular conductor and therefore it obeyed Ohm's law. The nearer its characteristic is to a straight line, the more closely does the conductor obey Ohm's law.

Finding the characteristic of a conductor

To obtain a full characteristic for a conductor we need a voltage that can be increased smoothly. Figure 14.7.1 shows a suitable test circuit.

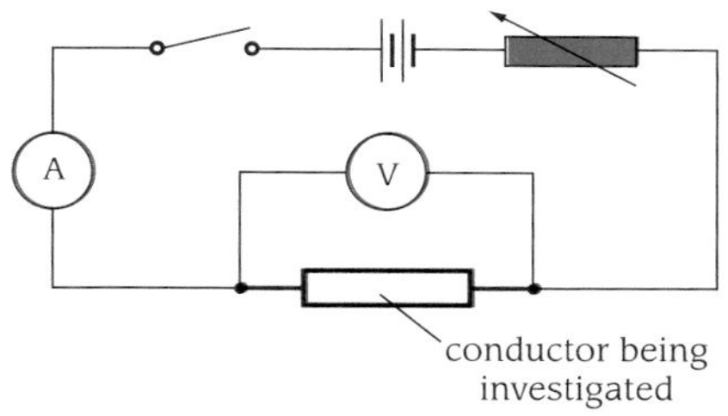

▲ **Figure 14.7.1** Circuit to find conduction characteristics. A protective resistor may be connected in series with the conductor being investigated.

- Choose the voltage of the battery and the ranges of the ammeter and voltmeter to suit the particular conductor or device to be tested. When in doubt about the size of the current, it is wise to start with a high-range ammeter, say 0–10 A or 0–1 A. If the current is found to be small, drop down to more sensitive ranges. This avoids overloading a sensitive ammeter with a large current and damaging it.
- Wire up the circuit and, by adjusting the variable resistor, obtain a set of readings from the two meters.
- By changing over its connections, turn the conductor round in the circuit and repeat the readings.
- Turning the conductor round in the circuit sends current through it in the reverse direction.
- Plot the two sets of results (for the current in opposite directions) in opposite quadrants of the graph, as in Figure 14.7.2.

We give the current and voltage positive values in one direction and negative in the other.

a) Ohmic conductor

The straight-line characteristic is symmetrical in both directions and passes through the origin of the graph. This conductor closely obeys Ohm's law:

- $I \propto V$
- R is constant.

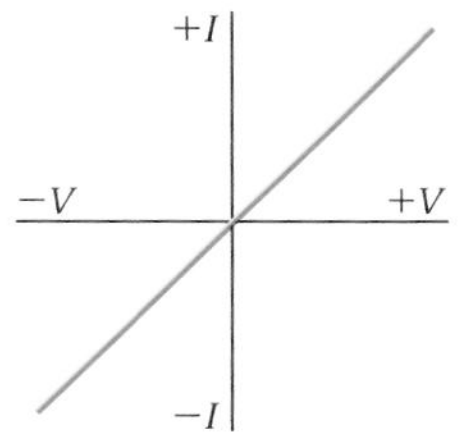

▲ **Figure 14.7.2** Conductor characteristic for an ohmic conductor

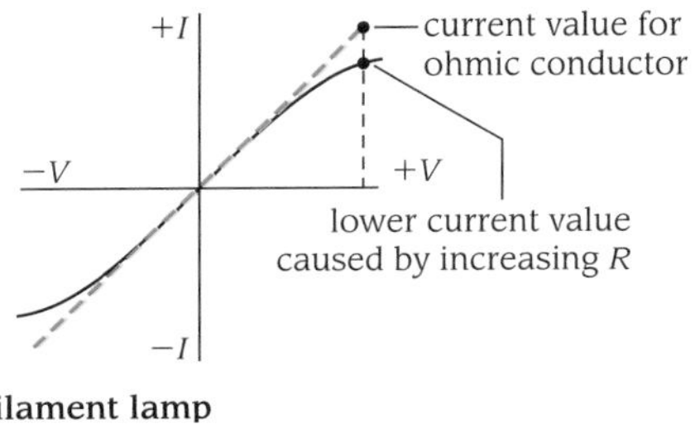

▲ **Figure 14.7.3** Conductor characteristic for a filament lamp

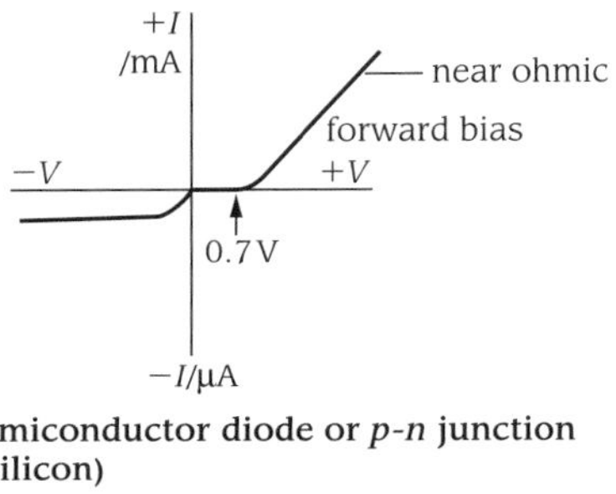

▲ **Figure 14.7.4** Conductor characteristic for a semiconductor diode

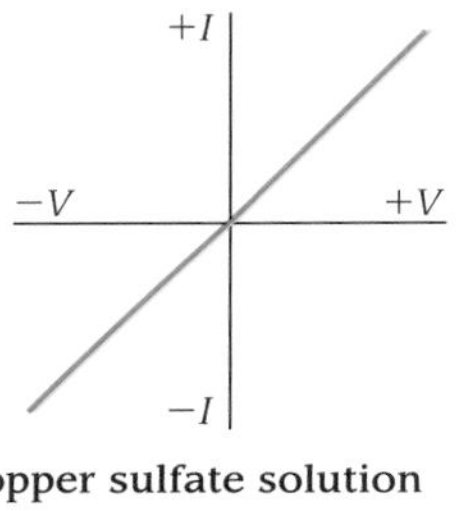

▲ **Figure 14.7.5** Conductor characteristic for copper sulfate solution

b) Filament lamp

At low currents the characteristic may be fairly straight but as the current rises, producing more heat, the temperature rise increases its resistance. So at a particular voltage when the filament temperature has risen, the current value is lower than it would be for an ohmic conductor.

- Resistance increases as temperature rises.
- The characteristic is curved.

c) Semiconductor diode (silicon)

This common device has a very distinctive characteristic.

Only a very small current flows in the reverse direction, indicating that its reverse resistance is very high.

In the forwards direction almost no current flows until a voltage of about 0.6 or 0.7 V is reached.

Above 0.7 V the current rises steeply and the device has a low resistance.

- A diode conducts well in one direction only. It is an electronic valve or one-way device.
- Conduction is by electrons and 'positive holes'.

d) Copper sulfate solution

Copper sulfate solution in water is called an electrolyte.

The copper sulfate breaks down into two charged particles called ions. There are positive copper ions and negative sulfate ions, which can carry electric charge through the solution.

- As the graph is straight, conduction through the electrolyte using copper electrodes is ohmic.
- The resistance of the solution is high compared with metallic conductors because the ions in the solution are less mobile than the electrons in a metal.
- Conduction is by means of copper and sulfate ions.

Things to do

Ohmic conductor

Using values from the table in 'Measuring resistance by a simple method' (at the start of D14.6), plot a graph of I against V. Use this graph to find the value of R.

Key fact

Remember: the gradient of a graph of I (y-axis) against V (x-axis) gives a value for $1/R$. (Resistance is found from V/I, and the gradient gives I/V.)

Summary questions

1 Sketch a graph of I against V for an ohmic conductor.

2 What happens to the resistance of a filament lamp as temperature increases?

3 Name one non-ohmic semiconductor device.

D14.8 Circuit calculations

Objectives

By the end of this topic you will be able to:

- recall and use the equations for finding the equivalent resistance of several resistors connected in series or in parallel
- calculate the currents in circuit components when connected in series or parallel with the supply
- calculate the voltage across components in a circuit when they are connected in series or in parallel.

The following stages form a plan for solving circuit problems.

1 Draw a circuit diagram and label it with the values given for each component; this will help you to see what is going on.

2 Decide whether the resistors in the circuit are all connected in parallel with the battery or supply.

3 Calculate the total resistance in the circuit.

4 Calculate the current in the circuit.

5 Calculate the voltage across circuit components.

Parallel circuits

When a circuit diagram has been drawn, if all the resistors are in parallel across the supply and if the voltage across them is known, then the current through each one can be calculated separately using $I = V/R$. There is no need to find their total resistance, unless this is asked for. If, however, the resistance of the supply or battery has to be included, then this is in series with the other parallel resistors and the total circuit resistance must be calculated first.

Parallel circuits are very common as is shown in the first worked example, which is about the parallel circuits used at home.

Worked example

Finding the currents in parallel circuits

A lamp of resistance 440 Ω, an electric fire of resistance 13.75 Ω and a vacuum cleaner of resistance 27.5 Ω are connected in parallel across the mains supply of 110 V. Calculate the current through each appliance and the total current supplied by the mains. See Figure 14.8.1 for the circuit diagram.

In this example the only resistors mentioned are in parallel. Each has the full 110 V mains supply connected across it and can be used independently. The current through each resistor can be calculated separately and there is no need to find the total circuit resistance.

For the lamp $I = \frac{V}{R_L} = \frac{110}{440} = 0.25\text{ A}$

For the fire $I = \frac{V}{R_F} = \frac{110}{13.75} = 8.0\text{ A}$

For the cleaner $I = \frac{V}{R_C} = \frac{110}{27.5} = 4.0\text{ A}$

Total current $= 0.25 + 8.0 + 4.0 = 12.25\text{ A}$
(Addition of the currents by Kirchoff's first law)

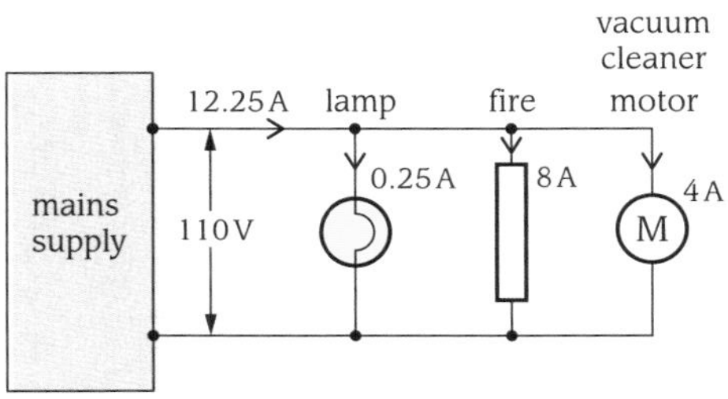

▲ **Figure 14.8.1** Conductors connected in parallel across the mains each receive the same p.d. of 110 volts. The total current from the mains, 12.25 A, equals the sum of the separate currents through the parallel conductors.

Resistors connected in series

In series circuits we need to find the total circuit resistance before we can calculate the current in the circuit.

- The p.d.s or voltages add up in a series circuit.
- The current through resistors in series must be the same.

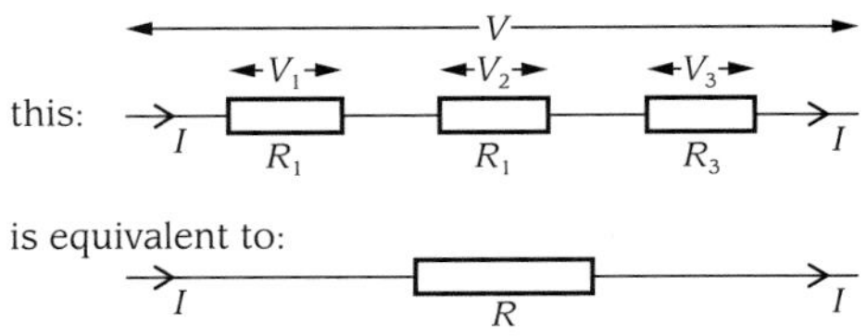

▲ **Figure 14.8.2** Equivalent resistors (series)

Worked example

Resistors connected in series

If three resistors of 2 Ω, 5 Ω and 7 Ω are connected together in series, what value single resistor could replace them and allow the same current to flow?

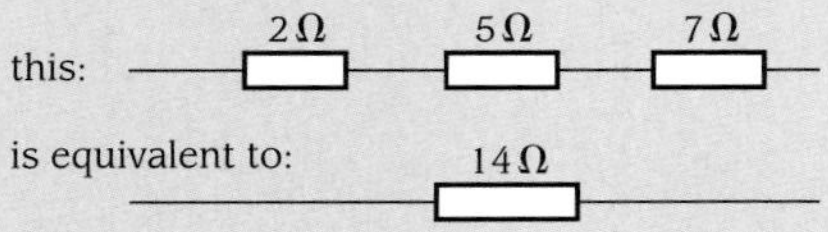

▲ **Figure 14.8.3**

$R_S = R_1 + R_2 + R_3$
$R_S = 2\,\Omega + 5\,\Omega + 7\,\Omega = 14\,\Omega$

Worked example

Calculate the current in the circuit shown in Figure 14.8.4.

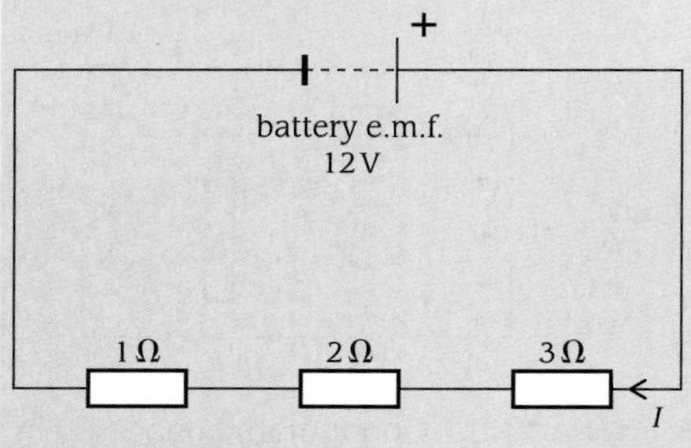

▲ **Figure 14.8.4**

This is a series circuit so we first find the total circuit resistance.
For the total circuit:
$R_S = R_1 + R_2 + R_3$
$R_S = 1\,\Omega + 2\,\Omega + 3\,\Omega = 6\,\Omega$
Now we apply the formula for current to the whole circuit:

$$I = \frac{V}{R_S} = \frac{12}{6} = 2\,\text{A}$$

Adding up the voltages.

$$V = V_1 + V_2 + V_3$$

We can use $V = IR$ so for each resistor

$$V = IR_1 + IR_2 + IR_3$$

$$\therefore \quad V = I(R_1 + R_2 + R_3) \qquad (1)$$

and for the equivalent resistor of resistance R_S we have

$$V = IR_S \qquad (2)$$

By comparing equation (1) with equation (2), since V and I are the same, we can see that for series resistors

$$R_S = R_1 + R_2 + R_3$$

For resistors in series, add all their resistances.

The effect of combining resistors in series is to increase the total circuit resistance, and to decrease the current throughout the circuit.

Calculating the current in a series circuit

Since every bit of resistance in a series circuit reduces the current in the whole circuit, the current in a series circuit is calculated from the total applied voltage and the total resistance in the circuit (including any resistance in the supply or battery itself).

The equations $V = IR$, $I = \frac{V}{R}$ and $R = \frac{V}{I}$ can be used for individual resistors, for groups of resistors or for whole circuits, but their use in each case must be consistent. This means that the values of R, V and I used in a formula must all apply to the same thing, e.g. a single resistor.

Worked example

Currents in a series circuit

Three 8 ohm resistors are connected in series with a battery. If the voltage across one of the resistors in the circuit is 4.0 volts:

a) What is the current through this resistor

b) What is the current in the whole series circuit

c) What is the battery voltage?

a) Applying the equation to the single resistor:

$$I = \frac{V}{R} = \frac{4.0}{8.0} = 0.5\,\text{A}$$

b) In a series circuit the current is the same all round it: here it is 0.5 A.

c) Applying the equation,
$V = IR$, to the whole circuit and adding the three resistances:
$V = IR_S = 0.5(8 + 8 + 8) = 12\,\text{V}$.
The battery voltage is 12 V.

Resistors connected in parallel

Referring to the circuit in Figure 14.8.5, the voltage across the single equivalent resistor of resistance R_P must also equal the voltage across each of the parallel resistors.

From Kirchhoff's first law we know that the current I divides up so that:

$$I = I_1 + I_2 + I_3$$

The current in each resistor is given by

$$I = \frac{V}{R}$$

$$\therefore \frac{V}{R_P} = \frac{V}{R_1} + \frac{V}{R_2} + \frac{V}{R_3}$$

As all the voltages are equal we can divide through the equation by V and so we get the equation for resistors connected in parallel:

$$\frac{1}{R_P} = \frac{1}{R_1} + \frac{1}{R_2} + \frac{1}{R_3}$$

For resistors in parallel,
add the reciprocals of the resistances
to give the reciprocal of the equivalent resistance.

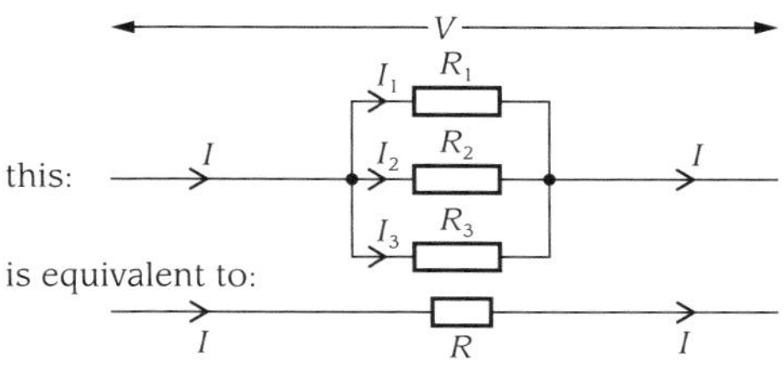

▲ **Figure 14.8.5** Equivalent resistors (parallel)

For two resistors in parallel

Some people prefer to use an alternative form of this equation for only two resistors in parallel. It is easier to use (if you are not using a calculator with a reciprocal key) and it gives the combined resistance rather than its reciprocal, but it only works for two resistors. By rearrangement the equation becomes:

$$R_P = \frac{R_1 R_2}{R_1 + R_2}$$

Worked example

Resistors connected in parallel

If a 6 Ω resistor is connected in parallel with a 3 Ω resistor as in Figure 14.8.6, what is their equivalent combined resistance?

$$\frac{1}{R_P} = \frac{1}{R_1} + \frac{1}{R_2} = \frac{1}{6} + \frac{1}{3} = \frac{1+2}{6} = \frac{3}{6} = \frac{1}{2\,\Omega}$$

Which gives: $R_P = 2\,\Omega$

Remember when using this equation, the value of the equivalent resistance, R_P is the reciprocal of your answer.

(Use the $1/x$ key or the x^{-1} key on your calculator.)

Alternatively using: $R_P = \frac{R_1 R_2}{R_1 + R_2} = \frac{6 \times 3}{6 + 3} = \frac{18}{9} = 2\,\Omega$

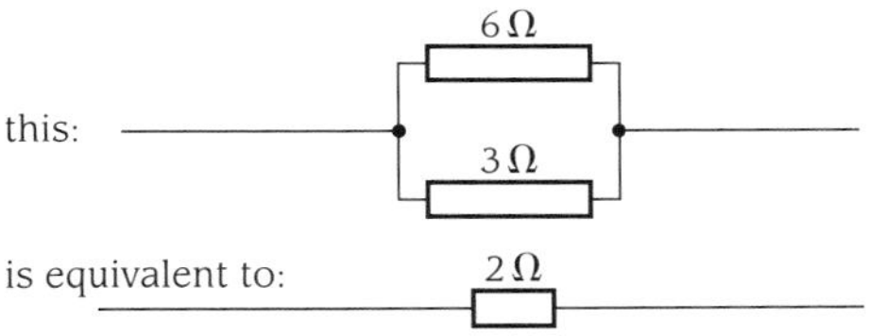

▲ **Figure 14.8.6**

Worked example

Resistors in parallel

Three resistors of values 24 Ω, 12 Ω and 8 Ω are connected together in parallel. Calculate their total combined resistance.

$$\frac{1}{R_P} = \frac{1}{R_1} + \frac{1}{R_2} + \frac{1}{R_3}$$

$$\frac{1}{R_P} = \frac{1}{24} + \frac{1}{12} + \frac{1}{8} = \frac{1+2+3}{24} = \frac{6}{24} = \frac{1}{4}$$

Total resistance, $R_P = 4.0\,\Omega$.

Key fact

- The p.d. or voltage across parallel connected conductors is the same.
- Connecting conductors in parallel provides more ways for the current to flow. This makes it easier for the current to flow, and makes the combined resistance less than each separate resistance.
- Resistors connected in parallel have a smaller combined resistance and conduct a larger total current than they do separately.

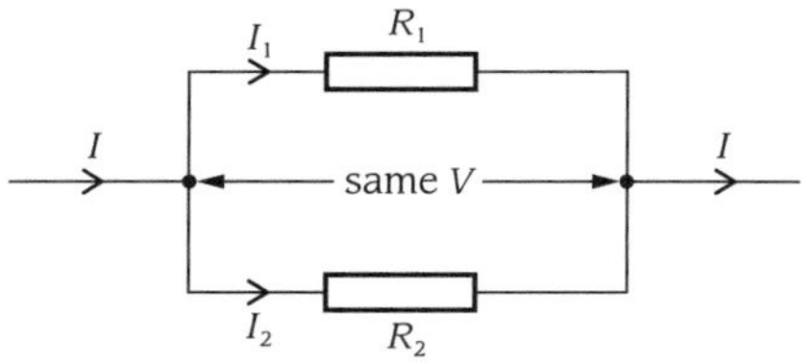

a Current dividing through two parallel branches of a series circuit, $I = I_1 + I_2$

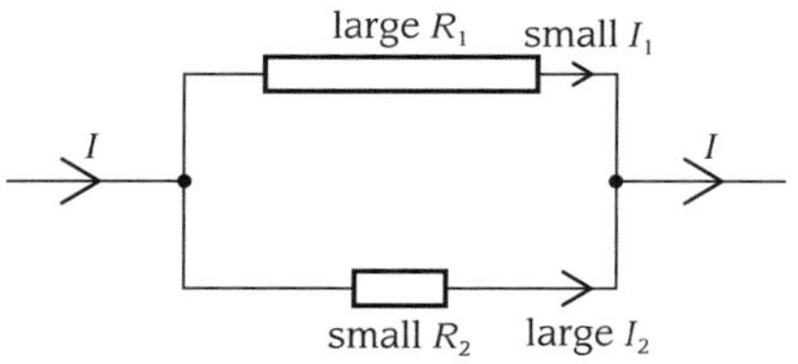

b For parallel resistors the currents are in the inverse ratio of the resistances:

$$\frac{I_1}{I_2} = \frac{R_2}{R_1}$$

▲ **Figure 14.8.7** Currents in parallel conductors

Calculation of current in parallel branches of a circuit

Figure 14.8.7a shows the current I dividing up through two parallel resistors of resistance R_1 and R_2.

We know from Kirchhoff's first law that: $I = I_1 + I_2$.

Resistors in parallel must have the same voltage V across them.

From the equation: $I = \frac{V}{R}$ we can write for R_1 and R_2:

$$I_1 = \frac{V}{R_1} \text{ and } I_2 = \frac{V}{R_2}$$

Dividing the first equation by the second and cancelling V,

we get:

$$\frac{I_1}{I_2} = \frac{R_2}{R_1}$$

As Figure 14.8.7b shows, the current I divides up so that, in proportion, there is more current through the smaller resistor and less current through the larger one.

The ratio of the currents in parallel resistors
is the inverse of the ratio of their resistances.

If the parallel resistances are equal then the current divides up equally, with half of the total circuit current going through each resistor.

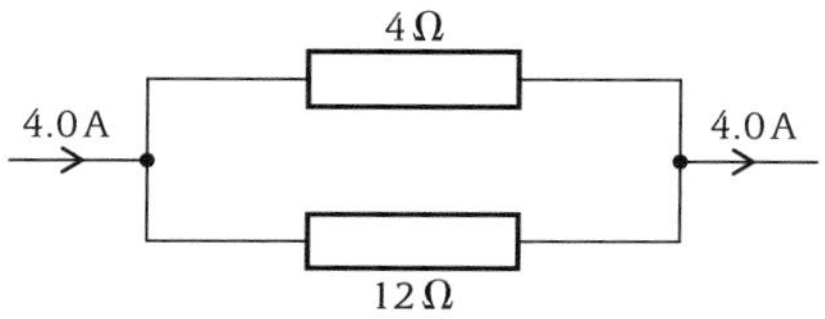

▲ **Figure 14.8.8**

Worked example

A pair of resistors of values 4 Ω and 12 Ω are connected together in parallel in a circuit in which the total current is 4.0 amperes (Figure 14.8.8). Calculate the current through each of the parallel resistors.

The current of 4 A divides up unequally through the parallel pair of resistors

so that $\frac{I_1}{I_2} = \frac{R_2}{R_1}$

$= \frac{12}{4} = 3$

So we have $I_1 = 3 \times I_2$

Also, by Kirchhoff's first law: $I = I_1 + I_2 = 4.0\,\text{A}$

So: $I = 3I_2 + I_2 = 4I_2 = 4.0\,\text{A}$

This gives $I_2 = 1.0\,\text{A}$ and $I_1 = 3.0\,\text{A}$.

Alternative solution

The equivalent resistance of the two resistors is given by:

$$R_P = \frac{R_1 R_2}{R_1 + R_2}$$

$$= \frac{4 \times 12}{4 + 12}$$

$$= \frac{48}{16} = 3\,\Omega$$

The voltage across the combination, $V = IR = 4.0 \times 3 = 12\,\text{V}$.

The current through each resistor is given by:

$$I_1 = \frac{V}{R_1} = \frac{12}{4} = 3.0\,\text{A} \text{ and } I_2 = \frac{V}{R_2} = \frac{12}{12} = 1.0\,\text{A}$$

Summary questions

1. Give the equation to find total resistance for resistors in series.
2. Find the total resistance when two resistors of 6 ohms and 2 ohms are connected in parallel.
3. Which of the above resistors will have the larger current flowing through it?

D14.9 Cells and batteries

Types of cell

Primary cells use a chemical reaction that converts stored chemical energy into electrical energy in a process that cannot be reversed. These cells only have one useful life and should be disposed of carefully or recycled, if possible.

Secondary cells can be reused, because they can be *recharged* many times. The chemical reaction that gives out electrical energy can be reversed by connecting the cell to a charger. **Rechargeable batteries** are secondary cells. Secondary cells are also sometimes called *storage cells* or **accumulators**. Although they are usually more expensive to buy than primary cells, they last much longer, so are usually cheaper in the long term.

Warning: Never try to recharge an 'ordinary' battery. It will get very hot and may explode.

A **solar cell** converts light energy directly into electrical energy.

A **thermocouple** converts heat energy into electrical energy.

Basic ideas about cells and batteries

- All cells have two terminals (or electrodes), a positive (+) and a negative (−).
- A battery is two or more cells connected together to increase the voltage.
- Conventional current flows out of the + terminal, round an external circuit and in to the − terminal. Inside the battery conventional current flows from − to +. The current is actually a flow of electrons in the opposite direction.
- Every cell acts like a resistor to the current flowing through it. This internal resistance of the cell is usually small enough to be ignored.
- When a very large current is needed, for instance for the starter motor to start a car, the internal resistance of 'ordinary' cells is too large. Car batteries (often called accumulators) are specially designed to have a very low internal resistance so they give a very large current. But they use liquid acids that are less safe than the chemicals in 'ordinary' batteries.
- The voltage (e.m.f.) of a cell depends mainly on the metals used for the electrodes.

The dry cell

The simplest primary cell is copper and zinc electrodes in dilute sulfuric acid. The chemical reaction causes hydrogen gas to collect at the positive electrode, which quickly stops this cell working. This is called polarisation.

In about 1860 Georges Leclanché invented the earliest form of the zinc–carbon dry cells we use today. In a dry cell, the chemicals are in the form of paste, so they do not spill. The cell is safer and portable. A zinc–carbon dry cell has a zinc electrode and a carbon electrode.

When new, a zinc–carbon cell has an e.m.f. of 1.5 V. This voltage falls as the cell is used. Over time, the zinc gradually dissolves, so the cell has a 'shelf life', and this may be less than a year. There are several types of primary cell, but a common type of modern dry cell is the 'alkaline battery'.

Objectives

By the end of this topic you will be able to:

- draw a diagram of a zinc–carbon cell and explain how it works
- draw a diagram of a rechargeable secondary cell and a circuit diagram of its recharging circuit
- compare primary and secondary cells, explaining their relative advantages and disadvantages.

Key fact

A battery is two or more cells connected together.

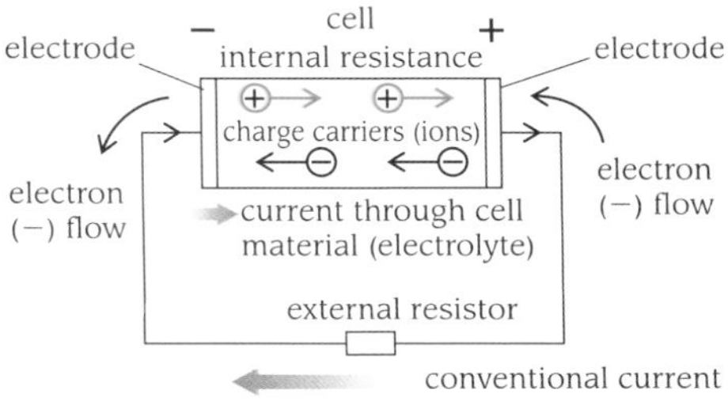

▲ **Figure 14.9.1** A cell

▲ **Figure 14.9.2** A 12 V car battery is made from six 2 V cells. Each cell has lead plates in sulfuric acid.

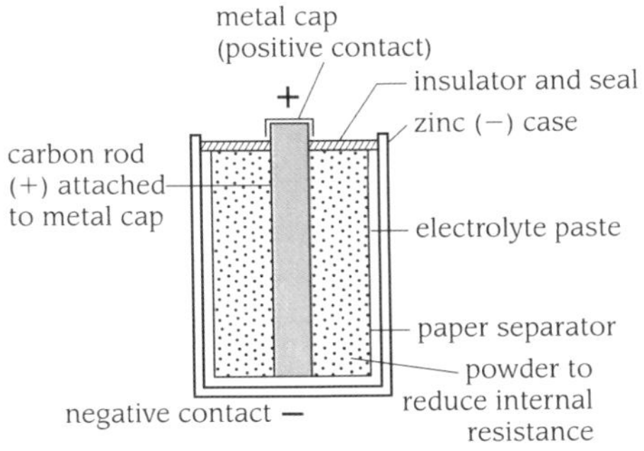

▲ **Figure 14.9.3** A zinc-carbon dry cell with outer case removed

The internal resistance of a dry cell

The internal resistance of a cell is the resistance of the cell itself. It forms part of the total resistance in a circuit, so it limits the maximum current that can flow in a circuit. You can measure approximately the maximum current by connecting a thick piece of copper wire across the terminals. This is called short-circuiting the cell and makes it go flat very quickly. The maximum current for a typical dry cell is about 1.0 A.

Key fact

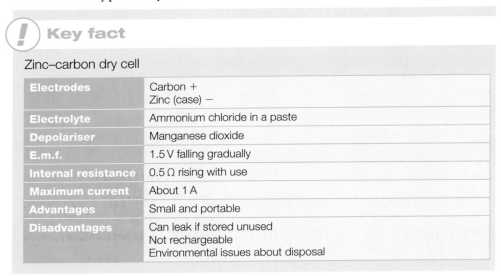

Zinc–carbon dry cell

Electrodes	Carbon + Zinc (case) –
Electrolyte	Ammonium chloride in a paste
Depolariser	Manganese dioxide
E.m.f.	1.5 V falling gradually
Internal resistance	0.5 Ω rising with use
Maximum current	About 1 A
Advantages	Small and portable
Disadvantages	Can leak if stored unused Not rechargeable Environmental issues about disposal

The lead–acid accumulator

Key fact

Lead–acid accumulator

Negative electrode –	Grey lead plate when charged
Positive electrode +	Brown lead(IV) oxide (PbO_2) coating on lead plate when charged
Electrolyte	Sulfuric acid
E.m.f.	2.2 V initially, Constant at 2.0 V for a long time
Internal resistance	Lower than 0.01 Ω
Maximum current	Up to 400 A
Advantages	Rechargeable Can supply a very large current, e.g. to operate the starter motor of a car
Disadvantages	Portable but usually heavy and bulky Acid may need topping up with distilled water
Charging connections	Connect the negative terminal of the battery to the negative terminal of the charging supply then connect the two positives together. Great care must be taken to avoid connecting together the two leads.

In 1860, Gustav Planté invented the lead–acid accumulator. A piece of cloth, soaked with dilute sulfuric acid and rolled up between two strips of lead was found to be able to store electrical energy. The energy is put into the cell by passing a current through it in one direction. Afterwards the cell gives up its energy by passing a current in the opposite direction. This is a *secondary* or *storage cell*, which only delivers energy to a circuit if energy has previously been fed into the cell.

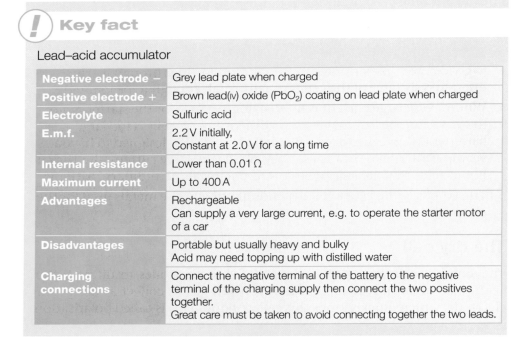

Making a lead–acid storage cell

Charging

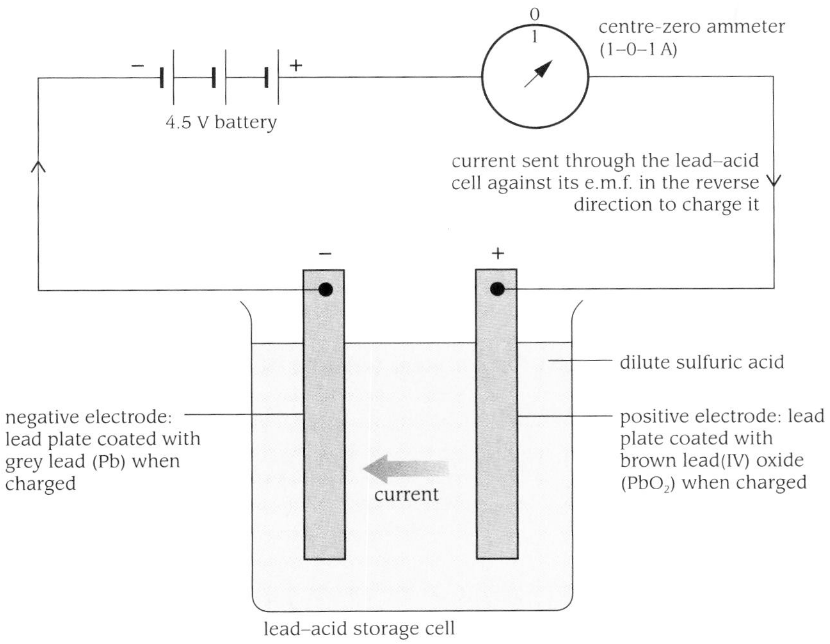

◀ **Figure 14.9.4** Charging a lead–acid storage cell, storing energy

- Set up the charging circuit shown in Figure 14.9.4.
- The power supply must be direct current (DC).
- A centre-zero ammeter shows the direction of current flow during charging and discharging.
- Allow the charging current to flow for about 5 minutes then look carefully at the lead plates.

Rechargeable batteries may need charging for several hours. For example, a car battery may need charging overnight. Much research is being done to develop rechargeable batteries that recharge faster.

Discharging

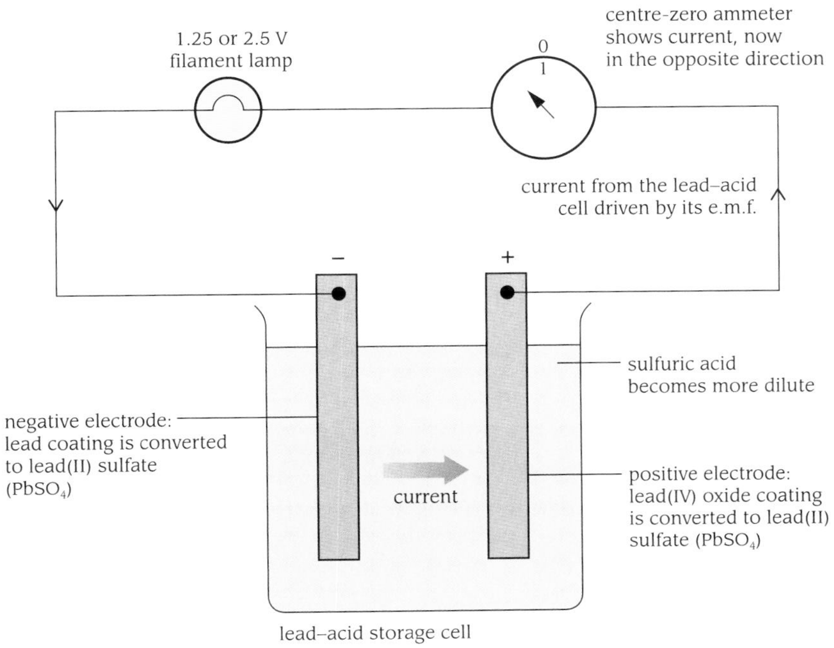

◀ **Figure 14.9.5** Discharging a lead–acid storage cell, supplying energy

- Replace the battery with a filament lamp, as in Figure 14.9.5, and watch what happens.
- Repeat the charging process for a longer time, then reconnect the lamp. What difference has this made?

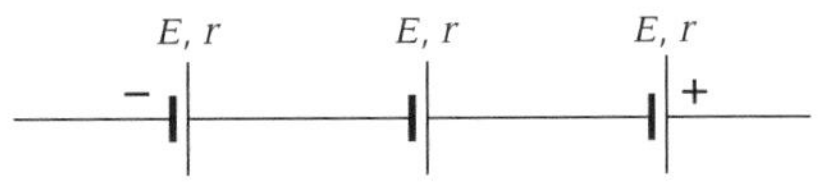

a Cells in series: total e.m.f. = $3E$, combined internal resistance = $3r$

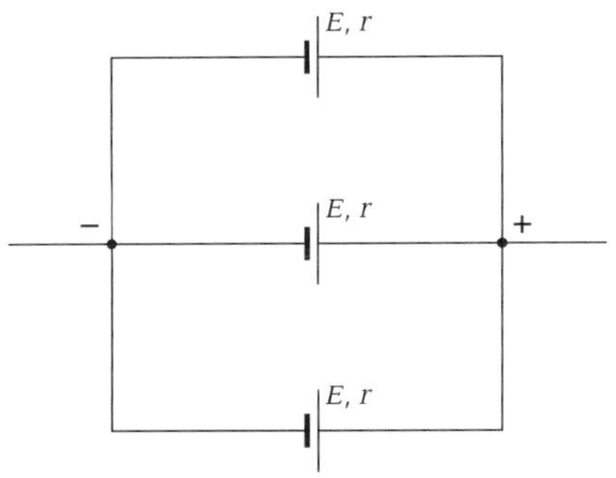

b Cells in parallel: total e.m.f. = E, combined internal resistance = $\frac{1}{3}r$

▲ **Figure 14.9.6** Cells in batteries

Cells in batteries

When cells are connected together to form a battery, they can be connected in series or in parallel.

In series:

- The individual e.m.f.s add up, so the voltage of the battery is higher.
- The internal resistance is high.
- The current produced is higher but the battery goes flat quicker.

In parallel:

- The voltage of the battery is the same as the voltage of an individual cell.
- The internal resistance is lower.
- The current produced is lower but the battery lasts longer.

Cells should not be left connected in parallel when not in use. A cell with a higher voltage will 'push against' a cell with a lower voltage, driving current through it the 'wrong way' and flattening the cells. For this reason, some types of cells, such as NiCd secondary cells, should never be connected in parallel.

Things to do

Make a lemon cell

- Insert two thin strips or rods of different materials into a lemon or other citrus fruit. Connect a voltmeter to these two electrodes using leads with crocodile clips.
- Electrodes that could be used are: zinc, copper, tin, lead, carbon, iron and aluminium.
- The best voltmeter range would be 0 to 2 volt, but 0 to 5 volt is more likely to be available.
- Complete a table of e.m.f. and polarity for each pair of electrodes and decide which pair gives the largest e.m.f.

Summary questions

1 State the difference between a cell and a battery.

2 What is a secondary cell?

3 Give the energy changes happening in a solar cell and a thermocouple.

D14.10 Alternating currents

DC or AC?

- Direct current or DC is the current supplied by batteries. It always flows from the positive terminal to the negative terminal.
- Alternating current or AC is current that changes direction many times a second. The magnitude of an AC current changes continuously from positive (current flowing one way), reaching a positive peak and then decreasing to zero. The current then becomes negative (current flowing the other way), reaching a negative peak then returning to zero. The current then becomes positive again.
- Much electrical equipment is designed to work on either DC or AC, not both.
- Some equipment (such as radios, phones, computers) is designed to work on DC (often using built-in rechargeable batteries), but can be plugged into the AC mains supply using an adaptor. Adaptors convert AC to DC and reduce the voltage to a lower value. If you connected such equipment directly to the mains supply, it would break and might be a fire risk too.

Comparing AC and DC

- AC electricity is easier and cheaper to generate than DC.
- When electricity is transmitted over long distances, it is easy to convert AC to very high voltages. This reduces the energy lost from the transmission wires. Transformers at the power station change the AC to a very high voltage. Transformers at electricity substations change it to the lower voltage used in our homes.
- It is easier to obtain varying voltages for AC than DC, using transformers. AC to DC adaptors contain transformers and rectifiers (see D16.1).
- The frequency of an AC supply is very precisely controlled. Electric motors and clocks can be synchronised to the frequency of the AC supply, so they run at a very precise speed.
- All heating equipment, such as electric cookers, kettles and irons work equally well on AC or DC so are connected directly to the mains supply.
- All modern electronic equipment requires DC, so these devices must use an AC to DC adaptor.

▶ **Figure 14.10.2** Transformers at an electricity substation

Objectives

By the end of this topic you will be able to:

- recognise that AC reverses direction rapidly
- draw graphs of current–time or voltage–time for AC and DC
- find the period and frequency from graphs of AC
- use $f = \frac{1}{T}$

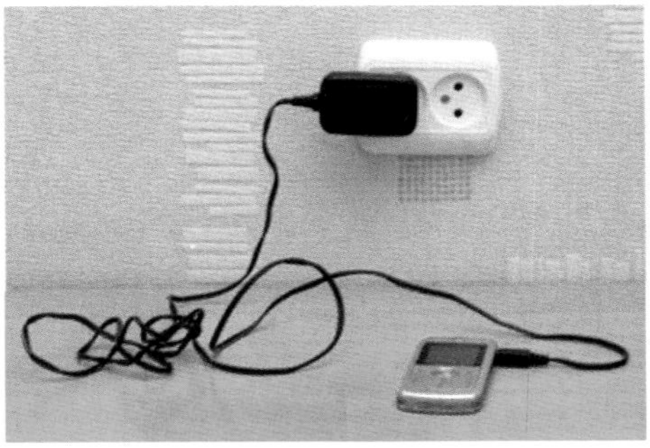

▲ **Figure 14.10.1** Most portable electrical devices, such as mobile phones, can work on rechargeable low voltage batteries. The recharging unit is a transformer fitted with a rectifier circuit, which converts the AC mains into a steady, low voltage DC supply.

! Key fact

Frequency

The frequency, f, of an alternating current is the number of complete cycles it goes through in 1 second.

A cycle includes current in both directions.

Period

The period, T, of an alternating current is the time for one complete cycle.

$$\text{frequency} = \frac{1}{\text{period}} \qquad f = \frac{1}{T}$$

Also $T = \frac{1}{f}$

Voltage of an AC supply

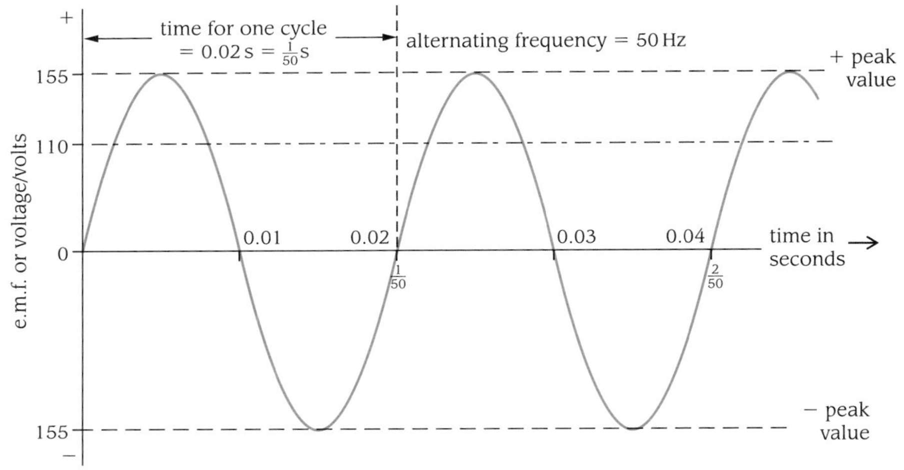

▲ **Figure 14.10.3** Alternating voltage

The graph in Figure 14.10.3 shows how the alternating voltage of the mains supply goes through a cycle, which takes it from zero to a peak voltage of +155 V, back through zero to another peak of −155 V and again back to zero.

The time for one complete cycle, called the period, T, is $\frac{1}{50}$ second or $\frac{1}{60}$ second depending upon which country you are in.

The graph of alternating current against time looks exactly the same but its peak values depend on the resistance of the circuit.

Peak and r.m.s. values

The peak value of an AC voltage or current is the maximum value (positive and negative) that the voltage or current reaches. The peak value in Figure 4.10.3 is 155 V.

The r.m.s. value is an *average* value. It is the size of the direct voltage or current that would transfer the same power to a device. The r.m.s. value is 0.71 of the peak value. All AC voltages are given as the r.m.s. value unless it is stated otherwise.

Worked example

The frequency of a mains supply is quoted as 60 Hz. Calculate the period of this supply.

$T = \frac{1}{f} = \frac{1}{60} = 0.0167\ \text{s}$

Worked example

An alternating signal has a period of 0.001 s.

a) What is its frequency?
b) How many times per second will the current change direction?

a) $f = \frac{1}{T} = \frac{1}{0.001\ \text{s}} = 1000\text{Hz}$

b) Because, in a full cycle of 0.001 s, the voltage changes polarity from + to − and back to +, i.e. twice, the number of direction changes of the current in 1 second will be 2000.

Summary questions

1 Sketch a diagram to show how voltage changes for an AC supply.

2 Name one appliance that would work equally well on AC or DC.

3 What is meant by the r.m.s. value of an AC supply?

Practice exam-style questions

1 In the circuit below, if ammeter A_1 reads 0.5 A, what will be the reading on ammeters A_2 and A_3?

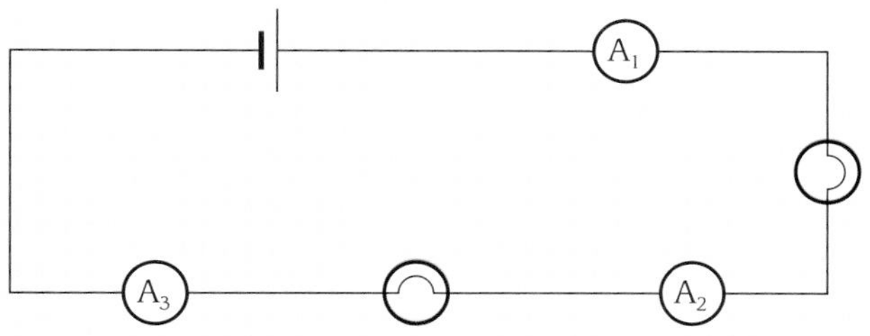

2 A current of 6 A is maintained through a conductor for 2 minutes. What is the total charge that flows through the conductor?

3 How long will it take for a total charge of 960 C to flow through a conductor if a steady current of 4 A is passed through it?

4 What current would circulate a total charge of 3600 coulombs round a circuit in 20 minutes?

5 The figure below shows the sizes and directions of the currents, at a junction J, in an electric circuit. Calculate the size and direction of the current recorded by the ammeter in the wire JX.

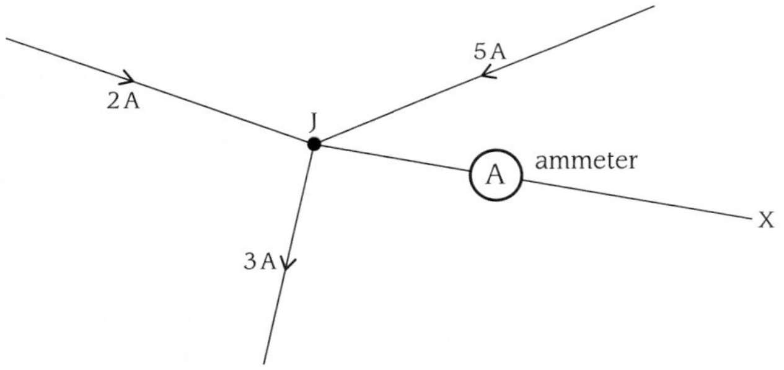

6 The figure below represents a junction in a continuous circuit. Ammeter A reads 4 A and ammeter B reads 1 A. Which of the following could be the reading shown by ammeter C?

i) 1 A **ii)** 3 A **iii)** 5 A

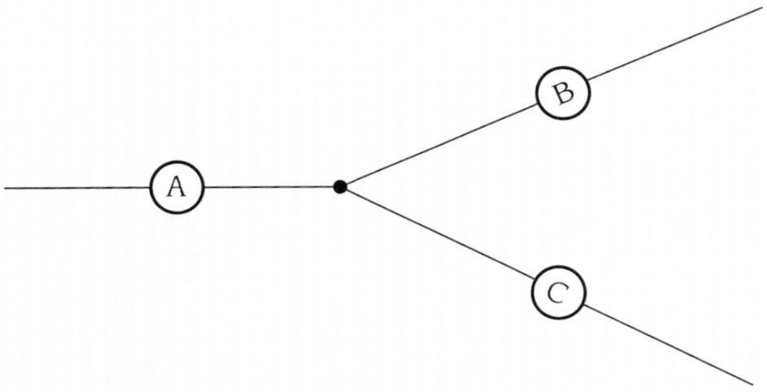

7 The figure below shows a completed electrical circuit containing an ammeter, a fuse, two lamps, a power supply, a resistor, a switch and a voltmeter. Draw the circuit diagram represented by the components.

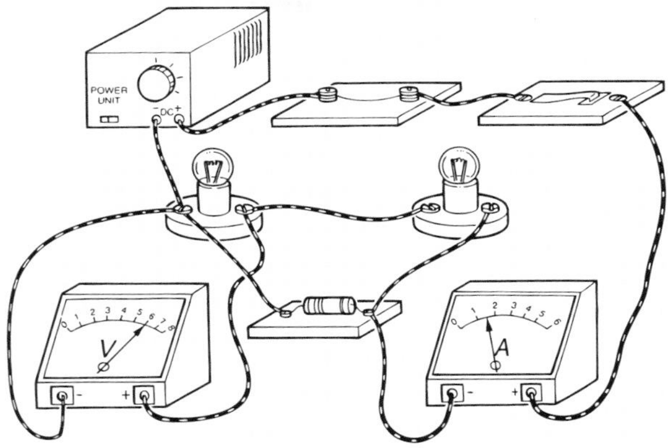

8 A conducting body carries a positive charge of 0.0048 C and is insulated from earth. When it is connected to earth by a wire, it becomes completely discharged. The average current during the discharge is 0.012 A.
a) How long would it take for the body to discharge completely if the current was a steady 0.012 A?
b) In which direction do electrons flow during the discharge?

9 If a 12 volt car battery circulated 500 coulombs round a circuit, how much energy did the battery supply?

10 If 660 joules of work was done by a battery in moving 110 coulombs of charge through a lamp, what was the voltage across the lamp?

11 A charge of 1200 coulombs flowing through a heater converted 14.40 kJ of energy into heat. If the current was 4.80 A, calculate the time for which the heater was switched on and the voltage across the heater.

12 What is the potential difference or voltage required to produce a current of 2.5 A through a conductor of resistance 12.5 Ω?

13 Three resistors of 8.0 ohms are connected in series with a 12 volt battery.
a) Draw the circuit diagram.
b) Calculate:
i) the current in the circuit
ii) the voltage across each resistor
iii) the charge circulated by the battery in 1 minute
iv) the energy converted into heat in each resistor in 1 minute.

14 A cell, a resistor and an ammeter are connected in series. If the voltage, V, of the cell is 1.5 V and the ammeter reads 0.25 A, calculate the resistance of the resistor in the circuit.

15 The mains voltage of 220 V supplies a current of 11.0 A to an electric kettle. What is the resistance of the kettle's heating element?

16 a) Describe, with the aid of a circuit diagram, how you would investigate the relationship between the current, *I*, in a filament lamp and the potential difference, *V*, applied between its terminals.

b) Sketch the graph you would expect to obtain from this investigation if *I* were plotted against *V*.

c) What conclusion can be drawn from the graph about the resistance of a filament lamp as it gets hotter?

17 A sealed box with two terminals may contain one of the following: a wire coil, a filament lamp or a diode.

a) Draw a circuit diagram to show how you would measure the *I–V* characteristic of the device in the box.

b) Briefly describe the experiment you would perform to obtain the *I–V* characteristic.

c) Sketch the *I–V* graphs you would expect to obtain for each device. Label your sketches clearly.

18 Two resistors of 560 Ω resistance are connected in series with a supply of 336 V. An additional unknown resistor is then connected in parallel across the first of the two 560 Ω resistors. If the voltage across the second 560 Ω resistor rises to 280 V, find the value of the unknown resistor.

The following steps will help you do this calculation:

a) Find the current through the second resistor.

b) Find the voltage across the parallel pair of resistors.

c) Find the total resistance of the parallel pair.

d) Rearrange the formula

$$\frac{1}{R_{\text{Total}}} = \frac{1}{R_1} + \frac{1}{R_2}$$

to calculate R_2, the unknown resistance.

19 The figure below shows four combinations of resistors. Find the total or equivalent resistance of each combination.

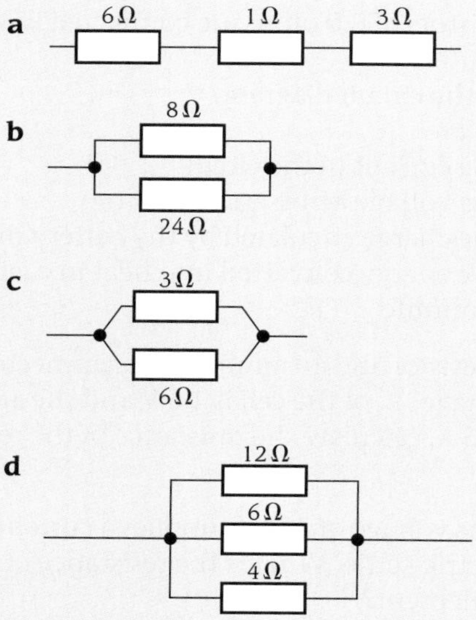

20 The figure below shows two combinations of resistors in a mixture of series and parallel connections. Calculate the equivalent resistance of each combination.

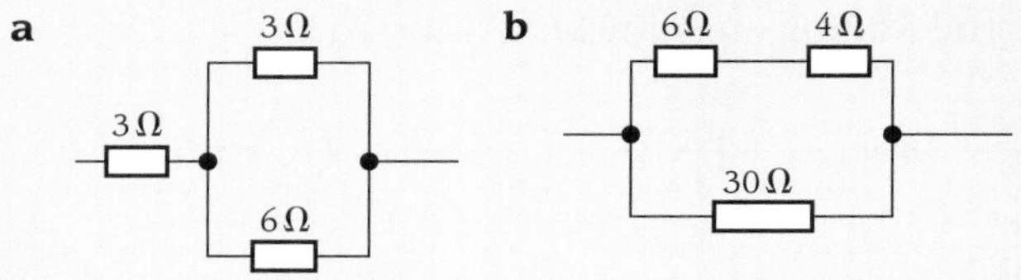

21 The figure below shows how three resistors, P, Q and R are connected together. If the values of their resistances are 2 Ω, 3 Ω and 4 Ω, find which resistor should have which resistance for the combination shown to have:

a) the minimum resistance

b) the maximum resistance.

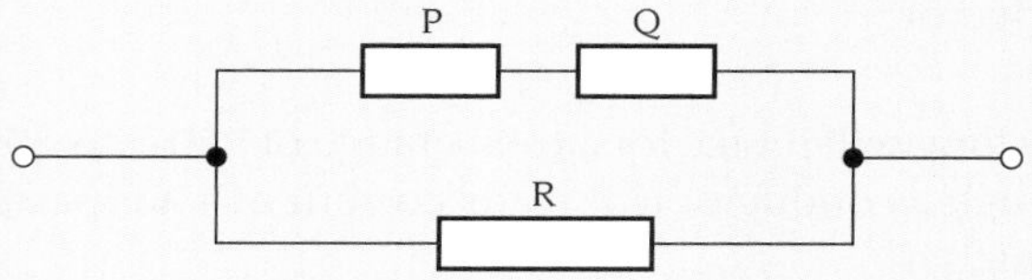

22 Three resistors of values 2 Ω, 3 Ω and 5 Ω are connected in series with a battery of voltage 6.0 V. Calculate the current through each of the resistors, and the current through the battery.

23 Calculate the reading of each of the ammeters in the circuit below.

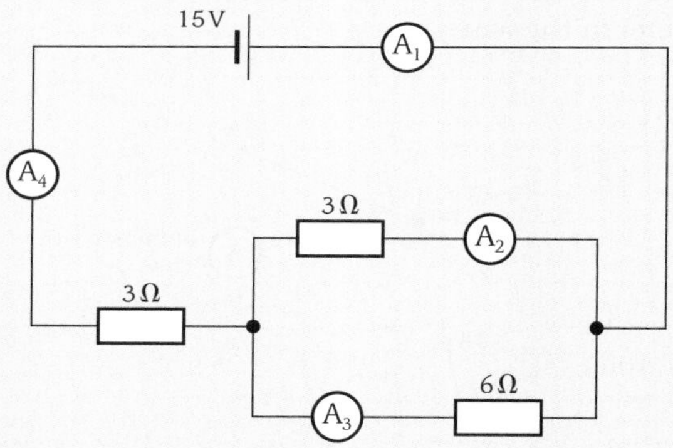

24 The figure below shows a series circuit.

a) If voltmeter V_1 reads 4 V, what is the reading of ammeter A_1?

b) If X = 3 Ω, what is the reading of voltmeter V_2?

c) If voltmeter V_4 reads 12 V, what is the value of Y?

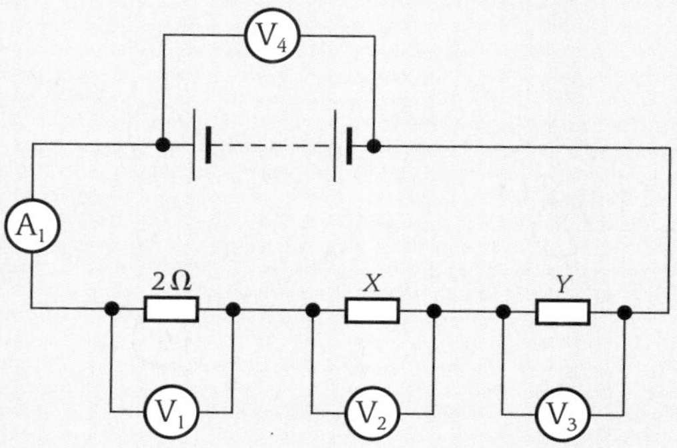

25 The circuit below contains three identical resistors connected in parallel and a 2 volt power supply.

a) What is the p.d. across each resistor?

b) If there is a current of 0.5 A in one resistor, what current will be taken from the power supply?

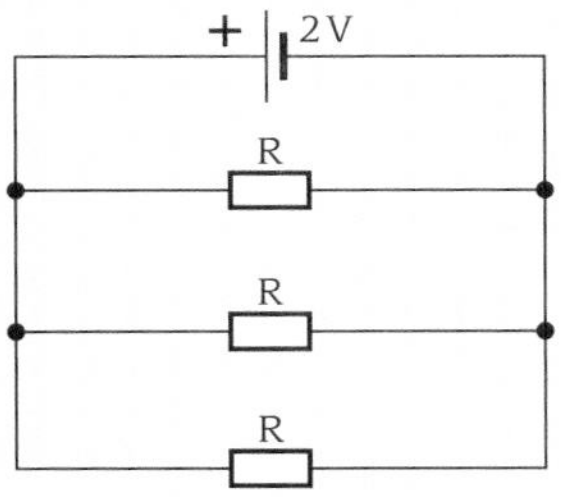

26 What is meant by the resistance of an electrical component? Describe an experiment to measure the resistance of a length of resistance wire. Your account should include a circuit diagram, a list of measurements you would make and a clear statement of how these measurements would be used to calculate the final result.

27 The figure below represents an electrical circuit containing a battery, an ammeter of negligible resistance and three resistors with the resistances shown.

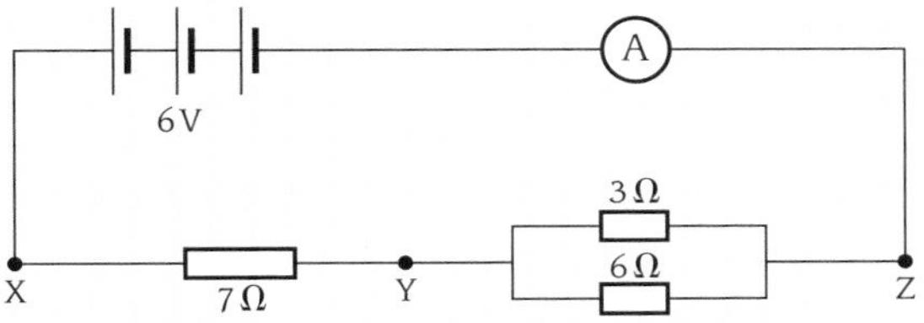

a) What is the resistance of the parallel combination of resistors between Y and Z?

b) What is the resistance of the circuit between X and Z?

c) Assuming that the battery has negligible internal resistance, what reading would you expect on the ammeter?

d) What is the potential difference between X and Y?

e) What is the current in the 3 Ω resistor?

28 The graph below shows the p.d. across a filament lamp plotted against the current through the lamp.

a) Draw a labelled circuit diagram of the apparatus you would use to obtain such a set of readings.

b) Explain why the graph indicates that the filament of the bulb does not obey Ohm's law.

c) What can be deduced from the graph about the resistance of the filament of the bulb?

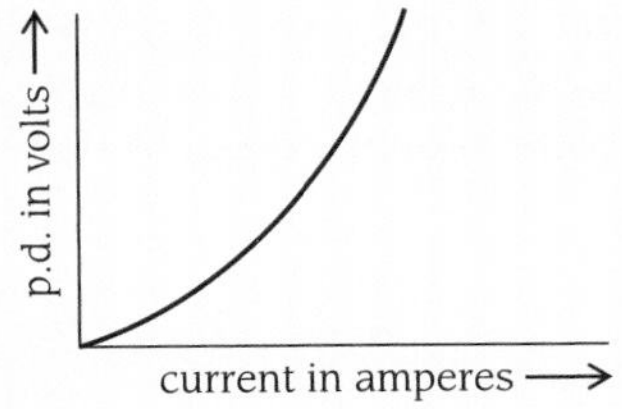

29 Some mains electricity supplies are described by the following data:
Frequency = 50 Hz
r.m.s. voltage = 220 V

a) Calculate the period for ONE cycle of this supply.

b) Calculate the peak voltage reached.

c) How many times does the voltage reach ± the peak value every second?

30 Two resistors, one of resistance 6.0 ohm and the other of unknown resistance, are connected in parallel. This combination is then placed in a circuit and the current passing into the combination is measured for various potential differences across the combination. The results of the experiment are given in the table.

Potential difference/V	1.5	3.0	4.5	6.0	7.5
Current/A	0.37	0.75	1.12	1.50	1.90

a) Draw a labelled diagram of the circuit you would use to perform the experiment.

b) Plot a graph of current against potential difference.

c) From the graph, calculate the total resistance of the combination of resistors, explaining clearly how the graph was used.

d) Using the resistance of the combination obtained in **c)**, calculate a value for the unknown resistance.

31 By copying and completing the table below, show that you understand the difference between a dry cell that would be suitable for using in a torch and a battery suitable for use in a car.

Description	Dry cell	Car battery
Typical voltage of each cell		
Typical voltage of whole battery		
Typical size of current available from battery in amperes		
Is it rechargeable?		
What is the positive electrode made of?		
What is the negative electrode made of?		

32 A car battery is connected to a starter motor and a current of 400 A flows. While the starter motor is being operated, the battery terminal voltage falls from 12.0 V to 8.0 V and the voltage across the starter motor terminals is also only 8.0 V.

a) Calculate the resistance of the wire of the coils in the starter motor.

b) The car battery is connected to the windscreen wiper motor and a current of 6.0 A flows. Calculate the voltage across the terminals of the battery when connected to the windscreen wiper motor.

33 a) Copy this diagram of a dry cell and label it.

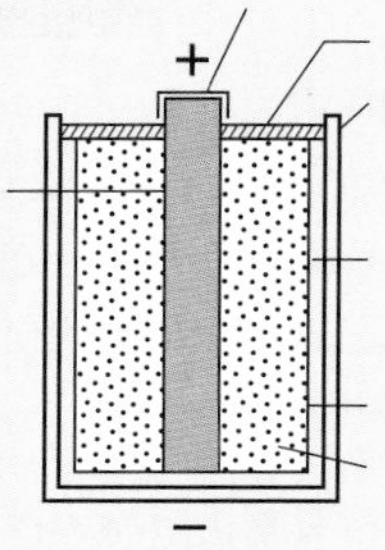

b) State what you understand by polarisation and say how it is reduced in a dry cell.

34 An electric circuit contains a lamp, a cell, a rheostat, two ammeters and two voltmeters, as shown in the figure below.

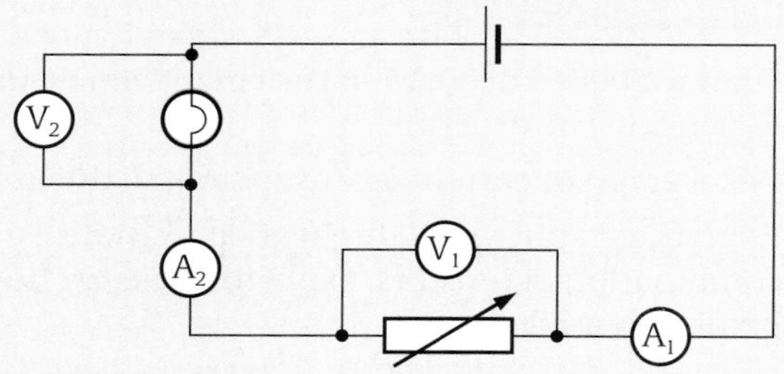

a) How will the readings of ammeters A_1 and A_2 compare? Explain.

b) What difference will it make to the reading of A_1 if the resistance of the rheostat is increased? Why?

c) What difference will it make to the reading of V_1 if the resistance of the rheostat is increased? Why? (It may be assumed that the voltmeters draw negligible current and that the ammeters have negligible resistances.)

d) What is the resistance of the lamp when A_2 reads 0.3 A and V_2 reads 1.5 V?

35 a) Draw a labelled circuit diagram showing how you would recharge a car battery.

b) When fully charged, a car battery can deliver 5 A at 12 V for 16 hours before it becomes fully discharged. Calculate, in kW h, the energy stored when the battery is fully charged.

c) If the battery can undergo 100 complete charge–discharge cycles before it fails, calculate in kW h the total energy it can supply during its 'lifetime'.

36 a) Explain why it is usual for electricity to be distributed around a country as an **alternating** supply.

b) Describe some advantages of using alternating electricity.

37 The frequency of a mains supply is 50 Hz.

a) What is the time period of a single cycle of the alternating current?

b) How many times does the current change direction in 1 second?

c) How many complete cycles occur in 1 minute?

38 The mains supply to a factory is quoted as 220 volts. What is the maximum or peak voltage that occurs during each cycle of this supply?

39 a) Draw a voltage against time waveform for the electricity supply to a Caribbean home, which is quoted as 110 volts, 50 Hz. Show two complete cycles.

b) Mark on your graph:

i) the peak values of the voltage

ii) the time period of the voltage variation.

40 The graph below shows the alternating voltage output from a generator.

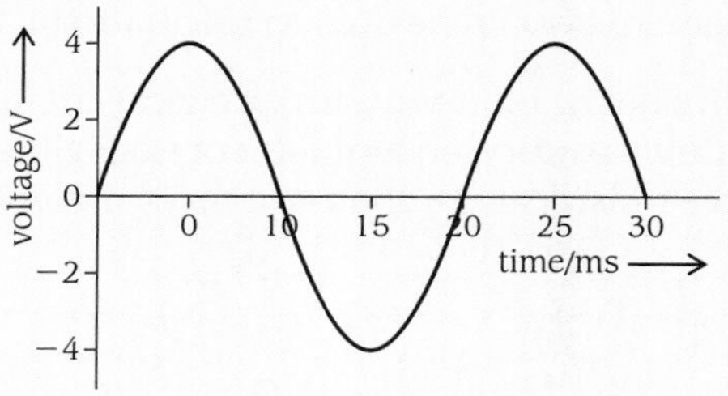

a) From the graph, read the value of the peak voltage.

b) Calculate the r.m.s. value of the voltage.

c) From the graph, find the period of the alternating voltage.

d) Calculate the frequency of this supply.

41 a) A current of 5 mA is used to charge a rechargeable cell. If the current flows for 10 minutes how much charge will the current transfer?

b) Rechargeable batteries usually give the charge they store in milliampere hours (mA h) where 1 mA h is the charge transferred by a current of 1 mA flowing for 1 hour.

i) How many coulombs (C) is equivalent to 1 mA h?

ii) A rechargeable battery holds 1200 mA h of charge. Assuming the charging process were 100% efficient, how long would it take for the 5 mA current to fully charge the battery?

iii) Assuming 100% efficiency, what size charging current would be needed to fully charge the battery in 12 hours?

c) Rechargeable batteries get warm while they are charging. What effect do you think this has on the charging time? Explain why.

D15 Using electricity

Calculating the energy conversion in an electrical circuit can tell us how much heat an electric fire will supply, how much work an electric motor will do in a certain time or even the kinetic energy gained by an electron in a cathode ray tube. In this chapter we see how electricity makes machines work and does work for us.

D15.1 Electrical energy and power

Objectives

By the end of this topic you will be able to:

- understand the relationship between energy and power:

$$\text{power} = \frac{\text{energy}}{\text{time}} \qquad P = \frac{E}{t}$$

- recall and use the equations: $P = VI$ and $P = I^2R$ to solve problems.

The heating effect of an electric current

Whenever a current flows through a wire, there is a heating effect. It is this heating effect that makes the heaters in electric kettles, irons or hairdryers work and that causes some electrical equipment to feel warm when it is switched on. The equipment in Figure 15.1.1 can be used to investigate the factors that affect the heat produced. The temperature rise of the water is directly proportional to the heat supplied by the wire, provided that no heat is lost to the surroundings.

Measurements of the water temperature can be taken as the time of heating, the size of the current and the length of the wire are changed. Values can be plotted on graphs of temperature rise against the quantity being changed. Remember: only change one factor at once, keeping others constant.

- Keeping the current and the length of wire constant shows that:
  temperature rise is directly proportional to time for which current flows.
- Keeping time and length of wire constant shows that:
  temperature rise is directly proportional to the magnitude of the current.
- Keeping current and time constant shows that:
  temperature rise is directly proportional to the length of resistance wire.
- For a wire of uniform cross-sectional area, the resistance of the wire is directly proportional to its length. So:
  the heating effect of a current flowing in a wire is directly proportional to the resistance of the wire.

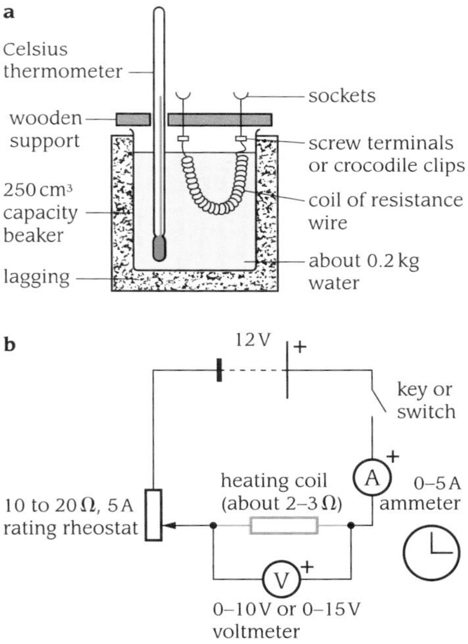

▲ **Figure 15.1.1** Investigation of the heating effect of an electric current

How does the heating effect depend on resistance?

- The same current must flow for the same time through several coils of different resistances. Use the same beaker refilled four times with the same mass of cold water (about 0.2 kg) and use each of the coils in turn.
- Use the rheostat to adjust the current to exactly the same value each time. The maximum convenient current should be used, say 3.5 A or 4.0 A.
- Record the initial and final temperatures for each coil and calculate the temperature rise ΔT.
- Plot a graph of temperature rise against length of wire in the coil.

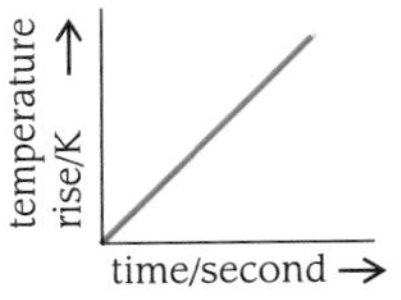

initial temperature θ_1 = °C constant current = A		
t in minute	θ_2/°C	$\Delta\theta$/K
2		
4		
6		
8		
10		

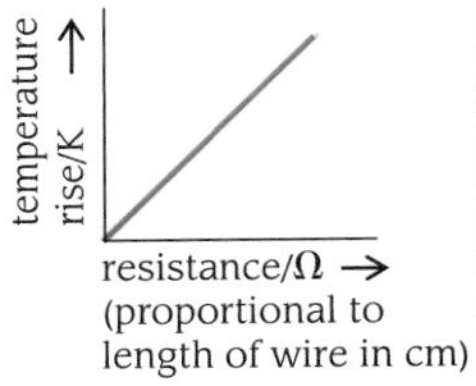

constant current = A constant time = s			
length of wire in cm	θ_1/°C	θ_2/°C	$\Delta\theta$/K
10			
20			
30			
40			

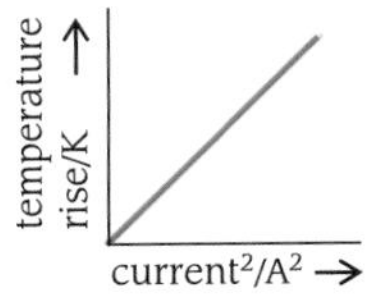

constant time = s				
I/A	I^2/A²	θ_1/°C	θ_2/°C	$\Delta\theta$/K
1.0				
2.0				
3.0				
4.0				

▲ **Figure 15.1.2** Factors affecting the heating effect

Key fact

The unit of power is the **watt (W)**.
1 watt = 1 joule per second.

Energy and power equations

Energy	Power
$E = Pt$	$P = \frac{E}{t} = \frac{W}{t}$
$E = I^2Rt$	$P = I^2R$
$E = IVT$	$P = IV$
$E = QV$	
$E = \frac{V^2}{R}t$	$P = \frac{V^2}{R}$

The heat produced is directly proportional to the temperature rise, and the resistance of the wire is directly proportional to its length. So, the heat produced is directly proportional to the resistance of the coil when the current and the time are the same.

Electrical energy and power

When an electric current flows through a resistance wire, the wire gets warm. Some of the electrical energy transferred from the power supply by the current is converted to heat energy. The resistance wire in electric heaters is a device for converting electrical energy into heat energy. Other devices convert electrical energy into sound energy, or light energy, or mechanical energy. A powerful device is one that rapidly converts electrical energy into other forms. So a powerful heater gives out more heat in any given time than a less powerful heater, a powerful light gives out more light than a less powerful light and so on.

Power is the rate of energy conversion or the rate of doing work.

$$\text{power} = \frac{\text{energy}}{\text{time}} \text{ or } \frac{\text{work}}{\text{time}} \quad P = \frac{E}{t} \text{ or } P = \frac{W}{t}$$

Worked example

Energy and power

A 5 kW immersion heater is used to heat water for a bath. If the heater heats the water for 40 minutes, how much electrical energy is converted into heat energy?

$P = 5\,\text{kW} = 5 \times 10^3\,\text{W}$
$t = 40\text{ minutes} = 40 \times 60\,\text{s}$
$t = 2400\,\text{s}$
$E = Pt$
$E = 5 \times 10^3\,\text{W} \times 2400\,\text{s}$
$E = 1.2 \times 10^7\,\text{J} = 12\,\text{MJ}$

Electrical energy and power equations

More equations can be used when calculating electrical energy or power. Starting from $P = \frac{E}{t}$, we know (from D14.4) that $E = QV$ and (from D14.3) that $Q = It$ so:

$$P = \frac{E}{t} = \frac{QV}{t} = \frac{ItV}{t} = IV$$

The equation $P = IV$ is useful because it can be used to calculate the current through a device of known 'wattage', such as a 1200 W kettle when it is connected to the mains voltage. Knowing the current enables the correct size fuse to be fitted.

Alternatively we can write equations for energy converted, *E*, in terms of the resistance *R*.

Start from $E = Pt = IVt$.

We know $R = \frac{V}{I}$ (from D14.6). Rearranging gives $V = IR$ and $I = \frac{V}{R}$.

Putting these into $E = IVt$, gives $E = \frac{V^2}{R}t$ and $E = I^2Rt$.

Worked example

Calculating electrical energy converted

If a current of 4.0 A is passed through a thin cable for 1.0 hours and its resistance is 20 Ω, how much electrical energy will be converted to heat energy in the cable?

$t = 1.0 \times 60 \times 60\,\text{s} = 3600\,\text{s}$

Using electrical energy converted, $E = I^2Rt$

$E = (4.0)^2 \times 20 \times 3600 = 1.15 \times 10^6\,\text{J} = 1.15\,\text{MJ}$

Calculating electrical energy conversions

Electrical energy into mechanical energy

Electric motors convert electrical energy into mechanical energy. If an electric motor is used to lift a known mass, m, through a given height, h, this can be used to calculate the efficiency of the electric motor.

The electrical energy supplied to the motor, $E = Pt = IVt$

The energy output of the motor is the work done to lift the mass. This can be calculated from:

work done = force × distance moved in the direction of the force, so

work done, W = weight × height lifted $= mgh$

$$\text{The efficiency of the motor} = \frac{\text{mechanical work output}}{\text{electrical energy input}} \times 100\%$$

Worked example

The efficiency of an electric motor

An electric motor, rated at 500 W, was used to raise a load of mass 16.0 kg a vertical height of 125 m.

If it took the motor 50 s to raise the load, calculate (as a percentage) how efficient the motor was in converting electrical energy into mechanical energy. ($g = 10\,\text{N kg}^{-1}$)

The mechanical work done by the motor is given by mgh.

$W = mgh$

$= 16.0 \times 10 \times 125 = 2.00 \times 10^4\,\text{J}$

The electrical energy supplied to the motor is given by Pt.

$E = Pt$

$= 500 \times 50.0 = 2.50 \times 10^4\,\text{J}$

The efficiency of energy conversion, as a percentage is

$$\text{efficiency} = \frac{\text{mechanical work output}}{\text{electrical energy input}} \times 100\%$$

$$\text{efficiency} = \frac{2.00 \times 10^4}{2.50 \times 10^4} \times 100 = 80.0\%$$

Worked example

Current and power

An electric fire has an element rated at a power of 1 kW. Calculate the current that will flow through the element when it is connected to the 110 V mains supply.

Using $I = \frac{P}{V}$ or, in units,

$$\text{amps} = \frac{\text{watts}}{\text{volts}}$$

$$I = \frac{1000}{110} = 9.09\,\text{A}$$

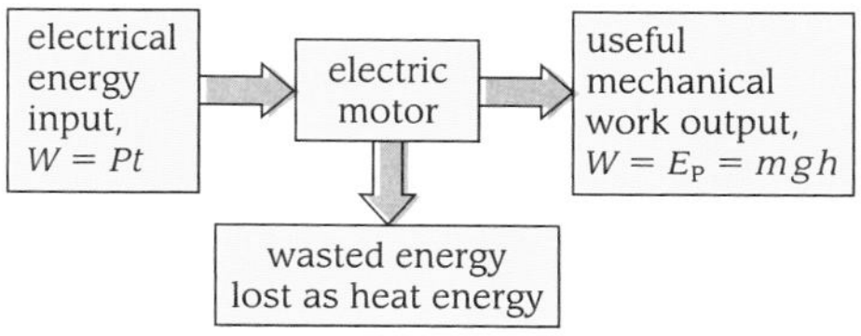

▲ **Figure 15.1.3** Converting electrical energy into mechanical energy

Worked example

A lift motor connected to a mains supply of 110 V has a current of 20 A flowing through it. If the motor is 60% efficient and takes 12 s to raise the lift and its passengers a height of 2.5 m, calculate the mass of the lift and its passengers. ($g = 10\,\text{N kg}^{-1}$)

Electrical energy supplied,

$E = IVt = 26\,400$

If this motor is 60% efficient, 60% of this energy is used to raise the lift $= 26\,400 \times 0.6 = 15\,840\,\text{J}$

This is the work done, W.

W = weight × height lifted $= mgh$

$$\text{so } m = \frac{W}{gh} = \frac{15\,840}{10 \times 2.5}$$

$= 633.6\,\text{kg}$

So, the mass of the lift and its passengers is 634 kg (3 s.f.).

Electrical energy into heat energy

Wherever an electric current flows through a resistor, electrical energy will be converted to heat energy. When the heat is used to heat something like a kettle full of water we can calculate the heat energy produced using the equation:

$E_H = mc\Delta T$ (See B8.6.)

The energy equation for an electric heater is:

electrical energy input → heat energy gained by an object + heat energy lost

$Pt = mc\Delta T +$ heat energy lost

Worked example

Conversion into heat energy

When an electric kettle is connected to the 110 V mains supply, the current through it is 20 A. If the mass of water is 2.0 kg and its temperature is 20 °C, calculate the temperature of the water after 1 minute.

Assume no heat is lost.
The specific heat capacity of water, $c = 4.2\,\text{kJ}\,\text{kg}^{-1}\,\text{K}^{-1}$.
$E = IVt = mc\Delta T$
where ΔT is the rise in temperature of the water that is to be found.
Electrical energy input, E is:
$IVt = 20 \times 110 \times 60 = 1.32 \times 10^5\,\text{J}$
(where t must be in seconds).
Heat energy gained, E_H is:
$mc\Delta T = 2.0 \times 4.2 \times 10^3 \times \Delta T$
$1.32 \times 10^5\,\text{J} = 8.4 \times 10^3\,\Delta T$
$\therefore\ \Delta T = 15.7\,°\text{C}$
The water temperature will reach 20 °C + 15.7 °C = 35.7 °C.

Summary questions

1 What happens to the heating effect when the current through a wire increases?

2 Give a definition of power.

3 Give an equation relating electrical power to voltage and current.

4 A voltage of 12 V causes a current of 4 A to flow for 10 s. How much energy is transferred?

D15.2 Electricity at home

The mains supply to houses

The electricity supplied to our homes has:

- an alternating frequency of 50 or 60 hertz, i.e. the alternating current flows in each direction 50 or 60 times every second
- a peak voltage of ±155 V (or 311 V in a few places)
- an r.m.s. ('average') voltage of 110 V (or 220 V).

Advantages of an AC supply at home

- The frequency of the supply is very precisely controlled, so we can use AC electric motors that synchronise their rotation to the mains frequency. This gives them a very accurate speed. Such motors are sometimes used in electric clocks.
- The 110 V supply can be transformed down to a low, safe voltage, say 12 V or 5 V, for operating toys, electric bells and electronic devices like computers and for charging batteries.

Disadvantages of an AC supply at home

- Some appliances and electronic devices require a DC supply. Examples include electronic equipment such as radios, computers and battery chargers. These devices are fitted with a circuit called a rectifier circuit, which converts the alternating supply into a direct one. However, all electric heating appliances including kettles, cookers and irons would work equally well on an AC or DC supply.
- Many devices requiring a DC supply will be damaged if connected to AC.

Colour codes for wires in the home

Figure 15.2.1 shows the colour code for the separate wires inside a cable used to connect an appliance to a power socket at home, or for the wires inside the cables that connect light switches and sockets to the fuse or circuit-breaker box in your home.

The international colour code is given in the table. Old appliances may still have wires colour-coded red (live), black (neutral) and green (earth).

▼ The international colour code for wires in a cable

Wire	Colour code
live	brown
neutral	blue
earth	green/yellow stripe

▼ Comparing supply voltages

110 V	220 V
• Used for all low power circuits e.g. lights, T.V. and most domestic equipment	• Used for high-power equipment, e.g. air conditioning and washing machines
• Safer than 220 V	• More dangerous
• $P = I \times 110\text{V}$	• $P = I \times 220\text{V}$
• Higher current for same power	• Lower currents for same power
• Need thicker wires for same power	• Can use thinner wires for same power
• Plugs and sockets with two flat pins and sometimes a round earth pin	• Plugs and sockets with three rectangular pins

Why are three wires often used?

All appliances need two wires to form a complete circuit from the supply through the appliance and back to the supply.

- The live wire (brown) delivers the power at the high voltage, which alternates between r.m.s. values of +110 V and −110 V.
- The live wire is therefore the dangerous one, capable of giving a serious electric shock.

Objectives

By the end of this topic you will be able to:

- understand the reasons for parallel connection of domestic appliances
- explain the purpose of a fuse or circuit-breaker and state where it should be connected
- select a fuse or circuit-breaker of suitable rating for a particular appliance or circuit
- explain the purpose of the earth wire and show how it is connected to appliances
- recall the international colour code for cable insulation
- connect wires to 110 V and 220 V plugs
- explain the adverse effects of connecting appliances to incorrect or fluctuating voltage supplies
- understand the relationship between the energy units: joules and kilowatt hours
- calculate the cost of electrical energy.

▲ **Figure 15.2.1** Mains cable

- Switches and fuses in circuits must be fitted in the live wire so that switching off disconnects the high voltage from an appliance.
- The second, neutral wire (blue) completes the circuit with the power supply, allowing current to flow in a closed circuit.
- The third wire (green/yellow) is the earth wire, which is a safety device used in some circuits.

Earth wires

The earth wire is the one coloured yellow and green. Its purpose is to protect people from electrocution if there is a fault in an appliance. The earth wire is connected to the metal case of appliances such as washing machines or fridges. It forms a low resistance path between the metal case and earth. If a fault in the appliance causes a live wire inside the appliance to touch the case, the case will become 'live'. Without the earth wire, a person touching the case would be electrocuted, which might be fatal. With the earth wire, a high current flows through the earth wire to earth. This should blow the fuse in the live wire, disconnecting the appliance from the mains supply.

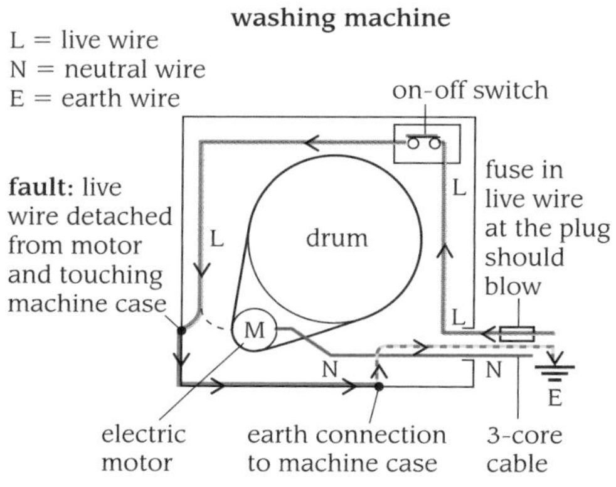

The earth wire protects any person who touches the machine. The circuit is completed from the loose live wire through the machine case and the earth wire.
The large current should blow the fuse and cut off the supply. The arrows show the path of the circuit.

▲ **Figure 15.2.2** Protection by an earth wire

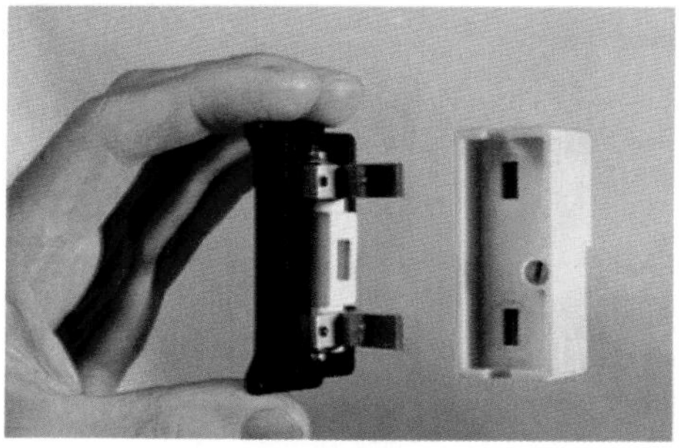

▲ **Figure 15.2.3** Cartridge fuse

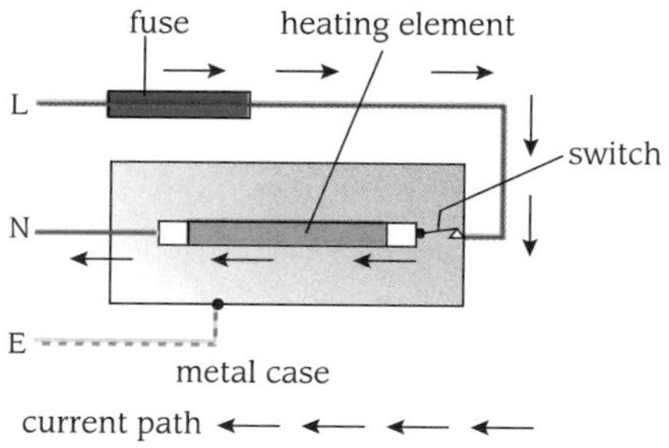

▲ **Figure 15.2.4** The position of a fuse in a circuit

The 'other end' of an earth wire is connected either to the metal protective casing of the incoming mains supply cable, or to a metal water pipe or a copper stake going into the ground.

It is dangerous to use 2-core cables for an appliance needing an earth connection. They must be connected to a 3-pin plug and fuse.

Fuses and circuit breakers

Fuses

A fuse is a safety device that disconnects an appliance if a fault in the appliance causes the current flowing to become too large. This is important because a current that is too large may cause the appliance to overheat, starting a fire. The fuse contains a piece of very thin wire that melts, or 'blows', when too much current flows through it, so breaking the circuit.

Fuses are labelled in amps, giving the size current that can flow without them melting. It is important to choose the right size fuse. The fuse should always be the smallest size that allows the operating current of the appliance to flow. For example, for an operating current of 2 A you would choose a 3 A fuse, not a 5 A fuse.

Worked example

Fuses come with ratings 3 A, 5 A, 15 A. Which fuse would you use for a 500 W food mixer connected to a 110 V mains supply?

The current can be found from $P = IV$, so $I = 500/110 = 4.5$ A.
So a 5 A fuse is the correct fuse to use.

Circuit breakers

A fuse has to be replaced each time it 'blows'. Circuit breakers are devices that disconnect the supply when a rated current is exceeded. They can be reset when a fault has been investigated and repaired. Earth leakage circuit breakers (e.l.c.b.) or residual current devices (RCD) also do the same job as fuses, but they measure the current in the live and neutral wires. Any difference means some current must be flowing to earth either through the earth wire, or through something else. If the difference is more than about 25 mA, the circuit breaker opens a 'trip switch'. This stops the current flowing before it flows for long enough to harm a person. The switch can then be reset after the fault has been repaired. So a circuit breaker does not have to be replaced each time it 'trips'.

Key fact

Fuses and circuit breakers

- To 'fuse' means to melt.
- Fuses or circuit breakers are fitted in all circuits to prevent a dangerously large current from flowing.
- A fuse is a short fine piece of wire with a fairly low melting point, which becomes hot and melts as soon as the current through it exceeds its rated value.
- A melted or 'blown' fuse stops the current like a switch, and protects against the fire risk caused by the heat in an overloaded cable or appliance.
- A miniature circuit breaker (m.c.b.) is a modern alternative to fuses and has several advantages.
- An m.c.b. can be reset quickly by a switch or button as there is no melted wire to replace.
- More importantly, it can break an overloaded circuit in less than 0.01 s, which is much less time than it takes for a fuse wire to melt.

Double insulation

Many appliances such as electric drills can be operated safely without an earth wire because they are double insulated. They are marked with the symbol ⧈. They are designed so that the appliance is totally enclosed in a plastic case with no direct electrical connections between the inside and the outside. So all metal screws, handles and attachments are insulated from wires and metal parts inside by plastic or rubber parts.

Key fact

Cars need fuses too!

- All circuits, except the starter motor's high-current circuit, are protected by a fuse.
- A typical fuse value is 30 A.
- The high-current values of the fuses are necessary because the circuits operate on only 12 volts.
- For example, a single headlamp requires a current of over 4 A to produce 50 W of power.
- The fuses are very necessary because of the fire risk in a car. A worn or loose wire may cause a short circuit and result in a fire.

Connecting a wire to a power plug

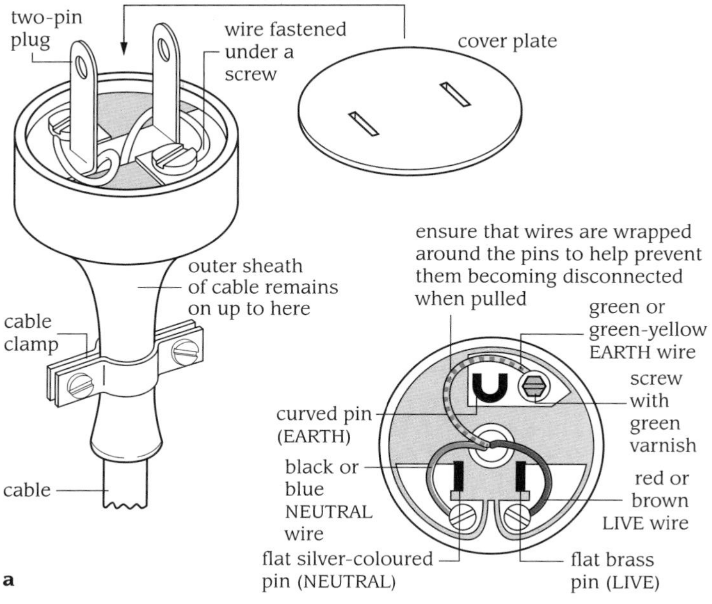

b Plan view of three-pin plug with earth connection

▲ **Figure 15.2.5** Wiring a 2-pin plug

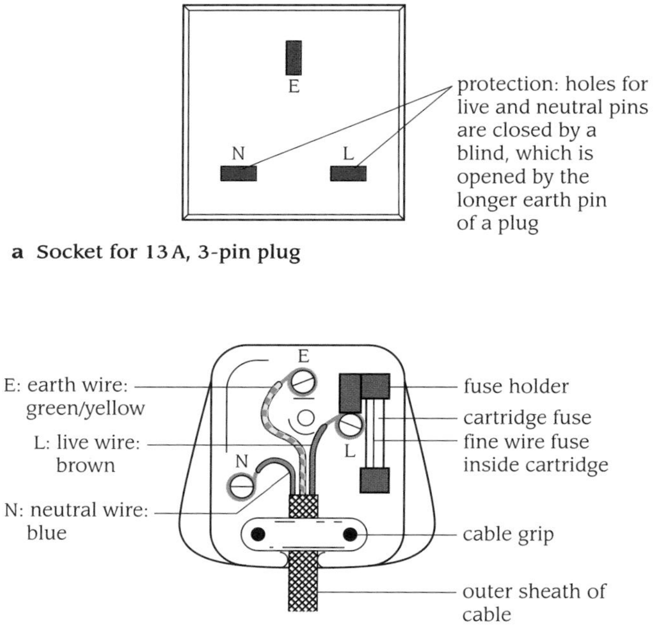

a Socket for 13 A, 3-pin plug

b Wiring a 13 A, 3-pin plug

▲ **Figure 15.2.6** Diagram of a 13 A socket and plug

- Remove the cover from the plug and estimate the length of wire needed to reach the screws.

Remember that the outer sheath of the cable must be firmly held by the cable grip and care should be taken not to remove too much of the outer sheath.

- Cut away the outer sheath being careful not to cut into the coloured insulation on the inner wires.
- Remove one or two centimetres of the coloured insulation from each of the inner wires.

Be careful not to cut off any of the fine strands of wire and leave enough insulation on each wire to protect it right up to the connector.

- Twist the fine strands in each wire together so that no stray strands are left loose inside the plug.
- If the plug has wrap-round screw terminals, bend the end of each wire clockwise round in the direction of tightening of the screw.
- Fit the wires to the correct terminals according to the colour code.
- Tighten the cable-grip and test to see that the cable will not pull out.
- Replace the cover of the plug.

Household wiring

Electricity comes into a home through one mains cable. This passes through a mains fuse, then an electricity meter, then into a distribution unit. In the distribution unit the current from the incoming mains cable is distributed to all the different circuits around the house: lighting circuits, **ring main** circuit for sockets, circuit to electric cooker, circuit to electric shower and so on. All these circuits are in parallel so that, for example, a fault in the electric cooker doesn't stop the lights working.

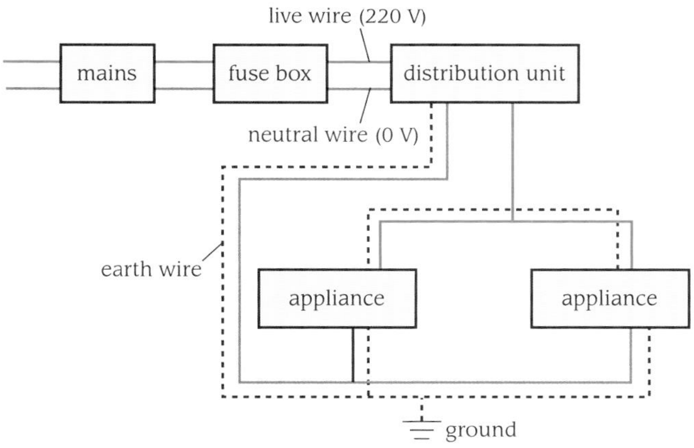

▲ **Figure 15.2.7** A house wiring diagram

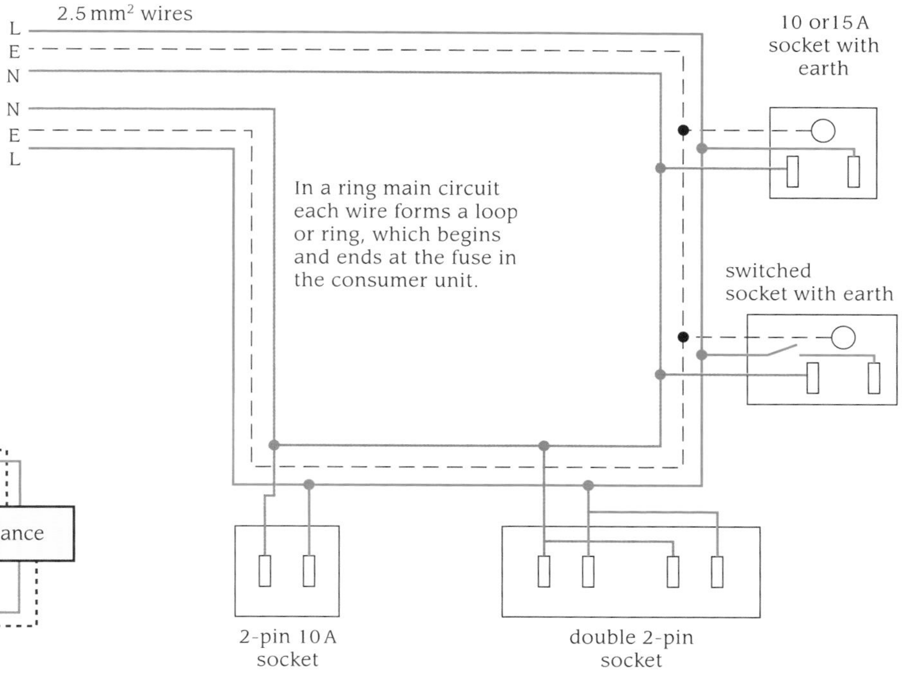

▲ **Figure 15.2.8** Power sockets on a ring main circuit

The distribution unit contains a separate fuse for each of the circuits around the house, and also a mains switch that can switch off all the circuits in the house. This is a double-pole switch, breaking the connection in both the live wire and the neutral wire.

The electricity meter

The meter records the electrical energy converted in the whole house in kilowatt hours (kW h). It may have either dials or a digital read-out.

Home lighting and power circuits

Lighting circuits

Figure 15.2.9 shows the important differences between the lighting and power socket circuits in a home. The current in a lighting circuit is quite low, only $\frac{1}{2}$ ampere for each 60 W lamp. So a single twin cable can supply all the lights in a house. In some houses, one cable supplies the upstairs lights and another supplies the downstairs ones. Each lamp is connected in parallel using a junction box at a convenient point along the cable. A separate spur cable supplies each lamp via a single-pole switch connected in the live wire.

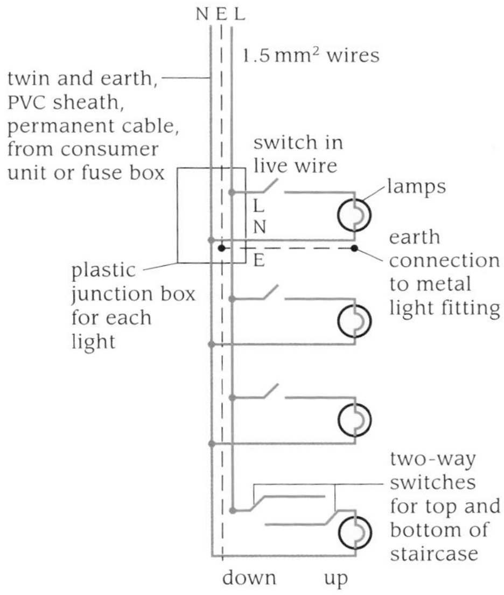

▲ **Figure 15.2.9** House lighting circuits

Parallel connection

All appliances are connected in parallel to the mains supply at home. This ensures that:

- each appliance is connected to the full 110 V mains supply voltage.
- each appliance can have a separate on/off switch.
- if one appliance is faulty or disconnected, all the other appliances can still work.
- large currents can be supplied to high-powered equipment like electric cookers and small currents to lights. (In a series circuit the current would be the same through all appliances.)

What happens if you connect an appliance to the wrong supply?

- If the supply voltage is too high, say 220 V instead of 110 V, the appliance will be damaged by an excessive current.
- If the supply voltage is too low the appliance will not work, a light will be too dim or a motor will run too slowly.
- If the supply voltage fluctuates the brightness of lamps will vary but data on computers can be corrupted. Computers should be connected via circuits that stabilise the supply voltage and protect against voltage surges.

The unit of electrical energy

We pay for the energy used or converted in our homes. The amount of energy converted depends on the power of the appliances and the time for which they are switched on:

$$\text{energy converted} = \text{power} \times \text{time}$$

The SI unit of energy, the joule (1 watt × 1 second) is too small for the large amounts of energy used in a modern home. The unit of energy for which we pay is the kilowatt hour (kW h):

$$\begin{aligned} 1\text{ unit} = 1\text{ kilowatt hour} &= 1000\text{ watts} \times 1\text{ hour} \\ &= 1000\text{ watts} \times 3600\text{ seconds} \\ &= 3.6 \times 10^6\text{ joules} \\ &= 3.6\text{ MJ} \end{aligned}$$

Calculating the cost of electricity

The number of 'units' used or converted by an appliance is given by the relation:

$$\text{number of kW h units} = \text{number of kilowatts} \times \text{number of hours}$$

The cost of the electricity used or converted by an appliance is given by the relation:

$$\text{cost} = \text{number of kW h units} \times \text{price per kW h unit}$$

Worked example

The cost of electricity

a) How many kW h units of electrical energy will be used in a day by each of the following, assuming they are each on for 24 hours:
  i) a 3 kW electric kettle
  ii) a 60 W electric lamp
  iii) a battery charger rated at 6.5 W?

b) The price of a unit of electricity is \$6.35. What will each appliance cost to run?

---

a) The number of units = kilowatts × hours
  i) The kettle will use: 3 kW × 24 h = 72 kW h
  ii) The lamp will use: $\frac{60\text{ W}}{1000} \times 24\text{ h} = 1.44\text{ kW h}$.
  iii) The battery charger will use: $\frac{6.5\text{ W}}{1000} \times 24\text{ h}$ $= 0.156\text{ kW h}$

b) The cost = kW h units × price per unit
  i) The kettle will cost 72 × \$6.35 = \$457.20
  ii) The lamp will cost: 1.44 × \$6.35 = \$9.14
  iii) The battery charger will cost 0.156 × \$6.35 = \$0.99

The electric kettle will use 72 units of electricity costing \$457.20 compared with the lamp, which will only use 1.44 units in a full day, costing as little as \$9.14 or the battery charger costing only 99 cents.

Key fact

Electrical safety

- Switch off and disconnect appliances when not in use, and always before starting any repair work.
- Learn how to fit plugs correctly and safely.
- Do not expose any wiring unless it is disconnected or unplugged.
- Replace fuses with new ones of the correct rating.
- Do not fit plugs that are damaged or have no cable grip.
- Do not overload circuits and sockets with too many appliances plugged into multi-way adaptors.
- Do not take mains appliances, for example hairdryers, into bathrooms where holding with wet hands can be dangerous.
- Do not use appliances requiring an earth lead on a 2-pin socket or a lighting circuit.
- Do not replace a fuse until the fault in the circuit or appliance has been found and removed or repaired.
- Do not leave long cables trailing across a room.

Electricity in the car

How do cars use electricity?

Modern cars have many things that use electricity: music systems, electric windows, air conditioning, lights and so on. But the most important use of electricity in cars is to produce the spark that ignites a petrol and air mixture in a petrol engine or, in a diesel engine, the heater that pre-heats the cylinders before starting the engine to make it quicker to start (and easier, in colder climates).

Car batteries

A car battery has to supply a very large current. It has to supply enough power to the starter motor to start the engine moving from stationary, and the larger the current the larger the power for any given voltage.

Once the engine is running, it turns an alternator, which generates electricity that recharges the battery all the time the engine is running.

Summary questions

1 Give the colour code for domestic wiring.

2 What is the purpose of an earth wire?

3 What is the unit of the 'units' of electrical energy that appear on an electricity bill?

Things to do

Look at some appliances at home:

- Find the label that gives the power rating of some of the following: electric kettle, hairdryer, vacuum cleaner, electric power tool, electric iron, fan, electric toaster or electric food mixer.
- What power rating is stated on the label?
- Calculate the current that the appliance will conduct. (Use $I = P/V$ and $V = 110$ V.)

Use a circuit board to wire up a lamp controlled by two 2-way switches.

D15.3 Energy at home

Objectives

By the end of this topic you will be able to:

- describe and calculate how energy is used at home
- suggest how energy can be saved at home.

Energy use at home

Find out what kinds of energy are used at home.

- How is the water heated?
- Look for energy-using equipment and note the kind of energy supplied in each case.
- Find out the annual consumption of each kind of energy by your household. You can do this by looking at the bills received over a recent 12-month period.
- Find the total number of units of each kind of energy used.

As each type of energy is measured in different units it is necessary to convert them all to a common unit for comparison. Use the information in the table to convert the energy units to joules or megajoules.

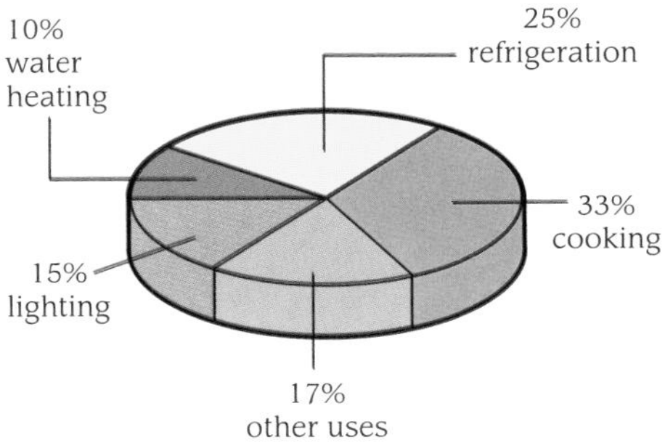

▲ **Figure 15.3.1** Use of energy in a Caribbean home

Electricity bills

The electricity bill shown in Figure 15.3.2 states that 270 kilowatt hours (kW h) of energy have been used (Usage column).

The fuel charge is based on the number of kilowatt hours used.

This customer has been charged as **follows**:

100 units at \$6.35 costs	\$635.00
170 units at \$14.52 costs	\$2468.40
Total cost of kW h units	\$3103.40

Additional charges, including a further charge of $26.54 per unit, increase the total bill to $10 877.50.

CURRENT CHARGES FOR METER # 835240

Billing Cycle	No. of Days	Billing Exchange Rate	Base Exchange Rate	Deposit	Multiplier
09	31	97.11	87.50	$2,000.00	1

From: 14-Feb-2013 To: 17-Mar-2013

Register Type	Reading Type	Current Reading	Previous Reading	Description	Current Usage	Rate	Current Period Charges
KWH	Actual	51585	51315	Energy 1st	100	6.350	$635.00
				Energy Next	170	14.520	$2,468.40

Cust Charge			$322.50
SUBTOTAL			$3,425.90
F/E Adjust @ 8.344 %			$285.86
Fuel & IPP Charge	270	26.540	$7,165.80
Total Current Electricity Charges Before Tax			**$10,877.56**
GCT @ 0.00% on Electricity Charges			$.00
TOTAL CURRENT CHARGES			**$10,877.56**

▲ **Figure 15.3.2** Electricity bill

The total energy used by a household in the Caribbean can vary over a wide range but usually most of the energy will be supplied as electricity. Most of the electricity will have been generated from oil used in diesel–electric generators. Some houses will have a supply of gas, especially in Trinidad where there is an abundance of natural gas. Alternatives include liquid petroleum gas and kerosene. Wood and charcoal are also used for cooking. Increasingly solar energy is used to produce hot water by roof-mounted solar panels.

Key fact

Energy units

Energy source	Unit of supply	Equivalent/joules
Electricity	kilowatt hour	3.6×10^6 J = 3.6 MJ
Gas	therm	1.1×10^8 J = 110 MJ
Coal	1 tonne = 1000 kg	2.8×10^{10} J = 28 000 MJ
Oil	250 gallons	4.4×10^{10} J = 44 000 MJ
Oil	1 litre	3.8×10^7 J = 38 MJ

Worked example

Calculate the electrical energy used in 1 month by a refrigerator if its compressor pump switches on for 8 hours every day.

The power requirement of the refrigerator is 250 watts.

Number of hours $= 8 \times 31$ days $= 248$

Number of kilowatts $= \dfrac{250}{1000} = 0.25$

Number of kilowatt hours $= 0.25 \times 248$

$= 62$ units

This is equivalent to 223.2 MJ.

Saving energy at home

Air conditioning

Air conditioning used for many hours per day can use more energy than either cooking or refrigeration.

The use of air conditioning can be reduced by:

- designing buildings that keep direct sunlight from reaching the windows
- using the air conditioning only at the hottest time of day
- using more cooling fans instead.

Solar water heating

Solar water heating is 'free' once the installation has been paid for and is not charged to the energy supply account. Solar panels can supply all the hot water needs of a home.

▲ **Figure 15.3.3** Solar water-heating panel mounted on the roof of a house in Kingston, Jamaica

Refrigerators and freezers

Energy used by refrigerators and freezers depends greatly on:

- the room temperature
- the amount of air circulation
- the position of the cabinet in the room
- the frequency of opening of the door.

A large saving can be made in the costs of refrigeration and air conditioning if steps are taken to help keep a house cool.

1 Reduce absorption of radiant solar energy. Avoid dark-coloured external walls and roofs. Ideally they should be white. Covering the external surface of a flat roof with white pebbles or light coloured tiles can reduce the heat absorption by more than half.

2 Reduce heat entering through windows by shading devices. External shading that prevents the sunlight reaching the windows at all is most effective. Internal shading using Venetian or roller blinds can make a significant improvement. The inside surface of a glass window can also be given a reflective coating.

▲ **Figure 15.3.4** This Caribbean home has white-painted walls and shades over the windows to keep the sunlight out. Both of these features help keep the house cool.

Other energy saving ideas

- Use full loads of washing in a washing machine and use low-temperature washing powder and programmes.
- Do not put more water in a kettle than you need for your hot drinks (as long as the element is covered). Do not leave the kettle boiling.
- Do not put warm food or liquids into a fridge or freezer. It increases the amount of heat pumping that the cooling system has to do and so uses more electricity.
- Switch off all unnecessary lights and use fluorescent or energy-saving lighting where it is acceptable.
- Plan cooking to make full use of a heated oven and put lids on pans.

▲ **Figure 15.3.5** A modern energy-saving light bulb produces much less waste heat than an ordinary filament bulb.

Summary questions

1. Calculate the number of joules of energy in a kilowatt hour.
2. Calculate the electrical energy used in a week by a 500 W air conditioning unit turned on for 5 hours each day.
3. Give one way to reduce the electrical energy used by a refrigerator.

Practice exam-style questions

1 An electric current produces heat in an element of resistance 40 ohms. Calculate:

a) the power of the element if the current in it is 5.0 amperes

b) the heat produced in 1 hour

c) the voltage across the element.

2 An electric lamp is labelled 150 W, 220 V. Calculate the current through it when working.

3 A 1 kW heater is fitted with a 35 W indicator lamp and a 15 W fan.

All three components of the appliance are connected directly to the 110 V mains supply and are switched on and off together. When the appliance is operating, calculate:

a) the total power

b) the total current

c) the energy used in 4 hours.

4 a) Explain what is meant by the inscription '110 V, 100 W' on an electric light bulb.

b) Sketch a circuit diagram showing how THREE such bulbs would normally be connected in a domestic circuit so that each bulb could be operated independently by its own switch.

c) The bulbs used for Christmas tree lights are often labelled 12 V, 0.3 A, yet are used with a 110 V domestic supply.

i) Sketch a circuit diagram to show how this is possible.

ii) What is the minimum number of such bulbs that can be used safely at the same time? Explain your reasoning.

iii) What is the main disadvantage of such an arrangement?

5 You have available fuses of the following values: 1.0 A, 2.0 A, 5.0 A, 10.0 A and 13.0 A. In the table below, select a suitable fuse for use with each of the following appliances when connected to a 220 V power supply.

Appliance	Fuse rating
2.0 kW electric kettle	
100 W lamp	
500 W electric drill	
A refrigerator	
A washing machine	
A battery charger	

6 The figure below shows an incorrect attempt to wire three sockets A, B and C to the mains supply. When a mains electric heater is plugged into anyone of the three sockets, there is no current in the circuit. When similar mains heaters are plugged into each of the sockets simultaneously, there is a current in the circuit but the heaters give out much less heat than they were designed to do.

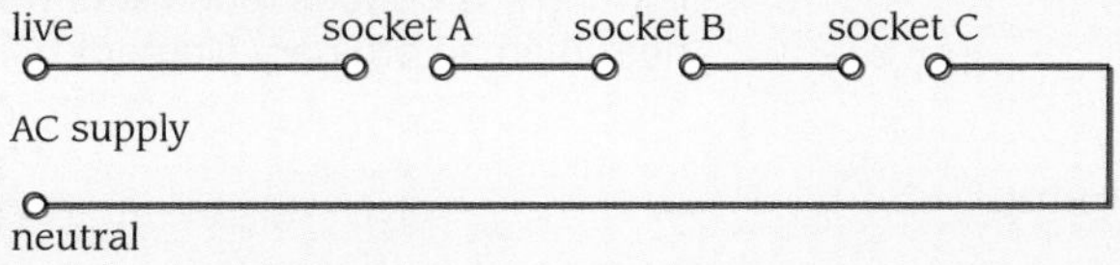

a) Explain these observations.

b) Draw a circuit diagram to show the three sockets correctly wired to the mains supply so that the three heaters can operate normally. Include a fuse and an earth wire in your circuit diagram.

c) Explain clearly why a fuse and an earth wire are used in a mains wiring circuit.

7 Describe briefly THREE features of a domestic electric wiring system that help to make the system safe, making clear the advantage of each feature.

8 This question is about using electric cables correctly.

a) Copy and complete the table below giving the correct colour code information.

	Live wire	Neutral wire	Earth wire
Standard modern colour code			
Old colour code			

b) Some devices can be connected to the mains supply with a twin-wire cable.

i) Which of the three wires in the table is omitted?

ii) When is it safe to use only two wires?

9 A 100 W lamp bulb and a 4 kW water heater are connected to a suitable 110 V supply.

a) Calculate:

i) the current in each appliance

ii) the resistance of each appliance.

b) Explain the difference you would expect to find between the wiring used to connect the bulb to the mains supply and that used to connect the water heater.

c) Calculate the time taken for the temperature of an electric iron to rise by 150 K when connected to a suitable electrical supply. The iron is rated at 1200 W and its heat capacity is $600\,J\,K^{-1}$.

d) Why, in practice, would the time be greater than you have calculated?

10 If the cost of electricity is $6.35 per unit, calculate the cost of using the following appliances:

a) a 2.5 kW kettle for 4.0 hours

b) a 100 W light bulb for 1 day

c) a cooling fan of resistance 55 ohms, connected to a supply of 110 V for 1 week of continuous use.

11 a) Each of the cells shown in the figure below has a potential difference of 2 volts. Draw connecting wires on copies of the two diagrams to show six cells connected:

i) in parallel

ii) in series.

In each case, state the total potential difference across the six cells.

Which arrangement is used for a car battery?

b) A 36 W car lamp is run from a 12 V battery.

i) How much energy is used by the lamp each second?

ii) What is the current in the heated lamp filament?

iii) What is the resistance of the heated lamp filament?

iv) How much heat is produced by the filament in 10 seconds?

		total potential difference
in parallel	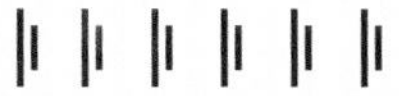	....
in series		....

12 An electricity account shows that a household has used 1400 units of electrical energy during a 3 month period. Calculate:

a) the number of joules of energy used in this time

b) the average number of joules of energy used per day

c) the average power consumption in watts

d) the cost of electricity in this 3 month period if each unit costs $6.35.

13 The figure below shows a simple arrangement to demonstrate the generation of hydroelectric power.

a) Draw a diagram to show the additional apparatus required to measure the electrical power developed in a lamp bulb connected to the output terminals of the generator. Make clear how the power is calculated from the readings taken.

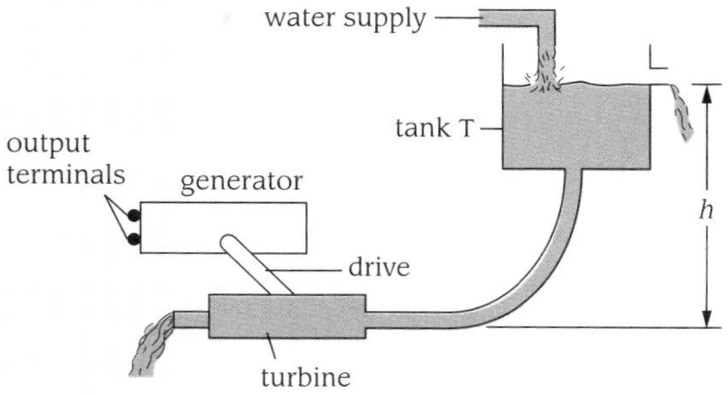

b) Given that the potential energy lost when 1.0 kg of water falls 1.0 m is 10 J, what measurements must be made in order to calculate the power provided by the falling water? Show how to calculate this power.

c) The efficiency of this model generating system is equal to:

$$\frac{\text{output power in the bulb}}{\text{input power of the falling water}} \times 100\%$$

Identify THREE sources of energy loss that cause the efficiency of the model to be less than 100%.

D16 Electronics

In the modern world, electronics is a major industry with many important applications. Electronic devices have a huge impact on our lives. Here we have only a brief look at two aspects of electronics. One is the important process of converting alternating electrical supplies to direct current, a process called rectification. The other provides a small insight into the fascinating world of digital systems through the basic building blocks of logic gates. All computers are built from these gates.

D16.1 Semiconductors

Objectives

By the end of this topic you will be able to:

- describe how a semiconductor diode can be used in half-wave rectification
- sketch *V–t* graphs to compare the variation of voltage with time, with and without rectification
- distinguish between the direct current from a battery and rectified alternating current by comparison of the *V–t* graphs
- describe a simple test to determine whether a p-n junction diode is defective.

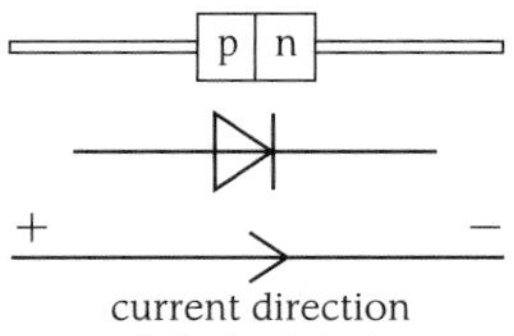

In practical diodes it is the negative end that is marked.

▲ **Figure 16.1.1** Diodes

Semiconductors are materials that conduct electricity better than insulators but not as well as conductors. Semiconductors are the basis of modern electronics, such as the 'chips' in computers. Silicon is a common semiconductor material, so occasionally you may still hear people talking about 'silicon chips'. There are two types of charge carriers in semiconductor materials: electrons (negatively charged), and 'holes', which are 'missing' electrons, so behave as positive charges moving in the opposite direction to the direction an electron would move in. Different types of semiconductor materials can be used together to create devices that, for example, only allow current to flow in one direction, or only allow current to flow if light shines on the device.

The semiconductor diode

A semiconductor diode acts like a switch or a one-way valve. The diode only conducts current when the voltage across the diode is 0.6 V or higher, and only conducts current in one direction, called the forward direction or forward bias. If the diode is connected the other way round, called reverse bias, no current flows.

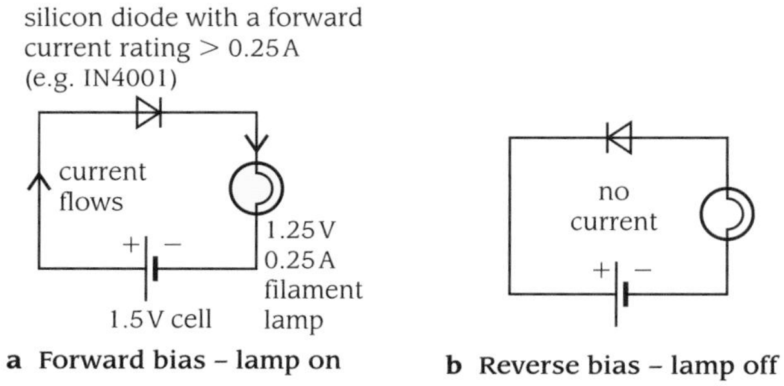

▲ **Figure 16.1.2** Diodes conduct in one direction only

- Connect a diode as shown in Figure 16.1.2a, with the negative end of the diode (the end that is usually marked with a band) to the lamp, which is then connected to the negative terminal of the cell.

The lamp lights, a current flows and this is called forward biasing. Current is conducted through the diode by electrons flowing in one direction (−ve to +ve) and 'holes' flowing in the opposite direction (+ve to −ve).

- Reverse the connections to the diode as shown in Figure 16.1.2b, where its negative end is joined to the 1 terminal of the cell.

This is called reverse biasing. No current can flow through the diode, which acts like an insulator.

Other semiconductor devices

LEDs (light-emitting diodes) are diodes that emit light when a current flows through them. The current supplies energy to the atoms in the semiconductor material and the atoms give this energy out as light. The colour of the light depends on the chemicals in the semiconductor material. Coloured LEDs are used as indicator lights. White LEDs make good lamps because they give a very bright light with a very small current, so they are very efficient. This means that batteries in LED torches or bike lights will last a long time.

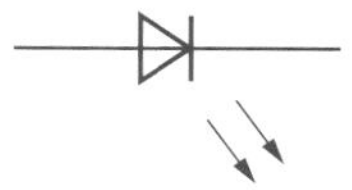

▲ **Figure 16.1.3** Symbol for an LED

LDRs (light-dependent resistors) are semiconductor resistors, where the resistance decreases as the light shining on them gets brighter.

Thermistors are also semiconductor resistors. They have a resistance that decreases as the temperature increases.

Worked example

Protective resistor for an LED

Look at the circuit shown in Figure 16.1.4. If a safe voltage drop across the LED is 1.4 V and a safe current to flow through the LED is 20 mA, calculate what size the protective resistor needs to be for the LED to operate safely.

Supply voltage = 5.0 V

Voltage drop required across protective resistor = 5.0 − 1.4 = 3.6 V

$$\text{The required protective resistance } R = \frac{V}{I}$$

$$= \frac{3.6}{0.02} = 180\,\Omega$$

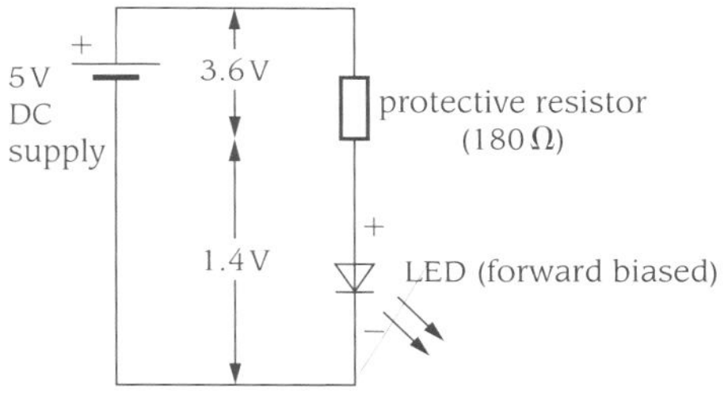

▲ **Figure 16.1.4**

Rectification: using diodes to convert AC to DC

The one-way conduction of a diode can be used to convert AC to DC. This process is called rectification.

The simplest form of rectification is half-wave rectification. Figure 16.1.5 shows how this happens. A resistor is connected across the 12 V output of an AC supply. An oscilloscope is connected across the resistor, so the oscilloscope trace shows how the voltage across the resistor changes with time. The oscilloscope traces in Figure 16.1.5 show how the voltage across the resistor varies when a diode is connected in series with the resistor. The current flowing in circuits **b** and **c** is said to be half-wave rectified.

The size of the half-wave rectified current varies, unlike the DC current from a battery, which would show a straight horizontal line on the oscilloscope trace.

Key fact

Why do we need a load resistor?

- A load resistor represents any device that the transformer might be expected to send a current through.
- The current through this load resistor will alternate at a frequency of 50 Hz, which is too fast to see on a DC ammeter.
- The voltage across the load resistor, which is always directly proportional to the current through it, will follow the same changes of direction at the same times.

Key fact

OBSERVATIONS

Circuit a

The alternating voltage waveform displayed on the screen shows how the voltage varies between + and − values as the current through *R* reverses direction.

Circuit b

When the diode is connected in series with *R* any current through *R* must also flow through the diode. The diode only conducts in one direction, so current flows through *R* in only one direction. The diode end of *R* becomes positive as current flows through it, which is why the positive (top) halves of the waveform appear on the screen.

Circuit c

The negative (lower) halves of the waveform show that the same end of the resistor becomes negative as it conducts in the opposite direction.

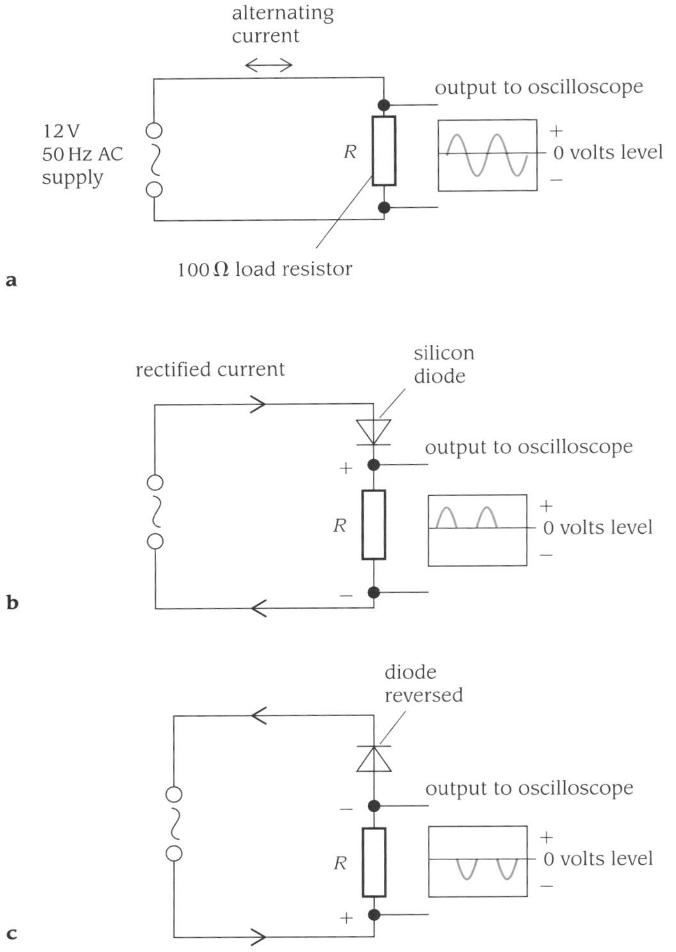

▲ **Figure 16.1.5** Half-wave rectification by a diode

Half-wave rectified current

The oscilloscope screen displays current against time graphs ($I \propto V$) for the load resistor *R*. The current flowing in both circuits Figure 16.1.5b and 16.1.5c is said to be **half-wave rectified**. The current is now direct current but, although it flows in one direction only, it is not a steady current like the current from a battery. The graph of a steady DC current would be just a horizontal straight line.

Full-wave rectification and smoothing

By using three more diodes, it is possible to use both cycles of the AC current, so that the DC current becomes **full-wave rectified**. The oscilloscope trace then looks like the trace in Figure 16.1.6. Adding capacitors can smooth out the 'ups and downs' so that the final trace looks like that in Figure 16.1.7.

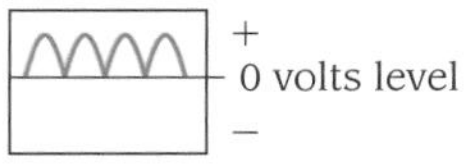

▲ **Figure 16.1.6** Full-wave rectification

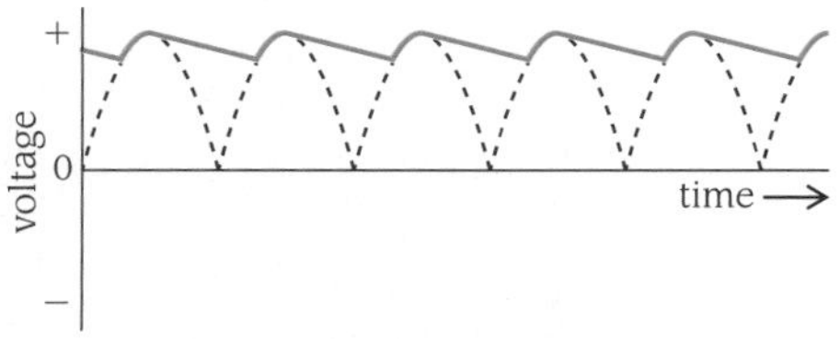

▲ **Figure 16.1.7** Full-wave rectification – smoothed

Summary questions

1 Sketch the circuit symbol for a diode.

2 How does a light-emitting diode (LED) work?

3 What is meant by 'half-wave rectification'?

D16.2 Logic gates

Objectives

By the end of this topic you will be able to:

- recall the symbols and truth tables for AND, OR, NOT, NAND and NOR logic gates
- state the function of each of these gates with the aid of its truth table
- analyse circuits involving the combinations of not more than three logic gates using truth tables.

What does digital mean?

Electronics have a huge impact on our daily lives. Electronic systems appear all around us, from the laptop or desktop computers we use, to phones to washing machines to televisions to microwave ovens. Anything that is 'programmable' in any way has electronics in it. At the very simplest level all these things use digital information. Digital information is information (usually in the form of voltages) that comes in set values only (like whole numbers). Analogue information is information that can come in a wide range of values (like all the values between whole numbers). The simplest, and most common, form of digital values used is just 'on' or 'off'. These are often referred to as **logic 1** (on) and **logic 0** (off). Logic 1 often means a voltage of 5 V and logic 0 a voltage of 0 V.

Binary codes

Form of binary code	Logic 0	Logic 1
Switch	open	closed
Magnetism on floppy disc	memory not magnetised	memory magnetised
Laser-burnt hole on CD	hole not burnt	hole burnt
Voltage on the pin of a chip	0 volts	5 volts

Key fact

How to remember logic gates

- The name of a gate describes how it makes its decisions.
- The small circle at the output end of some gate symbols is the inverting or NOT symbol. This makes the output the opposite of what it would be without the small circle.
- Remember the key line in the truth table, which is the odd one out. For example, in the NAND gate table, the only line that gives a logic 0 output is the case when both inputs are logic 1.
- The special or key lines in the truth tables are coloured.

Logic gates

Electronic circuits use integrated circuit boards, which contain very complicated circuits, often with hundreds of 'chips' on them, each chip containing complicated, microscopic circuits. But the basic building block of all these 'chips' is the logic gate. A logic gate is really just a very high speed switch. The logic gate output switches between 0 and 1 depending on the values of the inputs. Logic gates come in several different types, designed to do different things to the input values.

The simplest type of logic gate is called the NOT gate. Its output is high if the input is NOT high.

Truth tables

A truth table is a simple way of describing all the possible combinations of inputs and the output decisions produced by a particular logic gate or group of connected gates. In the truth tables shown, A and B are inputs and Y is the output.

Key fact

The simplest 'chips' will contain four logic gates. The pins or legs of the chip connect to the inputs and outputs of each logic gate with two more pins connecting to a power supply. The most complicated computer chips can contain hundreds of millions of logic gates. Two of the pins will still be for the power supply.

Logic gate	Symbol	Is equivalent to	Truth table	The output is high, logic 1 when:
NOT	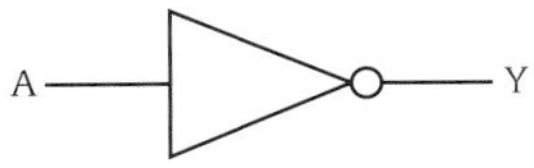	INVERTER	input: A / output: Y 0 / 1 1 / 0	input A is **NOT** high (output is the input inverted)
OR	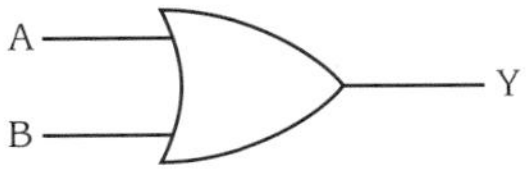	(inclusive) OR	A B Y 0 0 0 0 1 1 1 0 1 1 1 1	input A **OR** input B is high (or both are high)
NOR	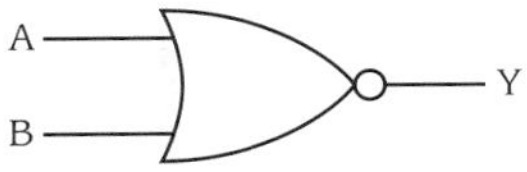	OR-NOT	A B Y 0 0 1 0 1 0 1 0 0 1 1 0	neither input A **NOR** input B is high
AND	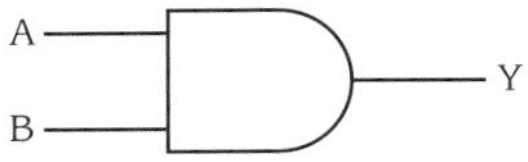		A B Y 0 0 0 0 1 0 1 0 0 1 1 1	input A **AND** input B are high
NAND	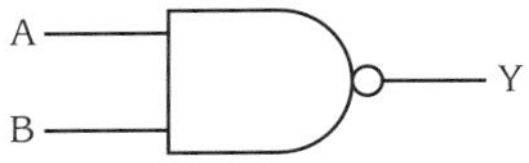	AND-NOT	A B Y 0 0 1 0 1 1 1 0 1 1 1 0	input A **AND** input B are **NOT** both high

▲ **Figure 16.2.1** Logic gates

Combinations of logic gates

Manufacturers put several identical gates on a chip, usually NAND gates or NOR gates. Combinations of these can be made that are equivalent to NOT, OR and AND gates as shown in Figure 16.2.2. Also logic gates can be combined to make more complicated logical decisions.

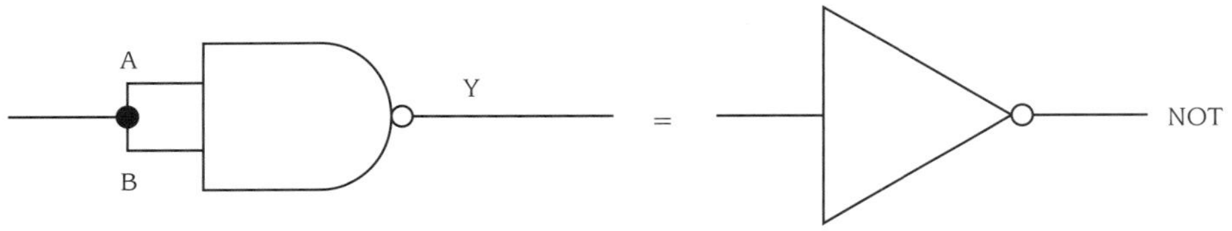

A	B	Y
0	0	1
1	1	0

A and B joined must be the same

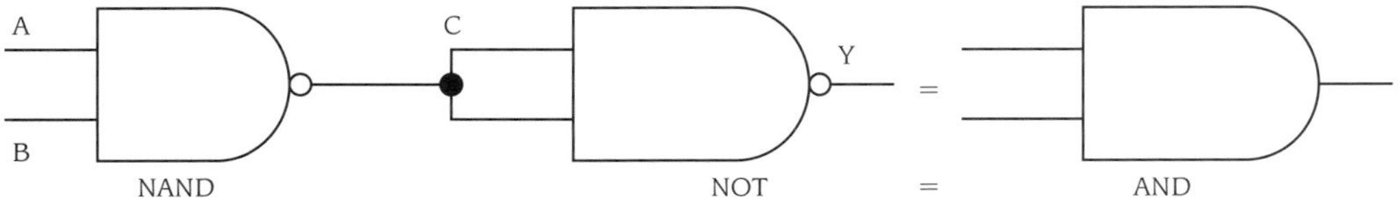

A	B	C	Y
0	0	1	0
0	1	1	0
1	0	1	0
1	1	0	1

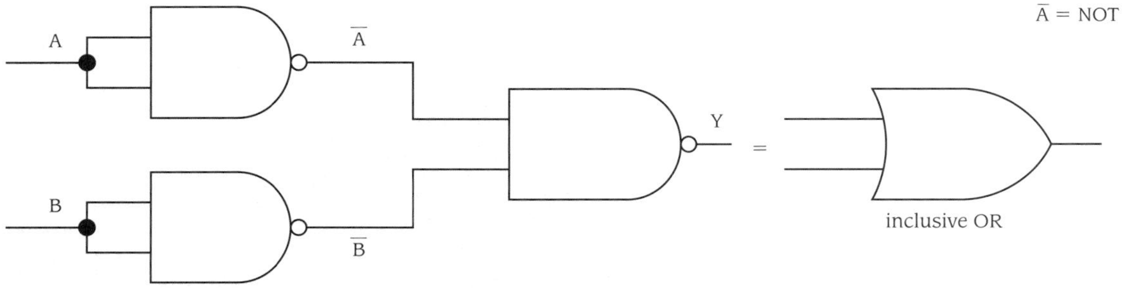

$\overline{A}$ = NOT A, $\overline{B}$ = NOT B

A	B	$\overline{A}$	$\overline{B}$	Y
0	0	1	1	0
0	1	1	0	1
1	0	0	1	1
1	1	0	0	1

Add another NOT gate to make a NOR gate

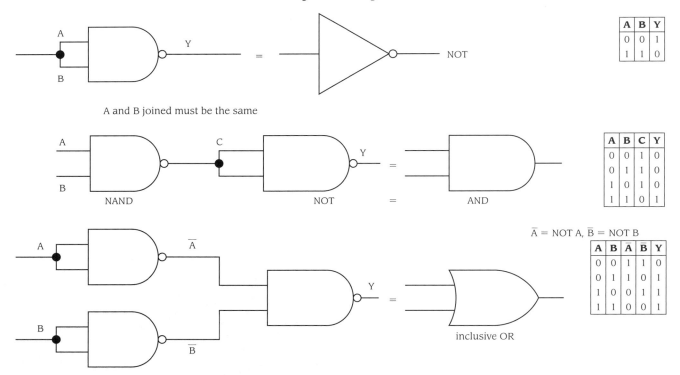

▲ **Figure 16.2.2** Building gates from combinations of gates

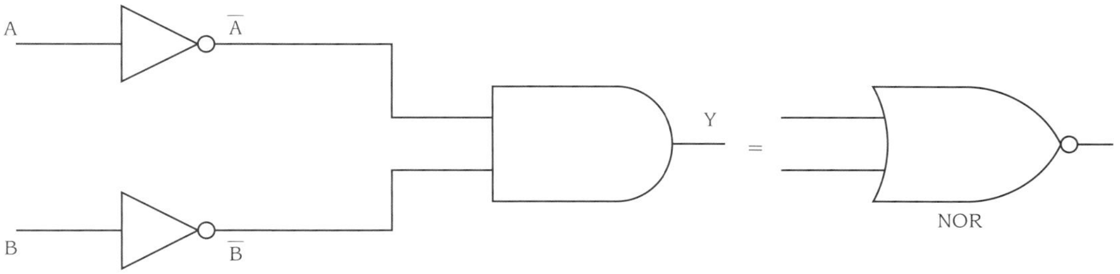

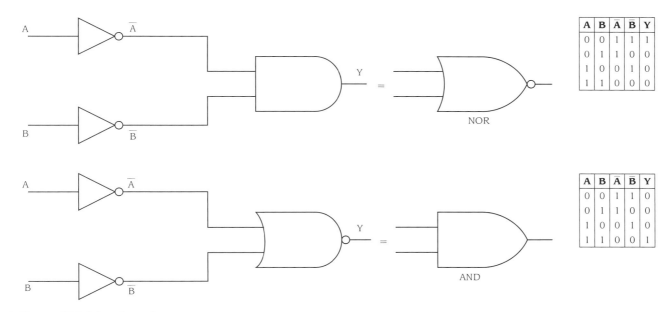

A	B	$\overline{A}$	$\overline{B}$	Y
0	0	1	1	1
0	1	1	0	0
1	0	0	1	0
1	1	0	0	0

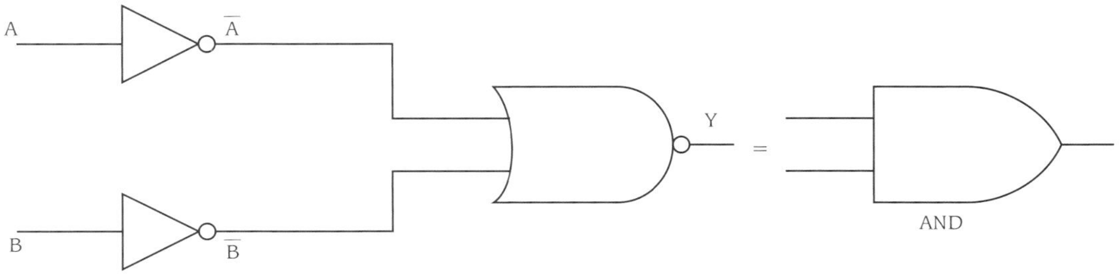

A	B	$\overline{A}$	$\overline{B}$	Y
0	0	1	1	0
0	1	1	0	0
1	0	0	1	0
1	1	0	0	1

▲ **Figure 16.2.2** (continued)

Simple alarm circuits that use logic gates

A night-time rain alarm

In the dark, the light sensor L gives a 0 output to the NOT gate, which becomes a logic 1 supplied to the final AND gate.

The moisture sensor M gives a logic 1 output when it gets wet.

The two logic 1 inputs together produce a logic 1 output from the AND gate, which sets off the alarm.

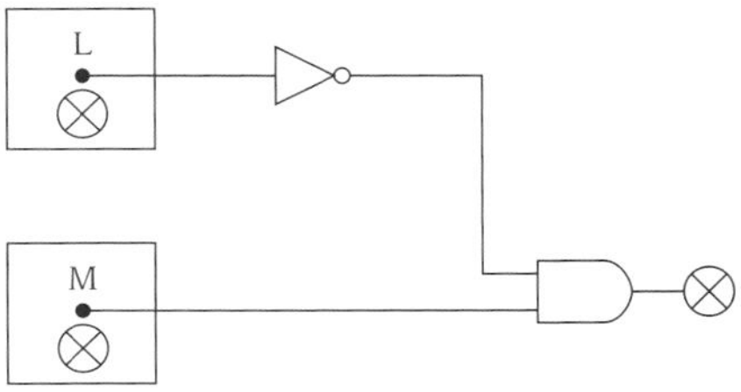

▲ **Figure 16.2.3** A night-time rain alarm

A low temperature warning alarm

When the temperature sensor T falls below a certain value its output becomes logic 0. The NOT gate inverts this to logic 1.

A logic 1 input to the OR gate produces a logic 1 output and sets off the alarm. To test that the alarm is working while the temperature is high, pressing the test switch connects the other input of the OR gate to 5 V, i.e. it provides a logic 1 input that should also set off the alarm.

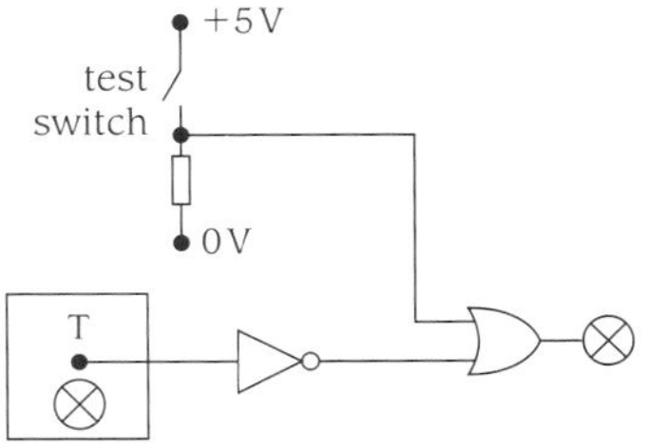

▲ **Figure 16.2.4** A low temperature warning alarm

A bank security lock

To unlock the door the output of the top AND gate must be high at logic 1 to operate a security solenoid, which withdraws a bolt (Figure 16.2.5). The AND gate requires both buttons A AND B to be pressed at the same time to connect both inputs to 5 V, i.e. logic 1.

Button A should be concealed behind the manager's desk inside the bank and button B is by the door, outside the bank.

If button B is pressed alone the warning buzzer sounds, alerting people inside the bank.

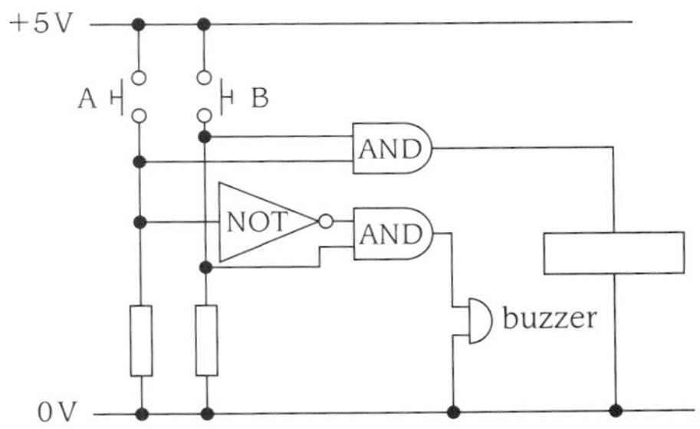

▲ **Figure 16.2.5** Circuit for a security lock

Circuits for sensors

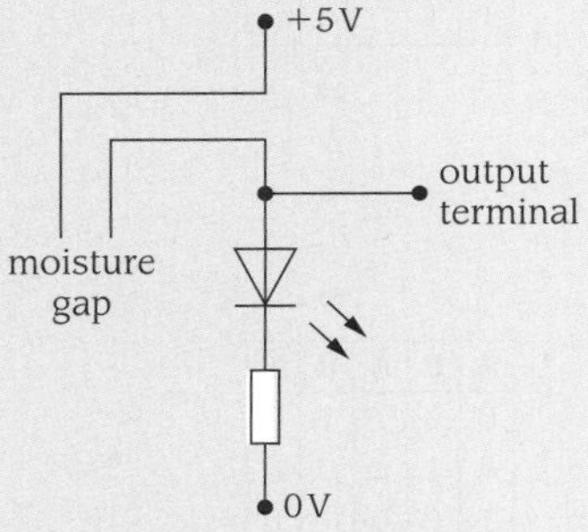

When the gap becomes wet it conducts and joins the output terminal to +5V. The LED indicator also lights.

▲ **Figure 16.2.6** Moisture sensor M

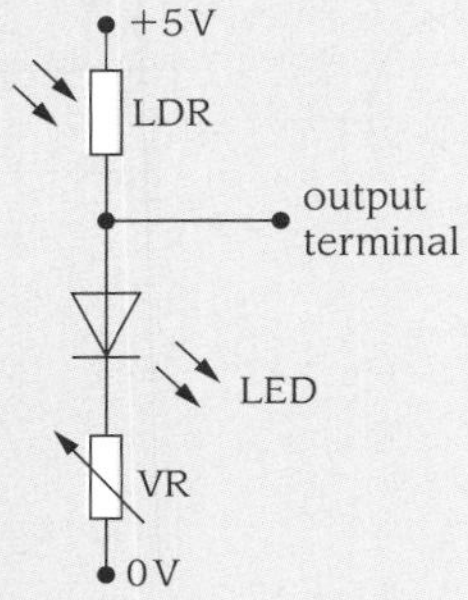

The LDR (light dependent resistor) is one half of a voltage divider circuit. When light shines on the LDR, its resistance falls. The voltage at the output terminal rises and the LED lights.

▲ **Figure 16.2.7** Light sensor L

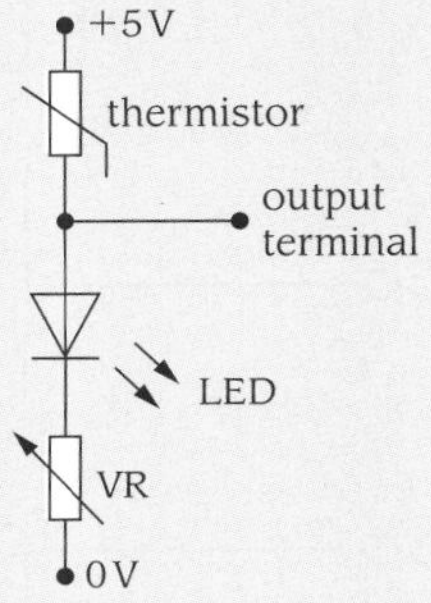

The thermistor and variable resistor VR form a voltage divider. When the temperature drops the resistance of the thermistor rises, making the voltage at the output terminal fall and become logic 0.

▲ **Figure 16.2.8** Temperature sensor T

Summary questions

1 Sketch the circuit symbol for a NOR gate.

2 Write out the truth table for a NAND gate.

3 Is the voltage high or low for a logic level 1?

Practice exam-style questions

1 a) Draw a circuit diagram to show how a single diode can be used to produce half-wave rectification of an alternating current from an AC supply.

Show clearly where in the circuit you would connect a DC electric motor, which could run using this rectified current.

b) Sketch a graph to show how the current through the DC electric motor would vary with time.

2 Draw a truth table for each of the systems **a** and **b** shown in the figure below and state the logic function that each possesses.

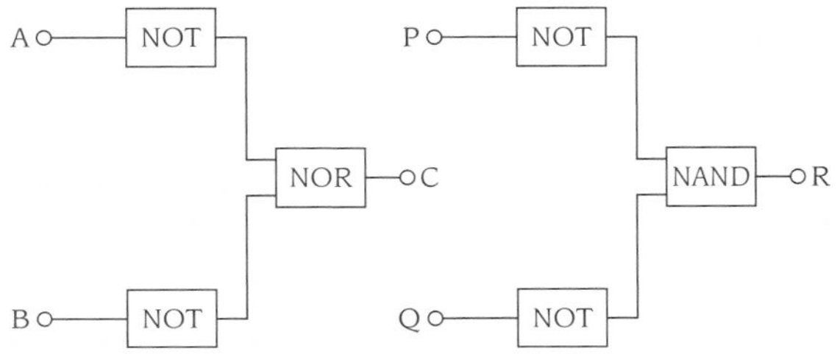

a **b**

3 Copy and complete the truth table for the system of logic gates shown in the figure below.

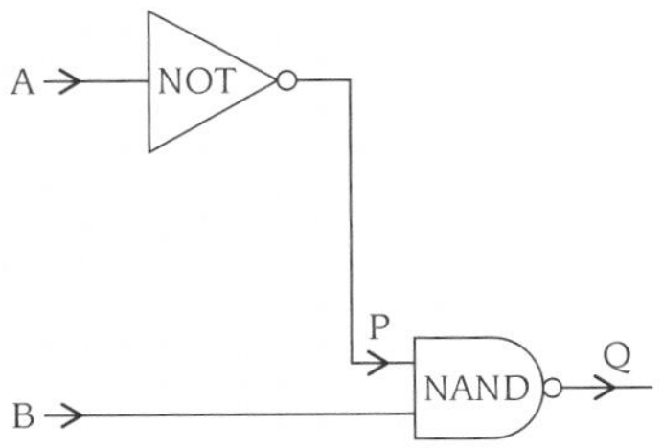

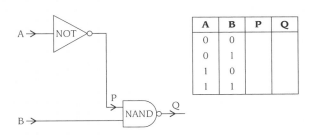

A	B	P	Q
0	0		
0	1		
1	0		
1	1		

4 Copy and complete the table below.

Name	Symbol
	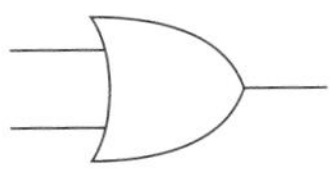
	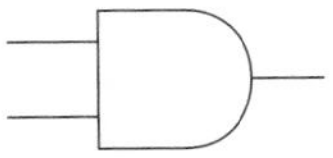
NOT	

5 The circuit symbol and truth table for a two-input NAND (NOT AND) gate is shown in figure **a** below.

In the design of logic circuits, the NAND gate is a basic 'building block' of the circuit, as shown in figure **b** below.

a) Copy and complete the truth table (figure **c**) for this circuit.

b) The output of a logic circuit can be displayed using an LED and associated series resistor, as in the circuit shown in figure **d** below.

i) When the LED is lit, what is the logic state at A?

ii) The LED has a potential difference drop of 2 V across it and a current of 10 mA through it when it is lit. What is the p.d. across resistor R when the LED is lit?

iii) Calculate the resistance of R.

iv) Why is the resistor R needed?

a

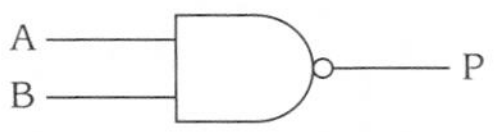

A	B	P
0	0	1
0	1	1
1	0	1
1	1	0

b

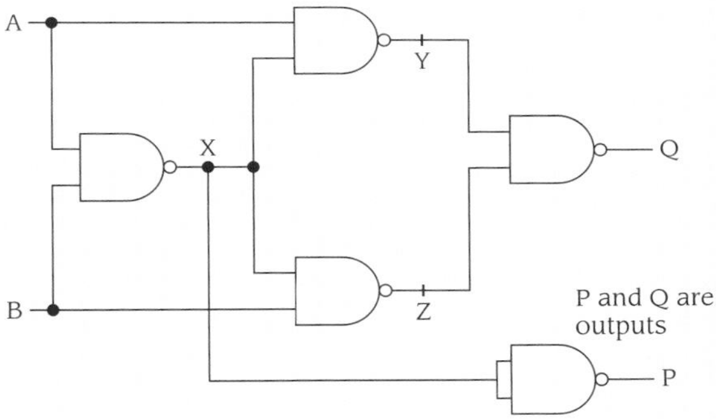

c

A	B	X	Y	Z	P	Q
0	0	1				
0	1	1				
1	0	1				
1	1	0				

logic level 1 = +5 V
logic level 0 = 0 V

d

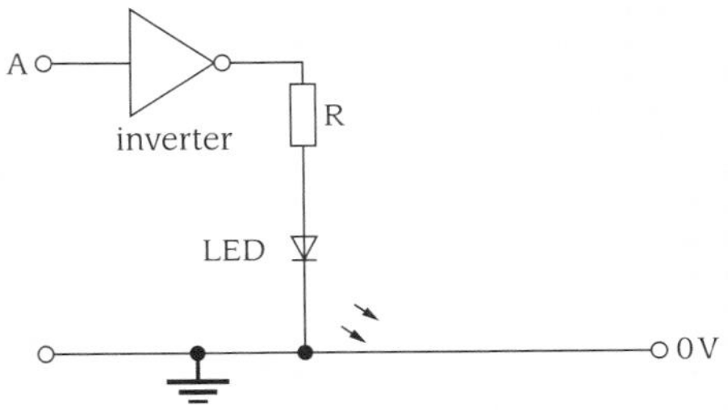

6 Copy and complete the truth table for the two connected logic gates shown in the figure below.

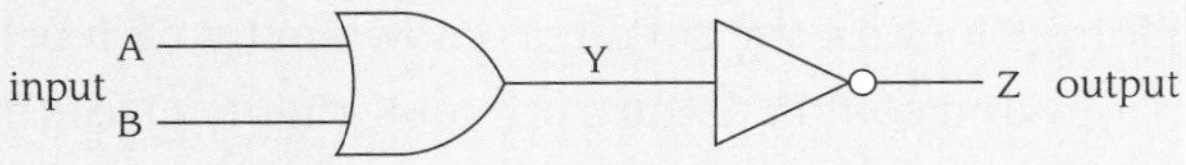

Inputs A B	Y	Output Z

7 A gas-fired central heating boiler has an alarm system that flashes a lamp if the boiler temperature becomes too high or if the flame goes out. The block diagram shows the system.

The temperature sensor gives a logic 1 when it is too hot and a logic 0 when it is normal.

The flame sensor gives a logic 1 if the flame is on and a logic 0 when the flame is out.

The lamp is switched on by logic 1.

a) Name logic block 'X'.

b) Name the logic block 'Y' and explain why it is needed in this system.

c) Name the logic block 'W' and explain how it is used to make the lamp flash when the alarm is triggered.

d) Copy and complete the truth table for the alarm system.

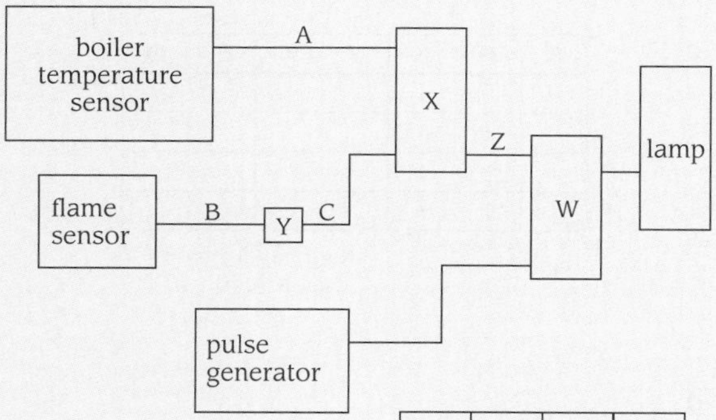

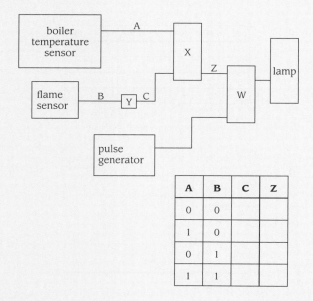

A	B	C	Z
0	0		
1	0		
0	1		
1	1		

8 The logic circuit shown below sets off an alarm if a car driver forgets to turn his headlights off when leaving the car.

When he turns off the ignition switch a logic 0 arrives at logic gate P.

When he closes the car door, a switch sends a logic 1 to logic gate R.

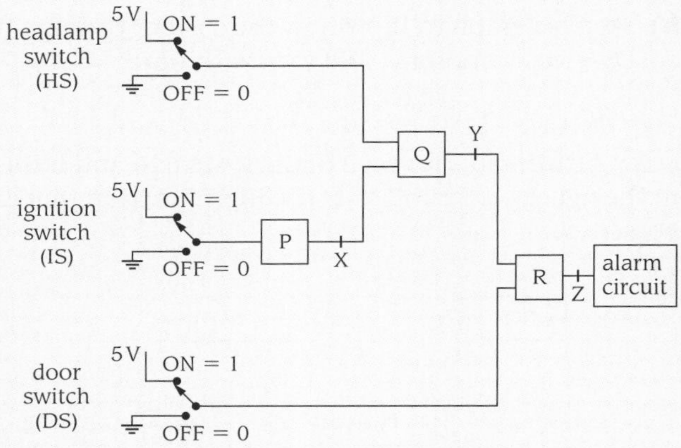

a) By studying the truth table below, deduce the types of logic gate being used at P and Q.

INPUT			OUTPUT		
HS	**IS**	**DS**	**X**	**Y**	**Z**
0	0	0	1	0	
0	0	1	1	0	
0	1	0	0	0	
0	1	1	0	0	
1	0	0	1	1	
1	0	1	1	1	
1	1	0	0	0	
1	1	1	0	0	

b) If the alarm is to sound when he closes the car door, what logic gate is required at R?

c) Copy and complete the truth table.

D17 Magnetism and electromagnetism

We live on a planet that is a large electromagnet. Many of the machines we use every day depend on the magnetic effects of electric currents and magnetic materials. Before we explore the variety of electromagnetic machines and try to understand how they work, we shall first investigate the properties of magnetic materials and the laws that describe how magnetism and electricity interact.

D17.1 Materials and magnets

Permanent magnets

The simplest way of finding out which materials are strongly affected by magnetism is to test them with another material that is already magnetised. Material that keeps its own magnetism for a long time is called a **permanent magnet**.

- Place a selection of objects made of different materials on the bench top for testing. It is important to find samples of as many different metals and alloys (mixtures of metals) as possible.
- Bring a permanent magnet up to each material in turn and note whether you can see or feel anything happening.
- Make a list of strongly magnetic materials (those attracted to the magnet) and non-magnetic materials (those quite unaffected by it).

The special class of materials that, like iron, are strongly affected by magnetism are called ferromagnetic materials (*ferrum* is Latin for iron).

Investigating the properties of magnets

All magnets have two poles

- Roll a magnet in some iron filings or small pins and see where and how they stick to the magnet. (You can use plasticine to remove the iron filings from the magnet afterwards.)

There are always two places on a magnet to which magnetic materials are attracted, as shown in Figure 17.1.1. These are called the poles of the magnet. The poles are near the ends of a bar or horseshoe-shaped magnet but some magnets, made for special applications, have poles in unsuspected places.

All magnets, having two poles, are called **magnetic dipoles**.

The two poles are always labelled N and S for north and south because, as we shall see, they are attracted to the north and south magnetic poles of the Earth.

Objectives

By the end of this topic you will be able to:

- differentiate between magnetic and non-magnetic materials
- distinguish between materials used to make permanent and temporary magnets
- describe how to identify the poles of a magnetic dipole
- describe experiments which show that like poles repel and unlike poles attract each other
- state the effect of separation of magnets on the magnitude of the force between them
- explain how a magnet can attract an unmagnetised object.

Key fact

Materials that are strongly attracted to magnets:
- iron and steel
- other alloys containing iron, cobalt or nickel
- alloys containing a mixture of iron, cobalt and nickel.

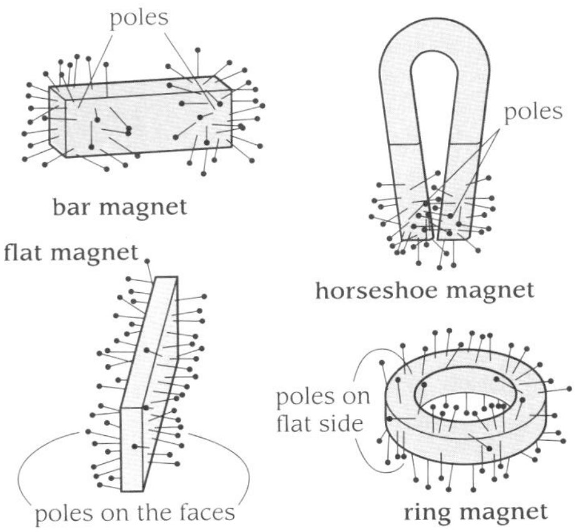

▲ **Figure 17.1.1** Iron filings or pins show where the poles are on some magnets.

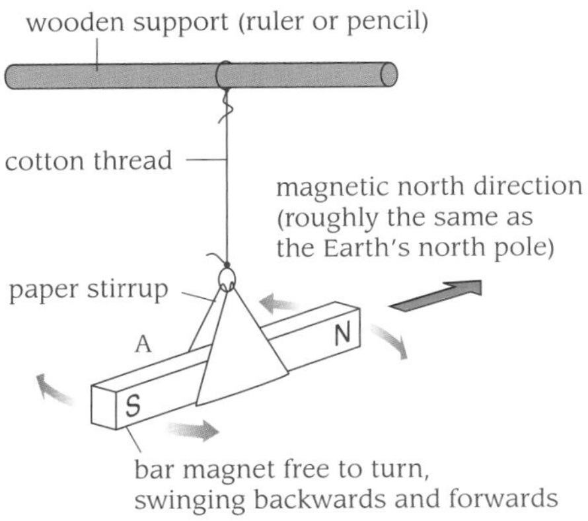

▲ **Figure 17.1.2** A suspended bar magnet

The poles of a magnet are north-seeking and south-seeking

A suspended magnet always settles with its poles pointing the same way.

It is important to place this experiment well away from all objects containing iron such as steel pipes or girders in the frame of a building and also not too near to electric cables or other magnets.

- Suspend a bar magnet using cotton thread from a wooden (non-magnetic) support so that it is balanced horizontally and is free to turn (Figure 17.1.2).

The magnet swings or oscillates slowly about a particular direction until it comes to rest with its poles always pointing exactly the same way. One pole of the magnet always points towards a place at the northern end of the Earth and so we call it a north-seeking pole, or just the north pole (N pole) of the magnet. Similarly the other pole of the magnet, called the south-seeking pole (S pole) always points towards the southern end of the Earth. This discovery is used in the magnetic compass to help sailors and travellers find their direction. A steel needle or pointer is magnetised with a N pole at the pointing end and is mounted so that it can turn freely and point to the magnetic north of the Earth.

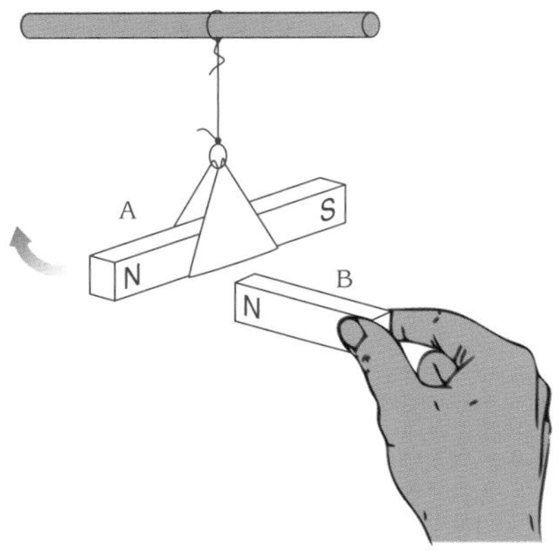

a Repulsion between like poles (two north poles or two south poles)

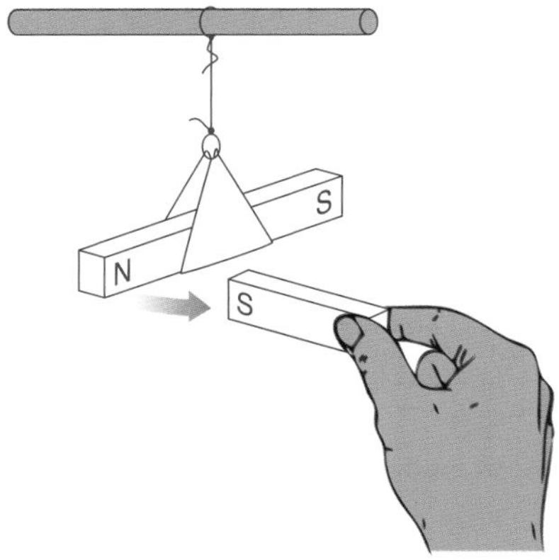

b Attraction between unlike poles (one north pole and one south pole)

▲ **Figure 17.1.3** Forces between magnets

Forces between magnets

- Suspend a bar magnet A horizontally so that it can turn freely as before and label its poles N and S.
- Bring the north pole of another similarly labelled bar magnet B slowly towards one pole of magnet A (Figure 17.1.3).
- Repeat with the other pole of magnet A and then again, bring the S pole of the hand-held magnet B towards each pole of magnet A.
- Record the action in a table.

The force rule we discover is very similar to the one we found for two objects with electric charges (see D13.1).

Like poles repel and unlike poles attract.

We also notice that the forces of attraction and repulsion both get stronger as the magnetic poles get closer together.

The same experiment can be used to test whether a piece of metal such as an iron bar or large nail is magnetised and to identify its poles.

We may find that both ends of the iron bar are attracted to both ends of the magnet. Repulsion never occurs. From this observation we learn that to prove the existence of a particular magnetic pole in another iron object we have to show repulsion between like poles. Attraction may occur whether an iron object is magnetised or not. When a magnet is brought near to a piece of iron, magnetic induction can produce opposite poles in the iron, which are attracted to the magnet.

Pole of suspended magnet A	Pole of hand-held magnet B	Action	End of suspended iron bar	Pole of hand-held magnet	Action
N	N	repulsion	X	N	attraction
S	N		Y	N	
N	S		X	S	
S	S		Y	S	

Magnetic induction

When an unmagnetised ferromagnetic material is brought near to a magnet it is attracted to the magnet. This is a result of temporary magnetism being induced in the material.

- Scatter some small iron nails, pins or paperclips on the bench top and slowly lower a magnet towards them (Figure 17.1.4a).
- Repeat this test with an unmagnetised iron bar to show that it has no effect on the iron nails.
- Hold the magnet above the nails so that the iron bar can pass between the magnet and the nails (Figure 17.1.4b).

In both cases the unmagnetised iron nails are attracted and move while they are still some distance away.

For attraction to occur between the iron bar and the nail the bar must become magnetised while under the influence of the permanent magnet above it. We say that there is induced magnetism in the iron bar. In fact there is also induced magnetism in the iron nails and this happens before they are attracted to the magnet or the iron bar. Figure 17.1.4c shows how the induced magnetic poles are always arranged so that unlike poles result in attraction.

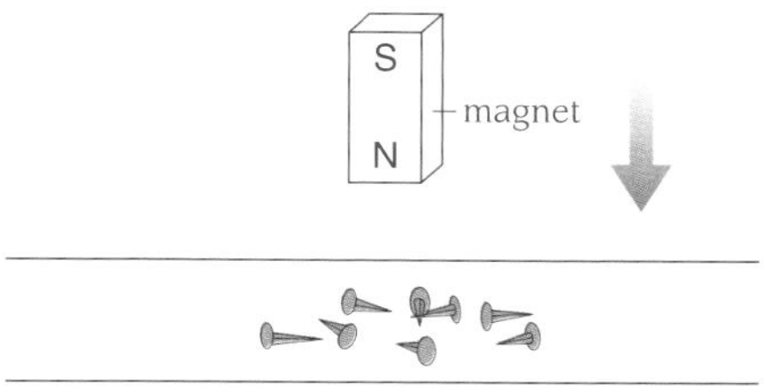

a

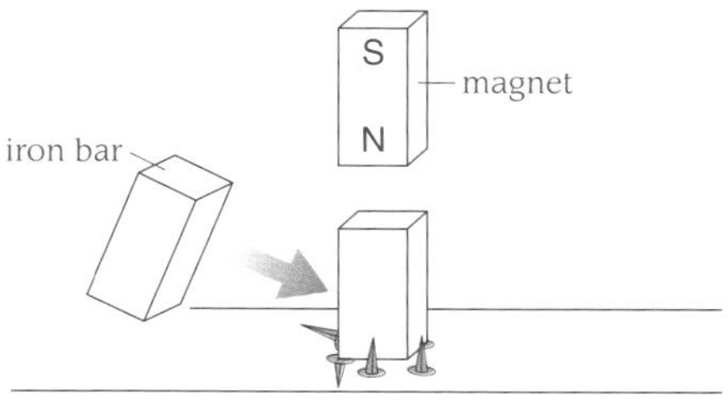

b An iron bar picks up nails under the influence of the permanent magnet

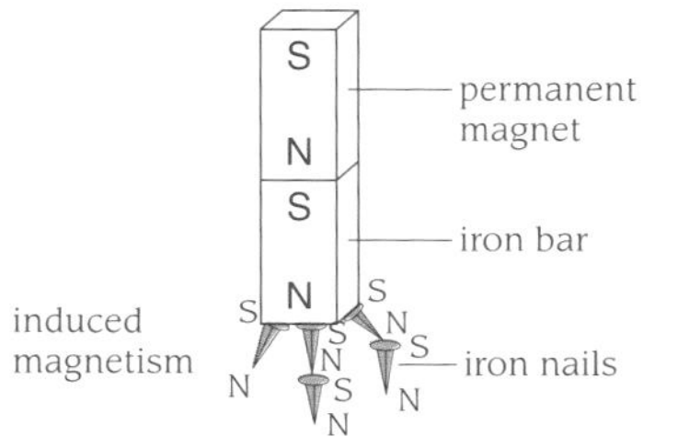

c Induced unlike poles attracted to the magnet

▲ **Figure 17.1.4** Action at a distance

Permanent and temporary induced magnetism

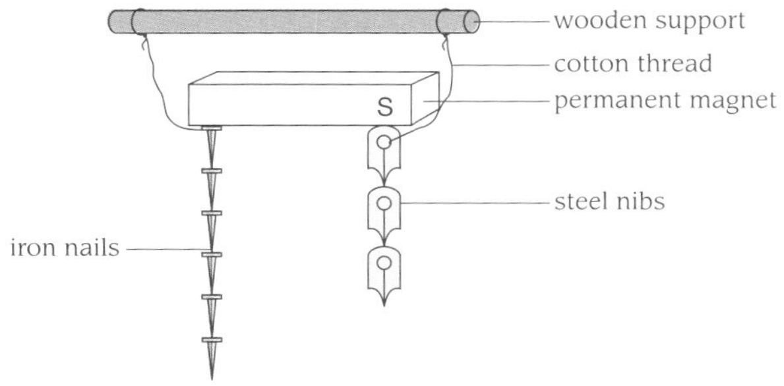

a With a permanent magnet

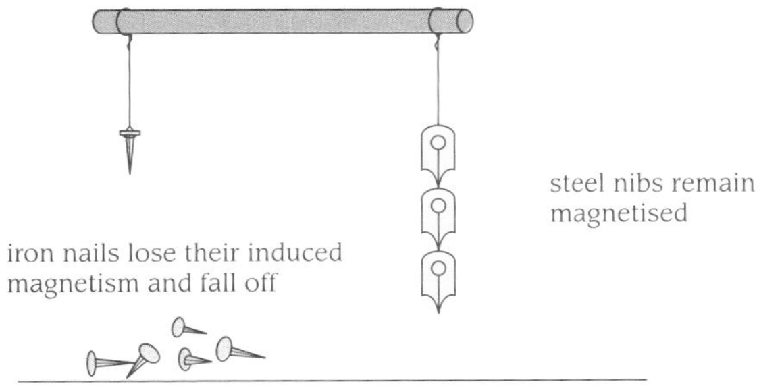

b Magnet removed

◀ **Figure 17.1.5**

- Select some small objects such as nails or paperclips made of iron, and some other objects of a similar size made of steel. Steel objects may be more difficult to find but pen nibs or small safety pins are usually suitable.
- Attach a fine cotton thread to the first iron nail and first steel nib so that they can hang from a wooden pencil or ruler.
- Now pick up these objects with a bar magnet as shown in Figure 17.1.5 and carefully add more nails and nibs in a chain until no more will stay attached by the induced magnetism.
- Carefully separate the top nail and top nib from the magnet allowing the chains to hang on the cotton thread.
- Remove the magnet completely.

! Key fact

- The force of attraction acts from a distance.
- Magnetic induction happens at a distance.
- An *unlike* pole is induced nearer to the permanent magnetic pole causing the magnetic induction.
- Magnetic induction never results in *repulsion*.
- There is always a *pair* of induced poles.

Key fact

Magnetic hardness	SOFT	HARD
Example	iron	steel
Magnetised	easily	less easily
Induced magnetism	temporary	permanent

Magnetic materials	Composition	Properties
steel Alcomax Alnico Ticonal	alloys of iron with aluminium, nickel and cobalt	strong permanent magnets: HARD
Magnadur	ceramic, made from metal oxides	very strong permanent magnets: VERY HARD
Stalloy: soft iron	iron alloy: 96% iron 4% silicon	temporary magnets used for electro-magnets: SOFT
mu-metal	nickel–iron alloys	easily worked into sheets, temporary magnets used for magnetic shielding: SOFT

Things to do

- List uses of permanent magnets at home, at school, in the car or anywhere else that you know about.
- Find out what a lode stone is.
- Explain how you would distinguish between three metal objects, one made of brass, one made of iron and the third one a magnet. You may use a small magnetic compass.

Observations

- The iron nails very quickly lose their induced magnetism and drop off the chain.
- The steel nibs retain their induced magnetism and continue hanging in a chain without the magnet.
- The steel nibs become permanently magnetised themselves.
- It may also be found that more iron nails than steel nibs could be picked up in a chain by the magnet. This is because it is usually harder to magnetise steel than iron and so the magnetism induced in steel nibs may be weaker.
- Ferromagnetic alloys like steel that are harder to magnetise are called **hard magnetic materials**. Those that are easier to magnetise such as the iron used in nails and paperclips are called **soft magnetic materials**, often referred to as **soft iron**. (The words 'soft' and 'hard' originally referred to the physical hardness of the metal, but they are now used in this magnetic sense to describe the ease with which a material can be magnetised.) The table in the margin summarises these properties.

Magnetising a steel bar by magnetic induction

A simple method of making a magnet from a steel bar is shown in Figure 17.1.6. (A steel knitting needle or screwdriver can be used.)

- Stroke the bar with one pole of a permanent magnet so that the pole passes along the bar in the same direction many times. Between strokes the magnet should be raised high above the bar.
- Test the poles induced in the steel bar by bringing them close to a magnetised compass needle. The pole that repels the N pole of the compass will also be a N pole.

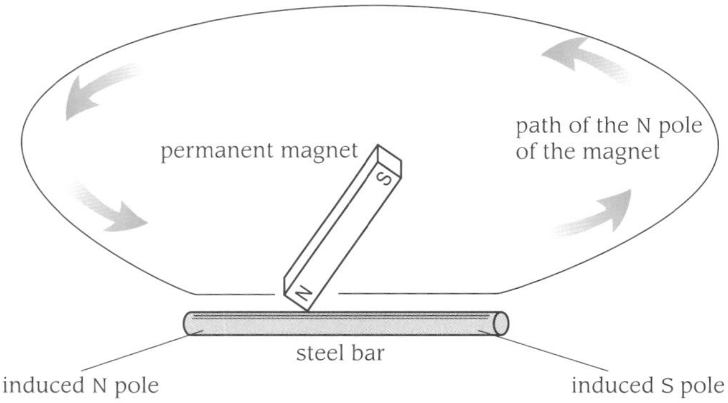

▲ **Figure 17.1.6** Making a magnet by magnetic induction

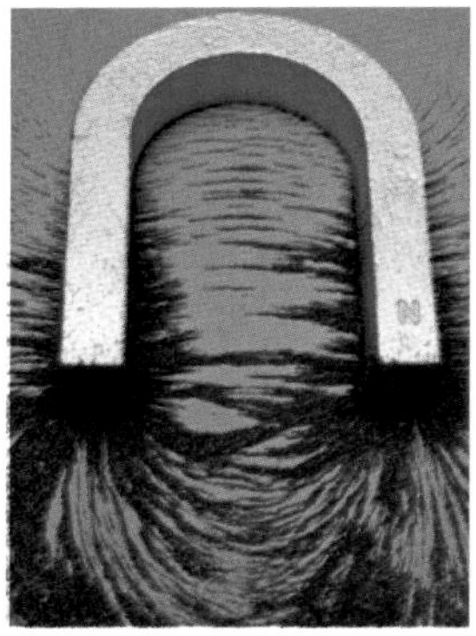

▲ **Figure 17.1.7** Using iron filings to show the magnetic field

Summary questions

1. What test can be used to distinguish between a magnet and a magnetic material?
2. Would you make an electromagnet from a hard magnetic material or a soft magnetic material?
3. Describe one method to magnetise a steel bar.

D17.2 Magnetic fields and forces

Definition

The direction of a magnetic field at a particular place is the direction of the force it produces on a 'free' magnetic north pole.

But remember that single magnetic poles do not really exist!

What is a magnetic field?

A magnet can pick up an iron nail or turn the magnetic needle of a compass while it is still some distance away. There is a magnetic force in the space around a magnet that moves these objects. An iron bar held a short distance away from a magnet becomes temporarily magnetised without touching the magnet. The magnetism is said to be **induced** in the iron by the magnetic field of the permanent magnet. The result of the induced magnetism is that the iron bar is attracted to the magnet.

The magnetic field around a magnet is the region in which forces act on other magnets and on magnetic materials by inducing magnetism in them.

Finding the direction of a magnetic field

The magnetic field points in different directions at different places around a magnet. The simplest way of showing the direction is to place a small compass needle in the field. The needle points in the direction of the magnetic field. A compass needle, however, has two magnetic poles and magnetic forces will act on both poles to line it up with the magnetic field. Figure 17.2.1 shows how we can find the direction of the magnetic force on a single magnetic pole, which is free to move in a magnetic field. By using a very long magnet, like a magnetised steel knitting needle, we can keep one pole far enough away for it not to be affected by the magnetic field being investigated.

- Use a cork to float the magnetised needle with its N pole at the same level as the bar magnet.
- Place the floating needle near the N pole of the magnet and watch what happens.

The needle moves round in a curved path from the N pole to the S pole of the bar magnet. It moves in the direction of the force acting on it, so this path shows the direction of the magnetic field of the bar magnet.

Objectives

By the end of this topic you will be able to:

- define a magnetic field as the region in which a magnetic force may be exerted
- describe the properties of a magnetic field
- map the magnetic field:
  a) of a single strong magnet
  b) between two strong magnets
- draw diagrams to show how permanent magnets can be used to create a uniform magnetic field.

Key fact

- The forces acting in a magnetic field, like all forces, are vectors and have both magnitude and direction.
- Since all magnets are dipoles, both the poles of a magnet cause a force to act on the magnetic materials in its field.

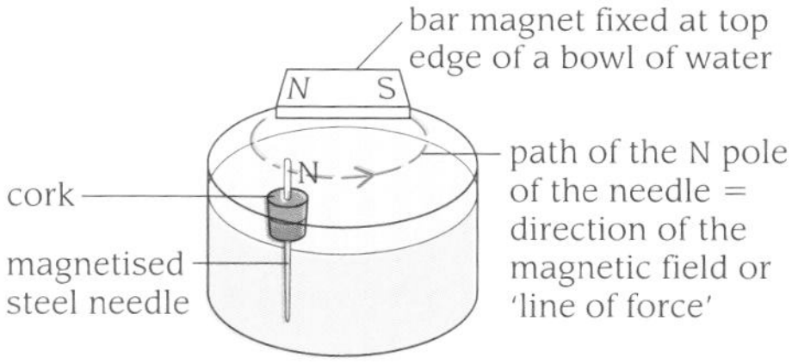

▲ **Figure 17.2.1** Finding the direction of a magnetic field using a floating magnetised needle

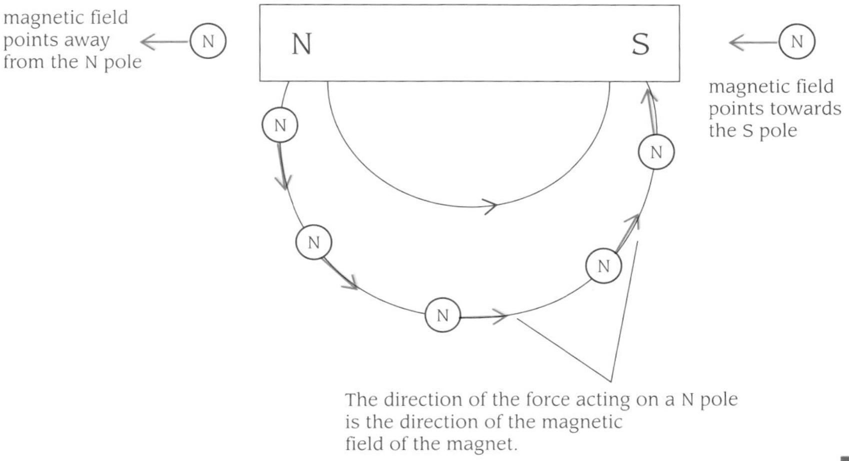

▶ **Figure 17.2.2** Finding the shape of the magnetic field

Key fact

- The magnetic field points out of, or away from, the N pole of a magnet and into, or towards, its S pole.
- The force on a N pole placed in a magnetic field is in the same direction as the magnetic field. The force on a S pole is in the opposite direction to the magnetic field.
- A compass needle aligns itself so that its N pole points in the direction of a magnetic field. The opposite forces acting on its poles pull the needle into the line of the magnetic field.
- **Magnetic field lines never cross each other.**
- In the absence of other magnetic fields, a freely-moving magnet aligns with the Earth's magnetic field.

Things to do

Compare the direction of a magnetic field with the direction of an electric field: Electric fields go from a + charge to a − charge. See D13.3.

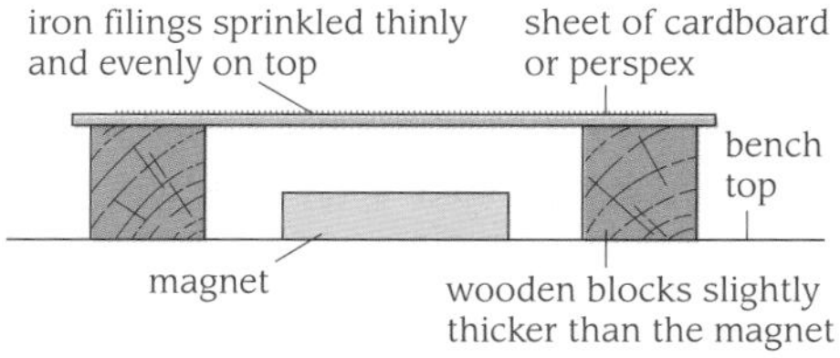

▲ **Figure 17.2.4** Using iron filings to show the shapes of magnetic fields

Magnetic field lines or lines of force

The lines we draw to show the direction of a magnetic field are called **magnetic field lines** or lines of force.

Mapping magnetic fields using a plotting compass

A plotting compass is a simple magnetic compass; a small magnet is supported between two glass faces so that it can turn freely in a horizontal plane.

- Place a bar magnet on a sheet of paper and draw round it.
- Make a dot on the paper near the N pole of the magnet ① (Figure 17.2.3).
- Position the plotting compass so that the curved S pole end of its needle surrounds the dot.
- Make the next dot ② near the N pole end of the plotting compass needle.
- Now move the plotting compass so that its S pole is over dot ② and mark another dot ③ near its N pole.
- Continue to plot points in the direction indicated by the N pole of the compass needle until you reach the S pole of the magnet.
- Join up the dots to show the magnetic field line.

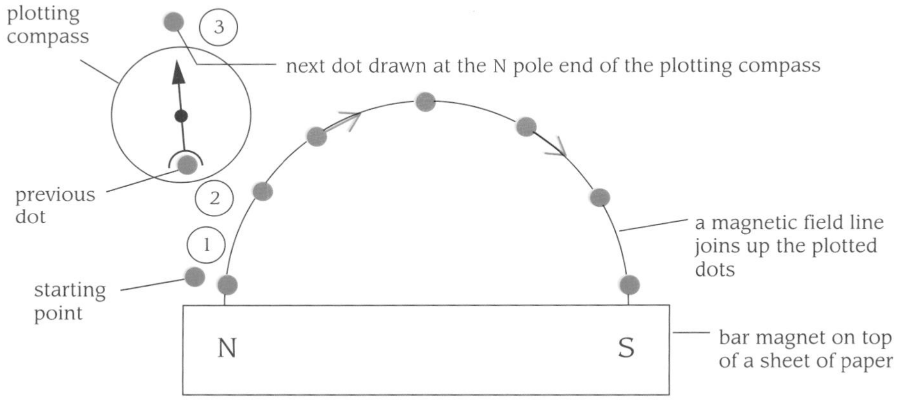

▲ **Figure 17.2.3** Using a plotting compass to map out a magnetic field

A complete map of the magnetic field of the magnet can be made by plotting field lines from several different starting points around the N pole of the magnet.

Mapping magnetic fields using iron filings

- Arrange a sheet of cardboard or transparent Perspex over the top of a magnet (see Figure 17.2.4).

Non-magnetic materials such as wooden blocks or aluminium rings can be used to support the sheet so that it is slightly raised above the magnet.

- Using a pepper pot, sprinkle iron filings thinly and evenly over the top of the sheet and then gently tap the sheet with a pencil.

The iron filings become magnetised by magnetic induction in the magnetic field, forming small magnetic dipoles. Tapping the sheet allows them to move and turn to line up with the direction of the magnetic field. As the filings have to become magnetised, this requires a strong magnetic field. Permanent records of iron filings field maps can be made by spraying the filings with a fixer such as hair lacquer.

Maps of magnetic fields

Drawing magnetic field maps

Figure 17.2.5 shows the basic structure of a typical magnetic field map. This is not a complete map. Rather it shows how to draw one by planning the main features first. The order to work in is as follows:

① Draw the magnet shape(s) and label the magnetic poles.

② A line of force will leave the N pole and one will enter the S pole at the end of each magnet.

③ Lines of force will curve round from the N pole to the S pole on both sides of each magnet.

④ When there are two magnets a line of force will reach across from the N pole of one magnet to the S pole of the other if unlike poles are nearby.

⑤ Look for any places where either lines of force pass in opposite directions or like poles of two magnets are nearby and mark an X between them for a neutral point.

⑥ Draw in extra lines of force to complete the map.

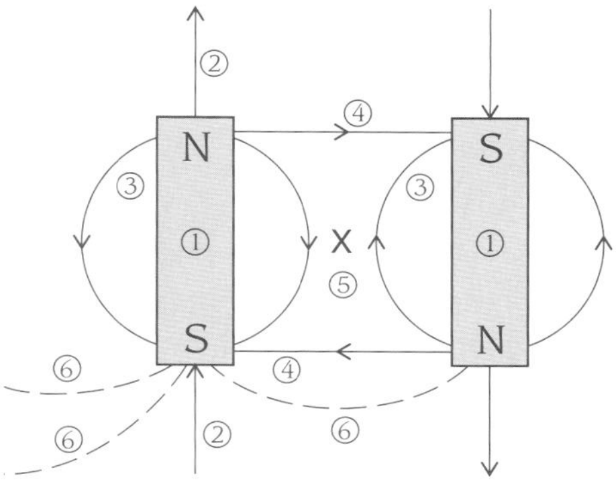

▲ **Figure 17.2.5** Drawing a magnetic field map

Note that:

- Arrows should be drawn to show the field direction (N to S).
- The magnetic poles are not at the very ends of a bar magnet.
- **Lines of force should never cross each other.**
- The magnetic field is strongest where the lines of force are closest together.

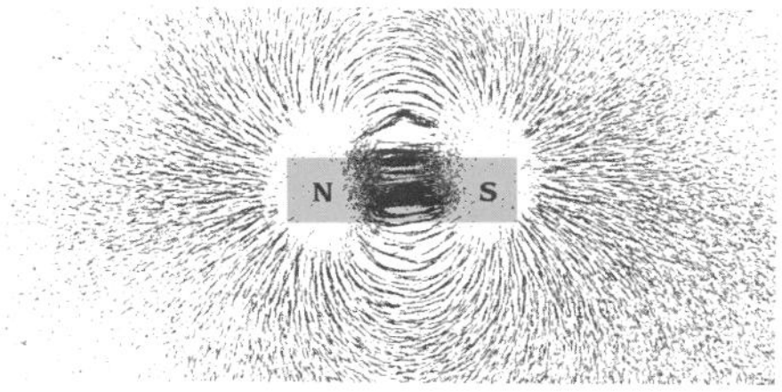

The magnetic field of a single bar magnet.

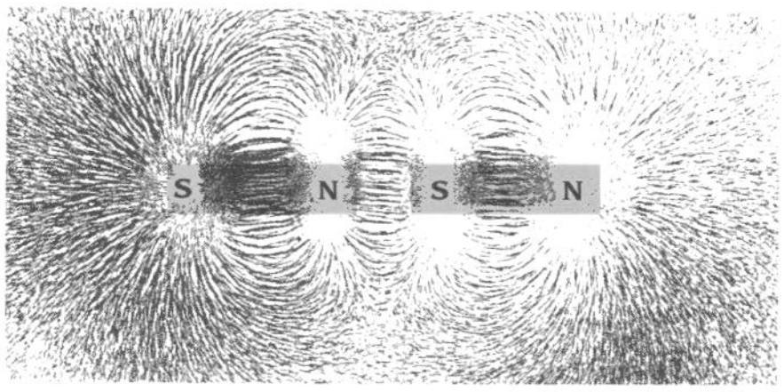

A pair of bar magnets in line with unlike poles together.

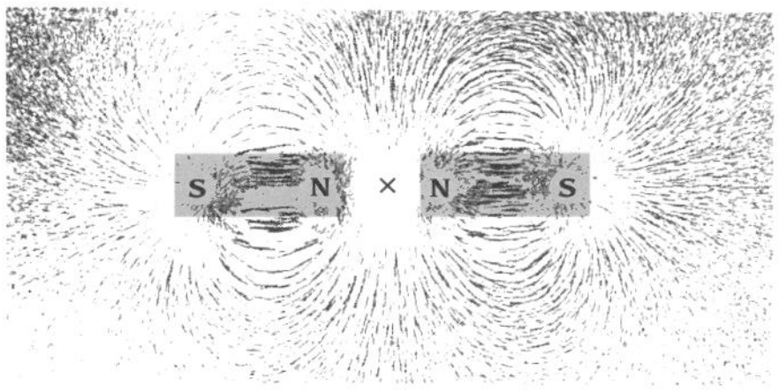

A pair of magnets in line with like poles together. There is a position called a neutral point (marked X) between the two like poles where the two magnetic fields cancel or neutralise each other.

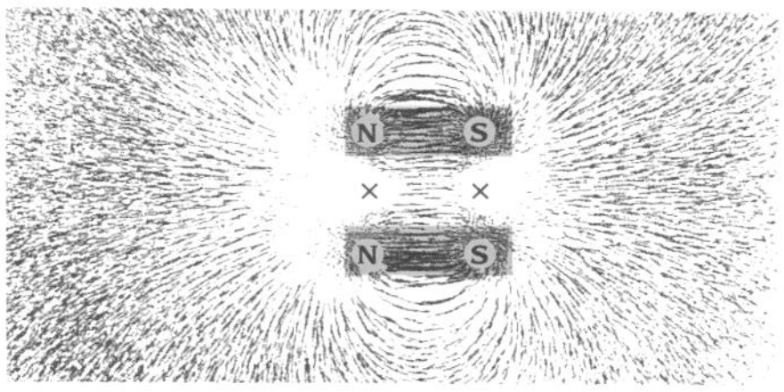

A pair of bar magnets side by side with like poles together. There are two neutral points (marked X) midway between the opposing poles.

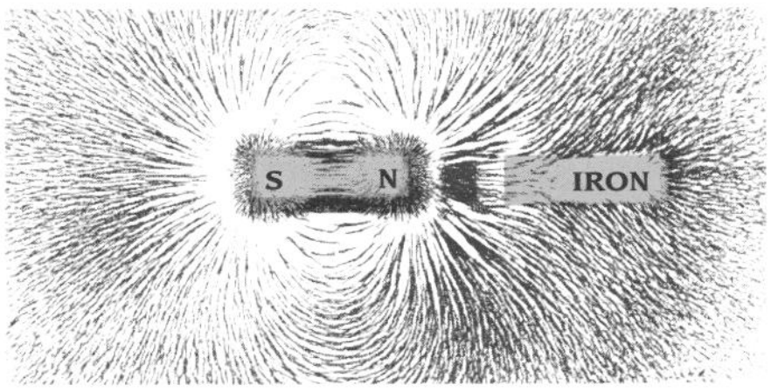

Induced magnetism produced in an iron bar placed in the magnetic field of a permanent magnet. The iron bar draws the magnetic field lines towards it and concentrates the magnetic field through the iron, so producing induced magnetism in it.

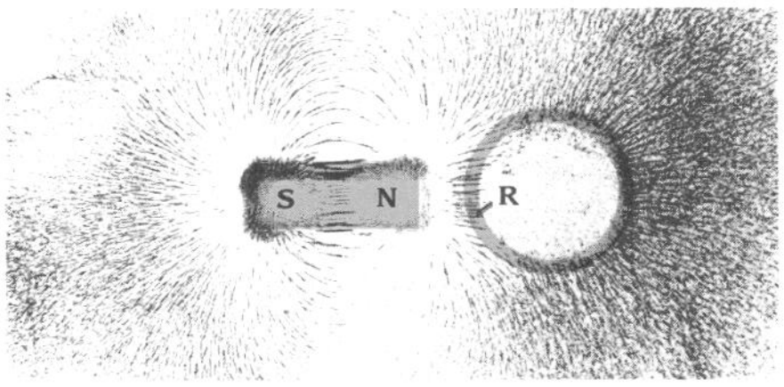

Magnetic shielding by a soft iron ring R. The magnetic field lines are attracted to the soft iron ring and induce magnetism in it, but the region enclosed by the ring is shielded from the magnetic field on the magnet. Soft iron boxes are sometimes used to shield sensitive electrical instruments from magnetic fields.

▲ **Figure 17.2.6** Features of some magnetic fields

Summary questions

1. What is a magnetic field?
2. Sketch the magnetic field lines around a bar magnet.
3. State two ways to show the magnetic field around a magnet.

Objectives

By the end of this topic you will be able to:

- describe experiments to investigate the magnetic field pattern around current-carrying conductors including straight wires, flat coils and solenoids
- apply rules that predict the direction of the magnetic field
- construct an electromagnet.

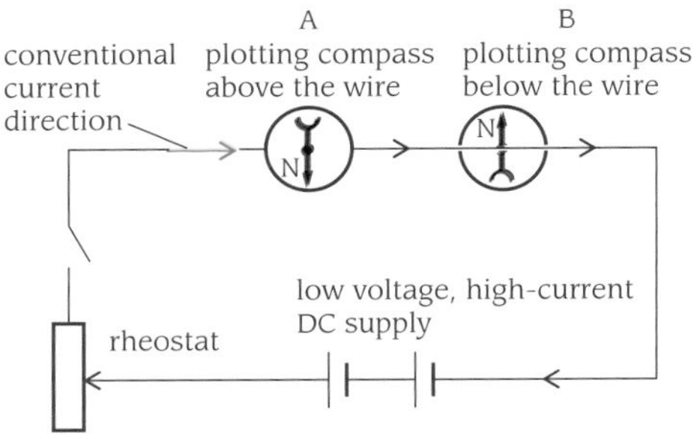

▲ **Figure 17.3.1** Oersted's discovery

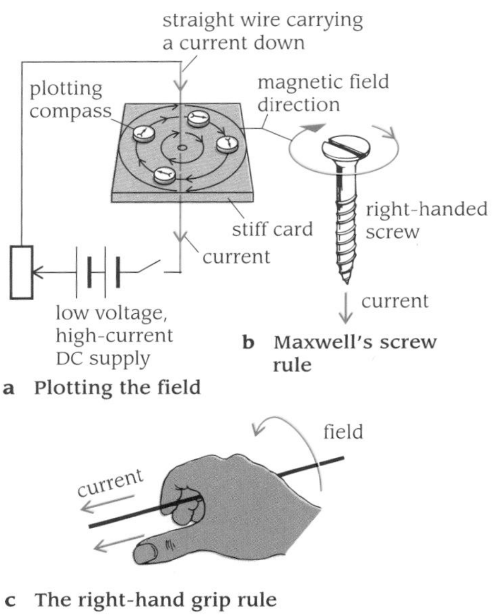

▲ **Figure 17.3.2** The magnetic field round a wire

D17.3 Magnetic effects of electric currents

Oersted's experiment

- Connect a thick copper wire to a low-voltage power pack that can supply several amperes of current. If an accumulator is used, a rheostat of 5 A or 10 A rating should be included in the circuit to protect it.
- Before switching on the current, place a plotting compass at various places around the wire and note the direction of the magnetic field (the direction of the N pole of the needle).
- Now switch on the current and place the plotting compass above and below the wire and note the direction of the magnetic field.
- What happens when the current direction is reversed?

Ampere's swimming rule

Ampere invented a rule to predict the direction of the magnetic field near a wire carrying an electric current.

Imagine you are swimming along the wire in the direction of the current. When you are facing the compass, the N pole of the needle will point to your left.

In Figure 17.3.1, the compass at A is above the wire, the swimmer is facing up out of the page and their left side is towards the bottom of the page. The compass at B is below the wire, the swimmer is facing into the page and their left side is towards the top of the page.

The magnetic field pattern around a straight wire

- Support a stiff card horizontally with a thick straight copper wire passing vertically through its centre (Figure 17.3.2a).
- Pass a large current through the wire vertically downwards.
- Place a plotting compass at various positions around the wire and note the direction of the magnetic field.
- Note the effect of reversing the current.
- Now sprinkle iron filings thinly and evenly over the card.
- With the current on, tap the card gently until the iron filings show the magnetic field pattern.

These experiments show that there is a magnetic field which goes in concentric circles round a wire carrying a current.

The direction of the field around a wire

Maxwell's screw rule: If a right-handed screw is turned so that it moves forwards in the same direction as an electric current, its direction of rotation gives the direction of the magnetic field due to the current (Figure 17.3.2b).

The **right-hand grip rule**: If a wire carrying a current is gripped with the right hand and with the thumb pointing along the wire in the direction of the current, the fingers point in the direction of the magnetic field around the wire (Figure 17.3.2c).

The magnetic field due to the current in a flat coil

- Make a flat circular coil by winding 10 or more turns of wire round a cylindrical former such as a length of plastic pipe or a cardboard tube of diameter about 4 cm or more.
- Push the turns of wire close together and slide them from the former onto a piece of stiff card as shown in Figure 17.3.3a.
- Connect the coil to a low-voltage, high-current supply.
- Sprinkle iron filings over the card both inside and outside the coil.
- Switch on the current and tap the card until the magnetic field pattern shows up.
- Use a plotting compass to find the direction of the magnetic field at various points around the coil.

It is helpful to compare the magnetic field around each side of the coil where it passes through the card with the field of a single straight wire.

Note the direction of the current at each side and apply a direction rule to check the direction of the magnetic field.

Note that the circular lines of force around the wires become squashed together inside the coil. The magnetic field is stronger inside the coil.

The magnetic field pattern due to a solenoid

- Make another coil, this time stretching out the turns to form a long coil, called a solenoid, about 10 cm long and 4 cm or more in diameter.
- Mount the solenoid on a stiff card or hardboard as in Figure 17.3.4.
- Again using a plotting compass and iron filings, obtain a map of the magnetic field showing both its shapes and direction.

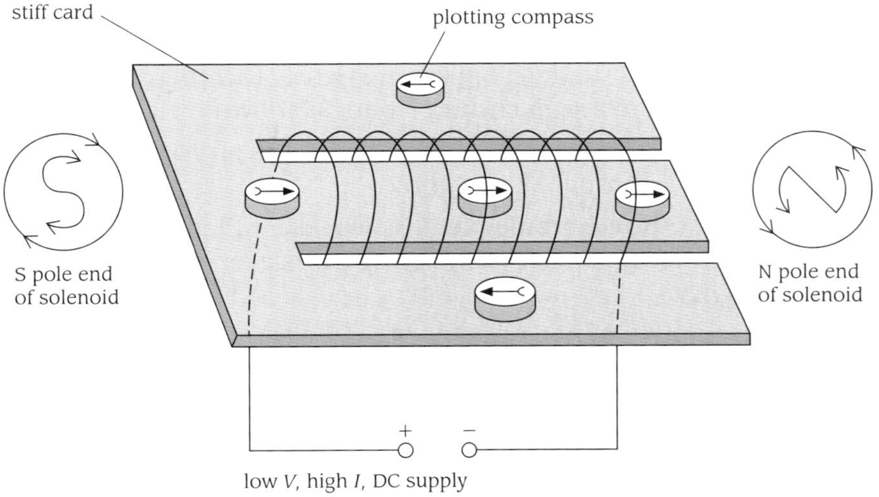

▲ **Figure 17.3.4** A practical arrangement for plotting the magnetic field due to a solenoid

Note the following:

- The direction of the magnetic field inside is opposite to the direction outside the solenoid.
- The clarity of the iron filing pattern shows that the magnetic field is stronger inside the solenoid than outside.
- This magnetic field map is similar to that of a bar magnet (Figure 17.3.5).

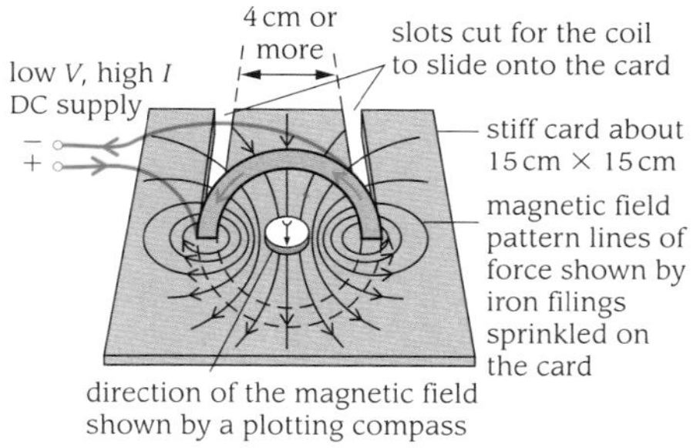

a Drawing the field:
- The magnetic field points out of the coil in the diagram towards us.
- The face of the coil we see with the current flowing anticlockwise round it produces a N pole.

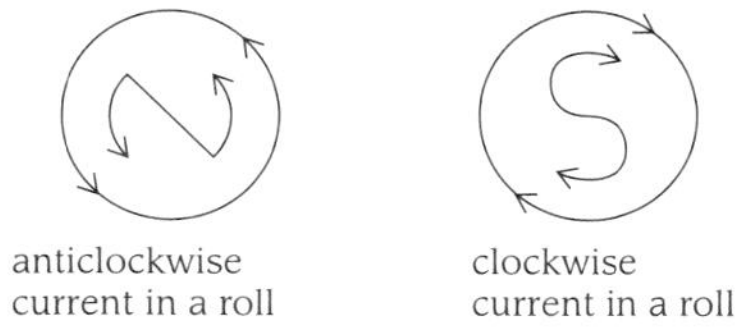

b Rule for the magnetic poles of a coil:
- The pole is given by the letter, which points in the same direction as the current.
- A coil will always have the opposite pole on its other face because the current direction is reversed when seen from the other side.

▲ **Figure 17.3.3** The magnetic field due to a flat circular coil carrying a current

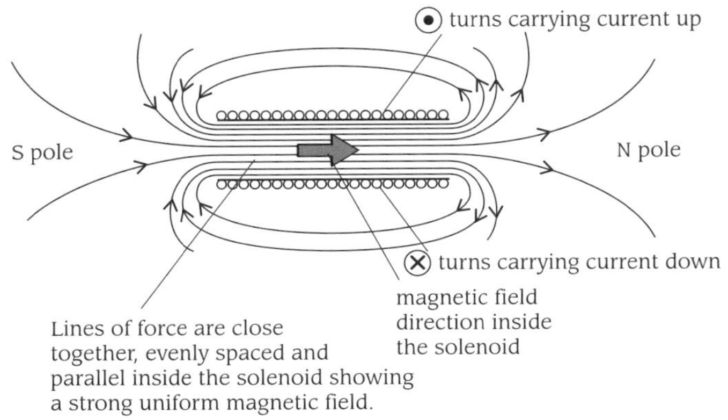

▲ **Figure 17.3.5** Map of the magnetic field pattern of a solenoid

The electromagnet: a solenoid with an iron core

The solenoid has a magnetic field, which is very similar to that of a bar magnet and we can fit an iron bar inside the solenoid where its magnetic field is strongest. A bar of soft iron inside a solenoid is called its core. The magnet produced by a current in a solenoid with a soft iron core is called an electromagnet. When the current in the solenoid is switched off the temporary magnetism in the soft iron core quickly disappears. Consequently, the magnetism of an electromagnet can be switched on and off.

Investigating the strength of an electromagnet

The factors that affect the strength of an electromagnet are:

- the current in the solenoid
- the number of turns of wire on the solenoid
- the shape of the iron core.
    - Clamp a soft iron nail or iron rod, about 10 cm long in a wooden holder as in Figure 17.3.6.
    - Wind 10 turns of insulated copper wire tightly together round the nail and connect to a high current circuit as shown.
    - Switch on the current and adjust the rheostat to give a particular current, say 2 A, through the solenoid.
    - Dip the end of the electromagnet into a beaker full of small iron nails, panel pins or paperclips by lifting the beaker up to the electromagnet.
    - Count the number of nails attached to the electromagnet.
    - Switch off the current and note that most, if not all of the nails fall off the electromagnet.
    - Repeat the experiment for different values of the current or number of turns on the solenoid.

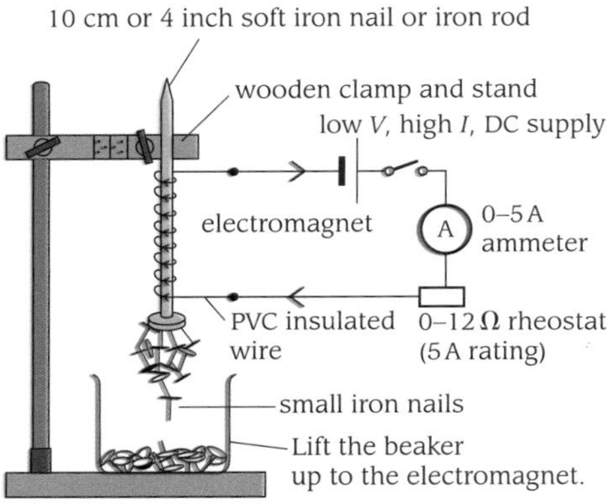

▲ **Figure 17.3.6** Testing electromagnets

Key fact

- The strength of an electromagnet increases with the current and the number of turns.
- After a certain current and number of turns is reached, further increases in current or turns do not make the electromagnet any stronger. (The iron core becomes saturated with magnetism.)
- Using a C-core or horseshoe-shaped core makes a stronger magnet because both poles can be used for lifting.

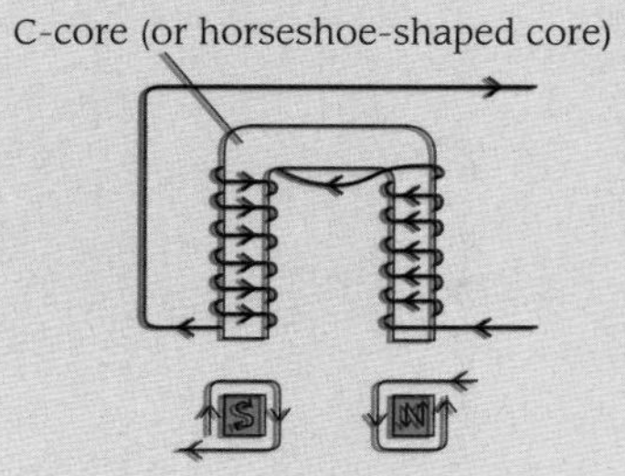

Summary questions

1. State one rule that can be used to find the direction of the magnetic field around a current-carrying wire.
2. What shape is the magnetic field around a solenoid?
3. State the factors that affect the strength of the magnetic field of a solenoid.

D17.4 Electromagnets at work

Objectives

By the end of this topic you will be able to:

- describe a commercial application of an electromagnet
- explain the action of a simple magnetic relay.

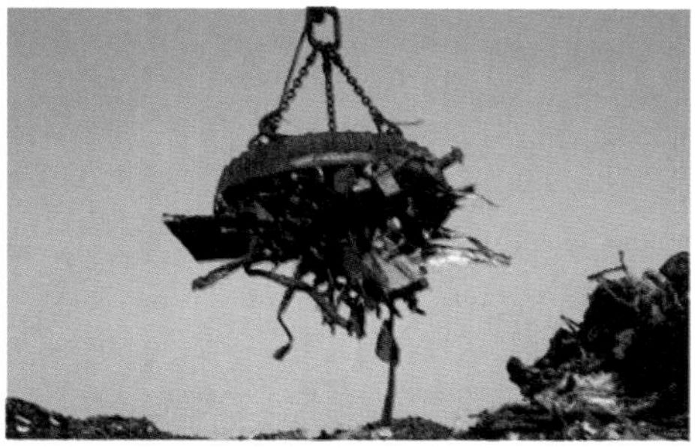

▲ **Figure 17.4.1** An electromagnet is useful for picking up filings and small pieces of iron or steel. It will leave behind metal fragments of copper, brass, aluminium and lead and all other rubbish.

▲ **Figure 17.4.2** An array of electromagnets provides an effective way of lifting single sheets of iron or steel. No hooks or chains are needed and the sheet metal can be released just by switching off the current.

Electromagnets for lifting

Electrical machines that use the magnetic effect of an electric current usually have a coil or solenoid which acts as an electromagnet. Electromagnets can be switched on and off and can be varied in their strength by the electric current.

An electromagnet can be made more powerful by:

- using a soft-iron core inside the coil or solenoid
- having a large number of turns on the coil
- passing a large current through the coil
- using a core shape that brings both magnetic poles close together
- forming a closed loop of soft iron from the electromagnet core and the steel object being lifted so that there is an 'iron circuit' for the magnetic field lines.

Figure 17.4.3 shows a design for a lifting electromagnet that uses all these ideas to make it very powerful.

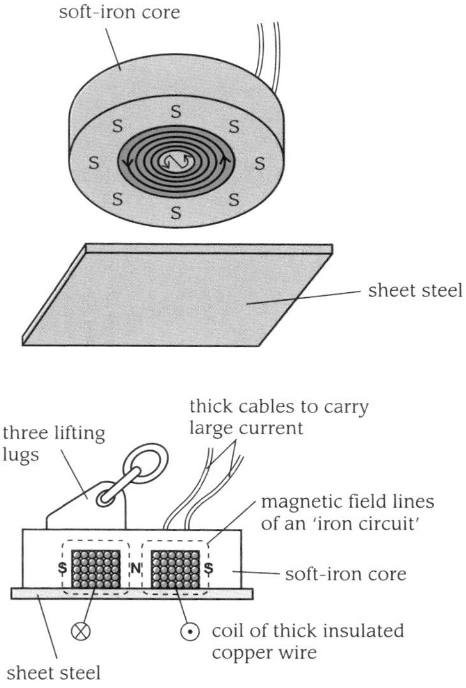

▲ **Figure 17.4.3** An electromagnet for lifting

Uses of electromagnets

Electromagnets are particularly useful in industry for:

- lifting steel plates and slabs that are difficult to handle or attach hooks and chains to
- lifting large quantities of loose iron and steel, e.g. scrap metal
- separating ferromagnetic metals from others such as copper, brass, aluminium and lead.

Making permanent magnets

A bar of steel, a weak magnet that needs re-magnetising, or a steel knitting needle can be used.

A solenoid with a large number of turns is required.

- Connect the solenoid in series with a switch and a supply of direct current capable of passing several amperes through the solenoid (Figure 17.4.4).
- Place the steel object fully inside the solenoid and switch the direct current on and off.

A high current is needed only for a short time to produce the maximum level of magnetisation. Longer times will not increase the strength of the magnet but may overheat the solenoid.

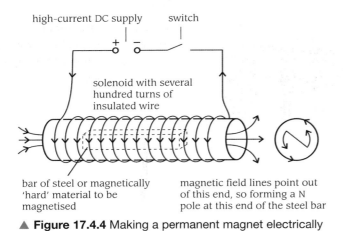

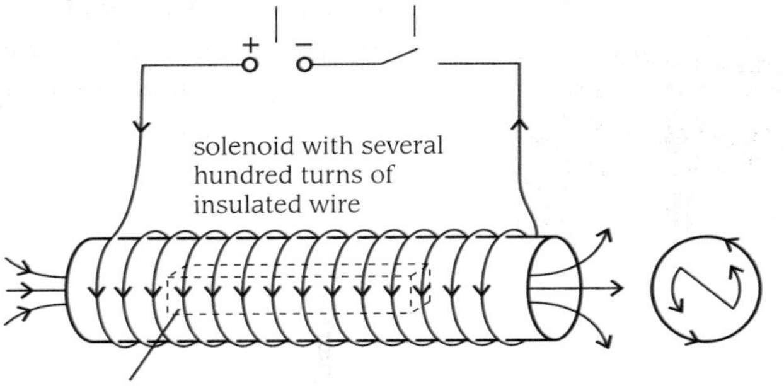

▲ **Figure 17.4.4** Making a permanent magnet electrically

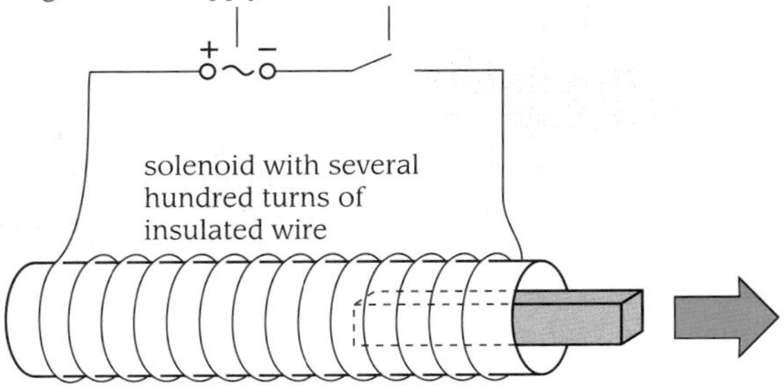

▲ **Figure 17.4.5** Demagnetising

Demagnetising, removing magnetism

Key fact

How demagnetisation works

- The alternating current will flow in both directions round the solenoid 50 or 60 times every second. Consequently the magnetic field inside the solenoid will change direction twice as often.
- As the steel object is slowly removed from this magnetic field the strength of the field will gradually weaken. The effect is to reverse the magnetisation of the object repeatedly, but at a slightly weaker strength every time the field reverses. Thus the strength of the magnetisation gradually reduces step by step.

- Use a similar solenoid to the one used for magnetising a steel bar but this time connect it to a supply of alternating current (Figure 17.4.5). (A transformer stepping the mains supply down to 12 V and capable of supplying about 8 A is suitable.)
- Place the magnetised object fully inside the solenoid and switch on the alternating current.
- With the current still on, slowly pull the object out of the solenoid and remove it well away from the magnetic field.
- Check to see whether the material is completely demagnetised by trying to pick up some unmagnetised pins. If the material is not completely demagnetised, repeat the process.

◀ **Figure 17.4.6** A computer hard disc. A small electromagnet, mounted in the read/write head on the end of the metal arm, is used to magnetise and demagnetise the magnetic coating of the hard disk. Digital data is stored in a binary code as very small dots of magnetisation on the surface of the hard disk.

The electric bell

Electric bells and buzzers often use an electromagnet in a simple way to attract a soft-iron bar called the armature. For a bell to ring continuously an automatic mechanism is needed to switch the current off and on again rapidly. The circuit in Figure 17.4.7 shows how this mechanism works in many electric bells. Follow the path of the current round the complete circuit and see if you can predict the poles on the electromagnet. Then read the next section.

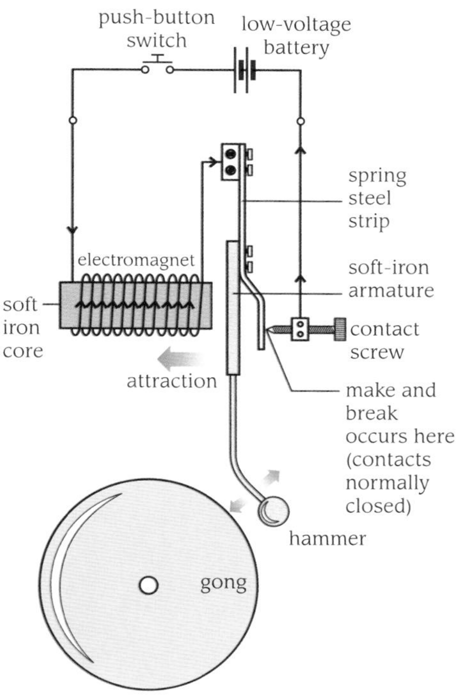

▲ **Figure 17.4.7** The electric bell

How the electric bell works

a) When the push-button switch is closed there is a complete circuit (the contact screw and spring strip are normally closed in the rest position of the armature).

b) A current flows through the electromagnet, so magnetising the iron core.

c) The electromagnet induces magnetism in the soft-iron armature, which is attracted to the pole of the electromagnet.

d) The hammer strikes the gong.

e) The spring strip contact moves away from the screw contact and breaks the circuit, switching off the current.

f) The electromagnet, no longer magnetised, releases the armature, which springs back to its starting position.

g) The spring strip contact now touches the screw again, remakes the circuit and switches on the current.

The cycle repeats rapidly from b) to g) for as long as the push-button switch is closed.

- The hammer strikes the gong repeatedly making a continuous ringing sound. The spring strip and screw contacts, where the current is automatically switched on and off, are often called a 'make and break' mechanism, because it 'makes' and then 'breaks' the circuit.

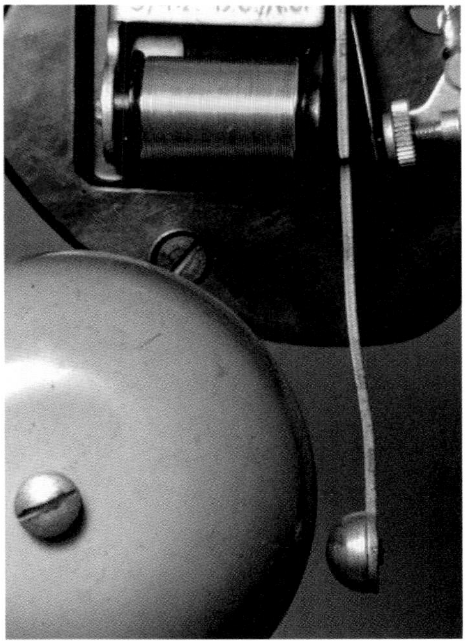

▲ **Figure 17.4.8** The inside of a battery-powered doorbell

Relays

A relay is a switching device that uses an electromagnet (Figure 17.4.9).

How a relay works

- A relay has two or more completely separate circuits.
- The input circuit (terminals 1 and 2) supplies current to the electromagnet.
- Only a very small current is needed to operate the electromagnet, which attracts one end of a soft-iron armature.
- The armature is pivoted so that its other end acts as a lever. This lever opens or closes contacts in the second or output circuit, by pushing a spring metal strip.
- The spring strips and contacts can be arranged so that they are normally open or normally closed and several sets of contacts can be operated by the same armature lever.

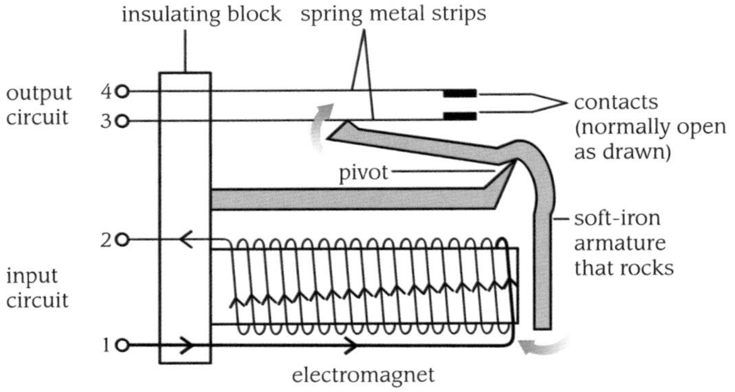

The contacts are made of precious metals such as silver or gold, which last for 10 to 100 million operations.

▲ **Figure 17.4.9** A relay

The purpose of a relay

- One circuit can be used to control (switch on or off) another circuit (or several circuits) without any direct electrical connection between them.
- The input circuit can work on a low-voltage (safe) supply and control another circuit on a high-voltage (dangerous) supply.
- A small current in the input circuit can switch a large current in the output circuit. For example, in the car ignition circuit, a low current through the ignition switch operates a relay, which closes a circuit so passing a very large current through the starter motor.
- Similarly a transistor switch using a very small current can control a relay that switches much larger currents in other circuits.
- The relay can be considered as a mechanical current amplifier when it is used as described above.
- The relay can be used as a level sensor. Only when the current through the electromagnet reaches a precise level will the armature swing and the output circuit operate. The input current level at which this happens can be made to represent the level of some quantity being measured.

Summary questions

1 State two uses of electromagnets.

2 Describe how an electric bell works.

D17.5 The Earth's magnetic field

The Earth as a magnet

▲ **Figure 17.5.1** These migrating birds have magnetic sensors in their heads, which help them find their direction by using the Earth's magnetic field.

Birds, animals and humanity use the Earth's magnetic field for navigation. The Earth's magnetic field also protects the Earth from charged particles from space, which would disrupt our communications systems. The Earth's magnetic field is probably caused by electric currents within the Earth's core, which contains large amounts of molten iron. Movements in the molten core mean the Earth's magnetic field changes, and the Earth's magnetic north pole moves slowly over the years. It can be hundreds of kilometres from 'true north'. The Earth's 'true North Pole' does not move; it is the north end of the Earth's axis of rotation.

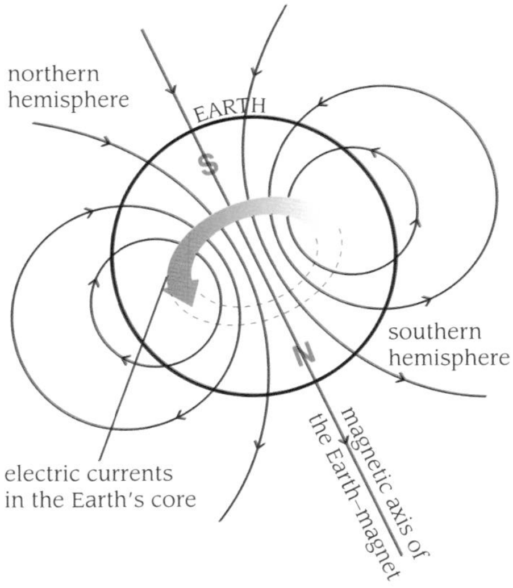

▲ **Figure 17.5.2** The magnetic field of the Earth, explained by electric currents in the core

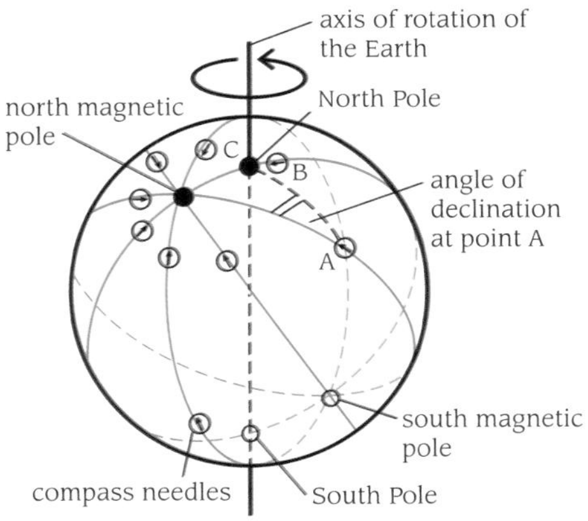

▲ **Figure 17.5.3** The horizontal components of the Earth's magnetic field as shown by compass needles

A compass works because the compass needle is a freely-moving magnet that lines up with the Earth's magnetic field, so that the 'north' pole of the compass points to the Earth's magnetic north.

Summary questions

1 Describe briefly what is thought to cause the Earth's magnetic field.

2 How does a compass work?

Practice exam-style questions

1 The figure below shows two permanent bar magnets placed so that unlike poles are facing each other.

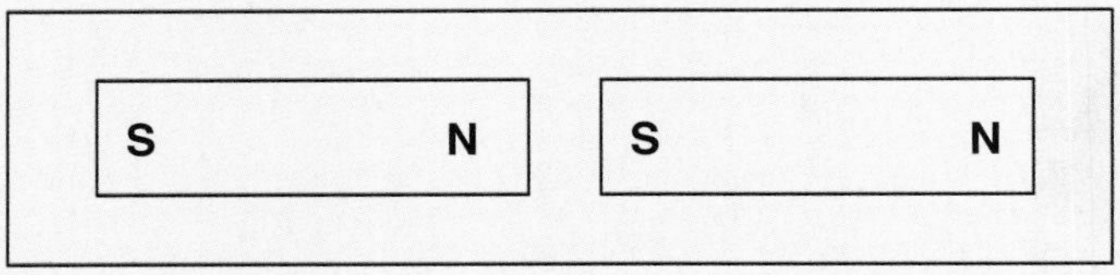

a) Copy the diagram and sketch the magnetic field around and between the magnets.

b) Name a suitable material from which these magnets could be made and state why it is suitable.

2 The figure below shows two bar magnets with their north poles facing each other.

a) Copy the diagram and sketch the magnetic field between the magnets.

b) What happens at the point roughly midway between the two facing north poles?

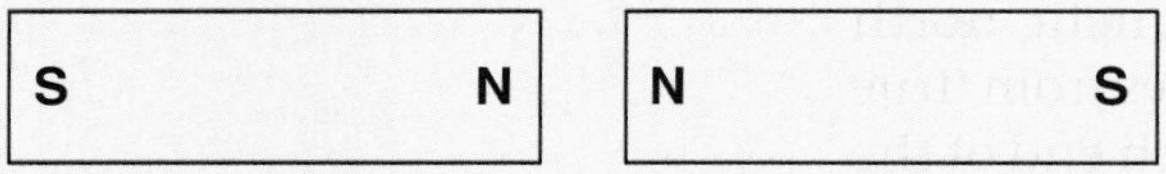

3 To make an electromagnet, a coil of insulated wire is wound around a U-shaped core AB and connected to a battery, as shown in the figure below.

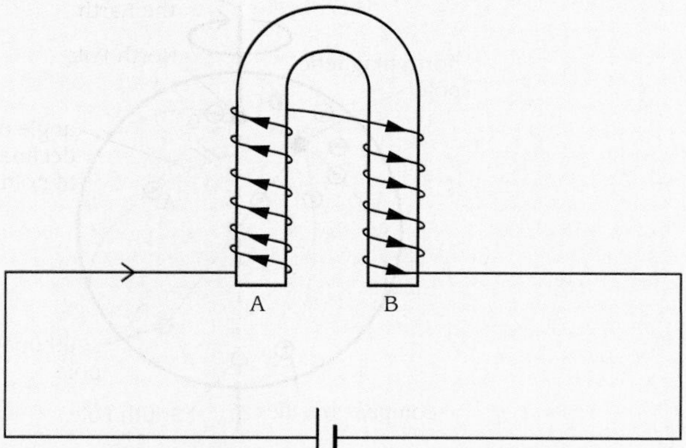

a) State the polarity of end A and draw a diagram to show how you deduced this.

b) Describe TWO ways of increasing the strength of this electromagnet.

c) Why must the wire be insulated?

d) What material would be used for the core and what are its properties that make it suitable?

4 Many small pieces of soft iron, identical in size and shape are held just below end A of the arrangement shown in the figure below.

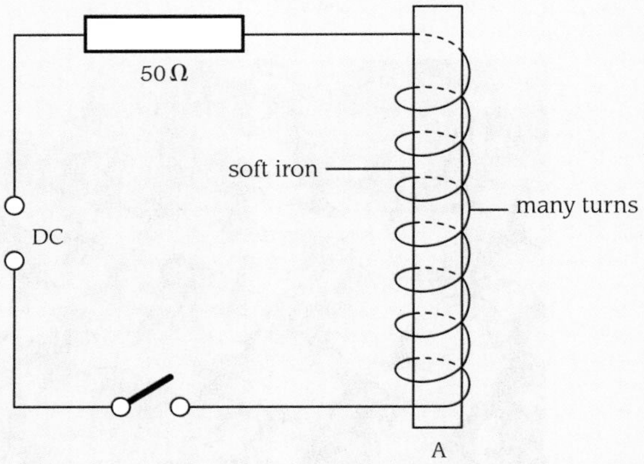

a) Describe and account for what happens when the switch is closed and then opened again.

b) Compare these results with what would happen if pieces of hard steel of identical size and shape were used instead of the soft iron.

5 a) Figure **a** below shows a wire XY carrying a steady electric current in the direction shown. Copy the diagram and sketch magnetic field lines in the horizontal plane indicated. Mark the direction of the field lines.

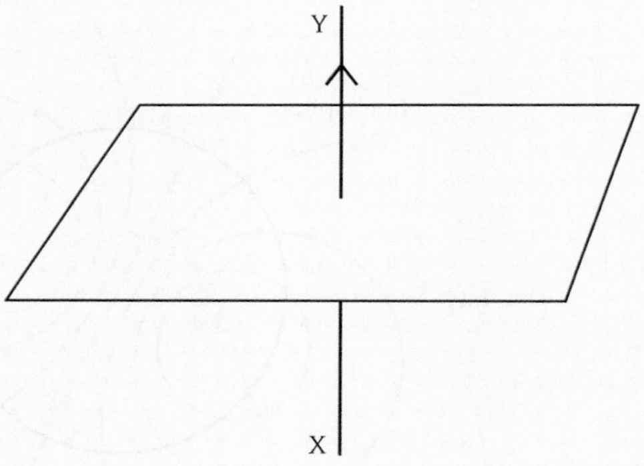

a

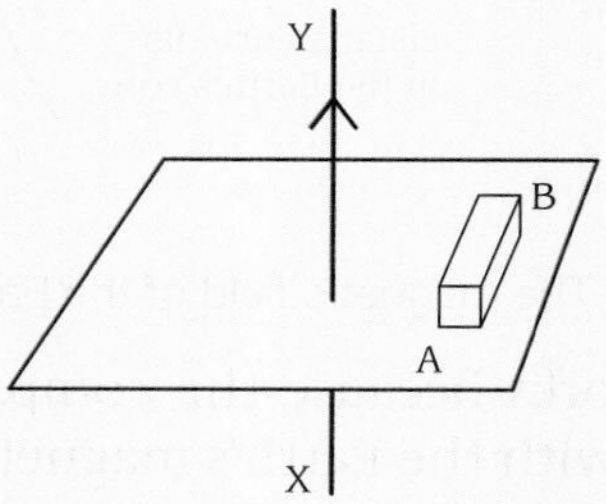

b

b) With the current switched off, a short piece of unmagnetised soft iron, AB, is placed alongside the wire in a horizontal plane, as shown in figure **b** above. The current is switched on again. State the effects produced in the soft iron by the current.

6 A solenoid is a long coil of wire often wound around a tube.

a) Draw a diagram to show the shape of the magnetic field both inside and outside the solenoid created by passing an electric current round the coils of the solenoid. Mark the directions of the electric current and the magnetic field.

b) By sketching another diagram, compare the shape of this magnetic field with that of a bar magnet.

c) State ONE way in which the magnetic field of the solenoid is different from that of the bar magnet.

7 **a)** State THREE factors that affect the strength of an electromagnet.

b) Describe an experiment that you could carry out in a school laboratory to demonstrate these three factors.

8 The figure below shows a cross-section through a current-carrying solenoid. The dot in a circle represents the current coming up out of the plane of the paper.

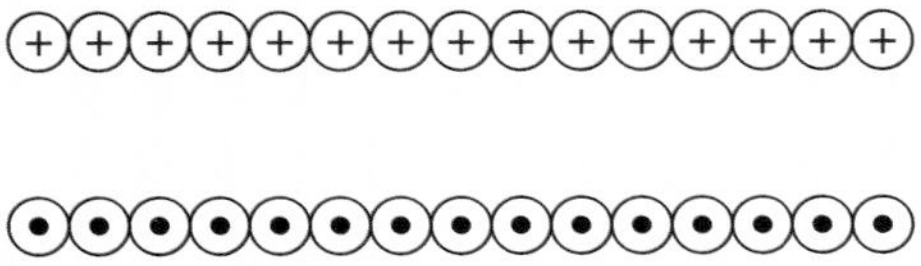

a) Copy the diagram and draw lines to represent the magnetic field both inside and outside the solenoid. Indicate the direction of the field lines.

b) Draw a circle to represent the left-hand end of the solenoid. On it, indicate the direction of the current around this coil of wire and the magnetic pole that appears on this end face of the solenoid.

9 Copy and complete the table below, which compares properties of magnetic and electric fields.

	Magnetic fields	Electric fields
The field lines leave …		
The field lines arrive at …		
Two field lines never …		
The field lines give the direction of the force on …		

10 The figure below shows a horizontal cross-section through a flat circular coil set in a vertical plane. The current directions in the coil are indicated by the dot (upwards) and cross (downwards).

a) Copy the diagram and on it draw lines with arrows to indicate the shape and direction of the magnetic field around the coil.

b) Where is the magnetic field strongest?

11 The Earth has a magnetic field with a pole in northern Canada.

a) Is the pole in northern Canada a magnetic north pole or a magnetic south pole? In your answer refer to the fact that magnetic compass needles point towards this pole.

b) Explain how a traveller would know that she was exactly above one of the Earth's magnetic poles.

12 Some of the following list of materials may be used for making magnets of various kinds.

Metals: iron, copper, nickel, cobalt, zinc.

Alloys: steel, brass, Ticonal, Alnico, Stalloy (soft-iron alloy).

a) Select TWO materials suitable for making a permanent magnet.

b) Select TWO materials suitable for making an electromagnet.

c) Select TWO materials that cannot be used for making magnets.

13 The figure below shows a reed switch. The iron reeds inside the switch become magnetised temporarily when the current is switched on via terminals 1 and 2 of the solenoid.

a) Explain why the switch, connected to terminals 3 and 4, closes when the solenoid current is switched on. In your explanation refer to the magnetic poles that will be induced in the iron reeds.

b) Give ONE example of an application for a reed switch.

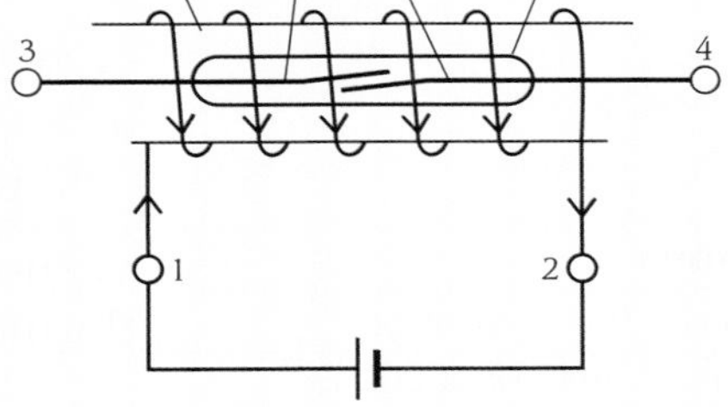

14 The figure below shows an electric bell operated by a battery.

a) Look at this diagram and explain the function of the parts labelled:

i) core

ii) S

iii) A

b) Explain why the bell will operate from a DC supply and does not require an AC supply.

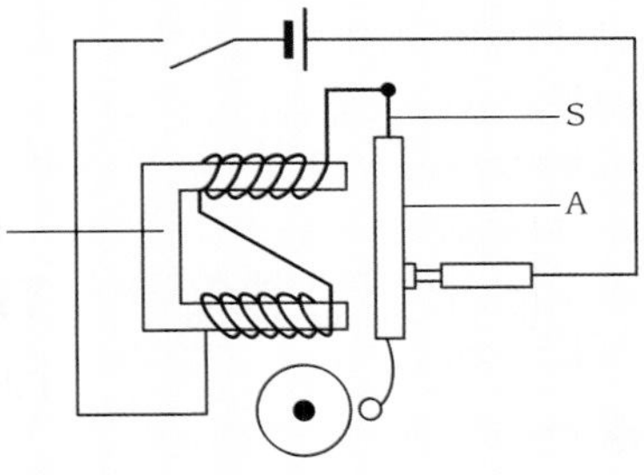

D18 Using magnetism

Objectives

By the end of this topic you will be able to:

- describe an experiment that demonstrates the force acting on a current-carrying wire in a magnetic field
- sketch the resultant magnetic flux pattern where a current-carrying wire is placed perpendicular to a uniform magnetic field
- apply Fleming's left-hand (motor) rule to predict the force and motion resulting when a current-carrying wire is perpendicular to a magnetic field
- recall that the magnitude of the force depends on the strength of the field and the current
- explain how a moving-coil loudspeaker works and draw a diagram showing how its coil moves to reproduce sound.

! Key fact

Observations

- When either the current or the magnetic field direction is reversed the direction of the movement of the wire is reversed.
- The wire is thrown out of the magnetic field as if the field had been stretched like a piece of elastic in a catapult, which is suddenly let go.
- The catapult force acts sideways or at right angles to both the current direction and the magnetic field direction.

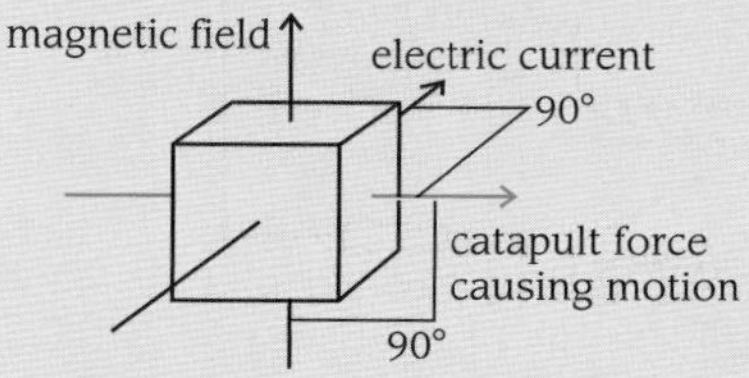

▲ **Figure 18.1.2**

The interactions of electric currents and magnetic fields are very varied and provide many applications that are essential to most of the devices and machines on which we depend in today's world. Generators, electric motors, transformers, relays and loudspeakers all use the dynamic links between magnetic field, electric current and force, which makes all these devices work.

D18.1 Electric currents in magnetic fields

The force on a current-carrying wire

- Attach two magnadur flat magnets to an iron yoke with unlike poles facing to provide a strong magnetic field.
- Mount two stiff, straight lengths of copper wire or brass rod parallel and horizontal on an insulating support as shown in Figure 18.1.1.
- Sit a length of copper wire or brass rod across the parallel wires so that it can move smoothly and freely along them. (Make the wire long enough that it does not fall off the rails as it moves.)
- Connect a low-voltage, high-current supply to the ends of the parallel wires so that a complete circuit is formed.
- With the magnets in place, switch on the current and watch what happens.
- Repeat the test with the current direction reversed and then the direction of the magnetic field reversed.

We notice that the wire is thrown or catapulted out of the magnetic field of the magnets (Figure 18.1.3).

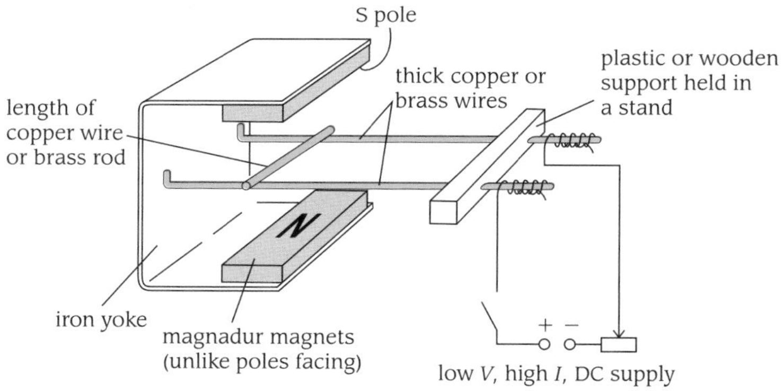

▲ **Figure 18.1.1** The force acting on a wire carrying a current in a magnetic field

The shape of the field producing the catapult force

Observations

- The two separate magnetic fields combine.

- If we imagine that the lines of force are lengths of elastic under tension, we see that the field of the permanent magnet is stretched and acts as a catapult trying to throw the wire sideways.
- The direction of the force is always at right angles to both the magnetic field and the electric current.
- **The force or thrust acting on the wire depends on:**
  1. **the magnitude of the electric current**
  2. **the strength of the magnetic field**
  3. **the length of conductor in the magnetic field.**
- **The force is greatest when the current and the field are perpendicular to each other.**

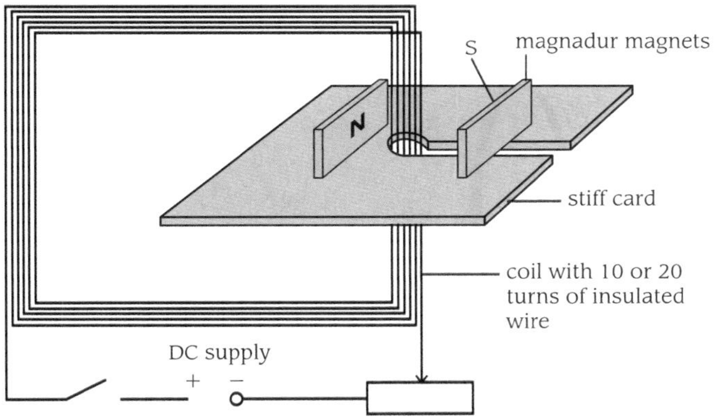

a

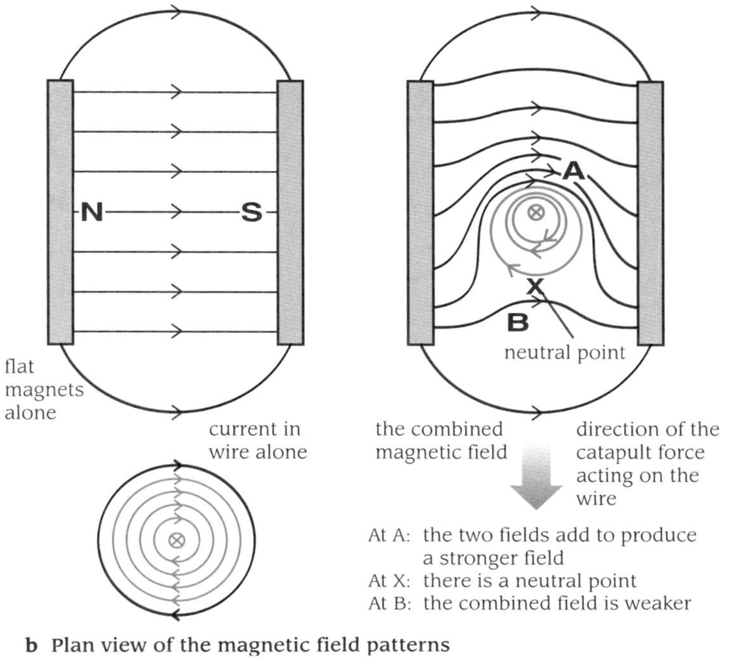

b Plan view of the magnetic field patterns

▲ **Figure 18.1.3** The field producing the catapult force

- Stand two magnadur magnets with unlike poles facing on a horizontal board on either side of a vertical wire.
- Sprinkle iron filings on the board between the magnets.
- Switch on the current and gently tap the board.

Fleming's left-hand rule: the motor rule

J. A. Fleming devised a rule for quickly predicting the direction of the catapult force (Figure 18.1.4).

Hold the thumb and first two fingers of your left hand at right angles to each other.

- Point your **F**irst finger in the direction of the magnetic **F**ield (N to S pole).
- Point your se**C**ond finger in the direction of the **C**urrent.
- Your **Th**umb now points in the direction of the **Th**rust.

An alternative (and easier) way to hold your hand for Fleming's left-hand rule is with your hand flat.

- Your **F**irst finger still points in the direction of the **F**ield.
- Your **Th**umb still points in the direction of the **Th**rust.
- And you have to remember that **P**ositive charges (conventional current) leave your **P**alm.

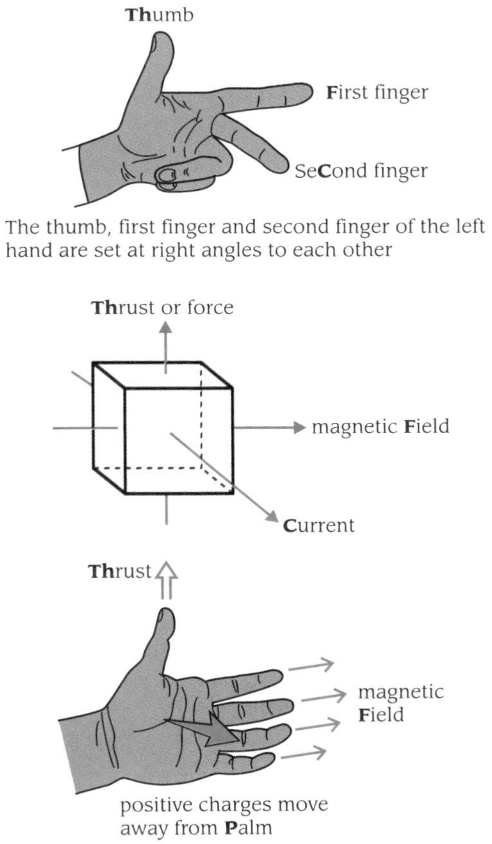

▲ **Figure 18.1.4** Fleming's left-hand rule

A moving-coil loudspeaker

The most common type of loudspeaker uses a moving coil to cause the motion that reproduces sound waves in the air.

The moving coil is attached to a flexible paper cone, which moves the air molecules to produce sound. The coil fits into a cylindrical magnet that has a centre S pole surrounded by a N pole as shown in Figure 18.1.5b. The coil is free to move in and out of the cylindrical gap in the magnet where the magnetic field lines point radially inwards.

Rapidly changing currents from an amplifier are passed through the speaker coil and as the current direction reverses, the movement of the coil and cone changes direction. You can check the direction of the catapult force using Fleming's left-hand rule.

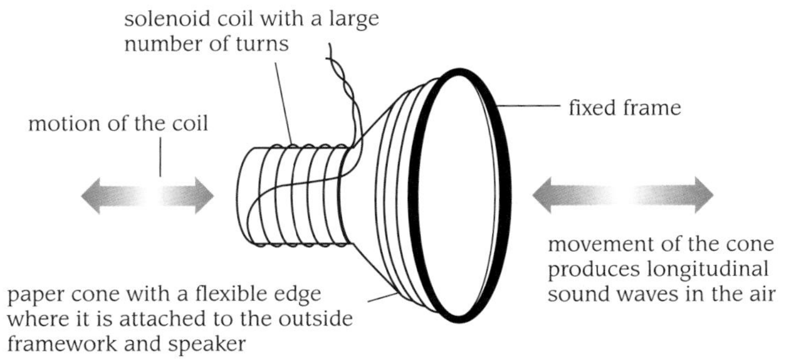

a Cone and coil

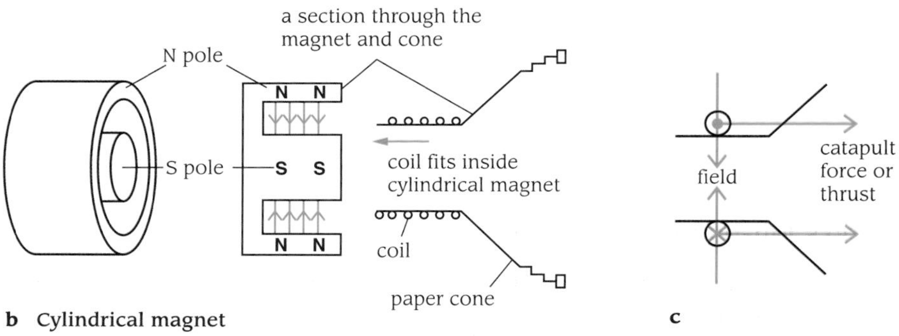

b Cylindrical magnet

c

▲ **Figure 18.1.5** A moving-coil loudspeaker

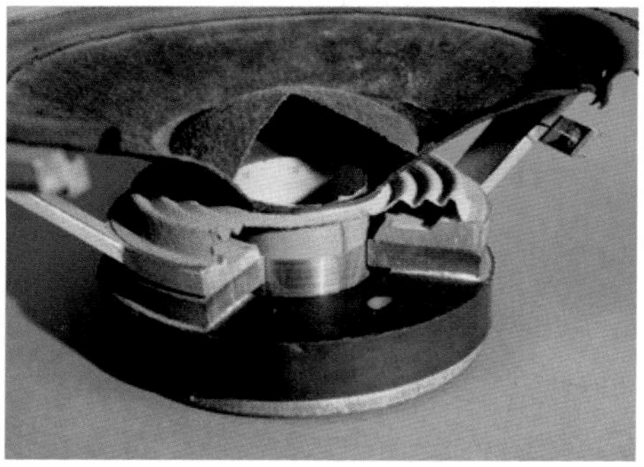

◀ **Figure 18.1.6** This cut-away image of a moving-coil loudspeaker shows the following details. The permanent magnet is black and at the base of the construction. The moving copper wire voice coil is in the centre. The flexible, corrugated circular structure holds the moving coil in place. The upper, grey diaphragm is attached to the moving coil and produces sound waves in the air when the coil moves.

Summary questions

1 What happens to a current-carrying wire at right angles to a magnetic field?

2 What does Fleming's left-hand rule show?

3 What factors affect the size of the force on a current-carrying wire?

D18.2 The motor effect

Coils can be made to twist and turn in different ways in a magnetic field. Electric motors can be made to run on direct current or alternating current and with or without brushes. The amazing variety of ways in which the motor effect is now used is a tribute to the inventiveness of electrical engineers over the last 100 years and to the fascinating nature of these machines.

The direct current motor

Making a simple direct current motor

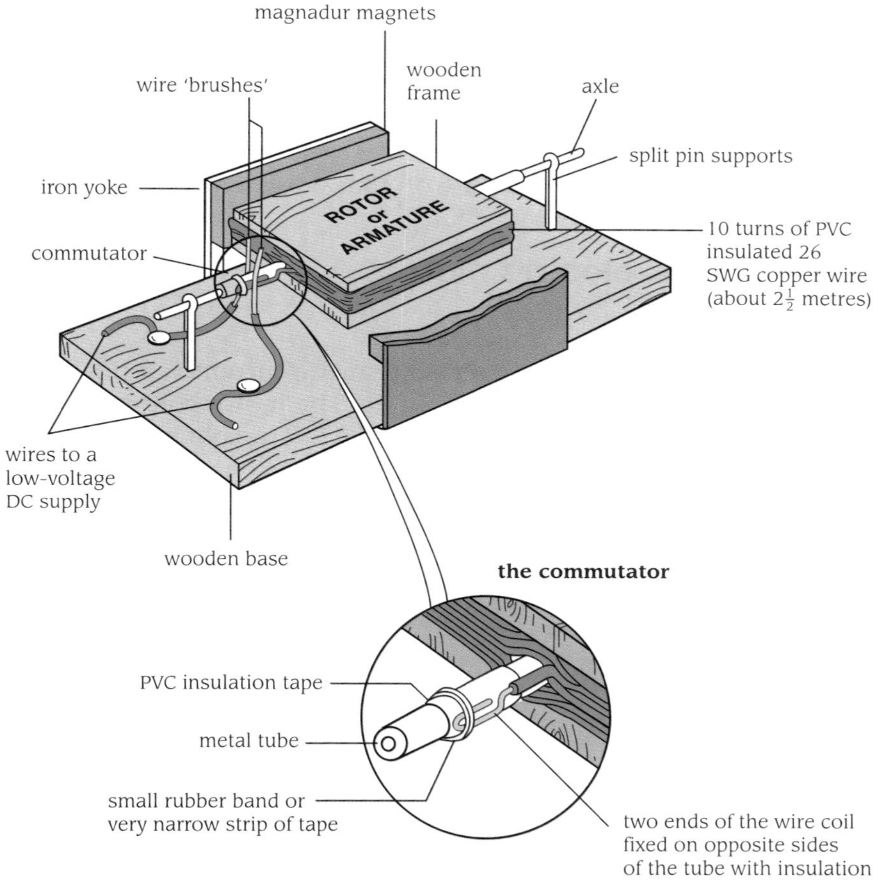

▲ **Figure 18.2.1** A model DC motor

- Using a wooden frame with a channel round its edges, wind 10 turns of thin (26 SWG) PVC-insulated wire around it so that the ends lie on either side of one end of the axle.
- Strip about 2 cm of the insulation from both ends of the wire coil and bend these into two flat U-bends (see inset details of the commutator in Figure 18.2.1).
- Press the two bared wire ends against opposite sides of the insulated tube and fix them there using a small rubber band (cut from rubber tubing) or with a very narrow strip of tape.
- Assemble the rotor on an axle supported by split pins as shown in Figure 18.2.1.
- Make two wire brushes by stripping about 2 cm of insulation from two short lengths of wire, which will form the contacts with the commutator as it rotates.

Objectives

By the end of this topic you will be able to:

- explain the action and draw a diagram of a DC electric motor.

Key fact

- The rotor is the coil that rotates in an electric motor.
- The commutator is the device that supplies the current to the rotor.
- The commutator also acts as an automatic current-reversing switch for DC motors.

Things to do

- Explain why the two halves of the commutator should be on the sides of the metal tube, rather than the top and bottom, when the rotor frame is horizontal.
- Explain what happens at the commutator when the rotor has turned to the vertical position.
- Work out the directions of the current in the coil and the catapult force on each side of the rotor coil when it is horizontal.
- Explain what would happen if the direction of the current in the rotor coil did not reverse twice in every revolution.

▲ **Figure 18.2.2** Small electric motor with multiple coils of wire and multiple sets of brushes to connect to the power supply

- Fix the wire brushes to the base board with drawing pins so that they press against the two sides of the commutator. They should make electrical connection when the armature is horizontal.
- Fit the magnadur magnets on their iron yoke around the armature making sure that the rotor is free to turn.
- Connect the brushes to a low-voltage DC supply and switch on. Some adjustment of the brushes may be necessary to get the motor running smoothly.

Working out which way the motor will turn

To work out which way a motor will rotate, we need to know which way the force acts on each side of the coil. Use Fleming's left-hand rule for the force on a current-carrying conductor in a magnetic field. Look at one side of the coil of wire. Point your **F**irst finger in the direction of the magnetic **F**ield (field points from N to S). Point your se**C**ond finger in the direction of the **C**urrent (conventional current flow from +ve to −ve). Your thu**M**b will point in the direction of the **M**ovement of the wire on that side of the coil.

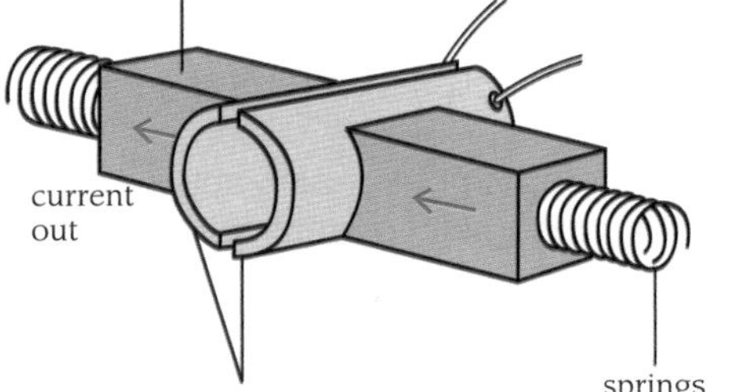

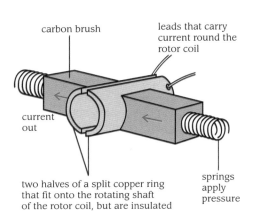

▲ **Figure 18.2.3** A split-ring commutator used in DC motors

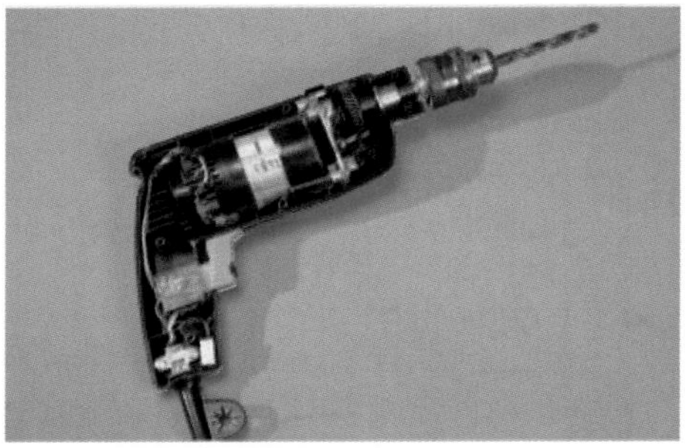

▲ **Figure 18.2.4** The inside of an electric drill shows the brushes and commutator on the left of the rotor coils. The gears that reduce the speed of revolution of the drill are on the right.

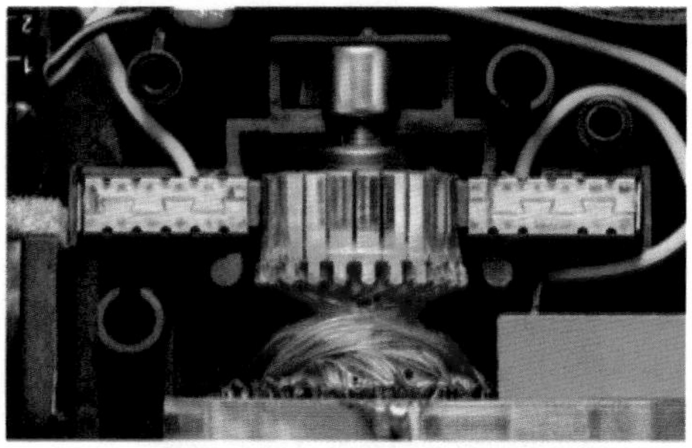

▲ **Figure 18.2.5** The split-ring commutator has a commutator in the centre made up of many segments. Two brushes press against the commutator as it rotates, feeding the direct current into and out of the rotor coils.

Commercial DC electric motors

Split-ring commutators

Commercial DC motors are designed so that the current can flow through the motor coil for as much time as possible. The motor coil wire ends in a split-ring commutator, as shown in Figure 18.2.3. The split in the ring allows the direction of the current through the coil itself to change direction as the coil turns over, so the coil keeps spinning in one direction instead of back and forth. The power supply flows through carbon brushes that are held in place by springs to make a good connection. The carbon brushes wear as the motor runs, but are cheap and easy to replace.

Designing commercial electric motors

In a commercial motor, the simple design of one flat coil is improved in the following ways:

- The flat magnets are replaced by curved magnets, so that even when the coil turns it is still at right angles to the magnetic field.
- The flat coil is replaced by lots of coils at different angles, so the whole of the space between the magnetic poles is filled with current-carrying coils.
- Electromagnets are used instead of permanent magnets. The motor speed can be varied by changing the size of the magnetic field, or changing the current.
- The rotor is made of soft iron to increase magnetic field for a given current through the electromagnet.

Summary questions

1. Describe briefly how a loudspeaker works.
2. What happens to the direction of rotation of a motor if the current is reversed?
3. What happens to the speed of a motor if the magnetic field is decreased?

D18.3 Electromagnetic induction

We have already seen examples of induced electric charge and induced magnetism. There is a third kind of induction in which electric currents are induced in wires by magnetic fields; this is called electromagnetic induction.

Cutting lines of force with a wire

- Fit two magnadur magnets to an iron yoke with unlike poles facing to form a strong U-shaped magnet (Figure 18.3.1). The lines of force cross horizontally between its poles from N to S.
- Connect a loop of copper wire in series with a sensitive galvanometer or centre-zero milliammeter.
- Move the wire up and down between the poles of the magnet and watch the meter.

We notice that an electric current flows through the meter. This current must have been *induced* by the magnetic field, because there is no current source in the circuit itself. As the wire moves through the magnetic field, a force acts on the electrons in the wire. This produces the current.

This effect is known as the **dynamo effect** or **generator effect**.

- Investigate which way the induced current flows when the wire is moved (a) upwards and (b) downwards.
- Investigate how the induced current is affected by the speed with which the wire is moved.
- What happens when the wire is moved horizontally across the gap from N pole to S pole, so that it slides in between the lines of force?
- Try reversing the magnetic poles and also moving the magnet instead of the wire.

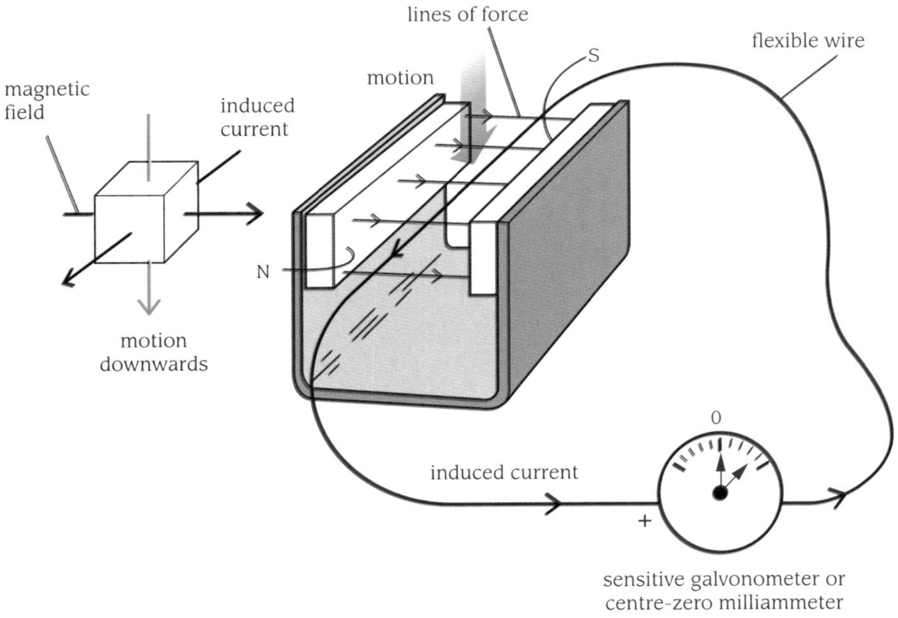

▲ **Figure 18.3.1** 'Cutting' a magnetic field

Objectives

By the end of this topic you will be able to:

- describe and perform simple experiments that demonstrate an induced current and e.m.f. caused by cutting or changing magnetic flux, including a coil and magnet and two coils
- describe and perform experiments to show how the magnitude of the induced e.m.f. in a conductor depends on the rate of change of magnetic flux experienced by the conductor
- predict the direction of the induced current from the direction of relative motion of the conductor and magnetic field.

Key fact

Observations

- When the current is directed into the terminal of the meter labelled + or coloured red, the pointer moves to the right.
- The direction of the induced current depends on both the direction of the motion of the wire and the direction of the magnetic field.
- It makes no difference whether the wire moves or the magnet moves because it is their relative motion that causes an induced current.
- The magnitude of the induced current depends on how quickly the magnetic field lines (or lines of force) are cut by the wire.
- If the wire moves parallel to the field and does not cut the lines of force no current is induced.

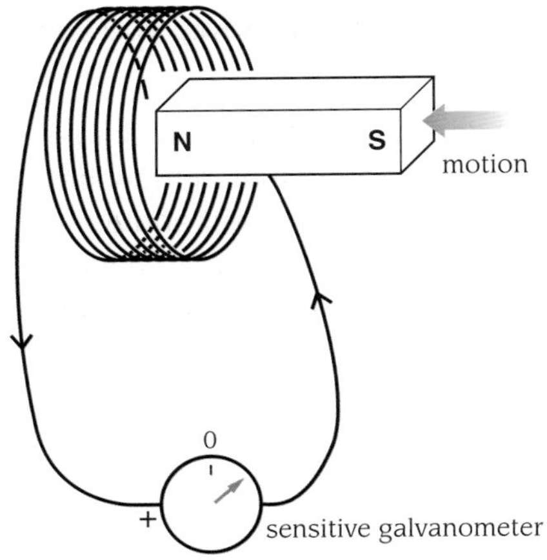

▲ **Figure 18.3.2** Moving a magnet into a coil

Electromagnetic induction using a coil and a magnet

- Connect a coil with a large number of turns in series with a sensitive meter (Figure 18.3.2).
- Move the N pole of a bar magnet in and out of the coil and watch the meter. Also try moving the coil.
- Investigate how the direction of the induced current depends on the pole of the magnet used and the direction of motion of either the magnet or the coil.
- Investigate how the magnitude of the induced current depends on (a) the speed of the relative motion, (b) the strength of the magnet and (c) the number of turns on the coil.

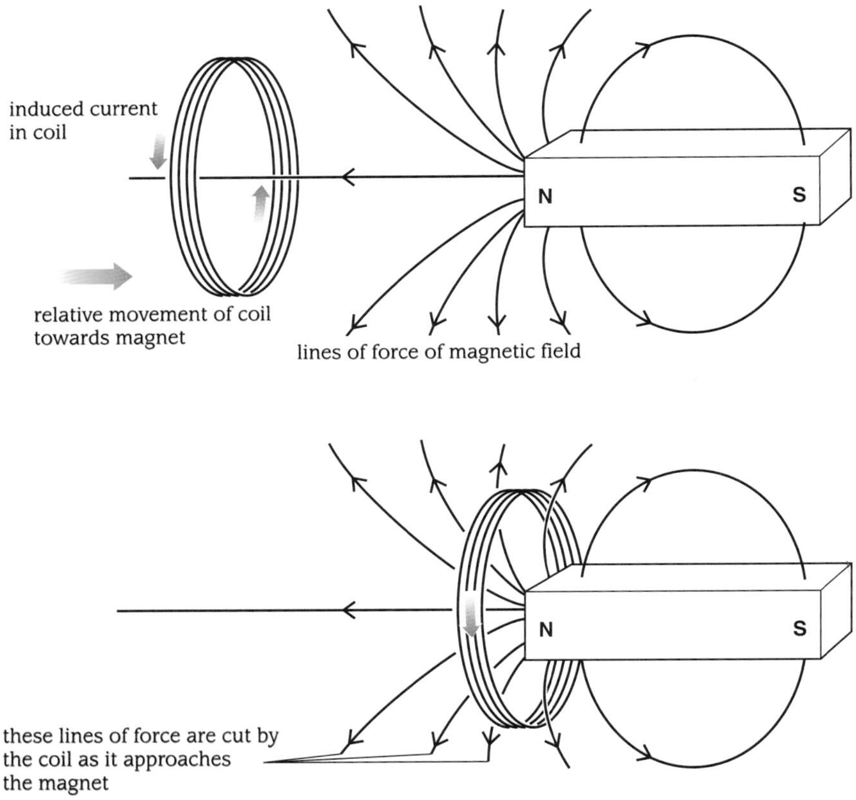

▲ **Figure 18.3.3** Moving the coil cuts lines of force

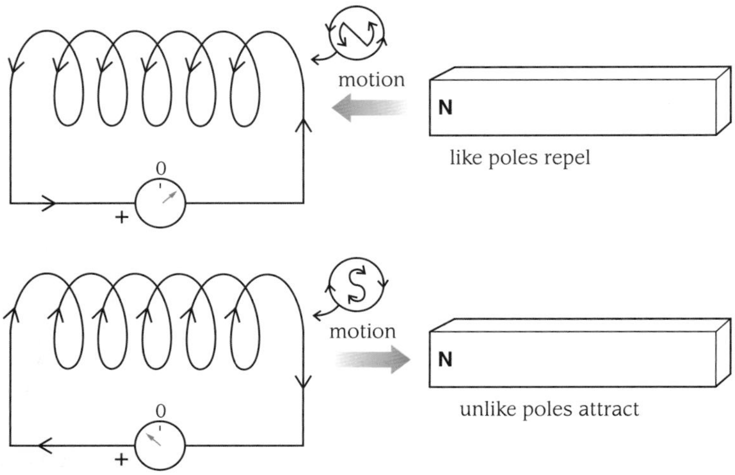

▲ **Figure 18.3.4** The induced current opposes the motion

Key fact

- The coil of wire moving towards the magnetic pole of the magnet cuts lines of force all round the coil (Figure 18.3.3). This is because the magnetic field spreads out into and out of the paper as well as in the plane of the paper.
- An alternative way of looking at this effect is to say that the magnetic field through the coil of wire changes from a weak field to a stronger field as the magnet and coil are brought closer together.
- Figure 18.3.4 shows how the current induced in the coil produces a magnet pole at the end of the coil, which opposes the motion of the magnet. As the N pole of the magnet approaches, the N pole caused by the induced current in the coil repels it and thereby opposes its motion. The reverse effect happens when the magnet is moved away: a S pole caused by a current induced in the opposite direction attracts the magnet's N pole, so preventing it from moving away.

Electromagnetic induction using two coils

The magnet in Figure 18.3.4 can be replaced by a second coil carrying a DC current. Whenever there is movement between a current-carrying coil and a second coil, a current will be induced in the second coil. This is because the current-carrying coil has a magnetic field around it. Moving either coil causes the magnetic field to change around the second coil without a current. This induces a current in that coil. The direction of the induced current is always such as to oppose the movement.

The direction of the magnetic field around the current-carrying coil can be found using the right-hand grip rule. Grip the coil so that your fingers wrap round in the direction of the current flow. Your thumb points to the N pole of the 'magnet'.

The current-carrying coil does not even have to be moved. Switching the current on or off, or changing the size of the current will change the magnetic field around this coil and so have the same effect as moving the coil. So they cause a current to be induced in the second coil.

If the DC current in the current-carrying coil is replaced with AC, an AC current will be induced in the second coil. The continually changing AC current produces a continually changing magnetic field, which acts like a continually moving magnet thereby inducing a current. The induced current is AC too because the changing direction of the AC current in the current-carrying coil means it acts like a magnet being continually moved towards the second coil, then away, then towards, and so on.

The laws of electromagnetic induction

The observations from the two previous experiments are summarised in the laws of electromagnetic induction. These were formulated by the English scientist, Faraday and the Russian scientist, Lenz.

Faraday's law of electromagnetic induction

You will have seen experimentally that the size of the induced current is greater when:

- the magnet or coil moves faster
- the magnet used is stronger
- the coil of wire has more turns
- the magnet moves along the central axis of the coil, and less when it moves at an angle.

Faraday's law explains this by saying:

The magnitude of the induced e.m.f. between the ends of a wire or coil is directly proportional to the rate at which it cuts magnetic lines of force or the rate at which the magnetic flux through it changes.

The induced e.m.f., and therefore the induced current, is larger when the coil moves faster through the magnetic field lines. This happens when the coil moves faster, or when there are more lines because the magnet is stronger or the coil has more turns. If the coil moves parallel to the magnetic field, it doesn't cut any field lines so there is no induced current.

Lenz's law and conservation of energy

Lenz's law predicts the *direction* of the induced current.

Lenz's law states that the direction of the induced current always opposes the change producing it.

Lenz's law is a direct consequence of the law of conservation of energy.

The induced current transfers energy. The law of conservation of energy states that energy cannot be created from nothing. So the energy in the induced current must come from the movement of the magnet. Therefore the energy of the magnet must be getting less, so it must be slowing down. Therefore the direction of the induced current opposes the motion.

Electric motors without brushes and commutators

Carbon brushes and commutators transmit current into the motor coils, but carbon brushes wear out. Most commercial motors, particularly large industrial ones, avoid the need for brushes by using AC currents in coils around the motor coil to induce the current in the motor coils. This makes the electric motor last longer and need less maintenance.

Summary questions

1. Describe a simple experiment to demonstrate electromagnetic induction.
2. What happens if a current-carrying coil is moved towards a second coil?
3. A magnet is moved towards a coil of wire. What changes would increase the induced current in the coil?

Objectives

By the end of this topic you will be able to:

- describe and explain the action of a simple dynamo or AC generator
- sketch graphs to represent the output from a simple AC generator.

D18.4 The dynamo effect

Making electricity by moving a magnet

- Wind a coil of about 20 turns of insulated copper wire round an iron C-core and connect the coil to a centre-zero meter (Figure 18.4.1a).
- Move a bar magnet towards and away from the C-core as shown in the figure and watch the meter. Can you explain why the induced current has the direction shown?

Using the iron C-core greatly increases the strength of the magnetic field, which changes through the coil and induces a larger current.

Figure 18.4.1b shows how a magnet can be rotated between the 'poles' of the iron C-core. A small powerful permanent bar magnet can be attached to an axle using glue or tape.

What do you notice about the induced current recorded by the meter?

The iron C-core has induced magnetism, which reverses as the permanent magnet rotates. So the direction of the induced current in the coil reverses as often as the induced magnetic poles are reversed.

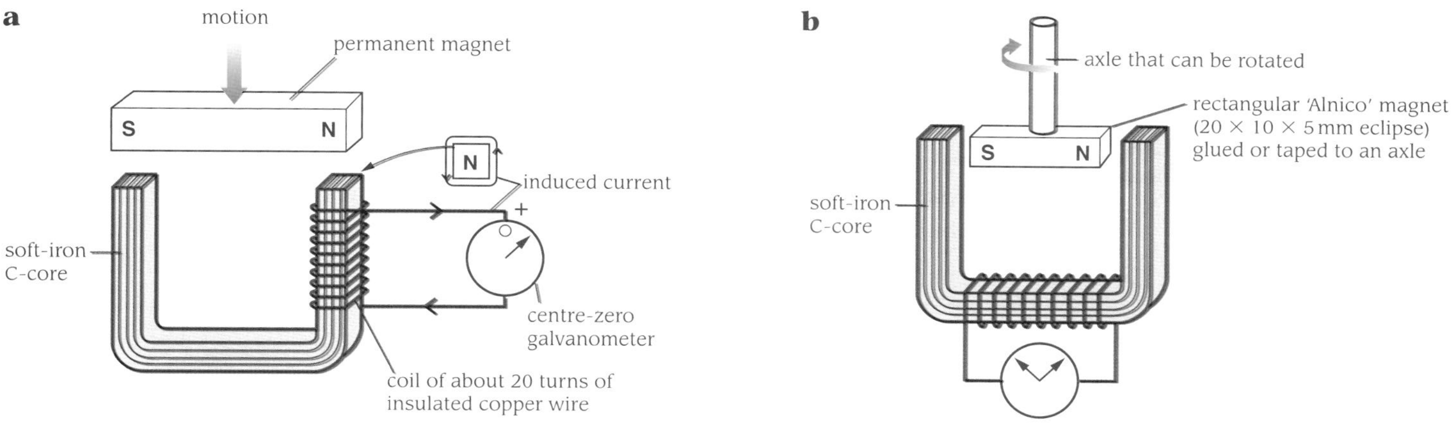

▲ **Figure 18.4.1** Making electricity by moving a permanent magnet

A rotating magnet and a stationary coil are used in the practical application of a bicycle dynamo. The rotor magnet is in the form of a cylindrical permanent magnet with its poles on opposite sides of the cylinder. The iron core of the stationary coil has concave poles shaped to fit closely round the rotor. An advantage of this type of design is that there are no brushes and no commutator to wear out.

What kind of current is produced by this type of dynamo?

Fleming's right-hand dynamo rule

- Hold the thumb and first two fingers of your right hand at right angles to each other.
- Point your **F**irst finger in the direction of the magnetic **F**ield.
- Point your thu**M**b in the direction of **M**otion of the wire.
- Your se**C**ond finger points in the direction of the induced **C**urrent.

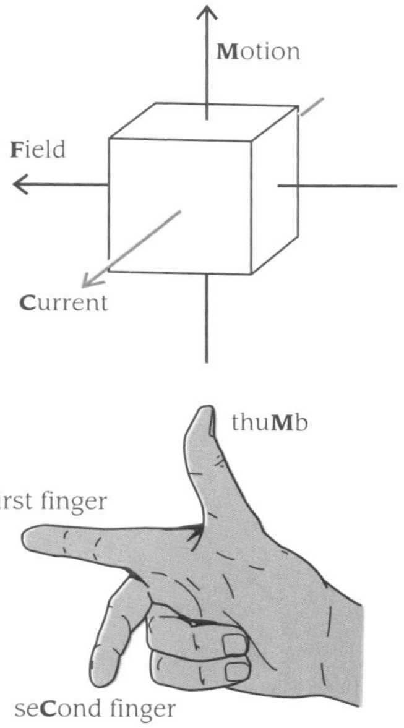

▲ **Figure 18.4.2** Fleming's right-hand rule

A bicycle dynamo

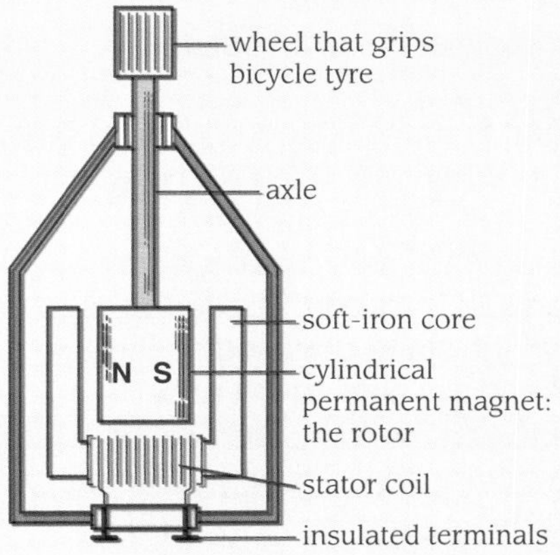

▲ **Figure 18.4.3** How a bicycle dynamo works

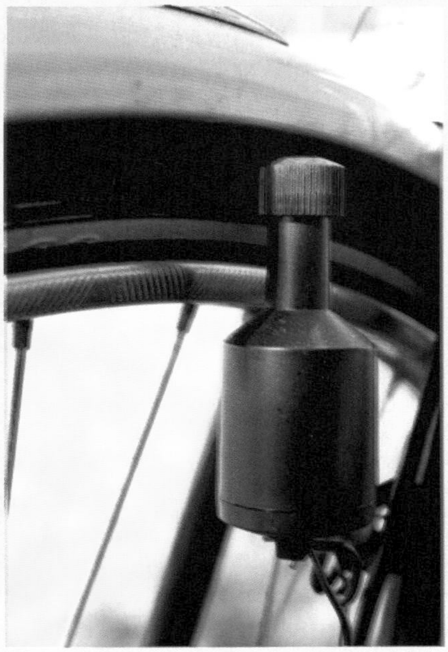

▶ **Figure 18.4.4** A bicycle dynamo

Key fact

Now you know that there are two rules from Fleming:

- The **left-hand rule** is used for the **electric motor** and helps us predict the direction of the thrust and motion.
- The **right-hand rule** is used for the **dynamo effect** and helps us predict the direction of the induced current.

It is important to use the correct hand because they give exactly opposite predictions if you use the wrong hand!

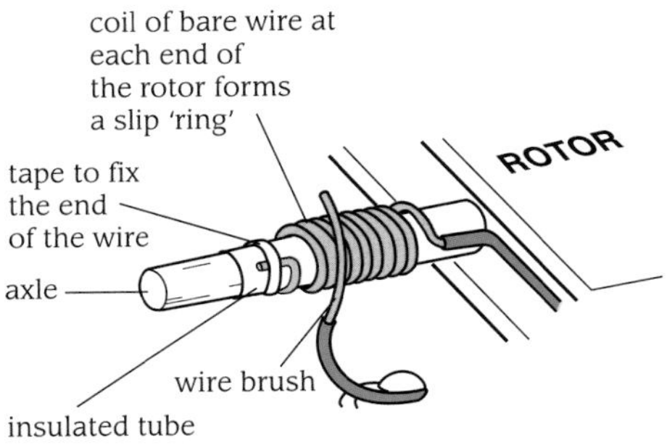

▲ **Figure 18.4.5** A slip-ring commutator for a model alternator

Things to do

Answer these questions:

- What do you notice about the current?
- What happens if the rotor spins quickly?
- What kind of electric current is produced?
- Does it make any difference if the rotor spins in the opposite direction?

Generating electricity by rotating a coil

Most generators of electricity are designed to produce alternating current. AC dynamos are called alternators.

To convert your model DC electric motor (page 313) to an alternator you need to change the type of commutator so that it does not reverse the current direction at all. This type of commutator is called a slip-ring commutator.

- Unfasten your split-ring type of commutator and adjust the ends of the wire coil on the rotor so that the two wire ends finish at opposite ends of the rotor.
- Insulate both ends of the tube through which the axle passes.
- Wind the bare wire ends of the rotor coil round each end of the tube in two compressed coils to form two slip rings.
- Fix the wire ends with tape or rubber bands so that they do not unwind (Figure 18.4.5).
- One wire brush is needed at each end so that the same brush is in continuous contact with the same slip ring.
- Connect the brushes to a centre-zero meter and spin the rotor slowly, watching the meter.

Your motor is now an AC dynamo, converting the mechanical work you put into it into electrical energy.

The meter needle swinging to both sides of the central zero shows that the induced current changes direction rapidly, i.e. it alternates. At faster speeds the meter needle and moving coil cannot swing fast enough from side to side, and so stay near to the central zero.

! Key fact

What changes are made to the design of an alternator to improve its efficiency and power output?

- The permanent magnet is replaced by a DC electromagnet.
- The DC electromagnet becomes the rotor and works like the rotating permanent magnet in a bicycle dynamo.
- The generated alternating current is obtained from the stator (stationary) coils. This improvement means that the large induced current does not have to pass through a commutator and brushes.
- A small fraction of the generated output is fed back as a direct current through slip rings to power the electromagnet of the rotor. This current is much smaller than the main AC output from the stator coils and so there is less difficulty in passing it through brushes and slip rings to the rotor.
- Sometimes a smaller DC generator is mounted on the same shaft as the main alternator. The output of the DC generator is used to supply DC to the electromagnet rotor of the alternator.

AC generators or alternators

The simplest design for an alternator is shown in Figure 18.4.6. A coil with a large number of turns of wire is rotated between the poles of a permanent magnet. The alternating current is picked up by the two brushes, which rub against the two commutator rings. The output and usefulness of this design is limited by the strength of the permanent magnet and the wearing of the brushes.

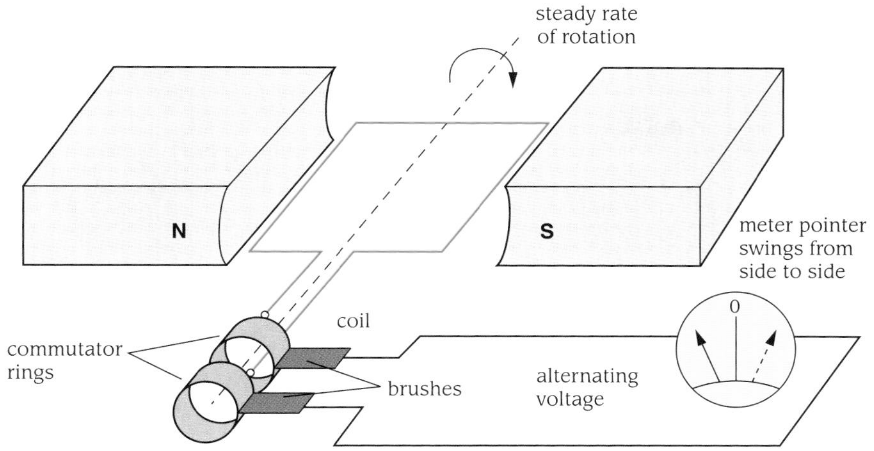

▲ **Figure 18.4.6** A simple AC generator

Alternators that are used to generate electricity in the power industry have improved designs for greater efficiency and power output (Figure 18.4.7). You saw in your experiments to create an induced current, that it does not matter whether the coil or the magnet rotates. In Figure 18.4.7 the central coil wound on a soft iron core is rotated by the turbine, inside an iron outer ring. This generates an induced AC current in the stator coils wound on this iron ring. Real generators or alternators have many coils with hundreds or thousands of turns each.

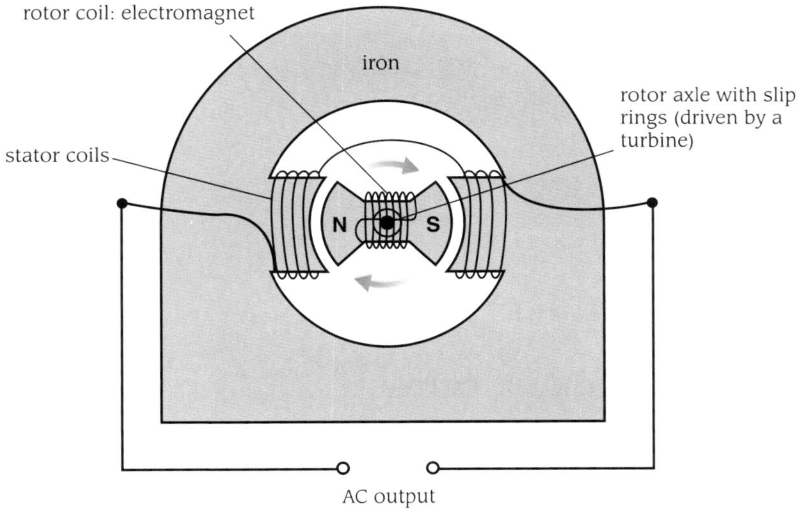

▲ **Figure 18.4.7** A practical alternator

Displaying the output of an AC generator

Switch on the time base of an oscilloscope to scan across the screen once while the rotor makes two or three revolutions.

The oscilloscope works as a voltmeter (displaying a voltage–time graph), so the trace on the screen shows how the output e.m.f. of the generator varies with time.

The e.m.f. induced in the rotor coil is constantly connected via the slip rings to the oscilloscope and can be seen to alternate. The e.m.f. induced in the rotor coil alternates from a positive value, through zero to a negative value and back through zero to a positive value again for each complete revolution of the rotor coil.

Key fact

Peak values

- The peak value of an alternating current or voltage is the maximum value in either direction. This occurs each time the generator's coil is in the positions shown in Figure 18.4.8a. These peak values are labelled (a) on the voltage–time graph (Figure 18.4.9).
- The peak value of an alternating voltage (or current) is only reached momentarily, twice for every revolution of the alternator rotor coil, and is therefore greater than the effective value of the supply.
- When the coil is in the positions (b) shown in Figure 18.4.8b, the output voltage is zero.

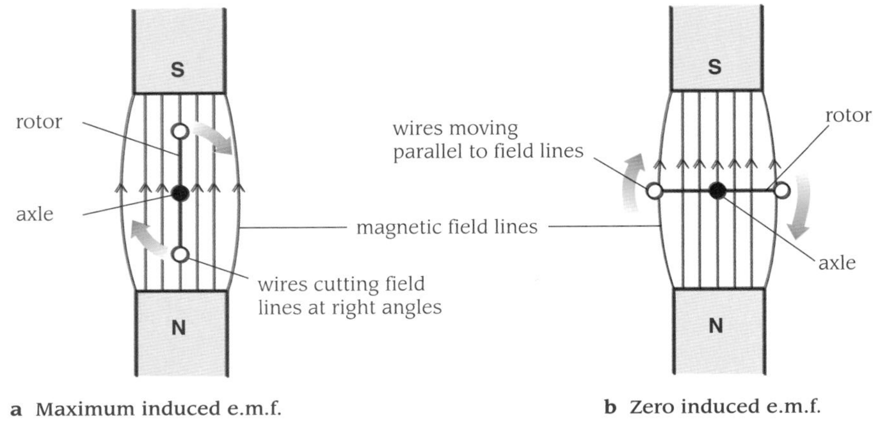

▲ **Figure 18.4.8** Investigating the output e.m.f. of an AC generator

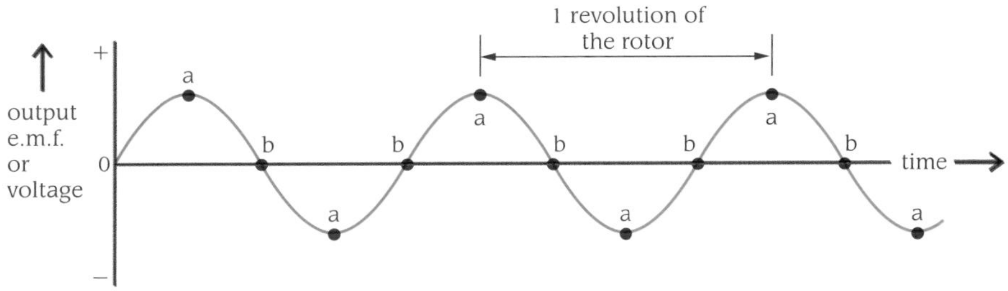

▲ **Figure 18.4.9** The output e.m.f. of an alternator

Summary questions

1 Sketch the output voltage of an alternator.

2 A simple generator has a rotating coil in a straight magnetic field. When will the induced current be zero?

Objectives

By the end of this topic you will be able to:

- describe how a transformer works and draw a diagram
- describe the features of a transformer that improve its efficiency
- understand that for an ideal transformer, $P_{out} = P_{in}$
- demonstrate and use the equations:

$$\frac{V_s}{V_p} = \frac{N_s}{N_p} = \frac{I_p}{I_s}$$

D18.5 Transformers

Two coils and a direct current

- Wind about 10 turns of insulated copper wire onto two iron C-cores as shown in Figure 18.5.2.
- Connect coil ① to a low-voltage DC supply and include an ammeter in the circuit to show the current.
- Switch on the current.
- Connect the second coil ②, to a centre-zero meter.
- With a steady direct current flowing in ① bring the two iron C-cores together so that they form a closed iron loop and watch the meter.
- Now separate the C-cores and then bring them together again.
- Note what the meter indicates while:
  a) the cores are held apart
  b) the cores are moving together
  c) the cores are held together
  d) the cores are moving apart.

▲ **Figure 18.5.1** Transformers

Coil ① forms an electromagnet. When it is moved so that its magnetic field lines are cut by the turns of wire on coil ②, the induced e.m.f. in the coil ② sends a current through the meter. The effect is exactly the same as when a permanent magnet was moved up to a similar coil (page 319). When the two coils are held together and a steady direct current flows in coil ①, the meter shows zero induced in coil ②.

- Clip the two iron C-cores together and watch the meter while:
  e) the direct current in coil ① is switched on,
  f) the direct current in coil ① is switched off,
  g) the rheostat is used to change the current in coil ①.

The effect of changing the current in coil ① is the same as moving the coil. When the current changes, the magnetic field that it produces in coil ① also changes, so that its magnetic field lines cut the turns of coil ②. When the current in coil ① is switched on or off, the current and the magnetic field change very rapidly. The rapid change of the magnetic field through coil ② induces a large e.m.f. in its turns, which lasts for a short time and shows up as a flick of the pointer on the meter. When the rheostat is used to produce a more gradual change of the current in coil ① the induced e.m.f. in coil ② is much smaller but lasts longer.

Electromagnetic induction can be used to transfer electrical energy from one circuit to another by means of a magnetic field that links the two coils. The two coils are called the primary coil and the secondary coil. Only when there is a change of current in the primary coil does an induced e.m.f. appear in the secondary coil.

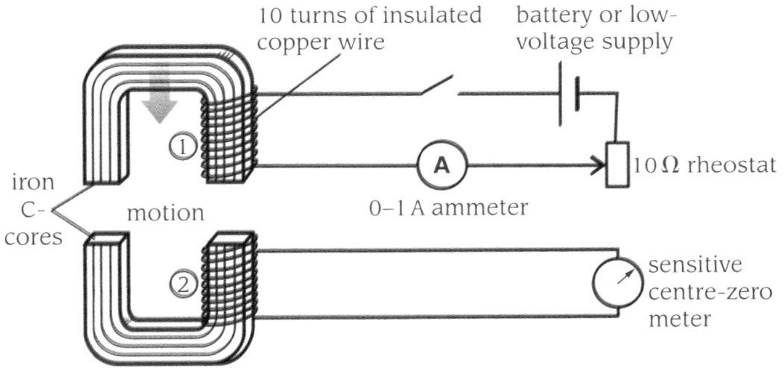

▲ **Figure 18.5.2** For induction to occur with a direct current we need motion, or a changing current

Making a transformer

- Wind a primary coil of 10 turns of insulated wire onto one arm of a C-core (Figure 18.5.3). Connect this coil to a low-voltage AC supply (1 V AC, high-current power unit.)
- Wind a secondary coil of 10 turns on another C-core, leaving some extra wire for winding more turns.
- Connect the secondary coil in series with a small filament lamp (2.5 V, 0.3 A) (Figure 18.5.3a).
- Replace the lamp with a centre-zero meter (Figure 18.5.3b).

Things to do

Answer the following questions while you test your transformer:

a) How does the brightness of the lamp change when the number of turns on the secondary coil is increased or decreased?
Why is the lamp brighter when there are more turns on the secondary coil?
What effect do you think more turns on the primary coil would have?

b) Why is the centre-zero meter unable to give a reading even though there is a current through it?
(The current is alternating at a frequency of 50 Hz.)

c) What does the vertical height on the oscilloscope graph measure?
How does this quantity depend on the number of turns on the secondary coil?
(The oscilloscope displays a voltage–time graph.)

▼ **Figure 18.5.3** Making a transformer

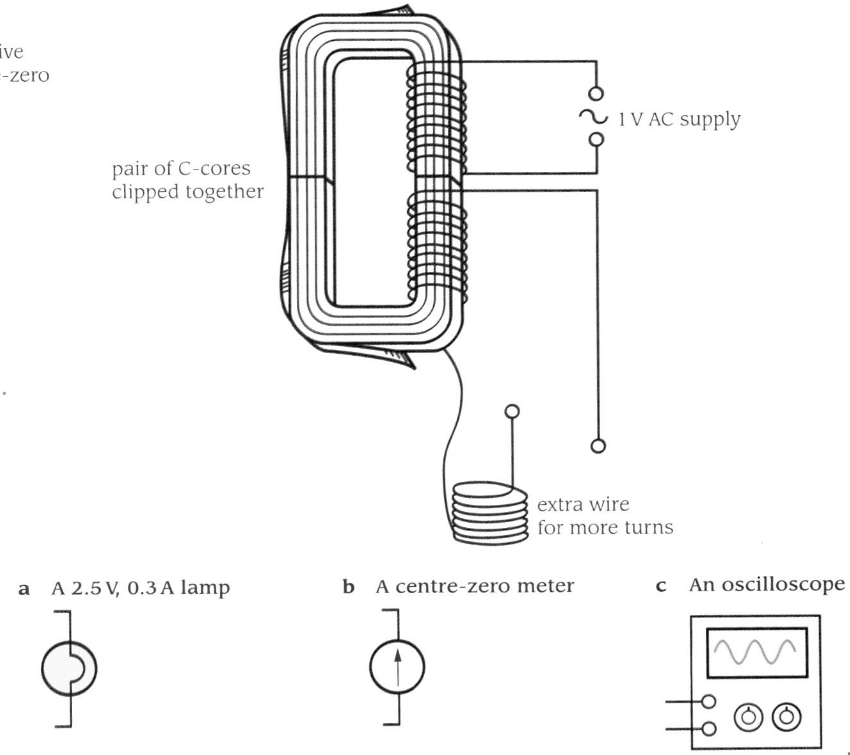

▲ **Figure 18.5.4** This small transformer (bottom left of photo) provides low voltages inside a portable radio.

- Connect an oscilloscope in place of the meter (Figure 18.5.3c). Connect the two ends of the secondary coil to the input terminals of the oscilloscope. Switch on the internal time base and adjust the control until a wave graph can be seen on the screen.
- Investigate the effect of changing the number of turns on the secondary coil.

The transformer

The transformer is a very common and very important electrical machine. Every mains-operated television and hi-fi system has one. Battery chargers and model train sets depend on transformers; the whole system of distribution of electricity across the country also depends on them. The transformer transfers electrical energy from one circuit to another by electromagnetic induction between two coils. This is sometimes called mutual induction, because it takes place between two coils.

While transferring the energy, the transformer enables us to change or transform the voltage to a larger or smaller value. High voltages are very dangerous and can kill people. By transforming the voltage of an electrical supply we can produce lower, safer voltages for everyday applications. This is one of the transformer's most important uses.

Step-up and step-down transformers

Worked example

A step-down transformer

A transformer is required to step down the mains voltage of 110 V to provide a 12 V supply for an electrical toy.

If the primary coil is wound with 1000 turns of wire, calculate the number of turns required for the secondary coil.

Using the equation

$$\frac{n_2}{n_1} = \frac{V_2}{V_1}$$

$$\frac{n_2}{1000} = \frac{12\,\text{V}}{110\,\text{V}} \quad n_2 = 109 \text{ turns}$$

A secondary coil with 109 turns would provide an alternating voltage output from the transformer of 12 V.

Worked example

A step-up transformer

An alternator generates an output voltage of 500 V. This output must be stepped up for transmission across the country. It is connected to a series of step-up transformers. If the first transformer has 800 turns on its primary coil and 16 000 turns on its secondary coil, what output voltage will it produce?

Using the equation

$$\frac{V_2}{V_1} = \frac{n_2}{n_1}$$

$$\frac{V_2}{500} = \frac{16\,000}{800} = 20$$

$$V_2 = 20 \times 500 = 10\,000\,\text{V}$$

The output voltage will be 10 000 volts.

Using more turns on the secondary coil of a simple transformer increases the brightness of a lamp and produces a larger amplitude graph on the oscilloscope screen. Each turn on the secondary coil has an e.m.f. induced in it, and these e.m.f.s add up to a higher total voltage as the number of turns increases.

If the number of turns on the primary coil is increased, the opposite effect occurs and the lamp becomes dimmer. We find that the voltage induced across the secondary coil depends on the ratio of the number of turns on the two coils as follows:

$$\frac{\text{secondary voltage}}{\text{primary voltage}} = \frac{\text{secondary turns}}{\text{primary turns}} \qquad \frac{V_2}{V_1} = \frac{n_2}{n_1}$$

- V_1 = the alternating input voltage to the transformer, (the primary voltage)
- V_2 = the alternating output voltage from the transformer, (the secondary voltage)
- n_1 = the number of turns on the primary coil
- n_2 = the number of turns on the secondary coil

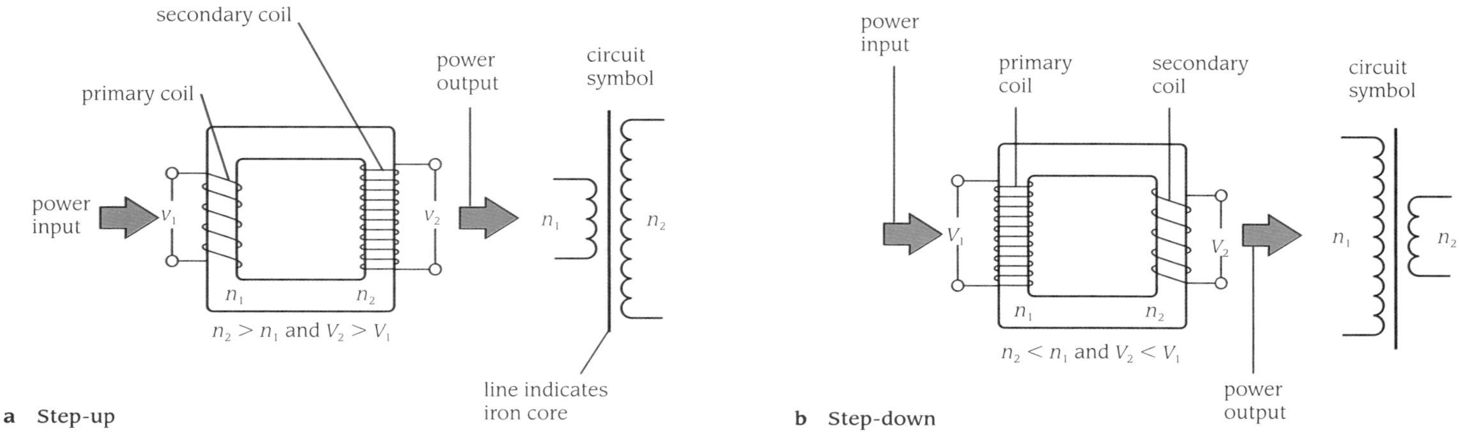

▲ **Figure 18.5.5** The transformer formula

Figure 18.5.5a shows a step-up transformer, which changes a voltage to a higher value, i.e. $V_2 > V_1$. This transformer has more turns on the secondary coil than the primary coil in the ratio of the voltage step-up required.

Figure 18.5.5b shows a step-down transformer, which changes a voltage to a lower value, i.e. $V_2 < V_1$. Here $n_2 < n_1$ in the required ratio for the voltage reduction.

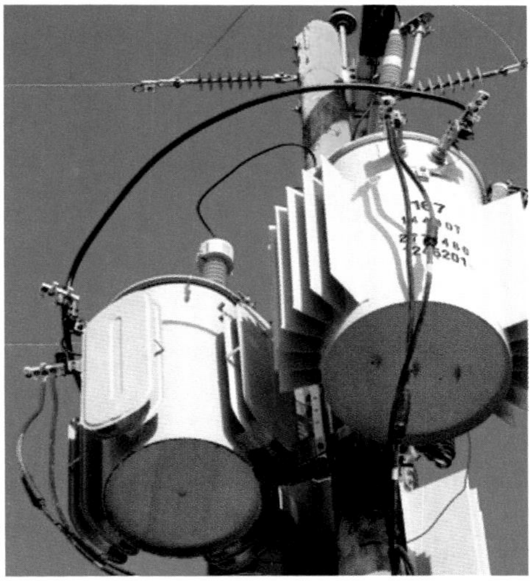

▲ **Figure 18.5.6** Local step-down transformers are an everyday sight on poles in Kingston, Jamaica. The transformers step the voltage down to 110 volts for use in homes.

Key fact

Transformers

- Transformers change both voltages and currents, increasing one while decreasing the other proportionally.
- Transformers can be used to step-up or step-down AC voltages.
- Transformers work by electromagnetic induction but involve no motion.
- To work efficiently, transformers need to have their coils wound round, but insulated from, a laminated iron core formed into a closed loop of iron.
- Transformers are a vital component of all electrical energy transmission systems in all countries.

Power transfer in a transformer

The law of conservation of energy means that it is impossible to get more power out of a transformer than is put into it. If a transformer was 100% efficient, with no power wasted, then the electrical power from the secondary coil would be equal to the electrical power input to the primary coil. In practice no transformers are 100% efficient. Some energy is always wasted as heat.

Figure 18.5.7 shows how these two powers can be measured. The ammeters and voltmeters must be special ones suitable for measuring alternating currents and voltages. For each coil the ammeter reads the current in the coil and the voltmeter reads the e.m.f. or voltage across the terminals of the coil.

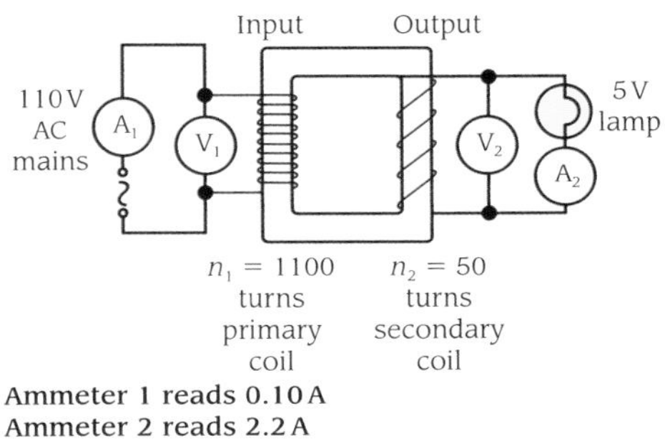

▲ **Figure 18.5.7** Transformer power

Electrical power is given by the formula: power = current × voltage

For the transformer in Figure 18.5.7

input power = $I \times V = 0.10 \times 110 = 11$ watts

output power = $I \times V = 2.2 \times 5 = 11$ watts

For this ideal transformer, the power output equals the power input. As the voltage is stepped *down* by a factor of 22, so the current is also stepped *up* by a factor of ×22.

Assuming 100% efficiency in this ideal transformer

$$\text{output power} = \text{input power}$$

$$V_s I_s = V_p I_p$$

Rearranging this gives:

$$\frac{V_s}{V_p} = \frac{I_p}{I_s}$$

Combining this with the equation we met earlier gives:

$$\frac{V_s}{V_p} = \frac{n_s}{n_p} = \frac{I_p}{I_s}$$

Reducing power losses in transformers

	Cause of power loss in a transformer	Design features that reduce power loss
1	Heating effect of the current in the copper wires of the coils: Power loss = I^2R	Thick copper wires of low resistance are used. The cost of copper and weight of the transformer limit the wire thickness used.
2	Heating effect of currents (called eddy currents) induced in the iron core. Currents induced in the iron core are not wanted.	Iron core must be laminated. The thin layers of iron, clamped together, offer greater resistance to induced currents than solid iron.
3	Energy used in the process of magnetising the iron core and reversing this every time the current alternates its direction.	Iron core, made from soft iron, holds only temporary magnetism. Soft iron is easily magnetised and demagnetised with low energy losses.
4	'Leakage' of the magnetic field, which should link both coils: some lines of force escape, missing one of the coils.	The core is shaped so that the magnetic field is concentrated in closed rings of iron from which very few field lines escape.

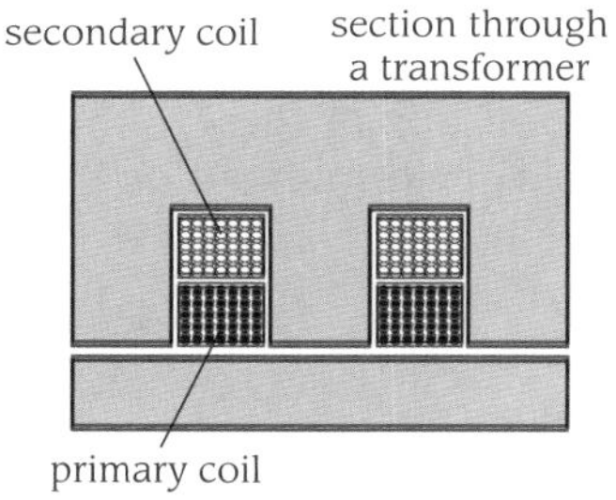

◀ **Figure 18.5.8** In this step-down transformer, the primary coil has a large number of turns of a thin gauge of wire and the secondary coil has a much smaller number of turns of thicker wire to carry a larger current.

The efficiency of a transformer

Real transformers always give a lower output power than the input power as some energy is inevitably wasted as heat in the coils and core of the transformer.

The efficiency of a transformer is given by:

$$\text{efficiency} = \frac{\text{output power}}{\text{input power}} \times 100\% = \frac{I_2 V_2}{I_1 V_1} \times 100\%$$

Worked example

Transformer power and efficiency

A step-up transformer has 10 000 turns on its secondary coil and 100 turns on its primary coil. The alternating current in the primary coil is 5.0 A when connected to a 12 V AC supply. Calculate:

a) the power input to the transformer

b) the e.m.f. induced across the secondary coil.

What is the maximum current in a circuit connected to the secondary coil if:

c) the transformer is 100% efficient

d) the transformer is 90% efficient but produces the same e.m.f. across the secondary coil as the ideal one?

---

a) input power $= I_1 \times V_1 = 5.0\,\text{A} \times 12\,\text{V} = 60\,\text{W}$.

b) The secondary coil voltage, V_2 is found using:

$$\frac{V_2}{V_1} = \frac{n_2}{n_1}$$

So $V_2 = V_1 \times \frac{n_2}{n_1} = 12 \times \frac{10\,000}{100} = 1200\,\text{V}$

c) When 100% efficient, output power = input power = 60 W.

output power $= I_2 \times V_2$

$$I_2 = \frac{60\,\text{W}}{V_2} = \frac{60\,\text{W}}{1200\,\text{V}} = 0.05\,\text{A}$$

d) Using: efficiency $= \frac{\text{output power}}{\text{input power}} \times 100 = 90\%$

output power $= \frac{90}{100} \times$ input power $= \frac{90}{100} \times 60\,\text{W} = 54\,\text{W}$

output power $= I_2 \times V_2$

$$I_2 = \frac{54\,\text{W}}{V_2} = \frac{54\,\text{W}}{1200\,\text{V}} = 0.045\,\text{A}$$

The maximum current through the secondary coil is 0.05 A at 100% efficiency, and 0.045 A at 90% efficiency.

Worked example

Transformer efficiency

A transformer input power is 5.0 A at 110 V. If the transformer is 95% efficient, find:

a) the maximum useful output power available

b) the power wasted by the transformer

c) the energy wasted and converted into heat by the transformer in 1 h.

Input power $= IV = 5.0 \times 110 = 550\,\text{W}$

a) Maximum output power available $= \frac{95}{100} \times 550 = 522.5\,\text{W}$

b) Power wasted $= 550\,\text{W} - 522.5\,\text{W} = 27.5\,\text{W}$

c) Energy wasted = power × time $= 27.5\,\text{W} \times 60 \times 60\,\text{s} = 99\,000\,\text{J}$

99 kJ of energy are converted to waste heat every hour.

Worked example

Currents and voltages are in inverse ratios.

An ideal transformer has an input voltage of 110 V and an output voltage of 12 V. If the current in its secondary circuit is 2.2 A, calculate the current in its primary coil.

Using the inverse ratios of the currents and voltages:

$$\frac{I_1}{I_2} = \frac{V_2}{V_1}$$

$$I_1 = \frac{V_2}{V_1} \times I_2 = \frac{12}{100} \times 2.2$$

$$I_1 = 0.264\,\text{A}$$

Worked example

Efficiency

The input current and voltage for a mains transformer are 0.24 A and 110 V respectively.
If its output voltage is 12 V and it is supplying a current of 2.0 A, calculate its efficiency.

$$\text{input power} = I_1 \times V_1 = 0.24\,\text{A} \times 110\,\text{V} = 26.4\,\text{W}$$

$$\text{output power} = I_2 \times V_2 = 2.0\,\text{A} \times 12\,\text{V} = 24.0\,\text{W}$$

$$\text{efficiency} = \frac{\text{output power}}{\text{input power}} \times 100\%$$

$$\text{efficiency} = \frac{24.0}{26.4} \times 100\%$$

$$\text{efficiency} = 91\%$$

Summary questions

1. Describe briefly how a transformer works.
2. What is a step-down transformer?
3. Give the equation used for transformer calculations.
4. For a 100% efficient transformer, with 4000 turns on the primary coil, how many turns would the secondary coil need to step-down a voltage from 200 V to 50 V?

D18.6 Transmission of electrical power

Objectives

By the end of this topic you will be able to:

- explain why electricity is transmitted at high voltages over long distances
- state the advantages of and reasons for using AC for transferring electrical energy
- explain where and why we need transformers in our electricity supply system.

Power stations that generate electrical energy are connected by cables to all the places where electricity is used. The cables arriving at factories, offices and homes are carried overhead by lines of poles along the roadside or are buried underground. Towns and villages are linked by a grid of wires that carry the electricity the long distances from the power stations to the consumers. The grid also allows for the sharing of power from different power stations.

Reducing power loss in transmission lines

Figure 18.6.1 shows how the power fed into a transmission line P_{in} divides into two parts. Most of the power output, P_{out}, should reach the end of the line where it is used by a consumer, but some of the power loss, P_{loss}, is wasted by the resistance of the wires, producing heat.

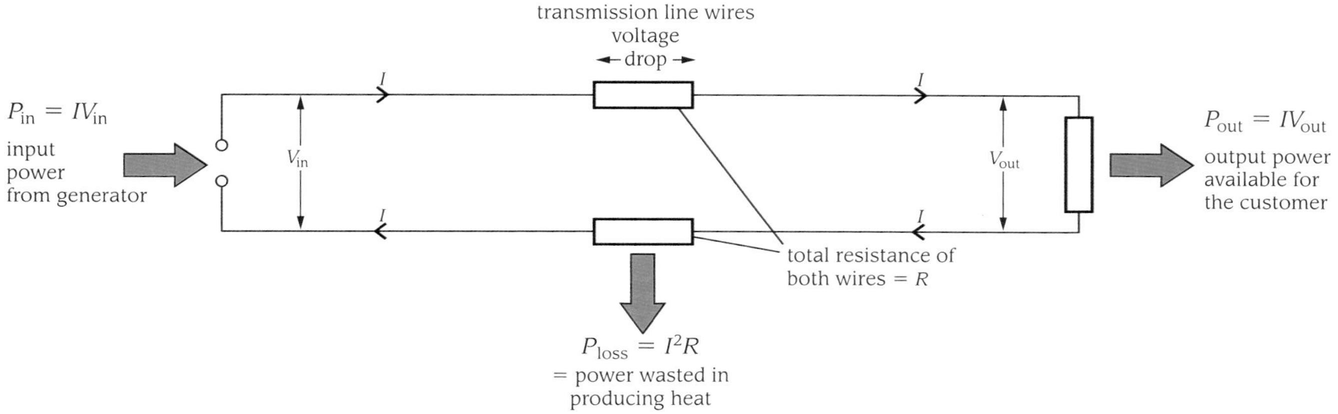

▲ **Figure 18.6.1** Power loss in transmission lines

The power in a wire at any point is given by the equation:

$$\text{power} = \text{current} \times \text{voltage} \quad \text{or} \quad P = IV$$

The power loss is due to the heating effect of the current in the wire, which is I^2R, where R is the resistance of the wire in the transmission line.

$$P_{out} = P_{in} - P_{loss} \quad \text{So,} \quad IV_{out} = IV_{in} - I^2R$$

As the same current, I flows all round the circuit we can divide through by I giving:

$$V_{out} = V_{in} - IR$$

where IR is the voltage drop along the wire.

The power loss is kept to a minimum by keeping the voltage drop along the wire as low as possible. As the voltage drop equals IR, it is clear that both I and R should be kept as low as possible. The resistance of the wires R is kept low by using thick wires with a large cross-sectional area. Aluminium alloys are used because they are cheaper and much lighter than copper.

> **Key fact**
>
> The same power can be carried in a wire at low current if the voltage is made high.
> In the example of the model power lines, 24 W of power was supplied.
> At 12 V, the current in the wires is:
>
> $$I = \frac{P}{V} = \frac{24\,\text{W}}{12\,\text{V}} = 2.0\,\text{A}$$
>
> At 240 V, the current in the wires is:
>
> $$I = \frac{P}{V} = \frac{24\,\text{W}}{240\,\text{V}} = 0.1\,\text{A}$$
>
> When the current is 20 times smaller the power loss as heat in the wires (I^2R) is 400 times smaller. This shows how effective it is to transmit electrical power at a high voltage.

Transmission lines

- Wires must have a low resistance to reduce power loss.
- Electrical power must be transmitted at low currents to reduce power loss.
- To carry the same power at low current we must use a high voltage.
- To step up to a high voltage at the beginning of a transmission line and to step down to a low voltage again at the end we need transformers.
- **Transformers only work when they are supplied with alternating current.**
- We can now understand why electrical power is transmitted as an alternating current at a very high voltage.

Calculating power loss in transmission lines

Power loss in any wires is due to the heating effect of the electric current in them.

Power loss in wires = I^2R

In this equation, R is the resistance of just the wires themselves, but I is the current in the wires and in the load.

The grid system

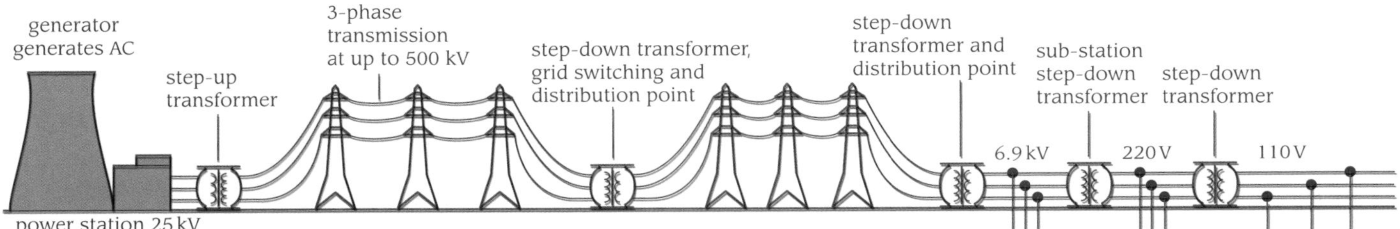
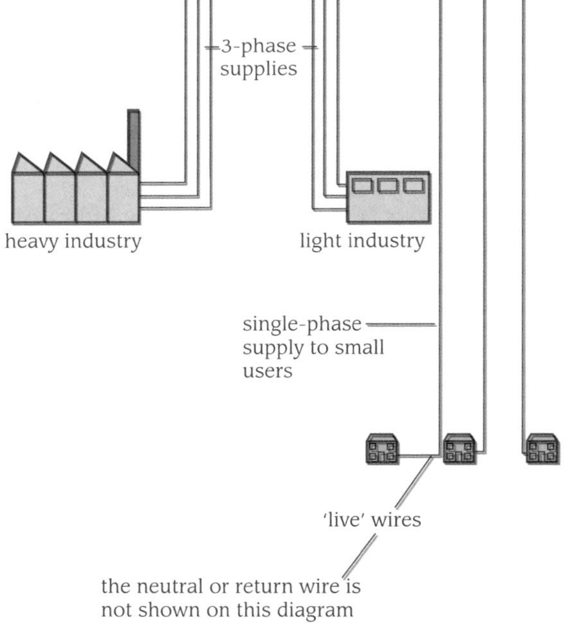

▲ **Figure 18.6.2** The grid system

▲ **Figure 18.6.3** Power lines

Key fact

The grid

- The generators at a power station produce alternating electric current at a fairly high voltage, typically 25 kV (Figure 18.6.2).
- A higher voltage is desirable for long-distance transmission, so a step-up transformer immediately steps up the voltage to a higher value.
- In countries where the power has to travel hundreds of kilometres this voltage can be as high as half a million volts.
- A series of transformers and switching stations, known as sub-stations, step the voltage down to the safer values used by industry and people in their homes.
- Industrial consumers use 220 volts or higher.
- Small users such as houses receive a supply at 110 volts.

Summary questions

1 Which reduces the power loss in transmission, increasing current or increasing voltage?

2 Where are step-up transformers used in the grid system?

3 Give an equation for the power loss in wires.

Practice exam-style questions

1 A wide horseshoe magnet is placed on the pan of a sensitive balance. A fixed piece of wire, connected to a switch and power supply, passes midway between the poles of the magnet. The apparatus is illustrated below.

a) In what direction is the force on the wire when the switch is closed?

b) State whether the reading on the balance will increase, decrease or remain the same and explain your answer.

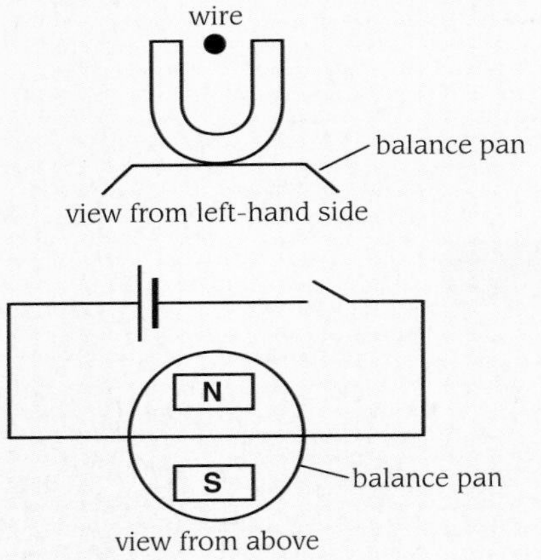

2 a) State the two laws of electromagnetic induction, one law relating to the size of the induced e.m.f. (Faraday's law) and the other relating to its direction (Lenz's law).

b) Describe a simple experiment, one in each case, which illustrates the truth of each of these laws. Explain how each law can be deduced from the observations made in the experiment.

3 Lenz's law, it is said, is a direct consequence of the law of conservation of energy.

a) Explain how the induction of an electric current in a circuit must involve energy associated with it.

b) In a demonstration of Lenz's law, in which a magnet is inserted into a coil of wire, how do we explain that work is done to supply the energy required? Refer to the force against which another force must be applied to do work.

c) How does the direction of the force against which work must be done confirm that the induced current flows in a direction that opposes the applied force?

d) How does the full explanation confirm that energy conservation lies behind the origins of Lenz's law?

4 The figure below shows a section through a moving-coil loudspeaker.

a) Copy the dark-shaded part and indicate on your sketch:

i) the position and name of any magnetic poles

ii) the shape and direction of the magnetic field.

b) Describe and explain what happens to the coil and what is heard when:

i) a dry cell is attached to the terminals of the loudspeaker and the current is switched on and then off

ii) a 200 Hz alternating voltage is applied to the terminals.

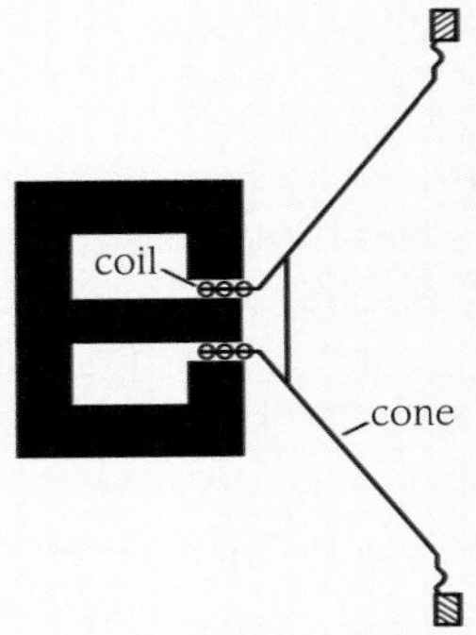

c) When the loudspeaker is emitting a sound, how does the movement of the coil alter if the sound becomes:

i) louder

ii) of higher pitch?

5 The figure below shows a rectangular plane coil ABCD with several turns of wire located in the magnetic field between the N and S poles. The magnetic field lines are parallel to each other and evenly spaced in the region of the coil. The coil is free to rotate on the horizontal axle XY.

a) When a current is passed through the coil in the direction ABCD the coil starts to turn, and eventually comes to rest. With the aid of diagrams, show:

i) why the coil begins to turn

ii) in which direction it begins to turn

iii) why it eventually comes to rest

iv) the position in which it comes to rest.

b) With the aid of a diagram, explain what essential modification is required to convert this coil into a working DC motor.

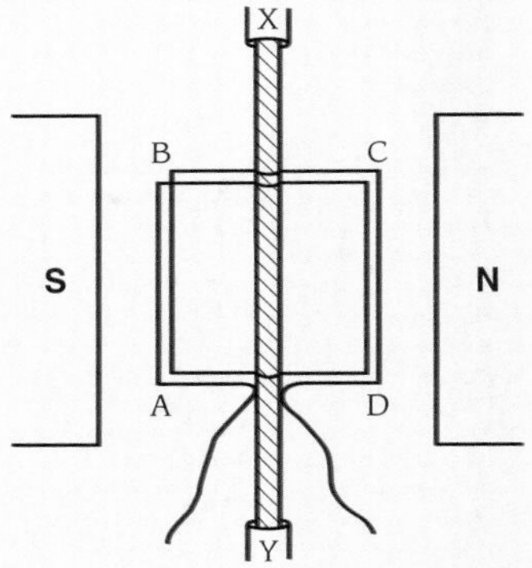

6 a) Describe an experiment that demonstrates the direction of the force acting on a wire, which is at right angles to a magnetic field and carries an electric current.

b) Rotation of the coil of a DC motor is produced by forces exerted on conductors in a magnetic field. To investigate the performance of such a motor it is necessary to measure:

i) the electrical power input from the DC source driving the motor and

ii) the rate at which the motor does work in lifting a load at a constant speed.

With the aid of diagrams, describe experiments by which you could measure these two quantities.

7 a) Draw a labelled diagram of a simple DC electric motor.
b) State THREE ways in which the forces on the coil, and hence the power of the motor, could be increased.
c) Name ONE other electrical device that works on the same principle as the motor.

8 Draw a diagram showing the main components of a simple AC generator. Briefly describe how the generator works and explain why it produces alternating current. Describe the energy changes taking place in the generator.

9 The figure below shows a simple generator.

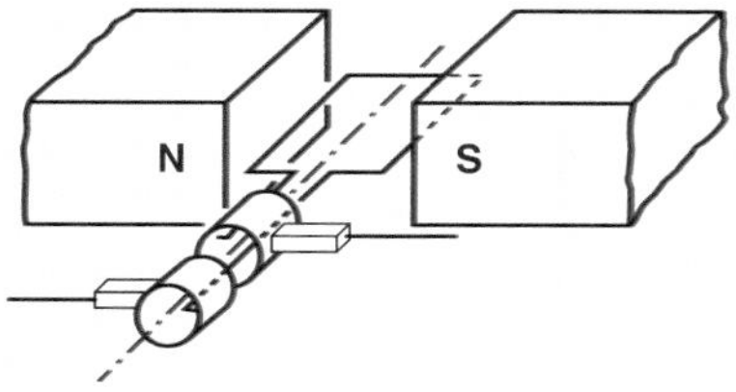

a) i) Explain why an e.m.f. is produced between the ends of the coil when it is rotated.
ii) Draw a sketch graph showing how the e.m.f. between the ends of the coil varies with time over at least ONE revolution of the coil. Relate the positions of the coil to the values shown on your graph.
iii) Draw a second sketch graph showing what you would expect if the speed of rotation of the coil were doubled.
iv) Draw a third sketch graph showing what you would expect if, in addition to rotating at twice the speed, the coil contained twice as many turns.
b) The output from the generator is found to be unsuitable for charging a car battery. Why is this? What modification to the generator would be necessary to enable this to be done?

10 A power station generator produces an e.m.f. of 33 000 V at a frequency of 50 Hz. The supply to your home is 110 V at 50 Hz. Explain how the output of the power station is modified for use in your home.

11 Figure **a** below represents a transformer with a primary coil of 800 turns and a secondary coil of 88 turns.

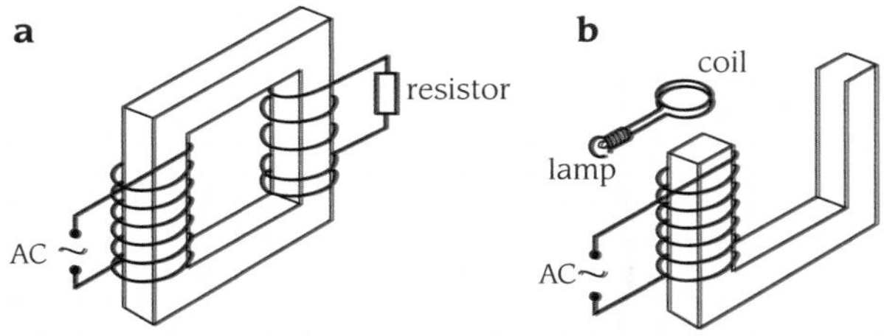

a) If the primary coil is connected to the 110 V AC mains supply, what will be the secondary voltage?
b) Calculate the efficiency of the transformer if the primary current is 0.5 A and the secondary current 5.0 A.
c) The secondary coil is removed and a small coil connected to a low-voltage lamp is placed as shown in figure **b** above. Explain the following observations:
i) the lamp lights
ii) if the coil is moved upwards, the lamp gets dimmer
iii) if a soft-iron rod is now placed through the coil, the lamp brightens again
iv) the lamp will not light if a DC supply is used instead of an AC one.

12 Copy and complete the following table, explaining how power and energy losses in a transformer can be reduced:

Cause of power loss in a transformer	Design features that help to reduce power losses
Heating effect of currents in the wires of the transformer coils	
Heating effect of induced eddy currents that arise in the iron core of the transformer	
Energy losses from the repeated rapid processes of magnetising and demagnetising the iron core	
Energy losses caused by some of the magnetic field lines failing to link the two coils of the transformer together	

13 Two cylindrical soft-iron bars are placed side-by-side inside and parallel to the axis of a horizontal solenoid of circular cross section. The figure below shows a cross section through the solenoid.

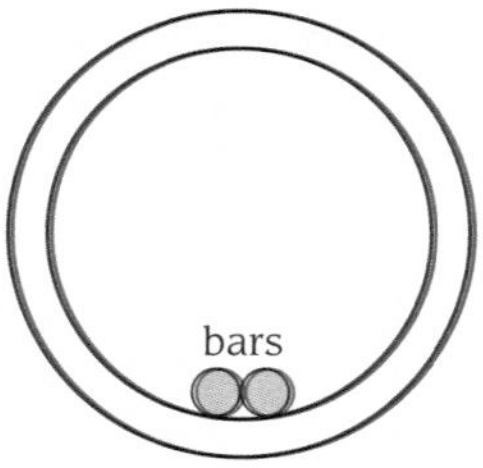

a) Describe and account for what you would see happen to the bars if a direct current is switched on in the solenoid and is then switched off.
b) What difference would it make if instead the bars were:
i) placed end to end in the solenoid
ii) made of hard steel?
Give reasons for your answers.

14 a) The primary and secondary coils of a transformer have 2200 and 240 turns, respectively. If the primary is connected to a 110 V AC supply, calculate the voltage across the secondary.
b) A person wishes to illuminate a shed 100 m from their house using a 12 V lamp connected to a mains supply of 110 V through a suitable step-down transformer. Explain, giving your reasons, whether it is more efficient to connect the transformer so that it is near the mains supply in the house or in the shed.

15 a) Draw a labelled diagram showing the main features of a voltage step-up transformer.

b) State the law of electromagnetic induction on which the working of the transformer depends.

c) Use the law stated in your answer to part **b)** to explain how the transformer works.

16 When a 110 V electrical supply is connected to the primary winding of a transformer, it produces a current of 100 mA in the circuit. The secondary winding is connected to a 5 ohm resistor in which a current of 1.4 A is produced. Calculate:

a) the power supplied to the transformer

b) the power dissipated in the 5 ohm resistor

c) the efficiency of the transformer.

17 a) The figure below shows a voltage step-down transformer connected to a 250 V AC supply. When a 5 ohm resistor is connected between terminals 1 and 2, the current in the resistor is 0.5 A, and when the same resistor is connected between terminals 2 and 3 the current is 1.0 A.
Assuming that the transformer is 100% efficient, calculate:

i) the potential difference between terminals 1 and 2

ii) the potential difference between terminals 2 and 3

iii) the number of turns on the secondary coil between terminals 1 and 2

iv) the number of turns on the secondary coil between terminals 2 and 3

v) the potential difference between terminals 1 and 3

vi) the current in the 5 ohm resistor when connected between terminals 1 and 3.

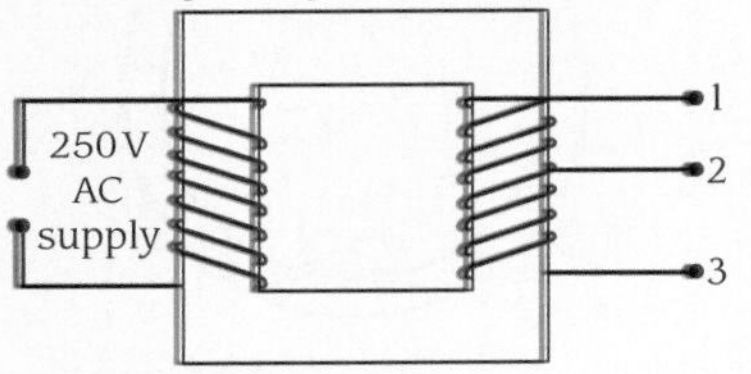

b) In practice, the potential difference between any two of the terminals is less than calculated in part **a)**. State why this is so and explain how the difference is kept to a minimum in a modern transformer.

18 The figure below shows a step-down transformer. The primary coil consists of 2200 turns and is connected to a 110 V AC mains supply. The secondary coil supplies a current of 5.0 A at 12 V AC. The transformer may be assumed to be 100% efficient.

a) What material is usually used for the laminated core of the transformer?

b) Why is the core laminated?

c) How many turns are there on the secondary coil?

d) What is the power taken from the mains supply?

If the transformer is only 90% efficient:

e) For the same useful power output, what power will be required at the input?

f) What current will be taken by the primary coil if the supply voltage remains at 110 V?

Another identical lamp is connected in parallel with the first, across the secondary coil of the 90% efficient transformer:

g) What input power will be required to light both lamps at full brightness?

h) What will limit the number of such lamps that could safely be connected to the transformer secondary?

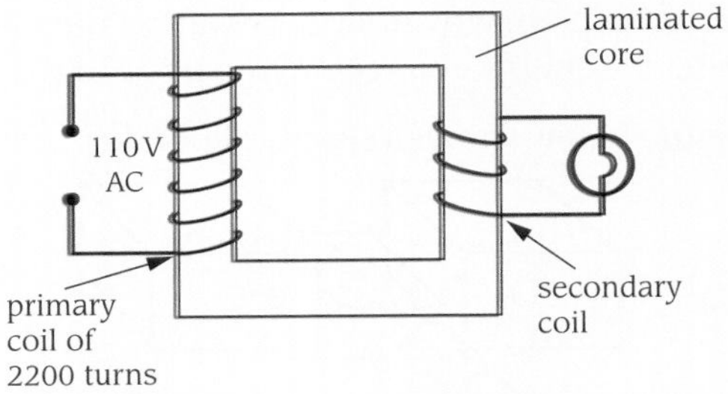

19 a) State the magnetic pole produced on face A of the solenoid by a steady direct current as shown in the figure below.

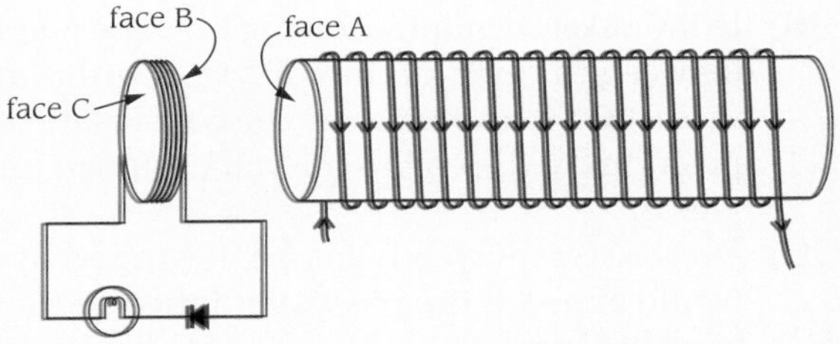

b) When the current in the solenoid is steady, what can you say about the other circuit containing the coil, the diode and the lamp?

c) The current in the solenoid is switched off.

i) What magnetic poles would you expect to find on faces B and C of the coil?

ii) Why would these poles appear only briefly?

iii) State what happens to the lamp.

d) The steady direct current is switched on again in the solenoid. What difference will this make to your answers given in part **c)**?

20 a) Calculate the power wasted by a cable of resistance 0.2 ohm when 20 kilowatts is to be transmitted through the cable:

i) at 110 volt

ii) at 200 000 volt.

b) Explain how energy is wasted in the cable.

21 a) Electrical energy is distributed by the overhead wires, which transmit alternating current at very high voltage. Explain why:

i) a very high voltage is necessary

ii) alternating current is used.

b) A generator capable of producing 200 kW of power is connected to a factory by a cable with a total resistance of 5.0 ohm. If the generator produces the power at a potential difference of 5000 V, calculate:

i) the maximum current in the cable

ii) the voltage drop along the cable

iii) the voltage supplied to the factory

iv) the maximum power available to the factory.

E19 Describing atoms

When something is too small to see, finding out what it is like is bound to be difficult. In the space of just a few years at the beginning of the 20th century, more by imagination and instinct than anything else, a few men gave us a model of the atom, which is the basis of our understanding of much of modern science.

E19.1 Models of atoms

Objectives

By the end of this topic you will be able to:

- describe the work done by Thomson, Rutherford, Bohr and Chadwick in establishing modern models of the atom
- describe the Geiger–Marsden experiment, which established the nuclear structure of the atom
- describe a model of the nucleus, which contains positively charged protons and neutral neutrons of roughly equal masses.

Before 1897	Atoms were thought to be very small indivisible particles.
1897	Joseph John Thomson (1856–1940) provided evidence that the cathode rays come from all elements and that, being particles much smaller than atoms, are common constituents of all atoms.
1902	Lord Kelvin and J. J. Thomson independently suggested a 'plum pudding' atom model.
1906	Ernest Rutherford observed alpha particles passing through a thin sheet of mica without making holes in it. Could alpha particles pass through the atoms themselves?
1911	Hans Geiger and Ernest Marsden fired alpha particles through gold foil and found evidence for the nuclear model of the atom, as proposed by Rutherford.
1913	Niels Bohr (1886–1962) found the link between atomic spectra, quantum theory and Rutherford's nuclear model of the atom. Bohr was awarded a Nobel Prize in 1922. Bohr's new model had electrons in stable orbits around the nucleus, like planets around the Sun.
1932	James Chadwick (1891–1974) identified the neutron as a neutral particle found in the nucleus of atoms, along with protons. Chadwick was awarded the Nobel Prize for Physics in 1935.
Today	There are now many more models of the atom involving new theories and particles. It is still helpful for many purposes to think of the atom with its very small and very dense nucleus surrounded by a cloud of very small negative electrons. The location of any one electron as a particle in an atom is now thought to be uncertain as it also exhibits wave characteristics.

J. J. Thomson

Joseph John Thomson was born in Manchester, England in 1856.

He studied at Owen's College Manchester and at Cambridge.

In 1897 he announced his discovery of the electron. In 1904 he gave lectures at Yale University in which he made important new suggestions about the structure of the atom.

In 1906 he was awarded the Nobel Prize for physics.

Thomson was President of The Royal Society from 1916 to 1920.

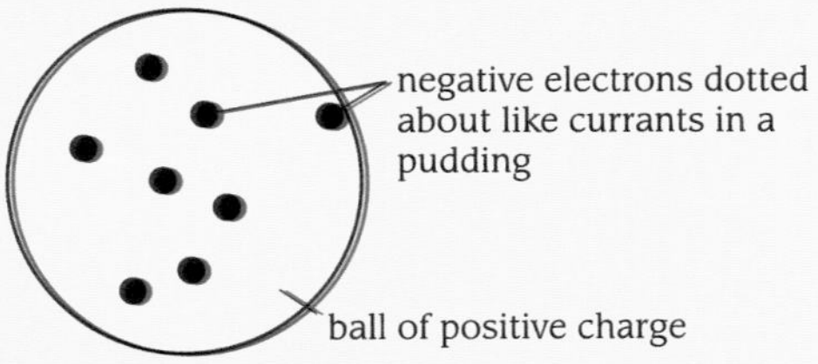

▶ **Figure 19.1.1** 1902: Thomson's plum pudding model

Sir Ernest Rutherford

Sir Ernest Rutherford was born in Nelson, New Zealand in 1871. He went to England in 1895 but also worked in Montreal, Canada.

He became Langworthy Professor of Physics at Manchester University, England in 1907.

In 1910, Rutherford's investigations into the scattering of alpha particles led him to propose that atoms have a very small central core or nucleus.
When he died in 1937, he had been awarded the Nobel Prize in Chemistry (1908), had been President of The Royal Society (1925–1930) and, as well as receiving numerous prizes, had written several books.

Niels Bohr

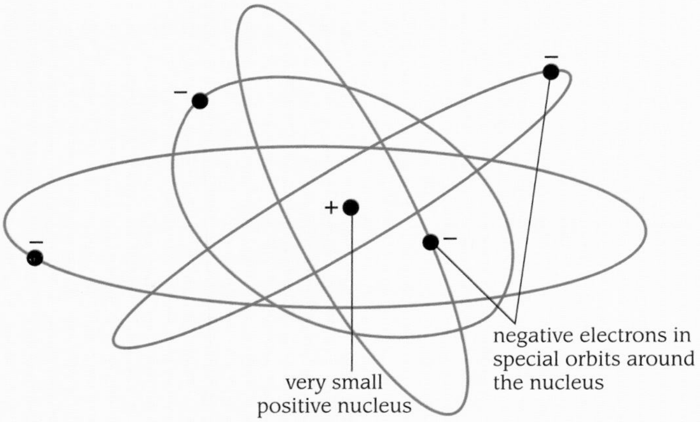

Figure 19.1.2 1913: Rutherford–Bohr model. Electrons orbit a nucleus, like planets orbiting the Sun.

Niels Bohr was born in 1885 in Copenhagen, Denmark.

Bohr studied with Ernest Rutherford at Manchester in England.

In 1913 Bohr published a theory of the structure of the atom, which was a development of Rutherford's nuclear model. Bohr imagined the negative electrons in orbit around the positive nucleus. He also suggested that the electrons existed in certain special orbits and could jump between these while emitting or absorbing radiation. This theory was later developed into Quantum Mechanics by other scientists.

James Chadwick

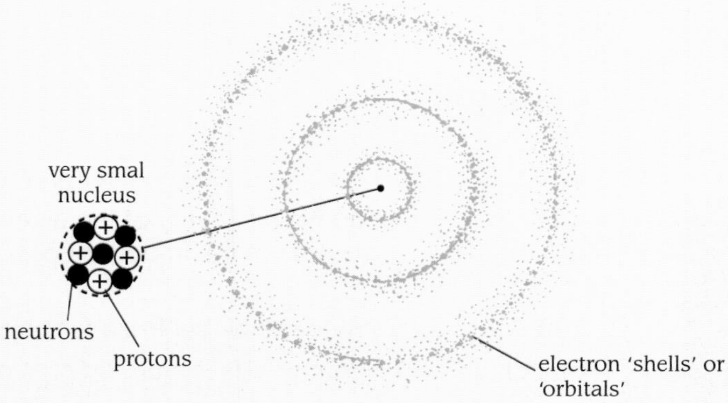

Figure 19.1.3 Today: The atom still has a nucleus but the electrons exist somewhere in regions called 'orbitals' or 'shells' around the nucleus. The electrons may be represented as 'waves' or 'clouds' around the nucleus.

James Chadwick was born in Cheshire, England in 1891.

He studied at Manchester and Cambridge under Ernest Rutherford.

Chadwick hypothesised the existence of the neutron, a nuclear particle with no charge, to explain anomalies in the existing theories of the atom. In 1932 the mass of the neutron was measured experimentally, and in 1935 Chadwick was awarded the Nobel Prize for Physics for his work on the neutron. Later he did some of the theoretical work assessing the feasibility of an atomic bomb, and worked as an adviser to the United Nations.

The 'plum pudding' model

The discovery of cathode rays, positive rays and radioactivity around the beginning of the century began to cause doubt about the atom as an indivisible particle. They provided evidence that particles smaller than atoms existed and that these had electric charges. This led both Kelvin and J. J. Thomson independently to the idea that perhaps atoms were solid balls of positively charged matter in which negative electrons were dotted about like currants in a pudding. There needed to be enough negative electrons to make the whole pudding electrically neutral.

Rutherford's nuclear model

Scattered alpha particles provide a clue

In 1906, Rutherford fired positively charged alpha particles (given off from radioactive materials) at thin sheets of mica. He discovered that although some alpha particles were deflected, most just passed straight through.

These results led Rutherford to suggest atoms had a very small, electrically charged, central nucleus, which deflected alpha particles passing close to it, surrounded by a large area that was mostly empty space, but had an opposite electric charge to the nucleus.

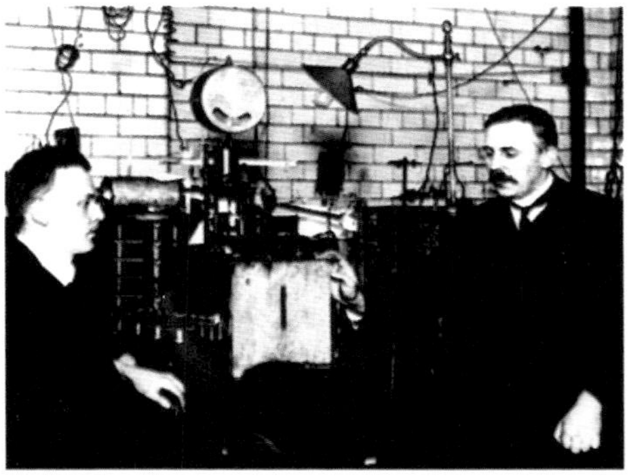

▲ **Figure 19.1.4** Ernest Rutherford and Hans Geiger at work in their Manchester laboratory

The experiments of Geiger and Marsden (1909–11)

Figure 19.1.5 shows the apparatus used by two of Rutherford's assistants, Hans Geiger and Ernest Marsden, to investigate how alpha particles were scattered by metal foils.

A narrow beam of alpha particles from a radioactive radium source passed through platinum, silver and gold foil. A zinc sulfide screen gave a small flash of light when an alpha particle hit it.

During their experiments, Geiger and Marsden counted over 100 000 flashes of light while looking down the microscope. They counted alpha particles deflected by angles in the range 5° to 150° from the straight-through direction.

Alphas are scattered backwards

Most of the alpha particles passed straight through the metal foils. The number deflected fell off quickly as the angle of deflection increased. A very small fraction, about 1 in 8000 (for platinum), were deflected by angles greater than 90°, i.e. they bounced back towards the source (Figure 19.1.6). This result was so surprising that Rutherford commented:

> 'It was about as credible as if you had fired a 15 inch shell at a piece of tissue paper and it came back and hit you.'

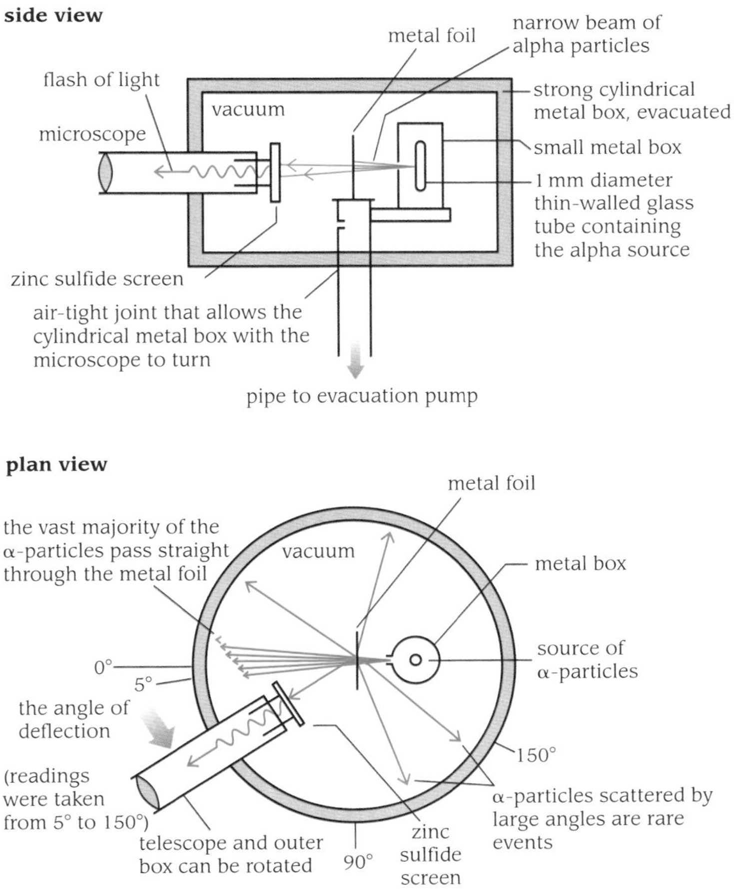

▲ **Figure 19.1.5** The layout of the experiments of Geiger and Marsden

Key fact

The size of the nucleus

- Rutherford estimated that the closest approach of an alpha particle to a gold nucleus in a head-on collision was about 10^{-14} m. So the gold nucleus could be no larger than this.
- The diameter of a single atom, (which varies from one kind of atom to another) is only a few tenths of a nanometre, somewhere between 10^{-9} m and 10^{-10} m.
- The diameter of the nucleus is only 1/10 000 of the diameter of the whole atom.
- The nuclear atom model is almost entirely empty except for this very tiny dot in the centre where all its positive charge and almost all of its mass is concentrated (Figure 19.1.7).
- The scale of the nucleus compared with its atom can be compared with a walnut at the centre of Sabina Park, Kingston.

Details of the nuclear model of the atom

- The nucleus has a positive charge. A deflected alpha particle is repelled by the nucleus of a single metal atom by the repulsion between the like (positive) electric charges of the alpha particle and atomic nucleus.
- The repulsion obeys the inverse-square law of the force between two charged objects and will become very strong as they approach very close.
- The charge on the nucleus of the atom depends on its relative atomic mass. This was confirmed by the experimental results for different metal foils. We now know that the size of the positive nuclear charge depends on the number of protons in the nucleus of the atom.

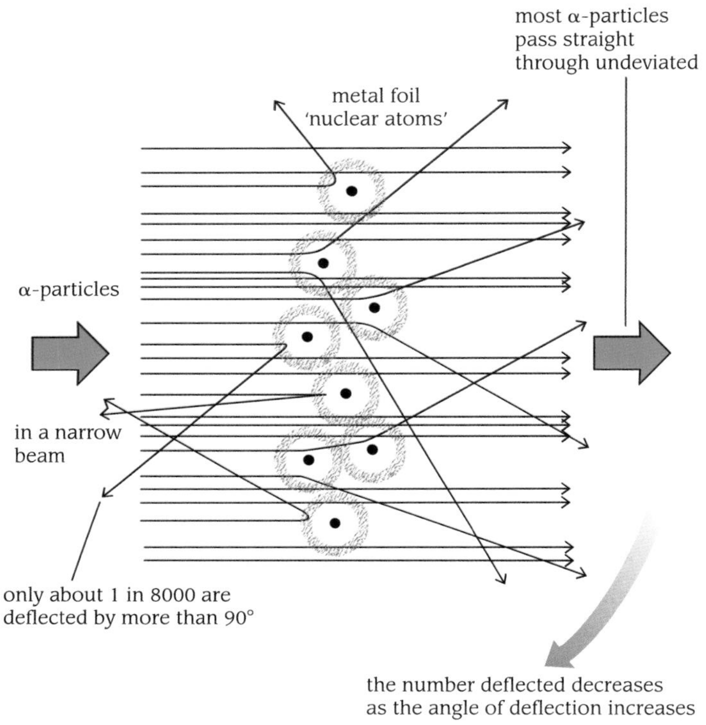

▲ **Figure 19.1.6** Alpha particle scattering

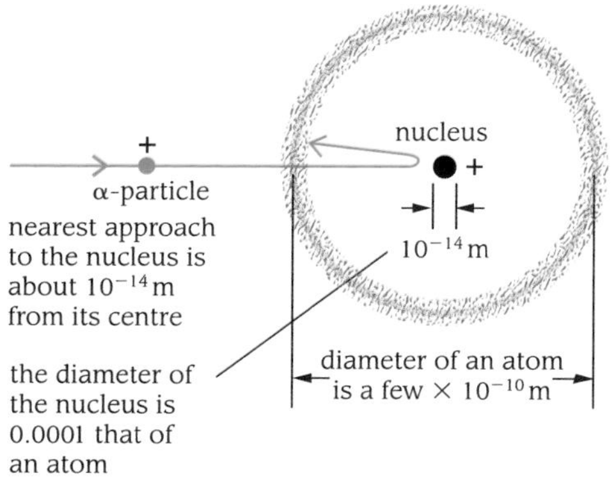

▲ **Figure 19.1.7** Comparing atomic and nuclear sizes

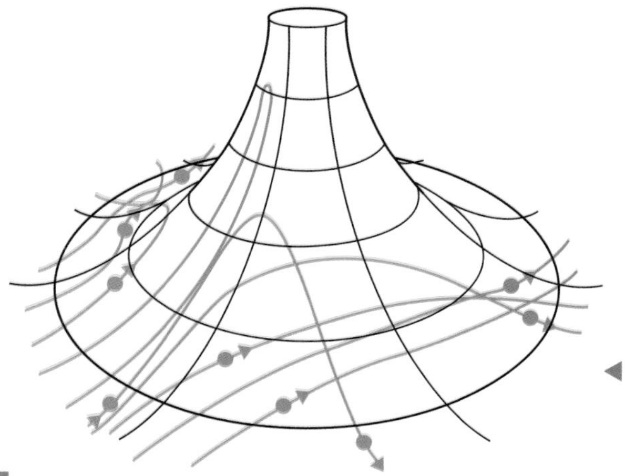

◀ **Figure 19.1.8** Firing an alpha particle at an atomic nucleus is like rolling a marble up a conical-shaped hill. As an α-particle gets nearer to the positively charged nucleus the force of repulsion increases in the same way as the conical hill gets steeper towards its peak.

The Bohr model of the atom

The Danish physicist Niels Bohr took Rutherford's nuclear model of the atom very seriously and he tried to find solutions to the problems posed by this new model. While Rutherford had been able to estimate the size of the atomic nucleus, there was no theory yet that could explain why the radius of the atom, as a whole, was so much greater than that of the nucleus. It seemed that negative electrons should just fall into the positive nucleus because of the attractive forces. As they accelerated inwards they should emit electromagnetic radiation. Rutherford's nuclear atom needed a fixed atomic radius and some form of stable structure.

In 1913, Bohr saw a formula invented by a Swiss schoolmaster called Johann Balmer. Years later Bohr said: 'As soon as I saw Balmer's formula the whole thing was immediately clear to me.' Balmer had noticed a pattern in the frequencies of the spectral lines from a discharge through hydrogen gas. His formula showed that the frequencies of light emitted from a hydrogen atom fitted a precise mathematical series.

Bohr now imagined the electrons to be in orbits around the atomic nucleus with precise radii that fitted the Balmer formula. However, for Bohr's new model of the atom to work, he had to propose some new rules about what electrons were allowed to do in atoms.

Chadwick finds the neutron

In 1920, Rutherford predicted the existence of a neutral particle in the nucleus of the atom. He proposed the name **neutron** for this new neutral particle, and suggested that it should have a mass very slightly greater than that of the proton.

In 1932, James Chadwick showed that radiation emitted from an experiment in which alpha particles were fired at beryllium must be particles fitting Rutherford's description. The neutron is now known to exist as a basic constituent of matter and the nuclei of all atoms, except hydrogen, contain neutrons as well as positive protons.

Today's model of the atom

We still think of the atom as having a very small nucleus composed of protons and neutrons, but our view of the nature of electrons has changed. The main objection to Bohr's model is that it pinpoints electrons in definite orbits with definite positions. We have evidence that electrons have a wave-like nature similar to light. We believe that the allowed orbits are the regions that can contain a whole number of electron 'waves'. This idea is similar to the way in which sound waves can be seen to fit into the stretched string of a musical instrument.

The electron structure of the atom is now described by very advanced mathematical theories known as wave mechanics.

Summary questions

1 Describe the 'plum pudding model' of atoms.

2 How did Rutherford's alpha scattering experiment show the plum pudding model to be wrong?

3 Describe today's model of the atom.

Objectives

By the end of this topic you will be able to:

- describe diagrammatically the structure of simple atoms
- compare the mass and charge of the electron with the mass and charge of the proton
- explain why an atom is normally neutral and stable
- recall and use the relationship: $A = Z + N$
- use the standard notation for representing a nuclide: ${}^{A}_{Z}X$
- explain 'isotopes'
- relate the shell model of the atom to the periodic table and understand that any element in the periodic table has one more proton than the element before it in the table.

Key fact

Definitions

- The proton number or atomic number Z of an element is the number of protons in the nucleus of every atom of that element.
- A neutral atom has exactly the same number of electrons as protons.
- The number of neutrons in the nucleus of an atom is known as the neutron number N.
- The number of nucleons in the nucleus of an atom is called its nucleon number or mass number A.

nucleon number or mass number = proton number or atomic number + neutron number

$$A = Z + N$$

E19.2 Particles in the atom

The atomic number, or proton number Z

An atom is normally electrically neutral and since the proton (+) and the electron (−) each have the same amount of charge, there must normally be equal numbers of protons and electrons in atoms. However, atoms can gain or lose electrons and become ions without changing into a different substance or element. So the number of electrons is not a reliable guide to the type of atom. The number of protons in the nucleus of an atom is the only factor that determines to which element an atom belongs.

Atoms of a particular element are labelled by a number called their **atomic number** or **proton number**, which is given the symbol Z.

Neutron number N and mass number A

The nucleus of an atom contains protons and neutrons. These are both referred to as nucleons, i.e. particles that belong in the nucleus of an atom. The number of nucleons in the nucleus of an atom is called its **nucleon number** or **mass number**, symbol A.

The number of neutrons in a nucleus is similar to the number of protons Z, but is often greater than Z, particularly for large atoms. The main effects of the number of neutrons in the nucleus of an atom are on its mass and its stability. Neutrons, having a mass very similar to that of a proton, make a great difference to the total mass of an atom. The number of neutrons in the nucleus is called the **neutron number**, symbol N.

Elements are identified by their proton number, Z

Atomic number or proton number Z	Element	Neutron number N	Mass number or nucleon number $A = Z + N$	Nuclide symbols and isotopes
1	hydrogen	0	1	${}^{1}_{1}H$ hydrogen
		1	2	${}^{2}_{1}H$ deuterium
		2	3	${}^{3}_{1}H$ tritium
2	helium	1	3	${}^{3}_{2}He$
		2	4	${}^{4}_{2}He$
3	lithium	3	6	${}^{6}_{3}Li$
		4	7	${}^{7}_{3}Li$
4	beryllium	5	9	${}^{9}_{4}Be$
5	boron	5	10	${}^{10}_{5}B$
		6	11	${}^{11}_{5}B$
6	carbon	6	12	${}^{12}_{6}C$
		7	13	${}^{13}_{6}C$
		8	14	${}^{14}_{6}C$

Isotopes and nuclides

If two atoms have the same number of protons they are atoms of the same element.

Sometimes two atoms, with the same proton number, have different numbers of neutrons. These atoms are of the same element but they have different nucleon numbers or mass numbers. We call these atoms isotopes (a name obtained from two Greek words: *isos* meaning same, and *topos* meaning place). Isotopes occupy the same place or position in the table of elements because they are of the same element.

Isotopes are atoms with the same proton number Z but different nucleon numbers A.

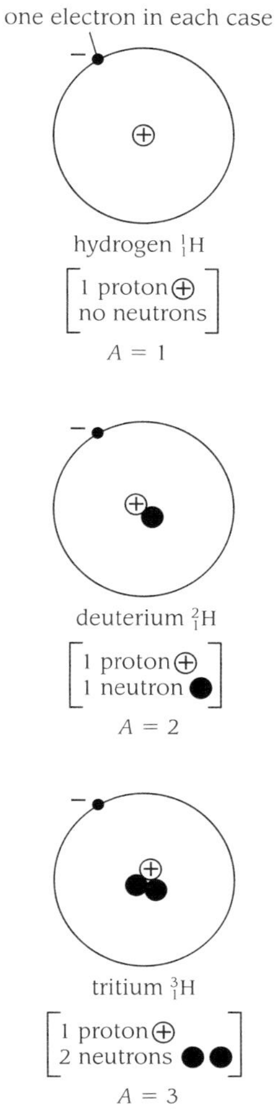

▲ **Figure 19.2.1** Isotopes of hydrogen

The nuclide symbol

$$^{A}_{Z}X$$

X is the symbol for the element

A = the nucleon number

Z = the proton number

N, the number of neutrons is given by $N = A - Z$

Figure 19.2.1 shows the different numbers of neutrons (and hence different nucleon numbers) in the three isotopes of hydrogen.

In the case of hydrogen, the isotopes also have special names: hydrogen, deuterium and tritium.

The table on the preceding page shows some common isotopes of the first six elements. These isotopes are not found in equal proportions, and in most cases nearly all of the atoms are of one particular isotope. For example, 98.9% of carbon atoms have the nucleon number 12.

When we wish to talk about one particular isotope of an element we use the word nuclide to refer to atoms with the same nucleon number as well as proton number.

The word nuclide describes a species of atoms of which every atom has the same proton number (atomic number) and the same nucleon number (mass number).

So we would say that hydrogen has three *isotopes* but when we talk about just one of them, say deuterium, we should refer to the *nuclide*, which has one proton and one neutron in its nucleus.

Nuclei that have too few or too many neutrons are found to be unstable. This means that they are prone to breaking up and shooting out fragments in a process known as radioactive decay.

Worked example

Using $N = A - Z$

$^{235}_{92}U$ is a nuclide of uranium.

How many neutrons and how many protons does it contain?

By reading the symbol we find that its proton number $Z = 92$, and its nucleon number $A = 235$. The number of neutrons $N = A - Z = 235 - 92 = 143$.

Particle	electron	proton	neutron
Symbol	e	p	n
Charge	$^-$e	$^+$e	neutral
Mass/u Symbol	0.00055 m_e	1.0073 m_p	1.0087 m_n
Relative mass	1 m_e	1836 m_e	1839 m_e
Location in the atom	in orbitals or shells around the nucleus	nucleons, i.e. particles found in the nucleus	

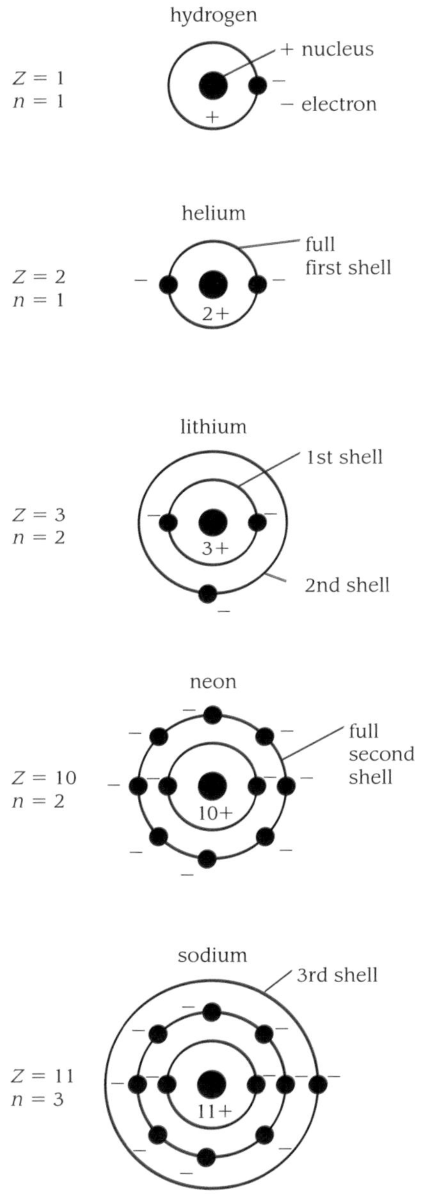

▲ **Figure 19.2.2** The shell structure of atoms

Atomic masses

The mass of an atom is almost equal to the mass of the nucleons it contains. However, as the masses of atoms and their nucleons are very small when expressed in kilograms, a more convenient unit of atomic mass was devised. This unit is approximately the same as the mass of the proton or the neutron.

The unit of atomic mass is called the **unified atomic mass unit**, symbol u.

1 u is equal to $\frac{1}{12}$ of the mass of the nuclide $^{12}_{6}$C.

So the mass of one $^{12}_{6}$C carbon atom is exactly 12 unified atomic mass units, written 12 u.

One $^{12}_{6}$C carbon atom has a mass of 2.0×10^{-26} kg,

so it turns out that

$$1\,\text{u} = \frac{2.0 \times 10^{-26}\,\text{kg}}{12} = 1.7 \times 10^{-27}\,\text{kg}$$

The masses of other atoms expressed in unified atomic mass units are not whole numbers.

The simplest hydrogen atom composed of one proton and one electron has a mass, m_H given by:

$$m_H = m_p + m_e = 1.0073\,\text{u} + 0.0005\,\text{u}$$
$$m_H = 1.0078\,\text{u}$$

The shell model of atomic structure

The Rutherford–Bohr model of the atom arranges all the elements in groups with electrons in certain allowed orbits. The orbits that electrons were allowed to occupy around atomic nuclei, were in groups of similar radii called shells.

There was a maximum number of electrons that each shell could hold given by the formula $2n^2$, where $n = 1, 2, 3$, etc.

- The first shell, nearest the nucleus, has only $2(1^2) = 2$ electrons.
- The second shell has $2(2^2) = 8$ electrons.
- The third shell has $2(3^2) = 18$ and so on.

Examples of the shell structure of some small atoms are shown in Figure 19.2.2. When one shell is full of electrons the next shell begins filling.

Neutral and stable

Most atoms are electrically neutral, because the number of protons is equal to the number of electrons, so the positive charge on the protons is 'cancelled out' by the negative charge on the electrons. If an atom loses or gains electrons for any reason, it is called an **ion** and it has an electric charge.

Most atoms are stable because although the positively charged protons repel each other (like charges repel) the nuclear force holding the protons and neutrons together in the nucleus is stronger than the repulsive electrical force. When this is not so, the atom becomes unstable and is said to be **radioactive**.

The periodic table

- The periodic table organises elements in order of their atomic number, (also called the proton number).
- Elements in the same vertical row have the same number of electrons in their outer shell. Those in Group 1 (column 1) have one electron in their outer shell. Those in Group 2 (column 2) have two electrons in their outer shell and so on.
- Elements in the same group, with the same number of electrons in their outer shell, have similar chemical properties.
- Elements in the right-hand column all have full outer shells of electrons. This makes them chemically unreactive, or inert.
- Elements with the same number of electron shells are in the same horizontal row, or period.
- The mass of elements increases across the period (horizontal row) from left to right.
- The number of electron shells increases as the elements go down each group (column).
- The elements are divided into metals, semi-metals and non-metals. Metals are in Groups 1 and 2.
- The noble or inert gases are in the right-hand group.

Summary questions

1 Write the nuclide symbol and state what the letters stand for.

2 What are isotopes?

3 What does the mass number of an element give?

Practice exam-style questions

1 Explain the following:

a) What you understand by the term 'atom'.

b) What you understand by the term 'element'.

c) What all atoms of the same element have in common.

d) What all atoms of a particular isotope of an element have in common, and what makes atoms of one isotope different from those of another.

e) What it is that protons and neutrons have in common that distinguishes them from electrons.

f) What it is that protons and electrons have in common that neutrons do not have.

2 Write down the number of each kind of particle in these nuclides:

a) ${}^{1}_{1}H$

b) ${}^{3}_{1}H$

c) ${}^{14}_{6}C$

d) ${}^{19}_{9}F$

e) ${}^{235}_{92}U$

3 Write down:

a) the nuclide symbol for an atom of chlorine (Cl), which contains 17 protons and 18 neutrons

b) the nuclide symbol for the isotope of uranium, which contains three neutrons more than the one given in question **2 e)** above

c) the symbol for the nuclide, $\frac{1}{12}$ of which is called 'the unified atomic mass unit'.

4 a) A particular atom of neon has an atomic number 10 and a mass number 20. How many protons and neutrons does this atom have?

b) Another atom of neon has a mass number of 22. In what ways is this atom similar to and different from the first atom?

5 Study the following list of nuclides:

${}^{235}_{92}U$ ${}^{40}_{18}Ar$ ${}^{40}_{19}K$ ${}^{238}_{92}U$ ${}^{40}_{20}Ca$ ${}^{39}_{19}K$

a) Select TWO nuclides that are isotopes of the same element.

b) Select TWO nuclides that have the same mass number.

c) Select the nuclide that has 22 neutrons.

d) Select the element that follows potassium in the periodic table.

e) Select the heaviest nuclide.

f) Select the lightest nuclide.

6 Write a paragraph (about 100 words) describing the main contribution made to our understanding of the structure of the atom by the following scientists:

a) Sir Ernest Rutherford

b) Joseph John Thomson

c) Niels Bohr

7 In some circumstances atoms will have the same number of two particles. Which two particles will have the same numbers in the following cases:

a) in a neutral atom

b) in a deuterium ${}^{2}_{1}H$ nucleus

c) in atoms of two isotopes of the same element?

8 When a narrow beam of alpha particles from a radioactive source is fired at a very thin gold foil in an evacuated chamber, most of the alpha particles pass straight through the foil without any change of direction.

a) Why does the chamber have to be evacuated?

b) If the gold foil is examined under a powerful microscope after the alpha particle bombardment, would you expect to find any holes in the foil? Explain your answer.

c) Very occasionally an alpha particle is found to bounce back from the foil. How can this observation be explained?

9 a) If the diameter of a gold atom is estimated to be about 3×10^{-10} m, calculate the number of gold atoms that an alpha particle will pass through when it penetrates a gold foil of thickness about 6×10^{-7} m. (If you assume that the gold atoms are arranged in layers, this will give a rough estimate of the number of layers of atoms in the gold foil.)

b) In an alpha-particle scattering experiment using this foil, one in 8000 of the alpha particles that hit the foil were thrown backwards and did not pass through it. Estimate the proportion of alpha particles thrown backwards by each layer of gold atoms.

c) Assuming that the proportion of the alpha particles thrown backwards by a layer of atoms gives an estimate of the proportion of the area of the layer that is occupied by nuclei, calculate a value for the diameter of a gold nucleus. (The area of the foil occupied by one gold atom, assuming all the atoms are square and are packed close together, is given by $(3 \times 10^{-10}\,\text{m})^2$. The diameter of the nucleus can be found by assuming that it also has a square area, the square root of which is the required estimate.)

10 The figure below shows the path of an alpha particle passing close to an atomic nucleus.

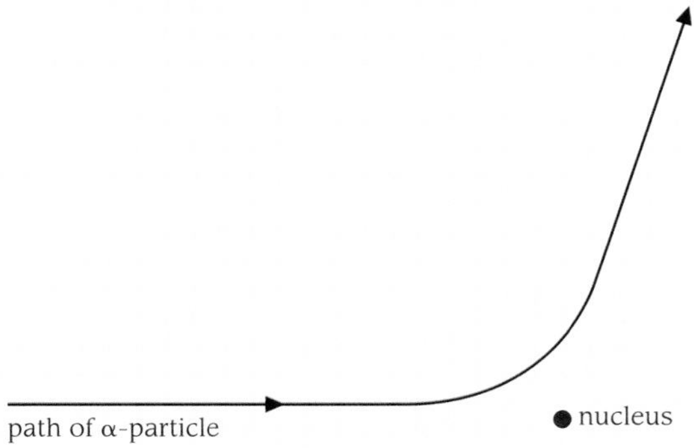

a) Explain why the alpha particle is deflected.

b) Copy the diagram carefully and on it mark the position where the force acting on the alpha particle is greatest. At this position, draw an arrow to show the direction of the force on the alpha particle.

c) On your copy of the diagram, draw the path that the alpha particle would take if the charge on the nucleus was greater.

11 Copy the diagram below and complete it by drawing the paths of the three alpha particles as they approach and are then scattered away from the nucleus of the metal atom shown.

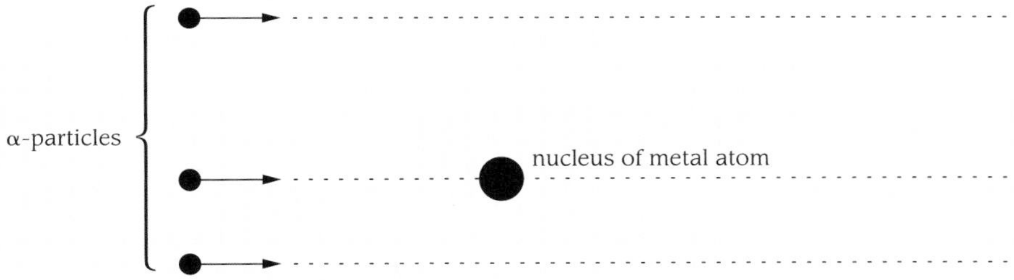

12 The figure below represents a neutral atom of lithium. Copy and complete the table for this atom.

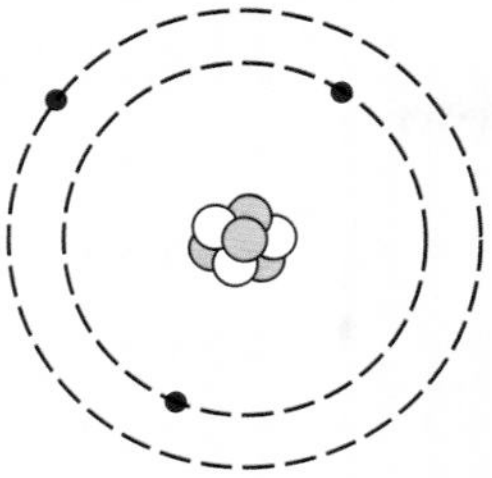

number of electrons	
atomic (proton) number	
number of neutrons	
nucleon (mass) number	

E20 Radioactivity

▲ **Figure 20.1.1** Maria Sklodowska 1867–1934, better known as Marie Curie

Natural radioactive decay of atoms has been happening on the Earth ever since it was formed, over 4000 million years ago. In 1896, Henri Becquerel discovered that some uranium salts emitted radiation that could pass through black wrapping paper and produce a dark silhouette on a photographic plate. Only then did we begin to explore what is now called radioactivity.

Discovering radioactivity

In 1896 Henri Becquerel discovered that radiation from uranium salts had caused an image of a metal key to form on photographic film wrapped in paper, even though no light had reached the film. He asked Marie Curie (born Maria Sklodowska) to investigate this invisible radiation. Marie Curie called this property of uranium radioactivity. She showed that the uranium gave out radiation all the time, and the activity only depended on how much uranium there was. She also showed that the radiation from uranium ionised the air around it, causing it to conduct electricity. Working with her husband Pierre, she discovered several new radioactive elements, including polonium and radium. She died in 1934 from the results of overexposure to radiation.

Objectives

By the end of this topic you will be able to:

- recall precautions to be taken while handling radioactive materials including the use of lead shields and tongs
- describe Marie Curie's work in the field of radioactivity
- recall the nature of the three types of emissions from radioactive substances
- describe the appearance of the tracks left by radioactive emissions in a cloud chamber.

E20.1 Three kinds of radiation

We now know that nuclear radiation or radioactivity happens because the nucleus of the atom is unstable and changes into a different nucleus, giving out radiation as it does so. Experiments showed that there are three kinds of radiation. These were called alpha (α), beta (β) and gamma (γ) radiation. Today we know that alpha radiation is the nuclei of helium atoms, beta radiation is fast-moving electrons and gamma radiation is very high-frequency electromagnetic radiation. The key fact box shows more characteristics of the three types of radiation.

! Key fact

The nature of α- and β-particles and γ-rays

	What is it?		Charge	Relative mass	Energy
Alpha α	particle	a helium nucleus (a helium atom that has lost two electrons) — 2 protons, 2 neutons	the charge of 2 protons: +2e	approx. 4 contains 4 nucleons	kinetic energy
Beta β	particle	a fast-moving electron emitted from a nucleus — e	the charge of an electron: −e	m_e: the mass of an electron, about of $\frac{1}{7000}$ of α	kinetic energy
Gamma γ	radiation	electromagnetic radiation of very high frequency, f and short wavelength, γ	no charge	almost none	photon energy $E = hf$

Safety precautions

All nuclear radiation can be hazardous. Figure 20.1.2 shows the hazard symbol for radioactivity.

▲ **Figure 20.1.2** The hazard symbol for radioactivity

The table below lists the safety precautions that apply to the use of all radioactive materials. No unauthorised person should ever handle radioactive materials.

1	Always use forceps or a lifting tool to move a source; never use bare hands. Strong sources should be handled with long tongs to keep the source further away from the body. When working with radioactive sources for an extended time, stand behind a lead shield and use remote handling equipment. See also Precautions for humans in E20.4.
2	Arrange a source so that its radiation window points away from your body.
3	Never bring a source close to your eyes for examination; it should be identified by a colour or number.
4	When in use, a source must always be attended by an authorised person and it must be returned to a locked and labelled store in its special shielded box immediately after use.
5	No eating or drinking must take place in a laboratory where radioactive materials are in use.
6	After any experiment with radioactive materials, hands must be washed thoroughly. (This applies particularly to the handling of radioactive rock and salt samples and all open sources.)

Detecting invisible radiation

The effect on photographic paper

A uranium ore such as pitchblende is suitable.

- Glue a few crystals of a uranium rock or salt to a small piece of paper about the size of a large coin.
- Place the radioactive material on top of a completely light-tight wrapped sheet of photographic paper.
- Leave it in a safe place where it will not be disturbed for several days.

The length of time depends on the amount and activity of the radioactive material and the type of photographic paper.

- Unwrap and develop the photographic paper in a dark room.
- Anyone who handles the radioactive material should wash their hands thoroughly afterwards.
- The uranium material leaves a dark patch or silhouette on the photographic paper where it has been. The radiation also causes certain materials to light up (fluoresce), so a fluorescent screen can also be used to detect the radiation.

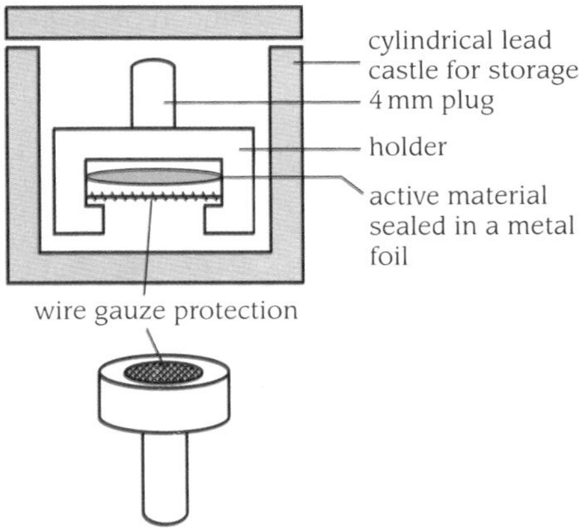

▲ **Figure 20.1.3** Radioactive sources must be handled with tweezers. A cobalt gamma source is shown here inside its shielding lead 'castle'.

The ionising effect of radiation

Radioactive materials emit radiation that causes ionisation of atoms and molecules of the air with which they collide. When a radioactive source is placed near an object that is charged with static electricity, its charge disappears. Ionised atoms and molecules in the air are positively charged and when they are attracted to the charged object they capture electrons from it, becoming neutral again themselves and discharging the charged object.

Measuring radiation

In 1928, Geiger and Müller devised a spark counter that could be used to count individual radioactive particles. The tube, known as a Geiger–Müller (G–M) tube, is the radiation detector. The whole counter, i.e. tube, power supply and pulse counter, is often called a Geiger counter.

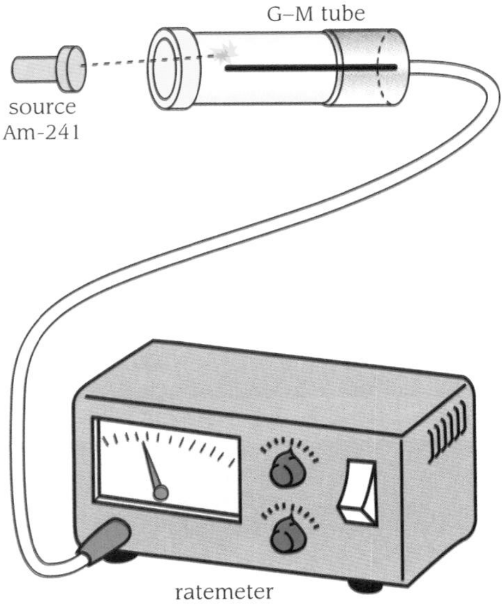

▲ **Figure 20.1.4** Diagram of a Geiger–Müller tube

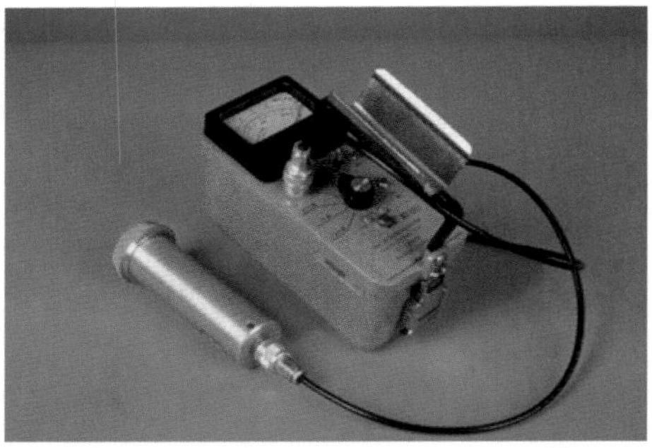

▲ **Figure 20.1.5** A Geiger-Müller tube

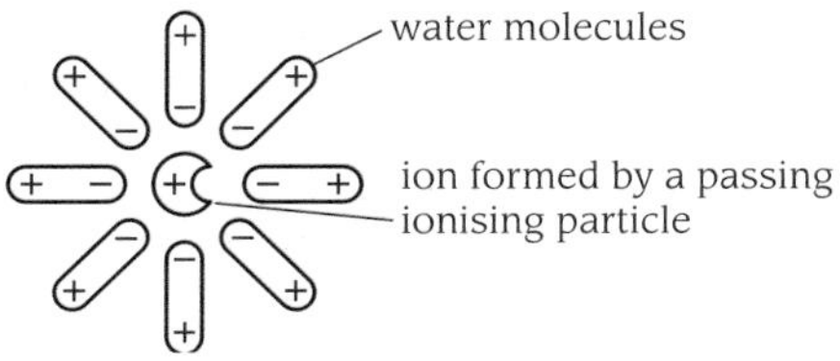

▲ **Figure 20.1.6** The formation of a water droplet around a positive ion

Radiation entering the G–M tube through the mica window ionises the gas inside so that it conducts electricity. So each radioactive particle causes a small pulse of electricity to flow between the metal case and the central wire. These pulses can be counted by a counter, and played through a speaker as a series of clicks.

Making particle tracks visible

A cloud chamber makes the tracks taken by radioactive particles show up as white lines. The cloud chamber is filled with supersaturated water vapour, with water molecules ready to condense on any suitable small particles. A radioactive particle passing through the cloud chamber ionises the air, leaving a trail of positive ions. Water molecules are attracted to these ions and condense on them, leaving a trail of tiny water droplets that show up as a white line.

Alpha particles cause the most ionisation, so show up as the thickest line. Gamma radiation is not charged, but the way it interacts with atoms causes a tiny amount of ionisation, leaving a very faint line.

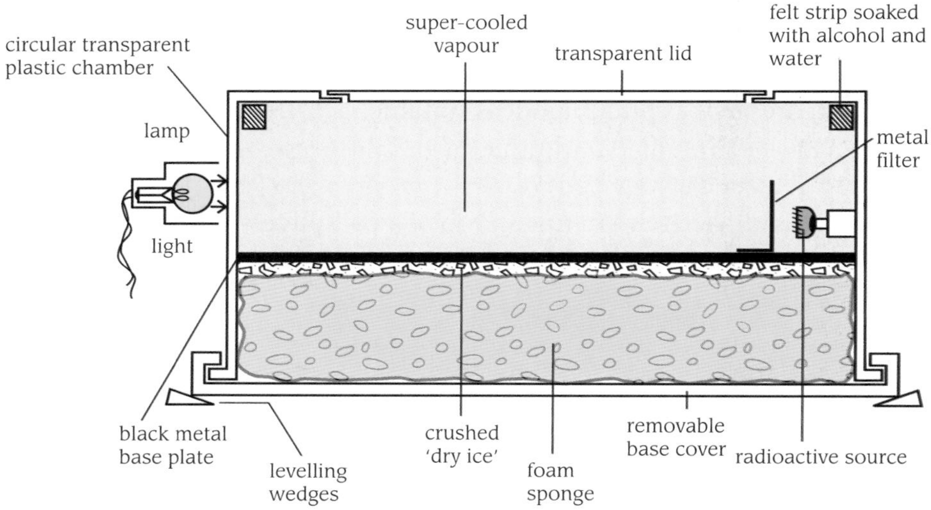

▲ **Figure 20.1.7** A cloud chamber

Cloud chamber tracks

Alpha particle tracks

The track left by an alpha particle in a cloud chamber is bold and straight. The tracks are bold because many tiny water droplets form around the many ions produced along the α-particle tracks. The tracks are very straight because the α-particle has a large mass and momentum compared with the electrons that it pulls off gas atoms as it passes them by.

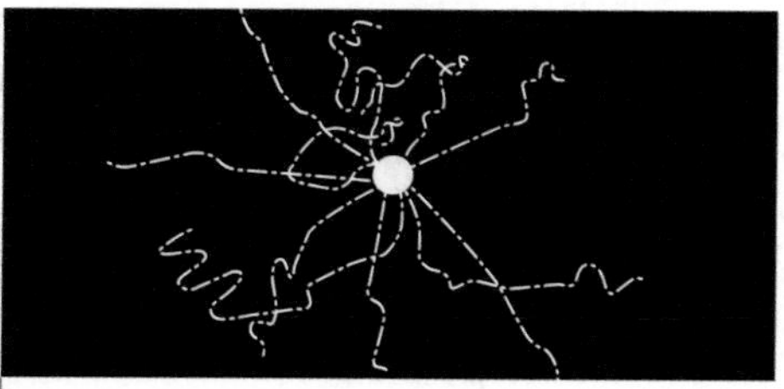

Beta particle tracks

The tracks of β-particles are much fainter than those of α-particles because of their much weaker ionising power. At slow speeds, however, the very light β-particle is easily deflected by the electrons of atoms in the air as it passes them close by. So β-particles suffer sudden changes of direction more frequently as they slow down.

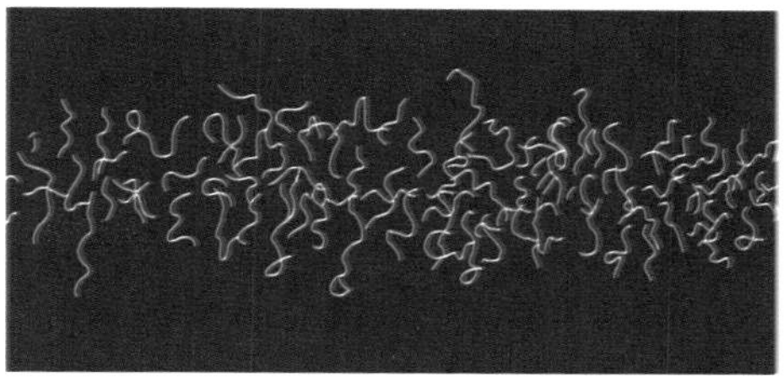

X-ray and gamma-ray tracks

There is no track along the path of an X-ray or gamma photon. However, in an intense beam of X-radiation or gamma radiation containing many millions of photons, occasionally a photon is stopped and absorbed by an atom. Then an electron is thrown out of the atom, producing a short faint and wandering track similar to that of a slow β-particle. The path of an intense beam of X-radiation or gamma radiation can produce many of these electron tracks, all of which start in the beam and wander out of it, creating the wispy image as shown in the diagram.

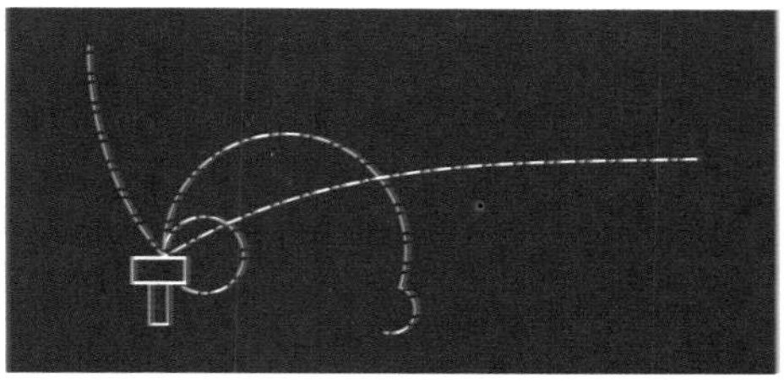

Beta particles in a magnetic field

The very low mass of the beta particles makes it easy to deflect in a magnetic field. The faster particles travel in gradual curves of large radius, while the slower particles travel in tighter circular curves. We can tell that β-particles carry a negative electric charge by the direction in which they are deflected in a magnetic field. The curved paths shown are caused by a magnetic field that is pointing vertically downwards at right angles to the page.

Summary questions

1 What type of radiation is the same as a helium nucleus?

2 What charge does beta radiation have?

3 What is gamma radiation?

E20.2 Properties of radiation

Objectives

By the end of this topic you will be able to:

- describe experiments to compare the ranges of α-, β- and γ-emissions in various media
- predict the effects of magnetic and electric fields on the motion of α- and β- particles and γ-rays.

Penetration and absorption of radiation

Set up an arrangement shown in Figure 20.2.1 with a radioactive source facing the mica window of a G–M tube at a fixed distance.

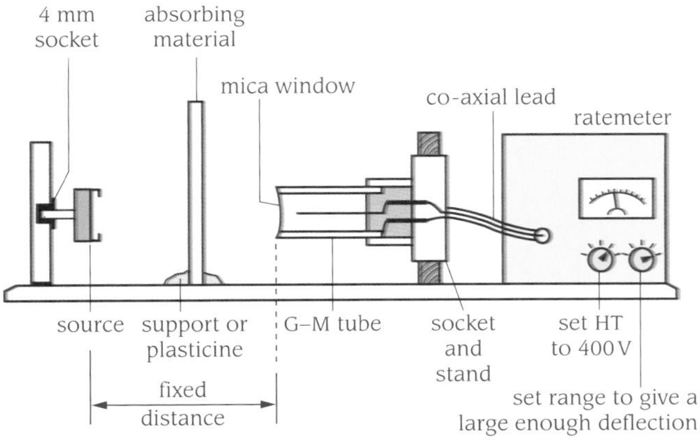

▲ **Figure 20.2.1** Penetration and absorption of α-, β- and γ-radiation

Taking a background reading

In all radiation experiments where counts or count rates are recorded, it is necessary to subtract from all the readings a background count rate. The background radiation count is always present due to natural radioactivity in the ground, bricks of buildings and the bombardment of the atmosphere by cosmic radiation.

Key fact

- α- and β-particles have definite maximum ranges.
- α-particles are totally absorbed by a thick sheet of paper, or a few layers of human skin.
- β-particles are absorbed by a few millimetres of aluminium.
- γ-radiation has no maximum range.
- About 1 cm of lead will absorb half of the γ-radiation, another 1 cm of lead will halve it again, allowing $\frac{1}{4}$ of the original radiation to pass through.
- So 5 cm of lead will halve the γ-radiation five times to $\frac{1}{32}$ of its original value.
- These facts are summarised in Figure 20.2.2.

- To obtain a background count rate, remove all sources some distance from the experiment and switch on the ratemeter with its range switch on the lowest range.

corrected count rate = count rate − background count rate

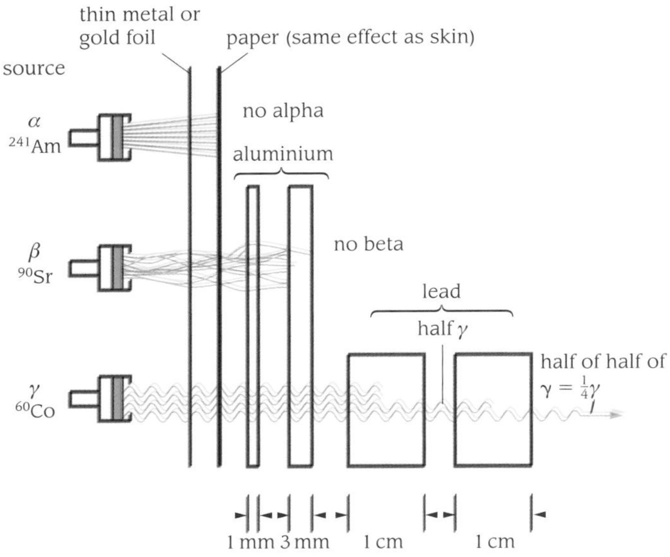

▲ **Figure 20.2.2**

The effect of distance on radiation

Alpha radiation

- To investigate how far α-particles travel in air, use the practical arrangement shown in Figure 20.2.1, but without the absorbing material.
- Move the G–M tube in 5 mm steps away from the source and record the count rate in each position.

Within a few centimetres all the α-radiation has been stopped by the air. The α-particles give up their kinetic energy as they form ions along their track. When all their energy has been used up in removing electrons from air molecules, α-particles pick up two electrons and become neutral helium atoms.

Beta radiation

The range of β-particles in air is difficult to measure because they can travel several metres before they come to rest. They give up their kinetic energy more slowly as they form far fewer ions along their tracks. A β-particle that has been stopped in its track is an electron.

Gamma radiation

- To investigate the effect of distance on γ-radiation it is better to turn the G–M tube with its side facing the γ-source as shown in Figure 20.2.3. Measure the distance d from the source to the side of the G–M tube. Suitable values of the distance d are shown in the table opposite.
- In each position, take a reading of the count rate.
- Record a reading of the background radiation count rate.

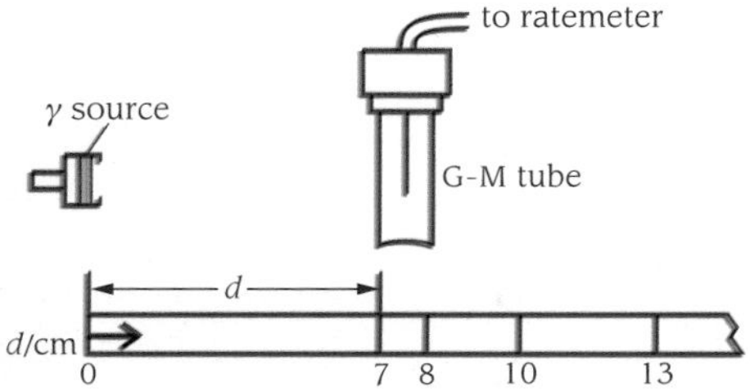

▲ **Figure 20.2.3** The effect of distance on gamma radiation

The count rate falls off rapidly as the G–M tube is moved away from the source, but it does not fall to zero. With γ-radiation, the drop in count rate is not a result of absorption of the radiation by the air, since γ-radiation has only a very weak ionising effect on air molecules. Rather the cause is the 'spreading out' or 'dilution' of the radiation as it gets farther away from its source.

The inverse-square law, which applies to light and all other parts of the electromagnetic spectrum, also applies to γ-radiation as it is part of that spectrum.

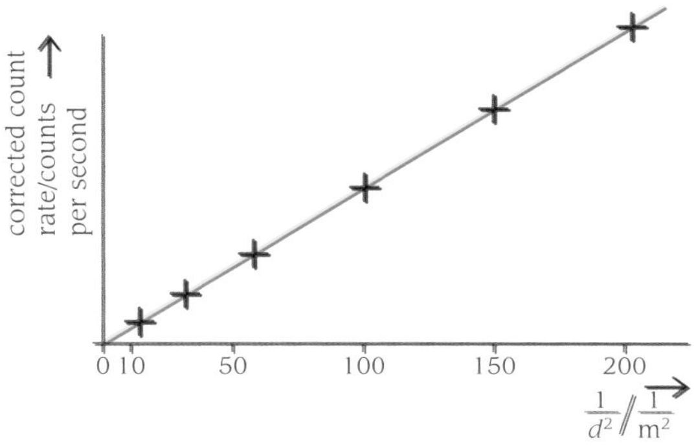

▲ **Figure 20.2.4** Graph of corrected count rate against $\frac{1}{d^2}$

The straight-line graph confirms that the count rate is inversely proportional to the distance squared.

Things to do

Test the inverse-square law for γ-radiation:

- Complete the table of results by calculating $\frac{1}{d^2}$ (d in metres)
  ($\frac{1}{d^2}$ is the inverse square of the distance of the G–M tube from the source.)
- Plot a graph of the corrected count rate against $\frac{1}{d^2}$ (Figure 20.2.4).

▼ Table for gamma radiation experiment results

d/cm	d/m	$\frac{1}{d^2} / \frac{1}{m^2}$	Count rate/counts s^{-1}	Corrected count rate/counts s^{-1}
7	0.07	204		
8				
10				
13				
20				
30	0.3	11		

Key fact

Why is it important to use long-handled tongs when handling a source of gamma radiation?

- A source held in the fingers 1 cm away, exposes them to concentrated or intense radiation.
- The radiation from the same source, held in 10 cm long tongs is reduced to $\frac{1}{100}$ of the intensity, simply as a result of being 10 times further away.

Key fact

- In 1900, Becquerel was the first person to deflect β-particles in an electric field.
- The information gained from deflecting β-particles in both a magnetic field and an electric field gave an estimate of the speed of β-particles and their charge-to-mass ratio.
- The results showed that the speed of some β-particles is about half the speed of light.
- The results also showed that the charge-to-mass ratio, *e/m* for β-particles was about the same as for the electron.
- More accurate experiments showed that at these high speeds the mass of the β-particles increased, as predicted by Einstein's theory of relativity. When the increase in mass of the β-particles is allowed for, the value of *e/m* agrees with that of the electron.
- Beta radiation is a stream of electrons, which are ejected from the nuclei of decaying atoms at speeds between 0.3 and 0.7 times the speed of light.

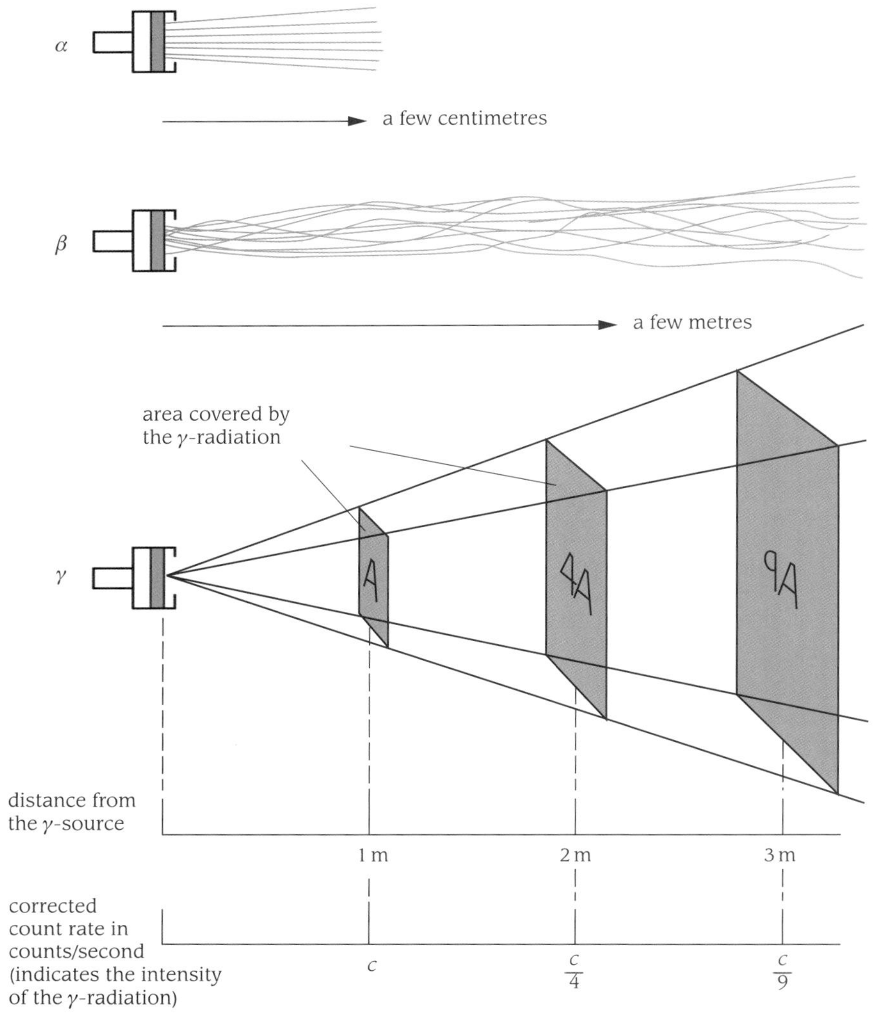

▲ **Figure 20.2.5** The range of α-, β- and γ-radiations in air

Figure 20.2.5 shows that γ-radiation gets weaker as the area it covers gets larger. The radiation is spread over an area A at a distance of 1 metre. At 2 metres it is diluted over an area $4A$ and at 3 metres over an area $9A$. As the area increases with the square of the distance, so the count rate C and the intensity of the radiation decrease according to the inverse-square law with distance.

Key fact

- For the same strength of magnetic field the deflection of alpha particles is negligible when the beta particles are bent into a tight circle.
- The alpha particle path bends the opposite way to the beta particle path.
- The gamma radiation is not deflected at all.

The effect of a magnetic field on radiation

Beta radiation

A β-source with a narrow slit in its aluminium housing should be used to produce a thin beam of β-particles. This is called a **collimated** source.

- Arrange this source so that the beam of β-particles enters the mica window of a G–M tube some 10 cm or 15 cm away, position A in Figure 20.2.6.
- Move the G–M tube to each side and check that most of the radiation is going straight ahead into the tube.
- Fit a pair of magnadur flat magnets to an iron yoke with their unlike poles facing. Using a magnetic compass, find out which pole is which and hence which way the magnetic field goes (N to S).

With the magnetic field in place, the count rate recorded by the ratemeter will fall down almost to background level.

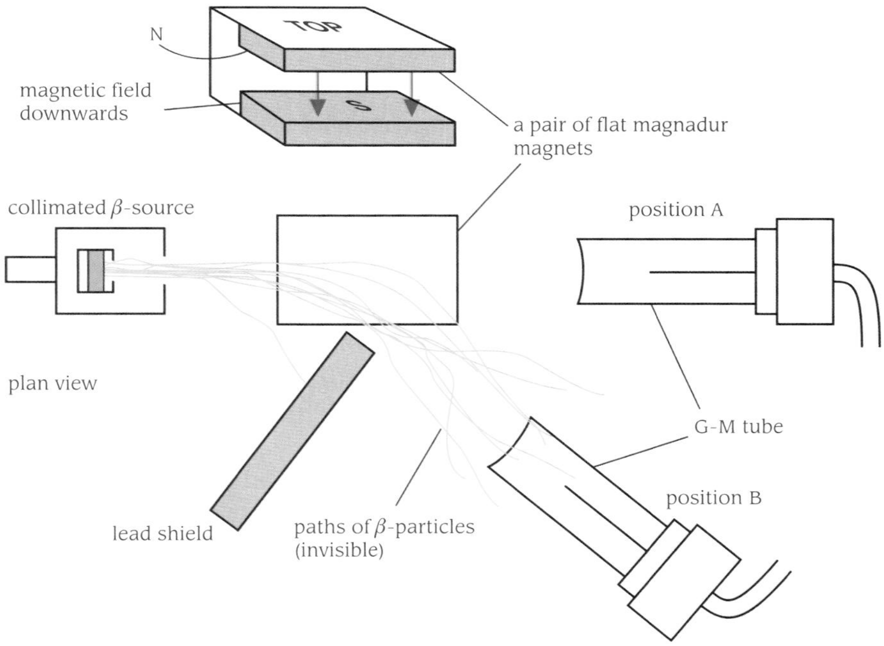

▲ **Figure 20.2.6** Deflection of β-particles by a magnetic field

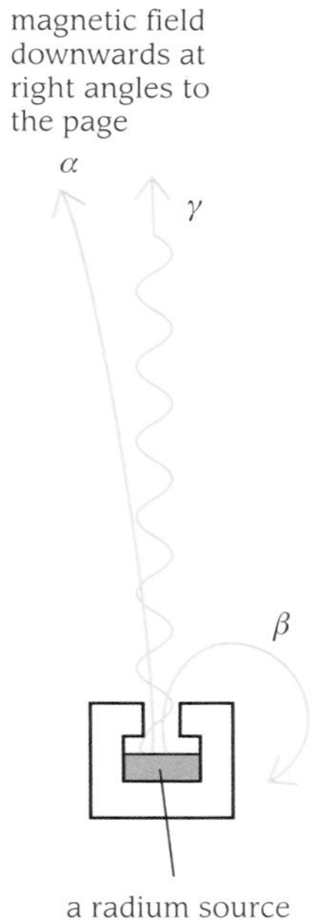

◀ **Figure 20.2.7** Radiation in a magnetic field

Figure 20.2.7 shows a summary of the effects of a magnetic field on alpha, beta and gamma radiation.

- Move the G–M tube to the sides until the count rate increases again, position B. Check that β-particles are not reaching the tube by a direct route by placing a lead shield in the way.

The tracks of the β-particles are definitely bent by the magnetic field. This shows that the particles carry an electric charge. Can you confirm (by the direction of bending) that these particles are the negatively charged electrons we believe them to be?

Alpha radiation

Alpha particles have about 7000 times the mass of beta particles, so are deflected less by magnetic fields. A stronger magnetic field is needed for the deflection to show up. Because they have the opposite charge to beta particles, they are deflected in the opposite direction.

Between 1903 and 1909, accurate measurements of the deflection of alpha radiation by magnetic and electric fields showed that it was a stream of helium nuclei, with a positive charge of twice the charge on an electron.

Gamma radiation

Gamma radiation, which carries no charge, is *not* deflected by magnetic fields of any strength. γ-radiation is electromagnetic radiation.

The effect of an electric field on radiation

Gamma radiation is not charged, so is not deflected by an electric field. Beta particles are deflected towards the positive, and alpha particles towards the negative. Again, because alpha particles are many times heavier (but only have twice the charge), they are deflected less by the same strength field.

Exam tip

The alternative version of Fleming's left-hand rule (described in D18.1) can be used to find out which way particles will deflect. Hold your left hand flat with your fingers pointing in the direction of the magnetic field. Turn your hand so that 'positive leaves palm' (so alpha particles coming out of your palm at right angles, beta particles going into your palm at right angles). Your thumb points in the direction the particles will move.

Summary questions

1. Which type of nuclear radiation is most penetrating?
2. What is the range in air of alpha radiation?
3. How is beta radiation affected by electric and magnetic fields?

Objectives

By the end of this topic you will be able to:

- understand that radioactivity is a consequence of nuclear instability
- describe an activity to demonstrate the random nature of radioactive decay
- describe an activity from which a radioactive decay curve can be obtained (including an analogue experiment such as throwing dice)
- represent and interpret the equations representing nuclear reactions
- define the term 'half-life', $T_{\frac{1}{2}}$
- use graphs of random decay to show that such processes have constant half-lives.

E20.3 Radioactive decay and half-life

The decay of radioactive substances is random and spontaneous. That means that we cannot tell when the nucleus of a particular unstable atom will break up and hurl out an alpha or beta particle. However, we find that, out of a large number of the same kind of unstable atoms, a constant fraction of them will decay in a certain time. It is easy to tell which atoms have decayed because they change into a different element.

A model of radioactive decay

Using a large number of dice or small wooden cubes to represent unstable atoms, we can build a model of radioactive decay. The wooden cubes can be made by carefully sawing cubes off a length of 1 cm × 1 cm square section hardwood. Paint one face of every cube. Several hundred cubes (or dice) are needed for each experiment.

- Shake and throw all the cubes onto a tabletop.
- Remove and count all the cubes with a painted face upwards (or dice with a 6 upwards.)

The cubes represent atoms. Those with a painted face upwards after each throw have 'decayed' or changed into a different kind of atom.

- Pick up all the remaining cubes (undecayed atoms) and shake and throw them again.
- Repeat the process, each time counting and removing the cubes with coloured faces upwards, until there are very few cubes left.
- Record your counts in a table.

The table shows a typical set of results.

- Plot a graph of the number of cubes remaining against the throw number (Figure 20.3.1).

▼ Specimen results from a radioactive decay model

Throw	Number of cubes removed (decayed atoms)	Number of cubes remaining (undecayed atoms)
Start	0	200
1	32	168
2	28	140
3	25	115
4	18	97
5	16	81
6	13	68
7	11	57
8	9	48
9	8	40
10	8	32
11	6	26

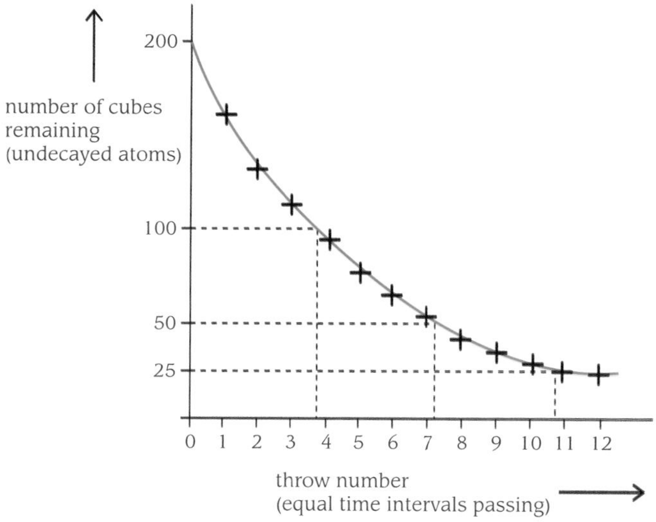

▶ **Figure 20.3.1**

This decay graph has a special shape. It is called an exponential curve. The graph gradually gets less steep and only approaches zero after a very long time. An important quantity for a radioactive substance is its half-life. The half-life is the time it takes for half of the radioactive nuclei present to decay. So after one half-life the activity will have halved, after two half-lives it will have halved again (to $\frac{1}{4}$ its original value), after threes half-lives it will have halved again (to $\frac{1}{8}$ its original value) and so on. In this model experiment the passing of time is represented by the number of throws.

- From your graph, find the number of throws that halved the number of cubes. You can find several values for the halving number of throws by halving the number of cubes several times, as shown.

After about $3\frac{1}{2}$ throws the number of cubes has halved. We find that the number of cubes remaining is halved after the same number of throws ($3\frac{1}{2}$), no matter how many cubes there are left. This is to be expected with six-sided cubes because there is a constant chance ($\frac{1}{6}$) of the painted face turning upwards. What we do not know before they are thrown is which particular ones will be the cubes to 'decay'. We can never say about any particular cube that it will 'decay' at the next throw. All we know is that it has a constant chance of $\frac{1}{6}$ of 'decaying' each time it is thrown. The moment when it will actually decay is unpredictable and happens randomly.

Key fact

Half-life

- The number of throws needed to halve the number of cubes represents the halving time of unstable atoms, called their half-life.
  The half-life of a sample of radioactive substance is the time taken for half of the unstable atoms to decay.
- However large the sample and however many unstable atoms of a particular kind it contains, the half-life is constant.
- Over a half-life, each atom has a 50% chance of decaying.
- The decay of atoms in a sample appears to be totally random in two ways:
  - we cannot tell *which* particular atoms are going to decay
  - we cannot tell *when* they are going to decay.
- For the very large number of atoms in the sample, the random decay of individual atoms is averaged out to give a constant half-life for the sample as a whole.
- **The value of a half-life is unaffected by all external changes such as temperature, pressure and even chemical reactions.**
- The half-life of some substances is very long. For example, thorium $^{232}_{90}Th$ has a half-life of 14 000 million years. We would have to wait rather a long time to notice any change in a sample of thorium.

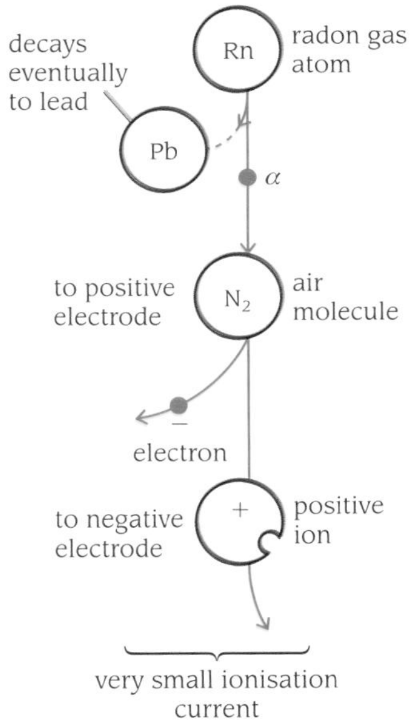

▲ **Figure 20.3.2** How the ionisation current is produced inside the ionisation chamber

Key fact

- Because of the random nature of radioactive decay, half-life values obtained experimentally may vary slightly.
- We take an average of the measured values.
- The half-life of radon is found to be 52 seconds.

Measuring the half-life of radon gas

Radon gas is separated from its parent thorium and collected inside a sealed ionisation chamber. Inside this metal chamber, the alpha particles emitted as the radon gas decays collide with air molecules and ionise them (Figure 20.3.2). The electrons and positive ions produced by the alpha particles allow a small current to pass through the chamber. This current may be displayed as a current, or as a number showing the activity, that is the rate of decay of the sample.

A graph of activity (or current) against time is plotted and a smooth curve drawn through the points (Figure 20.3.3).

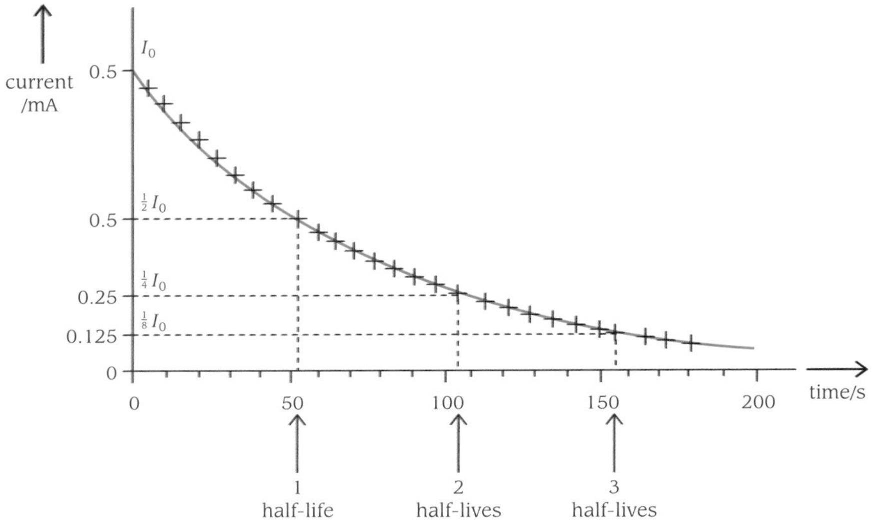

▲ **Figure 20.3.3** Decay graph for radon gas

By reading from the graph the time at which the current has fallen to $\frac{1}{2}$, $\frac{1}{4}$ and $\frac{1}{8}$ of its initial value we can obtain three values of the half-life of radon gas.

Worked example

Use the graph shown in Figure 20.3.3 to work out the half-life of radon gas.

Half the original reading is 0.5. This happens at time 50 s giving a half-life of 50 seconds.

We can check this value by finding the value for 2 half-lives and 3 half-lives.

After 2 half-lives, the activity will have fallen to $\frac{1}{4}$ of the original reading. This happens after time 100 s, giving 2 half-lives as 100 s, so one half-life as 50 s.

After 3 half-lives, the activity will have fallen to $\frac{1}{8}$ of the original reading. This happens after time 150 s, giving 3 half-lives as 150 s, so one half-life as 50 s.

So the graph in Figure 20.3.3 shows that the half-life of radon gas is 50 s.

Key fact

When a nuclide decays by emitting an alpha particle:

- its atomic number or proton number *Z* decreases by 2
- its mass number or nucleon number *A* decreases by 4.

When a nuclide decays by emitting a beta particle:

- the proton number *Z* increases by 1
- the nucleon number *A* does *not* change
- in the nucleus a neutron decays into a (+) proton and a (–) beta particle and conserves charge.

Nuclear changes

Atoms that have too many or too few neutrons in their nuclei are found to be unstable and prone to a spontaneous process of emitting radioactive particles from their nuclei. This decay process tends to make the atoms more stable although several decay processes may occur before a completely stable nuclide is reached.

When a radioactive atom decays, its nucleus breaks up, throws out an α-particle or β-particle with some energy, and forms a new atom of a different element. We can represent these events as a nuclear equation in which a parent nuclide X changes into a daughter nuclide Y.

Alpha decay

$^{A}_{Z}\mathrm{X}$	$\rightarrow$	$^{A-4}_{Z-2}\mathrm{Y}$	$+$	$^{4}_{2}\alpha$	$+$	energy
parent nuclide		daughter nuclide		alpha particle		

Uranium-238 decays by alpha emission

$^{238}_{92}\mathrm{U}$	$\rightarrow$	$^{234}_{90}\mathrm{Th}$	$+$	$^{4}_{2}\alpha$	$+$	kinetic energy
uranium parent nuclide		thorium daughter nuclide		alpha particle	$+$	gamma photon energy

When a nucleus emits an α-particle, some spare energy is released as kinetic energy of the particle and some as a γ-photon. When the particle is thrown out the new nucleus recoils so that momentum is conserved, but the nucleus has very little kinetic energy because of its low velocity.

The result of α-decay is that a new element is produced with a proton number two below its parent in the table of elements. For example, uranium ($Z = 92$) decays by α-emission to form thorium ($Z = 90$).

Beta decay

$^{A}_{Z}\mathrm{X}$	$\rightarrow$	$^{A}_{Z+1}\mathrm{Y}$	$+$	$^{0}_{-1}\beta$	$+$	energy
parent nuclide		daughter nuclide		beta particle		

Strontium-90 decays by beta emission

$^{90}_{38}\mathrm{Sr}$	$\rightarrow$	$^{90}_{39}\mathrm{Y}$	$+$	$^{0}_{-1}\beta$	$+$	kinetic energy
strontium parent nuclide		yttrium daughter nuclide		beta particle		

Gamma photons

Gamma photons are usually emitted at the same moment as either an α- or β-particle. When a nucleus ejects an α- or β-particle there is often some spare energy produced in the decay process. Decay leaves a nucleus in an excited state, i.e. it possesses more energy than it can comfortably hang on to. Almost instantly the spare energy is released in a quantum, i.e. as a single photon of gamma radiation. The size of this quantum puts it into the high-frequency, gamma part of the electromagnetic spectrum.

What makes a nucleus unstable?

A nucleus seems to be stable when it has the right balance of protons and neutrons. Having too many neutrons or too few neutrons makes it unstable and likely to break up. The unstable nucleus tends to decay by whichever process will bring it nearer to the correct number of neutrons for stability.

Summary questions

1. Describe an experiment to model radioactive decay.
2. What is meant by half-life?
3. A radioactive substance has a count rate of 3600. What will the count rate be after three half-lives?

Objectives

By the end of this topic you will be able to:

- describe the risks that radiation presents to humans and the precautions that must be taken by human beings.

E20.4 Radiation and people

Every day we are exposed to low levels of background radiation that we are unaware of and can do nothing about. But the artificial and very active sources of radiation, which have many valuable industrial and medical uses, also have considerable risks. When humans and radiation come together the risks and the benefits must be carefully assessed.

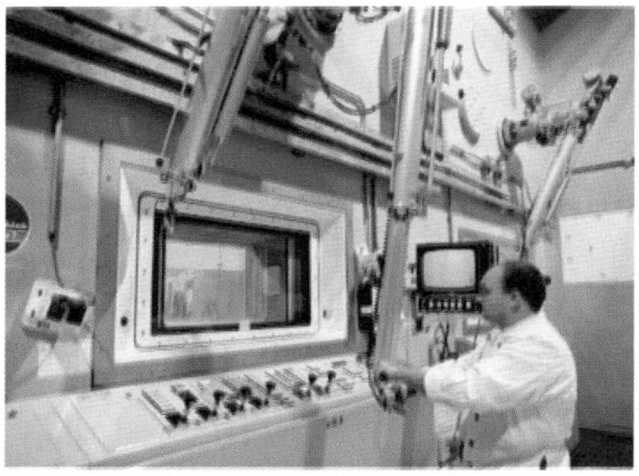

▲ **Figure 20.4.1** Remote handling of radioactive materials

What is ionising radiation?

Radioactivity can cause ionisation. This means it can cause some atoms or molecules to lose electrons and so split into positively and negatively charged ions. All radiation that can cause ionisation is dangerous to all animals including humans. This is because the ionisation can damage cells causing them to die or function incorrectly. Ionising radiation comes in many forms and from many sources. It includes the radiation from natural radioactive substances, i.e. α-, β- and γ-radiation, but it also includes radiation from artificial sources, such as X-ray machines and nuclear reactors.

X-ray machines produce X-radiation which, like γ-radiation, is high-frequency electromagnetic radiation. X-rays have the same properties and the same effects on humans as natural γ-radiation.

Nuclear reactors produce other kinds of radiation that are also harmful to humans. As well as large amounts of γ-radiation and radioactive waste materials, nuclear reactors produce large numbers of neutrons, which are released from the nuclei of uranium atoms as they break up in the process called fission. Neutrons fired out of atomic nuclei are also a form of ionising radiation that is dangerous to humans.

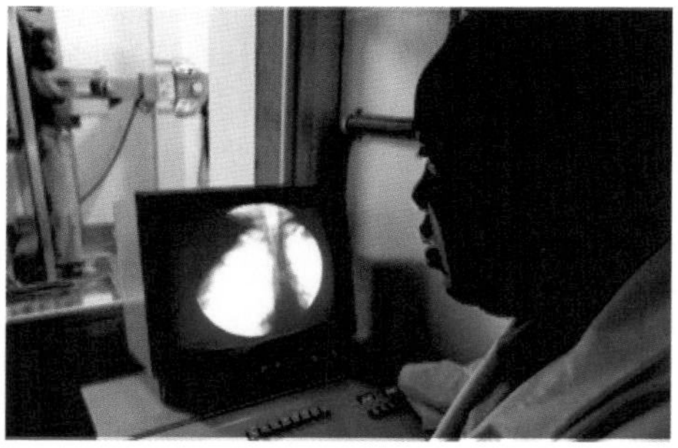

▲ **Figure 20.4.2** The radiologist stands behind a radiation-absorbing screen while the X-ray machine is operated.

Precautions for humans

The main risk from α- and β-radiation is when they enter a person's body. Since α- and β-particles do not penetrate very far into the body, the risk from external sources is quite small. However, care must be taken to avoid radioactive materials being eaten or inhaled from the air. So no eating or drinking is allowed where any radioactive materials are handled, and disposable gloves and protective clothing are worn. Masks are worn in mines where radioactive dust particles are airborne.

X-rays and γ-rays can be absorbed deep inside the body, and people exposed to external sources of X- and γ-radiation must be protected as much as possible.

The dose of radiation a person receives can be limited by:

- using shielding
- keeping a large distance between the person and the source
- keeping exposure times as short as possible.

People who work with ionising radiation wear a film badge that gives a permanent record of the radiation dose received.

Sources of ionising radiation

About 85% of the radiation we receive comes from natural sources. The natural background radiation comes mainly from space and from naturally occurring rocks. Gamma rays and radon gas come from radioactive materials in the Earth's crust. Some areas have a higher natural background radiation than others, due to different geology. Our atmosphere absorbs some radiation, so people in high-flying aircraft are exposed to higher levels of radiation from space than those on the ground.

Artificial radiation mainly comes from X-rays and radioactive isotopes used in medicine and industry.

The effects of radiation on people

When radiation is absorbed, it can damage or destroy living cells. The energy from high doses of radiation can cause 'burns' in which large numbers of cells can be destroyed, leading to organ failure and death.

Lower doses of radiation can cause cell changes leading to leukaemia and cancer. Damage to reproductive cells can cause deformities or hereditary defects in children or grandchildren. The genetic damage to future generations after exposure to radiation is hard to predict or measure.

▲ **Figure 20.4.3** Following the Chernobyl nuclear accident in 1986, there was an increase in births of malformed children in Belarus and the Ukraine.

Summary questions

1 Give one natural and one artificial source of radiation.

2 Why is ionising radiation harmful?

E20.5 Applications of radiation

Objectives

By the end of this topic you will be able to:

- describe and discuss useful applications of radioisotopes including tracers.

Smoke alarms

Smoke alarms use alpha particles. An alpha source inside the alarm gives out alpha particles, which cross a small gap and are detected by a detector also inside the alarm. Smoke particles absorb the alpha particles, causing the flow of charged particles across the gap to drop and setting off the alarm. Smoke alarms should be tested regularly and the battery replaced before it goes flat. Failing to do so can cost lives.

▲ **Figure 20.5.1** A smoke alarm

Radioactive materials in medicine

When radioactive materials are used in medicine they are chosen with care. The radioactive nuclide should have a short half-life so that any material remaining in the body quickly decays away. The radioactive substance used should also have a short biological half-life. This is the time taken for the body to get rid of half of the radioactive substance. In other words, the substance should be one that will pass through the body, or be filtered out of the blood as quickly as possible.

Radioisotopes are used in medicine both in diagnosis (finding out what is wrong) and in therapy (treating a disease).

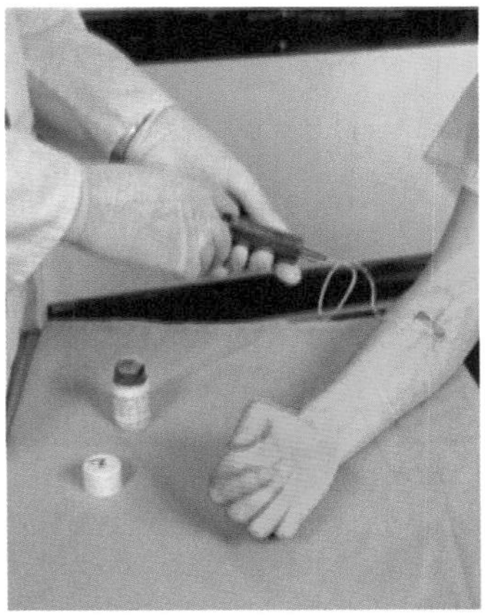

▲ **Figure 20.5.2** Patient being injected with a radioactive tracer before a gamma camera scan

Using radioisotopes as tracers or markers

Sodium-24 used as a tracer

Salt containing some atoms of the radioactive sodium-24 isotope is said to be labelled. If a patient eats some sodium-24 labelled salt, its progress through the body can be followed. A radiation detector moved over a patient's body shows where the labelled salt has reached and how much salt has been absorbed. While the radioactive salt behaves quite normally in its chemical role, the atoms of the radioisotope sodium-24 will decay while inside the body. They emit γ-rays, which pass out of the body to be detected.

Iodine-131 used to examine the activity of the thyroid gland

If a patient is given a dose of radioactive iodine-131 in solution, it finds its way to the thyroid gland and allows doctors to study how the gland is working.

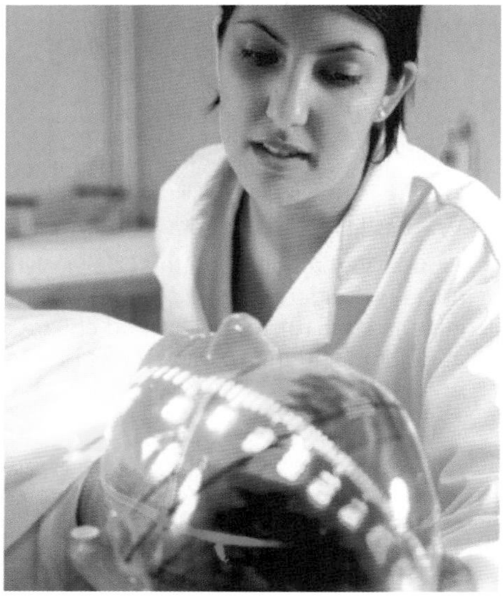

▲ **Figure 20.5.3** A patient being prepared for radiotherapy. A plastic mask holds the patient's head completely still. Laser cross-hairs line up so the radiation can be targeted very precisely on the tumour.

Technetium-99m used to study the working of the body

Technetium-99m is used for many purposes because it has the following advantages:

- It emits only γ-rays, which mostly escape from the body. No dangerous α- or β-radiation is produced.
- It has a short half-life of 6 hours.

Radioisotopes used to treat illnesses

Marie Curie was the first person to use some radium for the treatment of a cancer growth. As early as 1910 needles containing a few milligrams of radium were used to treat cancer.

Caesium-137 is sometimes used to give large local doses of γ-radiation to cancer growths inside the body.

Cobalt-60 is widely used to give patients a large dose of gamma radiation for the treatment of cancers. A restricted beam of γ-radiation is carefully directed at the cancer site from an external cobalt source. The source, a cube about the size of a sugar lump, is very radioactive and capable of giving a person a lethal dose if their whole body was exposed to its γ-radiation.

Uses of radioisotopes in industry and agriculture

Tracer applications

Fluid flow and leaks in pipelines

▲ **Figure 20.5.4** The technician is checking the join in a gas pipe line for flaws or poor welding. Photographic film is mounted on the inside of the pipe with a radiation source on the outside. The photograph was taken in Trinidad and you can see parasols used to provide shade for the workers.

Many industrial applications of radioisotopes use them as tracers. A radioactive substance added to a fluid in a pipeline can be used to measure the flow rate in the pipeline and to find leaks. Gamma radiation can pass out through the wall of a pipeline and so a radiation detector can follow the progress of a radioactive marker as it flows, mixed in with the fluid in a pipeline. Where fluid leaks out underground, the radioactive tracer will also be found to spread out away from the pipeline, so showing the position of the leak. Leaks in drainage systems can be found by this method. The isotope of sodium $^{24}_{11}$Na is useful in water pipelines and sewage systems because, in the form of salt, it is soluble in water.

Fertiliser uptake by plants

Tracers are used in agriculture to measure the uptake by plants of food from fertilisers in the soil. The phosphate ion in plant food can be labelled with the radioisotope phosphorus-32. As a plant absorbs this labelled food we can trace it to growing parts of the plant and learn about plant growth and improve our use of fertilisers.

Engineering applications

Checking welds in steel structures

The radioisotope cobalt-60 is used to check welds in steel structures and pipelines. Gamma radiation from a large cobalt-60 source placed on one side of a steel structure exposes a photographic plate at the other side, in the same way that X-ray images are produced. A flaw such as a bubble or crack inside a weld on a pipeline would be visible on the exposed film. An advantage of using a gamma source rather than an X-ray machine is that the gamma source is very portable and requires no electricity supply.

Measuring sheet thickness

Another common use for radioisotopes in industry is in the measurement and automatic control of sheet thickness. Sheets of plastic, paper and metal are manufactured to accurately controlled thicknesses. A radioisotope sends radiation through the sheet material as it comes off the production line. α- or β-radiation is used for thin sheets. A radiation detector on the other side of the sheet measures the intensity of the radiation passing through the sheet. Any small variation in sheet thickness produces a change in the count rate of the detector. This information can be fed back to the machinery to adjust the sheet thickness automatically.

▲ **Figure 20.5.5** Paper thickness gauge. This device uses a radioactive source to monitor the thickness of paper during manufacture. The source emits beta radiation, which is absorbed by paper relatively easily. By measuring the proportion of beta particles that penetrate the paper it is possible to measure and control the thickness of the paper as it is produced. Suitable beta sources are radioisotopes of promethium, krypton or strontium.

Radioactive dating

Radioactive substances with long half-lives stay around for a very long time. When a particular radioactive nuclide and its decay products become trapped as a rock solidifies or a plant or creature dies, they start a very slow radioactive clock. This clock tells us how much time has passed since the radioactive nuclide was trapped. The **carbon-14 clock** tells us how long ago something died.

As living plants grow, they take in carbon dioxide containing a small proportion of radioactive carbon-14 and animals eat some of these plants. The carbon atoms become trapped in the remains of a plant or animal at the moment of its death. At death, all plants and animals contain the same proportion of carbon-14 as is always present in the atmosphere. So at death, a radioactive clock is started as the trapped carbon-14 atoms decay and are not replaced by new ones from the atmosphere. Every 5730 years the number of carbon-14 atoms left in the fossil remains of plants and animals halves.

The fraction $\frac{\text{number of carbon-14 atoms}}{\text{number of stable carbon atoms}}$ reduces by half every 5730 years.

By measuring the fraction remaining today in a fossil and comparing it with the fraction when the clock started (one in 10^{12}), we are able to calculate how long the radioactive clock has been running.

Carbon dating isn't exact

When scientists give the date of something worked out using carbon dating, they always give a range of possible dates, not an exact figure. Several things make it impossible to give an exact date.

Worked example

The count rate from a piece of wood from a very ancient human settlement is found to be 150 counts per second. The count rate from the same mass of new wood is 600 counts per second. Use the half-life of carbon-14 to work out the age of the wood from the ancient settlement.

Count rate of the ancient wood is $\frac{1}{4}$ count rate of modern wood, so ancient wood is 2 half-lives old.

Half-life of carbon-14 is 5730 years, so the ancient wood is $5730 \times 2 = 11\,460$ years old.

- The proportion of carbon-14 in the atmosphere has changed slightly over thousands of years, so scientists can't tell exactly how much carbon-14 was present in a sample originally.
- The proportion of carbon-14 in the atmosphere at any given time is slightly different in different places.
- Scientists may be uncertain whether or not a sample has been contaminated by contact with material of a different age.
- Often only tiny samples are available, which make it harder or impossible to repeat measurements to check dates.

Dating using other isotopes

Carbon-14 is not the only radioactive substance used for dating. Uranium-238 has a very long half-life (4500 million years), and decays to lead, which is stable. Lead does not bond readily in the crystal structure of rocks, so igneous rocks form without lead. Any lead present in a sample can only have come from the decay of uranium atoms. So if there is one lead atom present for each uranium atom, the sample must be one half-life old (half the uranium has decayed). So the amount of lead in a sample can be used to date the rock very accurately.

Summary questions

1 What type of source is used in a smoke alarm?

2 Give one property of a radioactive substance used as a medical tracer.

3 Describe one engineering use of radiation.

Objectives

By the end of this topic you will be able to:

- describe how energy from the nucleus of atoms is released and controlled in a nuclear power station.

E20.6 Nuclear energy

The nuclear energy alternative

There is no doubt that the world's reserves of oil and coal and other non-renewable fuels are limited. It is inevitable that eventually the demand for oil will exceed the rate at which it can be supplied. Apart from predictions about a shortage of oil in the future, there are powerful arguments now for using oil for other purposes than as a fuel and source of energy. For example, oil is a basic raw material from which plastics and fertilisers can be made. This suggests that oil is too valuable as a raw material to be wasted by burning to produce electrical energy in power stations.

Fission and fusion

There are two very different ways in which a nuclear process can release energy. **Fission** involves the splitting up of large nuclei such as uranium or plutonium caused by neutron bombardment and the conversion of a very small amount of mass into energy. **Fusion** involves the building of larger nuclei from smaller ones. The following equation is an example:

$$\underset{\text{deuterium fuel}}{{}^{2}_{1}\mathrm{H}} + \underset{\text{tritium}}{{}^{3}_{1}\mathrm{H}} \rightarrow \underset{\text{helium}}{{}^{4}_{2}\mathrm{He}} + \underset{\text{neutron}}{{}^{1}_{0}\mathrm{n}} + \underset{\text{kinetic energy}}{3 \times 10^{-12}\,\mathrm{J}}$$

This fusion process requires very high temperatures to make the nuclei fuse together. While this process powers the Sun, and is the energy source of the hydrogen bomb, we have not yet succeeded in controlling this process for peaceful energy production on Earth. Nuclear power stations all use nuclear fission and not fusion as their energy source.

> **Key fact**
>
> The products of the fission of a single ^{235}U nucleus are:
> - two new elements, known as fission products
> - two or three fast-moving free neutrons with lots of kinetic energy
> - an average of 3.2×10^{-11} J of energy from each fission of a ^{235}U nucleus.
>
> Note that:
> - Most of the fission products are unstable and emit radiation.
> - The disposal of these radioactive fission products as waste material from the used uranium fuel is the cause of some difficulty with nuclear power stations.
> - The energy released by the fission process appears as the kinetic energy of the neutrons and as radiation. The kinetic energy of the neutrons is the source of the heat energy obtained from a nuclear reactor.

The main difference between a nuclear power station and a coal- or oil-fired station is that the heat which produces steam for the turbines is provided by nuclear fuel in a reactor, and not by oil or coal burnt in a furnace. So how does nuclear fuel produce heat?

Energy from the nucleus by fission

The nucleus of the uranium nuclide $^{235}_{92}U$ has the very rare property of splitting into two roughly equal halves when it captures a neutron. The splitting of the nucleus is known as **nuclear fission** (Figure 20.6.1).

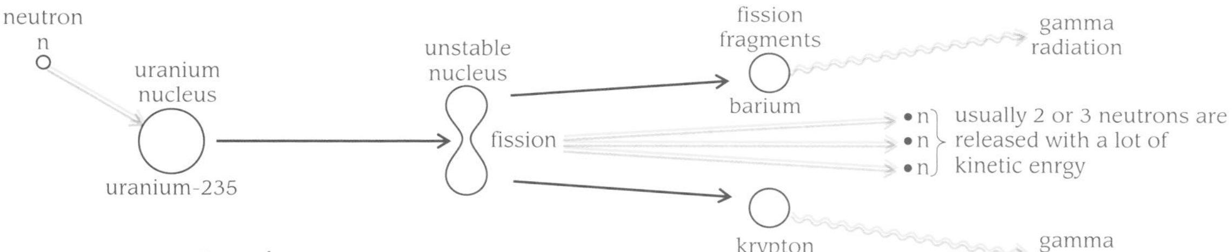

Example:

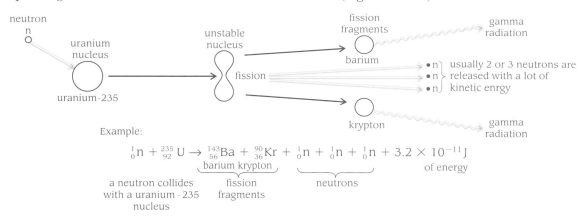

$$^{1}_{0}n + ^{235}_{92}U \rightarrow ^{143}_{56}Ba + ^{90}_{36}Kr + ^{1}_{0}n + ^{1}_{0}n + ^{1}_{0}n + 3.2 \times 10^{-11}\,J$$

a neutron collides with a uranium-235 nucleus; barium krypton: fission fragments; neutrons; of energy

(note that the *nucleon number* adds up to 236 on both sides of the equation and the *proton number* adds up to 92 on both sides of the equation)

Figure 20.6.1 Nuclear fission

Figure 20.6.2 Oldbury nuclear power station in Gloucestershire, England, UK, generated power from 1968 to 2012. Old nuclear power stations have to be decommissioned, i.e. shut down and dismantled safely.

Where has the energy released by fission come from?

The nuclear fission equation shows that the number of nucleons is conserved. But an accurate adding up of the total mass on each side of the equation would show that there is a small loss of mass on the right-hand side. This lost mass is converted into energy.

In 1905, Albert Einstein worked out the relationship between mass and energy in his now famous equation:

$$E = mc^2$$

The energy E released in joules can be found if the mass loss m is given in kilograms and $c = 3 \times 10^8\ \mathrm{m\,s^{-1}}$, the speed of light.

The fission of one ^{235}U nucleus gives off much more energy than would be released by natural radioactive decay.

Chain reactions

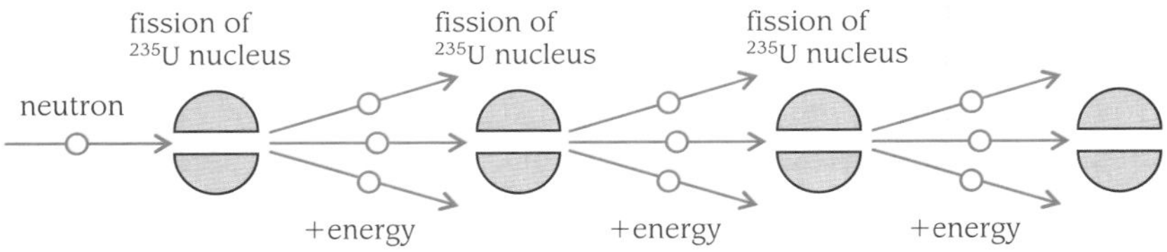

▲ **Figure 20.6.3** A chain reaction

If the neutrons that shoot out of the one dividing ^{235}U nucleus are captured by other nearby ^{235}U nuclei, then more fissions will occur, shooting out even more neutrons. In this way, it is possible to set up a chain reaction (Figure 20.6.3). About 85% of the nuclei that capture a neutron quickly undergo fission, shooting out two or three more neutrons. So we can see that if all these neutrons were captured by ^{235}U nuclei the number of fissions would rapidly increase, leading to a nuclear explosion. But this does not normally happen in a nuclear reactor where we can control the chain reactions.

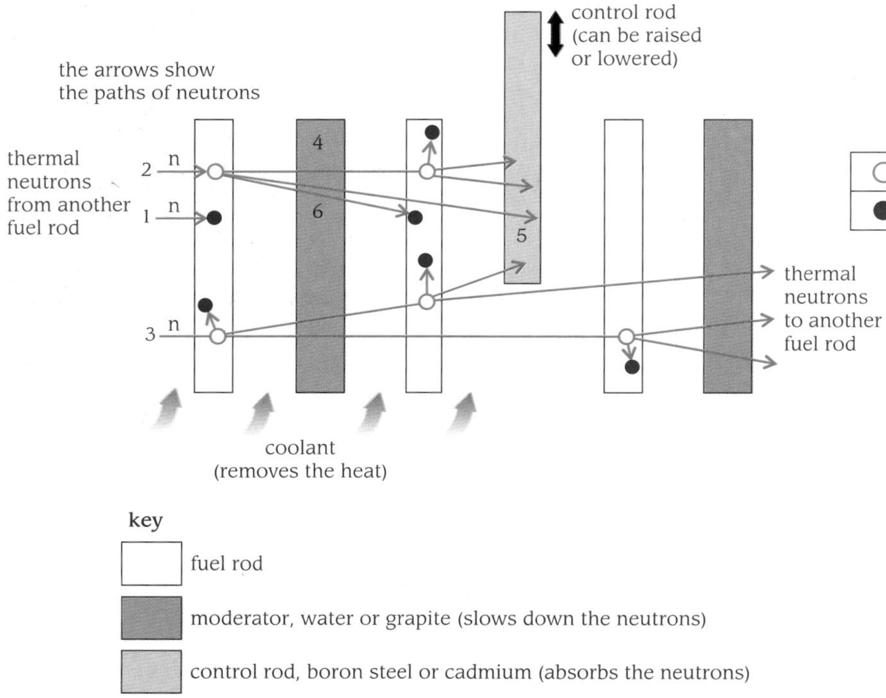

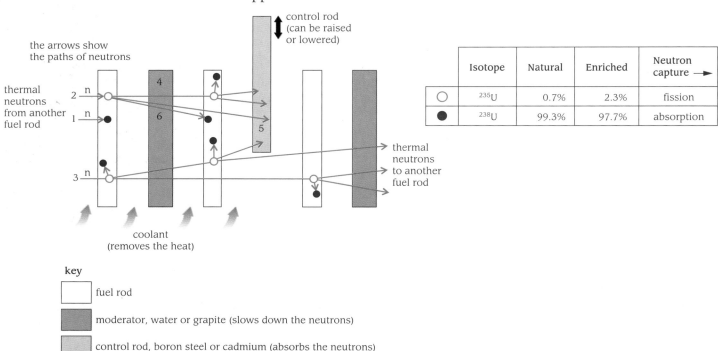

	Isotope	Natural	Enriched	Neutron capture ⟶
○	^{235}U	0.7%	2.3%	fission
●	^{238}U	99.3%	97.7%	absorption

▲ **Figure 20.6.4** Controlling chain reactions in a reactor core

Removing heat from the core of a nuclear reactor

To be able to use the heat produced by fission it must be removed from the reactor core. Heat is absorbed by a coolant, which may be a liquid or a gas. (Carbon dioxide gas, pressurised water and liquid sodium have been used.) The coolant is piped into the core where, as it passes close to the hot fuel rods and moderator, it absorbs much of the heat. The heated coolant then exchanges its heat with the water in a steam generator before it passes back into the reactor core.

▲ **Figure 20.6.5** A reactor core being charged with new uranium fuel rods

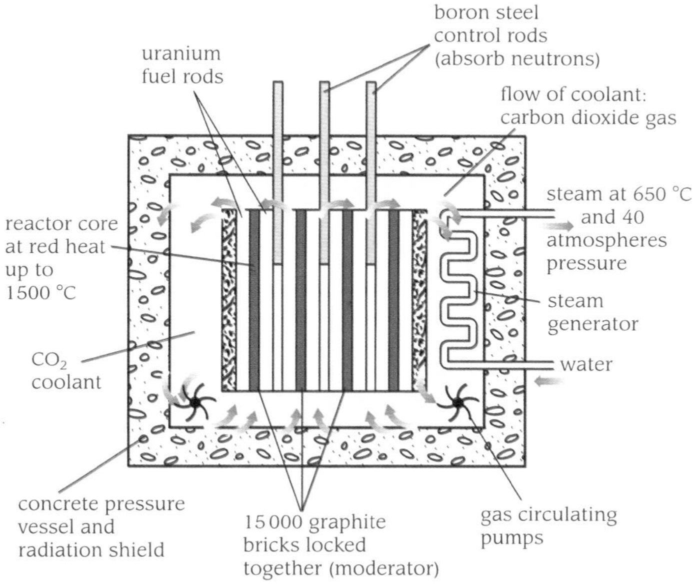

▲ **Figure 20.6.6** An AGR thermal reactor

Advantages and disadvantages of nuclear power

Advantages

- No greenhouse gases or smoke are produced. There is no contribution to the problem of global warming.
- Nuclear power stations can generate very large power outputs equivalent to thousands of wind generators.
- Nuclear fuel costs about the same as coal to produce so it is relatively cheap.

Disadvantages

- Radioactive waste products are difficult and expensive to process and store. Some waste material will remain active for many thousands of years.
- Extraction of natural uranium ores from which fuel rods are made involves environmental and health hazards.
- It takes about 10 years to build a nuclear reactor and they are very expensive too.
- Some people consider nuclear power stations to be a potential terrorist target.
- The history of accidents in which radioactive materials have escaped into the atmosphere is a cause for concern. People remember the incidents at Chernobyl and Fukushima, for example.

▲ **Figure 20.6.7** The Fukushima nuclear plant north of Tokyo in Japan began leaking radiation after it was damaged by a tsunami in March 2011. In 2013, radiation workers were still trying to bring the radiation leak under control.

Alternative ways of harnessing energy in the future

There are plentiful supplies of coal and there is more renewable energy available than we are ever likely to need, so why is there an energy problem? The main reason is that natural gas and oil, on which we rely heavily at present, are being used up rapidly and will have to be replaced. Also the burning of fossil fuels is a major contributor to the production of greenhouse gases.

When considering alternative ways of harnessing energy we should ask these important questions:

- Is the source renewable?
- Will the source produce greenhouse gases and/or smoke?
- How much energy could be provided by this method?
- How far developed is the necessary technology and how long is it likely to be before energy can be supplied?
- Are there any environmental consequences?
- How much would a scheme cost to develop and build and what is a likely price for the energy supplied?

Energy choices

An energy gap occurs when the demand for energy becomes greater than the supply. The effects of such a gap could be serious. Without sufficient energy the industrial societies of the world would be threatened. Energy prices would rise to levels that would deprive poorer people and nations of enough energy for their needs. The risk of war would increase as nations sought to control the world's main oil-producing regions.

Around the world, all countries will have to face the choice of how their electrical energy needs will be provided in the 21st century. Some countries will continue to have abundant supplies of coal; others will extend their hydroelectricity schemes. Other countries must choose between oil and gas at ever increasing prices as it becomes more scarce and difficult to obtain or adopt some of the alternatives available. One of those alternatives is nuclear power.

A balance is needed between cost, environmental damage, safety and health risks. It is even more difficult estimating our future energy needs because these are affected by the price of energy, the amount of economic growth and the more efficient use of energy resulting from conservation ideas that will be adopted.

It is clear that we should:

- improve energy conservation
- thoroughly investigate alternative ways of harnessing energy and keep all options open
- take precautions to protect our environment, especially the causes of global warming
- avoid action or inaction, which might lead to an increasd risk of war.

Albert Einstein
1879–1955

- Einstein was born of a German family.
- Einstein established that light had a dual nature: light was both corpuscles and waves at the same time.
- Einstein's equation for the photoelectric effect was particularly important because its success in explaining the effect provided support for his theory that light energy existed in small quanta or photons.
- His special theory of relativity had dramatic consequences:
  - The speed of light becomes a fundamental constant, which relates space to time in such a way that nothing can travel faster than light.
  - The mass of an object is no longer constant and increases with its speed, approaching infinity at the speed of light.
  - Mass and energy may be transformed according to the equation, $E = mc^2$.
- His general theory of relativity formulates the physical laws of the universe in a way that is valid for any reference system. The theory describes gravity in terms of space itself being curved. The theory predicted that light rays would be bent by a large mass such as the Sun.

Summary questions

1. What is the difference between fusion and fission?
2. Give the equation used to calculate the energy from fusion.
3. What is meant by a chain reaction?
4. Give one advantage and one disadvantage of nuclear power.

Practice exam-style questions

1 Emissions from radioactive sources can be detected by the ionisation the emissions cause in a gas. Explain what is meant by 'ionisation' in a gas.

2 A nuclear radiation detector is connected to a scaler that counts the number of particles detected. The scaler indicates 12 counts during a period of 1 minute. During two subsequent periods of 1 minute the scaler indicates 11 and 15 counts.

When a source of radioactive material is placed near the detector, the counts over three periods of 1 minute are: 1480, 1508 and 1496.

A piece of thick paper is placed between the source and detector and three counts over periods of 1 minute are: 1216, 1226 and 1230.

Finally, when a sheet of lead 5 mm thick is placed between the source and detector, the counts are 13, 11 and 14 over 1-minute periods.

a) Why is a count obtained without the source?

b) Why do the counts obtained in any group differ?

c) Which of the three types of radiation, α, β or γ, are emitted by the source?

3 A Geiger counter, G1, placed as shown in the figure below, at a distance of 25 cm from a radioactive source, S, records an average count of 250 per minute. A similar counter, G2, placed above G1 but also 25 cm from S, records three successive minute-interval counts of 21, 18 and 23. When a horseshoe magnet is suitably positioned, the count rate of G1 decreases to approximately half its former value and the count rate of G2 shows an appreciable increase.

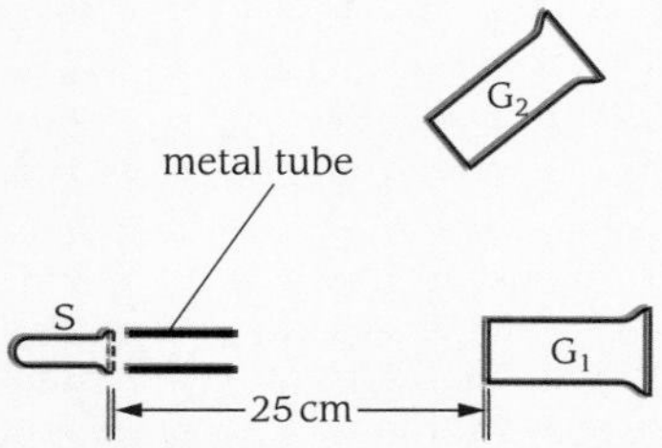

a) Account for the three successive minute-interval counts recorded by G_2 and explain why these figures are not constant.

b) Why, in experiments with radioactive sources, is a knowledge of these figures important? Indicate how they are used.

c) What is the nature of the radiation emitted by S? Give reasons for your answer.

d) Describe, as exactly as you can, the position of the horseshoe magnet. Show on a diagram the direction of its magnetic field.

e) Explain the purpose of the metal tube.

4 In an experiment to measure the half-life of a radioactive element the following results were obtained.

Count rate/counts per minute	2000	500	250
Time/seconds	0	55	80

From the results in the table, calculate:

a) two different values for the half-life of the element

b) the average half-life of the element.

5 You are required to show by experiment that beta particles are negatively charged.

a) State briefly how the beta particles are to be detected.

b) Draw a labelled diagram showing the arrangement of the apparatus you would use.

c) State the observations you would make and explain how you would use them to show that beta particles are negatively charged.

6 The graph below shows how the activity, measured in counts per minute, of a radioactive sample of $^{218}_{84}Po$ varied with time.

a) What do the numbers 218 and 84 represent?

b) Use the graph to calculate the half-life of $^{218}_{84}Po$. Explain how you have used the graph.

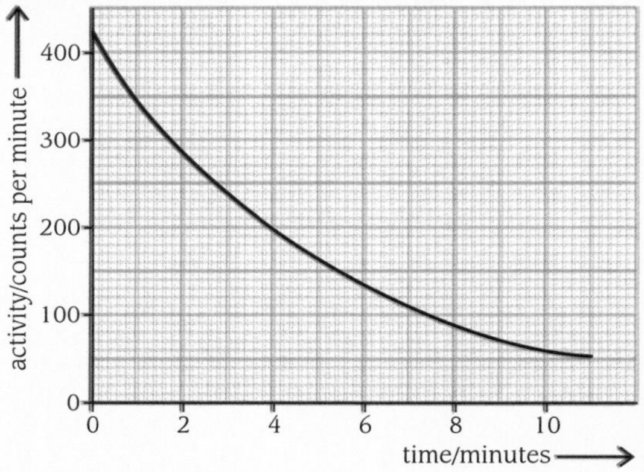

7 a) Explain what is meant by the spontaneous nature of radioactive decay.

b) Explain what is meant by half-life and how the concept depends on the random nature of radioactive decay.

c) A sample of a certain nuclide, which has a half-life of 1500 years, has an activity of 32 000 counts per hour at the present time.

i) Plot a graph of the activity of this sample over the period in which it will reduce to $\frac{1}{16}$ of its present value.

ii) If the sample of the nuclide could be left for 2000 years, what would be its activity then?

8 A Geiger–Müller tube attached to a scaler is placed on a bench in the laboratory. The following results were obtained:

- Over three consecutive minutes the scaler reads 11, 9 and 16 counts per minute for the background.

- When a radioactive source is placed near to the Geiger–Müller tube, the counts over three consecutive minutes are 1310, 1270 and 1296 per minute.
- When a piece of thick paper is placed between the source and the tube the counts are 1250, 1242 and 1236 per minute.
- When the paper is replaced by a sheet of aluminium 2 mm thick the counts are 13, 12 and 11 per minute.

a) What is meant by the 'background'?

b) Why do the three readings in any one group differ?

c) What can be deduced about the nature of the emission? Give reasons for your answer.

9 The decay of the radioactive isotope of carbon ${}^{14}_{6}C$ happens very slowly over thousands of years. The table below gives data for the number of radioactive carbon atoms remaining in a sample over a number of years. When reading from the graph, the numbers of atoms in the table should be multiplied by 10^{18} and the number of years should be multiplied by 1000.

Time in thousands of years, $t/10^3$ years	Number of ${}^{14}_{6}C$ atoms remaining, $N/10^{18}$
0	60
2	47
4	37
6	29
8	23
10	19
12	15.5
14	12.5
16	10.0
18	8.0
20	6.25
22	0.50
24	3.75
26	3.0
28	2.5
30	2.25

a) Plot a graph of $N/10^{18}$ against $t/10^3$ years and draw a good smooth curve through the points.

b) From the graph find at least THREE values for the half-life of the decay of ${}^{14}_{6}C$ and find an average value. Remember to multiply by 1000.

c) From the graph, find the number of radioactive atoms remaining after 11 000 years.

10 a) What do you understand by the 'half-life of a radioactive element'?

b) The graph below shows readings taken for the activity of a radioactive source at daily intervals. Use the graph to deduce the half-life of the source.

c) Find also:

i) the count rate after 5 days

ii) the time when the count is 300 per minute.

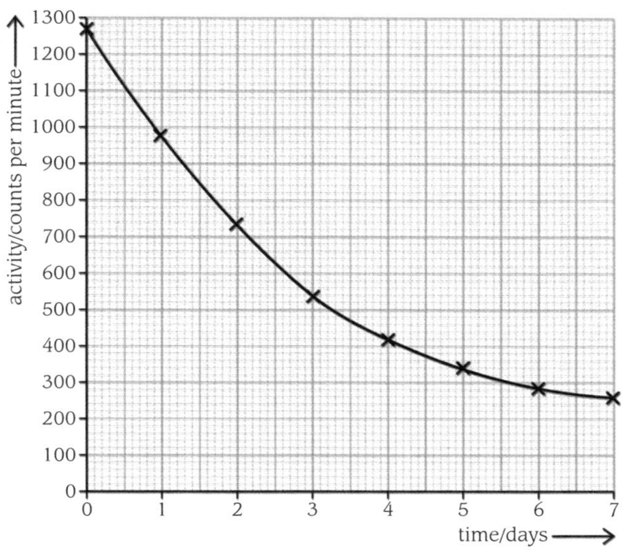

11 A nucleus of the radioactive isotope emits an α-particle when it decays to a nucleus of the element Po. Copy and complete the equation representing this event:

$${}^{222}_{86}Rn \rightarrow Po + He$$

12 The following symbols represent five different nuclides.

$${}^{58}_{29}A \quad {}^{54}_{27}B \quad {}^{59}_{29}C \quad {}^{58}_{30}D \quad {}^{59}_{30}E$$

a) Which nuclides are isotopes of the same element?

b) Which nuclide possesses most neutrons?

c) Which nuclide possesses least protons?

d) Which nuclide could be produced from which other by the emission of an alpha particle?

e) Which nuclide could be produced from which other by the emission of a beta particle?

13 A nuclide decays to become an oxygen nuclide by emitting an electron.

a) Write down an equation to show this process.

b) State the number of protons, neutrons and electrons in a neutral atom of the oxygen nuclide that is produced.

14 a) Make a list of FOUR effects that exposure to radiation can have on people.

b) State THREE ways in which the risk of exposure to radiation can be reduced for people who work with radioactive materials.

c) State TWO ways in which radioactive materials can be used in medical applications.

d) Describe TWO industrial or agricultural applications of radioactive materials.

15 The figure below shows energy conversions in a nuclear power station. The boxes represent forms of energy. The circles represent devices that convert energy into other forms. Copy the diagram and label the empty boxes and circles.

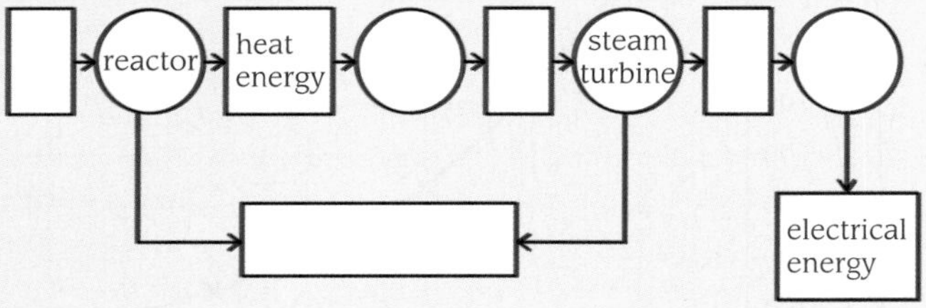

16 The Sun's source of energy is a nuclear fusion reaction in which mass is converted to energy. The energy, E, converted by a loss of mass, m, is given by the Einstein equation:

$$E = mc^2$$

c = speed of light in a vacuum = $3 \times 10^8\ \mathrm{m\,s^{-1}}$.
The Sun is losing mass at a rate of $2 \times 10^9\ \mathrm{kg\,s^{-1}}$.

a) Calculate the power output of the Sun.

b) If the total mass of the Sun is 2×10^{30} kg and it continues to lose mass at this rate, calculate its remaining life in years.
(Take 1 year to be 3×10^7 s.)

17 In a nuclear power station, the mass of the fuel decreases as energy is generated. Calculate the energy output when the mass of fuel decreases by 0.4 kg, assuming an overall efficiency of 30%.
c = speed of light in a vacuum = $3 \times 10^8\ \mathrm{m\,s^{-1}}$.

Index

Acknowledgements

Alamy/Andrew Lambert/LGPL 7, **/Deco** 27, **/epa European pressphoto agency b.v.** 38, **/Matthew Johnston** 45, **/Digital Focus** 97c, **/Frans Lemmens** 104t, **/Pierre Logwin** 105, **/Sciencephotos** 160t, **/David Hancock** 172, **/Sciencephotos** 199, **/Sciencephotos** 203, **/Nic Cleave Photography** 213cr, **/WoodyStock** 222b, **/Dr Ray Clark & Mervyn Goff** 225t, **/John Cole** 225c, **/Charistonne-images** 251tl, **/Steven Frame** 281t, **/Age Fotostock** 303tr, **/PRILL Mediendesign** 304, **/Jeff J Daly** 313, **/Interfoto** 336b, **/Ewing Galloway** 346, **/Zuma Press, Inc.** 365t; **Corbis/DK Stock/Rober Glenn** 121, **/DK Limited** 259, **/KYODO/Reuters** 365b; **Fotolia** 76, 162tr, 194, 273; **Frank Lane Picture Agency /Minden Pictures /Ingo Arndt** 114, **/Minden Pictures /Yva Momatiuk & John Eastcott** 307; **Getty Images** 50, **/Lars Klove Photo Service** 77, **/Vladimir Pcholkin** 91, **/Toronto Star 95b, /Time & Life Pictures** 96t, **/Universal History Archive** 112tl, **/Rischgitz** 112tr, **/AFP** 191, **/Noan Clayton** 213b, **/Time & Life Pictures** 367; **iStockphoto** 26, 81, 82, 97t, 125, 126t, 130c, 161b, 211, 225b, 248r, 281b, 359c; **PPL Photo Agency/Raymarine** 213t; **Robert Harding/Rolf Richardson** 281c; **Science Photo Library** 56, **/Martyn F. Chillmaid** 62tl, 66, **/NASA** 72, **/Dr. Arthur Tucker** 94b, **/Leonard Lessin** 99, **/Alex Bartel** 104c, **/David Nunuk** 125t, **/Patrick Dumas** 126C, **/Alexander Tsiaras** 161t, **/Martyn F. Chillmaid** 162 tl, **/David Parker** 162b, **/Martyn F. Chillmaid** 170, **/Berenice Abbott** 200, **/Andrew Lambert Photography** 202l, 202r, **/Paul Rapson** 214, **/Edward Kinsman** 219t, **/Giphotostock** 219b, **/Williams & Metcalf** 222t, **/Ted Kinsman** 231, **/Andrew Lambert Photography** 251tr, **/Shelia Terry** 274, **/Alex Bartel** 303tl, **/Andrew Lambert Photography** 312, 314c, **/Martyn F. Chillmaid** 314b, **/Andrew Lambert Photography** 324, **/Giphotostock** 326, **/Library of Congress** 335, **/Royal Astronomical Society** 336t, **/Science Photo Library** 336c, **/Prof.Peter Fowler** 337, **/Richard J. Green** 348, **/Steve Allen** 358t, **/Mauro Fermariello** 358b, **/Ria Novosti** 359t, **/Simon Fraser/Medical Physics, RVI, Newcastle Upon-Tyn**e 359b, **/Simon Fraser** 360t, **/David Nunuk** 360b, **/Martin Bond** 361, **/Skyscan** 363; **Shutterstock** 6, 46, 53, 62tr, 80, 86, 95t, 96c, 96b, 98t, 98c, 98b, 114, 130t, 130b, 135, 136, 154, 162tc, 221, 235, 239, 248l, 263c, 263b, 319, 322, 325, 330, 347